THE RULE OF BENEDICT

THE RULE OF BENEDICT

BENEDICT

A GUIDE TO CHRISTIAN LIVING

THE FULL TEXT OF THE RULE IN
LATIN AND ENGLISH WITH
COMMENTARY BY GEORGE HOLZHERR
ABBOT OF EINSIEDELN

Translated by Monks of Glenstal Abbey

FOUR COURTS PRESS

FRATRIBUS EREMI

The Latin text is taken, with the permission of Abbot E. Manning, from
H. Rochais and E. Manning, *Règle de Saint Benoît*, 2nd edn., Rochefort 1980
(now: Oelenberg Abbey, F–68950 Reiningue).
This book is a translation of *Die Benediktsregel: Eine Anleitung zu christlichem Leben*
© Benziger Verlag, Zurich, Einsiedeln, Cologne, 2nd edn., 1982.

Typeset by
Seton Music Graphics Ltd, Bantry, Co. Cork, for
FOUR COURTS PRESS LTD
Kill Lane, Blackrock, Co. Dublin, Ireland.

Translation © Glenstal Abbey 1994
ISBN 1-85182-121-X

A catalogue record for this book is
available from the British Library.

Printed in Ireland by
Colour Books Ltd, Dublin

PREFACE TO THE ENGLISH
EDITION

This chapter-by-chapter commentary on the Rule of St Benedict incorporates much of the analytical study of many scholars in recent decades, but, more importantly, it also provides a synthesis. That synthesis is based on the person of St Benedict himself. The reader will feel himself brought face to face with the Saint as he composed his Rule, leavening with his own wise and loving spirit the material available to him in his sources. Those who follow the Rule in the monasteries of our time will find here a welcome companion and support in daily life.

The rapid and wide success of the German original (now in its second edition) shows that many people outside the monasteries have found the book helpful as *A Guide to Christian Living*. The book has already appeared in a Polish edition.

The author has himself read and approved the English translation, and suggested some minor changes which have been included in the text.

Several options have been taken in the translation, notably with regard to the early sources so frequently quoted by Abbot Holzherr. It was judged best, in the interests of evenness and unity of style, to translate these directly from Abbot Holzherr's German renderings rather than use any existing English translations of the passages concerned. The very full references provided in the notes will enable the reader to judge for himself the accuracy and fidelity of the texts as given here.

With regard to the translation of the Rule itself, the English version offered here is a fresh translation from the Latin text followed by Abbot Holzherr. It is *not* therefore a translation of Abbot Holzherr's own German version, but a parallel one, following his layout and criteria and respecting his options wherever the text of the Rule is open to different interpretations. The needs of the hearers of the Rule as read aloud in our monasteries have been kept constantly in mind; for this reason also the traditional dates for reading the Rule in sequence have been inserted in the margin.

The German text of the Commentary was translated by Anselm Barry OSB and Cillian Ó Sé OSB; the Latin text of the Rule was translated by Placid Murray OSB, who also acted as editor of the book. The "user-friendly" layout of this edition is largely the concept of Henry O'Shea OSB. The index of keywords was computerized by Mary Kenny.

Glenstal Abbey
21 March 1994

CONTENTS

CONTENTS

CONTENTS

LIST OF ABBREVIATIONS

:	Parallels between RM and RB (in Notes on the relationship between one and the other)	R4P	Rule of the Four Fathers
		RB	Rule of Benedict
→	See: Commentary (Chapters and verses in Commentary or Introduction)	RBasRuf	Rule of Basil (Translation of Rufinus)
		RCaesVirg	Rule of Caesarius for Nuns
Conl	Conlationes (of Cassian)		
Dial	Dialogi (of Gregory the Great)	RF	Regula Ferioli (of Ferreolus)
Introd	Introduction	RM	Rule of the Master
Hist mon	Historia monachorum	RMth	RM theme (Baptismal catechesis)
Inst	Institutiones (of Cassian); Instituta (of Pachomius, Latin)	RMthp	RM theme-pater (Commentary on the Lord's Prayer)
Iud	Iudicia (of Pachomius, Latin)	RMths	RM theme-servitium operis (Commentary on the psalms)
Leg	Leges (of Pachomius, Latin)		
Lib	Liber (of Horsiesi, Latin)	T	Title (Chapter-heading)
		VAnt	Life of Antony
OM	Ordo monasterii (attributed to Augustine)	VHonor	Life of Honoratus
		VPJur	Life of the Jura Fathers
Praec	Praecepta (of Augustine = Rule of Augustine); Praecepta (of Pachomius, Latin)	VPach	Life of Pachomius (Latin)
2PR	Second Rule of the Fathers	VPatr	Vitae Patrum (Lives of the Fathers, Latin, 5 Books, with Hist mon and Verba Seniorum)
1QS	Rule of Qumrân	Prol	Prologue (of the RB)

INTRODUCTION[1]

1 *The Spirituality of the Rule*

Benedict's Rule is written for monks. However, it was composed long before there were 'Benedictines', 'Basilisans', or 'Augustinians'. The spiritual teaching of the Rule is to a great extent identical with the *spirituality of the ancient Church* as a whole. I think it important to make this available to committed Christians of our time.

The present *commentary* deals mainly with those sections of the Rule which are spiritually of significance.

The Rule is an epitome of Sacred Scripture. Benedict's aim is to form men according to the Beatitudes.[2] Christ is the prototype of monks. Monks are Christians who commit themselves fully to the ecclesial community. The Acts of the Apostles offer the perfect pattern of such commitment.[3] The early monastic Fathers and Benedict transposed this *biblical ideal* into a monastic rule of life, whose structures however remain variable. Every interpretation of the Rule of Benedict must take this biblical background as its starting point. A series of references in the margin of each chapter indicates biblical quotations, reminiscences, and allusions. The words and sentences printed in small capitals in the translation are intended to draw the reader's attention to this background. From time to time the commentary also gives hints in this direction.

In his last chapter Benedict points beyond his 'brief' Rule to the 'holy Fathers' on whom he had drawn. It is above all the *sources* of Eastern spirituality which poured themselves into his Rule. The spiritual teaching of the East had undergone further development in the West. Benedict achieved in the sixth century a synthesis combining the spirituality of East and West. The contact with these roots of Christian spirituality is still indispensable today.

The *Second Vatican Council* urges not only 'monks' and not only members of religious Orders, but Christians generally, to go to the Eastern sources on which Benedict draws: 'In the East are to be found the riches of those spiritual traditions which are given expression in monastic life especially. From the glorious times of the holy Fathers, that monastic spirituality flourished in the East which later flowed over into the Western world, and there provided a source from which Latin monastic life took its rise and has often drawn fresh vigour ever since. Therefore, it is earnestly recommended that Catholics avail themselves more often of the spiritual riches of the Eastern Fathers which lift up the whole man to the contemplation of the divine mysteries.'[4]

Jerome wrote in 404: 'Whoever is really interested in studying the coenobitical life should quench his thirst at the well itself and not take water which comes from further downstream.'[5] With this recommendation in mind my commentary illustrates the Rule with texts which I have newly translated from those Latin versions[6] which Benedict himself may have known. Besides, I occasionally quote Origen (d.253),[7] a writer so important for monasticism; I quote also the account of the life of Benedict from the pen of Pope Gregory the Great (d.604). Many editions of the Rule indicate the sources which open the way to *Benedict's own spiritual world*. A scholarly apparatus helps only a few readers, because the texts in question are scarcely available to them. If however the spiritual springs of Benedict's Rule do not flow, the Rule can easily give the impression of being a well long since dried up, or else will be expounded all too 'legalistically'. These reflections led me to write a commentary in the form here offered. I hope that from the roots of Benedict's Rule, the vital spiritual energies of the earlier, undivided Christendom may stream into our present time. I have tried to translate the ancient texts into the language and within the intellectual horizons of our time. Even when we cannot keep to the letter of what Benedict or his sources say, nevertheless these texts still convey a spiritual message. I do not explicitly discuss present-day problems; the present relevance of the ancient texts is generally obvious. Moreover, there is no shortage of recent works, which confront Benedict's Rule with current problems.[8]

2 A meditative Reading of the Rule

In Benedictine monasteries the Rule is read daily, but only a very short passage each day. The Rule is like an old, fully-bodied red wine; it is best enjoyed in sips. A person who exceeds moderation, or does not know how to drink with discernment, is to be pitied. Head and heart, soul and spirit ought to relish the words of the Rule, just as the eye is gladdened at the colour of the wine, while tongue, sense of smell and palate—each in its own way—savour the precious gift of God. If one has tasted on the tongue a maxim of Benedict's by repeating it over and over to oneself, one will reflect further, follow it up by meditating on biblical words, parables or characters which suggest themselves to us, or by meditating on the Person, the mystery, and the teaching of Jesus. This is the *'meditation method' of the ancient Church* of East and West; it will open out again and again into a spontaneous prayer.

The commentary illustrates the text of the Rule with quotations from the Fathers, which can help to open the eye and ear of the heart. I have deliberately avoided a systematically constructed commentary. Benedict himself does not write systematic treatises on theological problems, on grace for instance, or on Monophysitism (a much discussed question in his day), on eschatology, on martyrdom, or on the Church. Nevertheless, the Rule everywhere gives evidence of a markedly biblical and ecclesial understanding of the vital questions of Christian and monastic life. The commentary seeks to unfold Benedict's spiritual world, following his exposition step by step. In an unsystematic commentary the same theme admittedly turns up in various different passages. References to parallel passages, and a thematic index will facilitate *systematic* investigation.

The introduction and commentary give some basic information about the present state of research; but 'scholarship' is not the aim of this book. The commentary does not intend to heap up a mass of learned details. Rather, in the attitude of the spirituality of old, it wants the whole person to become, from the inmost centre, an eye and ear for God. The whole asceticism of the Rule is intended to prepare the ground for a *'theology* (vision of God) *of the heart.'*

In order to understand why certain texts of the ancient Fathers and monastic writers have been chosen for the commentary, it will be useful to take a look now at the antecedents of Benedict's Rule and at Benedict's own spiritual reading matter.

3 *Southern Gaul and the Jura Region the Seed-ground of Benedict's Rule*

It is now almost fifty years since it was first asserted that the anonymous so-called *'Rule of the Master'* was written before the Rule of Benedict. Thereupon an intensive study of the Rule began which brought about a certain clarification. Today the new thesis is generally accepted: one quarter of Benedict's Rule is—broadly speaking—taken over from this 'Master', two further quarters are strongly influenced by him; while one quarter shows no relationship to this 'Master'.[9] In addition to this first conclusion, F. Masai (d.1979) and E. Manning presume that the so-called 'Rule of the Master' originated in the Jura region and that Southern Gaul is its seed-ground.

The most important nursery of the monasticism of Southern Gaul was the island monastery of *Lérins* (off Cannes), founded about 410. Partly by way of the 'Rule of the Master' the influence of the following 'Fathers of Lérins' is discernible in Benedict:

— *Honoratus*, founder of Lérins, bishop of Arles (d.428/9);

— *Hilarius*, a pupil and biographer of Honoratus, bishop of Arles (d.449);

— *Eucherius*, bishop of Lyons (d.450/55);

— *Faustus*, bishop of Riez (d.490/500);

— *Caesarius*, bishop of Arles (d.542), author of a rule for nuns and one for monks, also of 'Sermons for Monks'. To his circle belonged

— *Ferreolus*, bishop of Uzès (d.581) author of 'Regula Ferioli', which is contemporary with Benedict.

From the Lérins sphere of influence there are a number of *writings* known to us which were made use of in the 'Rule of the Master', and thence found their way into the Rule of Benedict partly word for word:

—the '*Second Rule of the Fathers*' (*c.*426/7);[10]

—the '*Rule of the Four Fathers*' (*c.*460/70);[11]

—the '*Account of the Warfare of the Heart*' (actus militiae cordis);[12]

—a '*Rule of the Monastery*';[13]

—a treatise '*On Humility*'.[14]

A devout Christian named Romanus (d.*c.*463) who wished to found a monastery on his estate in the Jura, first of all became a monk in the monastery on the Rhone at Lyons,[15] in order to get to know the Rule and the life of the monks there. He then took appropriate writings[16] back with him, and began the founding of the first monastery in the Jura, followed soon by other foundations.[17] The writings which the founder had brought with him were worked over and furnished with supplements. In this way the so-called 'Rule of the Master' gradually came into being. We know the series of the most important monastic Fathers in the Jura:

—*Romanus* (d.*c.*463), the founder;

—*Lupicinus* (d.*c.*480), during his time there existed an early draft of the 'Rule of the Master', which became known in Southern Italy;[18]

—*Eugendus* (d.*c.*510), who carefully perfected the 'original regulations';[19]

—an *unknown author* wrote the 'Lives of the Jura Fathers' for the monastery of St Maurice in Valais (which was restored about 515) together with a Rule,[20] a reference which can only allude to the final version of the 'Rule of the Master'. Moreover the author rearranged the material which had by now become quite extensive.[21]

Benedict was presumably acquainted with an early draft of the 'Rule of the Master', perhaps at the stage it had reached under Abbot Lupicinus. It is possible that Benedict himself gives veiled references to the 'text of the Master'.[22] The anonymous text received morever the name '*Rule of the Master*', because all the chapters are constructed on the same set pattern: 'The disciple asks.—The Master (Magister) answers.' This pattern is already known from Basil (d.379), who always answers the questions put to him with quotations from Scripture and some explanations. Although Benedict starts from the 'Master', he by no means follows him slavishly. Unlike the Master, he does not present himself as a 'theologian', although he does not lack a theological outlook. One cannot find in Benedict any trace of the 'Master's' tendency to longwinded expositions, of his delight in ritualistic details, and his propensity towards a lack of proportion and to schoolmasterish attitudes.[23] Benedict not only abbreviated his source; he adjusted and completed it by a body of thought taken from other 'holy Fathers', and by his own sure eye, marked with a fine sense of proportion and a feel for ecclesial values.

The fact that Benedict took over many sections from the 'Master', or even that after Benedict's death *interpolations*[24] were inserted into the Rule, is no reason for not commenting on such passages or for not speaking of 'Benedict'.

4 The Roots of the Rule of Benedict in Africa, Egypt and Asia Minor

In his last chapter Benedict twice cites the 'holy Fathers'.[25] Just as for Holy Scripture,[26] they had become so familiar to him through close reading,[27] that their thoughts and turns of phrase flow into his pen, even when he is not directly excerpting from them. A passage from the 'Lives of the Monastic Fathers in the Jura'[28] gives us a picture of that collection of writings (in Latin translation) which could have been at the disposal of a monk of the sixth century: 'We do not wish in any way, out of an ill-timed arrogance to belittle the "Constitutions" written by the great Saint Basil, Bishop of the capital of Cappadocia, by the holy Fathers of Lérins, also by Saint Pachomius, an early abbot of the Syrians (!), and in more recent times by the venerable Cassian. We read their Rules daily, it is true, but we wish to keep to the following Rule which was introduced with an eye to the local climate and the requirements of work. We prefer this (following) Rule to those of the Eastern monks, because this Rule can be better and more easily observed, given the Gallic temperament and frailities . . . '
In this text we are struck by the deep respect for the 'Fathers of Lérins' already mentioned, and furthermore by the admiration for the Eastern monastic writings. This notwithstanding, preference was given in practice however to a Western Rule. The Rule referred to here is the 'Rule of the Master', although the manuscript is incomplete at this point.[29]

Other Fathers apart from those mentioned in the quotation from the 'Lives of the Jura Fathers' above, play a less important role in the Rule of Benedict.

Certain theological statements, especially on obedience, in sections stemming from the 'Master', remind us of *Irenaeus of Lyons* (d.*c*.202), a pupil of Polycarp of Smyrna in Asia Minor (d.156).[30]

The *Didascalia of the Apostles* (early third century), composed by a Jewish-Christian bishop in northern Syria appears to have influenced directly or indirectly the penitential code of our Rule (RB 1980).[31]

Cyprian, bishop and martyr in Carthage (d.258), was much read; and his Exposition of the Lord's Prayer is echoed in the 'Account of the Warfare of the Heart' and thence in the Benedictine Rule.[32] This is one of the ways by which the spirituality of the age of the martyrs found entrance into Benedict's Rule. A nostalgia for the age of the martyrs is no less marked[33] in Benedict than is his wistful longing for the early Church.[34]

Basil the Great (330–79), bishop of Caesarea in Cappadocia,[35] is the only author Benedict mentions by name. In the last chapter of his Rule he recommends the 'Rule of our holy Father Basil'.[36] Likewise the first sentences of the Prologue are taken from an 'Admonition' attributed to Basil.[37] Does

Benedict wish to put his Rule under Basil's patronage?[38] Be that as it may, Basil's influence is continually discernible throughout the Rule, above all his esteem for community life and his sense of proportion. Basil himself is strongly influenced by the ascetical movement which centred round Eustathius of Sebaste (d.after 377). Eustathius was more concerned about a reformation of the Church and of Christians than about monasticism as such. A synod of Gangra (340) condemned as being too one-sided the over-emphasis of the monastic dimension in the movement. Basil separated from Eustathius (with whom he had earlier visited the ascetics in Syria, Palestine and Lower Egypt); Basil shuns extremes and understands monasticism as an intensely lived Christianity.

Pachomius (d.347) likewise used to be read in the monasteries of the Jura.[39] A native of Egypt, he experienced as a young, overburdened soldier the active charity of a Christian community and so came to the faith. He founded the monastery of Tabennisi in the Thebaid on the Nile in Upper Egypt, then a further eight monasteries for men and two for women, so that he became abbot general of an enormous number of monks. His Rules are brief directives on questions of asceticism and organization.[40]

Horsiesi (d.c.380), the second successor of Pachomius, wrote a 'book',[41] which gives evidence of a scriptural spirituality and which hinges on the concept of 'koinonia' (community).

Augustine, bishop of Hippo (354–430) took the final step to the faith after the life of the Egyptian monk Antony (d.356) had been read to him. He became a monk, founded a monastery, and as bishop in Hippo (North Africa) gathered round himself a clerical community living in monastic fashion. He occupied himself frequently with the monasticism which flourished in North Africa (and which outlasted the Vandal invasions).[42] Benedict took from Augustine's Rule[43] the idea of the early Church of Jerusalem as the model concept for the monastery, especially in chapters in which he distances himself from the Master.[44] It was only under Caesarius (d.542), who represented a moderate Augustinianism that the monasticism of Southern Gaul became reconciled to the bishop of Hippo's teaching on grace. At first the monks had the impression that this teaching on grace dealt a body-blow to committed personal asceticism, and they inclined rather to Origen's teaching on grace.

Origen (c.185–253/4), a martyr's son who himself suffered for the faith, taught in the catechetical school in his native city of Alexandria. He promoted the knowledge of sacred Scripture, and a spirituality based on it,[45] and called for an ascetical struggle against evil,[46] without however denying the necessity of grace. This conception is also to be met with in the 'Rule of the Master', which cites 'a wise saying of Origen's'.[47] By way of the 'Master' this ancient teaching on grace found an entry into Benedict's Rule also.[48] In general, Origen's influence on monasticism was very great.[49]

Evagrius Ponticus (d.399) who was thoroughly familiar with Origen's writings expounded the teaching of the 'Ascent'. 'Faith strengthens the fear of God; this is strengthened by self-discipline (*enkrateia*), which in turn becomes imperturbable through perseverance (*hypomone*) and hope (*elpis*). From these is born freedom from emotions (*apatheia*), which has love (*agape*) as her daughter. *Agape* is the door of natural knowledge (*gnosis physike*) it is followed by knowledge of God (*theologia*), and at the end by blessedness (*makariotes*)'.[50] These dominant themes from the 'Ascent' exercised a formative influence on Cassian's works, and they have also left traces in the 'Rule of the Master' and in the Rule of Benedict.[51]

John Cassian (360–430/5) is deeply indebted to Origen's thought, through the influence, among others, of Evagrius. After a sound education Cassian set off as a young monk on travels that lasted fourteen years all told, to visit the monks in Egypt, above all the semi-eremitical settlements in the Nile delta, as well as the monks in Syria, Palestine, and Mesopotamia. During his travels he assimilated the thought of Origen (d.253) which still survived among the monks, but also the mysticism of Gregory of Nyssa (d.349), the brother of Basil (d.379). About 415 Cassian founded in Marseilles a monastery for men and also one for women, and wrote both his wide-ranging books.[52] In these *Conferences* and *Institutions*, which are twice recommended by Benedict,[53] Cassian disseminates the spirituality of Egyptian monasticism, although he wished it to be adapted to the climatic conditions of the West.[54] Benedict is often dependent on Cassian, e.g. in his view of the abbot as teacher,[55] or in his doctrine of 'discretio'.[56] 'Institutions' are not to be understood as those of Cassian exclusively.[57] Because Benedict is composing a concise rule for monks, and not a treatise, he does not fall into the doctrinal onesidedness of Cassian, who tends to reduce the Christian life to monastic life.

The *Lives of the Fathers* are recommended by Benedict,[58] and reminiscences of them often occur in his own work. The following are included among them in detail:

— the *Life of Antony* (d.356);[59]

— the *Life of Pachomius* (d.346);[60]

— the *History of the Monks in Egypt*;[61]

— the *Life of Honoratus* of Lérins (d.428);[62]

— the *Lives of the Jura Fathers* (written about 515);

— the *Sayings of the Fathers*.[63]

If Eastern monastic writings were translated in Rome in Benedict's time,[64] there obviously existed a circle of interested readers. Benedict must have been close to them.

5 Meeting Place of Western and Eastern Spirituality and a Gateway to the Future

Streams of tradition flowing from Egypt, Syria, from Greek-speaking Asia Minor, from North Africa, Southern Gaul and the Jura region, all come together and redouble in Benedict. Its roots reaching into all provinces and far back into the past explain the inner strength of the Rule of Benedict. On no account should we consider Benedict as an opponent of Eastern monasticism; nevertheless he made changes of emphasis of the greatest consequence; for example, he moderates the severe ascetical practices of earlier times and stresses the value and ethos of work.

Benedict was deeply rooted in the best spiritual tradition of a still undivided Christendom; this explains to a large extent the influence—which can scarcely be overrated—that the Rule exercised throughout western Europe. It is the *basic document* of monasticism and of religious life in the West. It became the educator of the young Germanic peoples. The Rule taught these peoples not only 'morals and behaviour',[65] but also 'pray and work', 'endure', and 'live in peace'. Benedict brought to these peoples a Christian understanding of community and authority, and taught them the duty of caring for the sick, the poor, and the stranger.

Even if Benedict's spirit was not accepted in everything by the *new peoples*, one cannot but be astonished at the way his Rule outstripped all earlier Rules and entered deeply into the thoughts and feelings of the new peoples. We have now to examine the causes of this development.

6 A Biographical Sketch as a Spiritual Message

About the year 593 Pope Gregory the Great (d.604) wrote his four books of 'Dialogues'. The dialogue form is reminiscent of Greek authors. In these books Gregory wants to show that it is not only in foreign lands, say the Egyptian desert or Gaul, that one can become a spiritual man, but even on Italian soil too. He tells of 'signs and wonders' wrought by numerous bishops and monks who were 'men of God'.

The whole second book of the Dialogues is completely devoted to one outstanding personality, namely Benedict (the 'Blessed'). Gregory wants to relate 'for the glory of the Redeemer, some of the miracles worked by the venerable man Benedict.'[66]

Given this avowed object, one must not look for the style of modern historical writing in Gregory's biographical sketch of Saint Benedict. With a storyteller's delight Pope Gregory weaves a garland of '*Fioretti*' round the saint's life. In order to proclaim a doctrine, he makes use of miracle stories which were readily listened to. He expounds moral and ascetical questions, and communicates a surprisingly many-sided experience—psychological, spiritual and mystical. I have included in the commentary many of Gregory's deep insights, which he may have brought with him from Constantinople.

Gregory's partner in the dialogue said of Benedict, 'This man was filled with the spirit of all the just'.[67] The miracles recounted were intended to ascribe to Benedict 'the spirit and power' of the apostles and prophets. Gregory explains vividly that Benedict was a man of the Church, who culti-vated a way of life in accordance with the Scriptures, and who, after early unsuccessful attempts exemplified and taught an *authentic* form of monastic life.

For this reason Gregory the Great assigns a singular place to the abbot of Montecassino within his four books of 'Dialogues on the Miracles of the Fathers of Italy'. In the second book Benedict alone takes the stage, as it were the central figure in a mosaic, surrounded by the many characters of lesser rank of the first and third books. The fourth book then shows that 'the soul lives on after death',[68] and as a description of Paradise constitutes at the same time the firmament over the whole mosaic.

Towards the end of his biographical sketch of Benedict, Gregory remarks, 'He writes, in a language flooded with light, a monastic Rule which is noteworthy for its sense of proportion'.[69] The high praise of *this abbot and his Rule* coming from the lips of Pope Gregory the Great decisively influenced the Germanic peoples in adopting this Rule of a 'Roman abbot'[70] in preference to all others.

7   *Historical Contours of Benedict's Life*

Pope Gregory's rhetorical narrative contains a long list of verifiable state-ments:

— definite places (Nursia, Rome, Subiaco, Terracina);

— persons and informants involved, whose existence is partly substan-tiated through other sources, and who were known to the Pope or his interlocutor;

— ancient temple buildings (the ruins of which are preserved);

— events such as the famine in Campania in 537–38.

Gregory would have shocked his readers as untrustworthy if he had openly invented the historical setting of Benedict's life, because they themselves were still acquainted with the persons, the places, and the circumstances. In view of the special literary genre of Gregory's narratives 'for the glory of the Redeemer', his assertions are indeed to be received with caution,[71] but they do make it possible to sketch Benedict's life in broad outline. Benedict was born as the son of parents of middle rank in the poor highland valley of Nursia (Norcia) in Umbria,[72] about the begin-ning of the sixth century.[73] According to Gregory's Dialogues[74] he could already have learned to know monasticism in the immediate surroundings of Nursia. As a young man Benedict comes to Rome for studies, but finds no way forward here. Disgusted, he flees from the decadent atmosphere of this city. His desire is 'to please God alone'.[75] It seems he then joined a group of ascetics in Enfide (Affile) in the Sabine hills. But soon—like many monks of his time—he begins a hermit's life. He seeks out the valley of Subiaco which lies about eighty kilometres east of Rome, and which is remarkable for the natural beauty of its wooded rocky slopes, its lake and the river Anio. Here he lives in strict solitude, and so sets out on the way of inner purification.

The young ascetic becomes known and begins to attract people who are seeking counsel and advice. Now the monastic community of *Vicovaro*(?), whose abbot has died, asks him to become superior. He hesitates to follow the call, because he has in mind the ideal of a strict monastic life. In fact he is unsuccessful in face of the opposition of these monks who are of a different cast of mind, and he goes back to *Subiaco* from Vicovaro. Here new disciples flock around him. He organizes a cenobitical life for them in 'twelve monasteries . . . each with twelve monks, according to the Statutes of the Fathers'.[76] One of the versions of the 'Rule of the Master' is perhaps referred to in this last expression 'Statutes of the Fathers'; Benedict certainly knew this Rule. It is not impossible that the one-sidedness of the 'Rule of the Master' was one of the reasons why Benedict ran into difficulties even in Subiaco (E. Manning).

The monasteries of Subiaco continued to exist, but Benedict himself moves to the heights of *Montecassino*, about 140 kilometres south of Rome. He destroys there an altar dedicated to Apollo, sets up two oratories, one in honour of St Martin, the other in honour of St John the Baptist, as well as the buildings of a monastery. It is here now that he writes his Rule. From experience he realizes that the pronouncedly 'vertical' trend in the 'Rule of the Master' needs a 'horizontal' complement; Christ is to be seen not only in the abbot, but also in the brother, in the poor man, in the guest, in the sick person. The influence of Augustine (d.430) is at work, and also the Greek influence significant at the time in Southern Italy.

8   *Within the Forces at Work in Church and Politics of the Sixth Century*

A glance at the world surrounding Benedict shows how he was involved in it and how he reacted to it. A first period of his life fell in the time of the *Ostrogoths* under King Theodoric (493–526). The occupying forces and the Catholic Romans at first lived together separately side by side. The Goths were tolerably Christianized and held to Arianism, therefore denying that Christ is of the same divine nature as the Father.[78] The intense Christocentric stance of the Rule of Benedict can be explained in part as a reaction against the Arians, likewise the strongly stressed reverence for the Trinity. On the other hand because of the Gothic occupation Catholics were able to enjoy an independent position towards the Emperor in Constantinople. Benedict himself may have experienced in his youth the sometimes bloody and long-drawn out turmoils of a Roman schism, when a pro-Byzantine minority had set up the anti-Pope Lawrence against the newly-elected Pope *Symmachus* (498–514), himself a doubtful enough figure. Symmachus conferred the primatial rights in Gaul and Spain on Caesarius of Arles (d.542). Pope *Hormisdas* (514–23) also writes to Caesarius, informing him of Church events. There existed then close relationships between Rome and the provinces of Southern Gaul, at that time an oasis of peace in a storm-ridden world. Contacts between a 'Roman abbot' and the monasticism of Southern Gaul should not in any event cause surprise. Hormisdas put an end to the Acacian schism with Constantinople during the reign of Emperor Justin I (518–27); Benedict's friend, Bishop Germanus of Capua (d.541) was in Constantinople about this time (519–20), acting as Apocrisiarius (Papal Legate).[79] Hormisdas had to deal with the complaints of Oriental (Syrian) monks about certain doctrinal questions (questions to do with the Trinity, among others). Many of these monks had emigrated to Italy.[80] The Byzantine East now begins visibly to gain influence in Italy, and accordingly the Gothic reaction becomes sharper.[81] King Theodoric bids Pope *John I* (523–6) defend the Arians (!) in Byzantium against encroachments; the Pope is received there with so much honour and respect that on his return to Theodoric in Ravenna he is treated with considerable suspicion; he dies soon afterwards in that very place. Pope *Felix III* (526–30), a kinsman of the later Gregory I (d.604), is elevated to the papacy at the command of the Arian king, contrary to the will of the Roman people and clergy. He supports Caesarius of Arles (d.542) in the controversy on grace and sends him an excerpt (*Capitula*) from the writings of Augustine (d.430). We know how considerably Benedict, under the influence of Augustine, altered earlier positions.[82] Felix III himself designated his successor, Boniface II (530–2), a son of the Goth Sigibald. This reminds one of the procedure laid down by the 'Master' regarding the choice of the abbot's successor, a method which proved unsatisfactory and was abandoned by Benedict.[83] How difficult the problem of succession could be in those times, is shown also by the unworthy, simoniacal election of *John II* (533–5).

The death of King Theodoric (526) and the assumption of office by Emperor Justinian I (527–65) of Constantinople introduce a new period, in which power and influence shift more and more to *Byzantium* as their centre of gravity. Pope *Agapetus* (535–6) at the behest of the Ostrogoth king, Theodahatus, pleads for peace in Constantinople, but without success.[84] Under pressure from Theodahatus, *Silverius* (536–7), a son of Hormisdas, is elected to be Pope. He surrenders Rome without a struggle to the Byzantine army commander Belisarius; but the latter deposes Silverius and has Vigilius (537–55) chosen as Pope.[85] As Pope, Vigilius at first stands up for the Council of Chalcedon (451), and so wards off the suspicion of Monophysitism. Called to Constantinople, he is subjected to alternate bouts of abuse and favour, and so made pliant for the deliberate religious policy of Emperor Justinian I (527–65) of having the Monophysites brought back to Church unity.[86] For a time in Constantinople Pope

Vigilius found an adviser in his deacon Pelagius, who strengthened him in his pro-Chalcedonian stand. Pelagius the deacon stayed in Byzantium from 535 onwards and journeyed about 538/9 to Gaza and Jerusalem. Here he supported the anti-Origenist and pro-Chalcedonian attitude of Abbot Gelasius in the monastery of St Sabas which was very influential throughout the whole of Eastern Christendom. At the instance of Pelagius, Justinian moreover condemned Origenism in 543, in which matter controversies arose, particularly in monastic circles.[87] Deacon Pelagius could have become acquainted at this point in time among monks with the collection 'Sayings of the Fathers', which he translated into Latin.[88] This translation by Pelagius of the 'Sayings of the Fathers' was very probably brought to Benedict's notice by his good friend Bishop Sabinus of Canusium[89] (who also had been a member of the papal delegation in Constantinople in 545) when he visited Benedict in 546, and spoke with him about the taking of Rome by Totila. At all events Benedict uses this translation. In spite of his contacts with churchmen involved in the theological problems, Benedict avoids every theological polemic in his Rule. Perhaps one could say: he has a feeling both for what belongs to the divine, as well as for what belongs to the human 'nature' in Christ and in the Christian life. Monophysite one-sidedness is not in his line. Justinian I (527–65) in his concern to bring about the religious[90] and the political unity of the Empire, invades Italy from 535 to 553, until he wins a complete victory over the Goths.[91] The population, especially that of Rome, suffered great hardship in the turmoil. It is possible that this war and its aftermath are the causes of that poverty of the monastery which is reflected in the Rule of Benedict.[92] Deacon Pelagius did his best to help the suffering people of Rome.

After the defeat of the Goths Benedict would have experienced a period of relative peace. Justinian I (527–65) raises *Pelagius I* (556–61; former deacon) to be Pope. As Pope he now accepts the 'Three Chapters'[93] which he had hitherto opposed. For this reason he is at first received with distrust by the Roman Church, then later accepted.[94] In the Rule of Benedict there is a regulation regarding the abbatial election which reflects a decree of Pelagius I (of February 559).[95] The decree itself is based on an Edict of Justinian I, who also gave Roman Law a unified form.[96] Justinian's norms for ecclesiastical and civil law found an entry into the Rule of Benedict.[97] The influence and presence of the Byzantines now make themselves everywhere felt. One notes in Italy many church buildings in Byzantine forms (sometimes also in Syrian), among others in Canosa, where Benedict's friend Sabinus was bishop. Benedict therefore, according to Gregory's account, had contact with representatives of the Church, who were well versed in Eastern theology, and also in the monasticism of the East.[98] We know that about this time many Eastern monks come to Italy. They bring spiritual vitality with them and set up their 'oratories'. Benedict could have come to know Eastern piety, directly or indirectly, through these circles.[99] The many newly erected 'oratories' of monks (often from the East) gave support to the faith of the people, and soon became bases for the evangelization of the Germanic tribes. At this time there was an increase in the number of churches for the pastoral care of the people in the countryside, while e.g. the episcopal see of Cassinum ceased to exist (G. Penco). Benedict at all events stands within the forces at work of his time, in his monastery certainly, but not aloof. According to Gregory's account he participates in the evangelization of the country folk, and has relations with foremost personalities in Rome,[100] in Cassinum,[101] and elsewhere.[102] All in all, Benedict was able precisely at this time to experience a late flowering of the best values of the Roman and Byzantine traditions, but also had to live through serious crises.

Benedict experienced the beginning of a fourth period, again a sombre one. From 568 onwards the invasions of the *Lombards* begin from the North-East. These Arians, for the most part scarcely converted from heathenism, were hostile and intolerant towards the people and the Catholic Church, sometimes going as far as acts of persecution, and reducing to ashes all the monasteries on their way. Pope *John III* (561–74) now brings the relics of the martyrs from the oratories lying outside Rome into the city itself. This reminds us of Benedict's veneration for the martyrs.[103] Many monks also seek refuge in Rome, as did the community of Montecassino. During the reign of Pope *Benedict I* (575–9), who had in vain petitioned for help in Byzantium against the Lombards, Montecassino was destroyed by these latter (577?). Benedict of Nursia had foreseen this destruction,[104] which was easily conceivable after the invasions of 568. During the siege of Rome by the Lombards, *Pelagius II* (569–90), a son of the Goth Wunigild, was elected Pope without any East-Roman involvement, and was immediately consecrated. He sends his deacon Gregory to Constantinople; the Apocrisiarius however obtains no help. As *Gregory I, the Great*, (590–604) he follows on the Chair of Peter, and in 593 writes the description of the life of Saint Benedict.

9 The Date of the Composition of the Rule and the Year of Benedict's Death

Benedict composed his Rule in order to sum up his experiences as monk and abbot, but he also had in mind the abbots, who, after his death, would be in charge of the monasteries founded by him:

—in *Montecassino* these were to be abbots Constantinus and Simplicius;

—in *Subiaco*, where Benedict continued to be venerated after his death, they were Maurus and Honoratus (about 593), who had previously been a monk in Montecassino;

—in *Terracina* Benedict founded a monastery (probably on the site of an ancient temple on high ground overlooking the sea) and himself supervised the construction;

—in the *Lateran* in Rome there arose (already in Benedict's time?) the monastery of St Pancratius, to which the monks of Montecassino withdrew after the destruction of their house by the Lombards (about 577/81). Valentinianus, who was a monk of Montecassino still under Benedict, became abbot here, and died before 593.

From these considerations which prove that the reforming abbot Benedict was a father figure for a series of monasteries, new light is thrown upon the problem of the year of Benedict's death. E. Manning, whom we follow here, came to the following conclusions:

— the foregoing lists of the abbots of Montecassino, of Subiaco, and of the Lateran, which reach as far as the time of the composition of Gregory's Dialogues, fall very short if, in accordance with the traditional assumption, Benedict himself had already died in 547;

— according to Gregory's account, Benedict himself had still known Bishop Sabinus of Canusium in Apulia, who died about 566, and Bishop Constantius of Aquino, who died about 570, and had known them when they were bishops;

— Exhilaratus, who had been a monk at Montecassino under Benedict, is still hale and hearty in Gregory's time, and Gregory's interlocutor still knew in 593 of Exhilaratus' conversion to the monastic state;

— the grandson of that priest or bishop Florentius, who—allegedly about 529—forced Benedict's withdrawal from Subiaco, by trying to poison him, and by sending naked girls to dance before the eyes of the monks, is only a subdeacon about 593.

These particulars fit in badly with 547 as the date of Benedict's death. E. Manning would therefore wish to bring forward the year of Benedict's death to about 575. In this way it is also easier to explain how Benedict was able to foretell the destruction of his monastery (577/81) by the Lombards, who were invading from the north from 568 onwards. Gregory writes about 593 that these events had taken place 'shortly before' (modo).[105]

Furthermore, the observances of the monasticism of Southern Gaul, which exercised a leading role at the time, and with which the Rule of Benedict shows close kinship, attained only towards the end of the century that *stage of development* which Benedict would allegedly have anticipated already before 547.[106]

A late date for Benedict's death, and a direct connection with the monastery in the Lateran, could, as E. Manning rightly observes, also explain the strikingly 'basilical' arrangement of the Divine Office and the relatively late stage of development of liturgy reflected in the Rule of Benedict.[107] Did Benedict himself draw up this arrangement in its fundamentals for a monastery already being established in the Lateran in his own lifetime? Or was this Order of the Divine Office inserted into the Rule by another hand only about 620?[108]

10   *A Future for the Rule*

The presence of the Rule of Benedict in the Lateran is of long-term significance for its diffusion. And the first appearance of the Rule outside Rome is more easily explained. Two groups of Roman monks travelled about this time as missionaries *through Gaul on their way to England*, the first about 596 (Augustine of Canterbury).

In Rome itself, only Gregory the Great (d.604) mentions that Benedict had written a Rule,[109] and he seems to quote it on one occasion.[110] For the rest we find no trace of the Rule of Benedict in Rome and its environs. It first surfaces in Southern Gaul, about 620.[111] Then we find it again and again in the Frankish empire among disciples of Columbanus, and indeed with and alongside the Rule of Columbanus and others (epoch of 'mixed Rules').[112] From 632 onwards the Rule of Benedict is cited for monasteries of this area,[113] even in excerpts.[114]

The oldest extant MS. of the Rule is the Codex Oxoniensis (Oxford), Hatton 48, written in the English Midlands (Worcester), about 700-10, which contains the short ending of the Prologue, and the so-called 'Interpolations'. In this way or that the Rule made its way *northwards*.[115]

The question is raised today, whether it was not the Anglo-Saxon Willibald (who spent the years 729-39 in Montecassino), who brought the first knowledge of the Rule to the community there. *Montecassino* had been refounded about 717 by Abbot Petronax of Brescia (and therefore not from the Lateran). (B. Steidle).

The *tradition* represented by Paul the Deacon holds that the monks of Montecassino brought the Rule with them on their flight to the Lateran, and that Pope Zacharias (d.752) gave it back to Abbot Petronax of Montecassino from the Lateran library about 750.[116]

At the request of Charlemagne (d.814) a copy is said to have come to Aachen; the reforming abbot Benedict of Aniane (d.821)[117] succeeded in various Synods (816–18) in having the Rule of Benedict declared to be the sole Rule of the Frankish Empire.

About 817, Abbot Haito of *Reichenau* sent the monks Grimald and Tatto to Benedict of Aniane in Aachen, to have them trained in the spirit of the Carolingian reform. At the request of Reginbert the librarian of Reichenau they made an exact transcription of the Aachen copy of the Rule mentioned above. It contains the longer ending to the Prologue.[118] A copy of the transcription made in Aachen for Reichenau came to *St Gall*. To this day it is preserved as Codex 914 in the Abbey Library. This Codex is regarded as being the most precious textual witness of the Rule of Benedict. It is at the basis of the modern Latin editions of the Rule (L. Traube–R. Hanslik–B. Steidle).

It was also from Reichenau that, about the same time, St Meinrad (d.861) brought the oldest exemplar of the Rule of our library (9th cent.) to *Einsiedeln*. One of the first abbots or monks inserted brief interlinear glosses into this text of the Rule. He obviously wished to meet a need for interpretation and explanation.

I hope that my commentary may also answer a need, and help many to understand the Rule, which W. Nigg calls 'one of the most important documents of Christendom'.

I was able to avail of valuable help for the translation as well as for the commentary, for which I must express my *thanks*. At every turn I have made use of the monumental, eleven-volume work of Dom Adalbert de Vogüé (La Pierre-qui-vire) and some individual articles of his, as well as the editions of the Rule by P. Basil Steidle, Beuron (d.1982), by H. Rochais–E. Manning (Rochefort/now: Ölenberg, F 68950 Reiningue), by Don Anselmo Lentini (Montecassino), and the 'RB 1980' (America).

NOTES TO THE 'INTRODUCTION'

1 The first edition was based on: '*Die Regel des heiligen Benedikt*, übersetzt und kurz erklärt von Dr. Pater Eugen Pfiffner, Dekan von Maria Einsiedeln, Benziger Verlag, Einsiedeln–Zürich'. 2 Cf. Matt.5:1–12. The RB quotes the Sermon on the Mount or refers indirectly to it about twenty-five times; the Beatitudes are referred to about five times. The Rule, above all in its spiritual part, wants to lead to the qualities mentioned in the Sermon on the Mount and in the Beatitudes. As the watermark guarantees the quality of a paper, without being visible at first glance, so the qualities praised by Jesus are a theme in our Rule, even though this is not expressly stated every time. 3 Cf. Acts 2:44–47; 4:32–37. The Rule always takes its bearings from the biblical and ecclesial model when there is question of the understanding of the community, or of services and the concept of service, of the performance of a task, of teaching and of spirituality. 4 Decree on Ecumenism, Art. 15. 5 Praef in Pach Reg 9. 6 Unfortunately, there is no German collection of the most important texts which would be easy of access. A practical 'Codex regularum' of this type exists in Italian: G. Turbessi, R*egole monastiche antiche* (Roma 1974).—In the case of the 'Liber Horsiesi', I was able to use a German translation for purposes of comparison: H. Bacht, *Das Vermächtnis des Ursprungs* (Würzburg 1972). 7 Based on H.U. von Balthasar, *Origines, Geist und Feuer* (Salzburg 1938). 8 Cf. D. Rees (ed.), *Consider your call* (London 1978).—G. Braulik (ed.) *Herausforderung der Mönche. Benediktinische Spiritualität* heute (Wien 1979).— The decree of the Council, 'Perfectae caritatis' (Art.2), not without cause requires 'adaptation to the altered circumstances of the times'. The necessity of this is not disputed, though our Commentary is concerned directly with the other demand mentioned by the Council in the same paragraph: 'A return to the sources of every Christian life and to the original spirit of the different Institutes'. 9 *The following passages have been taken word for word from the RM:* RB Prol. 5–45.50: 1.1–10: 2.1.18a.18b–25.30.35–37; 4.1–7.9–59.62–74; 5–7. *The following have no equivalent in the RM:* RB Prol. 46–47,49; 2,26–29,31–36; 3,12–13; 13,12–14; 16,5; 18,1–19,2; 20,4–5; 21,1.5–6; 22,2; 25,4; 27,2–3. 5–7; 29,1–2; 31,6–7.10–14.16–19; 34,1–7; 36,4–10; 38,5–7; 40,1–2; 41,2–5; 42,2–7; 44,5; 45,1–2; 46,1–4; 48,14–21; 49,1–3; 51,3; 52,1; 53,1–2.8–9.12.15–17.23–24; 55,1–3.7–12.20–22; 57,1–3; 52,1; 53,1; 53,1–2.8–9.12.15–17.23–24; 55,1–3.7– 12.20–22; 57,1–3; 58,5–7; 59,7–8; 60.8–9; 61,11–62,11; 63,10–19; 67,5–70,2; 70,4–7; 71,6–9; 73,1–9. Cf. A. de Vogüé, *La Règle de S. Benoît I: Sources Chrétienies 181* (Paris 1972) 174–185. 10 It was written by the deacon Vigilius of Lérins (A. de Vogüé). 11 These Fathers are called Serapion, Macarius, Pafnutius and another Macarius. The names are meant to indicate an Egyptian origin; but the Rule is more likely the product of a synod of abbots in Southern Gaul. This Rule precedes the Rule of the Master in the oldest manuscript (final version) of the latter. 12 Cf. RM 10.123. Parts of the Prologue and of Chapters 4–7 of the RB were originally located in this 'Account of the Warfare of the Heart'. 13 This 'Rule of the Monastery' originally included seven parts, as is clear from a title before RM 11: 1. Organization of the monastery; 2. Way of life; 3. Observance (of the times of the Hours); 4. Different ranks (abbot, deans, cellarer; the section on the abbot was later transplanted into the Actus militiae cordis, because the abbot must be the teacher of spirituality); 5. Possessions; 6. Supervision; 7. Moderation. This division exerts its influence even on the construction of the RB. 14 → 5.1–9 (Note 2). 15 Monasterium Interamne (Insula Barbara). This monastery was later entrusted to Benedict of Aniane (d. 821). 16 A book with the 'Lives of the holy Fathers' and the 'Institutions of the holy Abbots'. Cf. VPJur 11. 17 The monasteries were located in the Franche-Comté (the most important one in Condat) and in the Swiss Jura (Romainmôtier?). 18 Abbot Eugippus of Lucullanum near Naples (d. 533) uses a Rule of this

kind. He is a successor of St. Severinus (d. 482), who had founded monasteries in Noricum (in Passau, for example). These monks withdrew to Southern Italy. Abbot Eugippus had come to know the Eastern monastic spirituality (PL 62.1167–1170). He was also in contact with Dionysius Exiguus (PL 67.345–408; see below. Notes 60; 80). There is extant another manuscript of the Rule of the Master in its early form from the time of Eugippus (Paris, B.N. lat. 12364), the so-called Manuscript E. According to A. de Vogüé, it is only an excerpt from the final version of the RM with the original sequence of chapters. **19** VPJur 59. **20** The monks of St. Maurice requested the abbot and presbyter Marinus of Lérins for a Rule. He referred them to the Jura monasteries, where he affirmed that the Rule was available (VPJur 1–2). An unknown author from the Jura then sent them the 'Lives of the Jura Fathers'. In it he announces three times as forthcoming the 'Institutions of the Fathers' or the 'Rule' (cf. VPJur 174). By this he means the so-called 'Rule of the Master', because he had announced that he would produce 'the Acts, the Lives and the Rule' of the Jura Fathers; but the 'Rule of the Master' does in fact include parts that are entitled 'The Acts and the Lives of the monks' (cf. RM 1 T. and RM 10.123), and parts that are entitled 'Rule of the monastery' (cf. RM 11 T.). The extant manuscript of the 'Lives of the Jura Fathers' has a lacuna; for instead of finding the promised 'Institutions' or the 'Rule', we come on the remark: 'after we have contemplated the great sea of those Institutions', it says that the Lives are to be completed (VPJur 175).—There are also many parallels of content between the RM and the 'Lives of the Jura Fathers'. **21** There are extant two manuscripts of this final version of the 'Rule of the Master'. They are based on the manuscript written for St. Maurice (which was reformed in 515 under King Sigismund). These are: the MS. of Paris, B.N. lat. 12205, called P and written about 600 in Southern Italy, and the MS. used by Benedict of Aniane (d. 821) and preserved in Munich, Clm 28118.—This account is in accordance with the views of Masai-Manning, whereas A. de Vogüé assumes that the (final version of the) Rule of the Master was produced by a single author and in Southern Italy (cf. Note 18). **22** It is remarkable that he should begin the Prologue with: 'Hear and heed, my son, the Master's teaching (*Magistri*!)'. In the concluding chapter he uses the word 'describere' twice; it can mean 'to write down', but also 'to transcribe'. **23** Admittedly, if Benedict was dealing with an early phase of the redaction of the RM, it remains an open question whether he saw himself confronted with all the Master's digressions, with which we are familiar from the final version of the text. **24** Sections which were perhaps inserted into the Rule (E. Manning) only after Benedict's time (probably in the Lateran) are: RB Prol. 40–50; 8–18 (in part); 64,1–6; 65 (?). Different redactional strata can repeatedly be observed. **25** Cf. RB 73,2.4. **26** → 73,3 (in Note 33). **27** → 48,15–16. **28** VPJur 174. **29** See Note 20. **30** → Prol. 5–7; 5,1–9. The trichotomy of body-soul-spirit, emphasized in the 'Rule of the Master' (e.g. RM thp 28; 1,80; 81,18–19), which is mentioned in 1 Thess. 5:23 and familiar to the Fathers, was already known to Irenaeus, e.g.: 'The perfect man is the intimate union of the soul, which receives the Spirit of the Father, with the flesh, which is created in the image of God' (Adv haer 5,6,1). **31** It was translated at an early stage into Latin. **32** → 4,20–33.55–58; 72,11 etc. **33** → Prol. 28.47.50; 4,20–33.62–73; 5,10–13; 7,35–43; 9,8; 14,1–2; 58,1–4.13–16;72,7. **34** → Prol. 50; 1,2; 21,1–4, 33,6. **35** Caesarea (now Kaysari), then a Greek city, is in Turkey, east of Ankara. **36** RB 73,5. Rules in the question and answer style originate from Basil. Benedict was familiar with this 'Asketikon' in the Latin translation by Rufinus (345–510): 'Regula Basilii'. Rufinus reproduced an earlier version of the Asketikon. On reading the prologue to this Rule, one has the impression, for example, of looking at an address arising out of a special occasion, and recorded by a shorthand writer. It has indeed been falsely assumed that Rufinus arbitrarily stuck together Basil's 'longer' and 'shorter' Rules (a later phase of the 'Asketikon'). **37** → Prol. 1–4. **38** Basil was an unquestioned figure in the eyes of the church hierarchy, as he was in those of the monks. Cassian also mentions Basil by name (Inst, Praef 55), as does the author of the VPJur (174). It is conceivable that the abbot of Montecassino took Byzantium into consideration. → Introd. 8. **39** VPJur 174. **40** Jerome (347–419/20) translated these Rules into Latin. Their influence can be felt in the writings of Cassian (d. 430), Caesarius of Arles (d. 542) and Benedict (→ 21,1–4; 38,5–9 etc.) **41** This 'liber' was translated by Jerome, together with the Pachomian writings. **42** His work 'De opere monachorum' (about 400)—on the manual labour of the monks—is important. **43** 'Praeceptum' according to the rule: 'Haec sunt, quae ut observetis praecipimus . . .' **44** Cf. RB 33,6 (lack of possessions); 34 (individual needs); 63,13 & 72,10 (love and fear); 64,11 (hating the vice and loving one's brother); 64,15 ('to be more loved than feared'). **45** On a visit to the Church of Rome in 212 Origen came to know the local presbyter Hippolytus (d. 235), a pupil of Irenaeus of Lyons (d. about 200), from whom a line leads back to his teacher, Polycarp of Smyrna (d. 22 Feb. 156). **46** The ascetic combat is seen in analogy to the 'struggle' of Jesus against evil and to the 'struggle' of the martyrs: → Prol. 2.3.28.29–32.40.45; 4,55–58; 5,10–13; 7,35–43; 24,3; 48,17–18; 49,6–7. **47** RM 11,62; → 4,51–54 (in Note 79). **48** → Prol. 4,22–27.29–32.41–47.48–49; 1,3–5; 4,62–73. **49** He continued to have influence through Didymus of Alexandria (d. 398) and Gregory the Miracle-Worker (d. about 270). The latter influenced the spirituality of Cappadocia up to Basil's day. **50** Log. prak., prol. **51** → 72,11 (Note 53). **52** The 'Institutiones' or 'Institutions of the Fathers', or perhaps 'of the monasteries', on the subject of the monastic way of life (in Egypt) and of the eight Cardinal Vices; the 'Conlationes' or 'Conferences of the

Fathers' about the teaching on spirituality of the hermits of Lower Egypt. **53** Cf. RB 42,5; 73,5; Benedict does not however mention the name 'Cassian', perhaps because of Cassian's teaching on grace, which did not concur with Augustine's and brought him some accusations. **54** Cf. Conl 1,23. **55** → Prol. 8–11.45–50; 1,2; 2,1–10.11–15. **56** → Prol. 28; 2,4–6.7–11; 4,41–50; 7,44–48; 58,1–4; 64,17–19; 68,1–3; .4–5; 71,1–4. **57** See Note 20 above .**58** Cf. RB 42,3; 73,5. **59** The author is Athanasius of Alexandria (d. 373). **60** This *Vita* was translated by the Scythian (Gothic) monk Dionysius Exiguus (d. about 550), who lived in Rome. **61** Translation by Rufinus of Aquileia (d. 410), who had personal experience of Eastern monasticism. **62** The author is Hilary of Arles (d. 449). **63** Benedict repeatedly shows himself impressed by Eastern monasticism and considers his own Western practice to be a levelling down: RB 18, 25 (number of psalms); 40,6 (consumption of wine). The Latin translation of the 'Sayings of the Fathers', with which Benedict was familiar, is based on Greek versions: the 'Historia Lausiaca' by Palladius (d. before 431); the 'Historia monachorum in Aegypto' (a description of a journey from about 400); the 'Apophthegmata Patrum' (a collection of the sayings of the Fathers, arranged in part systematically, in part by author). These sayings of the Fathers mostly sound pithy and powerful, occasionally naive or idealistic. **64** The Latin translation of the 'Sayings of the Fathers' (Verba seniorum) is the work of Deacon Pelagius and Subdeacon John (the later Popes Pelagius I, 556–561, and John III, 561–574), and was probably produced about 543–545. Benedict was familiar with this translation. **65** Cf. 73,1. **66** Dial 1,36. **67** Dial 2,8. **68** Dial 3,38. **69** Dial 2,36. **70** The Verona text of the Rule (eighth century) calls Benedict 'romensis'. **71** Procopius of Caesarea in Palestine (d. after 562), historiographer under Justinian I, accompanied the Eastern Roman army commander Belisarius (d. 565) in Italy. He mentions various Italian churchmen, but nowhere at all Benedict. (B. Steidle). **72** The gravity of the way of life of this province was proverbial (austeritas Sabina: Nursina durities).—Gregory I, in his Dialogues, shows that he is very well informed about the ecclesiastical conditions in the province of 'Valeria'; he often receives visits from there (according to tradition, he had relations there) and describes its bishops and monks with loving care. Gregory entrusted his own monastery at the 'Clivus scauri' to Abbot Valentio (d. about 583) from 'Valeria'. **73** The traditional dating of Benedict's birth (480) and death (547) is too early. **74** According to Gregory I (Dial 3,14–15), 'in the first years of the reign of the Goths' (Theoderic 493–526) the hermits Spes, Eutitius and Florentius lived in the province of 'Valeria', about 10 km from Norcia, in a parallel mountain valley (Valle Castoriana). Their lauras (caves for hermits are still to be found) develop into *cenobia*. Gregory imputes to these monks features that are also to be found in the life of Benedict: Florentius lives in a cave for three years; Eutitius evangelizes shepherds (Dial 3,15); Spes dies standing up in the oratory while the psalms are being sung, and his soul leaves him in the shape of a dove, which shows, it is said, with what a 'simple heart he served God' (Dial 4,8).—Local traditions speak of 'Syrian' monks, who immigrated into Umbria. Their oratories have an Eastern character. **75** Dial 2 prol. **76** Dial 2,3. This description is meant to show that, under an abbot like Benedict, Moses' people of the twelve tribes and the Church of Christ founded on the Apostles, are realized anew in the cenobitic life.—Since a grouping of monasteries is presupposed here, the 'Precepts of the Fathers' that are mentioned were previously taken to be the Rules of Pachomius. **77** In theory he ruled in the name of the Byzantine Emperor, in reality he ruled independently, in Ravenna. His interests and those of the Byzantines often ran counter to each other. **78** The Arians had their own bishops and churches, e.g. in Ravenna and Rome. The church of S. Agata dei Goti in Rome was taken over for Catholic worship only under Gregory I (d. 604). **79** → Prol. 48–49. **80** Scythian (Gothic) monks came to Rome in 519 in the matter of the 'theopaschite' controversy. They wanted to have the following sentence sung in the Trisagion: 'one of the Trinity suffered for us'. In Rome they could count on Dionysius Exiguus, a Scythian, but found no official support. They were regarded as over-zealous 'simplificateurs'. Cf. also Note 74 above. Pope Gregory tells of the ardent zeal of a Goth: → 31,3–7. **81** Theoderic had for instance Boethius and Senator Symmachus publicly executed. **82** → Introd. 4. **83** Boniface II had the clergy commit itself to the deacon Vigilius as his successor, but had to reverse that arrangement. → 64,1–6, Note 1. **84** However, he was able to achieve the dismissal of the Patriarch of Constantinople, Anthimus, who was sympathetic to the Monophysites. The latter was a favourite of the Empress Theodora. **85** Empress Theodora had letters forged in order to bring down Silverius. Through Vigilius she sought to achieve the rehabilitation of Anthimus and thus a condemnation of the Council of Chalcedon (451). Vigilius had his predecessor handed over to him and sent him into exile on the island of Ponza, where Silverius died a broken man. **86** Pope Vigilius condemned, admittedly 'while maintaining the reverence due to the Council of Chalcedon', the 'three chapters'; these were statements of the theologians Theodore of Mopsuestia, Theodoret of Cyprus and Ibas of Edessa, who had been justified by that Council. When a storm of outrage arose against the Pope, he, supported by his deacon, Pelagius, reversed the decision in a new proclamation. Compromised by the Emperor through the publication of a secret agreement, and abandoned by his deacon, Vigilius issued a fresh condemnation of the 'three chapters' (533). Dishonoured and despised by all, he died on the journey back to Italy. **87** → Introd. 4 (in Notes 48–49). **88** → Introd. 5, Note 64. **89** Gregory, Dial 2,15. **90** He also sought to get rid of the remains of paganism. Thus, he dissolved the philosophers' school in Athens in the year 529 (the traditional date of the founding of Montecassino). **91** In 546 and 549 the Ostrogoths under Totila reconquered Rome. The Byzantine commander Belisarius and his successor Narses were however finally victorious over the Goths in 553 in the battle at Mount Vesuvius against King Teja. **92** Cf. List of Keywords: 'Poverty (of the monastery)'. **93** See Note 86 above. **94** The Pope's generosity in almsgiving and a public profession of faith made him acceptable to the people. Against that, the dioceses of Northern Italy, which under Vigilius had broken with Rome, did not renew ecclesiastical communion with Pelagius I. The continuing schism resulted in the Milanese liturgy developing in its own special way. The Roman Missal preserved prayers composed by Pelagius. **95** → 64,1–6; Note 7. **96** Codex 529/534; Digests (533); Laws (535–565). **97** → 3,1–3, Note 3; 58,19–20, Note 95; 22,3, Note 3. **98** See Notes 74 & 80 above; → 9,5–7, Note 13; 11,6–10, in Note 7. **99** See Notes 18; 60; 63; 77; 80 above.—Gregory I mentions the monk Romanus, about whom no further information is given, who taught the young hermit Benedict and himself lived 'not far away in a monastery under the Rule of the Father Adeodatus' (Dial 2,1).—We are reminded too of the themes in Byzantine art: Christ as the central figure (or also the 'Crux gemmata'), often surrounded by angels (cf. RB 7,13.28: 19,6). **100** Dial 2,3. **101** Dial 2,17.35. **102** Dial 2,26 ('vir illustris'); 2,15.35 (bishops): 2,23 (nuns from well-to-do homes); Dial 2,20 (novice from upper class family). It seems also that Benedict was allowed to carry out his foundations on public land, in buildings of a former villa belonging to Nero (Subiaco) and on State land (Montecassino) (A. de Vogüé). **103** → 14,1–2; cf. RB 58,19. In the 'Rule of the Master' the relics of the saints of the oratory are not yet mentioned. **104** Dial 2,17. **105** Ibid. **106** G. Holzherr, *Regula Ferioli* (Einsiedeln 1961) 74–75. **107** RB 8–18; cf. especially RB 13,10: 'as the Roman Church sings them' (an invitation to the monks, who had recently settled in the Lateran, to conform to the local custom?) **108** → 8,0 (E. Manning). **109** Dial 2,36. **110** In I Reg 4:70 (→ 58,1–4). **111** The Venerandus letter (extant only in a copy of the 15th century) mentions the Rule ('regulam s. Benedicti abbatis romensis') for the monastery of Altaripa in the diocese of Albi (northeast of Toulouse). **112** In the monastery of Romainmôtier ('Romanum' or 'Romenum monasterium'), reformed by Abbot Waldebert (629–670), a pupil of Columban, St. Wandregisil, for instance, made the acquaintance of 'Benedictine' spirituality (A. Borias). Columban conducted a correspondence with Gregory I, and could have received the Rule from him. **113** A mention of the 'Regula Sancti Benedicti' alone (without another Rule) is found in the records of a 'council' held by St. Leodegar, the bishop of Autun, 663–668 (No. 15). **114** Rule of Donatus of Besançon (660–665): Rule of Chrodegang of Metz (742–766). **115** There is evidence that the Rule existed in earlier times up there in Northumberland. Wilfrid of York, born in 634, had been in Rome and spent a longer period in Lyons; he was enthusiastic about everything 'Roman'. Around 660 he was Abbot of Ripon and introduced the Rule up there. He also preached down in the South of England, where he perhaps made it known as well. His friend, Benedict Biscop from Northumberland, was with Wilfrid in Rome in 653, and spent two years in Lérins (665–667). He returned to England with the Greek monk Theodore and the African, Hadrian (previously Abbot near Naples). Theodore became Archbishop and Hadrian Abbot in Canterbury. Biscop founded the monasteries of Wearmouth and Jarrow, where the Rule of Benedict was observed. The Codex Oxoniensis, which we have already mentioned, was produced in his time. It contains the 'interpolated text'. In a codex from Verona, also with the 'interpolated' version, the Rule is ascribed to the 'Roman' (romense), Benedict (cf. also Note 111 above).—It was under Wilfrid in Ripon that Willibrord (d. 739) was educated, who went as a missionary to France. For a time, Boniface (d. 754), later Apostle of the Germans, worked under him. The Anglo-Saxon monks spread the Rule of Benedict on the Continent (RB 1980). **116** Historia Langobardorum 4,17; 6,40; **117** Benedict of Aniane organized a collection of pre- and post-Benedictine Rules (Codex regularum) and a Rule concordance (Concordia regularum), in order to show that the Rule of Benedict was in harmony with the other monastic Rules. **118** RB Prol. 40–50 (with the definition of the monastery as a 'school'!—taken over from the Rule of the Master).

Rhine

JURA
MOUNTAINS
Reichenau
St Maurice
Lyons
Milan
Uzès
Arles
Lérins
Marseilles
Nursia
Subiaco
Rome
Montecassino
Terracina
Byzantium
Caesarea
Antioch
CHALCIS
Hippo
Carthage
Jerusalem
Alexandria
DESERT OF
SCETIS
Nile
THEBAID
Tabennisi

PROLOGUE

1 Jan
2 May
1 Sept
1 HEAR AND HEED, my son, the master's TEACHING
and BOW THE EAR of your heart.
Willingly take to yourself the loving FATHER'S ADVICE
and fulfil it in what you do.

Cf. Prov 1:8;4:1,20;
6:20; Ecclus 6:35;
51:21; Deut 6:4;
Mk 12:29

2 Thus, by laborious OBEDIENCE
will you return to him,
from whom you have withdrawn by idle DISOBEDIENCE.

Cf. Gen 3:17; Rom 5:19

3 To you my word is now directed, whoever you are,
if you renounce self-will
and grasp the tough, shining WEAPONS of obedience,
in order TO SERVE the true King, Christ, the Lord.

Cf. Rom 13:12;
2 Cor 6:7;
2 Tim 2:3–4,5;
Eph 6:13–17

4 First of all, with insistent prayer,
beg that he would bring to completion
every good that you set out to do.

5 Now that he has NUMBERED us with loving-kindness
AMONG HIS SONS,
he should never have to grieve over our bad lives.

Cf. Wisd 4:8;5:5;
Rom 8:15: Eph
1:5; 1 Jn 3:1–2

6 Rather we must obey him always
with his gifts which he has implanted in us,
so that, as an ANGERED Father, he will not some day
disINHERIT his sons;

Cf. Eph 2:3; 5:6;
Rom 8:17

7 still less, as a severe Lord,
grown angry by our misdeeds,
deliver us as GOOD–FOR–NOTHING SERVANTS
to eternal punishment,
because we did not wish to follow him to glory.

Cf. Mt 18:32;
25:30; Lk 19:22

2 Jan
3 May
2 Sept
8 Let us then at long last get up
because Scripture is calling us up with the words:
THE HOUR HAS COME TO RISE FROM SLEEP.

Rom 13:11

9 Let us open our eyes to the divine LIGHT,
and with startled ears
let us listen to what the divine VOICE is calling
  out every day,
urging us:

Cf. Ps 119:105;
2 Pet 1:17,19; Jn 8:12;
Ex 19:18–19;
Mt 17:5

10 TODAY, IF YOU SHOULD HEAR HIS VOICE,
HARDEN NOT YOUR HEARTS.

Ps 95:8

11 And furthermore: HE WHO HAS EARS TO HEAR, LET HIM HEAR   Rev 2:7;
   WHAT THE SPIRIT IS SAYING TO THE CHURCHES.   cf. Mt 11:15

12 And what is he saying? COME, O SONS, LISTEN TO ME,   Ps 34:12
   I WILL TEACH YOU THE FEAR OF THE LORD.

13 RUN WHILE YOU HAVE THE LIGHT of life,   Jn 12:35
   SO THAT THE DARKNESS of death MAY NOT OVERTAKE YOU.

3 Jan 14 The Lord proclaims this to the concourse of people,   Cf. Mt 20:1–6;
4 May   where he is looking for his WORKMAN, and he continues   1 Cor 3:9
3 Sept   further:

15 WHO IS THE MAN, WHO LOVES LIFE,   Ps 34:13;
   AND WANTS TO SEE GOOD DAYS?   cf. 1 Pet 3:10

16 If you hear this and answer 'I',
   then God says to you:

17 If you wish to have true and ETERNAL LIFE,   Cf. Mt 19:29;
   THEN KEEP YOUR TONGUE FROM EVIL   Ps 34:14–15
   AND YOUR LIPS FROM UTTERING LIES;
   TURN FROM EVIL AND DO GOOD,
   SEEK PEACE AND PURSUE IT.

18 If you do this,   Is 58:9; 65:24;
   MY EYES shall rest UPON YOU,   Ps 34:16
   and my ears shall hear your prayers,
   and BEFORE YOU CALL TO ME, I SHALL SAY: HERE I AM.

19 What sound could be sweeter, beloved brothers,   Ps 95:7; Jn 3:29;
   than this VOICE OF THE LORD, who is inviting us?   10:3–4,16; Rev 3:20

20 See, in his loving-kindness   Ps 16:11; Prov 6:23
   the Lord points out to us the PATH TO LIFE.

4 Jan 21 LET US GIRD ourselves then with FAITH,   Cf. 1 Thess 2:12;
5 May   let us fulfil our duty with all fidelity§   Is 11:5;
4 Sept   and, under the guidance of the GOSPEL   Eph 6:14–15;
           let us step forward on the ways of the Lord,   Lk 12:35;
           so that we may be given to SEE him,   Mt 5:8;
           who has CALLED us INTO HIS KINGDOM.   Ex 12:11

22 If we wish TO LIVE IN THE TENT of his kingdom,   Cf. Ps 15:1;
   we must hasten ahead with good deeds;   Lev 23:33; 26:11;
   otherwise we shall never get there.   Heb 9:11

§   The oldest MS. (the so-called 'interpolated' version) inserts here (instead of 'under
    the guidance of the Gospel') Eph. 6:15:
    'AS SHOES LET US PUT ON READINESS TO FIGHT FOR THE GOSPEL OF PEACE.'

23 But let us question the Lord with the prophet: Ps 15:1
LORD, WHO SHALL BE A GUEST IN YOUR TENT?
WHO MAY LINGER ON YOUR HOLY HILL?

24 Let us hear, brothers, what the Lord answers to this
question, as he points out to us the way to his tent.

25 He says: THE MAN OF BLAMELESS LIFE,   Ps 15:2–3
WHO DOES WHAT IS RIGHT;

26 WHO SPEAKS THE TRUTH FROM HIS HEART
AND DOES NOT SLANDER WITH HIS TONGUE;

27 WHO NEVER WRONGS A FRIEND
AND TELLS NO TALES AGAINST HIS NEIGHBOUR;

28 Who expels from the field of VISION of his HEART
the EVIL ONE, the devil, who is whispering something
to him, together with his suggestions,   Ps 15:4;
and BRINGS HIM TO NOTHING;   cf. Ps 137:9;
       1 Cor 10:4;
who GRASPS such devil's BROOD of thoughts   cf. Eph 1:18
and SHATTERS them on CHRIST;

29 who FEARS THE LORD   Ps 15:4; cf. Jn 15:5
and does not boast of his faithful service,
but rather believes that everything good
that is peculiarly his own,
exceeds his own POSSIBILITY and is the Lord's work;

30 such men GLORIFY THE LORD, who is AT WORK IN THEM,   Lk 1:46;
and they say with the prophet: 2:20;17:15;
       Mt 16:20; 1 Cor 12:6;
NOT TO US, LORD, NOT TO US,   Ps 115:1
BUT TO YOUR NAME GIVE THE GLORY.

31 Thus even the Apostle Paul in his teaching   1 Cor 15:10
did not ascribe anything to himself;
he says: BY THE GRACE OF GOD I AM, WHAT I AM.

32 And once again he says: 2 Cor 10:17;
IF A MAN MUST BOAST, LET HIM BOAST OF THE LORD.   cf. Jer 9:22–23

       Mt 7:24–25

5 Jan 33 That is why the Lord says in the Gospel:
6 May HE WHO HEARS THESE WORDS OF MINE AND ACTS ON THEM,
5 Sept I SHALL COMPARE HIM TO A WISE MAN,
WHO BUILT HIS HOUSE ON ROCK.

34 THE FLOODS CAME,
THE WINDS BLEW AND BEAT UPON THAT HOUSE,
BUT IT DID NOT FALL; IT WAS FOUNDED UPON ROCK.

35 WITH THESE WORDS   Mt 7:28
THE LORD CONCLUDES HIS DISCOURSE.

Now, day by day, he is waiting for us
to respond with deeds
to these holy urgings of his.

36 That is why   Cf. Heb 12:15
the days of this life are prolonged for us
as a reprieve to reform our evil ways—

37 the Apostle says so: DO YOU NOT KNOW   Rom 2:4
THAT GOD'S PATIENCE IS URGING YOU TO REPENT?

38 For in his goodness the Lord says: Ezek 33:11
I DESIRE NOT THE DEATH OF THE WICKED MAN,
BUT THAT HE RETURN AND LIVE.

6 Jan 39 Brothers, we have now asked the Lord,
7 May   who may live in his tent,
6 Sept   and we have learned what is demanded of a dweller;
if only we fulfil the duties of one who is to live in it.§

40 We must therefore get heart and body ready
for service under holy obedience
to these orders.

41 But because our NATURE does not have enough   Cf. Eph 2:3;
    strength for this,   Rom 3:24
let us ask the Lord,
to send us the help of his GRACE.

42 If we wish to escape punishment in the realm of death,
and attain to everlasting life,

43 we must, at present—   Cf. 2 Cor 5:6;
while our time lasts,   Jn 12:35
AS LONG AS WE ARE IN this BODY,
and can still fulfil all this IN THE LIGHT of this life—

44 HASTEN with rapid steps   Cf. 1 Cor 9:24:
and do what will help us for eternity.   2 Tim 4:7

7 Jan 45 We intend therefore   Cf. Mt 11:29
8 May   to found a SCHOOL for the LORD's service.
7 Sept

46 In its structures,   Cf. Mt 11:30
we hope to arrange nothing harsh, NOTHING OPPRESSIVE.

47 But if for some good reason
the requirements exacted be a trifle austere
in order to rectify faults and safeguard love,

§   In the oldest MS. (the so-called 'interpolated' version) the Prologue ends here with
the aphorism: we shall be heirs of the kingdom of heaven.

48 you should not, disconcerted by sudden fright,   Cf. Acts 16:17;
   shrink back from the WAY OF SALVATION,   Mt 7:14;
   which cannot but be NARROW at its opening.

49 But as for him who is who is making progress   Cf. Ps 119:32;
   in the religious life and in faith,   cf. 1 Pet 1:8
   HIS HEART OPENS WIDE,
   and with the JOY THAT IS TOO GREAT FOR WORDS
   and which comes from LOVE,
   HE RUNS AHEAD IN THE WAY OF GOD'S COMMANDMENTS.

50 So let us never let go of his instructions,   Cf. Phil 2:8;
   but rather HOLD FAST to his TEACHING in the monastery   Acts 2:42;
         2 Jn 9;
   UNTIL DEATH and SHARE in patience IN CHRIST'S   1 Pet 4:13;
         Col 1:24:
   SUFFERINGS SO THAT we may ALSO merit to have a share   Rom 8:17
   in HIS kingdom.
   Amen.
   (End of the Prologue)

INCIPIT PROLOGUS

¹OBSCULTA, O FILI, PRAECEPTA MAGISTRI, ET INCLINA AUREM CORDIS TUI ET ADMONITIONEM PII PATRIS LIBENTER EXCIPE ET EFFICACITER CONPLE, ²UT AD EUM PER OBOEDIENTIAE LABOREM REDEAS, A QUO PER INOBOEDIENTIAE DESIDIAM RECESSERAS. ³AD TE ERGO NUNC MIHI SERMO DIRIGITUR, QUISQUIS ABRENUNTIANS PROPRIIS VOLUNTATIBUS, DOMINO CHRISTO VERO REGI MILITATURUS, OBOE-DIENTIAE FORTISSIMA ATQUE PRAECLARA ARMA SUMIS. ⁴IN PRIMIS, UT QUIDQUID AGENDUM INCHOAS BONUM, AB EO PERFICI INSTANTISSIMA ORATIONE DEPOSCAS, ⁵UT QUI NOS IAM IN FILIORUM DIGNATUS EST NUMERO CONPUTARE, NON DEBET ALIQUANDO DE MALIS ACTIBUS NOSTRIS CONTRISTARI. ⁶ITA ENIM EI OMNI TEMPORE DE BONIS SUIS IN NOBIS PARENDUM EST UT NON SOLUM IRATUS PATER SUOS NON ALIQUANDO FILIOS EXHEREDET, ⁷SED NEC UT METUENDUS DOMINUS INRITATUS A MALIS NOSTRIS, UT NEQUISSIMOS SERVOS PERPETUAM TRADAT AD POENAM QUI EUM SEQUI NOLUERINT AD GLORIAM. ⁸EXURGAMUS ERGO TANDEM ALIQUANDO EXCI-TANTE NOS SCRIPTURA AC DICENTE: HORA EST IAM NOS DE SOMNO SURGERE, ⁹ET APERTIS OCULIS NOSTRIS AD DEIFICUM LUMEN ADTONITIS AURIBUS AUDIAMUS DIVINA COTIDIE CLAMANS QUID NOS ADMONET VOX DICENS: ¹⁰HODIE SI VOCEM EIUS AUDIERITIS, NOLITE OBDURARE CORDA VESTRA. ¹¹ET ITERUM: QUI HABET AURES AUDIENDI AUDIAT, QUID SPIRITUS DICAT ECCLESIIS. ¹²ET QUID DICIT? VENITE, FILII, AUDITE ME; TIMOREM DOMINI DOCEBO VOS. ¹³CURRITE DUM LUMEN VITAE HABETIS, NE TENEBRAE MORTIS VOS CONPREHENDANT. ¹⁴ET QUAERENS DOMINUS IN MULTI-TUDINE POPULI CUI HAEC CLAMAT OPERARIUM SUUM, ITERUM DICIT: ¹⁵QUIS EST HOMO QUI VULT VITAM ET CUPIT VIDERE DIES BONOS? ¹⁶QUOD SI TU AUDIENS RESPONDEAS: EGO, DICIT TIBI DEUS: ¹⁷SI VIS HABERE VERAM ET PERPETUAM VITAM, PROHIBE LINGUAM TUAM A MALO ET LABIA TUA NE LOQUANTUR DOLUM; DEVERTE A MALO ET FAC BONUM, INQUIRE PACEM ET SEQUERE EAM. ¹⁸ET CUM HAEC FECERITIS, OCULI MEI SUPER VOS ET AURES MEAS AD PRECES VESTRAS, ET ANTEQUAM ME INVOCETIS, DICAM VOBIS: ECCE ADSUM. ¹⁹QUID DULCIUS AB HAC VOCE DOMINI INVITANTIS NOS, FRATRES CARISSIMI? ²⁰ECCE PIETATE SUA DEMONSTRAT NOBIS DOMINUS VIAM VITAE. ²¹SUCCINCTIS ERGO FIDE VEL OBSERVANTIA BONORUM ACTUUM LUMBIS NOSTRIS (COD. O: . . . ET CALCIATIS IN PRAEPARATIONE EVANGELII PACIS

PEDIBUS PERGAMUS . . .), PER DUCATUM EVANGELII PERGAMUS ITINERA EIUS, UT MEREAMUR EUM QUI NOS VOCAVIT IN REGNUM SUUM VIDERE. ²¹IN CUIUS REGNI TABERNACULO SI VOLUMUS HABITARE, NISI ILLUC BONIS ACTIBUS CURRITUR, MINIME PERVENITUR, ²³SED INTERROGEMUS CUM PROPHETA DOMINUM DICENTES EI: DOMINE, QUIS HABITABIT IN TABERNACULO TUO, AUT QUIS REQUIESCIT IN MONTE SANCTO TUO? ²⁴POST HANC INTERROGATIONEM, FRATRES, AUDIAMUS DOMINUM RESPONDEN-TEM ET OSTENDENTEM NOBIS VIAM IPSIUS TABERNACULI, ²⁵DICENS: QUI INGREDITUR SINE MACULA ET OPERATUR IUSTITIAM; ²⁶QUI LOQUITUR VERITATEM IN CORDE SUO, QUI NON EGIT DOLUM IN LINGUA SUA; ²⁷QUI NON FECIT PROXIMO SUO MALUM, QUI OBPROBRIUM NON ACCEPIT ADVERSUS PROXIMUM SUUM; ²⁸QUI MALIGNUM DIABOLUM ALIQUA SUADENTEM SIBI CUM IPSA SUASIONE SUA A CONSPECTIBUS CORDIS SUI RESPUENS DEDUXIT AD NIHILUM, ET PARVULOS COGITATOS EIUS TENUIT ET ADLISIT AD CHRISTUM; ²⁹QUI TIMENTES DOMINUM DE BONA OBSERVANTIA SUA NON SE REDDUNT ELATOS, SED IPSA IN SE BONA NON A SE POSSE, SED A DOMINO FIERI EXISTIMANTES, ³⁰OPERANTEM IN SE DOMINUM MAGNIFICANT, ILLUD CUM PROPHETA DICENTES: NON NOBIS, DOMINE, NON NOBIS, SED NOMINI TUO DA GLORIAM; ³¹SICUT NEC PAULUS APOSTOLUS DE PRAEDICATIONE SUA SIBI ALIQUID INPUTAVIT DICENS: GRATIA DEI SUM ID QUOD SUM; ³²ET ITERUM IPSE DICIT: QUI GLORIATUR, IN DOMINO GLORIETUR. ³³UNDE ET DOMINUS IN EVANGELIO AIT: QUI AUDIT VERBA MEA HAEC ET FACIT EA, SIMILABO EUM VIRO SAPIENTI QUI AEDIFICAVIT DOMUM SUAM SUPER PETRAM; ³⁴VENERUNT FLUMINA, FLAVERUNT VENTI, ET INPEGERUNT IN DOMUM ILLAM, ET NON CECIDIT, QUIA FUNDATA ERAT SUPER PETRAM. ³⁵HAEC CONPLENS DOMINUS EXPECTAT NOS COTIDIE HIS SUIS SANCTIS MONITIS FACTIS NOS RESPON-DERE DEBERE. ³⁶IDEO NOBIS PROPTER EMENDATIONEM MALORUM HUIUS VITAE DIES AD INDUTIAS RELAXANTUR, ³⁷DICENTE APOSTOLO: AN NESCIS QUIA PATIENTIA DEI AD PAENITENTIAM TE ADDUCIT? ³⁸NAM PIUS DOMINUS DICIT: NOLO MORTEM PECCA-TORIS, SED CONVERTATUR ET VIVAT. ³⁹CUM ERGO INTERROGASSEMUS DOMINUM, FRATRES, DE HABITATORE TABERNACULI EIUS; AUDIVIMUS HABITANDI PRAECEPTUM; SED SI CONPLEAMUS HABITATORIS OFFICIUM (COD. O: . . . ERIMUS HEREDES REGNI CAELORUM. [END OF THE PROL.]). ⁴⁰ERGO PRAEPARANDA SUNT CORDA NOSTRA ET CORPORA SANCTAE PRAECEPTORUM OBOEDIENTIAE MILITANDA, ⁴¹ET QUOD MINUS HABET IN NOS NATURA POSSIBILE, ROGEMUS DOMINUM, UN GRATIAE SUAE IUBEAT NOBIS ADIUTORIUM MINISTRARE. ⁴²ET SI, FUGIENTES GEHENNAE POENAS, AD VITAM VOLUMUS PERVENIRE PERPETUAM, ⁴³DUM ADHUC VACAT ET IN HOC CORPORE SUMUS ET HAEC OMNIA PER HANC LUCIS VITAM VACAT IMPLERE, ⁴⁴CURRENDUM ET AGENDUM EST MODO QUOD IN PERPETUO NOBIS EXPEDIAT. ⁴⁵CONSTITUENDA EST ERGO NOBIS DOMINICI SCOLA SERVITII. ⁴⁶IN QUA INSTITUTIONE NIHIL ASPERUM, NIHIL GRAVE NOS CONSTITUTUROS SPERAMUS; ⁴⁷SED ET SI QUID PAULULUM RESTRICTIUS, DICTANE AEQUITATIS RATIONE, PROPTER EMENDATIONEM VITIORUM VEL CONSERVATIONEM CARITATIS PROCESSERIT, ⁴⁸NON ILICO PAVORE PERTERRITUS REFUGIAS VIAM SALUTIS, QUAE NON EST NISI ANGUSTO INITIO INCIPIENDA. ⁴⁹PROCESSU VERO CONVERSATIONIS ET FIDEI, DILATATO CORDE INENARRABILI DILECTIONIS DULCEDINE CURRITUR VIA MANDATORUM DEI, ⁵⁰UT AB IPSIUS NUMQUAM MAGISTERIO DISCEDENTES, IN EIUS DOCTRINAM USQUE AD MORTEM IN MONASTERIO PERSEVERANTES PASSIONIBUS CHRISTI PER PATIENTIAM PARTICIPEMUR, UT ET REGNO EIUS MEREAMUR ESSE CONSORTES. AMEN. EXPLICIT PROLOGUS.

COMMENTARY ON PROLOGUE

I **a.** The attempt has often been made to solve the puzzle, who the 'Master' might be who is mentioned at the beginning. The author deliberately expresses himself indeterminately. 'These words stem from me, but they are drawn from a divine source. I am communicating to you no new teaching, but rather what I have learned from the Fathers.' A writing attributed to Basil (d.379), which Benedict follows at the beginning of his Prologue, gives this information;[1] it puts on record, that the Rule does not intend to be a new creation, rather it is drawn from *Sacred Scripture*, in the way in which the latter has been interpreted by the *Fathers* and transferred to an ascetic life.[2]

b. Benedict begins emphatically with 'Hear and heed!' He is addressing a 'Hearer of the Word'. The Rule and what it describes must appear to be a creation of the Word. Especially in the Prologue Sacred Scripture enters on the scene, personified; it 'awakens', 'calls' and is perceived as the 'voice' of the Lord who invites.[3] Horsiesi (d.*c*.380) also begins his 'book' on Pachomian cenobitic life with the prophetic word:' Hear the commandments of life, O Israel'.[4] That is the beginning of the most important prayer of a devout Jew, the 'Sh'ma Israel': 'Hear, O Israel, the Lord, our God, is one Lord.'[5] An intensive 'listening' ought to correspond to this summons. For that, the 'heart' must 'bow'.

In these introductory words the fundamental attitude of humility is broached.[6] At the same time it becomes evident that the Rule directs itself to the whole man, body and soul, or in the biblical meaning, to the 'heart', that is to the total person and its conscience. One may say that the Rule wishes to develop a *'spirituality of the heart'*.[7]

c. Benedict is not satisfied with feelings, he urges on to *deeds*. The seed of the Word must bear fruit. Like every Christian the monk ought to live by the Word of God, but he should implement this Word in a particularly intensive manner.—With the 'teachings' or 'commands' of the 'Master'[8] attention is focused on the Rule itself.

2 a. In the first two sentences of the Prologue Benedict pithily sums up the 'Prologue' of the 'Rule of the Master'. In the 'Master' a 'teacher' calls upon the 'listener', urging him to listen to God's Word from this 'Scripture' and obey it, namely at the *'parting of the ways in one's own heart'*[9] to choose between the way 'to the Lord' or the way 'to ruin'. Benedict speaks in a concrete way of the 'return' out of estrangement from God. Listening and obeying are presupposed. Obedience is at first an ascetical 'labour'[10] for man; it is only towards the end of the Rule that Benedict characterizes obedience as something 'good' (bonum). Adam's guilt brings in its train first of all 'toil in the sweat of your face'.[11] 'The ancient Fathers used to say: "In those who are beginning monastic life, God seeks above all else a laborious obedience." '[12] Ancient monasticism did not pride itself on this 'toil' or ascetical working on oneself, to which listening to God leads. 'One of the ancient Fathers said: Without humility all toil is vain. Humility is the precursor of love'.[13]

The opposite of ascetical 'exertion' is 'sloth' or *'Acedia'* namely the lack of a sense for spirituality, i.e. a coldness towards religion.[14]

b. But the liberation from the human entanglement in guilt is not awaited from asceticism, but from Christ, the second Adam, to whom we must turn.[15] *Obedience* (hypakoe) to him leads to righteousness. Man must be 'obedient from the heart to the teaching'[16] which Christ proclaims. From this starting point Benedict develops his spirituality of the heart.[17]

3 a. *Renunciation* of a sterile introverted concern with self, and an acceptance of Christ, shed light on the deeper meaning of asceticism. It can only be understood from the attachment to this person: Jesus Christ. It is the personal

attachment to Jesus, and not doctrines, norms or practices, which gives enthusiasm for the following of Christ or for asceticism. As Benedict hints with controlled enthusiasm, this relationship goes far beyond the bonds of a soldier to his 'king'. Basil wrote: 'In this world a soldier is always prepared and willing to obey an order, wherever he is sent. He will not dare to excuse himself on account of his wife or children. All the more will a soldier of Christ not let himself be detained by anything from obeying the order of his king. A soldier of this world goes to war against a visible foe. But against you an invisible enemy will never cease to do battle.'[18]

The image which Benedict adopts of military service and of fighting for Christ and against the power of the Evil One stems from the Apostle Paul.[19] It announces the transfer of the outward, bloodstained battle of the martyrs to the *inner front*. The watchword which the martyr used before his judge is still valid: 'I serve Christ, the true King!' There is present unaltered in Benedict the outlook of Origen (d.253): 'Within yourself you must wage war. Inwardly there stands that wretched building which has to be pulled down. The enemy proceeds out of your heart.'[20]

b. Benedict's sentences also however summarize the *baptismal catechesis* of the 'Master'[21]. This stems from a spiritual tract entitled 'An account of the warfare of the heart' (actus militiae cordis) and which was in circulation in Southern Gaul about 440. If such a baptismal catechesis, which originally was intended for 'Christians', now forms the basis of monastic spirituality, then for the Master and Benedict the monk is simply a 'Christian'. In this baptismal catechesis the 'gracious voice' of the Lord invites to the 'refreshing fountain' of baptism those born of Eve or 'Mother Earth', who, 'burdened' with all the guilt of their father Adam, are going astray on the paths of a 'life in exile'. There, in the 'renunciation' of sin they free themselves of a 'deadly burden',[22] and newly-born of Christ they find in him a 'father', and in the 'law of Christ', i.e. in grace mediated by the Church, they find a supportive 'mother'. Benedict adopts this theology with the words about 'laborious obedience' and 'renunciation', which suggest the monk's profession—which, for its part, was seen as an analogy of baptism.[23] The baptismal renunciation of the 'pomp' of the Evil One is embodied in ascetical renunciation.[24]

c. This 'renunciation' is explained by Basil (d.379) in a positive way and wholly with New Testament words: 'He for whom *out of love for Christ* the whole world is crucified and who is himself crucified to the world, how can he make himself a slave to the problems and pressures of this world, since the Lord instructs him to deny himself for love of him'.[25] Benedict's mentor Cassian (d.430) wrote his works for those who 'renounce' (renuntiantes).[26] He systematizes 'the tradition of the Fathers combined with the authority of Scripture' and speaks of renunciation: 1. as the forgoing of money and property, 2. as a change of one's former lifestyle with its addictions, 3. as a change of direction from things present and material to things future and invisible.[27] The decision for Christ thus appears as a genuine alternative. In the radicalism, which Cassian describes as 'renunciation', it is indeed a matter of free choice, out of enthusiasm for Christ, and it is not obligatory on all Christians (a point on which Cassian is silent).

4 In the 'Rule of the Master' an explanation of the Lord's Prayer follows on the baptismal catechesis.[28] Benedict in this passage calls in a few words for prayer that precedes all activity. Before the summons to asceticism, he shows that the *grace of Christ* must carry all our striving.[29] Christ is not only the Lord who allots the tasks, but also the supportive Father. The formulation itself has a Semi-Pelagian, not an Augustinian ring: Man begins, God completes. But the controversy on grace is long over. So Benedict uses a formula close to practice: Make an effort, and God will help! Origen (d.253), Cassian (d.430), Caesarius (d.542) and the Fathers of Lérins expressed themselves in a similar manner. A theological reflection on 'prevenient' grace does not come within Benedict's purview.[30] He is perhaps influenced here by Basil's 'Admonition', the thinking of which he certainly shares: 'Do not ask, as it were, on the basis of your own merits; and when you yourself are conscious of a good deed, conceal it! If you are silent, then God will compensate you in many ways . . . Whatever work you begin, call first of all on the Lord, and do not cease from thanking him, when it is accomplished.'[31] Man is aware of his limitations; he waits for God to enable him to step out of such limitations.

5–7 Here begins a *psalm commentary*[33] taken word for word from the 'Rule of the Master'.[32] The plural 'we' of community takes the place of the inviting 'thou' form. At the outset there stands the theme of divine sonship. It recalls the 'love of God' which 'dwells in our hearts', the Spirit 'who makes us sons', 'heirs of God and fellow heirs with Christ'.[34] The theme of judgement forms the other side of the coin. According to Basil (d.379) we become our own judgement: 'If we refuse God's love . . . we shall inescapably fall under his anger[35] . . . No worse punishment can befall us, than to alienate ourselves from God's love.'[36] Biblical sequences of thought, strikingly similar to those of our Prologue are to be found in Irenaeus (d.*c*.220): 'Just as among men, disobedient sons disowned by the fathers, are still their sons according to nature, but no longer according to law, since they no longer inherit from their natural parents, in the same way those who do not obey God, will be disowned by him, and cease to be his sons. Therefore they can receive no inheritance from him.'[37]

8–11 a. The author depicts with many variations the biblical call to *watchfulness*. It has to strike 'ears' and 'heart'. While the author usually prefers phrases like 'every day', 'at all times', 'always', 'in every place', here he situates God's claim in 'today'. Benedict has purposely inserted this passage[38] into the 'Master's' text. Yet it has to remain clear, that we accept the call freely: 'He who has ears . . .'. 'Harden not your hearts.'
b. It is above all Eastern spirituality which repeatedly warns of the 'hardening of the heart', of a 'brittleness' or 'sclerosis' of the heart, that is of *deficient sensitivity*. But the Eastern Fathers were aware too of a remedy: 'Abbot Poimen was asked by someone about hardness of heart. The venerable father answered and spoke: water is by nature soft, stone on the contrary hard. But when the water drips continually on a stone, it hollows it out. So too, God's Word is delicate and mild, our heart on the contrary hard. Yet whoever hears the Word of God frequently and reflects on it, makes space within his heart for the fear of God, so that it can enter in.'[39]
c. A genuine inner sensitivity to the Lord's voice is necessary 'today'.[40] Here it becomes the *consoling message of the Spirit* to the 'Churches'.[41] The

communities, the local Churches, are thereby addressed. The monastery sees itself as an ecclesial community.[42]

d. To listening to God's Word there corresponds the *contemplation* of the divine light; there are echoes of Johannine theology at this point.[43] The statements about light stand here at the beginning of a psalm commentary, which alludes to baptism.[44] The Church has seen the 'light' in God's Word, but also has always understood baptism as illumination with the light of Christ.[45] The double theme of listening to God's voice, and contemplation of a divine light is especially familiar to Eastern mysticism. It starts from the divine appearances on Sinai and on Thabor[46] with their outward manifestations which produce simultaneously awe and fascination: light, the shining cloud, thunder, the voice exhorting to 'listen'.[47] This revelation of God in light and word now takes place in the 'heart'. Origen (d.253) explains it thus: 'That is sound teaching, that man himself cannot be the true teacher of virtue. 'He who teaches man wisdom', so it is said in the psalms, is none other than God. But God teaches by shining into the soul of him who is learning from him, and illuminates the mind with his own Word. And even when just men teach us, . . . it is in fact God who through them teaches us. Understanding itself and the opening of our heart to the reception of the divine teaching take place through divine grace.'[48] Irenaeus of Lyons (d.c.202) wrote: 'There is only one way; it leads all who see on high together, enlightened by the heavenly light.'[49] A glance at the Prologue of John's Gospel on the incarnation of the Word, which is the light that enlightens every man,[50] reveals the background of this theology.

e. Basil (d.379), in a Johannine way of looking at things, experiences not only the divine teaching, but especially the love between God and man as an indescribable inner light: 'I experience the *love of God* in a quite ineffable way. It can more easily be experienced than expressed. It is an indescribable light. If my speech wished to quote the comparison with lightning or thunder, the ear would not be able to bear it, to assimilate it. If you compare a blinding flash of light, the clear shining of the moon, the sunshine, all these are dark and gloomier than deepest night compared to this glory . . . With our bodily eyes we do not see this splendour, but soul and mind contemplate it. When this splendour permeates the soul and mind of saints, it drives deep into them the burning impulse to love it . . . "When shall I come and behold the face of God? My soul thirsts for God, the living God." '[51]

f. We contemplate then the divine light in the sacraments of faith, in which Christ addresses us and encounters us visibly under signs. We contemplate this light in the teaching of the Gospel and experience it in the gift of divine love.—The Old Testament psalms and 'prophets', for whom the author has a predilection, are to be read in this light. He himself speaks in the *language of imagery used by the Bible*, not in an abstract theoretical fashion. Thus he stimulates meditation. From the literal sense, from the images and parables of Scripture, we ought to rise up to the knowledge of the deeper realities of the faith and to the loving contemplation of God. A superficial glance easily overlooks the mystical depth of many texts of the Rule. According to Evagrius (d.399)[52] and Cassian (d.430), one should not pass on the holy doctrine indiscriminately to everyone; from many 'the secrets of the spiritual sense are to be veiled'.[53]

12–13   **a.** The psalm commentary expounds first of all *Psalm 34*, which used to be freely availed of in addresses to candidates for baptism, and which was also the favourite Communion chant of the ancient Church: 'Come, O sons, listen . . . O taste and see . . . and be radiant . . .'.[54] As is often the case in the Rule, the voice of the Lord who speaks here, is the voice of Christ. He calls and invites. Now in the psalm he is the 'Lord'. In him the God of the Old Testament is now present. To him the Christians pray with the words of the psalm, even though in a veiled manner. This view propagated by Origen, was treasured above all in monastic circles (B. Fischer). The 'Light' which divides from 'darkness' is Christ.[55]

b. When touched by God's Word, a person experiences 'fear' as a first reaction: *perplexity* about his inadequacy, his limitations and his guilt; anguish in face of the 'darkness', in which any sense of direction is lacking, and in face of a meaningless 'death'. Nevertheless this slavish fear[56] turns into reverence before the God who is holy. It leads to purification of the heart.[57]

14–15   God wills the salvation of man. He seeks him out, offers him *life and happiness*. He chooses him as an associate in the work of salvation:[58] in the work on his own person, and in the service of others.

16–17   The change from the plural to the singular implies that one is personally struck by the Word of 'God', which Christ directs to all. The response is a free and personal '*I*'. Whoever seeks the final meaning of life and its fulfilment in the beyond, ought never to overlook the demands of justice in relation to others. These demands are the pre-requisites of *peace*, of which the Rule often speaks,[59] in connection with which it often mentions 'peace and love' in one breath.[60] 'Seeking after peace' leads to 'love', which is named as the goal at the end of the Prologue,[61] similarly at the end of the chapter on the Tools of Good Works,[62] at the end of the chapter on Humility[63] and at the end of the whole Rule.[64] Seeking for 'peace' is in the last resort identical with 'seeking for God':[65] the monk's goal.

18–20   The inner experience of God's nearness precedes prayer and is consolatory. God is for us eye and ear, as we ought to be for him. He invites us to an intimate dialogue 'face to face'.[66] Benedict's piety like that of the Fathers generally is unostentatious; as soon however as there is question of the *'voice' of Christ*, then there is a spontaneous outburst, revealing a deep spirituality, scriptural and Christ-centred. It has a parallel in brotherly love.[67]

21   **a.** 'Not to ungird oneself'[68] means to watch, and to await in readiness the coming of the Lord, like men equipping themselves for the Exodus and for a long march through the desert.[69] The equipment for a Christian life, aware that it is on the march, is simple *faith*, which begets an awareness of the presence of God (the 'fear of God') and so makes possible perseverance in goodness.[70]

b. The *Gospel* must assume the 'guidance' of a Christian life. In the Prologue as in the final chapter, Scripture is simply presented as *the* norm. The Gospel ought not in this connection to remain an edifying private possession. It is to be proclaimed. The so-called 'interpolated' text of the Rule (the oldest manuscript) adds: '(Put on) as shoes, the readiness to fight for the Gospel of peace'.[71] Our life should make Christ visible. This apostolate is incumbent on every Christian. This presupposes that the Gospel has become second nature for us. 'Under the guidance of the Gospel' the monks became saints, and on that account also witnesses of the faith.[72] Their astonishing ability to radiate influence made them heralds of the faith, even when they were not wandering preachers.

c. The '*vision*' of God presupposes a 'clean heart', and for this reason also, ascetical purification.[73]

22–27 a. The *goal* has come into view. On the long road through the desert one must hasten, if one wishes to rach the goal and enjoy the intimate companionship of the tent or the loving care of hospitality.

b. The image of striding swiftly forward makes no reference to Rom 9:16 'So it depends not upon man's will or exertion, but upon God's mercy.' Without denying the necessity of grace, Origen (d.253) praised 'this running, which wants to reach the goal, in the urgency towards the good'.[74] Augustine (d.430) sticks to the same passage of Paul, one ought to 'ascribe everything to God, who prepares the goodwill of man for support, and after the preparation gives support'.[75] Here it seems the success of Christian endeavour is attributed solely to grace. Origen (d.253) on the other hand emphasizes also the significance of human co-operation: 'Our perfection does not take place without some co-operation on our part, but God does the most of it'.[76] The monastic Fathers have on occasion extolled in striking fashion the prospects of our *freedom* and of a powerful will: Abbot Allois said: 'If a man wills, he arrives in one single day, by evening time, to God's measure'.[77]

c. The Lord, who has called us to the way, is himself *the* dweller of the *tent*, towards which we are under way. 'He dwelt among us' (literally: 'set up his tent').[78] He is simply the man of the brotherhood. Are we worthy of brotherhood with Christ? Question and answer are in *Psalm 15*, which is now commented on. This Psalm also used to be a favourite text for expounding upon to candidates for baptism. The basic ethos of the monk is identical with the life programme of the Christian.

28 a. As in Scripture and in the literature of the early Church, e.g. in the Acts of the Martyrs or in the Lives of the Monastic Fathers[79] the *contest* with evil[80] is presented as a wrestling or a struggle for and with Christ[81] and against the devil.[82] Christ is the 'Rock',[83] on which everything opposed to God is smashed to pieces. Athanasius (d.373) describes in this point of view the climax of the 'struggle' of the thirty-five year old Antony (d.356) against evil: 'Jesus did not forget the struggle of his servant, and became his protector. When he raised his eyes, he saw from on high a pinnacle becoming visible. The shadows faded and the rays of light poured over him . . . Antony felt that the Lord was present and said: "Where were you, good Jesus, where were you? Why did you not stand by me from the beginning (in my struggle) and heal my wounds? Then he heard a voice which said: Antony, I was here all along, to see how you would emerge from the struggle. You did not give up wrestling manfully. Therefore I shall always be your helper." '[84]

b. The place of contest with the Evil One was for ancient monasticism the 'Desert' where Christ too was tempted. It is the region of solitude and isolation.[85] It conceals within itself the danger of loneliness and at the same time the opportunity of proving oneself personally. Here the monk has to face up to the demons of intemperance (in food and drink), of sexual licentiousness, of aggressiveness, of materialistic principles, of moods of depression, of timidity, of indifference, of a false elation and of selfish arrogance.[86] As it appears, people easily saw the personified Evil One in interior disturbances and difficulties of the soul, 'the wiles of the devil'.[87]

c. Jesus in his 'temptation'[88] is the prototype of this struggle with the Evil One. The martyrs too are prototypes; the 'Acts of Martyrdom' report how they withstood the Evil One even to shedding their blood. In their ascetic struggles the monks sought to emulate the martyrs. So it is said e.g. of Antony that 'in desire he was already a martyr'.[89] The introductory treatise on spirituality[90] in the 'Rule of the Master' is called the 'Account of the Warfare of the heart',[91] which is reminiscent of the concept of the Acts of the Martyrs. We must presuppose this view in Benedict, who offers a spirituality of the heart[92] and here speaks of 'promptings', which are perceived in the 'heart'. The contest with the Evil One is no longer enacted in the arena, but at the forum of the heart.[93] Cassian (d.430) says, we ought to take possession of every nook of our heart with positive forces, lest an evil spirit find them empty and with seven others return there.[94]

d. Alongside the reference to Jesus as helper in the combat, we frequently find *asceticism* mentioned *as a weapon* in the fight. Athanasius (d.373) writes in the *Life* of Antony: 'A pure life and the true, trusting faith in God are powerful weapons against the demons. Believe me, I know it from personal experience: Satan fears night vigils, prayer, fasting, mildness, voluntary poverty, scorn of conceited seeking for fame, humility, compassion, mastery of anger, and above all a God-fearing heart purified for the love of Christ.'[95]

e. The contest and the 'temptations were understood by Origen (d.253) as an opportunity for critical self-knowledge: 'everything that our soul absorbed into itself, and which is hidden from all except God, even from the soul itself, comes to light through temptation'.[96] For this clarifying interior struggle the gift of *'discernment of spirits'*[97] is important.[98] Origen has drawn up rules for it: 'Our soul is either made luminous by the true light which never fades, which is Christ himself, or if it has not this eternal light in itself, it must be illumined by an evanescent light, from him who "disguises himself as an angel of light" and lights up the sinner's soul with a false light, so that what is temporal and perishable may appear to him under the guise of what is good and valuable.'[99] 'A person however experiences the influence of the good Spirit, . . . when he is impelled and called to what is good, and made enthusiastic for what is heavenly and godly, . . . always indeed in such a way that it is left to the freedom and judgement of a man, whether he will follow or not. Therefore it is possible, to discern through manifest "discretion", in what way the soul is moved by the presence of the good Spirit, namely when it does not suffer the slightest darkening of the mind through the actual inspiration.'[100]

f. Patristic literature often gives the impression that these men were plagued with *fear of demons*. However we must remain aware, that they had the firm faith: where one gives scope to Christ, his Spirit, and his power, there evil loses all its power. Faced with a true believer, who is a bearer of the Spirit, all the devil's apparitions dissolve into nothingness.[101] According to Origen (d.253) only personal sin gives the Evil One entry into our inner self.[102] 'The Sign of the Cross and faith in the Lord are an impregnable rampart.'[103]

g. In Benedict we seldom find an allusion to the devil.[104] Obviously he did not want to countenance a false belief in spirits. Later, Gregory the Great (d.604) will portray Benedict as a *bearer of the Spirit*. Benedict sees through as non-existent, chimerical devilish illusions which frightened his monks.[105] He reads hearts and sees through secret faults of his monks.[106] Above all he has the gift of discernment and does not let himself be misled by any dissimulation. The Gothic king Totila (541–552) 'wanted to test whether the man of God really possessed a prophetic spirit'. He put one of his men, Ringgo by name, into 'kingly garments', gave him 'the Counts Wult, Roderick and Blidin' and 'armed men' as companions, and had him go thus to the monastery, while Totila remained concealed 'some distance away'. 'Benedict was seated on rising ground. As soon as he saw Ringgo coming and could be seen by him, Benedict called out 'Take off, my son, take off what is not yours!' The latter fell to the ground in fear, while the party of soldiers retreated in all haste back to Totila.[107] Benedict is then a bearer of the Spirit, possesses the gift of discernment, and works 'signs of power' as the apostles and prophets did once upon a time. He is proved to be a prophetic and apostolic man: 'This man was filled with the Spirit of all the just (that is to say, of the prophets and apostles).'[108] He exercised the gift of prophecy on one occasion among others when King Totila himself came to him and had to learn from Benedict that he, Totila, would 'march on Rome, pass over the sea, rule for nine years and in the tenth year die'.[109]

29–32 a. The *'fear of the Lord'*,[110] reverentially being gripped or startled by the holiness of God, manifests itself in 'faithful service', i.e. in 'good observance', in the fulfilling of duties and in asceticism.[111]

b. In a word that is deep and strong, the 'Master' and Benedict demand that we *'glorify the Lord, who is at work in us'*. That is faith in the primacy of grace before all the works of man. An attitude of humble praise, as was peculiarly Mary's,[112] is appropriate for this faith. The author does not use the abstract word 'grace', rather he gets the readers to direct the prayer of praise to 'the Lord who is at work in them'.[113] These sentences on the Lord as 'Worker' in our soul and on humble praise of God demonstrate Christ as present[114] in our ascetical striving, and lay the groundwork for the teaching on prayer, that will be developed later.[115]

33–34 For the sake of brevity, Benedict omits[116] the conclusion of Psalm 115, so that the transition to the following image of the 'unshakeable rock', which is Christ, is missing. A 'listener' to the Lord stands on firm ground.[117]

35–36 The Lord, who was speaking in the whole of this commentary on the Psalms 'concludes' his discourse with the final words of the Sermon on the Mount.[118] Now 'he is *waiting* in silence' for our response. 'Day by day' he is waiting for us, at prayer, at work, in the fulfilment of our duties. Like a father he is on the look-out for us.[119] But a 'reprieve' is appointed for us, urging us to conversion. This awareness is called the 'fear of God'.[120]

37–38 God is magnanimous in his 'patience' or *'forbearance'* (makrothymia). The forbearance is that of the farmer who confidently waits for the growth of the harvest.[121] The reprieve is appointed so that we may purify ourselves and remain alive. Here again there is an echo of Johannine theology: 'I came that they may have life, and have it abundantly.'[122]

39 The so-called 'interpolated text' (the oldest MS.) concludes the Prologue after 'if only we fulfil the duties of one who is to live in it' with 'we shall be heirs

of the Kingdom of heaven'.[123] The concept of living with God in his tent is valid both for the time of probation as well as for the *completion*. Origen (d.253) has a deep saying for this passing-over: 'God enters into the soul, and the soul emigrates into God.'[124]

40 The Rule develops a spirituality of the 'heart'.[125] It is not aiming thereby at mere inwardness, but at *being human* generally. The whole psychosomatic man is to be fitted out for 'service as a soldier'. In this formulation there lies once again the theme of the battle against the power of the evil spirit, which opposes the good tidings of Christ.[126] The whole man is expected to be present to himself in his 'heart' or conscience. He must not let himself be controlled by external practical pressures and should not fritter away his energies aimlessly. This is a whole programme in opposition to a chilly intellectualism and against a fragmentation of the person. When 'heart and body' find themselves together—inner 'recollection' as it is called—in order to submit obediently to God's guidance, a man will have no fear of losing his own centre in an environment that is complex and centrifugal.

41 This sentence is not to be understood in a Semi-Pelagian sense;[127] the author is alluding presumably to Eph 2:3 : he who belongs '*by nature* to the children of wrath'[128] is dependent on grace. We encounter here no illusion about a 'world that is sound' by nature. The writer is aware of the crises which beset human existence, but believes that this human world is open to God, that we are allowed to pray.

42–44 Themes already introduced are here gathered up together, in part only by being hinted at: death and life, light and darkness, a reprieve still open and definitive decision, existence in the body and new mode of being, fear and trust, the way and running to the goal.

45–50 This last paragraph of the Prologue is a formal presentation of the *monastery*. In the 'Master's' baptismal catechesis[129] were to be found the words: 'Learn from me; for I am gentle and lowly in heart, and you will find rest for your souls. For my yoke is easy and my burden light.'[130] To 'learn' from the Lord is equivalent to becoming his pupil. This corresponds to the invitation: 'Go therefore and make pupils (disciples) of all nations . . . teaching them to observe all . . .'.[131] This background should not be forgotten, when one sees that the Master's sentence about the 'school for the Lord's service'[132] has been taken over into this longer conclusion to the Prologue. In the 'Rule of the Master' the term 'school' stands ten times for the monastery. Benedict usually avoids this term (not the idea), presumably in order to guard against the schoolmasterish attitudes of the Master and the latter's idea of a competition of virtue among the 'pupils'.[133] The sentence about the 'school for the Lord's service' is given an explanation.[134] In this connection, with a clear reference to Matt. 11:29, it is explained that this school should not impose any heavy burdens. A further sentence of the 'Master's' forms the conclusion.[135]

45 a. In the sixth century '*School*' (schola) designated an official assembly room for soldiers, workers or pupils; then the members of this school, and finally the service itself, in this context the service of Christ.[136] This service includes 'holding fast to the teaching', as will be formulated later on with an echo of a phrase from the Acts of the Apostles.[137] Christ proclaims this teaching, and one 'serves' him. This service which he teaches, embraces hearing and

35

heeding his voice,[138] the renunciation of burdensome sin or a soldierly fight against it and acceptance of Christ,[139] as well as the practice of the service: training or ascesis.[140]

b. If the monastery is a 'school of the Lord', then its members belong to the *'circle of disciples of the Lord'*. These disciples acknowledge Jesus as their Master.[141] To this circle belonged the Twelve,[142] a group which followed him[143] or was sent out by him.[144] The number of the 'disciples' was large,[145] indeed finally the faithful are called in the New Testament 'disciples' or 'pupils'.[146] The monastery—admittedly in a conscious and unmistakable manner—makes a reality of the call to the circle of disciples, which is incumbent on all believers.— According to the words of the Rule the 'school for the Lord's service' is to be 'founded' and given 'structures'. Sacred Scripture offers the plan or an outline sketch for this foundation. The monastery is one definite realization of the plan, not the sole execution of the project or one that existed at all times.

46 Several times in our Rule we come across remarks which betray an apprehension about the decadent state of contemporary monasticism.[147] At the same time the misgiving reveals itself, that the Rule might be found too exacting for beginners. For that purpose it is first of all noted, that in the monastery hardships or difficulties are not cultivated for their own sake, neither from arbitrariness nor from a negative attitude or one that would be opposed to life. Precisely it is the Rule of Benedict which brings deliberate alleviations in comparison with earlier practice.[148] Moreover the monks endeavoured to make it understood, that only the lived *experience* shows how easily practicable the monastic way is, while doctrine and structures can at first appear oppressive. A certain person 'asked Abbot Moses for a word. The venerable father said to him: "Go, sit down in your cell, and the cell will teach you everything!" '[149] It is not theoretical discussions, it is not procrastination or a calculation of risks, but a resolute 'going' and the lived practice which lead forward on this way.

47 **a.** The 'austere requirements' which are to be predicted to the beginners,[150] are given a reason. The text is a reminiscence of Cassian (d.430). He warns against over-valuing charisms and powers of miracles. For all, the decisive question remains, 'whether they have rectified their faults'. This *purification* is 'granted according to personal effort through God's grace. It is "practical knowledge", which the Apostle calls by another name "Love" (caritas). It is to be preferred to all else . . . even to a glorious martyrdom'.[151]

b. As in Cassian (d.430) the effort for purification, and *love*, are presented as the substance of asceticism. Love directed towards action is called by Cassian 'practical knowledge' (as distinct from contemplation). This love stands higher than all other charisms. It must cost something. For its sake one must renounce genuine human possibilities.[152] Towards the end of the Prologue the goal of the Christian as well as of monastic life comes into view: love.

48–49 **a.** Transforming somewhat the Lord's phrase about the 'two ways'[153], the author restricts the 'narrowness' of the way to its 'beginning'. In the dilemma between decadence and over-taxing he finds the thought of progress and of *climbing* helpful.[154] There is the opportunity of seeing and making headway. Mere permissiveness is no genuine solution. But Benedict has very human feelings: the beginner is expected not to give up in face of difficulties, but rather 'to step out on the way—[155] and to arrive finally at perfection.'[156]

b. Man is called to a way of 'salvation'.[157] God takes the lead, as is stressed by Cassian (d.430), who as a rule emphasizes the prospects of human freedom: 'The Spirit of God prompted us with the first beginning of goodwill. It may be that he led us himself and without intermediary to the way of salvation; or that he roused us to it by a good person; or that he led us through a dispensation of Providence. The perfection of all positive powers in us is also God's gift to us. Our task is to carry out what God invites us to and helps us in, whether we do this with zeal or carelessness.'[158]

c. In any case there is no reason for 'shrinking back' in panic, or for 'flight'[159] in face of this way, when its difficulties become known. Trust in the help of God must be all the greater: Abbot David, of whom Cassian (d.430) writes, used to teach 'that the beginning of our conversion and of our faith, and the strength to withstand passions, is given to us by the Lord as a gift'.[160]

d. The phrase about the 'joy that is too great for words' echoes the scriptural phrase sealed with eschatological hope: 'Without having seen him you love him; though you do not now see him you believe in him and rejoice with unutterable and exalted joy'.[161]

e. The Fathers often speak of the 'heart that is wide'.[162] It is wide, because 'God's love has been poured into our hearts through the Holy Spirit.'[163] Ambrose (d.397) wrote: 'Let the way be narrow, the heart wide, so that it can sustain the indwelling of the Father, the Son and the Holy Spirit.'[164] The theme has been transformed in a variety of ways. Cassian (d.430)[165] holds the 'wide heart' alone capable of obtaining 'peace or rest'.[166] An impatient, faint-hearted or narrow-minded person succumbs to every 'sudden flood' of 'aggressiveness' or 'depression'. Through 'patience'[167] and 'love' on the contrary the 'open spaces' of a 'wide heart' are created, in which the 'sudden floods of the emotions' quickly ebb away.

The heart therefore is the place where *harmony* with God and the neighbour must focus, for it is also the place of the inner harmony of the person.— Hilary of Arles (d.449) writes about his predecessor Honoratus (d.428/9)— who likewise was a monk of Lérins—almost in the same breath that 'inner purity' and 'a wide love' were his characteristics. This inner harmony mirrored itself on Honoratus's face.[168] This will also be a major theme of the last chapter: love and peace among men and in God.

f. Gregory the Great (d.604) will later on take up the theme of the 'wide heart'. He describes a *mystical experience* of Benedict's on the death of his friend, Bishop Germanus of Capua. Standing praying at the window during the night, Benedict saw heavenly light shining clear as day over the darkness, and in it 'the whole world concentrated as if in a single sunbeam'. Gregory explains this mystical and at the same time cosmic experience: 'To a soul, that sees its Creator, everything created is small and narrow. If it is able to see even a little of the Creator's light, everything created becomes small for it. For in the light of the inner vision the innermost soul broadens out and expands itself in God to such a point, that it raises itself high above the earth. The seer's soul surmounts even itself. When it is seized by God's light and lifted high above itself, it dilates itself interiorly. Raised above everything it see itself far beneath and understands now how small everything is—what it could not grasp while it was still abased . . . When it is said, the world was concentrated before his eyes, that does not mean that heaven and earth and contracted. Rather, the seer's inner self had expanded. He was snatched away into God, and could effortlessly see everything that was beneath God. In the light which lit up the eyes of his body, the inner light was present. It laid hold of the seer's soul, raised it up and showed him in this way, how narrow and small are all things below.'[169] The theme of the 'wide heart' in this text of Gregory's passes on to a statement about the mystical vision of divine light and a *drawing near to God*, indeed even to a seeing together with him. According to Gregory's account, Benedict attained only for a brief moment to this highest peak of mysticism, and only after years of preparation and climbing. First of all, Benedict had to test himself and stand the test. He had to master the temptation of arrogance, the claims of sexual instinct and of aggressiveness. He had to become a teacher or spiritual father, and as a bearer of the Spirit to make visible the life of the prophets and apostles 'through signs of the Spirit and of power'. It is only on this height that his soul is for a moment snatched above itself, by God's light, into God (A. de Vogüé).

g. In general the ancient Church did not look on a *charismatic experience* as a rare exception. Irenaeus (d. *c*.202) writes thus: 'We hear of many brethren, that they have prophetic charisms ... The Apostle calls these 'spiritual' on account of their participation in the Spirit of Christ.'[170] That reminds one of the 'spirituals' (spiritales), which the 'Master' often uses instead of 'monk'.[171]

50   a. The final sentence of the Prologue is once again taken from the 'Master'. The phrase about 'persevering in the teaching of Christ' which fits in with the image of the 'Lord's school'[172] recalls the description of the *primitive Church* of Jerusalem.[173] One will not want to 'persevere' somewhere marginally, but rather right in the heart of the Church. For Irenaeus (d.202) too 'our *teacher*' is 'the Word'.[174] He is desirous that his readers 'follow none other than the true and faithful teacher, the Word of God, Jesus Christ, our Lord, who on account of his endless love became that which we are, so that he could make us perfectly that which he is.'[175]

b. Only now is the expression '*monastery*' (monasterium) heard. This concept is not found in Scripture. Only when the conformity of the structure to Scripture has been sketched, is the name introduced. The monastery appears as a community of the Lord's pupils and represents his circle of disciples.[176] Already Cassian (d.430) considers the monastery simultaneously 'a school and arena for our training'. The 'powers' of 'magnanimity' or 'forbearance' of 'unshakeable patience' or 'perseverance'[177] are to be developed. The 'Master' seems to have let himself be inspired by Cassian, who wrote 'Patience and the tireless fidelity with which they persevere in the "professio" once taken on, and never do their own will, makes of them daily, such as are crucified to the world'[178] and living martyrs.'[179] These themes are echoed in the formulation of the closing sentence of the Prologue. The Cross of Christ, his 'obedience unto death'[180] are central themes of the spiritual chapters of the Rule.[181] Origen (d.253) has developed these same themes, in which connection he sees the passage from the Cross to the Resurrection and to the newness of life in Christ, in the transition from fear to love.[182]

c. Like the martyrs, the Christian ought to conform himself to Christ. Jesus did not merely passively put up with suffering, but obediently concurred in it.

This active, voluntary entering upon the struggle of suffering is suggested in the concept of 'patience' which has to be understood positively as a trusting 'perseverance' or 'holding one's ground' in the sense of the New Testament 'hypomone'.[183] The believing Christian feels, to be sure, his limitations and weaknesses,[184] but from the union in faith with Christ there accrues to him an unsuspected 'power' (dynamis) or 'patience' or 'stamina' (hypomone), which showed themselves in a model way in the 'struggle' of the martyrs.[185] Power, patience and perseverance or forbearance are *gifts of the Spirit*. They belong to the new life in Christ.[186]

d. So there is condensed in the last sentence of the Prologue the longing of believing Christians for that union with Christ and those gifts of the Spirit, which were proper to the *martyrs*. We read e.g. in the 'Martyrdom of Polycarp' (d. 22 February 156): 'We wish so to love the martyrs as disciples and imitators of the Lord, as they deserve . . . , so that we also may belong to their fellowship (koinonia) and become their fellow-pupils.'[187]

e. Like the Church, the monastery is a 'school of the Lord', in which a 'war service' of the 'heart' is carried on, not a struggle with external persecutors. This school mediates *fellowship* with the Lord. He gives the circle of disciples the 'power' to 'witness' (martyrion). Horsiesi (d.*c.*380) cites in this regard the Acts of the Apostles:[188] 'With great power (dynamis) the apostles gave their testimony (martyrion) to the resurrection of the Lord Jesus.'[189] What is at stake is the interchange of the spiritual and vital powers of a new existence: 'Rejoice in so far as you share Christ's sufferings, that you may also rejoice and be glad when his glory is revealed.'[190]

NOTES TO COMMENTARY ON PROLOGUE

1 (Ps.) Basil, 'Exhortation to a spiritual son', Prooem.; Prol. 1–4 takes up formulations of the 'Exhortation' (Prooem., Ch. 11). 2 → 73.1–7—The concluding Chapter 73 contains a statement of intent; for that reason, it is better to read this epilogue and the related statement first. 3 Prol. 8.9.19. 4 Baruch 3:9. 5 Deut. 6:4. 6 → 7,62–66. 7 The concept of 'heart' appears in the Rule 31 times (22 times in those parts which correspond to the 'actus militiae cordis'). When one looks up parallels to the Rule of Benedict in the older monastic literature, one comes on the concept of 'heart' surprisingly often. A key concept! → Prol. 1.28.40.49–50; 7,1–4. Cf. List of Keywords: 'heart'. 8 Was this word 'master' (magister) consciously chosen, in order to point to the 'Rule of the Master'? → Introd. 3. One asks oneself too whether Benedict wanted to place the Rule so to speak under the patronage of Basil, by taking over the first words from him and mentioning him alone by name at the end (Goutagny; → Introd. Note 36). 9 RM pr 8–9; RB Prol. 1: RM pr 1.5.8.15.19.22; RB Prol. 2: RM pr 3.7.11; thp 6; RB Prol. 3: RM th 18.21.24–53; RB Prol. 4: RM thp 69–72.79; RB Prol. 5–44: RM ths 2–44; RB Prol. 45: RM ths 45; RB Prol. 50: RM ths 46.—The parallels (:) between RB and RM are noted in every chapter. The indications, somewhat simplified, are taken from: A. de Vogüé—J. Neufville. La Règle de S. Benoît, pp. 174–185. 10 Labor, kopos, ponos: → 71,1–4. 11 Gen. 3:17. 12 VPatr 5,14,15. 13 VPatr 7,13,7. 14 → 1,10–11; 7,10–13; 48,7–8.17–18.24–25. 15 Cf. Rom. 5:12–19. 16 Cf. Rom. 6:16–17. 17 Cf. Note 5. 18 Admonitio 11. 19 Eph. 6:13–17; → Prol. 3.28.29–32.40.45; 1,3–5; 4,55–58; 5,10–13; 7,35–43; 24,3; 48,17–18; 49,6–7; 73,4–7. 20 Origen, Jes Nave Hom 5,2. 21 RM thema; → 73,4–7. 22 → Prol. 45–50 (in Note 130). 23 → 58,12,17–23,26. 24 Cf. VHonor 1,5–8. 25 RBasRuf 4 (cf. Matt. 6:14; 16:24). 26 Conl 4,8. 27 Conl 3,6. 28 RM thp. It too comes from the 'Actus militiae cordis'. 29 → Prol. 35–41. 30 → Prol. 18. 31 Admonitio 11. 32 RM ths 2–46. Originally, the commentary on the Psalms belongs to the 'Account of the Warfare of the Heart'. 33 RB Prol. 5–45.50. 34 Cf. Rom. 5:5; 8:15–17. 35 Cf. Eph. 2:3; 5:6. 36 RBasRuf 2,33–44. 37 Adv haer 4,41,3. 38 V.10: cf. Matt. 13:19; Luke 18:15. The voice that is to be heard 'every day' is perhaps to be explained by the Invitatory Psalm 94, which is heard daily. 39 VPatr 7,29. 40 Cf. Matt. 11:15. 41 Cf. Rev. 2:7; cf. 1 Pet. 1:10–12. 42 → 7,67–70. 43 Cf. RB Prol. 9.13.43; → 21,4–6; 41,7–9. 44 → Prol. 3.12–13. 45 Photismos. Cf. Heb. 6:2,4; 10:32; Justin, Apol

61,12–13; 65,1; Thomas Aq., S. th. 3,67,1 ad 2: 'Baptism is not only a cleansing, but the power of enlightenment'. The present Order of Baptism speaks too of 'enlightenment' and is familiar with the symbolism of light. **46** Exod. 19:18–19; Matt. 17:1–9; 2 Pet. 1:17,19. **47** Cf. Origen, Matth Comm 12,43. **48** Job Fragm 22:2; cf. v. 10. **49** Demonstration of the apostolic preaching, Introd. 1. **50** John 1:14;9. **51** RBasRuf 2,24–30; cf. Ps. 42:3. **52** Logos praktikos 9. **53** Cf. Matt. 7:6; v. 11; Cassian, Conl 14,17; → 19,3–7; 73,3. **54** Ps. 34: 12,9,6; → Prol. 8–11. **55** Cf. John 1:5; → Prol. 8–11. **56** Cf. RB 7,67,69. **57** → 4,55–58; 7,10–30; 62–66; 31,10–12; 72,12; 73,2.—Benedict has inserted the words 'of life' and 'of death' into the verse John 12:35 (v. 13). In this way the Johannine theology comes through clearly. **58** → 4,78 (workshop); cf. RB 7,18 (the 'capable brother'). For his part, man 'seeks God' (RB 58,7). **59** RB 4,25.73; 34,5; 53,4–5. **60** RB 65,11; 4,71–73. **61** → Prol. 48–49. **62** → 4,73. **63** → 7,67–68. **64** → 72,8–11. **65** Cf. RB 58,7. **66** Cf. Exod. 33:11. **67** Benedict, on his own initiative, inserts into the Master's text in verse 19 the word 'dear' (carissimi) in addition to 'brothers'. **68** Luke 13:25. **69** Exod. 12:11. **70** → 7,10–30; 73,8–9. **71** Eph. 6:15. **72** Cf. Hors Lib 15. **73** Matt. 5:8. → 7,67–70. **74** Peri Archon 3,1,18–19. **75** Enchiridion 9,32. **76** Peri Archon 3,1,19. **77** VPatr 5,11,6. **78** John 1:14. **79** VAnt 4–5. **80** → 24,3. **81** → Prol. 3.50. **82** Benedict is discreet; he mentions the Devil three times, for instance, in contrast to the 'Master's' 37 times! Some monastic *vitae* also relish fantastic stories about the Devil.→ 25,4. **83** Cf. 1 Cor. 10:4; RB 4,50; 7,44. **84** VAnt 9. **85** Cassian, Conl 18,6. **86** Evagrius, Log prakt 6–44; Cassian, Conl 5,3; VAnt 21. **87** Cf. Eph. 6:11–12; VAnt 15; Cassian, Conl 5,16. **88** Cf. Matt. 4:1–11. **89** VAnt 23. **90** RM 1–10. **91** Actus militiae cordis (RM 10 expl.). **92** → Prol. 1. **93** → Prol. 3. **94** Conl 5,16; Cf. Matt. 12:43–45. **95** VAnt 17. **96** Peri euches 29,17. **97** VAnt 20. **98** → 64,19. **99** Judic Hom 9,1. **100** Peri Archon 3,3–4. On 'darkening' → 31,1–2; 72,1–3. **101** Cf. VAnt 10. **102** Judic Hom 3,4. **103** VAnt 8. **104** See Note 82 above. **105** Dial. 2,10. **106** Dial 2,12–13,30. **107** Dial 2,14. **108** Dial 2,8. **109** Dial 2,15. Because Totila penetrated into Rome in the autumn of 546, the conclusion was drawn that Benedict could have died at the earliest in 547. Thus the traditional date of his death: 21st March 547; see 'Introduction' 9. **110** → Prol. 12–13; 7,10–13. **111** By 'observance' is meant asceticism, as it is recommended in VAnt 17, for example (see Note 95 above). **112** Luke 1:46–55. **113** In v. 32 Benedict does not quote 2 Cor. 12:1, as the Master does (RM ths 28), but 2 Cor. 10:17. **114** → Prol. 28. **115** → 4,55–58; 8–20; 43,3; 49,4–5; 52,1–3. **116** 'He who does these things shall never be moved'. **117** Cf. Matt. 7:24–25; Prol. 1.28. **118** Prol. 33–34. **119** Cf. Luke 15:20; Prol. 3. **120** → Prol. 12–13.29–32; 5,1–9; 7,5–9.10–13.62–66.67–70. **121** Cf. Jas. 5:7; Mark 4:26–29 (the fruit grows in stillness!) **122** John 10:10. **123** Cf. Prol. 50. **124** Cant Comm 2,16. **125** → Prol. 1. **126** → Prol. 28. **127** → Prol. 4. **128** → Prol. 5–7. **129** → Prol. 3. **130** Cf. Matt. 11:29. → Prol. 3 (in Note 21). **131** Cf. Matt. 28:20. **132** Prol. 45; cf. Prol. 50; 2,11–15; 65,7–22. **133** In the so-called 'interpolated text', the concept of 'school' does not appear at all. It is to be found solely in the lengthier conclusion of the Prologue. There were doubts as to whether this lengthier conclusion is by Benedict himself or was inserted later (from the 'Rule of the Master'), in order to have the concept of the 'school of the Lord' for the monastery firmly anchored in the Rule of Benedict too. **134** Prol. 46–49. **135** Prol. 50. **136** → Prol. 3.28.40.45–50. **137** Prol. 50; cf. Acts 2:42. **138** → Prol. 1.3.8–13.18–20.21. 'Servant of God' (servus Dei) was a name for a monk. **139** → Prol. 3.28. **140** → Prol. 12–13. **141** In German and Yiddish a synagogue is called a (Jewish) 'Schul'. It is a house of instruction, in which one learns while praying. The instruction is concluded with a prayer (for the coming of the Kingdom). **142** Cf. Matt. 10:1; 12:1. **143** Cf. Matt. 8:21. **144** Cf. Luke 10:1. **145** Cf. Luke 6:17; 19:37; John 6:60. **146** Cf. Acts 6:1–7; 9:10–26. **147** RB 18,25; 40,6; 73,7. **148** RB 18,10; 35,13; 66,5—v. 46–49 are an insertion by Benedict into the RM. **149** VPatr 5,2,9. **150** RB 58,8. It cannot be overlooked that the author of the lengthier conclusion of the Prologue expresses himself much more mildly than Benedict does in Chapter 58. **151** Conl 15,2. **152** → 72,9–10; 73,8–9. **153** Matt. 7:14. **154** → 7,5–9; 4,1–9.55–58; 72,12; 73,8–9. **155** 'To stride onward': Prol. 2.13.22–27.44; 5,10. **156** → 73,9. **157** Cf. RB Prol. 20 & 5,11 ('way to life'; Prol. 48 'way of salvation'). **158** Conl 3,19. **159** Cf. RB 64,19. **160** Conl 3,15. **161** 1 Pet. 1:8; → 51,3 (in Notes 12–13). **162** Cf. Ps. 119:32. **163** Rom. 5:5. **164** Expl. Ps. 119:32. **165** Conl 16,27. **166** Cf. Matt. 11:28–29. **167** → Prol. 50. **168** VHonor 6,26. **169** Dial 2,35. **170** Adv haer 5,6,1. **171** RM 15,21 (quotes Gal. 6:1); 28,3; 56,1.15; 57,20.23; 61,5.12; 63,1; 78,25; 80,4; 81,20; 83,13; 85,3; 86,8. **172** → Prol. 45–50.45. **173** Acts 2:42; → Prol. 73,8–9. **174** Adv haer 1,1. **175** Adv haer 5 Prol. **176** → Prol. 45–50.45. The monastery will be defined straight away in the following Ch.1. **177** Conl 19,11; Cf. RB 3.1; 19,4. **178** Gal. 6:14. **179** Conl 18,7. **180** Phil. 2:8. **181** RB 5 (hear-obey); RB 7 (humility, self-denial, kenosis). **182** PsComm 118,20 **183** Cf., for instance, Matt. 24:13: 'He who endures (under persecution) to the end' . . . **184** The pagan Celsus mocks the weakness of the Christians, specifically their lack of stoical calm when they called to Christ for help before their martyrdom: 'Christ, help me, I pray you! Christ, have mercy on me, I pray you Christ, give me strength!' Human feeling speaks in these words, no fanaticism, but trustful faith. **185** In the letter of the Church of Lyons and Vienne about the martyrs of the year 177, for instance, there is no mention of 'andreia', the manly courage or self-confidence of the Greeks, but always of the 'hypomone' of the New Testament. **186** → Prol. 37–38; 7,35–43; 72,11. **187** 17,3. **188** Acts 4:33. **189** Lib 50. **190** Cf. 1 Pet. 4:13; → 72,12.

INCIPIT TEXTUS REGULAE.
REGULA APPELLATUR AB HOC QUOD
OBOEDIENTIUM DIRIGAT MORES.

It is called 'Rule', because it is a guiding rule of life for the obedient.

CHAPTER 1

OF THE TYPES OF MONK

8 Jan 1 It is clear that there are four types of monk.
9 May
8 Sept
    2 The first is that of the cenobites,
who serve under Rule and abbot
in the monastery.

    3 The second type are the anchorites or hermits.
After a long testing-time in the monastery
—not in the first fervour of a monk's life—

    4 they learned to fight against the devil
through the skill acquired from the support of many.

    5 They were well trained in the ranks of the brethren   Gal 5:9; Mk 7:21
for the single-handed combat of the desert.
Fearless and even without another's encouragement
they are able now, with God's help,
to fight against vices of flesh and thoughts,
unaided and alone.

9 Jan 6 A third, quite dreadful type of monk   Wisd 3:6; Prov 27:21
10 May   are the sarabaites.
9 Sept   never tested by a Rule,
never taught by experience,
they have never become like GOLD from the FURNACE;
instead they are in nature soft as lead.

    7 In their occupations   Cf. Ps 81:16; Acts 5:3
they still keep faith with the world
and openly LIE to God by their tonsure.

    8 In twos or threes or even singly   Cf. Ezek 34;

41

they live without a shepherd,
withdrawn within their own, not the Lord's,
SHEEPFOLDS.
What their appetites desire is for them the law.

9 All their own views and wishes they call holy;
what they do not want
they consider not to be allowed.

Ps 23;
Lk 15:4–7;
Jn 10:1–16

10 The fourth type of monk are those called gyrovagues.
Their whole life long they flit from country to country,
staying as guests for three or four days
in the cells of various monks;

11 always adrift and never stable
slaves of their own whims and the pleasures of the palate,
and in all points worse than the sarabaites.

12 Of the deplorable life of all these monks
let us rather keep silence than speak.

13 Let us disregard them,
and, with God's help,
set about to give the strongest type, the cenobites,
a way of life.

CAPUT I: DE GENERIBUS MONACHORUM

¹MONACHORUM QUATTUOR ESSE GENERA, MANIFESTUM EST. ²PRIMUM COEN-
OBITARUM, HOC EST MONASTERIALE, MILITÀNS SUB REGULA VEL ABBATE. ³DEINDE
SECUNDUM GENUS EST ANACHORITARUM ID EST HEREMITARUM, HORUM QUI NON
CONVERSATIONIS FERVORE NOVICIO SED MONASTERII PROBATIONE DIUTURNA, ⁴QUI
DIDICERUNT CONTRA DIABULUM MULTORUM SOLACIO IAM DOCTI PUGNARE, ⁵ET
BENE EXTRUCTI FRATERNA EX ACIE AD SINGULAREM PUGNAM HEREMI, SECURI IAM
SINE CONSOLATIONE ALTERIUS, SOLA MANU VEL BRACHIO CONTRA VITIA CARNIS
VEL COGITATIONUM, DEO AUXILIANTE, PUGNARE SUFFICIUNT. ⁶TERTIUM VERO
MONACHORUM TETERRIMUM GENUS EST SARABAITARUM, QUI NULLA REGULA
ADPROBATI, EXPERIENTIA MAGISTRA, SICUT AURUM FORNACIS, SED IN PLUMBI
NATURA MOLLITI, ⁷ADHUC OPERIBUS SERVANTES SAECULO FIDEM, MENTIRI DEO PER
TONSURAM NOSCUNTUR. ⁸QUI BINI AUT TERNI AUT CERTE SINGULI SINE PASTORE,
NON DOMINICIS SED SUIS INCLUSI OVILIBUS, PRO LEGE EIS EST DESIDERIORUM
VOLUPTAS, ⁹CUM QUIDQUID PUTAVERINT VEL ELEGERINT, HOC DICUNT SANCTUM,
ET QUOD NOLUERINT, HOC PUTANT NON LICERE. ¹⁰QUARTUM VERO GENUS EST
MONACHORUM QUOD NOMINATUR GIROVAGUM, QUI TOTA VITA SUA PER DIVERSAS
PROVINCIAS TERNIS AUT QUATERNIS DIEBUS PER DIVERSORUM CELLAS HOSPITAN-
TUR, ¹¹SEMPER VAGI ET NUMQUAM STABILES, ET PROPRIIS VOLUNTATIBUS ET
GUILAE INLECEBRIS SERVIENTES, ET PER OMNIA DETERIORES SARABAITIS. ¹²DE
QUORUM OMNIUM HORUM MISERRIMA CONVERSATIONE MELIUS EST SILERE QUAM
LOQUI. ¹³HIS ERGO OMISSIS, AD COENOBITARUM FORTISSIMUM GENUS DISPONEN-
DUM, ADIUVANTE DOMINO, VENIAMUS.

1 **a.** The 'Master', from whom the chapter, for the greater part, is taken[1], avoids almost always the concept '*monk*', and prefers the name 'brother'. Benedict does so too; yet in his usage the concept 'monk' sounds as an honourable name implying duties, which he uses in an important context. The first chapter begins emphatically with this expression, which denotes the 'individual'.[2] Augustine (d.430) takes the expression to be appropriate, because the monastery community is not a multitude, but '*one* heart and *one* soul'.[3,4] Tradition interprets the expression as seeking for the 'one thing necessary'[5] or as the image of divine Unity, which is the antithesis of fragmentation.

b. The 'Master' gets the enumeration of the types of monk in great measure from Cassian (d.430),[6] who for his part draws upon a description by Jerome,[7] dating from 384, of the types of monk in Egypt.

2 **a.** The '*cenobite*' lives in the 'koinobion',[8] i.e. in a 'life in common'. The author gives a paraphrase of this with 'Monasterium' (House of the monks).[9]

b. Other monastic Rules develop the idea of '*life in common*' right at the outset. It is the guiding principle of Pachomian monasticism. Pachomius (d.346) himself found the way to Christian faith and the vocation to the life of a monk through the experience of community virtues. As a twenty-year-old recruit in the Roman army, weakened by a journey and bad treatment, he had experienced the unselfish love of neighbour and the hospitality of the 'Christians' of an Egyptian city.[10]

His second successor Horsiesi (d.*c.* 380) not only speaks of the fact that 'Father (Pachomius) was the first to found koinobia',[11] he explains them also as 'circles of community' (koinonia): 'That our circle of community (*koinonia*) which binds us together, comes from God, the Apostle has taught us because he said "Do not neglect to do good and to share (koinonia) what you have, for such sacrifices are pleasing to God."[12] We read something similar in the Acts of the Apostles: "The company of those who believed were of *one* heart and *one* soul, and no one said that any of the things which he possessed was his own, but they had everything in common (koina). And with great power (dynamis) the apostles gave their testimony (martyrion) to the resurrection of the Lord Jesus."[13],[14] In this way the koinonia or Communio idea is the guiding theme of Pachomian spirituality.[15]

c. Cassian (d.430) adopts the presentation of the *primitive community of Jerusalem*[16] as a model: 'At that time the whole Church lived thus, while today only a few are to be found in the monasteries, who lead this life.'[17] In these words a certain nostalgia for the 'apostolic life' of the primitive Church is given expression. The idealized picture of the Acts of the Apostles inspires enthusiasm. There is also an unmistakable tendency in Cassian, to see Christian community life realized almost exclusively in the monasteries, because only here does he find community of goods.

d. The 'Rule of the Four Fathers'[18] lays stress on other aspects of community life, which are also mentioned in the Acts of the Apostles,[19] namely on unity of spirit, love and joy: 'the Holy Spirit says: "Behold, how good and pleasant it is, when brothers dwell in unity"[20] and likewise "God makes men of one mind to dwell in a house".[21] When this *Rule of Love* which is marked out and approved by the Holy Spirit, is established, then we can stride ahead, and give well-founded advice. We wish above all, that all the brethren live, all of

43

one mind, in one house, in which joy is at home.'[22] An ethos of unity of spirit, love and joy is the basis of a Christian community life.

e. These *biblical proofs* for community life are common property of the monastic writers. It will be sufficient to refer to Augustine (d.430),[23] for whom the community life of the primitive Church is *the* model of the monastery. Benedict himself appeals rather reservedly, and probably under Augustine's influence, to the community life of the primitive Church.[24] The theme of fraternal love will be fully developed by Benedict only in the concluding chapters, because love ought to appear as the goal of the way which leads to God.[25]

f. *'Doing service'* (militare) is part of the definition of the monastery. The word points to the ascetical effort, the struggle for Christ and against evil,[26] nevertheless in Benedict's time the original meaning of 'militare' has faded. It means 'to serve'. Even today we speak of 'doing service' meaning 'military service'. In some respects the thought of spiritual 'struggle' is audible in this 'service'.

g. The service is carried out *'under the Rule'*, which takes precedence over the abbot, who like all the others must keep to the Rule.[27] In his description of the 'cenobites' Cassian (d.430) does not yet mention the Rule: 'They live together in community and are led by an elder (senior) with the gift of discernment.'[28] The considerations which precisely in the monasticism of Southern Gaul led to allotting a prime importance to the Rule, are to be found in the 'Master' in a paragraph which precedes the chapter on the abbot:[29] 'The Lord has appointed to his Church . . . three grades for the preaching of doctrine: "first prophets, second apostles, third teachers".[30] The Churches (ecclesiae) and schools (scholae) of Christ are to be led by their doctrine and teaching . . . . Whoever hears the 'shepherds' and 'our teachers' hears Christ himself.[31] In this view 'Christ's doctrine'[32] is the basic law of the monastery. This 'doctrine'[33] has been in part incorporated into the written Rule, which continually leans on the 'God-given' words of Scripture.[34] The Rule is to be obeyed, as a sentence placed before the title of this first chapter does not allow us to forget. This is to accounted for by its character as an abridgement of the 'doctrine' of Sacred Scripture, and more specifically as a summary of the scriptural, spiritual and disciplinary tradition of preceding times (which Benedict himself develops further out of his own experiential knowledge), namely the 'Disciplina'.[35]

h. Of necessity then the abbot belongs to the structure of the monasteries. In the 'Master's' view the abbot ranks with the 'teachers' and 'pastors', who after the time of the Apostles preside over the 'schools', just as the bishops preside over the Churches.[36] The abbot's function is seen by analogy with the heads of the Churches; it is not derived from a secular or family model. The author remains consistent in his understanding of the monastery as a 'school of the Lord',[37] which is established[38] in the midst of the 'Church' and in which the abbot works as 'teacher' and 'pastor'.[39]

3–5   a. When the 'Master' and Benedict declare themselves in favour of the eremitical state, there is no doubt they are influenced by Cassian (d.430). The latter explained the rise of monasticism and of the hermits by the fact that the enthusiasm of the apostolic age remained alive in some Christians: 'After the apostles' death the multitude of believers began to grow cold in their zeal . . . But there were men, in whom the fire of the apostolic age glowed. In order to remain faithful to the original model, they left the cities and the society of those people, who believed that they themselves and the Church of God should be allowed to settle down without any ascesis into a comfortable life. Some therefore moved to the environs of the cities and into solitude. They began to observe for themselves the rules, which they knew that the apostles had drawn up for the whole body of the Church . . . On account of their solitary life without family they got the name of monks, that is "living as solitaries". Subsequently on account of their community life they were called "cenobites" . . . As flowers and fruit from a strongly growing root the holy hermits came forth from this form of life . . . They sought out solitude, neither from fear nor from an unhealthy excessive zeal, but because they longed for greater perfection and for contemplative surrender to God . . . With good reason then were they called "anchorites" or "men of the emigration". It was not enough for them, to be precise, to combat the persecutions of the Evil One victoriously in common with others, rather they looked for the open fight and the direct conflict with the demons. Therefore they push on fearlessly into the endless desert.'[40] In this enthusiastic and idealizing presentation it is again noticeable, that the 'struggle' stands in the centre.[41] In this connection the 'Master' speaks of the struggle against the 'vices of flesh and thoughts'. This is a restrictive interpretation. The Johannine concept 'flesh' denotes the natural and earthly self.[42] The struggle against bad 'thoughts' was originally directed against the psychic roots of sin. Origen (d.253) wrote: 'Bad thoughts are the root and beginning of every sin.'[43]

b. The preconditions for the eremitical life mentioned by the 'Master' and by Benedict are already to be found in Cassian (d.430).[44] It is remarkable, however, how much the avowed approval of the 'hermits'[45] becomes an indirect *praise of community life* because this procures: 1. 'Probation' which is more valuable than unenlightened zeal;[46] 2. 'Schooling',[47] 'good equipment' and 'qualification' for all conflicts, such as are possible only to a bearer of the Spirit;[48] 3. 'security' and 'support', namely trustworthy direction through the 'encouragement'[49] of others, in whom the possession of the Spirit is presupposed, or through fraternal 'consolation' in distress of body or soul; 4. the 'ranks of the brethren'· life in community[50] confers joy. 'Behold, how good and pleasant it is, when brothers dwell in unity!'[51] Augustine (d.430) says of this verse that it 'gave birth to monasteries'. Life in 'the ranks of the brethren' is not a mere impersonal coexistence, but rather a joint existence experienced with heart and soul. It provides a place of security. The model and pattern is the primitive community of Jerusalem,[52] not another sociological model. The religious and ecclesial core of monastic community life ought not to be overlooked. Anyone who only looks in the monastery for a 'cosy nest'—in the group psychology sense—will be disappointed. On the other hand one may say that energies of mutual support, such as monastic life releases, are operative in every ecclesial community, e.g. in the local Church, in the family.

c. Basil (d.379) had already dealt thoroughly with the question, whether it is better to lead a religious contemplative life alone and in solitude or together '*with brethren*' in an ecclesial community, without his having understood this concept exclusively of a 'monastery'. He holds fast to the principle: 'On many grounds it is better to lead a common life with likeminded people.' He mentions the following reasons: 1. Materially we are dependent on mutual help. 2. Because 'love does not insist on its own way'[53] it turns towards others. 3. Criticism from others is helpful. 4. The precepts of love of neighbour can be more efficiently realized in common: the care of the sick, hospitality . . . 5. Only as community are we '*one* body in Christ . . . and individually members one of another' and can 'rejoice with those who rejoice, weep with those who weep'.[54] 6. One individual cannot receive all the gifts of the Spirit.[55] In a *community of charisms* a person does not receive them fruitlessly, but can employ them communicatively for others. 7. The (thanksgiving-) prayer of a community is particularly precious, on account of the grace which rests upon each single one. 8. The solitary life has dangers: insufficient vigilance against evil; uncritical over-valuing of self; merely theoretical, instead of practical Christian life; impossibility of an ecclesial life in community in the scriptural sense.[56]

d. The 'Master' and Benedict emphasize that God's *grace* is indispensable, if a monk wishes to enter into absolute intimacy with God.[57]

6–9 **a.** According to Cassian (d.430) '*Sarabaites*' are degenerate cenobites. They are without superiors and without training, lapse easily into a false asceticism and remain entangled in material cares.[58] Historically indeed monasticism began with the early Christian ascetics, who lived alone or in very small groups.[59] This spontaneous, but vulnerable primitive form organized itself into cenobitic monasticism. Benedict sets limits to fanciful, secessionist or disruptive tendencies, when he demands that genuine monks hold fast to a Rule and accept the *living experiential knowledge* that is mediated through a superior.[60] The Rule wishes to hand on this spiritual and disciplinary experiential knowledge of the older ascetical and monastic tradition. To that extent the Rule is comparable—in a Christian context—to the 'Wisdom literature' of the Old Testament (RB 1980).

b. The 'Master' and Benedict pass severe judgement on the Sarabaites. They are monks imprisoned in their peculiar selfishness trimmed with religion. They revolve around their own self and its *supposed freedom*, which is only a lack of orientation. The individualistic quest for salvation, as also the group egoism of a monasticism concerned only with itself, and likewise a self-satisfied bourgeois Christian outlook are unmasked as living lies. This counter-image renders the positive traits of a genuine cenobitic life all more clearly visible.

c. The theme '*Shepherd and Flock*'[61] is to be understood with an eye to Christ, and defines the relationship of monastic life to him, from whom it awaits nurture, protection, and leadership and to whose voice it must listen.[62]

10–11 **a.** '*Gyrovagues*' are monks who 'wander about'. The 'Master' gave this fourth kind a name. Benedict succinctly sketches their egoism.[63] Cassian (d.430) calls the root of the evil which characterizes this type of monk: 'the evil spirit of acedia', i.e. the lack of a sense of spirituality, and shallowness. This religious boredom 'causes the monk to sit listlessly in his cell without the will to spiritual progress, or drives him out of it, and makes of him an unstable wanderer, shirking work, who visits the houses of the brethren and the monasteries, in order to be given board and lodgings'.[64] Cassian therefore rejects a monasticism without spiritual dynamism, as he does the shirking of work and the dodges of excuses, such as gadding about.

b. Along with the compensation which consists in a life devoted to pleasure,[65] Benedict rejects *instability* with particular determination. He does not enlarge upon the other dangers mentioned by Cassian, but emphasizes stability as he does in other passages.[66] There did indeed exist a wandering monasticism based on religious motives. We need only think of the heralds of the faith[67] or of ascetics, who sought for anonymity and inner peace in the pilgrim way of life.[68]

12–13 The concluding remark about the '*strong* kind of the cenobites' shows where Benedict's sympathies lie, and leads on to the chapter on the abbot.

NOTES TO CHAPTER 1

1 RB 1–9: RM 1,1–9: RB 1,10–11: RM 1,13–74: RB 1,12: RM 1,13: RB 1,13: RM 1,75. 2 In Greek: monazon. 3 Acts 4:32. 4 PsComm 132,6. 5 Luke 10:42. 6 Conl 18,8. 7 Ep. 22,34. 8 Cf. RB 5,12; in Greek: koinos (common), bios (life). 9 Cf. Cassian, Conl. 18, 9–10. [*Note in the German edition:* Since the corresponding German expression 'Münster' has undergone a change of meaning, 'Kloster' has to be substituted for it: that means literally the 'shut off' area of the monastery (cf. RB 4,78; 67,7).] 10 VPach(lat.) 4. 11 Lib 12. 12 Heb. 13:16. 13 Acts 4:32. 14 Lib 50, where the quotation of Ps. 133: 1 follows. 15 → 73,2. 16 Acts 4:32–35; 2:45. 17 Conl 18,15. 18 → 73,4–7. 19 Acts 2:46. 20 Ps. 133:1. 21 Ps. 67:7 LXX. 22 R4P 1,5–8. 23 For him, this verse, Ps. 133:1 (see Note 20 above) 'gave birth to the monasteries'. He quotes the verse at the beginning of his Rule (Praec 1,2–3) together with Ps. 67:7 LXX (see in Note 21 above). In the same place and in other places very frequently (cf. especially: sermo 356,1–2), he appeals to the example of the primitive Church: 'they were of one heart and soul' (cf. Acts 4:32–35). 24 → Prol. 50; 31,8–9; 33,6. 25 → 68,4–5; 70,6–7;71,1–4; 72. 26 → Prol. 3.28; 7,62–66. 27 RB 3,7,11; 7,55; 23,1; 37,1; 58,9.12.13–16; 62,4.7.11; 64,20; 65,17–18; 66,8; → 73. 28 Conl 18,4. 29 RM 1,82–92. 30 1 Cor. 12:28. 31 Cf. Luke 10:16. 32 RM 1,83. 33 Cf. Acts 4:32; → Prol. 50. 34 → 73,3. 35 → 1,6–9; 23,2–3 (Note 14) 36 RM 1,82–92. 37 → 45–50.45.50. 38 → Prol. 50; 1,2. 39 → 2,1–10; 5,1–9. 40 Conl 18,5. 41 → Prol. 28. 42 Cf. John 1:13: 'nor of the will of the flesh'. The 'flesh' and its 'aspiration' (cf. Rom. 8:5–6) can become a danger through the will of man. 43 Inst Comm 15,19; cf. Mark 7:21. 44 Inst 5,36: 'a very long period of probation in the monastery', the 'learning of the rule of patience and distinguishing the spirits' (→ Prol. 28,50; 64,19), as well as 'humility, lack of possessions and freedom from failings' (cf. RB 7; 33). 45 'Anchorite' = one who withdraws (ana-choreo). 'Hermit' from 'eremus' = desert, wilderness. 46 → 72,1–2. 47 → Prol. 45–50.45.50; 1,2. 48 → Prol. 28. 49 Paraklese, Consolatio. 50 → 1.2. 51 Ps. 133:1. 52 → Prol. 45–50.45.50; 1,2; 33,6; 34,6; 34,6; 34,1–2; see Note 23 above. 53 1 Cor. 13:5. 54 Cf. Rom. 12:5,15. 55 1 Cor. 12:8–9. 56 RBasRuf 3. 57 Verse 5. 58 Conl 18,7. 'Sarabaite': originally a non-pejorative, Coptic word for 'monastic people', probably from: sa(r) = '(people) of'; abet = 'monastery'. 59 Biblical parallels are to be found in the 'virgins' (1 Cor. 7) and the 'widows' (1 Tim. 5:3). Well-known ascetics were, for instance, Origen in Egypt and John Chrysostom in Syria. 60 Cf. Cassian, Conl 19,7: 'a long and practical schooling through experience' (experientia magistra); Conl 12,16; 2,11–15 (Note 24). 61 Cf. RB 2,7.10.32.39; 63,2,18. 62 Cf. Horsiesi, Lib 17; 40. 63 Verse 11. 64 Inst 10,5–6. 65 Cf. RB 4,12. 66 → 4,78; 58,13–16.17–18; 60,9; 61,5. 67 → Prol. 21; 67,6–7. 68 VPatr 7,32,6 7.

CHAPTER 2

WHAT THE ABBOT SHOULD BE LIKE

10 Jan
11 May
10 Sept

1 To be worthy to preside over the monastery,
let the abbot always be aware of what he is called;
let him make the name of 'superior' a reality
by his deeds.

2 Faith believes   Cf. RB 63,13
that he deputizes in the monastery for Christ,
since he is designated by a name proper to Christ,

3 as the Apostle says: Rom 8:15; Gal 4:6;
YOU HAVE RECEIVED THE SPIRIT OF ADOPTION OF SONS,   Mk 14:36
WHEREBY WE CRY: ABBA 'FATHER'.

4 Therefore the abbot has a duty
not to teach, set up or order anything
which deviates from the Lord's commandment,

5 rather what he orders and what he teaches   Cf. Mt 13:33;
should penetrate the hearts of his disciples   Mt 5:6,20;6,1, 33;
as a LEAVEN of divine JUSTICE.   Rom 1:17;3:22

6 Let the abbot constantly remember,
that at God's awe-inspiring judgement
both matters will be under scrutiny:
his teaching and the disciples' obedience.

7 And let the abbot know,   Cf. Jn 21:15–16;
that the responsibility falls on the shepherd,   Lk 14:21
when the HOUSEHOLDER discovers
a loss of yield among his sheep.

8 On the other hand it will be equally true: Cf. Mt 13:27; 21:33;
if the shepherd has bestowed all pastoral care   24:43
on a restless and disobedient flock,
and applied every healing skill
to their diseased ways of acting,

9 he will be acquitted at the Lord's judgement,   Ps 40:11; Is 1:2;
and may say to the Lord with the prophet: Ez 20:27
I HAVE NOT HIDDEN YOUR JUSTICE WITHIN MY HEART;
I HAVE DECLARED YOUR TRUTH AND YOUR SALVATION;
BUT THEY HAVE DESPISED AND DISDAINED ME.

10 And at last on the sheep,   Cf. Is 25:8 (VL)
who in disobedience set themselves in opposition

to his care,
the punishment will come: triumphant DEATH.

11 Jan
12 May
11 Sept

11 He therefore who assumes the name of 'abbot',
must lead his disciples with a twofold teaching;

12 that is to say: let him show what is good and holy   Cf Is 46:12 (lat.)
by deeds rather than by words.
To teachable disciples let him expound the Lord's
commands in words,
to the HARDHEARTED however, and the more simpleminded
let his deeds demonstrate God's precepts.

13 Whenever he has taught his disciples   1 Cor 9:27
that something is harmful,
let him show by his deeds
that one ought not do it.
Otherwise he could be PREACHING TO OTHERS
AND HIMSELF BE FOUND REJECTED.

14 And will not God say to him some day   Ps 50:16–17
on account of his sins:
WHAT RIGHT HAVE YOU TO RECITE MY STATUTES
OR TAKE MY COVENANT ON YOUR LIPS?
FOR YOU HATE DISCIPLINE,
AND YOU CAST MY WORDS BEHIND YOU.

15 And YOU SAW THE SPLINTER   Mt 7:3
IN YOUR BROTHER'S EYE,
AND DID NOT SEE THE TIMBER BEAM IN YOUR OWN.

12 Jun
13 May
12 Sept

16 Let him show no favouritism within the monastery.

17 Let him not love one more than another,
unless he finds one
who is better at good actions and obedience.

18 He who came from the status of freeman
should not have precedence over the monk
who came from the state of slavery,
except on some other basis that is reasonable.

19 If, on the basis of justice, the abbot decides to do so,
he may also do the same
for the rank of anyone at all.
If this be not the case,
let each keep his own place;

20 for WHETHER SLAVE OR FREEMAN   Eph 6:8;

IN CHRIST WE ARE ALL ONE,   Gal 3:28;
and under the same Lord   Rom 2:11;
BEAR the burden of the same duties of service;   cf. Jn 19:17
BECAUSE WITH GOD THERE IS NO RESPECT OF PERSONS.

21   For one reason only are we preferred by him,
     if we prove to be better than others in good works,
     and remain humble.

22   Let the abbot therefore show an equal love of all,
     let the same standards be set for all,
     in line with what each one deserves.

13 Jan   23   As a teacher,   2 Tim 4:2
14 May   let the abbot always follow the example of the Apostle
13 Sept   who says: REPROVE, ENTREAT, REBUKE.

24   That is to say: Cf. 2 Cor 3:1 ff
     let him vary sternness with affability
     according to TIME and circumstance,
     showing now the severe face of a master,
     and again the loving heart of a father.

25   The lawless and the restless therefore   Cf. Mt 5:4, 10
     he should sharply REPROVE,
     the obedient however, the MEEK, and the PATIENT
     he should ENTREAT to advance even still more.
     The careless and the disdainful
     he should REBUKE and punish:
     such is our advice.

26   He should not OVERLOOK THE SINS of the guilty,   Cf. Wisd 11:24;
     rather, immediately at the outset   1 Sam 2:11–4:18
     let him, as best he can,
     cut out these sins by the roots.
     Let him reflect,
     that otherwise the same danger threatens him
     which befell Eli the priest of Shiloh.

27   Those of upright and intelligent cast of mind
     he should, at the first and second warning,
     caution in words;

28   the shameless and the callous,   Cf. Prov 18:2;
     the proud and the disobedient   29:19 (VL)
     he should, at the first onset of sin,
     punish with the rod or with corporal punishment.

Surely he knows that it is written:
WORDS WILL NOT CORRECT A FOOL.

29 And again: BEAT YOUR SON WITH THE STICK   Prov 23:13–14 (VL);
AND YOU WILL SAVE HIS SOUL FROM DEATH.   cf. 13:24

14 Jan   30 Let the abbot constantly remember what he is;   Cf. Lk 12:48
15 May   remember the name he bears;
14 Sept   and let him know
               that THE MAN TO WHOM MORE IS GIVEN,
               OF HIM MUCH MORE IS REQUIRED.

31 Let him realize, what a difficult and toilsome task   Cf. Mk 10:45 par;
    he has taken on: Lk 22:27
    to be a leader of souls,
    a SERVANT of many characters:
    coaxing one,
    rebuking another,
    reasoning with a third.

32 Let him make himself congenial to all   Cf. Jn 17:12; 21:15–16
    and adapt himself to all
    according to each one's character and capacities,
    so that, in the flock committed to him,
    he not only suffers no loss,
    but may rejoice to see the good flock thrive.

15 Jan   33 Above all, he should not close his eyes to,
16 May   or underrate the salvation of souls entrusted to him,
15 Sept   by bestowing more care
               on things that pass,
               things of this earth,
               things that perish.

34 Rather let him ever keep before his mind   Heb 13:17
    that he has undertaken to lead SOULS
    FOR WHOM he will one day also have TO GIVE ACCOUNT.

35 And let him not make excuses   Mt 6:33
    because of what are perhaps insufficient means;
    let him remember the word of Scripture:
    SEEK FIRST THE KINGDOM OF GOD
    AND HIS JUSTICE,
    AND ALL THESE THINGS SHALL BE GIVEN YOU BESIDES.

36 And further: Ps 34:10

NOTHING IS LACKING TO THOSE WHO FEAR HIM.

37 Let him know that he who undertakes to lead SOULS, Cf. 1 Pet 3:15;
    must PREPARE himself TO RENDER AN ACCOUNT of them, Heb 13:17

38 Let him be quite certain Cf Heb 13:17;
    that, on the day of JUDGEMENT, 1 Pet 4:5
    he will have to give AN ACCOUNT to the Lord,
    FOR as many SOULS, as there are brothers under his care,
    and, beyond doubt, for his own soul too.

39 And so, always fearful of the coming scrutiny
    which he will have to undergo as shepherd
    for the sheep committed to his care,
    he is rendered watchful about his own statement of accounts,
    while he goes guarantor for those of others.

40 And while his words of advice
    help others to amend,
    he himself, in the process,
    sheds his own faults.

CAPUT II: QUALIS DEBEAT ESSE ABBAS

¹ABBAS QUI PRAEESSE DIGNUS EST MONASTERIO SEMPER MEMINERE DEBET QUOD DICITUR ET NOMEN MAIORIS FACTIS IMPLERE. ²CHRISTI ENIM AGERE VICES IN MONASTERIO CREDITUR, QUANDO IPSIUS VOCATUR PRONOMINE, ³DICENTE APOSTOLO: ACCEPISTIS SPIRITUM ADOPTIONIS FILIORUM, IN QUO CLAMAMUS: ABBA, PATER, ⁴IDEOQUE ABBAS NIHIL EXTRA PRAECEPTUM DOMINI QUOD SIT DEBET AUT DOCERE AUT CONSTITUERE VEL IUBERE, ⁵SED IUSSIO EIUS VEL DOCTRINA FERMENTUM DIVINAE IUSTITIAE IN DISCIPULORUM MENTIBUS CONSPARGATUR, ⁶MEMOR SEMPER ABBAS QUIA DOCTRINAE SUAE VEL DISCIPULORUM OBOEDIENTIAE, UTRARUMQUE RERUM, IN TREMENDO IUDICIO DEI FACIENDA ERIT DISCUSSIO. ⁷SCIATQUE ABBAS CULPAE PASTORIS INCUMBERE QUID-QUID IN OVIBUS PATERFAMILIAS UTILITATIS MINUS POTUERIT INVENIRE. ⁸TANTUNDEM ITERUM ERIT UT, SI INQUIETO VEL INOBOEDIENTI GREGI PASTORIS FUERIT OMNIS DILIGENTIA ADTRIBUTA ET MORBIDIS EARUM ACTIBUS UNIVERSA FUERIT CURA EXHIBITA, ⁹PASTOR EORUM IN IUDICIO DOMINI ABSOLUTUS DICAT CUM PROPHETA DOMINO: IUSTITIAM TUAM NON ABSCONDI IN CORDE MEO, VERITATEM TUAM ET SALUTARE TUUM DIXI, IPSI AUTEM CONTEMNENTES SPREVERUNT ME, ¹⁰ET TUNC DEMUM INOBOEDIENTIBUS CURAE SUAE OVIBUS POENA SIT EIS PRAEVALENS IPSA MORS. ¹¹ERGO, CUM ALIQUIS SUSCIPIT NOMEN ABBATIS, DUPLICI DEBET DOCTRINA SUIS PRAEESSE DISCIPULIS, ¹²ID EST OMNIA BONA ET SANCTA FACTIS AMPLIUS QUAM VERBIS OSTENDAT, UT CAPACIBUS DISCIPULIS MANDATA DOMINI VERBIS PROPONERE, DURIS CORDE VERO ET SIMPLICIORIBUS FACTIS SUIS DIVINA PRAECEPTA MONSTRARE. ¹³OMNIA VERO QUAE DISCIPULIS DOCUERIT ESSE CONTRARIA, IN SUIS FACTIS INDICET NON AGENDA, NE ALIIS PRAEDICANS IPSE REPROBUS INVENIATUR, ¹⁴NE QUANDO ILLI DICAT DEUS PECCANTI: QUARE TU ENARRAS IUSTITIAS MEAS ET ADSUMIS TESTAMENTUM MEUM PER OS TUUM? TU VERO ODISTI DISCIPLINAM ET PROIECISTI SERMONES MEOS POST TE, ¹⁵ET: QUI IN FRATRIS TUI OCULO FESTUCAM VIDEBAS, IN TUO TRABEM NON VIDISTI. ¹⁶NON AB EO PERSONA IN MONASTERIO DISCERNATUR. ¹⁷NON UNUS PLUS AMETUR QUAM ALIUS, NISI QUEM IN BONIS

ACTIBUS AUT OBOEDIENTIA INVENERIT MELIOREM. [18]NON CONVERTENTI EX SERVITIO PRAEPONATUR INGENUUS, NISI ALIA RATIONABILIS CAUSA EXISTAT. [19]QUOD SI ITA, IUSTITIA DICANTE, ABBATI VISUM FUERIT ET DE CUIUSLIBET ORDINE ID FACIET; SIN ALIAS, PROPRIA TENEANT LOCA, [20]QUIA SIVE SERVUS SIVE LIBER, OMNES IN CHRISTO UNUM SUMUS ET SUB UNO DOMINO AEQUALEM SERVITUTIS MILITIAM BAIULAMUS, QUIA NON EST APUD DEUM PERSONARUM ACCEPTIO. [21]SOLUMMODO IN HAC PARTE APUD IPSUM DISCERNIMUR, SI MELIORES AB ALIIS IN OPERIBUS BONIS ET HUMILES INVENIAMUR. [22]ERGO AEQUALIS SIT AB EO OMNIBUS CARITAS, UNA PRAEBEATUR IN OMNIBUS SECUNDUM MERITA DISCIPLINA. [23]IN DOCTRINA SUA NAMQUE ABBAS APOSTOLICAM DEBET ILLAM SEMPER FORMAM SERVARE IN QUA DICIT: ARGUE, OBSECRA, INCREPA, [24]ID EST, MISCENS TEMPORIBUS TEMPORA, TERRORIBUS BLANDIMENTA, DIRUM MAGISTRI, PIUM PATRIS OSTENDAT AFFECTUM, [25]ID EST INDISCIPLINATOS ET INQUIETOS DEBET DURIUS ARGUERE, OBOEDIENTES AUTEM ET MITES ET PATIENTES, UT IN MELIUS PROFICIANT OBSECRARE, NEGLEGENTES ET CONTEMNENTES UT INCREPAT ET CORRIPIAT ADMONEMUS. [26]NEQUE DISSIMULET PECCATA DELINQUENTIUM; SED UT, MOX UT COEPERINT ORIRI, RADICITUS EA UT PRAEVALET AMPUTET, MEMOR PERICULI HELI SACERDOTIS DE SILO. [27]ET HONESTIORES QUIDEM ATQUE INTELLEGIBILES ANIMOS PRIMA VEL SECUNDA ADMONITIONE VERBIS CORRIPIAT, [28]INPROBOS AUTEM ET DUROS AC SUPERBOS VEL INOBOEDIENTES VERBERUM VEL CORPORIS CASTIGATIO IN IPSO INITIO PECCATI COERCEAT, SCIENS SCRIPTUM: STULTUS VERBIS NON CORRIGITUR, [29]ET ITERUM: PERCUTE FILIUM TUUM VIRGA ET LIBERABIS ANIMAM EIUS A MORTE. [30]MEMINERE DEBET SEMPER ABBAS QUOD EST, MEMINERE QUOD DICITUR, ET SCIRE QUIA CUI PLUS COMMITTITUR, PLUS AB EO EXIGITUR. [31]SCIATQUE QUAM DIFFICILEM ET ARDUAM REM SUSCIPIT, REGERE ANIMAS ET MULTORUM SERVIRE MORIBUS, ET ALIUM QUIDEM BLANDIMENTIS, ALIUM VERO INCREPATIONIBUS, ALIUM SUASIONIBUS; [32]ET SECUNDUM UNIUSCUIUSQUE QUALITATEM VEL INTELLEGENTIAM, ITA SE OMNIBUS CONFORMET ET APTET UT NON SOLUM DETRIMENTA GREGIS SIBI COMMISSI NON PATIATUR, VERUM IN AUGMENTATIONE BONI GREGIS GAUDEAT. [33]ANTE OMNIA, NE DISSIMULANS AUT PARVIPENDENS SALUTEM ANIMARUM SIBI COMMISSARUM, NE PLUS GERAT SOLLICITUDINEM DE REBUS TRANSITORIIS ET TERRENIS ATQUE CADUCIS, [34]SED SEMPER COGITET QUIA ANIMAS SUSCEPIT REGENDAS, DE QUIBUS ET RATIONEM REDDITURUS EST. [35]ET NE CAUSETUR DE MINORI FORTE SUBSTANTIA, MEMINERIT SCRIPTUM: PRIMUM QUAERITE REGNUM DEI ET IUSTITIAM EIUS, ET HAEC OMNIA ADICIENTUR VOBIS, [36]ET ITERUM: NIHIL DEEST TIMENTIBUS EUM. [37]SCIATQUE QUIA QUI SUSCIPIT ANIMAS REGENDAS PARET SE AD RATIONEM REDDENDAM. [38]ET QUANTUM SUB CURA SUA FRATRUM SE HABERE SCIERIT NUMERUM, AGNOSCAT PRO CERTO QUIA IN DIE IUDICII IPSARUM OMNIUM ANIMARUM EST REDDITURUS DOMINO RATIONEM, SINE DUBIO ADDITA ET SUAE ANIMAE. [39]ET ITA, TIMENS SEMPER FUTURAM DISCUSSIONEM PASTORIS DE CREDITIS OVIBUS, CUM DE ALIENIS RATIOCINIIS CAVET, REDDITUR DE SUIS SOLLICITUS, [40]ET CUM DE MONITIONIBUS SUIS EMENDATIONEM ALIIS SUBMINISTRAT, IPSE EFFICITUR A VITIIS EMENDATUS.

1–10   **a.** The 'Master'[1] presents a well-thought out picture of the abbot, on the basis of a tradition that had already become general. Scriptural statements about Christ and the apostolic ministries are ingenuously applied to the abbot, because by analogy with the bishop he presides over an ecclesial community, namely the 'School of Christ'.[2] The theology of the abbot developed here is therefore capable of being transferred to every ecclesial superior, and generally to a Christian understanding of *authority*.

b. The real Abbot and Householder of the monastery is Christ. The abbot is, in the light of faith, his 'representative'. Without this religious context of meaning, authority and obedience in the monastery would be arrogance or an irresponsible renunciation of personal rights. He is '*Superior*' (maior). As the householder designates one of his servants 'maior-domus', and places him as his deputy over the rest of the domestics, so Christ in the 'House of God', namely in the Church or in the monastery, appoints the bishops and the clerics or the abbot and the officials. For Benedict the monastery is a 'House of God'.[3] In it the abbot has a function of service and mediation between Christ and the monks.

c. The abbot is understood to be a *spiritual father*, because like Christ in the circle of the disciples he 'manifests the Father'.[4] The abbot, in a certain sense, must also be defined from the standpoint of the community. The individuals, who bear the Spirit of Christ in themselves,[5] desire to see the fatherhood of God made present in their midst in a visible way.[6] By reason of the reception of the Spirit they call the abbot 'Abba-Father', and this with Christ in view. The belief that God, who bestows the Spirit on us, takes us for his own, gives the strength to accept ourselves, to accept and 'carry' the others, and to see in the abbot's authority the fatherly goodness of the Lord. In the ancient Church they were accustomed to see Christ as Father, because he mediates new life.[7] According to the Gospels Jesus called his disciples 'children'.[8] When in the primitive Church he is named 'Father', an ardent love of Christ expresses itself thereby. This is generally hinted at only in a veiled way in the written documents of the Age of the Martyrs, but it was a characteristic impulse particularly of popular piety. We catch an echo of it in the 'Master' and in Benedict.

In early times, for example, Irenaeus (d.*c.* 202) had very emphatically declared:' The father of the human race is the Word of God.'[9] And: 'The name of the Father is also that of the Son'.[10] Besides, the Christocentrism of the 'Master' and of Benedict reflects too an anti-Arian position.[11] Because Christ is in 'essence identical' with the Father, he may be addressed with the name of Father. Subsequently this name devolves also upon the one holding Christ's place in the monastery. Basil (d.379) recommends, to consider as 'father' those 'who have engendered someone through the Gospel'[12], and as 'brothers' those who have received the same 'Spirit, who makes (us) sons'.[13,14] Already in the Egyptian monasteries they used, for example, to call Pachomius (d. 346) 'our holy father'.[15] The 'spiritual father', around whom disciples begin to gather, is the prototype of the abbot,[16] for which the 'Lives of the Fathers' bring countless examples.

d. The abbot is a *teacher*, but only if, as it were, he lends his voice to Christ.[17] That he should teach nothing that is contrary to God's will or contrary to Scripture, is said also by Basil (d. 379).[18] Christ's doctrine is to be spoken in such a way, that it reaches the domain of the heart and can unfold itself there. The bond with the Lord and the warning about the shepherd's responsibility in face of God's judgment should prevent any false absolutism on the abbot's part.

e. By analogy with the *shepherds* of the Church the author alludes to Ezechiel's discourse to the shepherds,[19] as many monastic writers do in a similar manner, in order to put a curb on any autocratic system of government.[20]

f. The pastor's role as *physician* is often expounded.[21]

11–15 **a.** The abbot is a teacher by word and example. As spiritual father he imitates *Christ's teaching method.* Clement of Alexandria (died before 215) already spoke of this. In Egypt they began to call the monasteries 'schools', perhaps in memory of the 'didaskaleion' or the catechetical school. A 'senior' i.e. an older, more experienced ascetic instructs disciples, who place themselves under his authority. Cassian (d. 430) sought to promote in the West this conception of the monastery as a 'school'.[22] As a matter of fact in the Egyptian monasteries they wished to further all catechesis[23] and by a model practice.[24] Lérins took over the concept of 'school', Benedict rather represses it,[25] without detracting from the pre-eminent significance of knowledge of the Scriptures.

b. The distinction between 'capable' and 'more simple-minded pupils' (!)[26] is embedded in the admonition that the abbot must adapt himself to the individual character. The person with its individuality is to be accepted and respected in a community;[27] only thus can one integrate oneself in a community.

16–22 **a.** The precept of showing an equal love to all, and the prohibition of favouritism[28] are based on the Pauline teaching of the unity and equality of all in Christ.[29] That is the basic supposition of a genuine community life. Benedict inserts into the Master's text a remark of his own[30] on the question about the order of rank, a question to which he had given thought. He does not let social differences count as a reason for preference; he does however, of himself, mention other motives.[31] He deletes a remark of the Master's that God allows the earth to serve the good as well as the bad[32], because it might sound to him as too lacking in a sense of proportion.[33]

b. The phrase about *'bearing' the duties of service* is a discreet reminder of the 'carrying' of the Cross by Jesus,[34] who is the model not only for the abbot but for each and all.

23–25 The theme of adaptation to the *different individual characters* is based on a word of the Apostle's, which was a pointer for many monastic Rules. Once again, a directive for Church leaders is transferred to the abbot.[35] Benedict deletes[36] a paragraph of the 'Master's', which presents Jesus taking a child by the hand, in order to give an example of humility. He also deletes the Master's requirement of a fatherly as well as a motherly love to all. Origen (d.253) had already declared himself in favour of a well-balanced combination of kindness and stringency.[37]

26 Benedict introduced into the 'Master's text' this admonition to proceed immediately against faults. The reference to *Eli* is meant to warn against false complaisance.[38] In the later, second chapter on the abbot, the challenge to an immediate 'amputation'[39] of a fault is softened, because there a 'prudent and loving procedure' is suggested.[40] Basil (d.379) recommends to proceed as a father or doctor towards the sick son.[41]

27–29 These verses likewise inserted by Benedict treat again of *adaptation* to the individual character.[42] The tone of voice becomes stern in face of the 'hardhearted'[43] and of those who lack understanding.[44] Punishments which would be unbearable for sensitive natures, could be salutary for them.

30 The 'Master' refers again to the abbot's *responsibility*.[45]

31–32 **a.** This addition by Benedict on *adaptation* to the character of individuals[46] betrays a major concern of Benedict's which does him honour. In the whole context the abbot appears as bearer of the Spirit and pastor of souls.[47] Typical for this care of souls is the *concern for the individual*. It modulates from person to person, indeed it presupposes the 'knowledge of hearts'. The image of the first abbot of Lérins may have been a guide: Honoratus (d.428) 'could see into the special quality of each single person. If an individual improved, he adjusted the reprimand accordingly. He behaved sternly towards one, kindly towards another . . . He carried, as it were, the souls of each single one in his own soul.' He had at his disposal 'a God–given instinct', so that he was aware of the powers, the spiritual constitution, even the digestion and the sleep 'of each, one by one, reining in the enthusiastic, spurring on the sluggish'.[48] He knew how 'to mingle friendliness with strictness'.[49] The gift of the knowledge of hearts makes for a charismatic pastor of souls.

b. There are few direct parallels in the monastic Rules for the remark about the difficulty of the *cure of souls and of pastoral care*. Augustine (d.430) urges the brethren to obey spontaneously and thus render themselves a kindness(!) and simultaneously ease the responsibility of those in charge.[50] The image of the 'entrusted flock' is traditional.[51]

33–36 Scarcely any parallels are to be found in other mirrors for abbots for this admonition of Benedict's to safeguard *the priority of the spiritual*.[52] The abbot also carries the responsibility for the material well-being of all. The monks renounce personal property[53] and surrender themselves to a 'man of God', who represents the Providence of God.[54] As a spiritual man the abbot is expected to set the priorities right. He should 'lead the souls of the brethren upwards from earthly realities to the spiritual ones, by virtue of his supernatural gifts of love and truth'.[55] For the administration of the goods of the monastery, the gift of 'wisdom' is especially presupposed.[56] Since in the monastery everything belongs to a sacral sphere,[57] it is normal for Benedict, that the spiritual teacher should busy himself also with what is 'worldly'.[58]

37–40 This text of the 'Master's' is a further variation on the themes of care of souls, duties of the shepherd and responsibility.[59] The shepherd's service ought to lead to *inner purification*, i.e. to 'purity of heart' (apatheia), which is also the goal of the way of humility.[60] It makes room for the love of God, and is a presupposition for the vision of God.[61]

NOTES TO CHAPTER 2

1 Two-thirds of the chapter have been taken directly from the 'Rule of the Master': RB 2, 1–18a.20–25.30–37–40 = RM 2.1–21. 22–25.32–34.39–40. In the 'Rule of the Master', the chapter on the abbot follows immediately upon the statements about the 'Rule'. The abbot is the teacher of the Rule. The 'Master's' text about the abbot appeared originally in the 'Rule of the Monastery', a document that belongs to the same dossier as the 'Actus militiae cordis'. For practical reasons the chapters about the kinds of monks and about the abbot were later inserted into the spiritual 'Account of the Warfare of the Heart' (Manning). 2 → Prol. 45–50.45.50; 1,2; cf. RM 1,82–92. 3 Cf. RB 53,22; cf. RM 11,5–14. 4 Verse 3; cf. John 10:38; 14:8–12; 17:6. 5 Cf. also Acts 4:33: 'great grace was upon them all'. 6 RB 5,12: 'They desire to have an abbot rule them'. 7 Christ is the 'second Adam' (cf. 1 Cor. 15:45); → Prol. 3. It is for him that the messianic title 'Everlasting Father' is meant (Isa. 9:6). 8 Mark 10:24; John 13:33: 14:18; 21:5; especially: 1 John. 9 Adv haer 4,52,5. 10 Adv haer 4,17,6. This parallel to RB 2,2 is particularly striking: 'pronomine = 'sur-name' in the sense of title, form of address. Irenaeus quotes Matt. 11:27: 'no one knows the Father except the Son . . .' 11 → Introd. 8. 12 Cf. 1 Cor. 4:15–16; Gal. 4:19. 13 Cf. Rom. 8:15; Gal. 4:6. 14 RBasRuf 4. 15 Horsiesi, Lib 10. 16 Cassian, Conl 18,4: Inst 4,8–10. 17 Cf. RB 5,6, where Luke 10:16 is quoted: 'He who hears you hears me'. 18 RBasRuf 15. 19 Ezek.

34:2–5. The following are favourite quotations: John 21:15–17 (Hors Lib 17; RF 37); Heb. 13:17 & Acts 20:28 (Hors Lib 19.40); Heb. 3:15 (RF 37). **20** Hors Lib 7.9.10.11.13; Augustine Praec 7,1–3; R4P 5,11–17; RCaesVirg 35; RF 37. **21** E.g. Origen, Jes Nave Hom 7,6. Honoratus, the founder of Lérins, is described briefly as 'general medicine for all' (VHonor 6,27). → 2,26–29; 27,2–4; 28; 46,5–6; 64,12–15. **22** Conl 3.1. He relates that even old hermits had sought out the 'school of the disciples' in order to make real progress in the faith. **23** In Pachomian monasteries, the superior held a conference or catechesis three times a week (Pach Praec 20–21). **24** 'Abbot Hyperechios spoke: "He is truly wise who teaches the others by his deeds, not just through his words"'(VPatr 5, 12, 5). **25** → Prol. 45–50. **26** Verse 12. Cf. the distinction between *pneumatici* and others in the Alexandrine school. **27** → 2.31–32; 3.1–3; 31.3–7 etc. The monastic writers are familiar with this theme: Hors Lib 9.13; R4P 2.7; Augustine, Praec. **28** → 34. 1–2; 63, 1–9. **29** Cf. Hors Lib 9.16; Pach Inst 18; R4P 2.8; 5.11–12. **30** Verse 18–19. **31** → 63, 1–9. **32** Before Verse 22. **33** In Verse 22 he adds a remark that obscures the order of rank: 'as each deserves'. **34** 'baiulare' (John 19:17). **35** Cf RBasRuf 98 (choice of words!). **36** after Verse 23. **37** Verse 24. Origen points to God himself, who unites these characteristics in himself for our salvation. **38** A traditional warning: cf. Pach Inst 18; RBasRuf 122. **39** Cf. RB 33,1; 55,18. **40** RB 64.14. Perhaps under the influence of Augustine: Praec 7. **41** RBasRuf 23. On the image of the doctor, see Note 21 above. **42** → 2,23–25. **43** → Prol. 8–11. **44** Cf. RBasRuf 17. On the corporal punishments → 23,5; 28,1–5; 30,2–3; 45,3. **45** → 2.1–10. **46** → 2.11–15.23–25.27 29. The pairing of the concepts 'friendly words' — reprimand, is to be found, for instance, in RF 37. **47** → 27.5–6; 28,1–5; 41,5; 46,5–6. **48** VHonor 3,17–4,18. **49** Ibid, 6.26. **50** Praec 7,4; cf. RCaesVirg 35,4–8. **51** Cf. Hors Lib 17; see in Note 20 above. This comparison is to be met frequently in the liturgy too. **52** But cf. RCaesVirg 27.1. **53** Cf. Acts 4:35: '(they) laid it at the Apostles' feet'. **54** This ancient monastic view makes the abbot appear in a light different to that in which the bishop does. The latter does not have to concern himself directly with the material cares of his faithful. **55** R4P 2,4: cf. RM 11.94–106. **56** Cf. RB 31,2 (the Cellarer): RB 53,5–10 (the Guestmaster); 66, 1 (the porter). **57** → 31, 19–20. **58** RB 64, 17. **59** → 2,1–10.31–32. **60** → 7,67–70. **61** → Prol. 47; 4,55–58.

CHAPTER 3

ON CONVENING THE BRETHREN FOR CONSULTATION

16 Jan
17 May
16 Sept

1 Whenever there are matters of importance in the monastery,
let the abbot convene the whole community,
and himself state what is at issue.

2 And listening to the advice of the brethren
let him weigh it up in his own mind;
and when he has decided
what is the more useful course,
let him follow it out.

3 But the reason we have said   Cf. Mt 11:25
that all should be convened for consultation
is that the Lord often REVEALS the better thing
to a YOUNGER PERSON.

4 Let the brethren however give their opinion
with all the submission of humility,
nor let them presume
to defend their own point of view with insolence.

5 Let the decision DEPEND rather on the abbot,   Cf. Mt 22:40
and let all obey
what he will have judged to be
the more salutary course.

6 But just as it befits disciples
to obey the master,
so it is incumbent on him
to make all arrangements
with foresight and justice.

17 Jan
18 May
17 Sept

7 In all things therefore
let all follow the tutelage of the Rule,
nor let anyone defiantly
deviate from it.

8 Let no one in the monastery
follow the pull of his own heart,

9 nor let anyone presume to have words with his abbot
in an insolent manner,
or outside the monastery.

10 If he have presumed this,
    let him undergo the discipline of the Rule.

11 However, let the abbot himself do everything   Cf. Rom 14:12
    in the fear of God
    and with observance of the Rule,
    fully aware
    that he will have to RENDER AN ACCOUNT
    of all his decisions
    to GOD, the just judge.

12 If however some less important matters
    of the monastery's affairs
    have to be attended to,
    let him consult the seniors only,
    according to the word of Scripture:

13 DO EVERYTHING WITH CONSULTATION,   Prov 31:3 (VL);
    AND YOU WILL HAVE NO REGRETS   15:22; 24:6;
    WHEN THE DEED IS DONE.   Ecclus 32:24

CAPUT III: DE ADHIBENDIS AD CONSILIUM FRATRIBUS

¹QUOTIENS ALIQUA PRAECIPUA SUNT IN MONASTERIO, CONVOCET ABBAS OMNEM CONGREGATIONEM ET DICAT IPSE UNDE AGITUR. ²ET AUDIENS CONSILIUM FRATRUM TRACTET APUD SE ET QUOD UTILIUS INDICAVERIT FACIAT. ³IDEO AUTEM OMNES AD CONSILIUM VOCARI DIXIMUS, QUIA SAEPE IUNIORI DOMINUS REVELAT QUOD MELIUS EST. ⁴SIC AUTEM DENT FRATRES CONSILIUM CUM OMNI HUMILITATIS SUBIECTIONE, ET NON PRAESUMANT PROCACITER DEFENDERE QUOD EIS VISUM FUERIT; ⁵ET MAGIS IN ABBATIS PENDAT ARBITRIO, UT QUOD SALUBRIUS ESSE IUDICAVERIT, EI CUNCTI OBOEDIANT. ⁶SED SICUT DISCIPULOS CONVENIT OBOEDIRE MAGISTRO, ITA ET IPSUM PROVIDE ET IUSTE DECET CUNCTA DISPONERE. ⁷IN OMNIBUS IGITUR OMNES MAGISTRAM SEQUANTUR REGULAM, NEQUE AB EA TEMERE DECLINETUR A QUO-QUAM. ⁸NULLUS IN MONASTERIO PROPRII SEQUATUR CORDIS VOLUNTATEM. ⁹NEQUE PRAESUMAT QUISQUAM CUM ABBATE SUO PROTERVE AUT FORIS MONASTERIUM CONTENDERE. ¹⁰QUOD SI PRAESUMPSERIT, REGULARI DISCIPLINAE SUBIACEAT. ¹¹IPSE TAMEN ABBA CUM TIMORE DEI ET OBSERVATIONE REGULAE OMNIA FACIAT, SCIENS SE PROCUL DUBIO DE OMNIBUS IUDICIIS SUIS AEQUISSIMO IUDICI DEO RATIONEM REDDITURUM. ¹²SI QUA VERO MINORA AGENDA SUNT IN MONASTERII UTILITATIBUS, SENIORUM TANTUM UTATUR CONSILIO, ¹³SICUT SCRIPTUM EST: OMNIA FAC CUM CONSILIO, ET POST FACTUM NON PAENITEBERIS.

1–3 a. Out of rudiments in the 'Master'¹ Benedict develops a chapter of his own on the brethren in council. Benedict is progressive here. In earlier monastic Rules the institution is nowhere so clearly delineated.² Perhaps we have to reckon with the influence of the Eastern Roman state law for the Church,³ perhaps too with a later draft.

b. The weight which Benedict gives to this council of the brethren, shows that he takes seriously the solidarity and co-responsibility of all. Discussions in community are conducive to the well-being of the whole monastery.

c. When Benedict orders the convening of the brothers' council, he nevertheless holds fast to the abbot's *role of leadership*. The latter is competent and responsible for the presentation of the agenda and for the information of the brethren, who are expected to make use of their co-responsibility. The abbot leads the discussion, and after the process of circumspect and collegial formation of opinion, takes the decision.

d. The abbot has to listen to the advice of the brethren. God allots the charism of counsel as he wills. In order that this charism can be fruitful and that the will of God can be known, all are to be called to consultation. It is not a question of 'civil rights' or of democratic majorities.[4] Within the Church we do not think in categories of parties and majorities; we seek rather for a *'consensus'*, which ought to stem from the working of the Spirit in all members. Origen (d.253) once spoke of a 'consensus of the whole Church animated by the Spirit'.[5]

e. These considerations induce Benedict to call the *younger* also to consultation. Benedict mentions these frequently elsewhere too.[6] Much as early monasticism treasured the advice and guidance of the elders,[7] it was nevertheless prepared to recognize the working of the Spirit in the younger. Cassian (d.430) relates about Abbot Paphnutius: 'From early years on, he was, through grace, a particularly valuable member of the community. The best-known and most experienced among the elders of that time wondered at his gravity and his imperturbable constancy. In spite of his youth they placed him on a level with the elders on account of his virtue, and introduced him into their circle'.[8] In a religious perspective the generation conflict solves itself.

4–6 **a.** Good manners and a certain reticence are expected of all advisers. They are aware that good counsel is a *gift of grace*, and they know their own limitations. The following story demonstrates this pointedly: 'A brother in Scete was found guilty. The elders wanted to hold an assembly. They sent to Abbot Moses, and conveyed to him that he should come. But he did not want to come. Then the Presbyter sent to him and had it said to him: "Come! the multitude of the brethren is waiting for you." Then he stood up and came. But he took an old basket full of holes, filled it with sand and trailed it along behind him. Then they went towards him and asked: "Father, what does this mean?" The old man answered: "My sins are running behind me, but I can't see them. And have I to come today, to judge another's sins? When they heard this, they waived passing a sentence on the brother, and forgave him."'[9]

b. The abbot should let himself be guided by the gift of *discernment*. His sense of responsibility must be aimed at what is more 'salutary'. Cassian (d.430) could say on 'the gift of discernment': 'It avoids every exaggeration to right or left, and teaches the monk always to strike ahead on the golden way. It is neither in the habit—on the right—of over-excited achievement of virtues (by overstepping the bounds of a correct ascesis from excessive zeal or from too exalted an opinion of oneself), nor will it deflect to the left, and from laxity allow all faults to run to seed (i.e. to become spiritually lukewarm under the pretext of keeping the body in good trim).'[10] Moderation, which is not minimalism!

c. Benedict here urges a *reflective behaviour* on the abbot, in order thereupon to give the monks similar advice for their conduct towards the abbot.[11]

7–11   a. Benedict realizes that the abbot has faults and failings (the 'Master' never admits the like). On the other hand, Benedict endeavours to uphold the abbot's authority. But he must keep to the *Rule* as the basic law, just like all others.[12] With this proviso, Benedict entrusts the abbot with more discretionary freedom and power to make decisions than does the 'Master', who would regulate everything down to the smallest detail. The Rule of Benedict leaves much to the abbot's gift of discernment. One must not remain stuck in the letter of the Rule.[13] The Rule is so flexible that it can be adapted to new situations. It remains, however, a binding 'law',[14] because it wishes to be understood as a summary of Scripture, and it refers[15] to this latter as well as to the best tradition of the Fathers.[16] Even the literal sense of an obsolete individual directive from the sixth century can still be meaningful, when one keeps the author's intention in mind.

b. Benedict does not forbid differences of opinion in the monastery, but he certainly does forbid a self-centredness which is just out for conflict. The heart must become free from all aggressiveness and pride.[17]

12–13   This smaller 'council of seniors' seems to be totally a fruit of Benedict's own personal experience. Perhaps his community was considerably larger than that of the 'Master' and could not so often be called together 'for less important matters'. This practical reason may have led to the development of a new institution. Social structures are there to serve the good of persons and of the community. A smaller council of experienced and competent brethren can quickly go into action when urgent problems arise.

NOTES TO CHAPTER 3

1 RB 3,1–11: RM 2,41–50. The 'Master' discusses in the chapter on the abbot the question of the sale of monastic property. On this matter, the abbot consults the brethren assembled in council Cf. RF 36: Obtaining the consent of the brethren when bondmen are freed. It is possible that the text about the council of the brethren was inserted after the chapter on the abbot for the first time in the version P of the 'Rule of the Master'. Benedict would then follow an earlier version of the RM. 2 It will have to be accepted, however, that there were always discussions in common. In the community of Qumrân they took place under the leadership of the 'Supervisor of the Rabbiim' (1QS 6,8–14). Bishops were allowed, for instance, to dispose of Church property only with the consent of their colleagues in the ecclesiastical province. It was so stipulated by the Council of Agde, which was held under the chairmanship of Caesarius (506, can.7). 3 Justinian (d. 565) prescribes the involvement of all the monks when sales take place (Codex 1,2,17; Nov. 120,6–7; 123,6). 4 Cf. RB 64,1–6. 5 Jes Nave Hom 7,6: 'in uno consensu ecclesia universa conspirans' (→ 28,6–8, in Note 20). 6 Cf. RB 3,3; 4,71; 22,16; 30,5; 36,8; 63,8.10.12.15.16; 66,5; 68,4; 71,4. 7 Conl 2,2. 8 Conl 18,5. 9 VPatr 5,9,4. 10 Conl 2,2. 11 → 6,6; 64,17–19. 12 → 1,2 (Note 27). 13 → 18,22–25. 14 → 58,9–10. 15 → 1,2; 73,3.8–9. 16 → 73,2–4. 17 Cf. Luke 22:42: 'Not my will, but thine, be done.'

CHAPTER 4

THE TOOLS OF GOOD WORKS: WHAT ARE THEY?

18 Jan
19 May
18 Sept

1 First: TO LOVE THE LORD GOD
FROM A FULL HEART,
WITH THE WHOLE SOUL,
WITH ALL ONE'S STRENGTH. Mt 22:38; Deut 6:4; Mk 12:30; Lk 10:27

2 Then: THE NEIGHBOUR AS IF ONESELF. Lev 19:18; Mk 12:31; Mt 22:39–40; Lk 10:28

3 Then: NOT TO KILL.

4 NOT TO COMMIT ADULTERY. Mt 19:18–19; Lk 18:20; Rom 13:9

5 NOT TO STEAL.

6 NOT TO SIN BY CONCUPISCENCE. Ex 20:17; Deut 5:4; Rom 13:9

7 NOT TO BEAR FALSE WITNESS. Mt 19:18; Mk 10:19; Lk 18:20

8 TO RESPECT everyone. 1 Pet 2:17

9 And NOT TO DO TO ANOTHER
WHAT ONE DOES NOT WISH DONE TO ONESELF. Mt 7:12: Lk 6:31; Tob 4:15; cf. RB 61, 14; 70, 7

10 TO DENY ONE'S VERY SELF TO ONESELF,
in order TO FOLLOW Christ. Mt 16:24; 19:16; Lk 9:23

11 TO DISCIPLINE THE BODY. 1 Cor 9:27

12 Not to be enamoured of soft living.

13 To love fasting. Cf. Mt 4:2; 17:20; cf. Is 58:7; Mt 25:35–36

14 To give new heart to the poor.

15 TO CLOTHE A NAKED person. Mt 25:36; Tob 1:17

16 TO VISIT A SICK person.

17 TO BURY A DEAD person. Tob 1:17; 2:7–9

18 To be a support in time of TROUBLE. Is 1:17; James 1:27

19 To comfort one who is SADDENED. Cf. Is 61:2; 2 Cor 1:4: 1 Thess 5:14

19 Jan
20 May
19 Sept

20 To make oneself an OUTSIDER to the ways OF
THE WORLD. Cf. Rom 12:2; James 1:27

21 To put nothing above the LOVE for Christ. Cf. Mt 10:37

22 Not to bring anger to a head. Cf. Mt 5:22

23 Not to keep a time for an outburst of temper.

24 Not to retain DECEIT IN one's HEART. Cf. Prov 12:20

25 Not to offer an insincere PEACE. Cf. Jer 9:8

26 Not to be unfaithful to LOVE. Cf. 1 Pet 4:8

27 NOT TO SWEAR, lest one SWEAR FALSELY. Mt 5:33,34

28 TO UTTER THE TRUTH FROM HEART and MOUTH. Ps 15:2,3

29 NOT TO REPAY WRONG WITH WRONG.   1 Pet 3:9; cf. Rom 12:17

30 TO DO NO WRONG,   Cf. Mt 20:13; 1 Cor 6:7
but in fact TO SUFFER patiently
    WRONGS DONE TO ONESELF.

31 TO LOVE ONE'S ENEMIES.   Mt 5:44; Lk 6:27

32 NOT TO RETURN INSULT FOR INSULT,   Lk 6:28; 1 Cor 4:12;
TO RETURN rather A BLESSING.   1 Pet 3:9

33 TO SUFFER PERSECUTION FOR JUSTICE' SAKE.   1 Cor 4:12; 1 Pet 3:14;
         Mt 5:10

34 NOT to be ARROGANT.   1 Tim 3:3;
35 NOT A HEAVY DRINKER.   Tit 1:7

36 Not IMMODERATE in eating.   Cf. Ecclus 37.31

37 Not drowsy,   Prov 20,13

38 not LAZY,   Rom 12:11

39 not given to criticizing.   Cf. Wisd 1:11

40 not a DETRACTOR.

41 To entrust one's HOPE TO GOD.   Ps 40:5

42 On seeing something good in oneself,
to refer it to God, not to self;

43 realizing however always that evil was one's own doing,
and to impute it to oneself.

20 Jan 44 To fear JUDGEMENT DAY.   Mt 12:36
21 May 45 To be terrified of hell.
20 Sept 46 To yearn for eternal life with all spiritual longing.

47 To look death daily in the eye.   Cf. Mt 24:44;25:13; Lk 12:40

48 At every moment to keep guard over the
actions of one's life.

49 To know for certain everywhere that   Cf. Prov 15:3;
GOD IS LOOKING at one.   Ps 14:2

50 When bad thoughts slip into one's heart TO DASH them   Cf. Ps 136:9;
immediately against Christ   1 Cor 10:4;
and to reveal them to a spiritual elder.   cf. RB Prol 28

51 TO GUARD ONE'S MOUTH FROM EVIL or depraved TALK.   Cf. Eph 4:29

52 Not to love MUCH TALKING.   Prov 10:19

53 Not to speak FOOLISH or FACETIOUS WORDS.   Cf. Jer 10:15; Eph 5:6

54 Not to love much or loud laughter.

55 To listen with pleasure to the holy readings.

56 To prostrate oneself frequently in prayer.   Cf. Lk 18:1; 1 Thess 5:17

57 With tears and sighing   Cf. Mt 6:12

daily to confess your past SINS to God in prayer.

58 For the future to rectify these same faults.

59 NOT TO GRATIFY THE CRAVINGS OF THE FLESH. Gal 5:16

60 To hate SELFWILL. Cf. Ecclus 18:30

61 To obey the abbot's commands in everything, Mt 23:3
even were he himself—which God forbid—
to act differently;
remembering that command of the Lord:
'DO WHAT THEY TELL YOU,
BUT NOT WHAT THEY DO.'

62 Not to want to be called a saint,
before you are one;
first be so,
that you may be more genuinely called so.

21 Jan
22 May 63 Day by day
21 Sept to fulfil by deeds
what God commands.

64 To LOVE PURITY. Judith 15:11 (lat.)

65 To HATE NOBODY Cf. Lev 19:17

66 Not to entertain JEALOUSY. Cf. James 3:14,16: cf.

67 Not to indulge in rivalry. Phil 1:15;
1 Tim 6:4;

68 To have no craving for CONTROVERSY.

69 To shun pride.

70 And TO RESPECT THE ELDERLY. Cf. Lev 19:32

71 To love the younger.

72 Out of love for Christ TO PRAY FOR ONE'S ENEMIES. Cf. Mt 5:44

73 To make peace with an opponent BEFORE SUNSET. Eph 4:26

74 And never to despair of GOD'S MERCY. Cf. Lk 1:78

75 See, these are the tools of the art of the Spirit.

76 When, day and night they will have been acted on by us
without respite,
and accounted for on the Day of Judgement,
that reward will be paid out to us by the Lord
which he himself has promised:

77 EYE HAS NOT SEEN NOR EAR HEARD 1 Cor 2:9;
WHAT THINGS GOD HAS PREPARED FOR THOSE cf. Is 64:3
WHO LOVE HIM.

78 The monastery enclosure and stability in the community
constitute however
the workshop where we labour diligently at all these things.

CAPUT IV: QUAE SUNT INSTRUMENTA BONORUM OPERUM

[1]IN PRIMIS DOMINUM DEUM DILIGERE EX TOTO CORDE, TOTA ANIMA, TOTA VIRTUTE. [2]DEINDE PROXIMUM TAMQUAM SEIPSUM. [3]DEINDE NON OCCIDERE. [4]NON ADULTERARE. [5]NON FACERE FURTUM. [6]NON CONCUPISCERE. [7]NON FALSUM TESTIMONIUM DICERE. [8]HONORARE OMNES HOMINES. [9]ET QUOD SIBI QUIS FIERI NON VULT, ALIO NE FACIAT. [10]ABNEGARE SEMETIPSUM SIBI UT SEQUATUR CHRISTUM. [11]CORPUS CASTIGARE. [12]DELICIAS NON AMPLECTI. [13]IEIUNIUM AMARE. [14]PAUPERES RECREARE. [15]NUDUM VESTIRE. [16]INFIRMUM VISITARE. [17]MORTUUM SEPELIRE. [18]IN TRIBULATIONE SUBVENIRE. [19]DOLENTEM CONSOLARI. [20]SAECULI ACTIBUS SE FACERE ALIENUM. [21]NIHIL AMORI CHRISTI PRAEPONERE. [22]IRAM NON PERFICERE. [23]IRACUNDIAE TEMPUS NON RESERVARE. [24]DOLUM IN CORDE NON TENERE. [25]PACEM FALSAM NON DARE. [26]CARITATEM NON DERELINQUERE. [27]NON IURARE NE FORTE PERIURET. [28]VERITATEM EX CORDE ET ORE PROFERRE. [29]MALUM PRO MALO NON REDDERE. [30]INIURIAM NON FACERE, SED ET FACTAS PATIENTER SUFFERRE. [31]INIMICOS DILIGERE. [32]MALEDICENTES SE NON REMALEDICERE, SED MAGIS BENEDICERE. [33]PERSECUTIONEM PRO IUSTITIA SUSTINERE. [34]NON ESSE SUPERBUM. [35]NON VINOLENTUM. [36]NON MULTUM EDACEM. [37]NON SOMNULENTUM. [38]NON PIGRUM. [39]NON MURMURIOSUM. [40]NON DETRACTOREM. [41]SPEM SUAM DEO COMMITTERE. [42]BONUM ALIQUID IN SE CUM VIDERIT, DEO ADPLICET, NON SIBI. [43]MALUM VERO SEMPER A SE FACTUM SCIAT ET SIBI REPUTET. [44]DIEM IUDICII TIMERE. [45]GEHENNAM EXPAVESCERE. [46]VITAM AETERNAM OMNI CONCUPISCENTIA SPIRITALI DESIDERARE. [47]MORTEM COTIDIE ANTE OCULOS SUSPECTAM HABERE. [48]ACTUS VITAE SUAE OMNI HORA CUSTODIRE. [49]IN OMNI LOCO DEUM SE RESPICERE PRO CERTO SCIRE. [50]COGITATIONES MALAS CORDI SUO ADVENTIENTES MOX AD CHRISTUM ADLIDERE ET SENIORI SPIRITALI PATEFACERE. [51]OS SUUM A MALO VEL PRAVO ELOQUIO CUSTODIRE. [52]MULTUM LOQUI NON AMARE. [53]VERBA VANA AUT RISUI APTA NON LOQUI. [54]RISUM MULTUM AUT EXCUSSUM NON AMARE. [55]LECTIONES SANCTAS LIBENTER AUDIRE. [56]ORATIONI FREQUENTER INCUMBERE. [57]MALA SUA PRAETERITA CUM LACRIMIS VEL GEMITU COTIDIE IN ORATIONE DEO CONFITERI. [58]DE IPSIS MALIS DE CETERO EMENDARE. [59]DESIDERIA CARNIS NON EFFICERE. [60]VOLUNTATEM PROPRIAM ODIRE. [61]PRAECEPTIS ABBATIS IN OMNIBUS OBOEDIRE, ETIAM SI IPSE ALITER—QUOD ABSIT—AGAT, MEMORES ILLUD DOMINICUM PRAECEPTUM: QUAE DICUNT FACITE, QUAE AUTEM FACIUNT FACERE NOLITE. [62]NON VELLE DICI SANCTUM ANTEQUAM SIT, SED PRIUS ESSE QUOD VERIUS DICATUR. [63]PRAECEPTA DEI FACTIS COTIDIE ADIMPLERE. [64]CASTITATEM AMARE. [65]NULLUM ODIRE. [66]ZELUM NON HABERE. [67]INVIDIAM NON EXERCERE. [68]CONTENTIONEM NON AMARE. [69]ELATIONEM FUGERE. [70]ET SENIORES VENERARE. [71]IUNIORES DILIGERE. [72]IN CHRISTI AMORE PRO INIMICIS ORARE. [73]CUM DISCORDANTE ANTE SOLIS OCCASUM IN PACEM REDIRE. [74]ET DE DEI MISERICORDIA NUMQUAM DESPERARE. [75]ECCE HAEC SUNT INSTRUMENTA ARTIS SPIRITALIS. [76]QUAE CUM FUERINT A NOBIS DIE NOCTUQUE INCESSABILITER ADIMPLETA ET IN DIE IUDICII RECONSIGNATA, ILLA MERCIS NOBIS A DOMINO RECONPENSABITUR QUAM IPSE PROMISIT: [77]QUOD OCULUS NON VIDIT NEC AURIS AUDIVIT, QUAE PRAEPARAVIT DEUS HIS QUI DILIGUNT ILLUM. [78]OFFICINA VERO UBI HAEC OMNIA DILIGENTER OPEREMUR CLAUSTRA SUNT MONASTERII ET STABILITAS IN CONGREGATIONE.

1–9   **a.** Benedict has taken this chapter mainly from the 'Rule of the Master',[2] but long before the 'Master'[1] there existed similar sets of basic Christian precepts composed of the commandment of love, the Decalogue, and the Golden Rule. In its original form the chapter on the 'art of the Spirit'[3] is a *moral catechesis for lay folk* of the Church of antiquity. The fundamental duties of lay people and of monks are identical. Without these foundations there can be no 'art of the Spirit'. This catechesis was slightly worked over by Benedict for monastic use.[4]

b. Pachomius (d.346) placed at the head of a short collection of ethical norms,[5] dealing particularly with interpersonal relationships, the sentence: '*Love* is the fulfilment (pleroma) of the commandments.'[6]—Basil (d.379) begins his Rule for monks with the question about the greatest commandment.[7] He then explains the fundamental power of love: 'The power to love dwells in the soul from the first moment of its creation. To prove this no external evidence is necessary. I know it from my own experience. Everyone longs for that which is good . . . But what is as good as God himself? Indeed, what is good at all, other than God? What is so glorious, radiant or beautiful that from our very nature we are drawn to love it, as God is and as we must believe it about God? Where is there so much grace? What flame of love can set us on fire to our most secret depths as the love of God sets ablaze the secret abysses of the spirit?'[8]

c. Basil (d.379) anchors the twofold commandment of love in Christ and his love.[9] He then continues with a comparison which at once brings to mind our concept of the 'art of the Spirit': 'We must plan our actions according to his (the Lord's) will. All our dealings must, like a mirror, reflect the Lord. We should model our activity with our gaze always bent on him (the Lord), by fixing the eye of our heart continually on him. As the works of art from our human environment suggest that they have been inspired by an intellect and that the work of the hands has been directed by a concept of the mind, so too there remains for our undertakings this single basic plan and this single point of orientation, if we are to please God. When we put the commandments into effect, we must always orientate ourselves by this basic plan . . . while we are always mindful of God.'[10] According to Basil then all our undertakings are to be shaped from the model and pattern of the love of God and of Christ. That is the 'art of the Spirit'. Basil[11] puts love quite clearly at the beginning of the way; for him it is not merely the goal of the ascent.[12] It is also the reason for a separation from a 'world' alien to God, and for the union of believers in a common life.[13]

10–19   **d.** Benedict for his part calls special attention to two points: respect for the person of the other,[14] and the 'golden rule' of social corporate life.[15] Without the safeguarding of the dignity of the human person and the practical recognition of the *equality of rights* of others, there can be no Christian ethos. Without genuine humanity and a lived ethic, there can be no spirituality.

a. What follows[16] is likewise a tissue of Scripture passages. They treat of renunciation and of love and begin by pointing to *Christ*.

b. *Self-control* is a presupposition of the following of Christ. It has to be learned[17] by voluntary abstinence. In memory of Jesus, a special preference is given to 'fasting'.[18]

c. Fasting leads one's thoughts to the *poor*. Frugality based on unselfishness makes means available for those in need and opens our hearts to them. Jesus identified himself with them in his sermon on the Judgement.[19] In this perspective the corporal and spiritual works of mercy are enumerated.

d. *Charitable works* were held in high esteem by the early monks. Stories were often told how the loaves of bread for the poor increased in the hands of the monks.[20] From time to time there appears the wish to offer help with a view of self-help: 'A monk had a brother in the world who was badly-off. Everything that the monk earned he made a present of to his brother. But the more he gave him, the poorer his brother became. The monk went and reported this to an old Father, who said to him: "If you wish to take my advice, give him nothing further, rather say to him: Now, *you* begin to work, and bring *me* something of what you earn. Take in hand something that will bring you profit. If you know a stranger or a poor old man, give him something, and ask him to pray for you." The monk kept to this advice. When his secular brother came to him, he informed him of what the old Father had said. His brother went away downcast. But, lo and behold, one day he brought him some heads of lettuce from his garden. The monk passed them on to the old Fathers, and asked them to pray for his brother. The latter received the blessing and returned home. Later he brought more lettuce and three loaves of bread. The monk accepted them and did as before. The other received the blessing and returned. When he came the third time, he brought many victuals, wine and fruit as well. His brother was overcome with astonishment, sent for the poor and fed them. The monk said to his secular brother: "Do you need any bread?" He replied "No, sir! When I was still receiving gifts from you, they were like a devouring fire in my house. Now however, when I am not getting anything more from you, I have more than enough, and God blesses me."'[21]

e. Where monks lived in community, works of charity were organized. Cassian (d.430) for instance relates how lay folk had as it were competed with each other to have a 'tithe' of their incomes conveyed to Abbot John, 'who at that time because of his holy life had been chosen to oversee the *diakonia*.' In the selection they would have tried to find the best man. The one in charge of the diakonia had to deal with dividing the alms among the poor; the contributors he thanked with a 'word of encouragement', 'a spiritual present'.[22] This gift of a comforting word is specifically mentioned in our enumeration of the works of mercy.[23] The earliest generation of monks saw in the words of Scripture the decisive help for life, but a good word from a brother was also thought much of;[24] one expected such a spiritual present from a monk.[25]

20–33 a. The beginning of this section calls to mind an element of the baptismal rite: the renunciation of Satan and his 'pomps' ('the ways of the world') and the commitment to Christ.[26] This commitment is rendered[27] in an ancient Church formula passed on by Cyprian (d.258), which is to be found also in the 'biographical sketch of Antony' (d.356)[28] by Athanasius (d.373): 'His speech spiced with salt comforted the sad, taught the ignorant, reconciled the angry and contained for all the counsel, *to put nothing above the love of Christ*'. One is given a surprising insight into the deep love for Christ of a learned theologian of early times, namely Origen (d.253) the Scripture commentator, in his remark on St. John's Gospel: 'Only he can understand this Gospel who has laid his head on Jesus' breast and taken Mary as his mother.'[29] Union with Christ brings it about that the Spirit of Christ speaks from our word and the way we conduct our life. His Spirit can have no part with aggressiveness[30] or the behaviour of a 'false brother'.[31] Where the Spirit of Christ dwells, there remains in the heart no room for falsehood or malice. A saying of the Fathers puts it thus: 'He who hides a malicious deed in his soul's memory is like someone who conceals fire in straw.'[32] The heart should be open to love[33] and truth,[34] and not to malice whether hidden or apparent.

b. Further maxims[35] deal with the *vicious circle of evil*. Injustice begets further injustice, violence calls for violence. Fear endeavours to intimidate others, and provokes resistance. The Christian will not enter into these chain-reactions. 'Do not be overcome by evil, but overcome evil with good.'[36] The vicious circle can only be broken when love of one's enemies takes the place of hate, patience[37] the place of violence. Patience and steadfastness in persecution were the virtues of the martyrs and should also be those of every committed Christian: 'A monk begged a venerable Father: "Give me a word which I can hold to and so attain life!" The old Father answered him, "If you can bear an insult with patience, that is a great thing, and surpasses all demonstrations of strength".'[38]

34–40   a. This series of negative maxims is directed against the roots of sin. It begins with the warning against *arrogance*, for pride is *the* root of all evil.[39] 'An old Father said: "I prefer a defeat borne with humility to a victory achieved with pride."'[40] In the context[41] there follows the sentence against the 'heavy drinker'. The admonitions to *self-control*[42] ought not to be interpreted in a way which might be detrimental to bodily health. In ancient monasticism the warnings against overdoing things are frequent, notwithstanding all their recommendations of asceticism. Thus we read for instance in Cassian: 'Let us give to nature what it needs (of sleep), so that we are not obliged to take back during the daytime, what we withheld from the night (through watching). He who does not withhold from his "flesh" only a small part in reasonable measure, but rather tries to deny it every claim to sleep, will surely in the end concede everything to the "flesh". One should abstain from excess, not deprive oneself of what is necessary.'[43]

b. Benedict often speaks of 'grumbling',[44] by which he means a *fault-finding* peevishness. He rejects thereby a negative attitude, which feels obliged to run everything down.[45] Such an attitude betrays a disturbed relationship to one's environment, which may spring from an inferiority complex or from the fear of coming off a loser. One criticizes others mercilessly, because one does not accept one's own place.[46] There should be no room among Christians for this attitude.[47] It resembles the unappreciative rejection of Jesus' love[48] and the refusal to be led by God and Moses;[49] it is therefore one of the sins which is frequently mentioned.[50]

41–50   a. From now on there are fewer scriptural quotations than in the first part. There begins a series of ascetical and spiritual admonitions. In the middle of Chapter 4 the gaze is directed towards God.[51] This gaze wakens hope, which includes the thought of reward and recompense,[52] which of course are subordinate to love.[53] Contemplation of God evokes above all a deep trust. Everything that is good comes from him. Basil (d.379) advocates the same *optimism* of faith: 'The powers which we have received from God to fulfil all commandments, we bear in ourselves, they are implanted in us. Hence we experience no difficulty if something new or strange is demanded of us, but there exists for us no reason for presumption, as if we could offer to God something more than what we received from him at the creation of our nature. Our task is only to develop to a righteous work, as is fitting, what we were endowed with by God. Then we shall so live that people must regard us as a valuable source of strength. If on the other hand we let the good qualities of nature run to seed, we are turning to evil. Evil can thus be defined: Not to live according to the inspirations breathed into the soul by God. The definition of the positive attitude is: To live in accordance with the impulses breathed into the soul by God, i.e. to live according to God's commandment and our conscience.'[54]

b. After human responsibility has been taken note of, there follow maxims on Judgement, on punishment, and on eternal life, for which we ought 'to yearn with all spiritual longing'—as Benedict inserts into the Master's text.[55] The early monks did not seek to suppress the thought of death and of the *Last Things*; rather they saw in this thought a force for coping well with life. One adage of the Fathers runs: 'Ponder always on thy end, forget not the ever-lasting Judgment, then nothing dishonourable is in thee.'[56] Many tales speak of the open and uncomplicated attitude of ascetics in face of death: 'The news went abroad, that an old Father lay dying in the desert of Scete. Then the brethren came, stood around his bed, clothed him and began to weep. He however opened his eyes and laughed. He laughed once more, and again a third time. The brothers were astonished and asked him: "Tell us, Abba, why do you laugh, while we weep?" He answered: "I laughed once because you fear death, I laughed a second time because you are not prepared, I laughed a third time because leaving hard labour I am entering rest, and for this you weep!" Immediately he closed his eyes and died.'[57] Athanasius (d.373) tells how Antony (d.356) went forward to meet death composedly, even cheerfully. Before dying he had given away his few belongings as keepsakes, and ordered that no piece of his mortal remains be brought anywhere at all, but that his body be buried in a spot known only to the brothers.[58] Athanasius (d.373) adds: 'He looked smilingly at death.'[59] Benedict too, according to the account of Gregory the Great (d.604) faced death upright and unflinching: 'Six days before he died, he had his grave opened. Soon afterwards a fever seized him. The heat of the pains robbed him of his last ounce of strength. His condition worsened from day to day. On the sixth day he had himself borne into the oratory by his disciples. There he strengthened himself for his passing by receiving the Body and Blood of the Lord. Supported by his disciples, he held his feeble limbs upright. So he stood with hands raised to heaven, and in words of prayer breathed his last.'[60]

c. The strength for this trustful open attitude in face of death stems from the orientation to Christ which has become second nature. Neither death nor the devil[61] can effect anything against him. Cassian (d.430) explains it thus: 'We have to know in which direction our mind ought to be steadily aligned ... We will not take our eyes away from *Christ* for one instant. And if our eyes should wander from him in ever so small a degree, we shall turn back the eyes of our heart immediately to him again and steer the highest part of our soul clearly and directly towards him. All that happens in the deepest part of the soul. When the devil has been driven out, the kingdom of God is established in us there.'[62] This thought comes from the school of Origen (d.253). Thus, Evagrius Ponticus (d.399) for instance, says: 'The kingdom of heaven is the peaceful soul (apatheia psyches; tranquillity of spirit), filled with the knowledge of the true Being.'[63] When the 'eyes of our heart' look calmly into the 'eyes of God',[64] the Kingdom is there. The purification of the heart is a prerequisite, so that it becomes as it were an unclouded mirror into which God can look. We must therefore 'supervise' ourselves and 'guard'[65] ourselves so that God can reflect himself in the mirror of a pure heart. Abbot Poimen said: 'To watch oneself, to observe oneself carefully, and to practise the gift of discernment, that is asceticism of the soul.'[66] A self-critical conscience is a prerequisite for meeting God.

d. A life which unfolds under God's eyes or in God's presence, who sees through us,[67] thus appears as the beginning of the kingdom. The conscious experience of *God's presence*[68] leaves no room for 'bad thoughts'.[69] The Egyptian Fathers knew that not every spontaneous psychical passing fancy, not every 'bad thought creeping into the heart', is already a sin. A venerable Father said: 'We shall not be condemned if bad thoughts enter our minds, but only if we do bad things with them. Such thoughts can be the occasion of shipwreck or of winning the crown of victory.'[70] To a questioner who was plagued on all sides by temptations, a venerable father gave as answer—with a pastoral gift of discernment: 'Do not try to hit back in all directions simultaneously, but rather only in one.' He ought to reflect which was the chief of the temptations and defend himself against it.' In this way the remaining bad thoughts will be humbled.'[71]

e. Benedict counsels us to shatter evil thoughts on Christ, the 'Rock'.[72] He adds to the 'Master's text' that one should '*reveal them to the spiritual father*'.[73] 'The elders say, it is always a clear sign of a diabolical inspiration, when we were afraid to reveal our thoughts or plans to an elder.'[74] When a timorous monk opened his soul to Abbot Poimen and told him that he was continuously beset by thoughts, the old father ordered him to leave the cell and stop the wind blowing outside. 'That I cannot do,' answered the monk. 'If you cannot do that, then it is even less your fault that you are unable to hinder the thoughts from entering into you. But you can show yourself steadfast against them.'[75] The manifestation of conscience is met by the pastoral care of the 'spiritual father', his healing word that brings comfort and strength.

51–54 A short series of sentences deals with the *human word* and the sins of the tongue. In full accordance with Scripture they were taken seriously by the monks as a violation of the great commandment of the love of one's neighbour.[76] A saying of the fathers runs: 'Better to eat meat and drink wine than to eat the flesh of the brethren by slandering them.'[77] A person expresses himself in his word. Therefore the inflation of empty words[78] is rejected. The Master quotes a 'wise sentence from Origen': 'Better to throw a stone aimlessly than a word.'[79] Each is responsible for the witness borne against him by his own throwaway word. The saying of the fathers hints at this: 'Let your mouth speak no foul word, because the vine bears no thorns.'[80] In the same series of maxims, which are attributed to Abbot Hyperechios, emotional, uncontrolled speech is taken as a sign of a general unbridled instinct of the person: 'A monk who cannot restrain his tongue in a moment of anger, will never be able to control his bodily passion.'[81]

55–58 a. To the admonitions on the right use of speech, there is annexed the theme of *hearing and answering* God's Word. Cyprian (d.258) had already written: 'Be diligent at prayer and reading: speak to God, and then may God speak with you!'[82]

b. A monk of experience said to Cassian (d.430) when young: 'If in your striving after inner purity you feel driven to despair, then there is a speedy remedy, namely to read and study the spiritual Scriptures, and do that with the same energy with which you once read about worldly things (stories of war and frivolous tales).[83] The '*healing remedy of Scripture*'[84] is however only effective when the soul is not surfeited with 'Allotria' (every other thing).

c. The word of Scripture has not only a healing and purifying power, but also a unifying one. A source which Cassian (d.430) quotes says in this connection: 'Try in every possible way to cast aside earthly thoughts and cares, and to devote yourself with diligence and perseverance to holy reading, until this constant reading fills your spirit and forms you to its likeness. In this way your soul will become the chosen ark of the divine covenant and the royal priesthood . . . since it never leaves the sanctuary.'[85] This high regard for sacred Scripture on account of its *divinizing power* is characteristic of the Alexandrian tradition.[86] Clement of Alexandria (d. before 215) wrote: 'When someone forsakes his error in order to hearken to the voice of Scripture and to open his spirit to the truth, then he is no longer a mere man, he has in a certain sense become God.'[87] A fine example of the assimilation of Scripture is the Rule of Benedict itself, which is, as it were, a synopsis of the Old and New Testaments.[88]

d. The saying of the Lord: '*Pray without ceasing*'[89] is interpreted: 'To kneel down frequently in prayer.'[90] It seems that one may not translate it simply as 'to apply oneself to prayer'; for it was the custom after a spell of slow, half-audible reading, of repetition and 'meditative' murmuring to oneself of a text, to cast oneself down to an intensive 'ardent prayer'.[91] For such prayer the following was recommended: 'One should pray frequently, but briefly', lest by lingering too long, untoward thoughts might find their way into the heart.[92] The heart is the place of prayer: 'We pray in our 'inner room',[93] when we keep our heart completely at a distance from the turmoil of all thoughts and worries and expose our desires as it were under the seal of secrecy and trustingly to the Lord.'[94] Prayer must spring from the core of our being.

e. Since the dialogue with God takes place in the centre of our being, the heart must be pure and free from faults.[95] This again corresponds to the teaching of Cassian (d.430) on prayer: 'The whole aim of a monk and the *perfection of the heart* is to be sought for in persevering and uninterrupted prayer—and as far as human frailty allows—in the imperturbable inner quietness[96] and lasting purity. For the sake of this goal we give ourselves up to bodily labour and practise at all times compunction of spirit.'[97] This 'compunction'[98] manifests itself during prayer.[99]

f. This purity of heart is not a 'goal' resting in itself, not an end in itself. Rather it leads the one who prays to the vision of God, yes to a union with God in love. That is the teaching of Cassian (d.430) on prayer: Purity of heart enables us '*to look upon Jesus with the inner eye of the soul*, whether it be in the humility of his incarnation, or in his glory, or in his glorious, majestic second Coming . . . Only those shall see his Godhead with a pure heart, who rise above low and earthly works and ideas and betake themselves with him to the high mountain of solitude . . . Jesus can indeed also be seen in towns and villages . . . but not in the same radiant clarity, in which he appeared on the mountain . . . He withdrew "to the mountain, to pray there all alone".[100] His example teaches us. If we desire to pray to God with a pure and undivided heart, we must shun all vulgarities and the hectic rush of the market place, so that already in our earthly existence—if only in fragments and images—we come close to that glory, which is promised to the saints, so that for us "God is all in all".[101] Then that prayer of the Lord's will come fully true, which our Saviour offered to his Father for his disciples: "that the love with which thou hast loved me may be in them, and I in them"[102] and further: "that they may all be one; even as thou Father, art in me, and I in thee, that they also may be in us".[103] Then that perfect love, with which "he loved us first"[104] will also fill our heart and mind, and the Lord's prayer will be realized, that prayer of his which we believe can never remain unheard. These will be the signs of it: God will be our whole love, our yearning, the goal of our desires and endeavours, the context of our thoughts. We shall live for him, speak of him, breathe him in. God, that is that oneness which already exists of the Father with the Son and of the Son with the Father. It will be planted deep in our soul.'[105]

g. This teaching on prayer by Cassian (d.430) aspires to the summit of divine contemplation and to the depths of loving union with God. We remark once again how the image of ascent and of searching, which is painful at first, underlies Cassian's thought.[106] This teaching on the necessary conversion and a change for the better 'with tears'[107] is found in a saying of the blessed 'Amma' Synkletika: 'When a sinner desires to turn back to God, it costs him a hard struggle at the outset; later an inexpressible joy comes over him. If we want to kindle a fire, the smoke will at first irritate us and cause our eyes to smart. But in this way one reaches one's goal. It is written: "Our God is a consuming fire."[108] Hence we have to kindle the divine fire in us with labour and tears.'[109] Our gaze in doing so falls on Jesus who 'offered up prayers and supplications with . . . tears, to him who was able to save him from death.'[110] Every experience of God presupposes a conversion to him, and a personal feeling of being touched to the quick[111] by him. This experience is possible in the encounter with Jesus.

59–61 **a.** From the thought of purity of heart at prayer there follows the transition to exhortations to purity of desire, unselfishness regarding intentions, and to sincere, self-forgetting obedience. These fruits grow in a '*pure heart*' touched to the quick by the living experience of God;[112] at the same time they are indispensable presuppositions of the encounter with God.— 'Abbot Theonas declared: Our soul is shackled and held back from the vision of God, if carnal passions hold it in thrall.'[113]

b. Abbot Hyperechios said: 'The monk's jewel is *obedience*. Whoever has made obedience his second nature, his prayer will be heard. He stands full of confidence before the Crucified; for it was in this mind that the Lord went to the Cross: "Became obedient unto death"'.[114,115] Obedience here means the union of one's will with that of Christ and of God: 'Thy will be done!' Whoever prays in this disposition, prays in the Name of Jesus and will be heard. He bears in himself that power, of 'trustfulness' (fiducia, parrhesia) which was characteristic of the martyrs and can do all things, because Christ is present in the power of the Spirit. Benedict amplifies the sentence of his source: 'to obey the commands of the abbot',[116] by—as is his wont—entering into the possible subjective difficulties of obedience in the subjects, and indicating in what spirit the superior is to be encountered. The superior is considered as fallible, an idea which is foreign to the Master.

62–73 **a.** These final exhortations treat especially of relations to one's neighbour; a selfless love of God must bear fruit. The maxim on *pseudo-sanctity* and true holiness forms the introduction. Quite a number of maxims of this fourth chapter bear a remarkable likeness to the *Passio Iuliani*[117] in which the following explanation is to be found: 'He who does not wish to be called holy before he is so, is pleasing to God. Many allow themselves to be called so, when they are not . . . They live from the mere prospect of later becoming that which men now call them. This "certainty" leads them to become lukewarm and indifferent. They ought to strive to become that which they are called. There are in fact may saints, of whom nobody says that they are holy. These have no desire that others get to know that they are humble and full of grace. They will get the reward from him who knows what they are. While still living in this body they merit this great grace; later they will enter into intimate friendship with God. They have first received enlightenment from Christ, now they serve others with the gift of grace, which God has bestowed on them. They "win"[18] themselves first, then the others.' Holiness is therefore both a gift and a task; it stems from God and leads to him, not without bringing others along on its way.

b. The basic duty of every Christian and spiritual life is to fulfil *God's commandments*. 'A venerable father declared: God expects this from a Christian that he should so obey the divine Scriptures, that they animate his every word and deed, and that he live in full accordance with his superiors and the orthodox Fathers.'[119] We should note the nuances in this saying from the Fathers: to 'obey' God's Word in our deeds, to 'live in full accordance' with the Church and its legally entitled representatives. In the last resort obedience is paid to God and to him alone.

c. *Chastity* is a value worthy of our love.[120] Origen (d.253) looked upon chastity as a gift, which man and God present one to the other:[121] 'If we sacrifice our chastity to him (God), that is, bodily chastity, then we shall receive from him chastity of the spirit. If we offer our sensuality, then we shall receive from him his mind, as the Apostle says: "We have the mind of Christ."'[122, 123] Cassian (d.430) extols chastity as a gift of grace, which can only be experienced existentially, and cannot be analysed intellectually: 'The gifts which God daily bestows on his saints, gifts which are the work of his own hands, and which with supreme generosity he heaps on them, can only be perceived by *that* soul which is permitted to delight in them. This soul alone is in its conscience the secret witness of these gifts of grace, so that after she has returned from the fire of her love for God to the consideration of material and earthly things, she cannot find words to describe what she has experienced. Even intelligence and reflection are incapable of forming an idea of it.'[124]

Although Cassian (d.430) sees in chastity a gift of God's grace,[125] he is aware of the thoroughgoing commitment of the person, which chastity presupposes: 'The more room that kindness and patience find in the heart, the greater the progress of purity of body. The more a person can hold himself aloof from aggressive instincts, the more he persists in chastity . . . For the Saviour has pronounced this beatitude: Blessed are they who use *no violence*, for they shall inherit the land.'[126,127] Seen from this standpoint, chastity appears as a Christian alternative to lust for possessions and for power.[128]

Chastity cannot be preserved without the spiritual gift of *fortitude*: 'The story was told of Abbess Sarah, how for thirteen years she suffered the onslaughts of the demon of unchastity. She never prayed that the struggle should end, but only spoke this prayer: "Lord, give me fortitude".'[129]

d. The following maxims, in negative form, summon us to the love of our neighbour. Even in thought there must be no place for destructive hankering after power,[130] no bitter zeal,[131] and no arrogance.[132] Abbot Poimen declared: 'There is nothing greater than love,[133] and no one has a greater love than he who lays down his life for his neighbour.[134] When therefore someone hears bitter words and feels he could answer back in the same tone, let him resolutely master himself and not answer the other with insults. Or someone endures with forbearance harm done to him, without retaliating on the person who insults him or who has caused the harm—such a man lays down his life for his neighbour.'[135] In this text our attention is again drawn to the steadfast courage and patience of the martyrs.[136] This Christian valour is here identified with that heroic *love of neighbour*, which Christ demanded should be shown even to one's enemies.[137]

e. Benedict adds four maxims to the 'Master's' text.[138] In doing so, he goes into the relationship between '*young and old*' and handles the theme as in the chapter on the order of the community.[139] Natural age in years receives its relative importance, even if in a monastery or before the eyes of God other criteria than worldly questions of precedence hold good,[140] something which Benedict laid down expressly also in another passage.[141] A venerable father had a well-proven disciple. One day in a fit of depression he drove the disciple away. The disciple sat down outside and waited. When the venerable father opened the door and found him there, he did penance before the disciple and said to him: 'You must now be my "father", for your humility and manly patience far outdo my pettiness. Come in! From now on you are to be the "elder" and the "father", and I the "disciple" and the "pupil". For through your behaviour, you have shown yourself superior to me, the senior in age.'[142]

f. Before the conclusion of the whole moral catechesis, Christ is again set up as our model.[143] His Sermon on the Mount and his commandment of love have already formed the background of many maxims.[144] The injunction to *love one's enemies*[145] is given concrete shape: one prays for one's enemics with one's eyes on Christ, and with his love. Stephen is the model.[146]

g. The way is now free for reconciliation.[147] The 'Ministry of Reconciliation'[149] is incumbent on a Christian as a 'priestly'[148] duty. 'Blessed are the *peacemakers* for they shall be called sons of God.'[150]

74 The last maxim has again God as its focus point. The theme of the love of God, with which the chapter had opened, is echoed once more. He is the foundation of our *hope*.[151] Cassian (d.430) comments on St Paul's phrase of 'the helmet the hope of salvation'[152] as follows: 'The helmet protects the head. Our head however is Christ. We must always protect this head as with an unbreakable helmet, that is, with the hope of future goods, and do this in all temptations and persecutions, in which before all we preserve our faith in Christ without curtailment or reduction.'[153] In other words: eschatalogical hope belongs to the kernel of our faith in Christ.[154] The thought of the Last Things which await us, cannot be substituted for by any belief in 'progress' or by any futurology of this world.

75 a. That which the Master names also the 'holy art'[155] is here called the 'art of the Spirit'. The asceticism outlined here is at the service of spirituality. Though the 'doing of the Word',[156] 'spiritual men' are to be formed according to God's plan,[157] persons in whom God can show forth his power,[158] who work on themselves,[159] and allow the Lord to work in them.[160] The catechetical instruction from the fifth century contained in this chapter is a synthesis of morals and spirituality suitable for every Christian. It is put into the abbot's hand as a programme.[161]

b. The chapter on the 'art of the Spirit' begins, like the great monastic Rules, with the love of God and neighbour In the '*Account of the Warfare of the Heart*',[162] the 'art of the Spirit' follows after the baptismal catechesis, the explanation of the Our Father and the commentary on the psalms for those about to be christened. Faith, baptism, prayer, and grace are the roots of Christian morals and spirituality. In the 'Master' and in Benedict the chapters on the kinds of monks, on the abbot and on consultation break the original sequence of the 'Account' (Masai-Manning).[163]

76–77 a. All now stand without distinction of persons as 'We' before God, and in accordance with Scripture await the *reward*.[164] Benedict has an unwavering trust in God, who will pay out the heavenly reward.[165] The imaginative description of Paradise in the 'Master'[166] either was not yet to be found in the version of the 'Master's text' which Benedict had to hand, or he left it aside; he inserts a word from Scripture which names love as the goal.[167] Benedict does not wish to depict eternity, but rather the way and ascent to heaven.[168]

b. In comparison with the goal, which is love, the ascetical exercises are merely 'tools', not in themselves 'perfection'.[169] The Master adduces his own list of 'spiritual tools':[170] 'faith, hope, love,[171] peace, joy, gentleness,[172] above all humility, obedience, and reserve,[173] chastity of body, unsullied conscience, continence, purity, simplicity, kind-heartedness and goodness,[174] mercy, piety, temperance, watchfulness, sobriety, justice, fairness, truth, love, moderation, measure, and endurance to the end. This list of fundamental virtues omits those of the apostolate. The 'saint' by his very life gives an immense witness.

78 **a.** At the end of the chapter the *monastery* is represented as a 'workshop' of asceticism. Monastic asceticism is, apart from specific elements which confer on its own characteristic features, identical with Christian spirituality taken from sacred Scripture. For this reason an ecclesial moral catechesis has its place in the monastic Rule.
b. The definition of the monastery[175] has been formulated by Benedict with some modification of the Master's text. He names here two interrelated elements: the 'monastery enclosure'[176] and 'stability in the community'.[177] The 'workshop' should be a relatively undisturbed place, so that 'God's work' can be realized: the 'spiritual man'. The workshop itself is filled with the life of the community. In it and in its different members the Spirit of God is at work,[178] and precisely through the mutual support which each one finds here.

NOTES TO CHAPTER 4

1 We could mention the 'Didache', 1–6, written before 150, with its teaching of two ways; further, two declarations of a Council of Alexandria in 362: 'Syntagma' and 'Pistis'.—In the 'Account of the Warfare of the Heart' this moral catechesis followed on the exhortations to choose between the 'two ways' (→ Prol. 2). **2** RB 4,1–60.62–68.73–78 = RM 3,1–78; cf. RM 4–5. **3** RB 4,75. **4** Cf. V. 8 (Note 14 below). 40.50.61.69–72.78. **5** Pachomius, Iud. **6** Rom. 13:10. **7** RBasRuf 1. **8** RBasRuf 2. **9** John 14:21: 'He who has my commandments and keeps them, he it is who loves me.' **10** RBasRuf 2. **11** Just as for the 'Ordo monasterii' (OM) 1. **12** → Prol. 48–49; 4,1–9.55–58.76–77; 5,10–13; 6,2–5; 7,1–4.5–9.26–30.31–32.55; 72,9–10.12; 73,1.4–7.8–9. **13** RBasRuf 2. **14** Instead of 'honour father and mother', he writes 'honour all men'. He holds this dear; cf. RB 53,2; 63,17; 72,3. **15** It is mentioned in two further passages: RB 61,14 & 70,7. **16** Especially in Verse 40. **17** Verses 11–13. **18** Cf. Matt. 4:2; 6:16–18; 17:20. **19** Matt. 25:31–46. **20** E.g. VPatr 5,13,15. **21** VPatr 5,13,13. **22** Cf. Conl 21,1–2; → 1,3–5. **23** Verse 19. → 31,3; 46,5–6. **24** Athanasius writes: 'The holy Antony was asked by the assembled brethren to teach and instruct them. So, with prophetic frankness, he raised his voice and proclaimed that for the observance of all the commandments the Scriptures were sufficient; but it was also very good if the brethren comforted each other' (VAnt 15). **25** The exhortations to 'lend' and 'give alms' recorded in the 'Rule of the Master' (RM 3,20–21) are omitted by Benedict in Verse 19, probably because gifts other than material ones are expected from the individual cenobite. **26** A paragraph of the 'Passio Iuliani' (46) is couched in similar terms. The martyr proclaims that a truly Christian life is promised the demonstration of power. This paragraph of the Passio contains many parallels to the 'spiritual art'; by the latter is understood, *inter alia*, the capacity for wonderful demonstrations of the power of the spirit. **27** De or. dom. 15; → 72,11. **28** VAnt 13. The gift of 'comforting' (cf. RB 4,19) and the reconciling of the 'wrathful' (cf. RB 4,22) is at the same time mentioned here. **29** In Joh 1:4. **30** Verses 22–23; 72,1–3. **31** Verses 24–25; cf. Gal. 2:4. **32** VPatr 6,4–25. **33** Verse 26; → 71–72. **34** Verses 27–28. **35** Verses 29–33. **36** Rom. 12:21; cf. Matt. 5:44. **37** → Prol. 37–38.50; 4,20–33.62–73; 7,35–43; 31,3–7; 36,5–6; 48,17–18; 49,1–33; 58,1–4; 59,1–2; 72,1–3.4–12 (Note 14). 11 (Note 53). **38** VPatr 5,15,83. **39** Cf. RB 7. **40** VPatr 5,15,74. **41** Cf. Titus 1:7. Benedict goes into this question later in a restrained way: → 40,5–7. **42** Verses 35–38. **43** Cassian, Inst 4,8,3. **44** Verse 39; → 5,14–19. **45** Verse 40. **46** → 72,1. **47** Cf. 1 Cor. 10:10. **48** Cf. Luke 15:2; John 6:41.43. **49** Cf. Exod. 15:24; 16:7. **50** Similar series of faults, as of good works, are to be found in the 'Homilies to the monks', originating from the spiritual home of Lérins; see especially Hom. 9 (PL 50,855–856). **51** Verses 41–42.49. **52** Verses 44–47. **53** Cassian, Conl 11,6. **54** RBasRuf 2. **55** Verse 46. **56** VPatr 5,11,9. **57** VPatr 5,11,52. **58** VAnt 59. **59** VAnt 60; cf. VPJur 69. **60** Dial 2,37; → 51,3 (in Notes 12–13). **61** Verse 50; → Prol. 28. **62** Conl 1,13; cf. Luke 17:21. **63** Log prak 2. **64** Verse 49: God sees us. **65** Verses 48.51. **66** VPatr 5,1,12. **67** Cassian, Inst 8,4,2. **68** There is an obvious parallel here to the 'first stage of humility' (RB 7,10–30), where feeling the hand of God upon one appears as the basic stage of humility. **69** Verse 50; → Prol. 28. **70** VPatr 5,10,86. **71** VPatr 5,10,88. **72** → Prol. 28. **73** Verse 50 is formulated word for word in the same way by Cassian, Inst 4,9: 'not to conceal out of harmful shame any thoughts rising up in one's heart . . ., but to reveal them immediately to one's senior'. A custom general among the monks of antiquity; → 46,5–6. **74** Cassian. Inst. 4,9. **75** VPatr PG 65,329. 76 → 6; see Note 50 above. **77** VPatr 5,4,51. **78** Verse 53. **79** RM 11,62. **80** VPatr 5,4,50. **81** VPatr 5,4,49. **82** Eph. 1:15; → 9,5–6. **83** Conl 14,12. **84** RB 28,3. **85** Conl 14,10. **86** Origen recommended 'daily'

Scripture reading (Gen Hom 10,3). **87** Stromata 7,16. **88** → Prol. 1,1; 9,5–6; 73,3. **89** Luke 18:1; 1 Thess. 5:17; Rom. 12:12; Col. 4:2; → 16,1–3. **90** Verse 56. **91** → 8,3; 20,4–5. **92** Cassian, Conl 9,36; cf. Inst 2,10,3. **93** Cf. Matt. 6:6: 'into your room'. **94** Cassian, Conl 9,35. **95** Verses 57–58. **96** → 4,41–50; especially in Note 63. **97** Conl 9,2. **98** Cf. Ps. 51:19; → 20,1–3; 49,4–5. **99** Verse 57; → 20,1–3; 49,4–5. **100** Cf. Matt. 14:23. **101** 1 Cor. 15:28. **102** John 17:26. **103** John 17:21. **104** 1 John 4:10. **105** Conl 10, 6–7; when quoting John 17:21. Cassian omits the dimension of world-oriented witness ('so that the world may believe'). Since he emphasizes the duty of brotherly love very strongly in other places (→ 4,10–19), one ought not to be too hasty in accusing him here of one-sided flight from the world. **106** → Prol. 48–49; 4,1–9; 7,5–9; 72,9–10; 73,8–9. **107** Verses 57–58. **108** Heb. 12:29. **109** VPatr 5,13,16; → 20,1–3; 49,4–5. **110** Heb. 5:7. **111** According to Cassian, God can be experienced in 'compunction of heart' as in no other way. **112** → 7,23–25,31–34. **113** VPatr 5,11,12. **114** Phil. 2:8. **115** VPatr 5,14,11. **116** RM 3,67. **117** Passio 46. **118** Cf. 1 Cor. 9:19–22. **119** VPatr 5,14,13. **120** Verse 64. In spite of the high esteem expressed here, the Rule speaks only relatively seldom and discreetly of chastity; this is probably deliberate. → 22,7; 42,8–11. **121** Cf. Matt. 19:11. **122** 1 Cor. 2:16. **123** Num Hom 24,2. **124** Conl 12,12. **125** Conl 12,14. **126** Matt. 5:4. **127** Conl 12,6. **128** → 58,24–25. **129** VPatr 5,10; → 5,10–13; 58,1–4; 72,4–12 (Note 14). 11 (Note 53). **130** Verses 65.68. **131** Verses 66–67; → 72,1–3. **132** Verse 69; → 4,34–40; 7,1–9. **133** Cf. 1 Cor. 13:13. **134** Cf. John 15:13. **135** VPatr 5,17,10. **136** → Prol. 50. **137** Verse 72; → 4,20 33; cf. Prol. 31 (Matt. 5:44; Luke 6.22). **138** Verses 69–72. He repeats here the warning against presumption (cf. Verse 34); → 4,34–40. **139** → 63,10–12; see Note 4 above. **140** → 63,1–9. **141** → 3,1–3; 71; 72,4–12. **142** VPatr 5,16,17. **143** Verse 72. **144** Verses 64–68. **145** Cf. Verse 31; → 4,20–33. **146** Acts 7:55–56, 59–60. **147** Verse 73. **148** → 4,55–58 (see Note 85); 31,10–12; 35,15–18; 57,7–9. **149** Cf. 2 Cor. 5:18–19. For an example of readiness for reconciliation, see in Note 142 above. **150** Matt. 5:9. **151** Hope is also mentioned at the beginning of the second series of maxims (Verse 41), and now here at the end of that series. **152** 1 Thess. 5:8. **153** Conl 7,5. **154** → 4,41–50. **155** RM 3 Title. **156** Jas. 1:22. **157** → 4,1–9 (especially in Notes 12–13). **158** See Note 26 above. **159** Cf. RB Prol. 14; 7,49.70. **160** → Prol. 29–32 (in Note 105). **161** In the 'Rule of the Master', this 'art' follows immediately on the chapter on the abbot. **162** → Prol. 28 (especially in Note 91). **163** → See Note 1 above. **164** The image of the reward for works done by grace is especially frequent in Matthew: Matt. 5:12,46; 6:1–2,5,16; 10:41–42; 20:8. The Apostles are also familiar with it: 1 Cor. 3:8,14; 9:17–18; 2 John 8; Acts 11:18; 22:12. **165** RB 35,2; 36,5; 40,4; 49,9; 59,4; 64,6; → 4,74. **166** RM 3,84–94. **167** → 4,55–58 (especially in Note 105). **168** The Prologue (50) and Chapter 72 also conclude with the theme of selfless love, which leads to the gate of eternal life. **169** Cassian, Conl 1,7.—'Instrument' has perhaps the meaning of 'written direction': an 'instrument of work'. **170** RM 4. In the Rule of Benedict, this list does not appear, and neither does the parallel catalogue of vices. **171** 1 Cor. 13:13. **172** Gal. 5:22–23. **173** The three monastic virtues, 'humility, obedience, silence' (cf. RB 5–7) seem to have been inserted here from an older source. **174** Gal. 5:23. **175** Such a one is also to be found at a conclusion of the Prologue (Prol. 45–50). **176** → 66,6–7; 67,6–7. **177** → 2,10–11; 58,13–16.17–23; 60,9; 61,5. **178** → 1,2.3–5. The community will be the subject of the concluding chapters of the Rule (63–73) also.

CHAPTER 5

OF OBEDIENCE

22 Jan
23 May
22 Sept

1 The first step in humility
is to obey without delay.

2 This is appropriate for those
who value nothing dearer to themselves than Christ.

3–4 As soon as anything has been ordered by a superior,
just as if it were God's command,
they cannot brook a delay in carrying it out,
—because of the holy service they have professed,
or for the fear of hell,
and the glory of eternal life.

5 The Lord says of these: Ps 18:45
AT THE EAR'S HEARING
HE OBEYED ME.

6 And, besides, to teachers he says: Lk 10:16
HE WHO HEARS YOU,
HEARS ME.

7 Therefore, such as these   Cf. Mt 4:22;
IMMEDIATELY leaving aside what is their own,   1 Cor 13:5
and forsaking self-will

8 LEAVING UNFINISHED the work they were at,
with hands at the ready, and the step of obedience close by,
THEY FOLLOW DIRECTLY with deeds the voice of him who
commands.

9 And as it were in ONE second,
both things—the previously mentioned order of the master
and the completed task of the disciple—
are quickly finished together,
in the speed of the fear of God.

10 There presses on them
the love of advancing towards eternal life,

11 therefore they seize the narrow way,   Mt 7:14
about which the Lord says:
NARROW IS THE WAY THAT LEADS TO LIFE,

12 so that, resident in community monasteries,   Cf. Judith 16;
not living by their own free will,   Gal 5:16–17; Mt 6:10;
nor obeying their OWN DESIRES and pleasures,   cf. RB 4:59–61; 7:19–25

but walking by the judgement and orders of another,
they desire to have an abbot rule them.

13 There is no doubt that such as these
imitate that maxim of the Lord in which he says:
I HAVE COME NOT TO DO MY OWN WILL,
BUT THE WILL OF HIM WHO SENT ME.

Jn 6:38;
cf. Mt 26:39

23 Jan
24 May
23 Sept

14 But this obedience itself
will then be pleasing to God
and delightful to men,
if what is commanded, be done
not with fear,
nor with delay,
not half-heartedly,
nor with grumbling
nor with an unwilling answer,

Cf. Mt 21:29

15 because obedience shown to superiors is given to God.
He in fact has said:
HE WHO HEARS YOU,
HEARS ME.

Lk 10:16

16 And it ought to be given by the disciple
with good humour,
because GOD LOVES A CHEERFUL GIVER.

2 Cor 9:7;
cf. Ecclus 35:10–11

17 For if a disciple obeys with ill grace
and complains, not only by word of mouth,
but even in his heart,

18 though he should fulfil the command
nevertheless it will no longer be accepted by God
who is looking at his discontented heart.

19 And for such a deed he will obtain no grace.
Rather, he will incur the punishment due to murmurers,
if he does not amend with satisfaction.

Cf. 1 Cor 10:10;
Num 14:2,
36;21,5

CAPUT V: DE OBOEDIENTIA

¹PRIMUS HUMILITATIS GRADUS EST OBOEDIENTIA SINE MORA. ²HAEC CONVENIT HIS
QUI NIHIL SIBI A CHRISTO CARIUS ALIQUID EXISTIMANT. ³PROPTER SERVITIUM
SANCTUM QUOD PROFESSI SUNT SEU PROPTER METUM GEHENNAE VEL GLORIAM
VITAE AETERNAE, ⁴MOX ALIQUID IMPERATUM A MAIORE FUERIT, AC SI DIVINITUS
IMPERETUR, MORAM PATI NESCIANT IN FACIENDO. ⁵DE QUIBUS DOMINUS DICIT:
OBAUDITU AURIS OBOEDIVIT MIHI. ⁶ET ITEM DICIT DOCTORIBUS: QUI VOS AUDIT ME
AUDIT. ⁷ERGO HII TALES, RELINQUENTES STATIM QUAE SUA SUNT ET VOLUNTATEM
PROPRIAM DESERENTES, ⁸MOX EXOCCUPATIS MANIBUS ET QUOD AGEBANT

INPERFECTUM RELINQUENTES, VICINO OBOEDIENTIAE PEDE IUBENTIS VOCEM FACTIS SEQUUNTUR, ⁹ET VELUTI UNO MOMENTO PRAEDICTA MAGISTRI IUSSIO ET PERFECTA DISCIPULI OPERA, IN VELOCITATE TIMORIS DEI, AMBAE RES COMMUNITER CITIUS EXPLICANTUR. ¹⁰QUIBUS AD VITAM AETERNAM GRADIENDI AMOR INCUMBIT, ¹¹IDEO ANGUSTAM VIAM ARRIPIUNT, UNDE DOMINUS DICIT: ANGUSTA VIA EST QUAE DUCIT AD VITAM, ¹²UT NON SUO ARBITRIO VIVENTES VEL DESIDERIIS SUIS ET VOLUPTA-TIBUS OBOEDIENTES, SED AMBULANTES ALIENO IUDICIO ET IMPERIO, IN COENOBIIS DEGENTES ABBATEM SIBI PRAEESSE DESIDERANT. ¹³SINE DUBIO HII TALES ILLAM DOMINI IMITANTUR SENTENTIAM QUA DICIT: NON VENI FACERE VOLUNTATEM MEAM, SED EIUS QUI MISIT ME. ¹⁴SED HAEC IPSA OBOEDIENTIA TUNC ACCEPTABILIS ERIT DEO ET DULCIS HOMINIBUS, SI QUOD IUBETUR NON TREPIDE, NON TARDE, NON TEPIDE, AUT CUM MURMURIO VEL CUM RESPONSO NOLENTIS EFFICIATUR, ¹⁵QUIA OBOEDIENTIA QUAE MAIORIBUS PRAEBETUR DEO EXHIBETUR; IPSE ENIM DIXIT: QUI VOS AUDIT ME AUDIT. ¹⁶ET CUM BONO ANIMO A DISCIPULIS PRAEBERI OPORTET, QUIA HILAREM DATOREM DILIGIT DEUS. ¹⁷NAM, CUM MALO ANIMO SI OBOEDIT DISCIPLUUS ET NON SOLUM ORE, SED ETIAM IN CORDE SI MURMURAVERIT, ¹⁸ETIAM SI IMPLEAT IUSSIONEM, TAMEM ACCEPTUM IAM NON ERIT DEO, QUI COR EIUS RESPICIT MURMURANTEM. ¹⁹ET PRO TALI FACTO NULLAM CONSEQUITUR GRATIAM, IMMO POENAM MURMURANTIUM INCURRIT, SI NON CUM SATISFACTIONE EMENDAVERIT.

1–9 a. For Benedict obedience is a basic 'value', which consists essentially in a mutual listening and readiness to be of mutual help.¹ In this chapter however obedience is encountered first of all as 'the first step in humility'. It is question of the original 'first step of humility' from a treatise on humility which was in circulation in Southern Gaul even before the time of Cassian (d.430) and of the 'Master', and which was ascribed to Abbot Pinufius (Manning).² 'Obeying' is here almost identical with 'listening to' Christ, specifically to the Easter call to repentance, to faith and to baptism; such obedience is contrasted with Adam's disobedience.³ He who undergoes conversion, heeds the voice of the Lord, desires to follow him and to become the disciple of this teacher.⁴

b. Obedience therefore has its place within the ambit of *love for Christ*.⁵ This was a particular concern of the founder of Lérins, Honoratus (d.428): 'His continual aim was . . . lovingly to implant the love of Christ and of one's neighbour, . . . to renew the joy, and to let the yearning for Christ always burn as on the first day of conversion.'⁶ The love which Honoratus in exemplary fashion had lived out beforehand transferred itself to his disciples: 'The grace of the Holy Spirit has remained in his monastery and has been strengthened by the example and teaching of such an outstanding teacher. This is evident in the various charisms and gifts of grace, in humility and gentleness, in unfeigned love.'⁷ Thus did Hilary of Arles (d.449) write of his master.

c. Whoever wishes to follow Christ's voice, forsakes everything⁸ and seeks out a trustworthy *teacher*,⁹ who is capable of preaching the Lord's commandments. In the East as in the West, in the beginning, 'pupils' or 'disciples' gathered about an experienced 'elder' (senior) or 'father' who should instruct them in Christ's teaching by word and example and to whom they could reveal their failings. Hence the leitmotiv of this chapter: 'He who hears you, hears me.'¹⁰ The promise made to the apostles, usually understood of the bishops, is applied without hesitation to the 'teachers' in the monastery, since they are considered capable of passing on the Word of God.

d. It is understandable, that obedience in this view should be presented as a basic 'value'. It is *'humility'*, or the 'spirit of service'[11] in the sphere of action. Out of love for Christ,[12] one 'vows' him 'service'.[13] The eschatalogical motive of fear and reward accompanies the decision to conversion.[14]

e. Further it can be explained, how the content of a task given in obedience can be made equivalent to an *'order by God'*.[15] The psalm-verse too, in which the 'Lord' speaks: 'At the ear's hearing, he obeyed me'[16] points in the direction of a 'descending' order of obedience. At the top stands Christ. As 'Lord' he issues his commands through the 'teachers' he has appointed. The disciples obey.

f. In obedience towards the 'teachers' one aligns oneself on God and rises up towards him, indeed becoming like his image and sharer in his nature. The earliest Church writers understood obedience (hypakoe) in this *theological sense*. Irenaeus (d.*c*.202) writes: 'Every other thing therefore (that which is created) remains subject to God. Obedience to God means continuity and immortality; immortality however is the glory of the Uncreated One. By means of this disposition, harmony, and guidance, created man becomes the image and likeness of the created God, while the Father wills and ordains it, the Son brings it into being and shapes it, the Spirit provides nourishment and growth. Man gradually advances and arrives at perfection, that is, he approaches quite near the Uncreated. Contemplation of God is our goal and the cause of immortality.'[17] Here Irenaeus explains obedience as 'orientation to God'. In another context he gives the acceptance of God's Word as the reason for assimilation to God: 'The Word of God became man and the Son of God the Son of man, in order that man might receive God's Word into himself and as adopted child become God's son. For in no other way can we receive immutability and immortality, unless by becoming one with immutability and immortality.'[18] Irenaeus (d.*c*.202) presents Mary as the model of human obedience towards God's Word: 'Just as one (Eve) was seduced by the word of an angel so that she drew herself away from God and became deaf to his Word, so did the other (Mary) receive the message through the angel's word that she would bear God, because she was obedient to his Word. If one (Eve) was disobedient to God, then did the other (Mary) obey God willingly, so that the Virgin Mary became the advocate of the virgin Eve.'[19] In this early theology, as with Benedict, obedience is a *'value'*,[20] which leads man to God, makes him like God and bestows on him a share in his immortality. This God-orientated attitude of obedience is the deeper foundation for, and the justifying motive of the readiness to enter into a community as a free man, and to obey men, or to accept the providential dispensations of a way of life.

g. If one wishes *'to be converted'*, this 'vertical' obedience is indispensable,[21] later it will be filled out by the 'horizontal' perspective: The fathers of old 'teach, that no one is free from upsurges of aggressiveness, moods of depression, or sexual desires, nor can anyone arrive at true humility of heart, at constant unity with the brethren or strong and enduring unanimity, or even hold out for any length in the monastery, unless he has first learnt to put aside his own will'.[22] Genuine conversion presupposes a real change of soul, which however does not at all mean a loss of one's individuality.[23] To renounce 'self-will' means freeing oneself from those inner, cumbersome resistances and selfishness which absorb much spiritual energy and provoke tensions with one's fellow men. The goal is not to renounce one's individuality, it is rather openness towards the others and a willing insertion into the community, as is clearly expressed in the text of Cassian just quoted.

h. The tasks of teaching and *guiding* are not less exacting than obedience itself: 'The fathers explain: to guide others well or to let oneself be guided well is the prerogative of the wise. They explain it as a very great favour of grace and a gift of the Holy Spirit. No one can impart wholesome instruction to those entrusted to him, unless he himself is well versed in all questions of virtue. No one can obey a venerable father unless he is filled with the fear of God and perfect humility.'[24] This obedience is openness to guidance by the Holy Spirit. Such obedience can be understood only in the perspective of the Christian faith. It transcends by far functional obedience, such as is indispensable in a well-run organization.

i. The Lord himself, whose voice we love, is waiting for the answer of obedience. This obedience therefore is rendered *spontaneously*, quickly, and willingly.[25] The monastic writers love to tell of the immediate obedience of the scribe suddenly called from his work, who left the letter Omega unfinished in the middle of the circle in order to obey promptly.[26] They speak just as often of heroic obedience, which is occasionally compared to Abraham's obedience in faith,[27] and further, of the 'impossible obedience' to which Benedict will later devote a special chapter.[28]

10–13 a. These verses treat of the '*narrow way*' of the cenobites.[29] Obedience now appears as a progress, a search, or a swift striding onwards in the spirit of love.[30] The limitations of self are to be burst asunder in an *élan* of love'. It is not a mere question of a reliable orientation or of the 'sound' guidance of a teacher. The obedient man wishes rather to enter into Christ's self-offering and into his 'compelling love'.[31] One obeys out of free, inner spontaneity, not out of duress or after having weighed up the arguments for and against. The models are the martyrs' obedience in faith, the self-emptying and obedience of the Crucified,[32] the obedience of God's servant.[33] We might speak here of the obedience of love. Christ has shown us the way. By his self-abasement he became our Brother, and founded a new fellowship among humankind. It is into this dynamic movement that the cenobite wishes to enter.

b. The themes listed are to be found in Cassian (d.430) in a passage,[34] which resembles our text in various ways: 'the athlete of Christ, whose goal it is to succeed in the spiritual struggle according to the rules of combat and to receive from the Lord the laurels of victory, must first hasten to defeat this wild beast[35] (arrogance), which eats away all valuable energy ... The edifice of noble qualities of soul cannot be erected within us, unless the foundation of true humility has first been laid in our heart. Only this firm groundwork can "steadfastly" support the whole building of perfection and love up to the very ridge-piece of the roof. So then we have to ... encounter the brethren in a deep heartfelt sentiment of humility and may never let it happen that they become grieved or suffer hurt. We shall never achieve this, unless for *the love of Christ* we live in sincere self-renunciation, which consists in forgoing one's own possessions and in stripping oneself (like the Crucified), and accept with upright hearts the yoke of obedience, following no other will but the directions of the abbot ... which we consider as holy and God-given.'

14-19 **a.** The text of Cassian (d.430) just quoted speaks of obedience to the abbot, but also of a humble sentiment of obedience towards the brethren. In the text of the Rule the community comes into view by at least being hinted at, when there is question of an obedience which 'is delightful to men'. The 'orientation towards God' is not on that account revoked. Nevertheless the subjective attitude to obedience is clearly envisaged, which has its effects in the sphere of interpersonal relationships: opposition, ill-humour, or cheerful willingness are in fact plain to view. They are a burden to a community or they give it an uplift. One should then not overlook this community-orientated aspect of obedience, although our Rule begins with the relationship 'teacher-disciple'.

b. Some monastic Rules begin the other way round with this community orientation of obedience. For Pachomius (d.346) instant obedience[36] is indeed also the norm but he never speaks of seeking a 'teacher'. His guiding principle is that of '*Koinonia*', that is to say, fraternal love and community. The brethren, who have met to form a community, put themselves 'freely' and 'joyfully' under the superiors: 'But also all you brothers who have subjected yourselves under the constitution and in free willingness to serve, ought to "have your loins girded and bear burning lamps in your hands", after the example of "the servants who are waiting for their master . . . Blessed are those servants whom the Master finds awake when he comes"[37] . . ." "Rejoice in the Lord."[38] Be subject to the father in all obedience "without grumbling or questioning",[39] straightforward in heart, ready for every good work.'[40] Thus obedience is here a 'free willingness' to be at the service of the brethren in the community. This community obedience however is related to Christ, the Lord, who made himself the servant of all. It is a cheerful, not a grudging, obedience, which comes from a frank heart. Our Rule appeals to all these qualities: one obeys as a "cheerful giver",[41] without a "complaining heart".[42]

c. The Christian does not bear a 'heart of stone' within him, but rather 'a new heart' and 'a new spirit',[43] so that he can freely 'serve in the new life of the Spirit'.[44] A positive inner openness to the others sustains the community and spreads joy. *Murmuring*[45] is the opposite of this attitude. A constructive attitude is demanded with all emphasis by Basil, who seems to have influenced our text and its line of thought.[46] Basil (d.379) wishes for an obedience which 'pleases one's neighbour'[47] and not merely gratifies oneself,[48] an obedience without dissent[49] or murmuring[50] and without grieving a brother.[51] Basil even writes: 'Whoever murmurs, shall be a stranger to the community.' He 'must quite obviously be suffering from lack of faith'.[52] The community can in no way recognize its spirit, given to it by Christ, in a negative attitude of mind. Although Pachomius (d.346) and Basil (d.379) do not begin with the teacher-disciple relationship, but rather with the community and its needs, the duty of obedience is clearly held to, and is motivated by the example of Jesus. Thus Basil writes: 'It causes harm, if one lets everyone act in everything according to his own whim and fancy . . . One must accept the task laid on one by the superiors even if it is against the will of the person who receives the command, and this according to the example of the Lord, who says: "Father not my will, but thine, be done!"'[53,54]

d. For Benedict the bond joining us to community must give proof of a special 'stability'.[55] This suggests the will *to be identified* with the community in obedience. A 'faint-hearted, dawdling, sullen or listless obedience'[56] is incompatible with the basic purpose. Cassian (d.430) calls an obedience elicited under pressure 'a forced obedience'.[57] Identification with the community awakens the spontaneous readiness to acknowledge a superior. This is the view of Augustine (d.430): 'Obey the superior, as one obeys a father, and show him fitting honour, so as not to insult God through him.'[58] In community one feels that one belongs to a family which needs a 'father'. The monastic superior is obeyed, as one obeys in the family or in the Church.

e. An area of tension exists between unconditional obedience and personal responsibility. Benedict never suggests neutralizing the tension by abolishing one of the components. On the one hand he sees more in obedience than a mere sociological function of law and order. Obedience must be directed to God[59] just like Christ's obedience.[60] The 'Rule of the Four Fathers', which begins with the idea of community, sees the goal of the way of obedience in becoming like Christ: 'The highest point of the Cross is reached, when one practises obedience first and foremost and never acts according to one's own will but instead obeys the command of the superior.'[61] To gaze on the Cross does not hinder Christian joy, for the same Rule speaks of an obedience rendered with total submission 'as if to a command of the Lord's'.[62] According to Benedict's view the superior must come up to this high demand. He may not, that is, 'teach, set up or order anything which deviates from the Lord's commandment'.[63] Thus, in principle, on the other side—that of the person obeying—no *question of conscience* will arise. Perhaps that is the reason why Benedict passes over a text of the 'Master's'[64] which recommends one to unload all responsibility on to the superior and so relieve one's conscience. Quite the contrary: responsibility must be perceived in 'the heart',[65] that is to say at the centre of one's being, in the conscience. When the superior keeps to God's commandment, then a conflict of conscience is not to be feared.[66]

f. The closing sentence of the chapter, which comes from Benedict, takes up again the *theme of reward* and adds to it a threat, but nevertheless not without mentioning the opportunity of doing penance and amending one's ways.

NOTES TO CHAPTER 5

1 Cf. RB 71,1. Benedict adopts in this chapter the text of the 'Master', in an abbreviated form indeed, but mostly word for word. RB 5,1–9 = RM 7,1–9; RB 5,10–13.14–19: RM 7,47–51.67–74. 2 Cf. Cassian, Inst 4,32.—In RB 7,10 there also begins a 'first stage of humility', which originates from another tradition. 3 → Prol. 1.2.3. 4 → Prol. 2.8–1.18–20. 5 Verse 2; cf. RB Prol. 3.50; 4,10.21. 6 VHonor 4,18. 7 Ibid. 4,19. 8 Cf. Verse 7. 9 Verses 5–6. 10 Luke 10:16. Verse 6 and Verse 16. 11 → 7,49–50. 12 Verse 2. 13 Verse 3; → Prol. 45. 14 Verse 3; → Prol. 12–13.21; 4,41–50.74.76–77. 15 Verse 4. 16 Verse 5; Ps. 18:45. 17 Adv haer 4,38,3. 18 Adv haer 3,19,1. 19 Adv haer 5,19,1. 20 → 71,1–4 (Notes 3–5). 21 Verse 7; → 71,1–4. 22 Cassian, Inst 4,8. 23 Benedict often requires respect for the individual character: → 2,11–15.23–25.27–29.31–32; 5,1–9; 7,55; 23,5; 27–30; 34,1–2; 48, 9. 24 Cassian, Inst 2,3,4. 25 Verses 8–9. 26 Cassian, Inst 4,12; VPatr 5,14,5. 27 Cassian, Inst 4,10. 28 → 68,1–3. 29 Benedict has summarized RM 7,47–52. 30 → Prol. 48–49 (Note 155). 31 Cf. 2 Cor. 5:14; → 68,4–5. 32 Cf. Phil 2:8. 33 Verse 13: John 6:38; cf. Matt. 26:39; 'Not as I will, but as thou wilt.' → 4,59–61; cf. RB 3,5. 34 Inst 12,32. 35 An allusion to the (martyrs') combat with wild beasts in the arena. 36 Pachomius, Praec 30. 37 Cf. Luke 12:35–37. 38 Cf. Phil. 4:4. 39 Cf. Phil. 2:14. 40 Hors Lib 19. 41 Verse 16. 42 Verse 17. 43 Cf. Ezek. 11:19; 36:26; Jer. 31:33. 44 Rom. 7:6. 45 Cf. 1 Cor. 10:10 → 4,34–40. 46 Verses 14–19. 47 Rom. 15:2. 48 RBasRuf 68. 49 He quotes Luke 10:16, which in our chapter constitutes a repetition. 50 RBasRuf 70–71. 51 RBasRuf 72. 52 RBasRuf 71. 53 Luke 22:42. 54 RBasRuf 81. 55 →

4,78; 58,13–16. **56** Verses 14.17–18. **57** Inst 4,24,1. **58** Praec 7,1. **59** Verses 14.15.16.18. **60** Verse 13; →
7,10–30.34. **61** R4P 2,33. **62** R4P 1,12. **63** RB 2,4. **64** RM 7,53 56. **65** Verses 16–18. **66** Cf. RB 68.
Neither does Benedict here give a text (RM 7,57–66) about the difficulties comparable to martyrdom
(but cf. RB 7,38–40).

CHAPTER 6

OF RESERVE IN SPEECH

24 Jan
25 May
24 Sept

1 Let us do what the prophet is saying: Ps 39:2–3
I SAID: I WILL GUARD MY WAYS
SO AS NOT TO SIN BY MY TONGUE.
I PUT A GUARD AT MY MOUTH,
I FELL SILENT AND WAS HUMBLED
AND DID NOT SPEAK OF GOOD THINGS.

2 Here the prophet is showing
that if at times for reticence' sake
one must refrain from conversation that is good,
how much more,
because of punishment for sin,
ought one to cease from words that are bad.

3 Therefore, because of the serious nature of reticence,   Cf 1 Cor
let permission to talk be rarely granted to perfect disciples, 2:6;14:20
even for good, holy, and edifying conversations;

4 for it is written: Prov 10:19
IN MUCH SPEAKING
YOU WILL NOT ESCAPE SIN.

5 And in another passage: DEATH AND LIFE ARE IN   Prov 18:21
THE HANDS OF THE TONGUE.

6 To speak and to teach, indeed,   Cf. RB 3,6
befits the master;
to be silent and to listen
becomes the disciple.

7 Therefore,
if requests are to be made of a superior,
let them be asked for with all humility
and respectful submission.

8 Ribaldry however,
and idle words provoking laughter
we condemn everywhere with a perpetual ban,
nor do we allow a disciple to open his mouth for such talk.

CAPUT VI: DE TACITURNITATE

¹FACIAMUS QUOD AIT PROPHETA: DIXI: CUSTODIAM VIAS MEAS, UT NON DELINQUAM IN LINGUA MEA. POSUI ORI MEO CUSTODIAM, OBMUTUI ET HUMILIATUS SUM ET SILUI A BONIS. ²HIC OSTENDIT PROPHETA, SI A BONIS ELOQUIIS INTERDUM PROPTER TACITURNITATEM DEBET TACERE, QUANTO MAGIS A MALIS VERBIS PROPTER POENAM PECCATI DEBET CESSARI. ³ERGO QUAMVIS DE BONIS ET SANCTIS ET AEDIFICATIONUM ELOQUIIS PERFECTIS DISCIPULIS PROPTER TACITURNITATIS GRAVITATEM RARA LOQUENDI CONCEDATUR LICENTIA, ⁴QUIA SCRIPTUM EST: IN MULTILOQUIO NON EFFUGIES PECCATUM, ⁵ET ALIBI: MORS ET VITA IN MANIBUS LINGUAE. ⁶NAM LOQUI ET DOCERE MAGISTRUM CONDECET, TACERE ET AUDIRE DISCIPULUM CONVENIT. ⁷ET IDEO, SI QUA REQUIRENDA SUNT A PRIORE, CUM OMNI HUMILITATE ET SUBIECTIONE REVERENTIAE REQUIRANTUR. ⁸SCURRILITATES VERO VEL VERBA OTIOSA ET RISUM MOVENTIA AETERNA CLUSURA IN OMNIBUS LOCIS DAMNAMUS ET AD TALIA ELOQUIA DISCIPULUM APERIRE OS NON PERMITTIMUS.

1   The opening quotation gives a hint of the main themes of the whole chapter, which has been taken over in abbreviated form from the 'Master':[1] silence as a safeguard against sins of the tongue,[2] in order to create a sphere of quiet in which one can be oneself,[3] and as a proof of a humility which has its model in Jesus and his silence.[4] Whoever has turned to the Lord and is 'humble of heart'[5] will practise in word and deed the *humility* of the Lord,[6] namely in obedience[7] and in silence,[8] which according to Cassian are related[9] to humility and are treated of in three consecutive chapters of the Rule.

2–5   a. These sentences comment on the opening quotation from the psalm. There are similar admonitions in the chapter on humility.[10] There it is made clear that no inhuman mutism, *no 'deathly silence'* is the goal.[11] When Benedict explains what kind of talking is allowed, he replaces the 'Master's' expression 'holy' words by 'well-considered' words.[12] Benedict does not advocate a supra-ascetical ideal, unexperienced in the ways of the world. He allows conversation on matters other than purely religious ones, but desires a well-considered manner of speech. He specifies expressly how one should speak: in a friendly way, unassumingly, seriously or giving the reasons[13] for speaking. Within the community Benedict will later insist on dialogue and on an obedient 'mutual listening'.[14]

b. Basil (d.379) has shown more clearly than our rule, that there must be times of quietness and *times of the word*: 'Quietness and silence are good when they are appropriate to the persons and times . . . Silence is necessary in order to prevent sins of the tongue and provocative words. One should learn to speak as befits the situation, at the proper time and in a helpful way, as it is written: "Let your speech always be gracious, seasoned with salt, so that you may know how you ought to answer every one." '[15,16] From the earliest beginnings silence was provided for in the monasteries, for instance according to Pachomius (d.346), at meals,[17] during work,[18] or while baths[19] were being taken.

c. The warning word of James which is more than clear: 'No human being can tame the tongue—a restless evil, full of deadly poison',[20] leads to a conscious *reserve* in speech.[21] In the background there stands the example of Jesus, who remained silent, where others would have protested.[22] The demon

87

betrays himself in that he must 'cry out'.[23] Jesus commands the demons to be silent.[24] 'Perfect disciples',[25] as spiritual persons, bearers of the Spirit, ought not utter what would be even remotely 'demonic' evil words. In the word the person reveals himself.[26]

d. In the beginnings monks sought out the *desert*, in order that in silence and in solitude, free from sins, they might 'find rest for their souls'.[27] One wishes to keep one's distance and not let oneself be totally taken over by an intensely material environment, by the flood of information and the constraints of society. The word that Abbot Arsenios, a former official of the imperial court, heard is well-known: 'Arsenios ! withdraw! Be still! Calm down!'[28] Outward composure ought to make an inner dynamism possible, 'The venerable father Sisoes said: To be silent is to be a pilgrim.'[29] One does not wish to persevere passively, but rather to set out, not to lose oneself in things but rather to be on the way to a higher goal. The Spirit impels to it. Jesus himself went 'driven by the Spirit into the wilderness'.[30] More than once it is said of him, that he sought out a 'lonely place', 'in order to pray' or 'to rest'.[31]

e. A breath of the quietness and silence of the desert and something of its burning wind, the consuming ardour of the Spirit should be wafted through every monastery, every cell, and every heart. The 'Master' wished to establish a monastery of 'silence and of peace'.[32] Everyone must preserve for himself a *place of quiet*: 'The goal of his vocation, that is the pure contemplation of God which surpasses all else, he cannot reach otherwise than by silence, by keeping to his cell with perseverance and in meditation (of Scripture).'[33]

f. Quiet, stability and 'meditation' are then according to Cassian (d.430) indispensable on the way towards contemplation and *mystical prayer*, for which moreover he does not presuppose any special knowledge, and which also he does not regard as exceptional cases.[34] He lets this be understood in connection with his explanation of the Our Father: 'This prayer manifestly includes all perfection in itself. The Lord himself with all his authority has set us the example and given us the corresponding commandment. This prayer leads all who know it intimately to that condition already spoken of,[35] and which surpasses everything, namely to that ardent prayer (preces ignitae), which only a few know by experience and which is a really indescribable higher state of prayer. It is beyond the sense experience of humankind: no sound of the voice, no movement of the tongue, no spoken word! The soul is immersed, as it were, in the light which shines on it from above.[36] It makes no further use of human speech. All the powers of the affections rush forth like a rising wave. Prayer wells up from an overflowing fountain, springs onward to God and expresses itself wordlessly before him. In a flash and in an instant the soul understands so many and such great things, that she can scarcely express it, nor recall it to memory, when she returns to herself. Our Lord himself has sketched the image of this condition, namely in the manner of his prayer when he withdrew alone to the mountain and prayed in a lonely place[37] or when he sweated drops of blood in his agony,[38] an example of deep inner dedication that defies imitation.'[39]

g. This teaching on contemplative and mystical prayer is based on the Gospel. While Jesus was praying, he experienced the baptism of the Spirit[40] and the Transfiguration.[41] He prayed after he had finished teaching, late at evening, alone on the mountain;[42] he prayed in the early morning while it was still dark, *'even when everyone was searching for him'*.[43] His prayer is of an intimate character but is made for his apostles,[44] his disciples[45] and his mission.[46] The disciples try to be near Jesus when he is praying alone,[47] and he shares his experience of prayer with them. As Cassian's text quoted above shows, Jesus' teaching on prayer leads his disciples to mystical experience. In this way, *the Lord*, in the intimacy of his prayer, stands as *the model of contemplation* before the disciples.

h. *Christian meditation* can indeed also learn from the treasures of experience of *non-Christian monasticism*, from its methods of concentration and inner repose. The search for quietness and 'silence' is a fundamental human need. Such meditation does not yet become Christian through inner quiet or the freeing from all desire for property and power, but only through gazing on Jesus. Only in meeting the Crucified and Risen One do we experience more than a God of the philosophers, namely his Father. 'The Lord himself did not place the highest good in any, even good, work. "Only *one thing* is necessary"[48] says the Lord, namely that we arrive at the vision of himself: this vision is really only one and simple.'[49]

i. It is remarkable how in all Cassian's (d.430) texts, meditation merges into contemplation, into an intuitive and direct experience of God, which is possible only in his light and to the eyes of faith. Abba Bessarion's dying words were: 'The monk must be wholly eye like the cherubim and seraphim.'[50] Benedict never expressly mentions meditative silence or its function in relation to the experience of God. Nevertheless we can take it that silence means *more* for him *than a time without sound or noise*. silence makes possible that contemplative attitude, from out of which heart and mind are open to prayer.[51]

6–7 a. The Rule is written for 'beginners'.[52] It is no surprise therefore, that there is mention of a teacher–pupil relationship. In those chapters which he formulated himself, Benedict avoids the expression *'pupil'*[53], whereas the 'Master' employs it incessantly.

b. Benedict is anxious about the *humility* and unassuming attitude of the 'disciple' towards the superior.[54] Perhaps this betrays difficulties in his monastery,[55] or perhaps he merely wants to curb youthful rashness: 'A venerable father said: "I should rather be taught than be a teacher!" He said also: "Do not set yourself up as a teacher before the time, otherwise for the rest of your life you will only decrease in understanding." '[56]

c. As a 'pupil' the Christian wants to be a 'hearer of the Word'.[57] He goes to school to Christ and to the teachers appointed by him.[58] The Word is received in the depths of the heart in silence: 'All rests in the *depths of the soul.*'[59]

8 Basil (d.379) sees a link between *lack of self-control* and vulgarity in speech, laughter and behaviour. Inward joy is controlled in its expression.[60] Talking is worthwhile if it promotes faith[61] and does not wound charity.[62] In this context Benedict does not treat of the edifying power of a good word.[63] The avoidance of lack of self-control in speech is reckoned as a special effort of each individual in Lent.[64] For Benedict there are times and places where one keeps silence.[65] On other occasions one speaks,[66] this however is not expressly mentioned here.

NOTES TO CHAPTER 6

1 RB 6,1–6,8 = RM 8,31–33,35–36; 9,51; RB 6,7:RM9,1–50. **2** Cassian (Inst 4,41,2) recommends anyone who is provoked by injustice or insults to 'sing' Ps. 39:3 'to himself in his heart', so that he will not allow himself to be stung into making an uncharitable riposte. **3** It is in the word that the inner self expresses itself. → 4.51–54; 24,3. 'Seat and root of the soul is the heart.' (RM 8,7–11). According to the 'Master', the heart can establish contact with its environment through the eyes or the tongue. For that reason, it is emphasized, the control of the tongue is necessary. **4** Mark 1:23–24. **5** Matt. 11:29. **6** Cf. RB 7. **7** Cf. RB 5. **8** Cf. RB 6. **9** Inst 4,39,2. **10** RB 7,56–60. **11** → 72,1–2. **12** RB 7,60; see Note 3 above; → 31,3–7 (good and holy words). **13** RB 66,2–4 (the porter); 31,7 (the cellarer); 61,4 (a stranger monk). **14** → 68; 71,2; 72,6. **15** Col. 4:6. **16** RBasRuf 136. **17** Praec 31; 33–34. **18** Praec60; 116. **19** Praec68. **20** Jas. 3:8. **21** Verse 2: 'refrain even from good words'; Verse 3: to speak 'seldom'. **22** Matt. 26:62–63. **23** Cf. Mark 1:23–24; 66,6–7 (in Notes 9–10). **24** Cf. Mark 1:25. **25** Benedict elsewhere avoids the distinction, familiar to the 'Master', between 'perfect' or 'spiritual', and imperfect disciples. But cf. RB 2,12. **26** → 4,51–54; 24,3. **27** Matt. 11:29. **28** VPatr 5,2,3: 'fuge, tace, quiesce!' **29** VPatr 7,32,4. **30** Cf. Mark 1:12. **31** Cf. Mark 1:35; 6:31. **32** RM 21,14: 'sit monasterium taciturnitatis et pacis'. **33** Cassian, Inst 10,3. **34** → Prol. 48,49. **35** → 52,4. **36** Prol. 8–11.28. **37** Cf. Mk 9:2 ; Lk 5:16. **38** Cf. Lk 22:44. **39** Conl 9:25; → 19,1–3; 20 ; 52:4. **40** Cf. Lk 3:21. **41** Cf. Lk 9:29. **42** Cf. Mt 14:23 ; cf. Lk 9:18. **43** Cf. Mk 1 : 37. **44** He prays before he chooses them (Lk 6:12). **45** He prays before he teaches them how to pray(Lk 11:1). **46** Cf. Lk 3:21; 6:12; 9:29; 11:1. **47** Cf. Lk 9:18. **48** Cf.Lk 10:40–42 **49** Cassian, Conl 1,8. **50** VPatr 5,11,7. **51** 22,4–6;8,3. **52** Prol.46 ; 73,1. **53** Except : RB 36,10. **54** Verse 7 comes from Benedict himself, but summarizes RM 9,1–50 **55** → 67,6–7. **56** VPatr 5,15,81. **57** Prol.2 **58** Prol. 45–50.45.50 ; 1,2.3–5; 2,1–10.11–15; 5,1.9.14–19. **59** Cassian,Conl 1,13. **60** RBasRuf 8. **61** RBasRuf 40. **62** RBasRuf 41–45. **63** In this final sentence from the 'Master' he has inserted only 'in all places'. **64** RB 49,7. **65** RB 38,5; 42; 43,8. **66** RB 31, 13.

CHAPTER 7

OF HUMILITY

25 Jan
26 May
25 Sept 1 Sacred Scripture cries out to us, brothers. Lk 14:11; 18:14;
cf Mt 23:12
It is saying:
EVERYONE WHO MAKES HIMSELF GREAT
WILL BE HUMBLED,
AND HE WHO HUMBLES HIMSELF
WILL BE MADE GREAT.

2 In saying this therefore,
it shows us
that all aggrandizement
is of the nature of pride.

3 The prophet declares that he avoids this. Ps 131:1
He says:
LORD MY HEART IS NOT LIFTED UP,
MY EYES ARE NOT HAUGHTY,
NOR HAVE I WALKED IN GREAT THINGS
NOR IN MARVELS ABOVE ME.

4 But what will happen Cf. Ps 131:2
IF I DID NOT FEEL HUMBLY
IF I EXALTED MY SOUL?
LIKE A WEANED CHILD ON ITS MOTHER
SO YOU WILL PUNISH MY SOUL.

26 Jan
27 May
26 Sept 5 Now, brothers,
if we wish to reach the summit of highest humility
and if we want to arrive with speed
at that heavenly exaltation
to which one climbs
by the humility of the present life,

6 that ladder must be raised up Gen 28:12
by our mounting actions,
that ladder which appeared to Jacob
in the DREAM,
and on which were shown to him
ANGELS COMING DOWN AND GOING UP.

7 There can be no doubt

that that descent and ascent
is to be understood by us
as nothing else but
to come down by aggrandizement,
to go up by humility.

8   The ladder itself indeed raised up
is our life in the world,
which is raised up to heaven by the Lord,
when the heart has been humbled.

9   We say that our body and soul
are the sides of this ladder:
into these sides
the divine call has inserted
various rungs to be climbed
of humility and discipline.

27 Jan   10   The first rung of humility then is   Cf Ps 36:2;
28 May   if he absolutely avoids forgetfulness,   cf. Ps 101:3
27 Sept   11   always putting the fear of God before his eyes,   Cf. 1 Cor 2:9
always remembering everything that God commanded,
always turning over in his mind
that hell burns up for their sins
those who despise God,
and that eternal life is PREPARED
for those who fear God.

12   And keeping himself at every moment   Cf. Ps 12:2; Gal 5:16;
from sins and vices,   RB 4, 57–60
that is of thought,
TONGUE,
hands,
feet,
and self-will,
and the DESIRES OF THE FLESH too,

13   let a man consider   Cf. Ps 14:2; Prov 15:3
that he is WATCHED FROM HEAVEN
by God at every moment,
and that in every place
his deeds are seen
by THE EYE OF THE GODHEAD
and are reported at every instant by angels.

14 The prophet points this out to us   Ps 7:10
when he shows that God is ever present in our thoughts.
He says:
GOD IS SCRUTINIZING HEART AND LOINS;

15 and again: Ps 94:11
THE LORD IS AWARE OF MENS' THOUGHTS;

16 and again he says: Ps 139:2
YOU UNDERSTOOD MY THOUGHTS FROM AFAR;

17 and: Cf. Ps 76:11
BECAUSE MAN'S THOUGHT WILL MAKE CONFESSION TO YOU.

18 On the other hand,   Cf. Ps 18:24;
in order to be on the alert about his bad thoughts,   Ecclus 4:29
          (Lat.); Ps 14:3;
let the USEFUL brother   Mt 25:30;
always keep saying in his heart: Lk 17:10
Then SHALL I BE SINLESS BEFORE HIM
IF I SHALL HAVE KEPT MYSELF FROM MY INIQUITY.

28 Jan 19 We are accordingly forbidden to do our own will   Ecclus 18:30
29 May since Scripture says to us:
28 Sept AND TURN AWAY FROM THE ACTS OF YOUR WILL.

20 And similarly we ask the Lord in the Prayer   Mt 6:10
that his WILL BE DONE in us.

21 We are rightly therefore taught not to do our own will,   Prov 16:25;
when we avoid what Sacred Scripture says: 14:12
THERE ARE WAYS WHICH ARE THOUGHT BY MEN TO BE
STRAIGHT,
WHOSE END SWALLOWS UP IN DEEPEST HELL.

22 And when again we dread what has been said of   Ps 12:1
the negligent:
THEY HAVE BECOME CORRUPT AND ABOMINABLE IN THEIR WILLS.

23 And in the desires of the flesh   Ps 38:10
let us believe that God is always present to us in such
a way as the prophet says:
ALL MY DESIRE IS BEFORE YOU.

24 Evil desire must therefore be avoided,   Passio Sebastiani 4:14
because death is lurking at the threshold of delight.

25 This is why Scripture commanded: Ecclus 18:30
DO NOT FOLLOW YOUR LUSTS.

29 Jan
30 May
29 Sept
26 Therefore if THE EYES OF THE LORD ARE KEEPING WATCH   Prov 15:3
OVER THE GOOD AND THE BAD

27 and THE LORD IS EVER LOOKING DOWN FROM HEAVEN   Ps 14:2
ON THE CHILDREN OF MEN,
to see IF THERE BE ONE WHO IS WISE
AND SEEKS GOD,

28 and if the works we do   Cf. Heb 1:14
are reported to the Lord
daily, day and night,
by the angels assigned to us,

29 then, brethren,   Ps 14:3
as the prophet says in the psalm,
we must take care at every moment,
lest God see us at any moment
TURNED ASIDE to evil AND BECOME USELESS

30 and sparing us at present,   Ps 50:21;
because he is loving and waits for us to change   cf. Ecclus 2:13
  for the better,
he says to us in the future
THESE THINGS YOU HAVE DONE,
AND I KEPT SILENCE.

30 Jan
31 May
30 Sept
31 To be on the second rung of humility is
not to be in love with self-will,
not to be delighted
at fulfilling one's desires;

32 but to imitate in practice   Jn 6:38
that what the Lord says:
I HAVE NOT COME TO DO MY WILL,
BUT HIS WILL
WHO SENT ME.

33 Scripture also says: Passio Anastasiae 17
SELF-WILL GETS PUNISHED,
COMPULSION ENGENDERS A CROWN.

31 Jan
1 June
1 Oct
34 To be on the third rung of humility is   Phil 2:8
out of love for God
to submit oneself to a superior
in total obedience,
imitating the Lord, of whom the Apostle says:
MADE OBEDIENT UNTO DEATH.

1 Feb
2 June
2 Oct

35 To be on the fourth rung of humility
is to embrace patience,
silently and consciously,
if in the obedience itself
difficult and contrary things,
or even insults of whatever kind
are brought on,

36 and to bear up, not to grow weary or leave; Mt 10:22
Scripture has said:
WHOEVER HOLDS OUT TO THE END WILL BE SAVED.

37 Again: Ps 27:14
BE STOUTHEARTED AND WAIT FOR THE LORD.

38 And showing that the faithful one Rom 8:36;
ought to put up with everything, no matter how Ps 44:23
contrary, for the Lord,
it says in the person of those who suffer:
FOR YOUR SAKE WE ARE BEING SLAIN ALL DAY LONG;
WE ARE LOOKED UPON AS SHEEP TO BE SLAUGHTERED.

39 And certain of the hope of divine reward Rom 8:37
they go on with joy to say:
YET IN ALL THIS WE ARE MORE THAN CONQUERORS
BECAUSE OF HIM WHO LOVED US.

40 And again in another passage of Scripture: Ps 66:10–11
YOU HAVE TESTED US, GOD,
YOU HAVE REFINED US LIKE SILVER;
YOU LET US FALL INTO THE NET,
YOU LAID HEAVY BURDENS ON OUR BACK.

41 And to show that we ought to be under a superior, Ps 66:12
it goes on to say:
YOU PLACED MEN OVER OUR HEADS.

42 But fulfilling the Lord's precept Mt 5:39–41:cf. 27:42
by patience in adversities and insults
STRUCK ON ONE CHEEK THEY OFFER ALSO THE OTHER,
TO HIM WHO TAKES TUNIC
THEY LET HIM HAVE CLOAK AS WELL,
REQUISITIONED TO GO ONE MILE
THEY GO TWO.

43 In company with the Apostle Paul 2 Cor 11:26;
THEY PUT UP WITH FALSE BROTHERS 1 Cor 4:12; Lk 6:28
and ENDURE PERSECUTION,
and BLESS THOSE WHO CURSE THEM.

2 Feb
3 June
3 Oct

44 To be on the fifth rung of humility is
through a humble confession
not to conceal from one's abbot
all the bad thoughts that come to one's heart
nor the bad things one has secretly done.

45 Scripture urges us in this matter: Ps 37:5
LAY BARE YOUR WAY TO THE LORD
AND HOPE IN HIM.

46 And again it says: Ps 106:1; Ps 118:1
CONFESS TO THE LORD FOR HE IS GOOD,
FOR HIS MERCY IS FOR EVER.

47 And the prophet once more: Ps 32:5
I ACKNOWLEDGED MY SIN TO YOU,
MY GUILT I COVERED NOT.

48 I SAID:
ACCUSING MYSELF,
I WILL CONFESS MY OFFENCES TO THE LORD,
AND YOU FORGAVE THE GUILT OF MY HEART.

3 Feb
4 June
3 Oct

49 To be on the sixth rung of humility is   Cf. Lk 17:10;
for a monk to be content   Mt 23:11
with all that is cheapest and most marginal,
and in all that is enjoined on him,
to judge himself to be a bad workman,
an unworthy one,

50 saying to himself with the prophet: Ps 73:22–23
I WAS BROUGHT DOWN TO NOTHING
AND KNEW IT NOT;
I WAS LIKE A BRUTE BEAST IN YOUR PRESENCE;
YET WITH YOU I SHALL ALWAYS BE.

4 Feb
5 June
5 Oct

51 To be on the seventh rung of humility   Cf. 1 Cor 15:9;
is not merely to declare with one's tongue   1:28; Phil 2:3
that one is lower and of less account than all,
but even to believe it
in one's heart of hearts,

52 humbling oneself and saying with the prophet: Ps 22:7
BUT AS FOR ME, I AM A WORM AND NO MAN,
THE SCORN OF MEN
AND DESPISED BY THE PEOPLE.

53 I HAVE BEEN EXALTED AND HUMBLED AND CONFOUNDED. Ps 88:16 (Lat.)

54 And again:
   IT HAS DONE ME GOOD
   THAT YOU HUMBLED ME
   AND I MAY LEARN YOUR COMMANDMENTS.

Ps 119:71,73

5 Feb
6 June
6 Oct

55 To be on the eighth rung of humility
   is for a monk
   to do nothing except what is encouraged by
   the common rule of the monastery
   and the example of the superiors.

6 Feb
7 June
7 Oct

56 To be on the ninth rung of humility
   is for a monk to forbid his tongue to speak,
   and, maintaining reserve,
   not to speak until questioned.

Cf. Ps 34:14

57 Scripture shows that
   WHERE WORDS ARE MANY,
   SIN IS NOT WANTING.
   And:

Prov 10:19

58 'THE MAN OF TONGUE'
   DOES NOT FIND FOOTING IN THE LAND.

Ps 140:12

7 Feb
8 June
8 Oct

59 To be on the tenth rung of humility
   is to be not inconsiderately quick to laugh;
   because it is written:
   THE FOOL RAISES HIS VOICE IN LAUGHTER.

Ecclus 21:23

8 Feb
9 June
9 Oct

60 To be on the eleventh rung of humility
   is for a monk, when talking,
   to speak gently and without laughing,
   humbly and with seriousness,
   with good sense, in few words,
   and not in a noisy voice,

61 as it is written:
   A MAN IS RECOGNIZED AS WISE
   WHEN HIS WORDS ARE FEW.

Sextus, Enchiridion 145;
cf. Ecclus 20:5,7

9 Feb
10 June
10 Oct

62 To be on the twelfth rung of humility
   is for a monk to reveal to all who see him
   humility not only of heart,
   but of his very body.

63   That is, with head ever bowed and looks fixed   Cf. Jn 19:30
     on the ground,
    at the Work of God,
    in the oratory,
    in the monastery,
    in the garden,
    on the road,
    in a field,
    wherever he is sitting, walking or standing,

64   at every moment
    let him consider himself guilty on account of his sins,
    and already made present to the fearful Judgement,

65   saying always in his heart   Lk 18:13–14;
    what that tax-gatherer in the Gospel said   Mt 8:8
    with eyes fixed on the ground:
    LORD, I AM NOT WORTHY, I A SINNER,
    TO RAISE MY EYES TO THE HEAVENS.

66   And again with the prophet: Ps 38:7–9;
    I AM STOOPED AND BOWED DOWN PROFOUNDLY.   cf. Ps 119:107

67   Therefore, when he has climbed all these rungs   1 Jn 4:18
    of humility, a monk will immediately come
    to that LOVE OF GOD WHICH when PERFECT CASTS OUT FEAR.

68   By this love,
    without any trouble,
    as it were naturally, by habit,
    he will begin to keep everything
    which hitherto he used to observe
    not without fear,

69   no longer now by fear of hell
    but by the love of Christ,
    and the good habit itself,
    and the delight of virtues.

70   By the Holy Spirit   Cf. Rom 5:5
    the Lord will deign to demonstrate these things
    in his workman,
    clean from vices and sins.

CAPUT VII: DE HUMILITATE

¹CLAMAT NOBIS SCRIPTURA DIVINA, FRATRES, DICENS: OMNIS QUI SE EXALTAT HUMILIABITUR ET QUI SE HUMILIAT EXALTABITUR. ²CUM HAEC ERGO DICIT, OSTENDIT NOBIS OMNEM EXALTATIONEM GENUS ESSE SUPERBIAE. ³QUOD SE CAVERE PROPHETA INDICAT DICENS: DOMINE, NON EST EXALTATUM COR MEUM NEQUE ELATI SUNT OCULI MEI, NEQUE AMBULAVI IN MAGNIS NEQUE IN MIRABILIBUS SUPER ME. ⁴SED QUID, SI NON HUMILITER SENTIEBAM, SI EXALTAVI ANIMAM MEAM? SICUT ABLACTATUM SUPER MATREM SUAM, ITA RETRIBUES IN ANIMAM MEAM. ⁵UNDE, FRATRES, SI SUMMAE HUMILITATIS VOLUMUS CULMEN ADTINGERE ET AD EXALTATIONEM ILLAM CAELESTEM AD QUAM PER PRAESENTIS VITAE HUMILITATEM ASCENDITUR, VOLUMUS VELOCITER PERVENIRE, ⁶ACTIBUS NOSTRIS ASCENDENTIBUS SCALA ILLA ERIGENDA EST QUAE IN SOMNIO IACOB APPARUIT, PER QUAM EI DESCENDENTES ET ASCENDENTES ANGELI MONSTRABANTUR. ⁷NON ALIUD SINE DUBIO DESCENSUS ILLE ET ASCENSUS A NOBIS INTELLEGITUR NISI EXALTATIONE DESCENDERE ET HUMILITATE ASCENDERE. ⁸SCALA VERO IPSA ERECTA NOSTRA EST VITA IN SAECULO, QUAE HUMILIATO CORDE A DOMINO ERIGATUR AD CAELUM. ⁹LATERA ENIM EIUS SCALAE DICIMUS NOSTRUM ESSE CORPUS ET ANIMAM, IN QUA LATERA DIVERSOS GRADUS HUMILITATIS VEL DISCIPLINAE EVOCATIO DIVINA ASCENDENDO INSERUIT. ¹⁰PRIMUS ITAQUE HUMILITATIS GRADUS EST, SI TIMOREM DEI SIBI ANTE OCULOS SEMPER PONENS, OBLIVIONEM OMNINO FUGIAT ¹¹ET SEMPER SIT MEMOR OMNIA QUAE PRAECEPIT DEUS, UT QUALITER ET CONTEMNENTES DEUM GEHENNA DE PECCATIS INCENDAT ET VITA AETERNA QUAE TIMENTIBUS DEUM PRAEPARATA EST, ANIMO SUO SEMPER REVOLVAT. ¹²ET CUSTODIENS SE OMNI HORA A PECCATIS ET VITIIS, ID EST COGITATIONUM, LINGUAE, MANUUM, PEDUM VEL VOLUNTATIS PROPRIAE SED ET DESIDERIA CARNIS, ¹³AESTIMET SE HOMO DE CAELIS A DEO SEMPER RESPICI OMNI HORA ET FACTA SUA OMNI LOCO AB ASPECTU DIVINITATIS VIDERI ET AB ANGELIS OMNI HORA RENUNTIARI. ¹⁴DEMONSTRANS NOBIS HOC PROPHETA, CUM IN COGITATIONIBUS NOSTRIS ITA DEUM SEMPER PRAESENTEM OSTENDIT DICENS: SCRUTANS CORDA ET RENES DEUS; ¹⁵ET ITEM: DOMINUS NOVIT COGITATIONES HOMINUM; ¹⁶ET ITEM DICIT: INTELLEXISTI COGITATIONES MEAS A LONGE; ¹⁷ET: QUIA COGITATIO HOMINIS CONFITEBITUR TIBI. ¹⁸NAM UT SOLLICITUS SIT CIRCA COGITATIONES SUAS PERVERSAS, DICAT SEMPER UTILIS FRATER IN CORDE SUO: TUNC ERO INMACULATUS CORAM EO SI OBSERVAVERO ME AB INIQUITATE MEA. ¹⁹VOLUNTATEM VERO PROPRIAM ITA FACERE PROHIBEMUR CUM DICIT SCRIPTURA NOBIS: ET A VOLUNTATIBUS TUIS AVERTERE. ²⁰ET ITEM ROGAMUS DEUM IN ORATIONE UT FIAT ILLIUS VOLUNTAS IN NOBIS. ²¹DOCEMUR ERGO MERITO NOSTRAM NON FACERE VOLUNTATEM CUM CAVEMUS ILLUD QUOD DICIT SANCTA SCRIPTURA: SUNT VIAE QUAE PUTANTUR AB HOMINIBUS RECTAE, QUARUM FINIS USQUE AD PROFUNDUM INFERNI DEMERGIT, ²²ET CUM ITEM PAVEMUS ILLUD QUOD DE NEGLEGENTIBUS DICTUM EST: CORRUPTI SUNT ET ABOMINABILES FACTI SUNT IN VOLUNTATIBUS SUIS. ²³IN DESIDERIIS VERO CARNIS ITA NOBIS DEUM CREDAMUS SEMPER ESSE PRAESENTEM, CUM DICIT PROPHETA DOMINO: ANTE TE EST OMNE DESIDERIUM MEUM. ²⁴CAVENDUM ERGO IDEO MALUM DESIDERIUM, QUIA MORS SECUS INTROITUM DILECTATIONIS POSITA EST. ²⁵UNDE SCRIPTURA PRAECEPIT DICENS: POST CONCUPISCENTIAS TUAS NON EAS. ²⁶ERGO SI OCULI DOMINI SPECULANTUR BONOS ET MALOS ²⁷ET DOMINUS DE CAELO SEMPER RESPICIT SUPER FILIOS HOMINUM, UT VIDEAT SI EST INTELLEGENS AUT REQUIRENS DEUM, ²⁸ET SI AB ANGELIS NOBIS DEPUTATIS COTIDIE DIE NOCTUQUE DOMINO FACTORUM NOSTRORUM OPERA NUNTIANTUR, ²⁹CAVENDUM EST ERGO OMNI HORA, FRATRES, SICUT DICIT IN PSALMO PROPHETA, NE NOS DECLINANTES IN MALO ET INUTILES FACTOS ALIQUA HORA ASPICIAT DEUS ³⁰ET, PARCENDO NOBIS IN HOC TEMPORE, QUIA PIUS EST ET EXPECTAT NOS CONVERTI IN MELIUS, NE DICAT NOBIS IN FUTURO: HAEC FECISTI ET TACUI. ³¹SECUNDUS HUMILITATIS GRADUS EST, SI PROPRIAM QUIS NON AMANS VOLUNTATEM DESIDERIA SUA NON DELECTETUR IMPLERE, ³²SED VOCEM ILLAM DOMINI FACTIS IMITETUR DICENTIS: NON VENI FACERE VOLUNTATEM MEAM, SED

EIUS QUI ME MISIT. ³³ITEM DICIT SCRIPTURA: VOLUNTAS HABET POENAM ET NECESSITAS PARIT CORONAM. ³⁴TERTIUS HUMILITATIS GRADUS EST, UT QUIS PRO DEI AMORE OMNI OBOEDIENTIA SE SUBDAT MAIORI, IMITANS DOMINUM, DE QUO DICIT APOSTOLUS: FACTUS OBOEDIENS USQUE AD MORTEM. ³⁵QUARTUS HUMILITATIS GRADUS EST, SI IN IPSA OBOEDIENTIA DURIS ET CONTRARIIS REBUS VEL ETIAM QUIBUSLIBET INROGATIS INIURIIS, TACITE CONSCIENTIA PATIENTIAM AMPLECTATUR ³⁶ET SUSTINENS NON LASSESCAT VEL DISCEDAT, DICENTE SCRIPTURA: QUI PERSEVERAVERIT USQUE IN FINEM, HIC SALVUS ERIT. ³⁷ITEM: CONFORTETUR COR TUUM ET SUSTINE DOMINUM. ³⁸ET OSTENDENS FIDELEM PRO DOMINO UNIVERSA ETIAM CONTRARIA SUSTINERE DEBERE, DICIT EX PERSONA SUFFERENTIUM: PROPTER TE MORTE ADFICIMUR TOTA DIE, AESTIMATI SUMUS UT OVES OCCISIONIS. ³⁹ET SECURI DE SPE RETRIBUTIONIS DIVINAE SUBSECUNTUR GAUDENTES ET DICENTES: SED IN HIS OMNIBUS SUPERAMUS PROPTER EUM QUI DILEXIT NOS. ⁴⁰ET ITEM ALIO LOCO SCRIPTURA: PROBASTI NOS, DEUS, IGNE NOS EXAMINASTI SICUT IGNE EXAMINATUR ARGENTUM; INDUXISTI NOS IN LAQUEUM; POSUISTI TRIBULATIONES IN DORSO NOSTRO. ⁴¹ET UT OSTENDAT SUB PRIORE DEBERE NOS ESSE, SUBSEQUITUR DICENS: INPOSUISTI HOMINES SUPER CAPITA NOSTRA. ⁴²SED ET PRAECEPTUM DOMINI IN ADVERSIS ET INIURIIS PER PATIENTIAM ADIMPLENTES, QUI PERCUSSI IN MAXILLAM PRAEBENT ET ALIAM, AUFERENTI TUNICAM DIMITTUNT ET PALLIUM, ANGARIZATI MILIARIO VADUNT DUO, ⁴³CUM PAULO APOSTOLO FALSOS FRATRES SUSTINENT ET PERSECUTIONEM SUSTINENT, ET MALEDICENTES SE BENEDICENT. ⁴⁴QUINTUS HUMILITATIS GRADUS EST, SI OMNES COGITATIONES MALAS CORDI SUO ADVENIENTES VEL MALA A SE ABSCONSE COMMISSA PER HUMILEM CONFESSIONEM ABBATEM NON CELAVERIT SUUM. ⁴⁵HORTANS NOS DE HAC RE SCRIPTURA DICENS: REVELA AD DOMINUM VIAM TUAM ET SPERA IN EUM. ⁴⁶ET ITEM DICIT: CONFITEMINI DOMINO QUONIAM BONUS, QUONIAM IN SAECULUM MISERICORDIA EIUS. ⁴⁷ET ITEM PROPHETA: DELICTUM MEUM COGNITUM TIBI FECI ET INIUSTITIAS MEAS NON OPERUI. ⁴⁸DIXI: PRONUNTIABO ADVERSUM ME INIUSTITIAS MEAS DOMINO, ET TU REMISISTI IMPIETATEM CORDIS MEI. ⁴⁹SEXTUS HUMILITATIS GRADUS EST, SI OMNI VILITATE VEL EXTREMITATE CONTENTUS SIT MONACHUS, ET AD OMNIA QUAE SIBI INIUNGUNTUR VELUT OPERARIUM MALUM SE IUDICET ET INDIGNUM, ⁵⁰DICENS SIBI CUM PROPHETA: AD NIHILUM REDACTUS SUM ET NESCIVI; UT IUMENTUM FACTUS SUM APUD TE ET EGO SEMPER TECUM. ⁵¹SEPTIMUS HUMILITATIS GRADUS EST, SI OMNIBUS SE INFERIOREM ET VILIOREM NON SOLUM SUA LINGUA PRONUNTIET, SED ETIAM INTIMO CORDIS CREDAT AFFECTU, ⁵²HUMILIANS SE ET DICENS CUM PROPHETA: EGO AUTEM SUM VERMIS ET NON HOMO, OBPROBRIUM HOMINUM ET ABIECTIO PLEBIS. ⁵³EXALTATUS SUM ET HUMILIATUS ET CONFUSUS. ⁵⁴ET ITEM: BONUM MIHI QUOD HUMILIASTI ME, ET DISCAM MANDATA TUA. ⁵⁵OCTAVUS HUMILITATIS GRADUS EST, SI NIHIL AGAT MONACHUS, NISI QUOD COMMUNIS MONASTERII REGULA VEL MAIORUM COHORTANTUR EXEMPLA. ⁵⁶NONUS HUMILITATIS GRADUS EST, SI LINGUAM AD LOQUENDUM PROHIBEAT MONACHUS ET, TACITURNITATEM HABENS, USQUE AD INTERROGATIONEM NON LOQUATUR, ⁵⁷MONSTRANTE SCRIPTURA QUIA IN MULTILOQUIO NON EFFUGITUR PECCATUM, ⁵⁸ET QUIA VIR LINGUOSUS NON DIRIGITUR SUPER TERRAM. ⁵⁹DECIMUS HUMILITATIS GRADUS EST, SI NON SIT FACILIS AC PROMPTUS IN RISU, QUIA SCRIPTUM EST: STULTUS IN RISU EXALTAT VOCEM SUAM. ⁶⁰UNDECIMUS HUMILITATIS GRADUS EST, SI, CUM LOQUITUR MONACHUS, LENITER ET SINE RISU, HUMILITER CUM GRAVITATE VEL PAUCA VERBA ET RATIONABILIA LOQUATUR, ET NON SIT CLAMOSUS IN VOCE, ⁶¹SICUT SCRIPTUM EST: SAPIENS VERBIS INNOTESCIT PAUCIS. ⁶²DUODECIMUS HUMILITATIS GRADUS EST, SI NON SOLUM CORDE MONACHUS, SED ETIAM IPSO CORPORE HUMILITATEM VIDENTIBUS SE SEMPER INDICET, ⁶³ID EST IN OPERE DEI, IN ORATORIO, IN MONASTERIO, IN HORTO, IN VIA, IN AGRO VEL UBICUMQUE SEDENS, AMBULANS VEL STANS, INCLINATO SIT SEMPER CAPITE, DEFIXIS IN TERRAM ASPECTIBUS, ⁶⁴REUM SE OMNI HORA DE PECCATIS SUIS AESTIMANS IAM SE TREMENDO IUDICIO REPRAE-SENTARI AESTIMET, ⁶⁵DICENS SIBI IN CORDE SEMPER ILLUD, QUOD PUBLICANUS ILLE EVANGELICUS FIXIS IN TERRAM OCULIS DIXIT: DOMINE, NON SUM DIGNUS, EGO

PECCATOR, LEVARE OCULOS MEOS AD CAELOS. "ET ITEM CUM PROPHETA: INCURVATUS SUM ET HUMILITATUS SUM USQUEQUAQUE. "ERGO, HIS OMNIBUS HUMILITATIS GRADIBUS ASCENSIS, MONACHUS MOX AD CARITATEM DEI PERVENIET ILLAM QUAE PERFECTA FORIS MITTIT TIMOREM, "PER QUAM UNIVERSA QUAE PRIUS NON SINE FORMIDINE OBSERVABAT ABSQUE ULLO LABORE VELUT NATURALITER EX CONSUETUDINE INCIPIET CUSTODIRE, "NON IAM TIMORE GEHENNAE, SED AMORE CHRISTI ET CONSUETUDINE IPSA BONA ET DILECTATIONE VIRTUTUM. "QUAE DOMINUS IAM IN OPERARIUM SUUM MUNDUM A VITIIS ET PECCATIS SPIRITU SANCTO DIGNABITUR DEMONSTRARE.

1–4 a. At the end of the chapter on humility in the 'Master'[1] the phrase occurs: 'End of the Account of the Warfare of the Heart'.[2] The Rule wishes to propose a *spirituality of the heart*. In it the chapter on humility forms the heart of the matter. It concludes and sums up the doctrinal opening part. The style of the chapter is similar to that of the Prologue, for example in the direct address 'Brothers'. It is the style of the 'Actus militiae cordis'. The origins of the chapter on humility are sought in a 'libellus' known in Southern France already before Cassian's time (d.430) and ascribed to an Abbot Pinufius (A. de Vogüé challenges this thesis of Manning's).

b. Starting from a saying of the Lord's,[3] the way of humility is presented as a double movement of descent and ascent. To begin with, the first part of the Lord's saying is commented on: 'Everyone who exalts himself.' This is done with quotations from a psalm[4] on haughtiness or arrogance[5] and on the punishment[6] of pride. The psalm speaks of heart, eyes, senses and soul, that is of the whole person. Benedict often finds the notion 'heart' sufficient: it stands for the *innermost being of the person*, and denotes the whole self, the conscience.

5–9 a. The image of *ascent* is taken from tradition. Clement of Alexandria (d.before 215) already speaks of the ascent to knowledge (Gnosis) which is possible in this life, and in which the soul is led by the Word.[7]

b. The seemingly paradoxical statement reads: the ascent leads to the heights of lowliness. The Latin expression *'humilitas'* strictly means that 'which is near the ground (humus).' One ought not overlook the fact that this word originally suggested the lowest order of society and those deprived of civil rights. In Christian linguistic usage the word acquired a much more positive ring. It suggests the 'Anawim' of the Old Testament or Mary's humility.

c. The genuine 'ascent' extends over the descending movement of self-emptying.[8] We renounce pushing ourselves to the fore and fulfilling our will. Horsiesi (d.c.380) looks upon the renouncement of anxious care about oneself as an *act of emancipation*. Selflessness frees us from the urge to assert ourselves and from anxiety about oneself. We achieve as the 'highest' human possibility a partaking in Christ's self-renouncement (Kenosis) in the poverty of the Cross. That is the obedience of the Son, whom the Father takes up into the divine glory as his reward. Horsiesi writes: 'We are free. We have cast off the yoke of servile bondage to this world. Why should we turn back to our vomit![9] Why do we wish to retain belongings, to have to be once again in fear and anxiety of losing them . . . ! Everything is in common, at the disposal of all. Nothing can be harder than the Cross of Christ. Our fathers lived according to this norm. In this way they have set us firmly "upon the foundation of the apostles and prophets" and on the teaching of the Gospel. Everything is gathered together "in the cornerstone Jesus Christ".[10] If we want to follow him, we must come down from the death-bearing heights (of pride) into life-giving humility, by exchanging riches for poverty . . . Do not forget the decision you once made. Let us look upon the tradition of our father (Pachomius) as a ladder which leads to heaven.'[11,12]

d. Essential themes of the chapter on humility are intoned already in this text of Horsiesi (d.c.380), as well as the image of the ladder which is based on tradition. The pattern of ascent predominates also in the works of Cassian (d.430). For him humility is directed rather to the 'practical' 'active' ascesis concerned with deeds. It serves *purification*. Jesus demanded it for human life in common,[13] for the service by those who are the 'greatest'[14] and for prayer.[15] If one does not wish to fool oneself, it is only by the steps of humility that one can arrive at the height of 'Theoria', that is the contemplative vision of God.

e. The conception of 'steps'[16] used by Cassian (d.430) and *Jacob's ladder*[17] mentioned by Horsiesi are now used to illustrate the second half of the Lord's saying[18] mentioned at the outset: 'he who humbles himself will be exalted'. In the biblical view Jacob's ladder and the angels point to the presence of the God of holiness,[19] who reveals himself where least expected, and to begin with, sanctifies the insignificant spot. Benedict makes men climb this ladder and approach the all-holy God (A. de Vogüé).

The pattern of climbing is of a *dynamic* character. It implies a 'striding onwards and upwards'.[20] Antony (d.356) exhorted the brethren: 'Let this be the first commandment, binding on all: Let him be like the beginner, ever ready to augment the work he has begun, above all because in comparison with eternity the span of earthly life is brief and its space narrow.'[21]

f. The goal of the ascent is an eschatological one, heaven.[22] The Master therefore also at the end of the chapter on humility describes heaven in glowing terms. Benedict does not attempt any such description and indicates merely what can be attained in this life: the *home-straight*, the final stretch of the course immediately before the finishing line, love (caritas). The word 'love' has an almost mystical tone for the author. He speaks of it only at the end of the chapter on humility;[23] it also appears at the end of the Prologue[24] and at the end of the entire Rule.[25]

g. The image of *ascent and descent* indicates that the steps to the exalted goal should not be understood as following one another in chronological order, as if the goal might only be attained in old age. The monastic fathers insist that the juniors need formation,[26] but consider them capable of an inner maturity and wisdom, such as one expects only in old men. It was said of Honoratus (d.428), the founder of Lérins: 'He transcended every degree of age in the power of grace, and was always greater than himself.'[27] Gregory the Great (d.604) wrote of Benedict: 'Benedict, "blessed" in grace and name led a life which evoked admiration. From childhood on he bore within him a heart which would have done credit to an old man. More mature in character than in age, he never succumbed to sensual pleasure. During his life on this earth he despised the transitory nature of the world—which he might have enjoyed to the full—as if it were a flower already withered.'[28]

h. 'The ladder raised up is however our earthly life',[29] in so far as it *'raises itself up'* in a community of destiny with the Crucified. A profound saying of Abbot Hyperechios speaks not indeed of the 'ladder' but of the 'tree of life', which has to be climbed and which points to the Cross: 'The tree of life towers up on high. The monk, who lowers himself in humility, climbs on it to the heights'.[30] Only 'when our heart becomes humble'[31] can we enter into a life shared with Christ, to take a part in his Cross and his life. 'John of Thebes said: above all the monk must be humble. The first commandment of our Lord states in fact: "Blessed are the poor in spirit, for theirs is the kingdom of heaven."'[32,33]

i. The 'mind of Christ'[34] is the aim, and *not an emotional feeling of inferiority* when the monk speaks of 'humility'. The aged Amma Sarah let it be understood, that she did not suffer from a basic lack of self-confidence. When two respected elderly monks tried to upset her by a visit, in order to humiliate her, she did not let herself be intimidated but declared bluntly: 'In my sex I am a woman, but in my soul I have the courage of a man.'[35] Humility does not mean weakness. The man of the Beatitudes is humble. The Sermon on the Mount, this encouraging 'call from God': 'Blessed are you!' must penetrate 'body and soul', that is affect the whole person so that the attitude of humility is 'inserted'[36] into one's whole life.

10–13   a. The 'fear of God' which leads to purification is called the 'source and guardian of salvation' by Cassian (d.430).[37] For Basil (d.379) 'training' in the fear of God leads to the 'first steps' on the way of salvation.[38] The expression 'fear' sounds negative today. In ancient usage it had not got this tone. Origen (d.253) declares tersely: '"Blessed is the man, who fears the Lord!"[39] He who does not fear, is not blessed.'[40] When a person, *touched to the quick*, experiences the holiness and transcendence of God, he does not feel oppressed, but rather raised up and freed from the feeling of meaninglessness and the anguish of existence.

b. What is 'the fear of God'? The author describes it by its opposite image. *'Forgetfulness of God'* stands over against 'awareness of God's existence' in tradition. Whoever 'forgets'[41] God, has no fear of God. 'Forgetfulness of God' means practical atheism: being caught in what is practically possible and can be consumed, the evasion of the question of the meaning of life, and consequently self-alienation, the lack of antennae for the realm of the spirit (acedia) and a total conformity with prevailing public opinion. Basil (d.379) describes this practical atheism: 'A person sees that broad masses do not lead better lives than he himself does. He labours under the impression that he should not be different from the others, and cannot perceive that he is on the wrong path . . . This person is busy, even agitated just as life is. But apart from that: there is no room for the most worthwhile and greatest thing, namely for the awareness of God's presence. Because this awareness is missing and is driven out of the soul, he lacks that cheerful contentment that comes from God, and joy in the Lord departs from him.'[42]

c. *Practical atheism* shown itself quite specifically in that a person does not seek 'the one thing necessary', 'the kingdom and its righteousness',[43] but rather is driven in all directions. 'Intellect, will, tongue, hands, feet, instincts'[44] fall under an alien tyranny. Ideologies, the media, production, consumer attitudes, sex, become decisive.

A Christian can avoid these pressures, which pull in the most varied directions, if he enters into a bond with Christ and takes his Cross upon himself.[45] Cassian (d.430) quotes a 'profession homily' of Abbot Pinufius which almost shocks in its vivid statement: 'Our cross is the fear of the Lord. Whoever is crucified can no longer move his limbs at his own discretion and turn them in all directions. So we also ought to direct our will and our desires not towards fleeting pleasures, but towards the law of the Lord and its obligation.' Pinufius states that in fellowship with the Crucified One all superficial cares and passions and material bonds become irrelevant, while the 'eyes of the heart' are fixed on the future.[46] The eschatological outlook justifies the Cross. 'Whoever loses his life for my sake, will find it'.[47] It is in this perspective that we are to understand what the 'fear of God' means in our Rule, although the author points to the Lord and the Cross only with reserve. When it is said, not one's own will, but the will of God should 'be done', that calls to mind both the petition of the Lord's Prayer and Jesus' words on the Mount of Olives: 'Thy will be done!'[48] The whole physical person is brought into play. 'The flesh with its hankerings and desires'[49] must tremble before God.[50] In this kind of loving obedience to God, in poverty and renunciation, Pinufius and Cassian see the mystery of the Cross realized in the whole man.[51]

d. Many phrases of this 'first step' are reminiscent of the 'art of the Spirit',[52] and of the 'Visio Pauli'.[53] The advice to feel oneself continually under '*God's eye*'[54] was given to all Christians. But even the monks knew that the living, existential apprehension of God's presence is not something self-evident. 'Abbot Poimen related, how Abba Paizius was asked by someone: "I have become spiritually numb; my soul does not tremble before God. What should I do for it?" He answered: "Go, attach yourself to a God-fearing man! His company will teach you, how to become God-fearing yourself."'[55]

14–18 The fear of God leads to inner purity. Athanasius (d.373) speaks in the Life of Antony (d.356) of the wish, day after day, 'To appear worthy before God's eyes, to be pure of heart and ready to obey his will.'[56] This purity and candour enables our interior to become *an unclouded mirror for the image of God*, which should reflect itself in the depths of our being. Such purity is incompatible with 'dark thoughts'.[57] The question of 'sins of thought' is taken up once again in this paragraph.[58] All our desires and thinking should tremble and feel overcome by God's holiness as by the warm light which he radiates. Origen (d.253) refers to the saying of Jesus from the extra-biblical tradition: 'Whoever comes near me, come near fire.' Origen adds: 'Blessed are they therefore who are very near, and so near that the fire does not burn them, only enlightens them.'[59]

19–25 a. The statements on self-will want to strike at egoism and at an understanding of independence which allows only the ego as the valid norm. Whoever is entrapped in his own ego cannot be open to God or to his fellow men, indeed he becomes blind to God's instruction[60] and becomes indifferent or coarse.[61] Not seldom the 'self-will' of a *false asceticism* is pilloried, as for example in the Lives of the Jura Fathers (c.515). Lupicinus said to a monk who because of excessive asceticism had lost all his strength and could hardly move: 'Come, come, dear brother, give up your obstinacy. If you do not want to obey willingly, at least do not take scandal at my example. What you see me doing, you must imitate, surely in the name of obedience, which no discussion can annul. That is what the Rule demands.' Abbot Lupicinus (d.*c*.480) then began eating before the eyes of the almost starving monk, who had wanted to live on breadcrumbs alone, deflected him from his fatal self-will and put him back on his feet again.[62]

b. 'Self-will' is spoken of also in other passages of the Rule,[63] likewise the 'desires of the flesh',[64] among which aggressiveness, envy, sullenness, obsessions are to be understood.

26–30   a. At the end of the 'first step', immediately after words about the struggle with sexual desires,[65] an overall concluding view shows a serene picture of the fear of God: a life under God's eyes, joined to inner wisdom[66] and to the search for God.[67] The quest for the inner experience of God presupposes an ascetic striving for a '*pure heart*', so that God's image can be mirrored and seen in it.

b. Gregory the Great (d.604) will later present this basic conviction of the ancients in his biographical sketch of Benedict. Benedict flees from all *vain ambition*, the stir caused by his person. In Enfide his beloved nurse had borrowed a kitchen utensil from the women of the place. By mishap it broke to pieces. Benedict repaired it by the power of his prayer. Faced with the sensation attaching to himself and the beginnings of a personality cult Benedict takes flight to the rocky slopes above Subiaco. His turning away from all fuss about himself brings him near the people. They sense the saint in him. They seek him out and bring him food. He in return offers '*food for life*' which they 'take away in their hearts'.[68] In this way the monk and hermit becomes the apostle.

c. But people also become a temptation for him. A woman's 'beauty' and his own *sexual desires* threaten to take 'full possession of his heart'. Heavenly grace then helps him 'to come to his senses'. He 'throws himself naked into nettles and thorns, and rolls about in them there', until 'the burning outward pain quenches' the 'blaze of lust' within.[69] The renunciation of his own desire brings him to himself. He is now so settled and matured, that he can become a *teacher* for others.

d. The monks of Vicovaro summon him to be their abbot. He wants to teach them the 'monastic way of life', without tolerating 'deviations to right or left'. But the monks of Vicovaro feel themselves threatened and react *aggressively* and criminally with an attempted poisoning. The saint's blessing shatters the poisoned cup with a sign of the Cross. Benedict in this moment keeps 'a *tranquil mind* and a calm expression'. The self-control in face of aggressiveness leads to inner peace, which no emotions of fear or anger disturb.

e. 'Then he returns to his beloved solitude, in order to *dwell alone by himself under the searching eyes of God*.' Pope Gregory explains the meaning of his carefully chosen words: 'The venerable man "dwells by himself", because he is always circumspect in watching over himself, because he sees himself always under God's eyes, he examines himself and does not let his inner eyes rove about outside his own person.' After the tests and temptations arising from Benedict's own concupiscence, Gregory speaks of self-criticism under the searching eyes of God. Benedict really comes to himself, but under the eyes of God. He stands face to face with God, eye to eye. All this brings to mind our passage in the chapter on humility,[70] where the 'eyes of the Lord' are mentioned directly after words about wrestling with sensuality; immediately afterwards 'in-sight' and 'seeking-God' are spoken of. Subsequently there is talk of the ever-necessary examination of conscience.[71]

f. For Gregory the Great (d.604) the 'dwelling with oneself', the discovery of oneself follows on the toilsome struggle and examination of conscience, which Gregory calls 'to recollect oneself in one's heart'. These are the presuppositions for the hours of *contemplation*, which Gregory describes subsequently: 'We are taken out of ourselves in a twofold manner: either we sink to a subpersonal level by a lapse of our thought, or we are rapt above ourselves by the grace of contemplation . . . As often as the ardour of contemplation lifted (Benedict) above himself, without any doubt he left himself behind.'

g. Benedict then according to Pope Gregory (d.604) had to turn away from his own ego, from his desires and emotions, in order to come near to people and to reach the radiant 'heights' of the vision of God. Benedict's life, matured by renunciation, begins to bear '*fruit*'. Young people come to him. He founds 'twelve monasteries'.[72] The chapter on humility is to be understood in this way. Asceticism and candid examination of conscience are not an end in themselves.[73] They aim first of all at the 'composure' of the person and its powers, but then at a rising beyond oneself to God and to people.

31–33 a. On the basis of an ancient treatise on humility, which is found also in Cassian,[74] the 'Master' developed his 'twelve steps' of the ascent in humility. He makes a new 'first step' out of the fear of God and then begins, from the 'second step' onwards, the explanation of the 'ten signs' of humility, which are found in Cassian, and which for the 'Master' become 'steps'.

b. '*Self-will*'—as in other passages[75]—is seen in relation to the 'will of the flesh',[76] which is *the* obstacle to the reception of God's word and *the* opposite of the Son's readiness to obey for the sake of his mission.[77] Basil (d.379) stressed the incompatibility of 'self-will' and the putting oneself under the guidance of the Spirit of Jesus:[78] 'We all need the Holy Spirit as our leader on our way, who is to lead us on the way of truth, whether in thought, word or deed. Everyone is blind and lives in darkness, who lives without the Sun of Justice, i.e. without our Lord Jesus Christ, whose commands as it were shine into us and illumine us . . . Therefore we should in every way contribute to the edification of the others.'[79] To forsake self-will renders possible openness to God and his light, as also towards our fellow men and their salvation.

c. The renouncing of the '*will of the flesh*' and of 'self-will' is not to be equated with a lack of sexuality or a psychical weakness of will. An inner freedom in face of one's own wishful thinking, the pressures of the 'principle of enjoyment' or in face of addictions is indeed implied, but in the last resort the Pauline theology is here present: We may not hedge ourselves in with the 'sarx', i.e. the 'flesh' (understood as the natural drive of self-centredness) but ought to open ourselves to the 'Pneuma', i.e. the guidance and illumination of the Holy Spirit. This renders possible a positive social adjustment.

d. The sentence from a 'scripture', namely from the 'Passio Anastasiae' refers there to the martyr Irene (d.304), who declared that those who are forced to eat meat offered to idols or are compelled to prostitution without their consent, have a *crown* prepared for them (RB 1980).[80]

34   **a.** The quotation from St Paul on the *self-emptying* of the Word[81] shows *the* model of 'humility' in Christ's obedience to the Father. Origen (d.253) writes in admiration: 'We must dare to say this: A greater and more godlike bounty which really mirrors the Father's goodness became manifest in Jesus, when he "humbled himself and became obedient unto death, even death on a Cross".'[82] 'By his deeds he teaches forbearance and praiseworthy humility to those who are eager to learn.'[83] Basil (d.379) bases humility no differently: 'Have the same mind among yourselves, which was in Christ Jesus.'[84]

  b. This attitude of *humility* takes precedence over all asceticism: 'The holy Synkletika said: For our community, obedience is set high above all forms of asceticism. Asceticism can turn into arrogance. But obedience leads to genuine humility.'[85]

35–43   **a.** Obedience[86] to the superiors[87] and to all the brethren[88] is glorified here as a participation in *martyrdom*; therefore psalm verses are quoted which the martyrs are said to have recited. The 'Master' says expressly: 'In the monastery . . . they bear trials and judgement like martyrs.'[89] The Rule often alludes to a courage which was specifically that of the martyrs, and in so doing applies the corresponding biblical concepts: constant patience, fortitude, trust, endurance, steadfastness.[90] Such strength is a gift of grace from the Spirit for the ascetical 'combat' and 'struggle', which takes the place of the 'struggle' in martyrdom.[91] This surprisingly 'combative' ethos is rooted in the words of Jesus, the ultimate martyr, about the 'sword',[92] of the 'violence' which the kingdom of God 'suffers'.[93] As Jesus himself took the field against the power of the Evil One,[94] so the Christians have to fight out a 'spiritual combat' and wield spiritual 'weapons'.[95] In martyrdom they conquer 'in the Blood of the Lamb'[96] who triumphed in death and brings a peace which is not of this world. This peace consists of communion with God, of the light and of the contemplation of God, of the paradise of a life in God.[97] The stories of the martyrs' sufferings are therefore also quoted in our Rule,[98] because we believe we hear the Lord and his Spirit speaking through those who witnessed unto blood. Because the martyrs were venerated 'as disciples and imitators of the Lord on account of their unsurpassed love for their King and Lord',[99] the ascetics wished to imitate in their own way the 'combat' of Christ and the martyrs. Paul gave them the keyword for this, because he frequently draws a comparison between an athletic contest ('race')[100] and the Christian life,[101] especially in regard to frequent prayer[102] and apostolic service.[103]

  b. It cannot be denied that in primitive monasticism the will for 'combative' exertion sometimes shifted to questionable ascetical record-breaking achievements.[104] More in line with the future was the early appearance of the appreciation of work;[105] in Benedict's case one may speak of a shift of emphasis in the direction of an ethos of *work*, the ascetical character of which is stressed.[106]

  c. The strength characteristic of the martyrs to (endure) 'patience, fortitude, steadfastness, trust, forbearance'[107] should hold good not only in outward 'unjust treatment'[108] but also in *interior trials*: 'The fathers used to say: when a trial or temptation comes your way in the place where you dwell, do not abandon this place during the time of trial. If you run away, the difficulties you sought to flee from, will hasten ahead of you, wherever you go. Rather have courageous patience, until the trial has played itself out.'[109]

d. Patience in *times of illness* also ranks as a gift from God. 'A venerable father said: Do not be faint-hearted when an illness befalls your body. If God, the Lord, so wishes, that your bodily powers fail, who can take that amiss? Will not God think of all that is good for you? Can you live without him? Bear everything with patience, and beg him to give you what is for your salvation, that is to say, that you can do his will. Sit down in all patience, and in all love eat what is set before you!'[110] Patience and tolerance in bearing with others, their injustice and untrustworthiness, is the Sermon on the Mount lived consistently and without reservations.[111]

e. Notwithstanding all their zeal for asceticism, the ancients were not lacking in the gift of discerning what was genuine from what is false. 'Venerable father Mathois used to say: I prefer a mild but consistent effort to something spectacular achieved in a short time.'[112] With all esteem for an asceticism rightly understood, none of them wished to be a gloomy ascetic. Quite the contrary! Thus it is reported of Antony (d.356), the prototype of monks: His face was exceedingly *lovable*. This wonderful grace too he had received from the Redeemer. If a stranger, who wished to get to know him, came into the great assembly of the monks, no one needed to point out Antony to him; rather the stranger would immediately go up to Antony, without looking over the others. One could, that is to say, read from his face the purity of his soul; because he always had a cheerful countenance.'[113] Asceticism rightly understood does not trigger off psychical disturbances; rather it shapes a balanced personality, which radiates peace and joy.

44–48   **a.** *Unwholesome thoughts and feelings* have a negative and burdensome effect. The 'heart',[114] where the monk ought 'to be by himself',[115] becomes an alien's possession. It is confiscated property; no place remains for the yearning for God.[116] Basil (d.379) is of opinion that only by continual attachment to God is 'his image able to be engraved in the soul'.[117] It is general teaching that genuine experience of God and above all a prayer that is contemplative, is possible only for those who are 'pure of heart'.[118] 'One of the fathers said: Just as it is impossible to see one's reflection in troubled waters, so also the soul cannot pray to God in a contemplative way, if it is not purified from all thoughts which set it at variance with itself.'[119] The image of God ought to be able to imprint itself in the heart.

b. Frank confession of faults ranks as the best means of purification. Cassian (d.430) ascribes a liberating effect to a *discussion* of faults, above all of secret faults and of problems that weigh on the soul. The willingness to talk things out is a sign of the gift of discernment (discretio).[120] The ability to speak openly and trustingly is a gift of grace from the Spirit.[121] This holds good for the person who reveals himself as well as for the spiritual father who is to comfort him with a kind word.[122] The conversation carried out on either side openly and in the atmosphere of the Spirit relieves tensions and the shackles of fear. It develops a healing effect and establishes peace.

49–50   **a.** To this 'sixth degree' belong on the one hand a curbing of one's needs, and on the other a readiness to be of service. The *undemanding* person is quickly satisfied, even 'with the least'.[123] He is more likely to find his peace and to be accepted by others[124] than the demanding person, who 'infects others with his misery'.[125] There is an insatiability of desires, which cannot be appeased.

b. The monastic fathers cultivate *frugality*; with their eyes on Christ on the Cross they often extol absolute poverty: 'Abbot Evagrius told of a brother, who called nothing his own except a Gospel book. Even this he sold in order to feed the poor. He then spoke only one sentence, which it is worth keeping in mind: "I have sold even the Word itself", said he,' which commands: "Sell all and give to the poor!"'[126] Benedict, who is founding a coenobium, nowhere requires total destitution for the monastery; the want and misery of the poor are of no positive value, rather they are to be removed.[127] The individual member of the monastic community however renounces every right to raise a claim to private property.[128] In return Benedict will have it that individual needs be taken into consideration.[129]

c. *Readiness to serve* (the German word for humility—*Demut*—means a willingness to serve—*Dienmut*) must be a characteristic of those who are 'first'.[130] Even good servants ought to feel themselves as 'useless slaves' before God.[131]

51–54 **a.** The 'seventh degree' is a high point to which the foregoing degrees lead. One does not merely accept a humiliation with patience. The attitude of humility must be rooted 'in the *very depths of the heart*'[132] and become second nature. Only a strong personality is capable, of his own free will and without being plagued by feelings of an inferiority complex, to be content with a modest place,[133] without reacting with fear or resentment. It is the attitude of the person who is 'poor in spirit'.[134] Such a need for help is the preferred place for God's grace.[135]

b. Basil (d.379) adduces the Apostle as witness, that from humility one can esteem oneself less than others.[136] He cites too the saying of Jesus: 'Learn from me, for I am gentle and lowly in heart.'[137] For Basil therefore, the strenuous Apostle of the Gentiles and Jesus himself, who was free from all fear of men, are models of humility.[138] Christian humility is not *lack of self-confidence*, nor merely the unassuming reserve of the well-bred. It is magnanimous selflessness, generosity towards the other, 'greater love'.[139] The awareness of being on the same path with Jesus includes an 'uplifting' and confident hope.[140]

c. This attitude of humility must stand the test of practice. Humility cannot strike *roots*, if a person still wants to take the first place. The psalm quotations which are adduced by way of illustration point to Jesus as model; taken in themselves they sound drastic. A word handed down from Amma Synkletika speaks of the necessity of being firmly rooted in humility. Only the grain of seed, which surrenders itself, yields good fruit: 'The holy Synkletika said: Just as the seed cannot at the same time be a plant, is it equally impossible to enjoy worldly honours and at the same time yield heavenly fruit.'[141]

55 **a.** In the eighth to the eleventh 'degree' the inner attitude of humility reveals itself in practical rules of behaviour for life in the monastery, for human and monastic good manners.[142] With Cassian (d.430) it is a question of '*signs*' of humility, which he adduces in his list. Since these 'signs' are now built in as 'steps' into the model of ascent, this 'workaday holiness' (Heufelder) stands on the highest steps, immediately before the summit.

b. Cassian (d.430) in his 'sixth sign' spoke simply of the 'common Rule and the example of the elders'.[143] By that Cassian understood the monastic observance[144] which had become usual in Egypt, and the example of monastic Fathers like Antony (d.356), Pachomius (d.346), Basil (d.379). The 'Master' and

Benedict now speak of the common Rule '*of the monastery*'. This addition betrays a process of institutionalization. There is now in force the specific 'Rule' of a monastery, with the authority of its abbot, with the local traditions and usages, which are set as a model above all by the good example of the 'seniors' and 'superiors'. Humility makes possible a form of life of the monastery agreed to in common by many individual persons. In the strength of the good 'spirit' of a community, the individual is able to live the 'institutionalized' Rule freely and with joy, and not feel it as a law alien to himself.

c. Integration into the community and its activities protects one from an individual compulsion towards achievement and success and from the temptation to be *a star with a following of devotees*. 'A brother asked Abbot Mathois and said: "If I go somewhere and remain in a certain place: how should I conduct myself there?" The elder replied: "Wherever you will live, do not seek to attract attention in any way and to make a name for yourself, by declaring for instance: I'm not coming to this gathering of the brethren! Or: I don't eat this or that! In this way you can only make a pseudo-name for yourself. Afterwards you will suffer for it. When people hear of something so unusual, they will run there, you know".[145] The renunciation of almost compulsive seeking for recognition makes one free. It does not mean, that personal talents should not be developed. A monastery should rather be understood as a 'community of charisms', in which each person by his gifts contributes to the common upbuilding.[146]

56–58 Humility must be recognizable in the manner of speaking and in keeping silence.[147] The 'Master' and Benedict heighten Cassian's formulation, which ran: 'to control the tongue'. *The ability to be silent* is taken seriously. 'A brother asked a venerable father and said: "Father, how long must silence be kept?" The elder answered: "Until you are questioned! Wherever you are: if you safeguard the habit of silence, you will find rest."'[148]

59–61 Benedict has somewhat softened his source, because the 'Master' wanted to allow only 'short and holy words', while he opts for 'well-considered' words.[149] Neither is all laughing forbidden, only that which is unseemly. The frequently strict rejection of laughter[150] in the older monastic writings is to be explained partly from the will for a lasting sense of penance,[151] partly from an exaggerated interpretation of the Gospel, as is shown by the following passage from a monastic Rule of South Gaul (roughly contemporary with Benedict), which likewise is milder in tone than older Rules: 'I think it is fitting that monks should refrain from laughing, if not at all times, nevertheless frequently (!). If one of the brethren is seeking an example for this which he can read, let it suffice him what we learn through the witness of the Gospel: Our Lord Jesus Christ wept,[152] while we do not know whether he laughed.'[153] Jesus' 'Woe to you that laugh',[154] which was interpreted literally, also explains our text. More taboo than laughter however were 'sadness', a sad depressive mood[155] and unfriendliness. The exemplary monk is obliging, amiable and cheerful.[156]

62–66 a. The *fear of God* appears, as in the first,[157] so likewise in this 'twelfth degree of humility'. Cassian's 'ten signs of humility' are set within the framework of this basic conviction of the presence of the God who is holy. This consciousness must take possession of the whole person, 'heart' and 'outward appearance', and make itself known even in one's 'bodily bearing'.[158] There is an interaction between bodily and spiritual life. 'A venerable father said: If our outward person does not live in sobriety and watchfulness, it is impossible to preserve the inner man.'[159]

b. The concrete interpretation appears very literal. The monk must continually *bow* his *head*.[160] Perhaps we must reach back to a text of Basil's, to realize what is meant. To the question, in what way old and proven members of the monastery could help the newly entered, Basil answered by making a distinction: 'Those who are healthy and strong, can give a vivid example for a positive development (of the newcomers) by their commitment and the readiness for every service of which they are capable. Those however who are weak or sickly, can show in all their activity and behaviour and even by their appearance, that they are always consciously living in the presence of God, and in that love, which the Apostle describes: "Love is patient and kind . . . "'[161,162] The healthy vigour of a young man and the gentle goodness of an old monk, bowed with age, are here placed side by side, nor should one be played off against the other. Perhaps the almost pedantic stipulation of 'bowing the head' 'in all places' was meant originally to recall the manner of Jesus' death.[163] The disciples want to become like their Lord in his self-emptying and in his obedience to the Father. In their zeal many may have tried to practise that absolutely to the letter.

c. The existential perception of God's holiness leads to a reverential awe before him.[164] The consciousness of one's own sinfulness and of the thoughts of *judgement* are awakened.[165] The disciple is gripped by the awe-inspiring mystery of God, and scarcely has eyes for anything else. He has arrived at the 'highest degree of humility'.[166] He has a 'pure heart'.[167] In this disposition he directs fervent words of prayer to God, out of the consciousness of being 'poor' before him.[168]

67–70 a. The 'pure heart' is 'free from sins and failings'.[169] This is the Christian concept for the Greek '*Apatheia*' (peace of soul), which is not a kind of stoical quiet and imperturbability, but the aim of asceticism brought about by the Spirit: the 'pure heart'. It is that 'rest', which Jesus promises to those who have burdens to carry.[170] He proclaimed a 'Sabbath year' with the correponding liberation from ancient oppression.[171]

b. Now at the end of the ascent, there is heard at last, as if a mystical secret were being unveiled, the expression 'love' (caritas). The 'Master' and Benedict describe in almost the same words as Cassian (d.430),[172] how this '*perfect love* casts out fear',[173] how it becomes second nature, how without any constraint it does what is good, in love[174] and joy. Whoever has gone this way, has become a free man. God, the awe-inspiring mystery, is for this man the fascinating mystery as well.

c. 'One of the venerable fathers said: . . . humility is the forerunner of love . . . humility entices us to love, that is to God himself, for "God is love."'[175,176] Whoever is 'pure of heart', will 'see God'. According to Irenaeus (d.*c.*202) a 'human life' formed by God's word ' . . . is the *contemplation of God*'.[177] This contemplation is not reserved to 'visionaries'. Every committed Christian life should lead to a state of perfection, in which the fear of punishment and even the thought of reward fade from view, and man stands eye to eye before God.[178] There remains 'the grace of mutual ardent love'.[179] For Irenaeus also writes: 'The knowledge of God renews man.'[180]

d. As long as we tarry in this life, we cannot of course reach the goal that lies beyond, but we can reach the home straight. This presupposes that the Holy Spirit[182] is 'poured into our hearts',[183] so that they are 'free from sins and failings'.[184] Where the Spirit is, there indeed is 'freedom'.[185] This insight recorded in the last verse of the chapter on humility may have been influenced by Cassian: 'Love (caritas) inflames in us a holy ardour of love (amor) for Christ, and for the fruits which stem from the powers of the Spirit.'[186] Basil writes in a similar vein: 'We need the Holy Spirit as guide on our journey, so that he may lead us on the way of truth.'[187]

NOTES TO CHAPTER 7

1 RB 7 = RM 10. Benedict omits RM 10,20–29.91–122. 2 → Prol.28(in Note 91). 3 Verse 1: Lk 14:11. 4 → Prol.5–7. 5 → 4,34–40. 6 The comparison with the frightening treatment of a weaned child seeking again the maternal breast (VPatr 5,5,30) alters the original meaning of the psalm. 7 Stromata 2,134,2–4; cf. Irenaeus → 5,1–9(Note 17). 8 Cf. Phil 2:5–11. 9 Cf. 2 Pet 2:2. 10 Cf. Eph 2:20. 11 Cf. Gen 28:12. 12 Lib 21–22. 13 Cf. Lk 14:11. 14 Cf. Mt 23:11–12. 15 Cf Lk 18:14. 16 Inst 4,38; cf.4,23.39. 17 Gen 18:12. The image is also found in VPJur 123. 18 Lk 14:11(Verse 1). 19 Cf. RB 19,5–6. 20 Cf. Prol. 13. 21 VAnt 15. 22 Verse 8. 23 → 7,67–70. Benedict, unintentionally or intentionally, has already introduced the saying in RB 7,34. 24 Prol. 47.48–49. 25 → 72,8.9–10. 26 → 6,6–7(in Note 56). 27 VHonor 1. 28 Dial 2, Introduction. 29 Verse 8. 30 VPatr 5,15,49. 31 Verse 8. 32 Mt 5:3. 33 VPatr 5,15,23. 34 Cf. Phil 2:5. 35 VPatr 5,12,73. 36 Verse 9. One is reminded here of the Acts of the Apostles(2:36–37): The word about Jesus as the crucified Lord 'cut (them) to the heart'. 37 Inst 4,39,1. 38 RBasRuf 2 (with reference to Prov 1:7). 39 Ps 112:1. 40 Ps Comm 118, 128. 41 Verse 10. 42 RBasRuf 2. 43 Cf Mt 6:33; Lk 10:42. 44 Verse 12. 45 Cf. Mt 16:24. This passage is quoted by Basil (RBasRuf 2), as also by Pinufius in the following text. 46 Inst 4,34–35; → 5,1–9 (in Note 2). 47 Mt 16:25. 48 Verse 20:Lk 2:44. 49 Verse 23. 50 Cf. Ps 119:120. 51 Inst 4,34–35; → 5,1–9. 52 With verse 11 cf. RB 4,45; with verse 12 cf.RB 4,48; with verse 13 (God's eye) cf.RB 4,49; → 4,75; 4,41–50; 7,62–68; 19,1–2. 53 With verse 13 (report by the angels): cf. Visio Pauli 7; 10; cf. also: VAnt 37. 54 Verse 13. 55 VPatr 5,11,23. 56 VAnt 6. 57 VAnt 6. 58 Here RB 7,12 is explained in detail; still, Benedict omits the 'Master's' remarks about the sins of the 'tongue', the 'hands' and the 'feet' (RM 10,10–29). 59 Jes Nav Hom 4,3. 60 Verse 21. 61 Verse 22; on the concept of 'self-will': → 5,1–9. 62 VPJur 75. 63 Cf.RB 4,60 and RB 7,31–33 (second rung). 64 Cf.RB 4,59 and RB 7,31–33(second rung). 65 Verses 23–25. 66 Verse 27: 'intellegens'. 67 ib.: 'requirens Deum', cf. RB 58,7. 68 Dial 2,1. 69 Dial 2,2. 70 Cf. verses 25–26. 71 Verses 28–30. 72 Dial 2,3; → Introduction 7. 73 → 4,76–77. 74 → 5,1–9(Note 2). Cassian speaks of 'steps' to perfection; he calls the 'fear of the Lord' the 'beginning' (see Note 16 above) and speaks immediately afterwards of ten 'signs' of humility (Inst 4,38–39). 75 → 4,59–61; 7,19–25. 76 Cf. Jn 1:13. 77 Jn 6:38 is quoted in this connection. 78 RBasRuf 12. 79 RBasRuf 12; 15. 80 RM 10,44 and here RB 7,33 understand 'consent' as 'self-will' and compulsion as 'obligation' or 'bond'. 81 Phil 2:8. 82 Jn Comm 1,37. 83 Origen, Comment Series 113. 84 Phil 2:5; cf.RBasRuf 65. 85 VPatr 5,14,9. 86 The fourth and fifth 'signs' of humility according to Cassian, constitute here the 'fourth step' (Inst 4,39). 87 Verses 35–41. 88 Verses 42–43. 89 RM 7,59. 90 → Prol. 28,47; 4,20–33.62–73; 5,10–13; 72,11. 91 → Prol. 2.3.28.29–32.40.45; 1,3–5; 4,55–58; 5,10–13 (struggle); 7,26–30(wrestling); 58,1–4; 72,4–12(Note 14). 11(Note 53). 92 Cf. Mt 10:34. 93 Cf. Mt 11:12. 94 Cf. Mt 4:1–11; 12,27; Lk 11:18. Jesus triumphs in death over the power of the Evil One: Jn 12:31; 16:33. 95 1 Thess 5:8; Eph 6:11.13–17; → Prol.2.3.28.29–32.40.45; 1,3–5; 4,55–58; 5,10–13; 7,35–43; 24,3; 48,17–18; 49,6–7; 73,4–7. 96 Rev 12:11; 14:1–5. 97 Rev 21–22. 98 RB 7,24.33, perhaps in other passages also. 99 Martyrium Polycarpi 18. 100 For that reason, the ascetic is often called 'Athleta Christi' in the Lives. 101 Cf. 1 Cor 9:25; 2 Tim 2:5; Heb 12:1. 102 Cf. Rom 15:30; Col 4:12. 103 Col 2:1. 104 → 7,19–25.31–32. 105 → 4,55–58; 48,1–2,17–18. 106 → 4,55–58; 6,2–5; 16,1–3; 18,22–25; 31,3–7.10–12; 32,1–4; 33,6; 35,10–12.15–18; 39,6–9; 40,5–7; 41,2–4.5; 43,13–17; 48; 64,17–19. 107 Verses 35.36.37.38.39.42.43.50; see above, Note 91. 108 Verse 42. 109 VPatr 5,7,32. 110 VPatr 5,7,45. 111 Verse 42: Mt 5:39–41; → 25,1–2; 26,1–2 112 VPatr 5,7,11. 113 VAnt 40; → 2,31–32 (in Notes 48–49). 114 Verse 44. → 1.3–5; 4,41–50; 7,14–18. 115 → 7,26–30. 116 Cf. RB 58,7. 117 RBasRuf 2. 118 Cf. Mt 5:8. 119 VPatr 5,12,13. 120 Cf. Inst 4,9; Conl 2,11–13; → 46,5–6. 121 Cf. Verse 45: 'hope in him!' 122 → 4,10–19,20–23. 123 The writer is probably also thinking here of simplicity in dress; cf. VPJur 62: 'in vestitu vilitas; → 55,7–8. 124 → 61,1–4. 125 → 61,5–12(Verses 6–7). 126 Mt 19:21; VPatr 5,6,5. 127 → 5,10–19; 31,8–9. 128 → 33 129 → 31,3–7; 33,5; 34,1–2. 130 → Mt 23:11–12. 131 Cf:Lk 17:10; cf. RB Prol. 14; 7,70. 132 Verse 51. 133 ib. 134 Mt

5:3. **135** Cf. 1 Cor 15:9–10. **136** Cf. 1 Cor 15:9. **137** Mt 11:29. **138** RBasRuf 62. **139** Cf Jn 15:13. **140** Cf.RB 7,39. **141** VPatr 5,8,20. **142** → 4,51–54. **143** Inst 4,39,2. **144** → Prol. 29–32. **145** VPatr 5,8,11. **146** → 1,3–5. **147** Maxims in RB 4,51–54 and the whole of chapter 6 are devoted to these themes. **148** VPatr 7,32,3. **149** RM 10,80; → 6,2–5; 4,51–54. **150** e.g. RBasRuf 53. **151** → 49,1–3;6,8. **152** Cf. Lk 19:41; Jn 11:33.35. **153** RF 14. **154** Cf. Lk 6:25. **155** → 31,6–7. **156** → 53,3–5; 6,2–5; 7,35–43. **157** → 7,10–30. **158** Verses 62–63. **159** VPatr 5,11,45. **160** Verse 63; → Prol. 1 (especially in Note 6). **161** 1 Cor 13:4. **162** RBasRuf 86. **163** Cf. Jn 19:30. **164** → 7,14–18. **165** Verse 164. **166** Verses 5.66–67. **167** Cf. Mt 5:8. **168** Cf. Mt 5:3 → 49,4–5(Note 20). **169** Verse 70. **170** Prol.45–50 (in Note 130). **171** Lk 4: 19; cf. Isa 61:2. **172** Inst 4,39,3. **173** Cf. 1 Jn 4:18. **174** Verse 69: 'amor'. Benedict adds: 'for Christ'. **175** 1 Jn 4:8; → 51,3. **176** VPatr 7,13,7. **177** Cf. Irenaeus, Adv haer 4,20,7. **178** → 7,26–30. **179** Cassian, Conl 11,7. **180** Adv haer 5,12,4 (cf. Col 3:10). **181** → 7,5–9; 72,12 (in Note 57). Benedict refrains from the colourful description of the next world that the 'Master' adds here (RM 10,92–122). **182** Verse 70. **183** Cf Rom 5:5. **184** Verse 70. **185** Cf. 2 Cor 3:17; → 73,8–9. **186** Conl 11,6. **187** RBasRuf 12; cf. Jn 14:7.

CHAPTER 8

OF THE DIVINE OFFICES IN THE NIGHTS

10 Feb
11 June
11 Oct

1 In winter time,
that is from the first of November until Easter,
taking everything into due consideration,
they shall get up at the eighth hour of the night,

2 so as to sleep for a little more than half the night,
and rise
when digestion is completed.

3 The brethren who need to do so
shall employ the time over after Vigils
in going over the psalter or the readings.

4 From Easter however until November as mentioned
let the timing be such
that the brethren may go out for the necessities of nature
during a very brief interval after Vigils.
Lauds, which are to be celebrated at first light,
shall follow immediately.

CAPUT VIII: DE OFFICIIS DIVINIS IN NOCTIBUS

¹HIEMIS TEMPORE, ID EST A KALENDAS NOVEMBRES USQUE IN PASCHA, IUXTA
CONSIDERATIONEM RATIONIS, OCTAVA HORA NOCTIS SURGENDUM EST, ²UT MODICE
AMPLIUS DE MEDIA NOCTE PAUSETUR ET IAM DIGESTI SURGANT. ³QUOD VERO
RESTAT POST VIGILIAS A FRATRIBUS QUI PSALTERII VEL LECTIONUM ALIQUID
INDIGENT, MEDITATIONI INSERVIATUR. ⁴A PASCHA AUTEM USQUE AD SUPRADICTAS
NOVEMBRES SIC TEMPERETUR HORA, UT VIGILIARUM AGENDA PARVISSIMO INTER-
VALLO, QUO FRATRES AD NECESSARIA NATURAE EXEANT, MOX MATUTINI QUI
INCIPIENTE LUCE AGENDI SUNT, SUBSEQUANTUR.

o The spiritual part of the Rule, mostly borrowed literally from the 'Master', is
now at an end. There begins an *Order of the Divine Office*, which is in a completely different style. The liturgical vocabulary does not correspond to that of
the 'Master', even when there are certain points of contact. We can also identify
reminiscences of Cassian (d.430).¹ Within the liturgical Order of chapter 8–18
one comes upon a curiously imprecise and fluctuating terminology.²
  The 'Master' treats of the Divine Office within the framework of the *order
of the day*. With Benedict some fragmentary liturgical directions are found in

the chapters which deal with the order of the day.[3] The directions for the Divine Office which occur in those later parts of the Rule, suggest not a 'basilical' liturgy, but rather the situation of a poor, rural monastery. The monks are often compelled to work in the fields, with the result that certain Hours are not held in the oratory.[4] In chapters 8–18, on the other hand, a detailed model of an order for the Divine Office is presented, which leads one to think of the order in the *basilicas* of Rome or Arles. Comparison shows, however, that it was only in the first half of the seventh century that such a perfectly ordered Divine Office as the one presented here was developed in the Roman basilicas (C. Gindele). The author explains his order in every detail, no doubt because it is new to the addressees, and he justifies his position.[5]

All these observations have led to the conjecture that in chapters 8–18 *another hand* was at work after Benedict or was involved in the original composition, except perhaps in those sections with spiritual statements (E. Manning).[6]

The placing of this order of the Divine Office after the chapter on humility and before the order of the monastery, seems to indicate that the Divine Office presupposes a spiritual formation, above all the attitude of obedience, humility and reverence, and takes precedence of disciplinary questions. Whoever wishes to enter God's presence must be able to forget himself. The model is Jesus, who, praying 'with tears', 'learned obedience', and so was 'heard.'[7] The Rule of Benedict stresses the deference with which to encounter men[8] and God.[9] Before[10] and after[11] the order of the Divine Office, a *reverential awe* is spoken of. Prayer presupposes this atmosphere.

1–2 a. Compared with the 'Master',[12] who had the monks rise shortly before midnight, Benedict's Rule allows them to sleep until two hours after midnight. This is a carefully weighed innovation and *mitigation*. However the monks do not return to bed after the Night Office. That too is an alteration of the customs.[13]

b. The nightly rest varied in length according to *the season*. Around Christmas one of the twelve hours of the natural night lasted about seventy five minutes; if the monks slept from the first hour of the night[14] to the eighth hour, they could rest nearly nine hours by today's reckoning. In summer, a natural night hour lasted only about forty five minutes; the monks rested at night for only about five of today's hours.[15] Around the equinox they slept for about seven of today's hours (Lentini, RB 1980).

c. Already in the Qumrân community the night suggested itself for reading and prayer: 'The Rabiim keep common vigil during a third of the nights of the year, to read the "Book" and seek righteousness—and to render praise together.'[16] Good Christians and ascetics also cultivate prayer spontaneously at night-time,[17] while nocturnal liturgical celebrations of the whole Church were usual initially only in the Easter Vigil and before the feasts of martyrs. There is no lack of evidence of a heroic zeal for prayer on the part of individuals: 'They related of Abbot Arsenios that on Saturday evening, in the twilight before the Lord's Day, he let the sun go down behind him, then raised his hands in prayer to heaven, and continued until on the Lord's Day early in the morning the rising sun shone in his face.'[18]

3 a. The Night Offices or their parts are called '*Vigils*' (night watches) or 'Nocturns'. The two or three parts consist each of psalms (or songs of praise), of readings and responsories (antiphonal chants).

b. The 'rehearsing' (meditatio) of the psalter ought to make it possible for all to pray the psalms by heart at all times. Pachomius (d.346) requires that a passage of Scripture be '*meditated*' on when a person is not otherwise engaged,[19] or when he is at manual work.[20] In this connection, Pachomius—like many after him—refers to 'chewing the cud' (ruminare) of the word of Scripture:[21] one speaks it quietly in an undertone to oneself, repeats it, murmurs it to oneself. The Jewish tradition too is familiar with the 'sayer of psalms', who recites the whole psalter in sequence to himself, for example, while he is at work. Through constant repetition, the word becomes not only fixed in the memory, but also grows into second nature. Under Pachomius everyone had to read and learn 'by heart' at least the New Testament and the psalms.[22] Basil (d.379) recommends that the rest of the night should be devoted to meditation on the Scriptures.[23]

4 Benedict calls *Lauds* the 'morning praise'[24] or the 'morning celebration'.[25] The time of Prayer at the first light of day recalls the Resurrection of Christ.[26]

NOTES TO CHAPTER 8

1 Inst 2–3. 2 Even though the same rendering is meant, the expressions 'speak', 'sing' etc., alternate without apparent reason: dicere, cantare, legere, recitare, imponere, modulatis . . . 3 Cf. RB 42–47 and RB 50–52. 4 → 48,6.10–12.14. 5 RB 18, 22; cf. RB 13,10. 6 Cf. Introduction 3 (note 24); 9 (notes 107–108). 7 Cf. Heb. 5:7–8. 8 Cf. RB 4,8; 53,2; 63,10.17;72,4. 9 Cf. RB 11,9; 19–20; 63,13. 10 → 7,5–9.10–13.62–66. 11 → 19–20. 12 RB 8,1–2: RM 33,3–9; RB 8,3: RM 44,12–19; RB 8,4: RM 33,10–26 13 Cf. Cassian, Inst 3,4; RB 8,3. 14 Cf. RB 41,9. 15 The necessary counterbalance was provided by the 'siesta' (RB 48,5). 16 1 QS 6,7–8 ('glorify' = to sing psalms). 17 In the interminable winter nights an interruption of sleep must have been for good Christians an almost instinctive call to prayer. → 16,1–3 (in note 9). 18 VPatr 5,12,1. 19 On the way to the refectory; at the distribution of bread (Praec 28; 37). 20 Praec 116. 21 Praec 122. 22 Praec 139–140. 23 RBasRuf prooem. 24 Matutinae (i.e. laudes). 25 RB 12 T: 'matutinorum solemnitas'. 26 → 12,1–4.

re P116   cf Schillebeeckx *Christ*

P434 "They (the Apocalyp-
tists) do not really _quote_, but
actually _think_ in OT texts.

greater glory through the service of others. She made Freedom *(the right and the ability to choose what is judged the best in the sight of God)*; Justice *(seeing and acknowledging the image of God in every human being)*; Sincerity *(that which is genuine and true (sine cera))*, as the distinguishing marks of her followers. She predicted that "women in time to come" would do great things for God.

Her life was challenging and prophetic; her ideals were novel at that time and so were suspect. She suffered much in her lifetime, and was greatly maligned. She was accused of being a heretic, and was imprisoned in 1631. The Institute of the Blessed Virgin Mary was suppressed, and was not fully approved by the Church until 1877. In 1909 she was officially acknowledged as its Foundress. In this century Pope Pius X11 named her "that incomparable woman", and Pope John Paul 11 described her as a "prophet of hope".

CHAPTER 9

HOW MANY PSALMS ARE TO BE SUNG
AT THE NIGHT HOURS

11 Feb
12 June
12 Oct

1 In winter time, as defined above,
begin with the versicle,
to be said three times:
LORD, YOU WILL OPEN MY LIPS,
AND MY MOUTH SHALL DECLARE YOUR PRAISE.

Ps 51:17

2 To this shall be added Psalm 3, and *Glory be*.

3 After this, Psalm 94,
with antiphon,
or at least chanted.

4 Then shall follow an Ambrosian hymn,
then six psalms with antiphons.

5 When these have been said,
after the versicle,
the abbot shall give a blessing.
And all being seated on the stools
three lessons shall be read by the brothers in turn
from the book on the lectern;
three responsories to be sung between these readings.

6 Two responsories are to be said without *Glory be*,
after the third reading however
the chanter says the *Glory be*.

7 When the chanter intones this,
let all immediately rise from their seats
for the honour and reverence due to the Holy Trinity.

8 The books of divine authority,
as well of the Old as of the New Testaments
shall be read at Vigils,
as also the commentaries on them
which have been made
by renowned and orthodox Catholic Fathers.

9 After these three readings then,
the remaining six psalms are to follow,
to be sung with Alleluia.

10 After these,
   there shall follow
   a reading from the Apostle,
   to be said by heart,
   and a versicle,
   and the supplication of the litany, that is Kyrie eleison.
11 That is how Vigils end.

CAPUT IX: QUANTI PSALMI DICENDI SUNT NOCTURNIS HORIS

¹HIEMIS TEMPORE SUPRASCRIPTO, IN PRIMIS VERSU TERTIO DICENDUM: DOMINE, LABIA MEA APERIES, ET OS MEUM ADNUNTIABIT LAUDEM TUAM. ²CUI SUBIUNGENDUS EST TERTIUS PSALMUS ET GLORIA. ³POST HUNC, PSALMUM NONAGESIMUM QUARTUM CUM ANTEFANA, AUT CERTE DECANTANDUM. ⁴INDE SEQUATUR AMBROSIANUM, DEINDE SEX PSALMI CUM ANTEFANAS. ⁵QUIBUS DICTIS, DICTO VERSU, BENEDICAT ABBAS ET, SEDENTIBUS OMNIBUS IN SCAMNIS, LEGANTUR VICISSIM A FRATRIBUS IN CODICE SUPER ANALOGIUM TRES LECTIONES, INTER QUAS ET TRIA REPONSORIA CANTENTUR. ⁶DUO RESPONSORIA SINE GLORIA DICANTUR; POST TERTIAM VERO LECTIONEM, QUI CANTAT DICAT GLORIAM. ⁷QUAM DUM INCIPIT CANTOR DICERE, MOX OMNES DE SEDILIA SUA SURGANT OB HONOREM ET REVERENTIAM SANCTAE TRINITATIS. ⁸CODICES AUTEM LEGANTUR IN VIGILIIS DIVINAE AUCTORITATIS TAM VETERIS TESTAMENTI QUAM NOVI, SED ET EXPOSITIONES EARUM, QUAE A NOMINATIS ET ORTHODOXIS CATHOLICIS PATRIBUS FACTAE SUNT. ⁹POST HAS VERO TRES LECTIONES CUM RESPONSORIA SUA, SEQUANTUR RELIQUI SEX PSALMI CUM ALLELUIA CANENDI. ¹⁰POST HOS, LECTIO APOSTOLI SEQUATUR EX CORDE RECITANDA, ET VERSUS, ET SUPPLICATIO LITANIAE, ID EST QUIRIE ELEISON. ¹¹ET SIC FINIANTUR VIGILIAE NOCTURNAE.

1–4 **a.** The author begins with the distribution of the psalms.[1] In the process, he makes remarks about the rendering of the psalms, but his terminology is often unclear for us.[2] The Rule is acquainted with the simple *chanting of the psalms*, which in that case were chanted without interruption, and chanting with 'Antiphons'. In this latter case indeed one or more cantors sang the psalm, while those present joined in with a 'refrain', e.g. an 'Amen' or an 'Alleluia'. However, in Benedict's time the rendering of a whole psalm by a soloist was also possible. As well, the chanting of psalms choir against choir was popular; finally, the singing of the whole psalm by all together was practised too.[3]
b. The *hymn* at Vigils,[4] Lauds[5] and Vespers[6] is called 'Ambrosianum', presumably because that series of hymns was attributed to Ambrose or originated in Milan. 'Hymns' were usual in Milan, Lérins and Arles; by contrast, they were taboo in Rome until within the twelfth century, because they were not taken from the Bible.
c. Benedict reduces the number of psalms to the point that for the whole Night Office only twelve psalms were sung. They are distributed between the two parts (nocturns) of the celebration. Such a mitigation was known in

Lérins and Arles, where a conscious attempt was made to create an *agreeable climate for prayer*.[7] With the number twelve Benedict adheres to a norm which was allegedly given by an angel in order to prevent an excess of psalmody.[8]

5–7 a. To sit for the readings and responsories, as is not done during the singing of the psalms, represents a pleasant change after the first and second block of psalms. Each '*reading*' contained according to Caesarius (d.542), 'two or at most three pages',[9] it lasted therefore a fairly long time and presupposed competence in the reader.[10] In the responsory, God's word is relished to the full and is answered with prayer.

b. Previously it was not customary to sing the 'Glory be' so frequently.[11] A markedly *trinitarian piety* is explained by the anti-Arian attitude of the author and the relevant theological controversies.[12]

c. For 'lectern' we read the *Greek* term 'analogium'. The frequency of Greek expressions in the Rule and in this chapter[13] is traceable to the cultural content and to contemporary circumstances.[14]

8 a. The *reading of Scripture and of the Fathers* is one of the most essential features of monastic life. The monk wants to be a 'hearer of the Word'.[15] The silence of night lends itself especially to making oneself familiar with the Word of God. Athanasius (d.373) wrote of Antony (d.356): 'He listened so attentively to the Scriptures that he could forget nothing. He treasured all the commandments of the Lord, and this in the memory instead of in books.'[16] Cassian (d.430) recommends an interiorisation of Scripture: 'Frequent reading and constant contemplation of Scripture ought to be the occasion for us to become attuned to spiritual values.'[17]

b. The writings of the 'recognized and orthodox *Catholic Fathers*'[18] form, to a certain extent, a commentary on Sacred Scripture. The Rule of Benedict is the first to attest the reading of the Fathers in the Night Office. In Southern Gaul the Acts of the Martyrs were read on their feasts,[19] whereas, according to Roman usage, non-biblical readings were to be excluded from the services.

c. It is not impossible that Gregory the Great (d.604) praises the Rule of Benedict for its 'discretion' for the very reason that it recommends only '*orthodox*' Fathers,[20] and because the Rule avoids non-biblical quotations (except for some 'overlooked' ones) as well as theological controversies.[21]

9–11 The *second part* of the Night Office repeats the pattern of the first, but only a short reading. A litany, reduced to Kyrie responses and containing no intercessions, was usual in Rome.

NOTES TO CHAPTER 9

1 Cf. RM 33,27–34; 34,1–4. The numbering according to the Latin psalter is retained in the translation of Benedict's text. Otherwise we follow the now usual Hebrew numbering of the psalms. 2 Cf. RB 47,2–3: 'imponere, legere, cantare'. Elsewhere we find simply 'dicere'; → 8,0 (note 2). 3 → 17,6. 4 Verse 4. 5 RB 12,4; 13,11. 6 RB 17,8. 7 Cf. RCaesVirg 69,23. 8 Cf. Cassian, Inst 2,4–6; VPach 22; cf. RB 10,3; 11,2.4.12; 18,21. According to present-day studies, the 'Angel's Rule' applied originally not to twelve psalms, but to praying twelve times both by day and by night, thus to 'unceasing' prayer at all times (RB 1980). 9 RCaesVirg 69, 24. 10 → 38,2–4. 11 Cassian, Inst 2,8. 12 Verse 7; Introd. 8 (especially notes 78.80). 13 Analogium, antiphona, litania, Kyrie eleison, orthodoxis; Senpectae → 27,1–4 (note 10); Eulogiae → 54,1–5 (note 10). 14 → Introd. 8. 15 → Prologue 1,1; 4,55–58; 6,2–5.6–7; 48,14. 16 VAnt 3. 17 Conl. 1,17. 18 → 73,4–7; 4,62–73; 7,55. 19 RCaesVirg 69,20; RF 18. The so-called *Decretum Gelasianum*, composed at the beginning of the sixth century in Southern Gaul, seeks to have

the Acts of the martyrs excluded from the service, although the author of the *Decretum* values them. →
Prologue 28; 7,35–43. **20** Dial 2,36. **21** This was not self-evident in the Church of the sixth century, and
especially not among monks; → Introd. 8 (especially notes 80.87); 58,1–4 (notes 12–17).

CHAPTER 10

HOW THE NIGHT PRAISE IS TO BE CELEBRATED IN SUMMER

12 Feb 1   From Easter however until the first of November,
13 June   let the full quantity of psalmody be maintained
13 Oct   as said above:

        2   with the proviso
            that on account of the short nights
            the readings from the book are never read.
            Instead of these three readings
            one shall be said by heart from the Old Testament,
            to be followed by a short responsory.

        3   And all the rest shall be fulfilled as stipulated,
            that is,
            that not counting the third and ninety fourth psalms,
            never less than a quantity of twelve psalms
            shall be said at the night Vigils.

CAPUT X: QUALITER AESTATIS TEMPORE AGATUR NOCTURNA LAUS

¹A PASCHA AUTEM USQUE AD KALENDAS NOVEMBRES, OMNIS UT SUPRA DICTUM EST PSALMODIAE QUANTITAS TENEATUR, ²EXCEPTO QUOD LECTIONES IN CODICE PROPTER BREVITATEM NOCTIUM MINIME LEGANTUR, SED PRO IPSIS TRIBUS LECTIONIBUS UNA DE VETERI TESTAMENTO MEMORITER DICATUR, QUAM BREVIS RESPONSORIUS SUBSEQUATUR. ³ET RELIQUA OMNIA, UT DICTUM EST, IMPLEANTUR, ID EST UT NUMQUAM MINUS A DUODECIM PSALMORUM QUANTITATE AD VIGILIAS NOCTURNAS DICANTUR, EXCEPTIS TERTIO ET NONAGESIMO QUARTO PSALMO.

1–3   In the short summer nights,¹ a fixed number of psalms is maintained, which was also the Roman usage, whereas the 'Master'² is aware of changes according to the seasons. *Reductions* in the readings are provided for by Caesarius (d.542).³

NOTES TO CHAPTER 10

1 → 8,1–2. 2 RB 10,1–33: RM 33,35–41; 44,5–8. 3 RCaesVirg 69,25 (e.g. in the case of a delayed start); → 11,11–13.

CHAPTER 11

HOW VIGILS ARE TO BE CELEBRATED ON SUNDAYS

13 Feb
14 June
14 Oct

1 For Vigils on Sundays they shall rise earlier.

2 In these Vigils the structure to be maintained is:
six psalms and the versicle having been sung,
as we have arranged above,
and all being seated on the benches
in an orderly way,
by rank,
four readings with their responsories
shall be read from a book,
as we said above.

3 In this regard
the *Glory be* is to be sung by the chanter
only in the fourth responsory.
When he intones it,
all shall at once stand up,
respectfully.

4 After these readings
there shall follow the other six psalms in numerical order,
with antiphons like the preceding ones,
and a versicle.

5 After this
four lessons shall again be read,
with their responsories,
as arranged above.

6 After these let there be said
three canticles from the Prophets,
as selected by the abbot;
these canticles are sung with Alleluia.

7 A versicle also shall be said,
and after the blessing given by the abbot,
four other readings are read from the New Testament,
as arranged above.

8 After the fourth responsory
the abbot shall intone the hymn *Te Deum laudamus*.

9 When this is said through,
the abbot shall read the lesson from the Gospels,
while all stand
with respect and fear.

10 When this has been read
let all answer: *Amen*;
and the abbot follows on immediately
with the hymn *Te decet laus*.
And after the blessing let them start Lauds.

11 This order of Vigils
is to be kept identical in all seasons,
both of summer and winter,

12 unless perhaps—which God forbid—
they are late in getting up,
and the readings or responsories have to be somewhat
shortened.

13 Every precaution however is to be taken
that this do not occur;
but if it should occur,
let him through whose neglect it came about,
do fitting satisfaction for it to God in the oratory.

CAPUT XI: QUALITER DIEBUS DOMINICIS VIGILIAE AGANTUR

¹DOMINICO DIE TEMPERIUS SURGATUR AD VIGILIAS. ²IN QUIBUS VIGILIIS TENEATUR MENSURA, ID EST, MODULATIS UT SUPRA DISPOSUIMUS SEX PSALMIS ET VERSU, RESIDENTIBUS CUNCTIS DISPOSITE ET PER ORDINEM IN SUBSELLIIS, LEGANTUR IN CODICE, UT SUPRA DIXIMUS, QUATTUOR LECTIONES CUM RESPONSORIIS SUIS. ³UBI TANTUM IN QUARTO RESPONSORIO DICATUR A CANTANTE GLORIA; QUAM DUM INCIPIT, MOX OMNES CUM REVERENTIA SURGANT. ⁴POST QUIBUS LECTIONIBUS SEQUENTUR EX ORDINE ALII SEX PSALMI CUM ANTEFANAS SICUT ANTERIORES, ET VERSU. ⁵POST QUIBUS ITERUM LEGANTUR ALIAE QUATTUOR LECTIONES CUM RESPONSORIIS SUIS, ORDINE QUO SUPRA. ⁶POST QUIBUS DICANTUR TRIA CANTICA DE PROPHETARUM, QUAS INSTITUERIT ABBAS; QUAE CANTICA CUM ALLELUIA PSALLANTUR. ⁷DICTO ETIAM VERSU ET BENEDICENTE ABBATE, LEGANTUR ALIAE QUATTUOR LECTIONES DE NOVO TESTAMENTO, ORDINE QUO SUPRA. ⁸POST QUARTUM AUTEM RESPONSORIUM INCIPIAT ABBAS HYMNUM TE DEUM LAUDAMUS. ⁹QUO PERDICTO, LEGAT ABBAS LECTIONEM DE EVANGELIA, CUM HONORE ET TIMORE STANTIBUS OMNIBUS. ¹⁰QUA PERLECTA, RESPONDEANT OMNES AMEN, ET SUBSEQUATUR MOX ABBAS HYMNUM TE DECET LAUS, ET DATA BENEDICTIONE INCIPIANT MATUTINOS. ¹¹QUI ORDO VIGILIARUM OMNI TEMPORE TAM AESTATIS QUAM HIEMIS AEQUALITER IN DIE DOMINICO TENEATUR, ¹²NISI FORTE—QUOD ABSIT—TARDIUS SURGANT, ALIQUID DE LECTIONIBUS BREVIANDUM EST AUT RESPONSORIIS. ¹³QUOD TAMEN OMNINO CAVEATUR NE PROVENIAT; QUOD SI

CONTIGERIT, DIGNE INDE SATISFACIAT DEO IN ORATORIO PER CUIUS EVENERIT NEGLECTUM.

1–3   a. Before Sunday, which is called 'the Lord's Day', the author no longer has a full Vigil lasting the whole night. The 'Master' still observes the usage of this service lasting until 'second cockcrow',[1] as does his contemporary Ferreolus (d.581)[2] in Southern Gaul; he, however, has problems with tardy participants. Thus the Rule of Benedict attests to a considerable innovation; for from Saturday to Sunday (and, with the exception of Rome, also from Friday to Saturday)[3] the monks used always celebrate the full Vigil.
   b. The Vigil on Sunday, however, is distinguished still further in Benedict's case by a special, precisely structured form. It begins at an earlier hour, because, with its *twelve readings*, it lasts considerably longer. Here, too, the number of twelve psalms applies, which falls well short of the Roman number of 19 (?) psalms.[4]

4–5   The *second part* of the celebration exhibits the same 'order' or 'sequence' as the first.

6–10   This '*third nocturn*' consisting of three songs of praise (canticles of the prophets), which are sung with an Alleluia-antiphon, of readings, of the Gospel of the Resurrection, and of hymns, was usual in the Churches of Jerusalem,[5] Byzantium, Milan and Arles. In the case of the 'Master', this joyful celebration of the Resurrection, so accessible to the people, is lacking. The Rule of Benedict describes in detail this congregational celebration, which is something new for a monastic office.—Caesarius of Arles, too, mentions the 'Te Deum' in connection with this celebration.[6] The abbot reads from the book of the Gospels, something which at this celebration was reserved to the bishop. The 'Amen' after the Gospel—especially significant in relation to the pericope of the Resurrection—was usual in the Visigothic area, to which Southern Gaul also belonged. The hymn of venerable antiquity 'To Thee our praise is due'[7] is taken from Byzantium, where it is still to be found at the end of the 'Orthros (morning praise). Even with all the reductions the Sunday Vigil remains a protracted and uplifting celebration.

11–13   The number of twelve psalms is regarded as inviolable. Reductions are possible elsewhere.[8]

NOTES TO CHAPTER 11

1 RM 49. 2 RF 13: 'As often as a night Vigil is desired by devotion or demanded by a feastday . . .' 3 Cassian, Inst 3,8–9. 4 → 9,1–4. 5 Cf. Egeria (c.381–4), peregr. 24,9–10. 6 RCaesVirg 69,11. 7 Cf. Constit. apost. 7,48. 8 → 8,1–4;10,1–3. The 'Master' permits a reduction if necessary, either by having a psalm collect only after each third psalm (→ 20,4–5) or by having only a short passage read of each of the psalms prescribed (RM 33, 42–54).

CHAPTER 12

HOW THE SOLEMN MORNING OFFICE IS TO BE CELEBRATED

14 Feb
15 June
15 Oct

1 On Sundays at Morning Office
  Psalm 66 is to be said first,
  without antiphon,
  straight on.

2 After this, say Psalm 50 with Alleluia.

3 Then say 117 and 62.

4 Then the *Benedicite* and the psalms of praise,
  a reading from the Apocalypse, by heart,
  Ambrosian hymn,
  versicle,
  canticle from the Gospel book,
  litany,
  and so end.

CAPUT XII: QUOMODO MATUTINORUM SOLLEMNITAS AGATUR

¹IN MATUTINIS DOMINICO DIE, IN PRIMIS DICATUR SEXAGESIMUS SEXTUS PSALMUS, SINE ANTEFANA, IN DIRECTUM. ²POST QUEM DICATUR QUINQUAGESIMUS CUM ALLELUIA. ³POST QUEM DICATUR CENTESIMUS SEPTIMUS DECIMUS ET SEXAGESIMUS SECUNDUS. ⁴INDE BENEDICTIONES ET LAUDES, LECTIONEM DE APOCALIPSIS UNA EX CORDE ET RESPONSORIUM, AMBROSIANUM, VERSU, CANTICUM DE EVANGELIA, LITANIA, ET CONPLETUM EST.

1–4 a. *Morning Prayer* or Lauds is formed according to the Roman model.[1] *Benedictiones* is the name for the 'Benedicite', the 'Hymn of the Three Young Men'.[2] 'Psalms of praise' (laudes) are here the psalms 148, 149 and 150. The canticle from the Gospel Book (Evangelia[3]) is the 'Benedictus'.[4] Here, to all appearances, the Litany exists not only in an abbreviated form.
b. Morning Prayer is characterized by the themes of *praise and glory* to God, who gives the gift of the new light of day, and makes heart and spirit rejoice. The Church has taken over this celebration from the Temple liturgy by way of the synagogue,[5] and always recommended morning prayer to the faithful: 'We will pray early in the morning, in order to celebrate the Resurrection of the Lord with a morning prayer.'[6]

NOTES TO CHAPTER 12

1 Not therefore as in the 'Master's' text (RM 35,1; 39,1–5; 45,12), with which however terminological agreements exist. 2 Dan 3: 57–88. 3 Book of the Gospels. 4 Lk 1: 68–80. 5 → 8,1–2.4. 6 Cyprian, De or. dom. 35.

CHAPTER 13

HOW THE MORNING OFFICE IS TO BE SAID
ON FERIAL DAYS

15 Feb
16 June
16 Oct

1 On ferial days however the solemn Morning Office shall be
celebrated as follows:
Psalm 66 said without antiphon as on Sunday,
at a slightly slower pace,
so that all may be in for Psalm 50,
which is to be said with antiphon.

3 After this, two other psalms are said, according to custom, i.e.

4 Monday, 5 and 35;

5 Tuesday, 42 and 56;

6 Wednesday, 63 and 64;

7 Thursday, 87 and 89;

8 Friday, 75 and 91;

9 on Saturday however 142 and the Deuteronomy canticle
divided in two by *Glory be* said twice.

10 On the other days however
a canticle is to be sung,
each one to its own day,
as the Roman Church sings them.

16 Feb
17 June
17 Oct

12 Besides,
the Morning and Evening Office
should never come to a close
without the Lord's Prayer
being said in full
at the end
by the superior
in the hearing of all,
on account of the thorny scandals
which have a habit of springing up,

13 so that challenged by the promise
of the very Prayer itself
in which they say:
FORGIVE US AS WE FORGIVE,
they may purge themselves
of this kind of vice.

14   At the other Offices,   Mt 6:12–13
      let the final part only of the prayer be said aloud,
      so that all may reply:
      BUT DELIVER US FROM EVIL.

CAPUT XIII: PRIVATIS DIEBUS QUALITER AGANTUR MATUTINI

¹DIEBUS AUTEM PRIVATIS MATUTINORUM SOLLEMNITAS ITA AGATUR, ²ID EST, UT SEXAGESIMUS SEXTUS PSALMUS DICATUR SINE ANTEFANA, SUBTRAHENDO MODICE, SICUT DOMINICA, UT OMNES OCCURRANT AD QUINQUAGESIMUM, QUI CUM ANTEFANA DICATUR. ³POST QUEM ALII DUO PSALMI DICANTUR SECUNDUM CONSUETUDINEM, ID EST: ⁴SECUNDA FERIA QUINTUS ET TRICESIMUS QUINTUS; ⁵TERTIA FERIA QUADRAGESIMUS SECUNDUS ET QUINQUAGESIMUS SEXTUS; ⁶QUARTA FERIA SEXAGESIMUM TERTIUM ET SEXAGESIMUM QUARTUM; ⁷QUINTA FERIA OCTOGESIMUM SEPTIMUM ET OCTOGESIMUM NONUM; ⁸SEXTA FERIA SEPTUAGESIMUM QUINTUM ET NONAGESIMUM PRIMUM; ⁹SABBATORUM AUTEM CENTESIMUM QUADRAGESIMUM SECUNDUM ET CANTICUM DEUTERONOMIUM, QUI DIVIDATUR IN DUAS GLORIAS. ¹⁰NAM CETERIS DIEBUS CANTICUM UNUMQUEMQUE DIE SUO EX PROPHETIS, SICUT PSALLIT ECCLESIA ROMANA, DICANTUR. ¹¹POST HAEC SEQUANTUR LAUDES; DEINDE LECTIO UNA APOSTOLI MEMORITER RECITANDA, RESPONSORIUM, AMBROSIANUM, VERSU, CANTICUM DE EVANGELIA, LETANIA ET CONPLETUM EST. ¹²PLANE AGENDA MATUTINA VEL VESPERTINA NON TRANSEAT ALIQUANDO, NISI IN ULTIMO PER ORDINEM ORATIO DOMINICA, OMNIBUS AUDIENTIBUS, DICATUR A PRIORE PROPTER SCANDALORUM SPINAS QUAE ORIRI SOLENT, ¹³UT CONVENTI PER IPSIUS ORATIONIS SPONSIONEM QUA DICUNT: DIMITTE NOBIS SICUT ET NOS DIMITTIMUS, PURGENT SE AB HUIUSMODI VITIO. ¹⁴CETERIS VERO AGENDIS ULTIMA PARS EIUS ORATIONIS DICATUR, UT AB OMNIBUS RESPONDEATUR: SED LIBERA NOS A MALO.

1–11   a. In Rome it was the custom to have two psalms¹ after psalm 51(50), and then the canticle. The series of two psalms each time, which our Rule also provides for in the same place, corresponds to a large degree with the two psalms which were used in Morning Prayer on the Roman model. They are *morning psalms*, which are understood as referring to the light of the new day and to the Resurrection.
      b. The reference to the custom of the *Roman Church*,² which is given for the canticles from the Prophets, is all the more remarkable because Benedict does not name his sources elsewhere.³ Caesarius of Arles (d.542) also referred to Rome when he recommended that, in the case of attempts to interfere with the internal order of the monastery, 'the hallowed ordinances of his Holiness the Pope of the city of Rome' were to be adhered to.⁴

12–14   The recitation of the *Lord's Prayer* aloud at the end of Lauds and Vespers is a custom attested at that time in Spain.⁵ In Rome, a silent 'Our Father' instead of a concluding prayer was to be met with here and there. In this supplementary addition the author, in contrast to the 'Master's' position, declares himself for the recitation aloud. Cassian (d.430) tells of Christians who did not wish to utter the petition for forgiveness.[6] The reason given here points in that direction.

NOTES TO CHAPTER 13

1 Verse 3. The 'Master's' order is different: RM 35,1; 39:1–4. 2 Verse 10. → Introd. 9(in note 107); 8,0. 3 With an exception in the final chapter (RB 73). 4 RCaesV 64,2–4. 5 Council of Gerona I. (517) c.10. 6 Conl 9,22.

CHAPTER 14

HOW VIGILS ARE TO BE CELEBRATED ON BIRTHDAYS OF THE SAINTS

17 Feb
18 June
18 Oct

1 On the feasts of saints and on all solemnities,
do as we have said should be done on the Lord's Day,
2 except that
psalms,
antiphons, and
readings
appropriate to the day be said.
3 However, let the structure described above
be adhered to.

CAPUT XIV: IN NATALICIIS SANCTORUM QUALITER AGANTUR VIGILIAE

¹IN SANCTORUM VERO FESTIVITATIBUS VEL OMNIBUS SOLLEMNITATIBUS, SICUT DIXIMUS DOMINICO DIE AGENDUM, ITA AGATUR, ²EXCEPTO QUOD PSALMI AUT ANTEFANAE VEL LECTIONES AD IPSUM DIEM PERTINENTES DICANTUR; ³MODUS AUTEM SUPRASCRIPTUS TENEATUR.

1–2 The author attaches importance to the 'birthdays of the *saints*'.[1,2] The feast of a local martyr[3] and some feasts of other martyrs were celebrated.[4] Other 'feastdays' were in accordance with the custom of the Roman basilicas: Christmas, Epiphany, Easter, Ascension, Pentecost. The veneration of the saints, especially of the martyrs, is attested in the 'Lives of the Jura Fathers', which tell of pilgrimages to the grave of St Maurice.[5]

NOTES TO CHAPTER 14

1 Title. What is meant is the day of death, as a 'birthday' for heaven. 2 In the case of the Master, there follows straight on the discussion of the Sunday Vigil (RM 45,12–15) a remark – which does not constitute a special chapter—on the Vigil of Saints (RM 45,16–18). → Introd. 9 (under note 109); Prologue 28; 4,62–73; 7,35–43; 8,0; 52,5. 3 Cf RF 18. 4 Cf RCaesVirg 69,20. 5 VPJur 44.

CHAPTER 15

ALLELUIA: AT WHAT SEASONS IS IT TO BE SAID?

18 Feb
19 June
19 Oct

1 From holy Easter until Pentecost,
alleluia shall be said without exception
both in the psalms and in the responsories.

2 From Pentecost however until the beginning of Lent
say it every night
only with the last six psalms of Nocturns.

3 On every Sunday outside Lent
sing with Alleluia:
canticles,
Morning Prayer,
first Hour,
third Hour,
sixth Hour,
ninth Hour;
Evening Prayer on the other hand with antiphon.

4 Responsories are never to be said with Alleluia,
except from Easter to Pentecost.

CAPUT XV: ALLELUIA QUIBUS TEMPORIBUS DICATUR

¹A SANCTUM PASCHA USQUE PENTECOSTEN SINE INTERMISSIONE DICATUR ALLELUIA, TAM IN PSALMIS QUAM IN RESPONSORIIS. ²A PENTECOSTEN AUTEM USQUE CAPUT QUADRAGESIMAE, OMNIBUS NOCTIBUS, CUM SEX POSTERIORIBUS PSALMIS TANTUM AD NOCTURNOS DICATUR. ³OMNI VERO DOMINICA EXTRA QUADRAGEIMA CANTICA, MATUTINOS, PRIMA, TERTIA, SEXTA NONAQUE CUM ALLELUIA DICATUR, VESPERA VERO IAM ANTEFANA. ⁴RESPONSORIA VERO NUMQUAM DICANTUR CUM ALLELUIA, NISI A PASCHA USQUE PENTECOSTEN.

1–4 The question as to when '*alleluia*' is to be sung, was in dispute among the specialists in Benedict's time, and the usages were various.[1] In the monasteries, the 'servants of God' held themselves entitled, at variance with the usage of the 'churches', to sing 'alleluia' outside Eastertide too,[2] obviously because they regarded themselves as Easter people. Cassian (d.430) asserts that the Egyptians sang this acclamation: 'alleluia', i.e. 'praise the Lord' only to psalms with the alleluia-superscription.[3]

NOTES TO CHAPTER 15

1 RB 15,1: RM 45,1; RB 15,2: RM 44,2–7; RB 15,3: RM 45,12; RB 15,4; RM 45,1; cf 44,3. 7. 2 Cf. RM 28,47; → Prol 50. 3 Inst 2,11,3.

CHAPTER 16

HOW THE DIVINE OFFICES ARE TO BE CELEBRATED IN THE COURSE OF THE DAY

19 Feb
20 June
20 Oct

1 As the prophet says: SEVEN TIMES A DAY I HAVE GIVEN YOU PRAISE.

Ps 119:164

2 This sacred sevenfold number will be fulfilled by us, if
in the morning,
at the first Hour,
at the third Hour,
at the sixth Hour,
at the ninth Hour,
at evening
and at Compline time,
we acquit ourselves of the duties of our subject state,

3 because it was of these daytime Hours he said:
SEVEN TIMES A DAY I HAVE GIVEN YOU PRAISE.

Ps 119:164

4 For the very same prophet says of the night Vigils:
I ROSE AT MIDNIGHT TO GIVE YOU PRAISE.

Ps 119:62

5 Let us then at these times give PRAISE to our Creator
FOR THE JUDGEMENTS OF his JUSTICE,
that is,
at Lauds,
Prime, Terce, Sext, None, Vespers and Compline,
and AT NIGHT LET US GET UP, TO GIVE HIM PRAISE.

Ps 119:164, 62

CAPUT XVI: QUALITER DIVINA OPERA PER DIEM AGANTUR

¹UT AIT PROPHETA: SEPTIES IN DIE LAUDEM DIXI TIBI. ²QUI SEPTENARIUS SACRATUS NUMERUS A NOBIS SIC IMPLEBITUR, SI MATUTINO, PRIMAE, TERTIAE, SEXTAE, NONAE, VESPERAE CONPLETORIIQUE TEMPORE NOSTRAE SERVITUTIS OFFICIA PERSOLVAMUS, ³QUIA DE HIS DIURNIS HORIS DIXIT: SEPTIES IN DIE LAUDEM DIXI TIBI. ⁴NAM DE NOCTURNIS VIGILIIS IDEM IPSE PROPHETA AIT: MEDIA NOCTE SURGEBAM AD CONFITENDUM TIBI. ⁵ERGO HIS TEMPORIBUS REFERAMUS LAUDES CREATORI NOSTRO SUPER IUDICIA IUSTITIAE SUAE, ID EST MATUTINIS, PRIMA, TERTIA, SEXTA, NONA, VESPERA, CONPLETORIOS, ET NOCTE SURGAMUS AD CONFITENDUM EI.

1–3   **a.** The passages of Scripture quoted[1] purport to prove that a practice which had arisen in the course of a long historical development, is in conformity with Scripture. The deep *root* of the Church's hours for prayer is however the exhortation to pray always, without ceasing;[2] this point is rightly made by Cassian.[3]

b. Already in the 'Didache', a catechetical treatise of about A.D. 100, Christians are called upon to recite the Lord's Prayer *thrice a day*.[4] Clement of Alexandria (d.*c.*215) mentions the custom of praying at the third, sixth and ninth hour.[5] In the 'Apostolic Tradition', which is attributed to Hippolytus of Rome, praying at the third hour recalls the crucifixion of Jesus; at the sixth hour, his hanging on the cross; at the ninth hour, his return (home) into the reappearing light (an 'image of the Resurrection'). Hippolytus also invites to prayer before going to sleep, just as he does to prayer at midnight[6] and at 'cockcrow'.[7]

c. Cassian, whose work must be read critically in this connexion, reports that in Egypt there was prayer in common only in the evening, in the night and until morning, whereas *during the day* prayer was practised again and again, but in private. In the monasteries of Palestine, Mesopotamia and Syria the monks also came together for Terce, Sext, and None, he alleges.[8]

d. In the Church as a whole, Lauds and Vespers, that is *Morning* and *Evening Prayer*, became more and more widespread as communal services.[9] Prayer at the third, sixth, and ninth hours (Terce, Sect, None) continued to be commended to Christians, and its observance was motivated by reference to the command to pray without ceasing. The 'seven times' means perhaps originally the 'whole': a life and a day's work before God and in his presence. Special times of prayer established themselves first in the basilicas and the basilical monasteries,[10] then in the monastic communities generally.[11]

e. During the long process of consolidation of the 'Prayer of the Hours', at first there was still a clear awareness that the institutionalized communal prayer should stimulate, nourish, and, to a certain extent, guarantee 'prayer without ceasing'. Initially prayer was cultivated at work, which was always regarded as important, and at 'holy reading'.[12]

Later, the *times for prayer became autonomous* and a 'duty'[13] in their own right corresponding to the duty of work.[14] Simultaneously there came about in the monasteries an ever greater awareness of the 'ecclesial' character of the Office.

f. The roots of the times for prayer and the basic duty to pray unceasingly, ought never to be forgotten, however. 'The following message was sent to the venerable Epiphanius, bishop in Cyprus, by the abbot of his monastery in Palestine: "Thanks to your prayers, we do not neglect the rule, but celebrate zealously Terce, Sext, None, and Vespers." The former, however, transmitted to him the following reproof: "It is clear that you do not pray at other times; but a true monk must pray without ceasing; that means, therefore, to sing psalms in his heart."'[15] The saying of Evagrius Ponticus (d.399) points in the direction of the basic duty: 'We have no instruction to work, watch or fast unceasingly; but there exists for us the precept to pray unceasingly.'[16]

g. Already earlier Origen (d.253) had explained the Lord's words about unceasing prayer in the sense that the whole life of a Christian must have the character of worship: 'Jesus' words, "Pray without ceasing" . . . can be so understood that we say: a holy person's whole life is a single, great, continuous prayer, of which that which is usually called prayer is also a part.'[17] According to Origen, the whole life and all the doings of a Christian, motivated by faith, can be understood as prayer; such an activity lifts up to heaven: '"The lifting up of my hands is an evening sacrifice." I do not believe that, if someone lifts up or stretches out his hands to heaven, he has offered a sacrifice to God just by doing that. Let us examine, however, whether the word of God in this passage does not intend "hands" to be understood as deeds: he lifts up his hands who lifts up his works from the earth, and, while he is still on his earthly pilgrimage, his "citizenship" is already "in heaven".'[18] All the life and doings of the believer ought to lead to God and be a 'sacrifice'.[19]

h. Neither must it be forgotten that in St Paul the exhortation 'to pray without ceasing' occurs in a context that requires a climate of lasting joy, union with God and gratitude.[20] Common prayer ought to contribute to that, especially in a monastery as a 'house of God'.[21]

4 The author does not want the Night Vigil to be reckoned among the 'seven times of prayer in the day', no doubt in order with the number seven to be able to give a reason for the obligation of prime, which was in dispute.

5 a. The Office is not presented directly as the outstanding peak of unceasing prayer. It is however a *community prayer* for the sanctification of the periods and hours of the day. All the daily work of the individual and of the community thus becomes a prayerful response to God.

b. Praise and thanks refer to the mighty deeds of the '*Creator*'. We know that we are safe in his hand. We thank him. From him we receive all we have. Our life, too, comes from him, for there is nothing we are as little capable of giving ourselves as life. Our existence is a gift. We give thanks for the world about us, and in our praise of God we lend a voice to the dumb creation, so that it can proclaim the glory of God. Thus, at divine praise, the person praying is in living fellowship not only with his brethren but also, beyond that, with the whole of creation. The fact that the times for prayer are governed by the rhythm of natural light, is a clear sign of this cosmic fellowship of those who pray.

c. In communal celebration, 'we offer praise to our Creator because of his just judgements'. By these are meant the commandments and precepts of God's word which *Christ* mediates to us. At the Office, the community is 'assembled in the name of Jesus'. He is in the 'midst' of the brethren.[22] At worship they are 'taught to do all that' he 'has commanded' us. To them, then, applies the promise: 'Lo, I am with you always, to the close of the age'.[23] In the fraternal atmosphere of the Office in community, gathered about Christ, we sing psalms and proclaim the word of God. That is 'prophetic speech'.[24]

d. Outsiders also feel this grace and power which rests upon community prayer.[25] 'If an unbeliever or outsider enters,' it may often be as in Paul's time, 'falling on his face, he will worship God, and declare that God is really among you'.[26] This *prophetic power* of the Office was summed up in former days in the pithy saying: 'The choir is the pulpit of the monks.'

e. Praising God in community is a *free offering, which has its meaning in itself.* The wish to praise the 'Creator' has always led to a creative, artistic development of the service itself as well as to an artistic shaping of the spaces or the books and requisites used. The *unselfcentred beauty* of divine service on the other hand, is itself a silent sermon for many. It proclaims that here people have faith, and experience God as the centre of their existence.

NOTES TO CHAPTER 16

1 They are also to be found in the 'Master': RB 16,1–3: RM 34,1–3;RB 16,4: RM 33,1. 2 Cf. Lk 18:1; 1 Thess 5:17. 3 Inst 2,1; cf. 9,2.7; 10,10. Cf. RCaes Virg 21,7. 4 8,3. 5 Stromata 7,7. 6 → 8,1–2. 7 About A.D. 215. 8 Inst 3,1–3. 9 In the Pachomian monasteries we find as communal celebrations morning and evening service with a series of reading repeated several times and listened to sitting down, the Lord's Prayer (standing) and silent prayer (beginning with a brief prostration, then standing). The 'reading' was not necessarily a psalm (RB 1980). 10 In basilicas (cathedrals, people's churches) the participation of the people was taken into consideration. Christologically interpreted psalms were selected (not necessarily all the psalms in a week), richer ceremonies developed(light, incense, vestments), and catchy texts and hymns repeated (RB 1980). 11 In monastic communities, as well as Lauds and Vespers, Vigils were held, and then Terce, Sext, and None. It was in the urban monasteries that 'basilical' elements were first adopted. 12 → 4,55–58;48. 13 RB 50,4. 14 → 43,3; 4,55—58. 15 VPatr 5,12,6. 16 Log prakt 49. 17 Peri euches 12,2. 18 I Reg Hom 1,9. 19 → 31,10–12; 35,7. 20 Cf. 1 Thess 5:16–18. 21 Cf. RB 31,19;53,22;64,5. 22 Cf. Mt 18:20. 23 Cf. Mt 28:20. 24 Cf. 1 Cor 14:24 ('to speak prophetically'). 25 → 1,3–5 in note 56. 26 1 Cor 14:5.

CHAPTER 17

HOW MANY PSALMS ARE TO BE SAID
AT THESE HOURS?

20 Feb
21 June
21 Oct

1 We have already mapped out the order of psalmody for
Nocturns and Morning Prayer; let us now look at the remaining
Hours.

2 At the first Hour, say three psalms separately,
and not under one *Glory be*,

3 the hymn of the same Hour   Ps 70:2
after the verse DEUS IN ADIUTORIUM,
before the psalms are begun.

4 After the completion of the three psalms,
one reading is to be recited,
a versicle,
Kyrie eleison,
and dismissal.

5 The prayer of the third, sixth and ninth Hours
is to be celebrated also in this same order, i.e.
verse,
hymns of the same Hours,
group of three psalms,
reading,
versicle,
Kyrie eleison, and
dismissal.

6 If the community be more numerous,
the psalmody is done with antiphons,
if however smaller,
straight through.

7 The evening assembly however is limited to
four psalms with antiphons.

8 After these psalms a reading shall be recited,
then the responsory,
Ambrosian hymn,
versicle,

the canticle from the Gospel book,

litany,

and the Lord's Prayer before the dismissal.

9 Compline is limited to the saying of three psalms.
These psalms are to be said straight through,
without antiphon.

10 After these
the hymn of the same Hour,
one reading,
versicle,
and the blessing before the dismissal.

CAPUT XVII: QUOT PSALMI PER EASDEM HORAS DICENDI SUNT

[1]IAM DE NOCTURNIS VEL MATUTINIS DIGESSIMUS ORDINEM PSALMODIAE: NUNC DE SEQUENTIBUS HORIS VIDEAMUS. [2]PRIMA HORA DICANTUR PSALMI TRES SINGILLATIM ET NON SUB UNA GLORIA, [3]HYMNUM EIUSDEM HORAE POST VERSUM DEUS, IN ADIUTORIUM, ANTEQUAM PSALMI INCIPIANTUR. [4]POST EXPLETIONEM VERO TRIUM PSALMORUM RECITETUR LECTIO UNA, VERSU ET QUIRIE ELEISON ET MISSAS. [5]TERTIA VERO, SEXTA ET NONA ITEM EO ORDINE CELEBRETUR ORATIO, ID EST VERSU, HYMNOS EARUNDEM HORARUM, TERNOS PSALMOS, LECTIONEM ET VERSU, QUIRIE ELEISON ET MISSAS. [6]SI MAIOR CONGREGATIO FUERIT, CUM ANTEFANAS, SI VERO MINOR, IN DIRECTUM PSALLANTUR. [7]VESPERTINA AUTEM SINAXIS QUATTUOR PSALMIS CUM ANTEFANAS TERMINETUR. [8]POST QUIBUS PSALMIS LECTIO RECITANDA EST; INDE RESPONSORIUM, AMBROSIANUM, VERSU, CANTICUM DE EVANGELIA, LITANIA, ET ORATIONE DOMINICA FIANT MISSAE. [9]CONPLETORIOS AUTEM TRIUM PSALMORUM DICTIONE TERMINENTUR; QUI PSALMI DIRECTANEI SINE ANTEFANA DICENDI SUNT. [10]POST QUOS HYMNUM EIUSDEM HORAE, LECTIONEM UNAM, VERSU, QUIRIE ELEISON, ET BENEDICTIONE MISSAE FIANT.

1–4 The *number of three psalms* at the Hours during the day is also to be found in the Rule of the 'Master',[1] and was a general custom.[2] Prime established itself relatively late.[3] The expression 'missas'[4] probably means the 'dismissal', which is effected with a concluding prayer at the end of the Office.

5 Tradition attributes to the Hours of Terce, Sext, and None a symbolic meaning. *Terce* recalls the prayer at the descent of the Holy Spirit; *Sext* the prayer of Peter at that hour, and Jesus' Way of the Cross; *None*, Peter and John going to pray in the Temple, and the death of Jesus.[5]

6 The length or difficulty of the chant 'with Antiphons'[6] makes this form unsuitable for small communities.

7–8 a. For *Vespers* an old designation is brought into use: ('vespertina) synaxis.' Synaxis (like 'synagogue') means the 'meeting' or 'assembly', and emphasizes the communal character of the celebration. Synaxis and 'coming together' are extremely ancient designations for Christian worship.[7] As well as Vespers, Lauds are distinguished by a special title in another place: 'matutina sollemnitas' (morning celebration).[8] The structure of Lauds resembles that of Vespers. Both celebrations stem originally from Jewish services. In Lauds and Vespere a 'litany' is recited before the conclusion. In the petitions, the worshipper proclaims his solidarity with the Church, the world and people's needs. Prayer in divine service is always recited vicariously *for* all.[9]

b. Later, singing is prescribed for Vespers: ' . . . psalmorum modulatione canatur';[10] evening praise is celebrated with special ceremony. Pachomius (d. 346) already describes Vespers as a 'specially pleasant' celebration which is not tiring.[11] Of Abbot Eugendus (d.*c.*510) in the Jura region it is reported that he always remained praying in the oratory after the 'synaxis', and then joined the brethren 'beaming, with joyful mien'.[12]

c. The number of Vesper psalms is reduced to four.[13] The author, in contrast to contemporary sources, does not call Vespers 'Lucernarium' (celebration of light),[14] probably because no light is carried in.[15] As a celebration of light, Vespers were explained as referring to the resurrection of Christ.[16]

9–10 *Compline* is somewhat different to the other Hours as far as its structure is concerned. It is striking in its simplicity.[17]

NOTES TO CHAPTER 17

1 RM 35,2; RB 17,1–5:RM 35,2–3; RB 17,6:RM 55,6; RB 17, 7–8: RM 36,1–9; RB 17, 9–10: RM 37,1–2; cf. 42, 1–4. 2 Cassian, Inst 3, 3,1. 3 Caesarius provides for them only on Sundays: RCaesVirg 69,13–15. 4 Verse 4. 5 Tertullian, De or.25; De ieiunio 10; Cyprian, De or. dom. 34; Cassian, Inst 3, 2–7. 6 → 9, 1–4. 7 Acts 20:7; 1 Cor. 7:5; 11,17.34; 14,23, 20–33. Cassian uses the expression 'Synaxis' (Inst 2,10,1); cf.VPJur 64. 8 RB 12 T. 9 → 53, 23–24 (in note 30). 10 RB 18,12. 11 Leges 10; → 41,7–9 (Evening Prayer). 12 VPJur 130. 13 In contrast to the 'Master' (RM 36) and the Roman usage. 14 E.g. RM 36. 15 Everything is to take place by daylight; → 41,7–9. The Christian 'Lucernarium' has its counterpart in the Jewish ceremony on Friday evening. 16 Cf. Hippolytus,Trad.apost. 41. 17 In the Rule of the 'Master' the psalms at Compline were sung with antiphons, the third one with 'alleluia'. The abbot recited the 'Gospel' (the canticle of Simeon ?). Cf. RM 37:42.

CHAPTER 18

IN WHAT ORDER THESE PSALMS ARE TO BE SAID

1 To begin, Ps 70:2
say the verse:
O GOD, COME TO MY AID,
O LORD, MAKE HASTE TO HELP ME;
Glory be
then the hymn of the appropriate Hour.

2 Then at the first Hour, on Sunday,
four strophes of Psalm 118 shall be said.

3 At the remaining Hours, i.e. third, sixth, and ninth,
a group of three strophes
of the above-mentioned Psalm 118 is said.

4 On Monday, at the first Hour,
say three psalms, i.e. 1,2, and 6.

5 And so, each day up to Sunday, at the first Hour,
say three psalms in numerical order,
but with Psalm 9 and Psalm 17 divided in two.

6 And in this way, Sunday Vigils will always begin with the 20th.

7 At the third, sixth and ninth Hours of Monday,
the nine strophes which remain of 118,
are said in groups of three at these Hours.

8 Psalm 118 therefore being spread over two days, i.e. Sunday and Monday,

9 then on Tuesday at the third, sixth and ninth Hours,
sing groups of three psalms from 119 to 127, i.e. 9 psalms.

10 These psalms are to be repeated always at the same Hours
in the same way,
until Sunday;
the arrangement nevertheless of hymns, readings, and versicles
being maintained uniform each day.

11 And in this way,
we shall always begin on Sunday by 118.

23 Feb 12 Evening Prayer shall be sung daily with four psalms.

24 June 13 Beginning at 109 they go up to 147,

24 Oct 14 except those which are set aside for various Hours,
  i.e. from 117 to 127,
  and 133 and 142;

15 all the rest shall be said at Evening Prayer.

16 And because the total is three psalms short,
  therefore those of the aforesaid number which are longer
  are to be divided,
  i.e. 138, 143, 144;

17 but 116, being short, shall be joined to 115.

18 The order of evening psalms therefore being arranged, the rest,
  i.e. reading,
  responsory,
  hymn,
  versicle,
  and canticle
  shall be fulfilled as we have fixed above.

19 For Compline, however, the same psalms are repeated daily,
  i.e. 4, 90, and 133.

24 Feb 20 Having fixed the order of daytime psalmody,
(in Leap   all the other psalms which remain,
Year)   shall be divided equally
25 June   in the Vigils of the seven nights,
25 Oct
21 dividing those among them which are longer,
  and appointing twelve to each night.

22 We urge above all,
  that if by chance this distribution of the psalms
  should displease anyone
  let him arrange it otherwise if he judge better,

23 provided that at all costs he take care
  that every week the integral psalter of 150 psalms be sung,
  always taking up from the beginning again
  at Vigils on the Lord's Day.

24 Monks indeed who, in the course of a week,
  say less than the psalter and customary canticles,
  show up their vowed service as far too listless.
  If only we half-hearted ones

could get through in a full week,
what we read that our holy Fathers
strenuously fulfilled in a single day!

CAPUT XVIII: QUO ORDINE IPSI PSALMI DICENDI SUNT

'IN PRIMIS DICATUR VERSU: DEUS, IN ADIUTORIUM MEUM INTENDE; DOMINE, AD ADIUVANDUM ME FESTINA, GLORIA, INDE HYMNUM UNIUSCUIUSQUE HORAE. 'DEINDE PRIMA HORA, DOMINICA, DICENDA QUATTUOR CAPITULA PSALMI CENTESIMI OCTAVI DECIMI. 'RELIQUIS VERO HORIS, ID EST TERTIA, SEXTA VEL NONA, TERNA CAPITULA SUPRASCRIPTI PSALMI CENTESIMI OCTAVI DECIMI DICANTUR. 'AD PRIMAM AUTEM SECUNDAE FERIAE DICANTUR TRES PSALMI, ID EST PRIMUS, SECUNDUS ET SEXTUS. 'ET ITA PER SINGULOS DIES AD PRIMAM, USQUE DOMINICA, DICANTUR PER ORDINEM TERNI PSALMI USQUE NONUM DECIMUM PSALMUM, ITA SANE, UT NONUS PSALMUS ET SETPIMUS DECIMUS PARTIANTUR IN BINOS. 'ET SIC FIT, UT AD VIGILIAS DOMINICA SEMPER A VICESIMO INCIPIATUR. 'AD TERTIAM VERO, SEXTAM NONAMQUE SECUNDAE FERIAE NOVEM CAPITULA QUAE RESIDUA SUNT DE CENTESIMO OCTAVO DECIMO, IPSA TERNA PER EASDEM HORAS DICANTUR. 'EXPENSO ERGO PSALMO CENTESIMO OCTAVO DECIMO DUOBUS DIEBUS, ID EST DOMINICO ET SECUNDA FERIA, 'TERTIA FERIA IAM AD TERTIAM, SEXTAM VEL NONAM PSALLANTUR TERNI PSALMI A CENTESIMO NONO DECIMO USQUE CENTESIMO VICESIMO SEPTIMO, ID EST PSALMI NOVEM. "QUIQUE PSALMI SEMPER USQUE DOMINICA PER EASDEM HORAS ITIDEM REPETANTUR, HYMNORUM NIHILOMINUS, LECTIONUM VEL VERSUUM DISPOSITIONEM UNIFORMEM CUNCTIS DIEBUS SERVATAM. "ET ITA SCILICET SEMPER DOMINICA A CENTESIMO OCTAVO DECIMO INCIPIETUR. "VERPERA AUTEM COTIDIE QUATTUOR PSALMORUM MODULATIONE CANATUR. "QUI PSALMI INCIPIANTUR A CENTESIMO NONO USQUE CENTESIMO QUADRAGESIMO SEPTIMO, "EXCEPTIS HIS QUI IN DIVERSIS HORIS EX EIS SEQUESTRANTUR, ID EST A CENTESIMO SEPTIMO DECIMO USQUE CENTESIMO VICESIMO SEPTIMO ET CENTESIMO TRICESIMO TERTIO ET CENTESMIO QUADRAGESIMO SECUNDO; "RELIQUI OMNES IN VESPERA DICENDI SUNT. "ET QUIA MINUS VENIUNT TRES PSALMI, IDEO DIVIDENDI SUNT QUI EX NUMERO SUPRASCRIPTO FORTIORES INVENIUNTUR, ID EST CENTESIMUM TRICESIMUM OCTAVUM ET CENTESIMUM QUADRAGESIMUM TERTIUM ET CENTESIMUM QUADRAGESIMUM QUARTUM; "CENTESIMUS VERO SEXTUS DECIMUS, QUIA PARVUS EST, CUM CENTESIMO QUINTO DECIMO CONIUNGATUR. "DIGESTO ERGO ORDINE PSALMORUM VESPERTINORUM, RELIQUA, ID EST LECTIONEM, RESPONSUM, HYMNUM, VERSUM VEL CANTICUM, SICUT SUPRA TAXAVIMUS IMPLEATUR. "AD CONPLETORIOS VERO COTIDIE IDEM PSALMI REPETANTUR, ID EST QUARTUM, NONAGESIMUM ET CENTESIMUM TRICESIMUM TERTIUM. "DISPOSITO ORDINE PSALMODIAE DIURNAE, RELIQUI OMNES PSALMI QUI SUPERSUNT AEQUALITER DIVIDANTUR IN SEPTEM NOCTIUM VIGILIAS, "PARTIENDO SCILICET QUI INTER EOS PROLIXIORES SUNT PSALMI ET DUODECIM PER UNAMQUAMQUE CONSTITUENS NOCTEM. "HOC PRAECIPUE COMMONENTES UT, SI CUI FORTE HAEC DISTRIBUTIO PSALMORUM DISPLICUERIT, ORDINET SI MELIUS ALITER IUDICAVERIT, "DUM OMNIMODIS ID ADTENDAT, UT OMNI EBDOMADA PSALTERIUM EX INTEGRO NUMERO CENTUM QUINQUAGINTA PSALMORUM PSALLATUR, ET DOMINICO DIE SEMPER A CAPUT REPRENDATUR AD VIGILIAS. "QUIA NIMIS INERTEM DEVOTIONIS SUAE SERVITIUM OSTENDUNT MONACHI QUI MINUS A PSALTERIO CUM CANTICIS CONSUETUDINARIIS PER SEPTIMANAE CIRCULUM PSALLUNT, "DUM QUANDO LEGAMUS SANCTOS PATRES NOSTROS UNO DIE HOC STRENUE IMPLESSE, QUOD NOS TEPIDI UTINAM SEPTIMANA INTEGRA PERSOLVAMUS.

a. The whole chapter and the *distribution of the psalms* itself are a new creation. The most important innovation is that there is a partial departure from the traditional principle of reciting the psalms 'always in the order of the psalter'.[1] A number of psalms are deliberately selected for certain Hours.

b. In the psalms, the person at prayer identifies himself with the psalmist, who is regularly called 'the prophet'.[2] Whoever sings the psalms 'speaks *prophetically*'.[3] The one praying makes his own the praise and thanks, the trusting plea, rejoicing or bitter complaint and distress of the psalmist. In the psalms, the whole scale of man's basic moods is heard, so that the person at prayer can practise solidarity with humanity, with the Church, with Christ. Cassian (d.430) writes: 'Penetrated to the heart by the moods in which the psalms were sung or written down, we become their authors, as it were . . . We find every mood in the psalms. As in an unclouded mirror we see very clearly what happens to ourselves, and thus come to an insight which operates at a deep level. Our feelings become our teachers and educators for that which we not only hear, but intuitively experience.'[4]

1 When the Christian prays, not only can he say, 'I am praying,' but must confess: 'Prayer is taking place in me.' Because in fact the 'Spirit' of God 'helps us in our weakness; for we do not know how to pray as we ought, but the Spirit himself intercedes for us with sighs too deep for words.'[5] Out of knowledge of human weakness, Benedict has God's help called on at the beginning of the time of prayer. Cassian (d.430) claims to reveal the 'formula of piety', which 'was handed down to him 'from the few surviving Fathers of the primitive period': 'O God, come to my aid! O Lord, make haste to help me!'[6] This word, he says, 'is a calling on God in every need, a humble confession of piety, a sign of weak, reverent submission, a conscious expression of one's own weakness and of a trusting confidence in the support of an ever-present helper, a confidence in the certainty of being heard . . . It is the voice of burning, devoted love . . . '[7] This prayer motto, loved by Benedict,[8] is therefore, at the beginning of every Hour, an *Epiclesis* of the Holy Spirit over the praying community and over each individual. The Spirit's role is to stand by us, so that we, strengthened by the spiritual gift of *parrhesia* (confident freedom of speech) may freely call upon God.

2–6 For Prime a series of psalms was chosen which begins with Psalm 1 and, following Roman usage, belongs to the Sunday Vigil. Perhaps Benedict wishes to be able to begin the Sunday Vigil with Ps.21(20), because this psalm and the ones immediately following seem to him to be particularly suitable for the Day of the *Resurrection*.

7–11 A large part of Psalm 119(118), too, falls on the Lord's Day. This psalm offered nourishment for the *devotion to Scripture and the Word* and was a favourite.

12–18 In conformity with Roman usage, Vespers on Sunday begin with Psalm 110 (109). It opens the series of psalms at Vespers.[9] The number of four psalms for Vespers represents an innovation and abbreviation.[10] Departing from his models, Benedict, following Cassian (d.430), directs that longer *psalms should be divided*. Cassian wrote: The Egyptians 'think it more fruitful to sing ten verses attentively than to reel off a whole psalm'.[11]

19 These psalms were allotted to *Compline* in Rome too.[12]

20–21 The *number of twelve* psalms for the Vigil is important for our author.[13] The four times three psalms of the minor Hours during the day also give this number.[14]

22–25 Benedict gives evidence of a great *flexibility*. He allows each monastery a certain freedom in finding a suitable distribution of the psalms. This generosity is not surprising when one knows that the author himself is proposing a new model of the order of worship. On the other hand, he wants to ensure a *minimum* of liturgical obligation which may seem to us rather high, either because of the number of Hours demanded, or because of the number of 150 psalms which are to be recited in a weekly cycle. The author himself regards the proposed measure as pitched very low.[15] Perhaps the record performances of two superstars of monks impressed him; these are described, not without a certain quiet amusement, in the 'Lives of the Fathers': 'A senior came to one of the Fathers who was preparing a lentil purée. The latter spoke: "We will first set ourselves to prayer, then eat!" One of them recited the whole psalter; the other, however, said off by heart, like a reader, two of the major prophets. As morning dawned, the senior, who had come to visit, went his way. They had forgotten to eat!'[16] In fact, the Fathers often recited the psalter off by heart while at work.[17]

NOTES TO CHAPTER 18

1 The 'Master' emphasizes this order in eight passages: 'currente semper psalterio'. Other contemporary sources (e.g. RF 12) also witness to the custom of reciting 'the psalter always in its order'. The Eastern Church retained this custom. 2 RB Prol 23.30; 2,9; 6,1.2; 7,3.14.23.29.47.50.52.66; 11,6; 13,10; 16,1.4; 19,3. 3 → 16,5 (in notes 24.26). 4 Conl 10,11. 5 Rom 8:26. 6 Ps 70:2. 7 Conl 10,10; → 6,2–5. 8 → 35,15–18. 9 Pss 110–147. 10 The Master provides for six psalms (RM 36,1.7). In Rome five psalms were sung. 11 Inst 2,11,2; → 20,4–5. 12 The 'Master', too, seems to have been acquainted with the same three psalms for Compline. 13 → 9,1–4. 14 Cf. VPach 22. 15 → Prol 46; 40,6; 73,4–7. 16 VPatr 5,4,57. 17 → 4,55–58; 16,1–3.

CHAPTER 19

OF DISCIPLINED PSALMODY

24 Feb 1 We believe that the divine presence is everywhere   Cf. Prov 15:3
(25 Feb   and that THE EYES OF THE LORD ARE KEEPING WATCH
Leap   OVER THE GOOD AND THE BAD IN EVERY PLACE.
Year)
26 June 2 Most especially however let us,
26 Oct   without any hesitation,
    believe this when present at the Divine Office.

   3 Let us therefore always remember what the prophet says: Ps 2:11
    SERVE THE LORD IN FEAR.
   4 And again: SING THE PSALMS WITH WISDOM.   Ps 46:8 (lat.)
   5 And: IN THE SIGHT OF THE ANGELS   Ps 138:1
    WILL I SING A PSALM TO YOU.
   6 Let us therefore reflect
    what one should be in the sight of the Godhead and of his
    angels,
    and let us so stand at psalmody
    that mind and voice may be in tune.

CAPUT XIX: DE DISCIPLINA PSALLENDI

¹UBIQUE CREDIMUS DIVINAM ESSE PRAESENTIAM ET OCULOS DOMINI IN OMNI LOCO SPECULARI BONOS ET MALOS, ²MAXIME TAMEN HOC SINE ALIQUA DUBITATIONE CREDAMUS, CUM AD OPUS DIVINUM ADSISTIMUS. ³IDEO SEMPER MEMORES SIMUS QUOD AIT PROPHETA. SERVITE DOMINO IN TIMORE, ⁴ET ITERUM: PSALLITE SAPIENTER, ⁵ET: IN CONSPECTU ANGELORUM PSALLAM TIBI. ⁶ERGO CONSIDEREMUS QUALITER OPORTEAT IN CONSPECTU DIVINITATIS ET ANGELORUM EIUS ESSE, ⁷ET SIC STEMUS AD PSALLENDUM, UT MENS NOSTRA CONCORDET VOCI NOSTRAE.

1–2   a. Reverence for God, being gripped or startled by the presence of the God who is holy, and being certain that one lives *under God's eyes*, belong for Benedict to the foundation of a Christian life, and are prerequisites for the Office.[1] When a person stands praying before God, free of ulterior aim and purpose, the core of the Christian vocation is revealed; the priority of being to doing, the primacy of meaning over success.
b. Basil (d.379) writes in the same vein: ' "My eyes are ever toward the Lord."[2] We will always think of God, of his works, his blessings and gifts.'[3]

God, our Creator,[4] and his working upon us for salvation, are to be praised in the Office. In prayer, we have *eyes* only *for God*, whose gaze rests upon us.

c. Cyprian (d.258) also quotes the introductory saying from Scripture[5] and, in his treatise on prayer,[6] his formulation is similar to that of Benedict after him: 'We must remember that we stand under God's gaze.' With respect to prayer Cyprian says in the same context: 'Friendly and intimate prayer of God consists in our letting the prayer of his own Son rise up to him. The Father should recognize the *voice of his Son* when we pray. Let him who is in our breast be also in our voice.'

d. People showed a particular inclination to call on Christ himself with the words of a psalm; the *christological interpretation* of the psalms made these words especially dear to those praying them.[7]

e. Cassian (d.430) explains the 'Our Father' as the best prerequisite of ardent mystical prayer.[8] Immediately after his explanation of the 'Our Father', Cassian mentions psalmody as an occasion for mystical contemplation: 'When we sang the psalms together, it was not infrequent for some verse or other of a psalm to be for me the occasion of an *ardent prayer*. From time to time, the voices of the brethren and their melodious song induced a lively wonder in our spirit. According to our experience, the dignified and intelligible recitation of a psalm can help those present towards heartfelt prayer.'[9] Once again, 'mystical' prayer is not made dependent on special methods. The emphasis here is on the fraternal atmosphere of communal prayer. There is no doubt that, in this process, 'ardent prayer' rises up from the depths of each individual, and is not brought about just by the external solemnity.

3–7 a. Benedict quotes three passages from the psalms, which occur in a parallel context in the Rule of the Master.[10] *Reverence* is a fundamental postulate for Divine Service,[11] as Cyprian (d.258) had already emphasized: 'When one prays to the Lord, a careless presentation is an irreverence in the face of God's majesty, if, for instance, one's eyes are open while one's heart sleeps . . .'[12]

b. The summons, 'Sing psalms wisely'[13] was commented on by Basil (d.379): 'If someone concentrates with complete inner attention on the individual words of a psalm, then, just as the sense of taste is able to savour the special flavour (*sapor*) of a particular food, he realizes what is written: "Sing psalms wisely (*sapienter*)!"'[14] We ought not read on over the words of the psalms in a hasty and superficial way, but ought to savour them and sense their 'spiritual meaning';[15] we ought to listen for 'what the Spirit is saying to the Churches'.[16]

c. Prayer, especially prayer in fraternal community, during which Christ is in the midst of those assembled,[17] and the psalms are recited which are 'prompted by God' and proceed from the 'Holy Spirit',[18] is an intimate though reverent walking with God. It is *a piece of heaven on earth*, the 'presence of God and his angels', a piece of lost paradise, in which man dealt with God 'face to face',[19] a piece of the future divine praise by the blessed.

d. Cyprian (d.258) makes clear beyond all shadow of doubt that Christian prayer which is profoundly related to God must not result in an estrangement from the world of men and their necessities. He quotes biblical passages in support of the idea that angels bring our prayer before God,[20] and explains that what they bring are prayers accompanied 'by acts of charity, by fasting and alms-giving'. It is only such prayers that Cyprian calls 'fruitful': 'When we pray, we must not come before God with sterile and bare[21] requests. A prayer which is only sterile talk before God, cannot be effective. "Every tree that bears no fruit will be cut down and thrown into the fire."[22] Thus, to speak in God's presence is of no use, if it does not *become fruitful in action* . . . For Christ, who, on the Day of Judgement will distribute the reward for the works of charity, will also be a good listener, when someone comes before him with prayer and works.'[23] A Christian life, therefore, cannot consist exclusively of prayer; it must bear fruit in an attitude of readiness to serve.[24]

e. So that a Christian life can bear good fruit, the seed of the word of God must be sown and carefully ploughed into the field of the heart. Great attention is therefore to be paid to interior dispositions. The 'Master' warns against a 'piety of the lips', which allows God as far as the 'threshold of the mouth', but not into the 'dwelling of the heart'. 'In this task (of prayer) which is so meaningful, heart and tongue must reach harmony . . . Whoever recites psalms must take note in his heart of everything he pronounces . . . '[25] That is the teaching of Cyprian (d.258): 'God does not hearken to the voice, but to the heart.'[26] Benedict formulates this aim of the *'prayer of the heart'* tellingly in the final sentence. The formulation reminds one of a saying of Augustine's (d.430): 'What the voice pronounces should linger on in the heart.'[27] Benedict insists on the right dispositions for prayer. Every time he describes an external liturgical action, he indicates a corresponding internal attitude, especially reverence.[28]

NOTES TO CHAPTER 19

1 → 8,0 (in Notes 5–8). There is no parallel passage in the 'Rule of the Master'. 2 Ps 25:15. 3 RBasRuf 109. 4 → 16,5. 5 Prov 15:3. 6 De or.dom.4. 7 → 2,1–10; 4,20–33. 8 Conl 9,25; → 6,2–5; 20,4–5; 52,4. 9 Conl 9,26. 10 RM 47,4–8; RB 19,3–7: RM 47,1–24. RB 19–20 come perhaps originally from a special work circulating in Southern Gaul (E.Manning). One should however take note of the relationship in style and content of RB 20 with RB 49 and RB 52. Cf.A. Wathen, 'Licet omni . . . .' : *The American Benedictine Review* 38(1987) 71–83. 11 → 8,0 (in Notes 5–8); 19,1–2. 12 De or.dom.31. 13 Cf. Ps 47:8. 14 RBasRuf 110; cf. RCaesVirg 66,1. 15 Cf. Prol 8–11 (in Note 53); 18,12–18; 73,3. 16 Rev 2:7; → cf.Prol 8–11 (Notes 41.53). 17 → 16,5 (in Note 22); 17,7–8. 18 Cf. 2 Pet 1:21; 1 Pet 1,11; 2 Tim 3:16. 19 Cf. Gen 3:8; 4: 14. 20 Acts 10:30–31 (Cornelius); Tobit 12:12–35 (Raphael). 21 Cf. Rev 19:8. 22 Cf. Matt 3:10. 23 De or.dom. 32. 24 → 22,8. 25 RM 47,12.14–15. 26 De or.dom. 4. 27 Praec 2,3. 28 Cf RB 9,7; 11,3.9; 50,3.

CHAPTER 20

OF THE REVERENCE OF PRAYER

25 Feb 1 If, when wishing to make suggestions to men in power
(26 Feb we do not venture to do so,
Leap except with humility and deference,
Year)
27 June 2 how much more ought supplication be made   Cf. Est 4:17b
27 Oct to the LORD, GOD OF ALL
with all humility and pure devotion!

3 And let us realize that we shall be heard   Cf. Mt 6:7; 5:8
NOT IN MUCH SPEAKING, but in
PURITY OF HEART
and in COMPUNCTION and tears.

4 And that is why a prayer should be brief and pure,
unless perhaps it be prolonged
by an inspiration of divine grace.

5 In the assembled community however
a prayer shall be altogether shortened,
and at the signal given by the superior,
let all stand up together.

CAPUT XX: DE REVERENTIA ORATIONIS

¹SI, CUM HOMINIBUS POTENTIBUS VOLUMUS ALIQUA SUGGERERE, NON PRAESUMIMUS
NISI CUM HUMILITATE ET REVERENTIA, ²QUANTO MAGIS DOMINO DEO UNIVERSORUM
CUM OMNI HUMILITATE ET PURITATIS DEVOTIONE SUPPLICANDUM EST. ³ET NON IN
MULTILOQUIO, SED IN PURITATE CORDIS ET CONPUNCTIONE LACRIMARUM NOS
EXAUDIRI SCIAMUS. ⁴ET IDEO BREVIS DEBET ESSE ET PURA ORATIO, NISI FORTE EX
AFFECTU INSPIRATIONIS DIVINAE GRATIAE PROTENDATUR. ⁵IN CONVENTU TAMEN
OMNINO BREVIETUR ORATIO, ET FACTO SIGNO A PRIORE OMNES PARITER SURGANT.

1-3 a. This chapter on reverence at prayer deals with personal *interior prayer*,
perhaps in a special way with 'psalm prayer'.[1]
b. The Rule emphasizes here, as in many places, that an atmosphere of
reverence and humility is indispensable for prayer.[2] The teaching of the Rule
on prayer was deliberately connected with the chapter on humility.[3] Cyprian
(d.258), before the beginning of his explanation of the 'Our Father', refers to
the attitude of the Publican[4], and makes humility a basic condition for prayer.[5]

The comparison with appearing before 'powerful people' is often found, for example in the writings of Basil (d.379)[6] and Cassian (d.430).[7]

c. This '*prayer*' (oratio) seems to be directed to God, the Father. Also according to Evagrius (d.399), it must rise up to 'God, the Lord of the universe',[8] while the 'Master' teaches that the 'prayer' is directed to Christ, who is 'present' in the Spirit: 'One should pray reverently and earnestly. Whoever prays, embraces as it were the feet of Christ, who is present' (B. Fischer).[9]

d. In this chapter, the integrity or *purity of prayer* is mentioned three times. This purity of heart is that condition to which the ascent of humility must lead.[10] 'Purity' of heart, according to Evagrius (d.399), is freedom from distracting thoughts and imaginings (for God, too, is one and undivided). The soul raises itself to God and can then be filled with the light of the Trinity, in a condition of spiritual ecstasy, which Evagrius calls 'anaesthesia'.[11] In order to avoid misunderstandings,[12] an emotional element is referred to immediately in our Rule. 'Peace of soul' does not mean insensibility. The 'tears of self-abasement' are a possible affective accompaniment[13] of this state of earthly perfection, which, however, consists essentially in love.[14] Cassian (d.430), quoting the Song of Songs[15] in support, makes it clear that all asceticism is in vain, if it lacks that love,' which consists solely in purity of heart', by which in this context he means selflessness.[16]

e. Benedict's sentences recall the 'Admonition to a spiritual son' attributed to Basil (d.379): 'When you, my son, appear before the Lord to pray, cast yourself down in humility before his face. Ask for nothing as if trusting to your own merits . . . Do not pray to him with a loud voice, for he knows what is hidden. Instead, the *cry of your heart* should knock at his ear. Do not come before him with long, seemingly never-ending words, for it is not through many words, but through a prayer from an utterly pure soul that God is appeased.'[17]

f. The *experience of being stirred to the depths*[18] is not the core of Christian prayer.[19] It is regarded as a gift of God's, which cannot be deliberately extorted. In this regard, Basil (d.379) writes: 'This feeling of being moved (compunction) is brought about by a gift of God's. He wishes to arouse an interior desire to experience this feeling of being touched and moved, even in those with little zeal.'[20]

g. Ascetic struggle and renunciation are not an end in themselves, but instruments[21] to make the heart empty, open, and wide.[22] Prayer fills this 'emptiness' of the heart, which renunciation brings in its train. That 'rest of the heart', which the Lord has promised,[23] is not the rest of the dead or unfulfilled emptiness, but it is 'joy in the Lord' and the peace which prayer and the Divine Office give us in a special way.[24]

4–5 a. It would seem that here Benedict in his own words—which however mirror Cassian's (d.430) instructions[25]—explains the psalm prayers of the Egyptians. In other passages also, Benedict bears witness to the custom,[26] which Cassian describes in more detail. After the end of a psalm, or of a section of a psalm, they stood up to pray with outstretched hands, then they prostrated themselves briefly, 'as if to worship the divine mercy', stood up and 'persevered praying still with outstretched arms'.[27] The words of the Old Testament psalm, which have been taken in with an attentive ear, should now become the words of a Christian prayer in the individual heart.[28] Besides, the juxtaposition of formulated and personal spontaneous prayer was already known in the Synagogue. After the morning 'Sh'ma' prayer,[29] the worshipper threw himself down to pray and lay prostrate with his face to the ground (B. Fischer).[30] **b.** Obviously, this pause for prayer was easily endangered.[31] The *silence* was to be in no way disturbed, except if there chanced to be a charismatic utterance by a participant.[32] An 'ardent prayer', however, is[33] in itself wordless[34] and short.[35] It could be joined with the 'Glory be' or replace it, as was the case in Egypt. According to Cassian (d.430), a priest concluded the silent prayer of the individuals with a Collect.[36] All rose simultaneously with him.[37] Benedict specifies that the prostration to the ground should last only a short time.

NOTES TO CHAPTER 20

1 The corresponding chapter in the 'Rule of the Master' (RB 20,1–4: RM 48,1–14) makes a reference in this direction (RM 48,10–11). → 20,4–5; 52,4. 2 → 4,55–58; 6,2–5; 7; 7,35–43; 19,12.3–7. 3 → 8,0. 4 Cf. Lk 18:9–14. 5 De or.dom.6. 6 RBasRuf 108. 7 Conl 23,6. 8 Log prakt 11. 9 RM 48,12. 10 → 7,62–66.67–70; Cassian, Conl 10,11. 11 De orat.120. 12 Jerome (d.420) accused Evagrius of requiring the soul to become 'a stone or God' . The Coptic monks of the fourth century were very indignant that Evagrius should condemn the 'image' of God appealing to the senses; for they were accustomed to 'imagine' God, indeed to converse with the 'images' (as well as with angels and devils). The Greek monks accused the uneducated Copts of 'anthropomorphism'. Both sides accused each other of heresy in the 'Origenist' and the 'anthropomorphist' controversy (RB 1980). → 7,67–70; Introd. 8. 13 → 4,55–58; 6,2–5; 8,0. 14 → 7,44–48,62–66.67–70. 15 1 Cor 13:3–5. 16 Conl 1,6. 17 Admonitio 11. 18 Verse 3: 'Tears of Compunction'. Cf. Ps 34,19; 51,19; Cassian, Inst 4,43; see above, Note 13. 19 → Prol 4,56–58; 7,10–13.62–66; 49,4–5; 52,4. 20 RBasRuf 123. 21 → 4,76–77; 7,26–30. 22 → Prol 48–49. 23 Mt 11:28–29; → Prol 40.45–50. 24 → 17,7–8. 25 Inst 2,7–8.10. 26 RB 50,3 (They 'bend the knee' at the hour of prayer at the place of work, as is usual at the psalm prayer); RB 67,2 (the 'last prayer' of an Office presupposes earlier ones, i.e. the psalm Collects). 27 Cassian, Inst.2,7,1–2. The Master writes: 'when all apply themselves to prayer after finishing the psalms' (RM 14,1). In chapter 48 (On Reverence at Prayer) he mentions praying while prostrated on the ground (RM 48,10–11). 28 → 19,3–7 (in Note 15). 29 → Prol 1 (in Note 5). 30 Nowadays it is the custom of the Jews to hide the face in the arms while praying thus. Cf. Scholastica's prayer: → 51,3 (in Note 7) (B.Fischer). 31 Cf. RM 48,6–14. 32 Verse 4. Cf. Cassian, Inst 2,10: 'No other voice is heard but that of the priest concluding the prayer, except perhaps a voice that in a transport of the soul (mentis) escapes the lips, when that soul is enkindled by an uncontrollable spiritual ardour which exceeds all measure. . .' 33 → 6,2–5; 19,1–2; 52,4. 34 Cf. Mt 6:7. 35 It can consist in the 'Yes' of surrender and in the 'Amen' of faith, if the Spirit but prays in us (Rom.8:26). 36 Inst 2,10,1. This was customary more in basilicas than in early monastic communities (RB 1980). 37 Inst 2,7,4.

CHAPTER 21

OF DEANS OF THE MONASTERY

26 Feb
(27 Feb
Leap
Year)
28 June
28 Oct

1 If the community be on the large side,
let there be CHOSEN from among them
brothers of GOOD WITNESS and HOLY LIFE
and let them be appointed DEANS.

2 They shall take care of their deaneries
in all matters,
according to the commandments of God
and the orders of their abbot.

3 Let such be chosen as deans,
with whom the abbot can safely SHARE his BURDENS.

4 Nor let them be chosen by rank
but according to MERIT OF LIFE
and WISDOM and doctrine

5 As regards these deans,
if one of them, swollen by some pride,
be found blameable,
if he do not wish to amend
when corrected once and a second and a third time,
let him be deposed

6 and some one else who is worthy
be substituted in his place.

7 And we ordain the same about the prior.

Cf. Acts 6:3,5;
Deut 1:9–15;
Ex 18:21

Cf. Ex 18:13–17,
21–22

Cf. Deut 1:13–15;
Acts 6:3

Cf. Mt 18:16–17;
1 Tim 5:19–20

CAPUT XXI: DE DECANIS MONASTERII

¹SI MAIOR FUERIT CONGREGATIO, ELEGANTUR DE IPSIS FRATRES BONI TESTIMONII
ET SANCTAE CONVERSATIONIS, ET CONSTITUANTUR DECANI, ²QUI SOLLICITUDINEM
GERANT SUPER DECANIAS SUAS IN OMNIBUS SECUNDUM MANDATA DEI ET
PRAECEPTA ABBATIS SUI. ³QUI DECANI TALES ELEGANTUR IN QUIBUS SECURUS ABBAS
PARTIAT ONERA SUA. ⁴ET NON ELEGANTUR PER ORDINEM, SED SECUNDUM VITAE
MERITUM ET SAPIENTIAE DOCTRINAM. ⁵QUIQUE DECANI, SI EX EIS ALIQUA FORTE
QUIS INFLATUS SUPERBIA REPERTUS FUERIT REPREHENSIBILIS, CORREPTUS SEMEL
ET ITERUM ATQUE TERTIO SI EMENDARE NOLUERIT, DEICIATUR, ⁶ET ALTER IN LOCO
EIUS QUI DIGNUS EST SUBROGETUR. ⁷ET DE PRAEPOSITO EADEM CONSTITUIMUS.

1–4   **a.** The disciplinary 'Order of the Monastery'[1] begins here. The chapter treats of the 'deans', who support the abbot in his leadership role by assuming supervision of a ten-man 'deanery'. The division of larger communities into more easily supervised small groups usually imposes itself spontaneously. Thus, in Qumrân there were groups of ten people, and a rota was in operation.[2] The Roman army was organized in ten-man groups. Pachomius (d.346), who had served in the army, divided his large monasteries into groups,[3] and a rota was known.[4] 'Deaneries' with a 'senior' in charge are also known to us from other sources in Egyptian monasticism.[5]

b. Benedict mentions the 'choice' or appointment of the deans three times, and, in doing so, each time uses turns of phrase which occur in the Bible. Scripture relates that Moses appointed persons to help him in leading the people during the journey through the desert, and divided the people up into groups.[6] The Church used to invoke this model at the appointment of presbyters and deacons by the bishop. This *ecclesial* order is clearly the model for the organization of the monastery.[7] Benedict's choice of words in the enumeration of the deans' qualities is, however, also reminiscent of the appointment of the 'seven men' in the Acts of the Apostles.[8] It is clear that in establishing his monastery Benedict was not thinking of structural models from the sphere of politics or the family, but from that of the Bible and the Church: Moses, Christ's apostles, their helpers, the people in the desert, the primitive Church.

c. Benedict's chief concern is the '*spiritual*' qualities of his helpers; there is no regard for precedence conferred by age. Benedict demands from his helpers the same characteristics as are required in the cases of the abbot, priests, deacons and the prior.[9] Thus, the abbot can divide his responsibility and draw others into *co-responsibility* and co-operation. We may assume that, like the 'Master', Benedict envisages two deans in each group of ten monks.[10] Delegation of responsibility is provided for on a wide scale. The task of the deans is, on the one hand, a spiritual one, namely, good example and the individual help of the 'spiritual *Seniores*'; on the other, it is a disciplinary one, such as supervision at the place of work, at reading, in the dormitory or at table, because good order is very important for Benedict. Contemporary conditions, which were often semi-barbaric, could have prompted such a solution.

5–6   This procedure against an *unworthy* person is without parallel in the 'Rule of the Master'. The directives occur again in the chapter on the Prior, this time in a sharper and more tense tone.[11]

7   The author feels drawn to the old, traditional system of the deans, but must adapt to *new developments*. He is brief on the theme of deans, and refers to the office of Prior, which had grown in importance.[12]

NOTES TO CHAPTER 21

1 Title before RM 11. Cf. Introduction, Note 27. RB 21,1: RM 11,4; RB 21,2: RM 11,27–30; RB 21,3–4: RM 11,20–21. In comparison with the 'Rule of the Master', this chapter is kept unusually brief—a sign that the deanship no longer has the same significance as in the time of the Master. 2 1QS 6,3.11. 3 Jerome, praef in Pach Reg 2. 4 Horsiesi, Lib 7. 5 Jerome, ep 22,35; Cassian, Inst 4,17. 6 Dt 1:13–15; Ex 18:21. 7 The Master (RM 11:9–11) draws a parallel between the bishop with his priests and deacons on the one hand, and the abbot and the 'praepositi' (= superiors; cf. RB 65,12.18–21), i.e. deans, on the other. 8 Acts 6: 3.5. 9 Cf. RB 2,4; 62,1; 63,14; 64,2.20; 65,13. 10 They are also called

'(spirituales) seniores', i.e. (spiritual) seniors'; cf. RB 22,3; 23, 1–2; further: 3, 12; 4,50; 27,2; 46,5 ; 48,17; 58,6. **11** → 65,18–22; 23,2. **12** This verse 7, added on as a postscript refers to the office of 'Praepositus',which was introduced only later (RB 65).

CHAPTER 22

HOW MONKS SHALL SLEEP

27 Feb
(28 Feb
Leap
Year)
29 June
29 Oct

1 They shall sleep singly in single beds.

2 They shall receive bed-clothes
which are suitable to the monastic way of life
and are distributed by their abbot.

3 If possible, let all sleep in one place,
but if the large numbers do not allow this,
let them sleep by tens or twenties;
their seniors shall be with them to take care of them.

4 Let a LAMP be LIGHTING in the same cell
all the time
until morning.

Cf. Lk 12:35;
2 Pet 1:19

5 They shall sleep CLOTHED
girded with BELTS or cords
so as not to have their knives at their sides while asleep,
for fear they might wound a sleeper by a dream

Cf. Lk 12:35;
Rev 16:15

6 and so that the monks always be PREPARED.
And when the signal is given
let them get up without delay
and hasten to pass one another out to the Work of God,
with all seriousness however and restraint.

Cf. Lk 12:35–40;
Rev 16:15

7 The younger brethren shall not have their beds side by side,
but interspersed with those of the elders.

8 As they rise for the Work of God
let them gently urge one another on,
because of the excuses of sleepyheads.

CAPUT XXII: QUOMODO DORMIANT MONACHI

¹SINGULI PER SINGULA LECTA DORMIANT. ²LECTISTERNIA PRO MODO CONVERSA-
TIONIS SECUNDUM DISPENSATIONEM ABBATIS SUI ACCIPIANT. ³SI POTEST FIERI
OMNES IN UNO LOCO DORMIANT; SIN AUTEM MULTITUDO NON SINIT, DENI AUT
VICENI CUM SENIORIBUS QUI SUPER EOS SOLLICITI SINT, PAUSENT. ⁴CANDELA
IUGITER IN EADEM CELLA ARDEAT USQUE MANE. ⁵VESTITI DORMIANT ET CINCTI
CINGULIS AUT FUNIBUS, UT CULTELLOS SUOS AD LATUS SUUM NON HABEANT DUM
DORMIUNT, NE FORTE PER SOMNUM VULNERENT DORMIENTEM; ⁶ET UT PARATI SINT
MONACHI SEMPER ET, FACTO SIGNO ABSQUE MORA SURGENTES, FESTINENT INVICEM

SE PRAEVENIRE AD OPUS DEI, CUM OMNI TAMEN GRAVITATE ET MODESTIA.
⁷ADULESCENTIORES FRATRES IUXTA SE NON HABEANT LECTOS, SED PERMIXTI CUM
SENIORIBUS. ⁸SURGENTES VERO AD OPUS DEI INVICEM SE MODERATE COHORTENTUR
PROPTER SOMNULENTORUM EXCUSATIONES.

1–2 The *single bed* was, in Benedict's time in point of fact, a comfortable rarity.[1]
3 The 'cella', that is the small house or cell of the hermit or cenobite,[2] was
valued in ancient monasticism as a privileged place of recollection and for
being on one's own with God. Work in common, the celebration of all the
Hours in community, and the wish to control the inclination to personal
property as well as to bad morals, led at the beginning of the sixth century in
many places to an innovation.[3] At this point, the monastery possesses not only
a common dining room but also a common *sleeping room*, which will later
yield to single rooms (cells) under *one* roof.

4–7 a. Biblical allusions[4] bring to mind the faithful servants, who, like watchmen,
in the silence of the night[5] with 'lighted lamps', 'clothed', 'girt' and 'always
prepared' await the Day of the Lord, which brings the light. They are themselves children of the light[6] and shun the 'works of darkness'.[7] 'Everything' is
'to take place *in the light*': in daylight[8] or in the light of the lamp[9] which burns
until the break of day.—In veiled language,[10] the basic, eschatalogical motive of
monasticism and its relation to Christ is hinted at.—The monks hasten[11] to
the Opus Dei, i.e. to the Office, with 'gravity' or 'dignity' (gravitas); Benedict
often uses the concept of 'dignity'.[12]
b. The directions about the single bed,[13] the burning lamp[14] and about sleeping
fully clothed,[15] are aimed at the protection of chastity.[16] Celibacy and renunciation of unregulated affective relationships follow from the eschatological motive. Benedict is very reserved in these matters.[17]

8 In the same context Benedict urges *brotherly help*.[18] The Rule uses the word
'mutual' (invicem) about eight times in this connection and devotes the closing
chapters[19] to the monks' relationships as brothers. Here the Rule recommends
reserve, as is fitting for 'disciples'. Perhaps Benedict wishes especially to protect
the night silence, without making it an absolute rule, as the 'Master' does.[20]
Brotherly help is given above all by mutual good example.

NOTES TO CHAPTER 22

1 Cf. RM 11,109 (single bed). In the 'Rule of the Master' we find no parallel to verse 2 (bedding). RB
22,1: RM 11,109; RB22,3:RM 11,108; 29,2–4; RB 22,4: RM 29,5–6; RB 22,5: RM 11,111–112; RB 22,6:
RM 11,114; RB 22,7: RM 11,121. → 4,34–40; 8,1–2. 2 Cf. Jerome, praef in Pach Reg 2; → Prol 46;
6,2–5. 3 Cf. VPJur 170: Eugendus (d.510) had the individual small dwellings destroyed after a fire; to
the common dining room there was now added the common sleeping room with single beds. Emperor
Justinian issued regulations concerning the common dormitory with single beds, concerning the good
example of the older monks for the younger ones, and concerning the avoidance of an accident 'while
dreaming' (Nov.5, c.3 of 20 March 535; Nov.133 of 539 and Nov.123,c.36 of 1 May 546). The
similarities, word for word, are unmistakeable. Cf. RF 16. 4 Cf. Lk 12:34–40; Rev 16:15. 5 Cf. RB 42,1;
→ Prol 8–11. 6 → Prol 9; 42,7–9. 7 Cf. Rom 13:12–13; Eph 5: 8–14; 1 Thess 5:5–8. 8 RB 8,4; 41,8. 9
Verse 4. 10 → Prol 8–11 (in Note 53). The 'Master' had the lamp extinguished on occasion (RM 29,6).
11 → 43,3. 12 RB 6,3; 7,60; 42,11; 43,2; 47,4. 13 Verse 1; cf. VPJur 170; RF 23. 14 Verse 6; cf. VPatr
5,5,37. 15 It was not customary in antiquity. 16 Cf. RM 11,118–119. 17 Cf. RB 4,64; 33,4; → 4,62–73;
33,4; 42,8–11; 43,18–19; 58,17–18.24–25. 18 Without parallels in the 'Rule of the Master'. 19 RB 63;
68–72. 20 RB 42,11; RM 30,19.25–26; → 6; 7,56–58.

CHAPTER 23

OF EXCOMMUNICATION FOR FAULTS

28 Feb
(29 Feb
Leap
Year)
30 June
30 Oct

1   If any brother be found to be
     rebellious,
     or disobedient,
     or arrogant,
     or disputatious,
     or to be contrary to the holy Rule in some point,
     and despising the orders of his seniors,

2   he should, according to our Lord's command,   Cf. Mt 18:15–16
     be secretly admonished once and a second time by his seniors.

3   If he do not amend,
     let him be REPROVED publicly before all.   Cf. Mt 18:17; 1 Tim
                                          5:20; 2 Tim 3:6,14

4   If even thus he do not correct himself,
     let him undergo excommunication   Cf. 2 Thess 3:14
     if he understands what a punishment that is.

5   If however he be impudent,
     let him be subjected to physical punishment.

CAPUT XXIII: DE EXCOMMUNICATIONE CULPARUM

¹SI QUIS FRATER CONTUMAX AUT INOBOEDIENS AUT SUPERBUS AUT MURMURANS VEL IN ALIQUO CONTRARIUS SANCTAE REGULAE ET PRAECEPTIS SENIORUM SUORUM CONTEMPTOR REPERTUS FUERIT, ²HIC SECUNDUM DOMINI NOSTRI PRAECEPTUM ADMONEATUR SEMEL ET SECUNDO SECRETE A SENIORIBUS SUIS. ³SI NON EMEN-DAVERIT, OBIURGETUR PUBLICE CORAM OMNIBUS. ⁴SI VERO NEQUE SIC CORREXERIT, SI INTELLEGIT QUALIS POENA SIT, EXCOMMUNICATIONI SUBIACEAT; ⁵SIN AUTEM INPROBUS EST, VINDICATE CORPORALI SUBDATUR.

o   a. In the older monastic Rules there are hardly any *penitential Ordos* as comprehensive as those in the 'Rule of the Master'¹ and in that of Benedict. Basil (d.379) has defaulters warned, because wrong may not be indifferently passed over;² however, Basil does not want to make individual regulations, but declares: 'The timing and form of the correction are a matter for the superiors' judgement, because age and education make a great difference in questions of penance.'³ In the works of Cassian (d.430), too, we find only the rudiments of a penitential Ordo.⁴

b. Benedict's penitential Ordo begins here with the chapters about the *punishments*.⁵ The chapters about the form of satisfaction follow later.⁶ The Master deals with both questions jointly, but in a prolix and confused fashion. He offers, as it were, a collection of material, which connects with the chapters on the pedagogic and spiritual task of the abbot.[7]

1 a. For Benedict, the penitential Ordo is also a matter of *pastoral care for individuals*. It is significant that at the outset he is concerned with the interior dispositions of the penitents.

b. The attitude to the 'holy Rule' is specifically inquired about.[8] This expression is also found in the writings of Caesarius (d.542)[9] and already in the Life of Pachomius (d.346), where however the expression designates the whole monastic way of life: A boy of fourteen, for religious reasons, begins to distance himself from the feasting and riches of his home. During his studies, he already cultivates asceticism, as far as it is possible at that age. Then 'he begins to reflect whether he ought to go to a monastery and bind himself to the *holy Rule*'.[10]

2–3 Benedict adheres to the evangelical and ecclesiastical prescriptions regarding the *correction of a brother*,[11] which provide for an admonition in confidence, one before witnesses, and public correction.[12] The 'Disdascalia of the Apostles' (early third century) warns the bishops to take note of an erring brother's way of life (conversatio), and to warn him according to the Gospel[13] first privately, then before witnesses; because, 'where an exhortation is according to teaching, there also is discipline (a keyword of Benedict's!) and conversion of the erring'.[14]

4 a. Just as Benedict sees a connection between the 'conversion' to monastic life and baptism,[15] so he adopts as the model of the monastic penitential Ordo the penitential Ordo of the Church, which is often practised in the monastery, but, as it were, in miniature, to heal minor or major lapses. After the 'correction'[16] there follows, as a second element '*excommunication*', with its various punitive consequences.[17] It consists in a partial or complete exclusion from community life, not in expulsion from the monastery, which is treated of later.[18] The isolation of a brother is seem as a punishment. Life in community is treasured as a great value. The processes of 'doing penance' and of 'being received back into the community', which are also comparable to the ecclesial penitential Ordo, are discussed later.[19]

b. The 'Didascalia of the Apostles' (early third century) does not admit a refractory member to the community of the Church; here it follows the Gospel.[20] The possibility of 'conversion' remains open: 'If he promises afterwards to do penance (to convert)—just as we also admit the pagans into our assembly, if they wish to convert, promise to do so and proclaim "we believe"; we do this so that they may hear the Word, but in such a way that we practise no fellowship with them, until they receive the seal and are made perfect[21]—so we practise no fellowship with these (sinners), until they display the fruits of conversion . . . '[22] Penitential conversion is seen as analogous to baptismal: 'While all pray for him (the sinner) you (the bishop) lay your hand on him and bring him into the fellowship of the Church . . . ; either through baptism or the laying on of the hand one receives participation in the Holy Spirit.'[23]

c. The ancient ecclesiastical penitential Ordo,[24] the external structures of which have their origins in the Synagogue,[25] has fallen into disuse; for that reason, much in Benedict's penitential Ordo appears *off-putting* today, even though it may be understood that a community must have at its disposal some means to protect itself, and above all that it must concern itself with the healing of its members, if these should err. The community strives, as a circle of Jesus' disciples,[26] to be assembled in the Holy Spirit,[27] and cannot accept evil in its midst.

5 Benedict constantly wishes adaptation to the *individual character*. If the regular proceeding has no prospect of success with a 'rough' character, corporal punishment has to be considered something that was not unusual in those times.[28]

NOTES TO CHAPTER 23

1 RB 23,1–3: RM 12,1–2; RB 23,4–5: RM 14,79–86. 2 RBasRuf 122. He quotes: Mt 18:15–17; 1 Cor 5:2; 2 Cor 7:11. 3 RBasRuf 194. 4 Inst 2,15–16; 4,16. 5 RB 23–30. 6 RB 43–46. 7 RM 12–14. 8 → 1,2; 3,7–11; 4,75; 7,55. 9 RCaesVirg 62; 64. 10 VPach(lat.) 29. 11 Cf.Mt 18:15–17; 1 Tim 5:20. 12 Cf. RBasRuf 16; 122. 13 Mt 18 :15–17. 14 2,38,1–3; 58,9–10 (Note 51). 15 → Prol 3.12–13.22–27; 58,26. 16 Verses 2–3. 17 RB 24–25. 18 RB 28, 6–8. 19 RB 43–46. 20 Didascalia 2,38,2. 21 'Seal' and 'perfection' are designations for the Confirmation which completes a baptism. 22 Didascalia 2,39,6. 23 Didascalia 2,41,2. 24 Cf. Mt 18:15–18; 16:19; Jn 20:23. 25 As punishment for a fraud involving material goods, the Rule of Qumran mentions 'exclusion from the community of purity of the Rabiim for one year' (IQS 6,24) and similar penal provisions for sins of the tongue and spiteful words . . . 26 → Prol 45.50; 6,2–5. 27 → Prol 8–11; 3,1–3; 7,67–70. 28 Various councils imposed corporal punishments, e.g., for clerics who drink, for children instead of excommunication (Vannes,465,c.13; Agde,506,c.41; Epaon,517,c.15). Pachomius (Iud 4) provides for a triple reprimand for those who make difficulties; if they persist, they are to be whipped before the door of the monastery, and to be put fasting on bread and water.

CHAPTER 24

WHAT THE NORM OF EXCOMMUNICATION SHOULD BE

1 Mar
1 July
31 Oct

1 The degree of excommunication or of punishment   Cf. Deut 25:1
   should match the nature of the fault.
2 The nature of faults shall be left to the abbot's judgement.

3 If however some brother be found out in lighter faults,   Cf. 2
   let him be deprived of sharing at table.   Thess 3:14
4 This shall be the treatment for those deprived of
   sharing at table:
   he shall not sing a psalm or antiphon on his own in the oratory,
   nor read a lesson, until he has made satisfaction.
5 He shall receive his food alone, after the meal of the brethren:
6 for instance, if the brethren eat at the sixth hour,
   this brother shall do so at the ninth,
   if the brethren eat at the ninth,
   he shall do so in the evening,
7 until by fitting satisfaction he obtains forgiveness.

CAPUT XXIV: QUALIS DEBET ESSE MODUS EXCOMMUNICATIONIS

¹SECUNDUM MODUM CULPAE, ET EXCOMMUNICATIONIS VEL DISCIPLINAE MENSURA DEBET EXTENDI. ²QUI CULPARUM MODUS IN ABBATIS PENDAT IUDICIO. ³SI QUIS TAMEN FRATER IN LEVIORIBUS CULPIS INVENITUR, A MENSAE PARTICIPATIONE PRIVETUR. ⁴PRIVATI AUTEM A MENSAE CONSORTIO ISTA ERIT RATIO, UT IN ORATORIO PSALMUM AUT ANTEFANAM NON INPONAT, NEQUE LECTIONEM RECITET, USQUE AD SATISFACTIONEM. ⁵REFECTIONEM AUTEM CIBI POST FRATRUM REFECTIONEM SOLUS ACCIPIAT, ⁶UT, SI VERBI GRATIA FRATRES REFICIUNT SEXTA HORA, ILLE FRATER NONA, SI FRATRES NONA, ILLE VESPERA, ⁷USQUE DUM SATISFACTIONE CONGRUA VENIAM CONSEQUATUR.

1–2 The actual gravity of the faults is not the only criterion. There is no automatic process of punishment. The abbot ought always to have the possibility of *proceeding pastorally*.

3 This chapter¹ treats of the 'minor faults'. They, too, need correction.—Lesser and greater *threats of punishment* are numerous in the Rule of Benedict. Although three times shorter than that of the 'Master', it contains twenty seven threats of punishment, the latter only twenty one (A. de Vogüé). In many cases Benedict abbreviates the 'Master's' longwinded text, assigns the

settlement of the individual case to the abbot (which leads to a great flexibility) and ends abruptly with a threat of punishment, instead of bringing forward further arguments and motivations. If the process can be plausibly explained by Benedict's wish for a 'shorter' Rule,[2] yet the many threats are off-putting. However, it must not be forgotten that Benedict is writing in part for uneducated 'primitives' and that ancient monasticism intended to wage a struggle against evil in all its manifestations.[3] This struggle is reflected in Jesus' radical 'No' to evil, clearly witnessed in the Gospel. Thus, Basil (d.379), for instance, emphasizes that not one iota of the Law may be neglected[4] and not a single sin trivialized.[5]

4–7 The punishments which exclude from 'participation' in *community life*, show, as in a negative image, how great a positive value Benedict attaches to the community, for instance to the communal meal and even more to the communal liturgy. Basil (d.379) sees in the Apostle's warning not to consort with a refractory person,[6] a summons to break off sharing a common table with him.[7]

NOTES TO CHAPTER 24

1 RB 24 ,1–2: RM 12,4–7; RB 24,3: RM 13,60; RB 24,4: RM 13,66–67; RB,24,5–6: RM 13,50–52; RB 24,7: RM 13,61; → 44,9–10. Various passages of Benedict's penitential Ordo are reminiscent of a Law of Justinian's of 1 May 546: Nov.123, can.4 (RB 24,3; 44,9) can.5 (RB 24,1; 25,1–2; 28,2). 2 → 73,8–9. 3 → Prol 28. 4 Cf. Matt 5:18. 5 RBasRuf 17. 6 2 Thess 3:14. 7 RBasRuf 16.

CHAPTER 25

OF MORE SERIOUS FAULTS

2 Mar
2 July
1 Nov

1 That brother however who is entangled in the guilt
of a more serious fault,
shall be debarred from table, as well as from
oratory.

2 No one of the brethren shall join his company or   Cf. 2 Thess 3:6,14
converse with him.

3 He is to be alone at the work enjoined him,   Cf. 2 Cor 7:10
continuing in SADNESS AND PENANCE
aware of that frightening decision of the Apostle,
who says:

4 SUCH A ONE IS DELIVERED   1 Cor 5:5
FOR THE DESTRUCTION OF THE FLESH
THAT THE SPIRIT MAY BE SAVED FOR THE DAY OF THE
LORD.

5 He shall take his meal alone,
in the measure and at the time which the Abbot
shall foresee is fitting for him;

6 neither he nor the food that is given him   Cf. Ps 129:8
is to be blessed by anyone passing by.

CAPUT XXV: DE GRAVIORIBUS CULPIS

¹IS AUTEM FRATER QUI GRAVIORIS CULPAE NOXA TENETUR, SUSPENDATUR A MENSA,
SIMUL AB ORATORIO. ²NULLUS EI FRATRUM IN NULLO IUNGATUR CONSORTIO NEC IN
CONLOQUIO. ³SOLUS SIT AD OPUS SIBI INIUNCTUM, PERSISTENS IN PAENITENTIAE
LUCTU, SCIENS ILLAM TERRIBILEM APOSTOLI SENTENTIAM DICENTIS: ⁴TRADITUM
EIUSMODI HOMINEM IN INTERITUM CARNIS, UT SPIRITUS SALVUS SIT IN DIEM
DOMINI. ⁵CIBI AUTEM REFECTIONEM SOLUS PERCIPIAT, MENSURA VEL HORA QUA
PRAEVIDERIT ABBAS EI CONPETERE; ⁶NEC A QUOQUAM BENEDICATUR TRANSEUNTE
NEC CIBUM QUOD EI DATUR.

1–2 **a.** In comparison with the penitential practice of the Church of the time, the
monastic penitential Ordo of Benedict's time[1] punishes even relatively minor
faults as '*grave offences*'. According to Cassian (d.430), 'unauthorized excursions',
'open quarrelling' or 'improper familiarities with women' are thus catego-
rized.[2] While in the Church a penance was often postponed, in the monastery

it was imposed straight away, because the immediate healing of the sinner was desired. On the other hand, the penance did not last as long as in the Church. **b.** A mistaken complicity and fraternization with the one punished can produce the effect, according to Cassian (d.430), that 'his heart becomes more and more hardened', or that he 'feigns' amendment.[3]

3 The whole of a monk's life should be a continuous Lent', it says in the chapter on Lent.[4] In fact the monastic state was put in the same category as that of the penitents. For the monk, *readiness to convert* is a basic virtue.[5] For the 'salutary grief' mentioned here, Basil cites the Apostle Paul.[6] 'For godly grief produces a repentance that leads to salvation.'[7]

4 In Benedict's quotation from Paul,[8] the words 'deliver ... to Satan' are missing; either Benedict wanted to tone down the text for the purpose of a merely monastic excommunication, or he is following a different reading extant at the time.[9] The transference of the *major Church penance* to the situation inside the monastery is in any case problematic.

5–6 Exceptionally, Benedict goes into *detailed regulations*. The punishment consists in exclusion from the community.

NOTES TO CHAPTER 25

1 RB 25,1: RM 13,41–42; 62; RB 25,2–3: RM 13,43–45; RB 25,5: RM 13,50–53; RB 25,6: RM 13,46–47. 2 Inst 4,16,3. 3 Inst 2,16. 4 RB 49,1. 5 → Prol 2.3 6 2 Cor 7:10. 7 RBasRuf 50; → 7,59–61; 31,3–7; 72,1–3. 8 1 Cor 5:5. 9 Cf. on the other hand: Cassian, Inst 2,16. The 'Master' has no parallels; → Prol 28 (in Note 82).

CHAPTER 26

OF THOSE WHO WITHOUT PERMISSION
HAVE DEALINGS WITH THE EXCOMMUNICATED

3 Mar 1   Should any brother presume, without the abbot's   Cf. 2 Thess 3:6
3 July   permission,
2 Nov   to join an excommunicated brother
            in any way,
            or speak to him,
            or send him a message,
       2   he shall incur a similar sanction of excommunication.

CAPUT XXVI: DE HIS QUI SINE IUSSIONE IUNGUNT SE
EXCOMMUNICATIS

¹SI QUIS FRATER PRAESUMPSERIT SINE IUSSIONE ABBATIS FRATRI EXCOMMUNICATO
QUOLIBET MODO SE IUNGERE AUT LOQUI CUM EO VEL MANDATUM EI DIRIGERE,
²SIMILEM SORTIATUR EXCOMMUNICATIONIS VINDICTAM.

1–2   This chapter, with its severe ring, treats of the *accomplice* who confirms the
      brother who has been punished in his wrong attitude,¹ not of a brother who is
      acting in a pastoral sense.²

NOTES TO CHAPTER 26

1 Cf RM 13,54–56; → 25,1–2. 2 → 27,2–4

CHAPTER 27

WHAT THE ABBOT'S CARE
FOR THE EXCOMMUNICATED SHOULD BE

4 Mar
4 July
3 Nov

1   Since THEY THAT ARE IN HEALTH NEED NOT A PHYSICIAN,   Mt 9:12;
    BUT THEY THAT ARE ILL,   Lk 5:31
    the abbot must look after erring brethren
    with great concern.

2   And so, as a wise physician, he must use every remedy.
    He should send in *senpectae*,
    that is older, wise brethren

3   who may as it were secretly console the vacillating brother   2 Cor 2:7
    and move him to humility and satisfaction,
    and CONSOLE HIM,
    LEST HE BE SWALLOWED UP WITH OVERMUCH SORROW.

4   Rather, as the Apostle also says: 2 Cor 2:8
    LET CHARITY BE CONFIRMED TOWARDS HIM
    and let all pray for him.

5   For the abbot must exercise the greatest concern
    and move fast
    most tactfully and painstakingly
    lest he lose any one of the sheep entrusted to him.

6   Let him realize
    that he has undertaken
    the care of sickly souls
    not a violent rule of the healthy.

7   And let him fear the prophet's threat   Ez 34:3-4
    through which God is saying:
    WHAT YOU SAW WAS FAT, YOU TOOK,
    AND WHAT WAS WEAK
    YOU THREW ASIDE.

8   And let him copy the example of love of   Cf. Jn 10:11; Mt 18:12;
      THE GOOD SHEPHERD,   cf. Lk 15:4
    who LEFT THE NINETY-NINE SHEEP ON THE HILLS,
    and went away
    TO SEEK THE ONE SHEEP WHICH HAD STRAYED.

9   He took so much compassion on its weakness   Lk 15:4; cf. Mt 18:12;
    that he saw fit   Heb 4:15

to PLACE it ON his sacred SHOULDERS
and so return it to the flock.

CAPUT XXVII: QUALITER DEBEAT ABBAS SOLLICITUS ESSE CIRCA EXCOMMUNICATOS

[1]OMNI SOLLICITUDINE CURAM GERAT ABBAS CIRCA DELINQUENTES FRATRES, QUIA NON EST OPUS SANIS MEDICUS, SED MALE HABENTIBUS. [2]ET IDEO UTI DEBET OMNI MODO UT SAPIENS MEDICUS: INMITTERE SENPECTAS, ID EST SENIORES SAPIENTES FRATRES, [3]QUI QUASI SECRETE CONSOLENTUR FRATREM FLUCTUANTEM ET PROVOCENT AD HUMILITATIS SATISFACTIONEM ET CONSOLENTUR EUM NE ABUNDANTIORI TRISTITIA ABSORBEATUR, [4]SED, SICUT AIT ITEM APOSTOLUS: CONFIRMETUR IN EO CARITAS, ET ORETUR PRO EO AB OMNIBUS. [5]MAGNOPERE ENIM DEBET SOLLICITUNDINEM GERERE ABBAS ET OMNI SAGACITATE ET INDUSTRIA CURRERE, NE ALIQUAM DE OVIBUS SIBI CREDITIS PERDAT. [6]NOVERIT ENIM SE INFIRMARUM CURAM SUSCEPISSE ANIMARUM, NON SUPER SANAS TYRANNIDEM. [7]ET METUAT PROPHETAE COMMINATIONEM PER QUAM DICIT DEUS: QUOD CRASSUM VIDEBATIS ADSUMEBATIS, ET QUOD DEBILE ERAT PROICIEBATIS. [8]ET PASTORIS BONI PIUM IMITETUR EXEMPLUM, QUI, RELICTIS NONAGINTA NOVEM OVIBUS IN MONTIBUS, ABIIT UNAM OVEM QUAE ERRAVERAT QUAERERE. [9]CUIUS INFIRMITATI IN TANTUM CONPASSUS EST, UT EAM IN SACRIS HUMERIS SUIS DIGNARETUR INPONERE ET SIC REPORTARE AD GREGEM.

o   Apart from some suggestions of the 'Master',[1] this chapter and the following are the work of Benedict, and bear witness to his pastoral zeal and sensitivity. Several times he exhorts the abbot to behave with *pastoral care* towards the defaulters, in accordance with the Gospel. The emphasis is not on punishment, but on therapeutic help: 'Overcome evil with good'.[2] Benedict offers many possibilities of positive help, which are practically unknown in the 'Rule of the Master'.

1-4 **a.** The image of the *physician*[3] reflects the traits of Christ. Ignatius of Antioch (d.*c*.110) already called Christ 'the physician for body and soul'.[4] Origen (d.253) loves this image.[5] Basil (d.379) would like to see practised 'the goodness of a father or physician towards an ailing son,' especially if 'the treatment' should prove to be 'painful or severe'.[6] In the 'Lives of the Fathers', a monk who succeeds in advising and encouraging a confrère who is passing through a crisis because of sexual difficulties, is described as a 'wise physician'.[7] In a similar case, a monk is also called a 'wise physician' because he 'applied a healing plaster taken from the holy Scriptures on the soul' of a brother who was in despair and upset by the unenlightened severity of another monk, 'by explaining that the possibility of doing penance existed for those who turned to God in true love'.[8]

b. The 'Didascalia of the Apostles' (early 3rd cent.) also quotes the words 'of our Saviour . . . against the murmuring' of the Pharisees: ' "Those who are well have no need of a physician, but those who are *sick*." If people are found guilty of sin, and sick, concern yourselves with them, associate with them, care for them, speak with them, console them, receive them and lead them to repentance.'[9]

c. The sending in of 'senpectae' is an innovation on the 'Rule of the Master'.[10] In order to make possible fruitful and *individually adapted pastoral care*, the abbot delegates a part of his pastoral task, avails himself of the special charismata of others and shares the responsibility with them.

d. The punishment should not cause 'too great sadness'.[11] Cassian (d.430) speaks of a hopelessness which 'does not lead the offender to amend his life or correct his faults, but allows him to founder in *deadly despair*'.[12] The punishment must not damage the personality, but must have a medicinal character. Cassian continues by saying that salutary grief is 'humble' and stems 'from the love of God'.[13]

e. Benedict recommends this love straight away,[14] because the healing powers of love are obviously more important for him than any punishment. In this, he sees the *prayer of the brethren* as important. The prayer of the community for the penitents was an important part of the penitential Ordo in the early Church.[15]

5–6 a. Again Benedict warns the abbot. He must be a *pastor of souls*,[16] and like a shepherd, actively go searching on his own initiative. The Master has it the other way round: the offenders must seek out the abbot and plead for mercy.[17] Benedict will mention this reverse way later.[18]

b. Benedict warns the abbot against an authoritarian, tyrannical use of power. Later, he also comes to speak of the *misuse of power*.[19]

7–9 a. Partiality is particularly odious to Benedict.[20] The threats of Ezechiel against *bad shepherds* tend to be referred to the abbot in monastic literature.[21] The warning not to 'cast away' the 'weak' seems to put into question the (definitive) excommunication of offenders. The reflection that pastoral care does not aim to exclude or condemn anybody, is often found in monastic writings.[22]

b. Benedict expects, however, that the caring love of the 'good shepherd' will bear positive fruit. Regard for the weak does not dispense from initiatives to heal them. We already find this train of thought in Origen (d.253); he protests against members of the Church being left defenceless by their pastors in face of dangers: 'But those presiding over the Churches do that. They do not reflect that all we who believe form *one* body, have one God, who brings us together into one and supports us, namely Christ, for whose body you, who preside over the Church, are the eye. Therefore you must survey everything circumspectly, foreseeing also what is to come. You are a shepherd, you see the Lord's sheep, all unsuspecting, approaching an abyss . . . Thus you forget the Lord's mystery: he left the ninety-nine (angels) in heaven, to come to earth to find the *one* lost sheep (mankind) and carry it on his shoulders to heaven. Should we, in our care for the sheep, neglect completely to follow the example of the shepherd, our teacher?'[23] Pastoral care is no idyll. The 'one who presides' must be the *'eye' of the community*, look out over wide horizons and think ahead. In all things he has to orientate himself by Christ.

c. An account from the 'Lives of the Jura Fathers' illustrates the pastoral care of the abbot in respect of two 'wavering brothers':[24] Abbot Lupicinus (died *c*. 480) was praying one night in the oratory. 'Two brothers enter the oratory, having agreed to meet there', in order to discuss how they can run away from the monastery under cover of darkness. They do not notice the abbot, who suddenly speaks loudly out of the darkness: 'At least give me the parting kiss!'

They start up in fright. 'The holy man, however, addresses each by name, stretches out his hand, takes them affectionately by the chin, and kisses them. Then he says no more, but kneels down and, in his fatherly love, reaches for the weapon of prayer.' Both call on Christ for forgiveness and return to their beds, subdued and full of remorse, without any mention having been made of a further penance or punishment, for 'a loving father saw what a severe punishment for them their own humiliation was'.[25] When the healing powers of love and prayer are effective, *punishment becomes superfluous*.

d. Following the example of the 'Good Shepherd', the monks of old practised 'compassion'[26] beyond and outside the circle of their own brethren. A caring fellow-feeling and a religiously motivated 'sympathy' is applicable to all. In this regard, monks are quite often put on their guard against considering themselves better than people 'in the world'.

NOTES TO CHAPTER 27

1 RB 27,1: RM 14,12; RB27,4: RM 15,19–27; RB 27,8–9: RM 14,7–8. 2 Cf. Rom 12:21; → 4,20–33. 3 → 2,1–3.26–29; 28; 46,5–6; 64,12–15. 4 Ignatius, Eph 7,2. 5 Lev Hom 7,1–2; 8,1–4. 6 RBasRuf 23. 7 VPatr 5,5,4. 8 VPatr 5,10,85; → 4,55–58. 9 Didascalia 2,40. 10 From the Greek loan-word (Sympekte means 'playmate', from sym-paizein) Benedict wrongly deduces the Latin 'sen-iores' (elders) (B.Steidlc). 11 2 Cor 2:7. 12 Inst 9,11; → 7,59–61; 25,3; 31,3–7; 72,1–3. 13 Inst 9,11. 14 Verse 4. The quotation is lacking in the 'Master'. 15 → 23,4(in Note 23) 28,1–5; 44,1–3.4–5. 16 → 2,31–32.37–40 4,41–50. 51–54; 21,1–4; 23,1; 27; 28,1–5; 31,3–7; 41,5; 44,0.6–8; 46,5–6; 60,1–7; 62,2–7; 64,12–15. 17 RM 14,3–19. 18 RB 46,3. 19 → 65,1–10. 20 → 2,16–20; 34,1–2. 21 For instance in the contemporary RF (37), in which other warnings, valid for the pastors of the Church, are also applied to the abbot; → 1,2. The Ezechiel quotation is very free. 22 Cf Mt 6:12; 18,21–22; John 8:7 → 3,4–6 (in Note 9). 23 Origen, Ies Nave Hom 7,6. 24 Verse 3. 25 VPJur 79–81. 26 Verse 9 ('compassus'), → 28,1–5; 31,3–7.

CHAPTER 28

OF THOSE WHO, THOUGH OFTEN CORRECTED, DO NOT WISH TO AMEND

5 Mar
5 July
4 Nov

1 If any brother be frequently corrected for whatever fault,
if even excommunicated has not amended,
let a stiffer rebuke be given him,
that is let them proceed against him
with the punishment of rods.

2 But if even thus he do not amend,   Cf. 1 Tim 3:6
or perhaps—which God forbid—
CARRIED AWAY WITH PRIDE even wishes to defend what he did,
then let the abbot act the wise physician:

3 if he has applied poultices,
the ointments of exhortations,
the tonics of the divine Scriptures,
if in the last resort
the cautery of excommunication and of beatings with the rod,

4 and if now he sees
that all the pains he has taken
produce no result,
then let him bring on what is greater—
his own prayer and that of all—

5 so that the Lord who can do all things   Cf. Mt 19:26;
may heal the sick brother.   Phil 2:12

6 But if he be not cured even in this way,   1 Cor 5:13;
then let the abbot use the amputation knife,   cf. Mt 5:29–30
as the Apostle says:
PUT AWAY THE EVIL ONE FROM AMONG YOURSELVES

7 and again: 1 Cor 7:15
IF THE UNBELIEVER DEPART, LET HIM DEPART,

8 lest *one* diseased sheep infect the whole flock.

CAPUT XXVIII: DE HIS QUI SAEPIUS CORREPTI EMENDARE NOLUERINT

¹SI QUIS FRATER FREQUENTER CORREPTUS PRO QUALIBET CULPA, SI ETIAM
EXCOMMUNICATUS NON EMENDAVERIT, ACRIOR EI ACCEDAT CORREPTIO, ID EST UT
VERBERUM VINDICTA IN EUM PROCEDANT. ²QUOD SI NEC ITA CORREXERIT, AUT
FORTE—QUOD ABSIT—IN SUPERBIA ELATUS ETIAM DEFENDERE VOLUERIT OPERA

SUA, TUNC ABBAS FACIAT QUOD SAPIENS MEDICUS: ³SI EXHIBUIT FOMENTA, SI UNGUENTA ADHORTATIONUM, SI MEDICAMINA SCRIPTURARUM DIVINARUM, SI AD ULTIMUM USTIONEM EXCOMMUNICATIONIS VEL PLAGARUM VIRGAE, ⁴ET IAM SI VIDERIT NIHIL SUAM PRAEVALERE INDUSTRIAM, ADHIBEAT ETIAM, QUOD MAIUS EST, SUAM ET OMNIUM FRATRUM PRO EO ORATIONEM, ⁵UT DOMINUS QUI OMNIA POTEST OPERETUR SALUTEM CIRCA INFIRMUM FRATREM. ⁶QUOD SI NEC ISTO MODO SANATUS FUERIT, TUNC IAM UTATUR ABBAS FERRO ABSCISIONIS, UT AIT APOSTOLUS: AUFERTE MALUM EX VOBIS; ⁷ET ITERUM INFIDELIS SI DISCEDIT, DISCEDAT, ⁸NE UNA OVIS MORBIDA OMNEM GREGEM CONTAGIET.

1–5   **a.** This chapter on *backsliders* is also directed primarily to the abbot and recommends to him, in a way typical for Benedict,¹ all conceivable pastoral means of healing, even though thoroughly disapproving of arrogance. Basil (d.379) also speaks of the backsliders and advises that 'the true roots of guilt be cut out', that is, that 'healing be carried out with opposite and counteracting means'. Thus, in the case of 'persistent quarrels', their root, 'arrogance', should be treated by the offenders taking on 'very humble services'.²
b. For the case of insubordination, too, the abbot should first employ all pastoral care. Even the punishments³ must have medicinal character (in contrast to what we find in the 'Master'). Parallel expressions to the medical ones Benedict uses are to be found already in the writings of Origen (d.253), specifically following his words of warning for pastors.⁴ For Origen, Jesus himself is *the* physician; he applies a '*logotherapy*': 'Jesus, the physician, is at the same time the Word of God. Thus, he prepares medicines for his patients not from the juices of herbs, but from the mysteries of words . . . word-medicines.'⁵
c. The words about the 'experienced' or '*wise physician*'⁶ are applied to the Apostle Paul by Cassian (d.430). He is regarded as a 'spiritual physician', who seeks to cure the weaknesses of those entrusted to him by his mild and attractive word-therapy.⁷ The Word of God has a healing power. It blots out sin.
d. Benedict's texts about the *medical skill* of the abbot have points of contact with the imagery of many ecclesiastical texts, e.g. with the 'Didascalia of the Apostles' (early 3rd cent.), which warns the bishop:⁸ 'Therefore, heal all sinners like a sympathetic physician, employ all your skill and bring healing, in order to preserve their lives. Do not be ready to amputate members from the Church, but use the word as bandages, and mild reprimands and the plaster of prayer. For when an ulcer eats deep into the flesh, and the latter is decomposing, then treat it and even it out with salutary medicines. However, if it smells badly, then clean it with a cauterizing agent, that is, with the word of reproof. But if the flesh begins to swell, scrape it off and make it even again with an astringent medicine, that is, by the threat of judgement. If it is a cancerous ulcer, then burn it out with a cauterizing iron, that is, impose many fasts, and thus lance and clean the septic ulcer. However, if the cancer spreads and survives the cauterizing iron also, then come to the conclusion that the limb is gangrenous; confer with the physicians and reflect at length; then amputate that stinking limb, lest it destroy the whole body. Thus, do not be too quick to amputate, do not be in too much of a hurry to fetch a many-toothed saw, but first use the scalpel and lance the ulcer, that the cause of the hidden malady

may come to light, and it may become obvious what the sore is like inside, so that the whole body may remain free of pain. But if you see that a person is not doing penance and that there is no hope for him, then, in profound sadness, cut him off and throw him out of the community.'

e. As pastor[9] the abbot has to resort to the measures suited to individual cases. In the Jura monasteries too the rule prevailed that the abbot should first try all other means, a 'reprimand', or, when someone humbles himself, 'soothing words', and that he ought not to 'carry out surgery' exclusively or immediately.[10] The most important medicine, however, is *prayer*,[11] because healing comes from the Lord.

6–8 a. For the (definitive) exclusion from the monastic community[12] Benedict uses the harsh image of 'amputation', presumably thinking of those words of the Lord, according to which it is better to chop off 'a limb' than to allow the whole body to go to its destruction.[13]

b. Basil and Augustine have also concerned themselves with the question of the elimination of members who no longer share the spirit of a Christian community. For Basil (d.379), the 'relapsed' are above all arrogant and envious instigators of discord.[14] According to the Rule of the Gospel, an 'unrepentant sinner' is to be dealt with as follows: 'If he refuses to listen even to the Church, let him be to you as a Gentile and a tax collector.'[15] Augustine (d.430) wants to have the ecclesiastical procedure adhered to, with repeated warnings before witnesses,[16] before punishment by the superior and finally, in the case of obstinate resistance, '*expulsion*' are resorted to. 'Such a measure is not cruel; on the contrary, it stems from mercy; one individual should not ruin many others by his example, which is as contagious as the plague.'[17]

c. The example of the 'tainted sheep' is already cited by Origen (d.253) in the well-known passage on ecclesiastical superiors, who ought to act like shepherds and doctors.[18] As in a vision of the future, Origen describes in the continuation of this passage his own fate, so undeserved as it was. At the same time, his words are an unprecedented testimony for the Church and for himself. The fact that the Church later outlawed this very man is a warning against disproportionate *ecclesiastical measures*. Origen wrote: 'We do not wish to say that someone should depart because of a minor fault. If, however, someone is warned and corrected once, twice and three times because of his offence, without showing a sign of improvement, then we have to apply medical skill. If a hardened tumor does not shrink, even when we have anointed the spot with oil, and tried to heal it with plasters and soften it up with ointments, the only cure remaining is amputation. For thus says the Lord: "If your right hand causes you to sin, cut it off and throw it away!"[19] Does perhaps the hand of our body wish to seduce us, or does the Gospel say of this bodily hand, "Cut it off and throw it away!"? No, Jesus' words mean this: If I, who seem to be your right hand, who am called a presbyter and who have the task of proclaiming the word of God, if I should offend in any way against the ecclesiastical order and against the rule of the Gospel, so that I should become a seducer of you, the Church, then let the Church as a whole through its spiritually inspired, common decision (consensus) cut off me, its right hand, and throw me away.'[20]

NOTES TO CHAPTER 28

1 Only a few hints are to be found in the 'Rule of the Master' RB 28,1: RM 13,69; 14,87; RB 28,2–5:RM 15,19–27; RB 28,6–8: RM 13,70–73. **2** RBasRuf 22. **3** For corporal punishments: → 23,5 (in Note 28); 30,2–3. **4** → 27,7–9 (in Note 24): Ies Nave Hom 7,6. **5** Origen, Lev Hom 8,1. **6** → 27,1–4. **7** Inst 10,7; → 4,55–58. **8** 2,41,3–9. **9** → 2,31–32; 27,5–6; 41,5; 46,5–6. **10** VPJur 85–86. **11** Verses 4–5; → 23,4 (in Note 23); 27,1–4.7–9; 44,1–3.4–5. **12** Benedict quotes 1 Cor 5:13 in support of this, whereas he had cited 1 Cor 5:5 for the mere exclusion from the actions of community life (RB 25,4), although in Paul the context is identical. **13** Mt 5:29–30. **14** RBasRuf 25. **15** Mt 18: 17; RBasRuf 73. **16** Mt 18:15–18. **17** Praec 4,8–9. **18** → 27,7–9 (Ies Nave Hom 7,6). **19** Mt 5:30. **20** Ies Nave Hom 7,6.

CHAPTER 29

WHETHER BRETHREN WHO LEAVE THE MONASTERY SHOULD BE RECEIVED BACK AGAIN

6 Mar
6 July
5 Nov

1 Should a brother who leaves the monastery through his own
fault wish to come back,
let him first promise a full amendment
of the fault which led him to leave.

2 And so let him be received in the last place,
so that in this way his humility can be tested.

3 Should he go off again,
let him be received back in this way up to a third time,
knowing that after that
every avenue of return is closed for him.

CAPUT XXIX: SI DEBEANT FRATRES EXEUNTES DE MONASTERIO ITERUM RECIPI

¹FRATER QUI PROPRIO VITIO EGREDITUR DE MONASTERIO, SI REVERTI VOLUERIT, SPONDEAT PRIUS OMNEM EMENDATIONEM PRO QUO EGRESSUS EST, ²ET SIC IN ULTIMO GRADU RECIPIATUR, UT EX HOC EIUS HUMILITAS CONPROBETUR. ³QUOD SI DENUO EXIERIT, USQUE TERTIO ITA RECIPIATUR, IAM POSTEA SCIENS OMNEM SIBI REVERSIONIS ADITUM DENEGARI.

1–2 Even after a voluntary, culpable *withdrawal*, there still remains, according to the Gospel,¹ the possibility of pardon and return. Benedict, however, going further than the 'Master', demands a promise of a change of heart, and names humility as a decisive sign of the rediscovered monastic vocation.² Basil (d.379) recommends humility and the taking on of the most modest duties as compensating for faults committed.³ Pachomius (d.346) speaks of the loss of one's former rank.⁴

3 As a reason for pardon being offered *three times*, the 'Master'⁵ gives the three warnings of defaulters required by the Gospel.⁶ Benedict passes over this artificial reasoning, but stays with the number three as a rule of discretion. When Benedict rules out a later return, that does not mean that no ecclesial forgiveness of the guilt was possible.

NOTES TO CHAPTER 29

1 Cf. Mt 18:25–31; → 27,7–9. 2 → 7. 3 RBasRuf 22. 4 Praec 136. 5 RB 29,3: RM 64,1–4. 6 Cf. Mt 18:15–17; → 23,2–3; 28,6–8.

CHAPTER 30

HOW BOYS UNDER AGE ARE TO BE CORRECTED

1 Every age and mind
should have its own standards.

2 And therefore
as often as children or juniors
or those who cannot understand too well
how great a punishment excommunication is,

3 such as these, when they commit faults
shall have heavier fasts inflicted on them,
or be restrained with sharp beatings,
so that they may be healed.

CAPUT XXX: DE PUERIS MINORI AETATE QUALITER CORRIPIANTUR

¹OMNIS AETAS VEL INTELLECTUS PROPRIAS DEBET HABERE MENSURAS. ²IDEOQUE QUOTIENS PUERI VEL ADULESCENTIORES AETATE, AUT QUI MINUS INTELLEGERE POSSUNT, QUANTA POENA SIT EXCOMMUNICATIONIS, ³HII TALES DUM DELINQUUNT, AUT IEIUNIIS NIMIIS AFFLIGANTUR AUT ACRIS VERBERIBUS COERCEANTUR, UT SANENTUR.

1 Benedict establishes a maxim about adaptation to the *individual* character. He formulates more briefly and more generally than the 'Master',[1] who refers only to 'children up to the age of fifteen years'. The 'Master' wants corporal punishment excluded after the fifteenth year of age,[2] because it is not the body or bodily members which are the source of faults, but the heart.

2–3 At the end of the penal code, the *medicinal* character of every punishment is again referred to.[3]

NOTES TO CHAPTER 30

1 RM 14,79–86. 2 For 'youthful lack of understanding' (Pachomius, Iud 13) the Master permits strokes, otherwise however, exclusion, except in cases of theft or criminal behaviour (RM 14,89); → 23,5 (in Note 28). 3 → 28,1–5.

CHAPTER 31

OF THE MONASTERY'S CELLARER:
WHAT TYPE OF PERSON HE SHOULD BE

8 Mar   1   There shall be CHOSEN from the community   Cf. 1 Tim 3:2;
8 July   as the monastery's cellarer   Is 42:2; cf. Acts 6:5
7 Nov

a wise person,
of mature character
SOBER,
not a gross eater,
not carried away by pride,
not a TROUBLE MAKER,
not scornful
not sluggish
not a spendthrift,

2   but God-fearing.
He shall be like a father to the whole community.

3   He shall look after everything.
4   Let him do nothing without a direction from the abbot.
5   Let him keep to his orders.
6   Let him not grieve the brethren.
7   Should any brother perhaps
unreasonably demand some things from him,
let him not contemptuously sadden him,
but with good sense and humility
let him refuse the person's wrong request.

8   LET HIM KEEP GUARD OVER HIS SOUL   Tob 1:12 (Lat.);
always mindful of the apostle's saying: 1 Tim 3:13
that HE WHO WILL HAVE FULFILLED HIS OFFICE WELL
WILL ACQUIRE A GOOD POSITION FOR HIMSELF.

9   Let him take care of   Cf. Mt 18:5; 25:35
THE SICK, THE CHILDREN, THE GUESTS AND THE POOR
with total commitment,
knowing without a doubt
that he will be answerable for all of these
on the day of JUDGEMENT.

10 Let him look on all the utensils of the monastery   Cf. Zech 14:20
     and on the entire property
     as if on the CONSECRATED VESSELS OF THE ALTAR.

11 He shall not let slide any business as if unimportant.

12 Let him not put his mind to avarice
     nor be a spendthrift
     and a squanderer of the monastery's property,
     but let him do everything with due measure
     and in accordance with the abbot's orders.

9 Mar   13 Above all let him have humility,   Cf. Eph 4:29
9 July   and to the person to whom he has nothing to give,
8 Nov   let him offer a friendly reply,

14 as it is written: Ecclus 18:17
     A KIND WORD IS BETTER THAN THE BEST GIFT.

15 He should have under his care
     everything which the abbot shall have committed to him;
     he shall not presume on those areas
     which the abbot shall have forbidden him.

16 He shall offer the brethren   Mt 18:6; 25:40
     the regular allowance
     without any arrogance or delay,
     so that they be not scandalized,
     remembering the divine word
     about what is in store for the person
     THAT SHALL SCANDALIZE ONE OF THE LITTLE ONES.

17 If the community be larger,
     let assistants be given him,
     so that helped by them
     he himself may, with a quiet mind,
     carry out the office assigned him.

18 Things to be given out   Cf. Acts 2:45
     and things to be asked for,
     shall be given out and asked for
     at appropriate times,

19 so that in the HOUSE OF GOD   Cf. Ps 135:2;
     nobody be disturbed or distressed.   Zech 14:21

CAPUT XXXI: DE CELLARARIO MONASTERII QUALIS SIT

'CELLARARIUS MONASTERII ELEGATUR DE CONGREGATIONE SAPIENS, MATURIS MORIBUS, SOBRIUS, NON MULTUM EDAX, NON ELATUS, NON TURBULENTUS, NON INIURIOSUS, NON TARDUS, NON PRODIGUS, 'SED TIMENS DEUM; QUI OMNI CONGREGATIONI SIT SICUT PATER. 'CURAM GERAT DE OMNIBUS. 'SINE IUSSIONE ABBATIS NIHIL FACIAT. 'QUAE IUBENTUR CUSTODIAT. 'FRATRES NON CONTRISTET. 'SI QUIS FRATER AB EO FORTE ALIQUA INRATIONABILITER POSTULAT, NON SPERNENDO EUM CONTRISTET, SED RATIONABILITER CUM HUMILITATE MALE PETENTI DENEGET. 'ANIMAM SUAM CUSTODIAT, MEMOR SEMPER ILLUD APOS-TOLICUM, QUIA QUI BENE MINISTRAVERIT, GRADUM BONUM SIBI ADQUIRIT. 'INFIRMORUM, INFANTUM, HOSPITUM PAUPERUMQUE CUM OMNI SOLLICITUDINE CURAM GERAT, SCIENS SINE DUBIO, QUIA PRO HIS OMNIBUS IN DIE IUDICII RATIONEM REDDITURUS EST. 'OMNIA VASA MONASTERII CUNCTAMQUE SUBSTAN-TIAM AC SI ALTARIS VASA SACRATA CONSPICIAT. "NIHIL DUCAT NEGLEGENDUM. "NEQUE AVARITIAE STUDEAT NEQUE PRODIGUS SIT ET STIRPATOR SUBSTANTIAE MONASTERII, SED OMNIA MENSURATE FACIAT ET SECUNDUM IUSSIONEM ABBATIS. "HUMILITATEM ANTE OMNIA HABEAT, ET CUI SUBSTANTIA NON EST QUOD TRIBUATUR, SERMO RESPONSIONIS PORRIGATUR BONUS, "UT SCRIPTUM EST: SERMO BONUS SUPER DATUM OPTIMUM. "OMNIA QUAE EI INIUNXERIT ABBAS, IPSA HABEAT SUB CURA SUA; A QUIBUS EUM PROHIBUERIT, NON PRAESUMAT. "FRATRIBUS CONSTITUTAM ANNONAM SINE ALIQUO TYFO VEL MORA OFFERAT, UT NON SCANDALIZENTUR, MEMOR DIVINI ELOQUII, QUID MEREATUR QUI SCANDALIZAVERIT UNUM DE PUSILLIS. "SI CONGREGATIO MAIOR FUERIT, SOLACIA EI DENTUR, A QUIBUS ADIUTUS ET IPSE AEQUO ANIMO IMPLEAT OFFICIUM SIBI COMMISSUM. "HORIS CONPETENTIBUS ET DENTUR QUAE DANDA SUNT ET PETANTUR QUAE PETENDA SUNT, "UT NEMO PERTURBETUR NEQUE CONTRISTETUR IN DOMO DEI.

o   From thinking about the means of healing the soul[1] Benedict moves on to thinking about the needs of the body, about food and the relationship to mate-rial things, to their *administration* and to related questions of the daily routine.[2] It will become apparent that material questions, too, are approached in a spiri-tual perspective.

1–2   a. The 'cellarer', model and pattern for other office-holders, is the person charged[3] by the abbot to administer material goods. He looks after table, kitchen, cellar and storeroom.

b. The title and office are traditional from the time of Pachomius (d.346); Benedict takes over a great deal from the 'Master',[4] without making as many rules as he does. For Benedict, the basic attitude is more important. The 'Master' starts from the care of the Father in heaven, who places the whole earth at the disposal of his creatures, and especially everything necessary at the disposal of his servants.[5] The cellarer is the steward of these gifts of the heavenly Father.[6] Benedict indeed compares the cellarer with a '*father*', a designation which is otherwise reserved for the abbot,[7] who deputizes for the place of Christ.[8] The chapter on the cellarer thus resembles in many respects the second chapter on the abbot.[9] Like the abbot, the cellarer is a 'father', but in the mate-rial sector and subordinate to the abbot.

c. Benedict repeatedly speaks of the qualities of character that he expects in the cellarer. They are taken from the chapter on the 'Instruments of the spiritual art',[10] from the exhortations to the deacons in the Pastoral Epistles,[11] and from the prophetic image of the Servant of God.[12] Thus, the monastic *understanding of service* shows itself as spiritually, ecclesially and biblically inspired.

3–7 a. *Care* (cura)[13] for things and people, especially for those in need of help, is the dominant theme of this chapter and the following ones. Care of the brethren is for this reason especially importunate, because they do not have private means at their disposal.[14]

b. The exhortation 'not to grieve the brethren' and also not to 'offend' or 'turn away contemptuously' an 'unreasonable' petitioner,[15] which is without parallel in the 'Rule of the Master', gives evidence of Benedict's respect for the individual, who should receive a negative decision 'only accompanied by the reasons for it'. It shows his *humanity* and sensitivity for the feelings of others. Sadness should not reign in the monastery, and no one should feel weighed down or depressed. In the following chapters, this motif is echoed especially often.[16] Human realities are taken seriously. Feeling down, depressions, being out of sorts, 'black moods' occur only too frequently. A Christian, however, must go the paschal way[17] from fear and sadness to joy and peace. He tries to achieve freedom of heart,[18] which ought not allow itself to be dominated by moods.

c. An ancient Father was asked what was to be done when another, despite being reprimanded, did not make good a wrong, so that the former could not stop thinking of the wrong suffered. 'The venerable Father answered: "Get rid of these thoughts! Do not grieve your brother, for you are a *monk*!" '[19]

d. '*Sadness*' engrosses a person 'spiritually to too great a degree', says Basil (d.379).[20] In common with Paul[21] he distinguishes a 'sadness willed by God', which 'leads to conversion and salvation', and a 'worldly sadness', which 'leads to death'.[22] The latter has as its opposite 'joy in the Lord'.[23] Basil also deals expressly with 'offending a brother' and with 'murmuring',[24] both of which are anathema to Benedict.

e. Evagrius Ponticus (d.399) described this sadness from a *psychological* point of view: 'Sadness befalls one sometimes when affective demands are frustrated, or it occurs as a consequence of aggressiveness.' Frustrations appear when someone indulges in a kind of regression, looking backwards, recollecting 'things of the past', which are now lacking 'in his life'.[25] One should therefore not become attached to a sterile yearning,[26] or else one will feel unfulfilled and unhappy.

f. Evagrius' instruction was taken up and expanded by Cassian (d.430):[27] sadness 'keeps us from the contemplation of God, it makes us spiritually unsure and leads us away from an undisturbed interior life, into depression. It does not allow us to pray with our usual interior joy or to find a means of healing in reading Holy Scripture. It prevents us from meeting the brethren in peace and friendliness, and makes us impatient and dismissive . . .'[28] Like Evagrius, Cassian, too, sees fits of depression and moodiness as a consequence of aggressiveness, extravagant demands and disappointed wishful thinking.[29] Often, he thinks, no exterior reason for the depression is perceptible, and even meeting friendly people brings no improvement. 'That is a clear proof that the cause of our disturbances is not always to be found in the faults of others, but in ourselves. We carry in our own subconscious the sources of our disorders . . .'[30] Therefore God, who knows us, has commanded us not to avoid the company of brethren whom we have probably insulted, or by whom we have allegedly been offended. On the contrary, he wants us to placate them, conscious that perfection of heart is to be achieved not through separation from people, but by the power of *patience*'.[31]

g. Seeking encounters with people, seeking *dialogue*—these are concerns of Benedict[32] and of monastic writings generally. Their purpose is to show especially that encounters with 'spiritual' people, with 'bearers of the Spirit', has therapeutic power, brings joy and banishes sadness. Athanasius (d.373) writes: 'Christ has presented Egypt with a good physician. Whose sadness did not transform itself into joy on encountering Antony?'[33] Whenever Eugendus (d.*c*.510) heard that in his Jura monastery a monk was suffering from 'gnawing fits of depression', 'as can occur in natural human weakness' 'he unexpectedly joined him' and showed 'so much spiritual joy and so much friendliness, that his good and holy words rendered the dangerous poison of sadness harmless'.[34] It is said that Honoratus (d.428), the first abbot of Lérins, 'took unbelievable pains to ensure that no one was overshadowed by sadness'.[35]

h. Gergory the Great (d.604) wishes to show[36] that Benedict was filled with the same strength of the Spirit as the prophet Elisha.[37] In this connection Gregory reports that Benedict 'received' a Goth 'with great joy (into the monastery)'. When the latter, sickle in hand, with fiery zeal was clearing a field on the shore of the lake[38] from undergrowth, the sickle blade suddenly sprang from its socket and fell into the lake. When the Goth, troubled, looked for help, the blade—according to Gregory—in response to Benedict's prayer, miraculously returned to its socket. Benedict 'gave the tool back to the Goth and said: "Go to work and do not be sad!" '[39] As well as word therapy, *work therapy* is also helpful. Benedict, the man of God, wants no sad people about him. His concern for joy and peace shows itself in the countless warnings against anger, annoyance, offensiveness and murmuring.[40]

8–9 a. The scriptural quotation about '*serving*' (*diakonein*) is taken from the ecclesiastical Ordo for deacons.[41] It is said of the cellarer that he is 'chosen', as the 'seven men' for the 'service at table' were 'chosen'.[42] The Church's offices and her concept of service are Benedict's model for the services in the monastery.[43]

b. As the *deacon* stands by the bishop, in his charge to care for those in need of help and to see to the administration of the Church's goods for social and charitable purposes, so the cellarer helps the abbot and the brethren in a serving capacity in that same care. It includes the charitable and social activity of the monastery towards the outside world. Gregory the Great (d.604) relates that, 'during a famine in Campania', Benedict distributed the stores of the monastery to the needy. 'A small residue of oil was left over in a glass vessel.' When the subdeacon Agapitus from the surrounding area 'urgently asked for some oil', Benedict ordered the residue to be given to him. However, because of the monastery's own desperate state, the cellarer did not obey. Challenged, he admitted this. Then, 'in anger', Benedict ordered the vessel to be thrown out through the window, 'lest anything should remain in the monastery because of disobedience.' Although the glass vessel landed 'in the rocky precipice' in front of the monastery, it remained undamaged, and Benedict had it given to the petitioner.[44]

c. For the office of service or the diaconate, Christ is the model, who came as 'one who serves'[45] and who waited on the disciples at the Last Supper.[46] The passage about the 'Judgement'[47] points to the service of one of the least.[48] At the Judgement, a verdict will be given on preparedness to render this service.[49] Mutual *service* (*douleuein*),[50] or service to one's brother, the sick, the poor and guests is a service to Christ. It is essential in a 'school' for the 'Lord's service'.[51] The passage about 'service' is the main concept in these chapters.[52] Christ serves in those holding office; Christ is served in the brethren. The service is to be rendered in humility[53] and with an eye to the reward (A. de Vogüé).[54]

10–12 a. The comparison of the goods of the monastery with 'holy vessels of the altar' is traditional[55] and perhaps reminiscent of an eschatological promise of Zechariah,[56] who proclaims the removal of the difference between sacred and profane for the 'House of the Lord'.[57] Life and work in the monastery, which was a monastery of laymen, in interpreted as temple service[58] or as *priestly activity*.[59] Other eschatological motives are hinted at only in a veiled fashion.[60] The dignity of Christians is, in God's sight, their 'royal priesthood'.[61]
b. The spirituality of the ancient Church remains true to itself when it has this general priesthood exercised on the *'altar of the heart'*. Origen (d.253) writes: 'The altar, then, is the heart of man, which is regarded as the noblest part of him; vows and gifts are all that which is laid upon the heart. You make up your mind to say a prayer for instance: you lay the vow to say the prayer on your heart as on an altar ... The heart of him who is 'pure of heart' is an altar that sanctifies his vows.'[62] Here, according to Origen, a permanent priesthood is to be exercised: 'Listen: "there ought always to be fire upon the altar" ..., priest of God, ... for you too it has been said: a chosen, a royal priesthood, a people of election";—if you wish, therefore, to have the care of the priesthood of your soul, then let the fire never leave your altar.'[63] All of Christian existence is, according to Origen, priestly: 'You have a priesthood, then, since you are a "priestly people", and you must therefore "offer to God a sacrifice of praise": a sacrifice of prayer, a sacrifice of mercy, a sacrifice of chastity, a sacrifice of righteousness, a sacrifice of holiness.'[64] In this way Benedict, too, understands the 'priesthood' of the Christian not as an exclusively interior reality. All righteous action of a Christian is priestly, even the use of the tools of the monastery.
c. So much the more must the way people are treated be a priestly one. Pope Gregory (d.604) was to write later of Benedict that he had become a 'custodian of the sacred vessels' because 'the souls of the faithful are sacred (altar) vessels'.[65] 'Priestly' above all is *the work of reconciliation*[66] or of 'peace', which is the aim of monastic existence.[67] Contributing to peace means leading to God, for peace is in God.[68]

13–14 Benedict *repeats*—how often!—what is important to him: humility or preparedness to serve[69] and preparedness to converse, for a good word is a 'gift of the spirit'.[70] Parallel passages to these are not to be found in the 'Rule of the Master'.[71]

16–19 a. These sentences of Benedict's are without parallel in the 'Rule of the Master', except for the saying about the 'annona' or share of food and drink, which however was current. Augustine (d.430) turned his face in a very similar way against a false 'condescension' and against negligence,[72] a caricature of humility.

b. Sensitivity to people and their needs, for instance to the necessity for helpers[73] or for a clear order of the day,[74] goes together with *spiritual motives*: 'peace of soul' as a high, individual aim,[75] the prevention of all 'sadness',[76] and— as the comprehensive motive—the understanding of the monastery as a 'house of God'.[77]

NOTES TO CHAPTER 31

1 RB 23–30. **2** RB 31–42 **3** Verses 4.12.15. **4** RB 31,1–2: RM 16,62–66; RB 31,3–5: RM 16,32–37; RB 31,8: RM 16,53–56; RB 31,9.15: RM 16,27–37. Cf. Pachomius, Praec 137; RBasRuf 111–114.185–186; Augustine, Praec 5,9; R4P 3,22–26; RCaesVirg 30,42. **5** Cf. 6,31–33. **6** RM 16,1–45. **7** RB 3,5; 49,9. **8** → 2,1–10. **9** RB 64. **10** RB 4,34–36. **11** Cf. 1 Tim 3:2. **12** Cf. Is 42:2. **13** This word occurs fourteen times in RB, as well as the expression 'solicitude' (sollicitudo), which occurs seventeen times. **14** → 33. **15** Verses 6–7. **16** Cf. RB 31,19; → 34,3; 35,12–14; 36,1–4; 38,10–11; 41,5; 48,7–8. **17** Cf. Lk 24; Mt 28:5–8; Jn 20: 19–21. **18** → Prol 45–50.48–49 (in Note 166); 7,67–70; 20,1–3 (in Note 11). Texts about joy are to be found in parts of the Rule adopted from the Rule of the Master; → 49,6–7. **19** VPatr 3,170. **20** RBasRuf 8. **21** Cf.2 Cor 7:10 **22** → 7,59–61; 25,3; 27:1–4; 72,1–3. The doctrine of 'sadness according to God' was by Origen set in opposition to the shallow ethical understanding of happiness (eudaemonism) current in the world about him. In Lev hom 3,6; in Jer hom 20 (19), cf. Mt 5:4. **23** RBasRuf 50–51. **24** RBasRuf 71–72. **25** Log prakt 10. **26** Loc. cit. 19. **27** Inst 9. **28** Inst 9,1. **29** Inst 9,4. **30** Inst 9,5: 'reconditas in nobismetipsis habemus offensionum causas'. **31** Inst 9,7. **32** RB 31,7.13–14; 63; 68,2; 71,1–2; 72,6. **33** VAnt 55. **34** VPJur 150; → 6,2–5 (in Note 12). **35** VHonor 4,18. **36** Dial 2,8. **37** Cf. 2 Kings 6:7. **38** Of Subiaco ('Below the lake'). **39** Dial 2,6. **40** RB 31,13–14. 16–17. 19; 34,3.13; 36,4; 40,8–9; 41,2.5; cf. 5,16; 7,49; 27,3; 48,7; 49,6; 54,4. **41** 1 Tim 3:8–13. The saying is also quoted in R4P 3,26. 'Ministrare': RB 31,8; 38,6; 64,21. **42** Verse l; cf.Acts 6:2. **43** → 31,1–2 (in Note 11); 1,2; 5,1–9. **44** Dial 2,28. **45** Cf. Jn 6:38; Mt 20:28. **46** Cf. Jn13:15–17. **47** Verse 9; 36,2–3. **48** Cf. verse 16. **49** Cf. Mt 25: 31–46. **50** Cf. RB 35:6: Gal 5:13. 'Servire': RB 2,31; 35.1.6.13; 36,1.4 (twice); 53,18. **51** → Prol 45. **52** RB 31,8; 35,1.6; 36,1.4.7.10. **53** → 7,49–52. **54** Cf. Mt 25: 46; → 4,41–50.74.76–77; 5, 1–9.14–19; 19,3–7; 35,1–3; 36,1–4; 40,4. **55** Basil speaks of 'God's requisites' (RBasRuf 103–104); the Rule of the four 'Fathers' calls all things of the monastery 'holy', and forbids 'careless' treatment of them (R4P 3,27–28). Cf. Cassian,Inst 4,19–20. **56** → 14,20–21. **57** Verse 19. **58** Cf. also RB 53,14: 'within your temple'. **59** → 16,1–3; 17,5; 35,7. **60** → Prol 8–11; 22,4–7. **61** Cf. 1 Pet 2: 5,9. **62** Comm Series 18. **63** Lev Hom 4,6. **64** Lev Hom 9,1. **65** Dial 2,2. **66** Cf.2 Cor 5:18–19. **67** → Prol 48–49; 4,62–73; 72,8. **68** Cf. 1 Cor 14:33. **69** → 7,49–50. **70** → 4,10–19 (in Notes 22–23); 6,2–5.8; 27,1–4; 28,1–5; 31,3–7; 72,6. **71** Cf.Augustine, in Ps 103,1,19. **72** Verse 16; cf. Augustine, ep.22,6. **73** → 33,5. **74** Verse 18; → 47–48. **75** → 7,62–66. **76** → 31,3–7. **77** Verse 19; → 31,10–12 (in Note 47).

CHAPTER 32

OF THE IRON TOOLS
AND MATERIALS OF THE MONASTERY

10 Mar
10 July
9 Nov

1 For the monastery's possessions in iron tools and
clothing and articles of whatever kind, let the abbot foresee
brethren on whose life and character he can rely.

2 Let him assign each separate thing to them, as he judges fit,
for safe keeping and collecting.

3 The abbot should keep a WRITTEN LIST of these,   Cf. Ecclus 42:7
so that while
the brethren succeed one another in the allotted charges,
he may know what he is giving out and what receiving back.

4 Should anyone treat monastery material in a slovenly or
careless manner, he should be corrected;

5 if he do not amend, let him undergo the discipline of the Rule.

CAPUT XXXII: DE FERRAMENTIS VEL REBUS MONASTERII

¹SUBSTANTIA MONASTERII IN FERRAMENTIS VEL VESTIBUS SEU QUIBUSLIBET REBUS PRAEVIDEAT ABBAS FRATRES DE QUORUM VITA ET MORIBUS SECURUS SIT, ²ET EIS SINGULA, UT UTILE IUDICAVERIT, CONSIGNET CUSTODIENDA ATQUE RECOLLIGENDA. ³EX QUIBUS ABBAS BREVEM TENEAT, UT DUM SIBI IN IPSA ASSIGNATA FRATRES VICISSIM SUCCEDUNT, SCIAT QUID DAT AUT QUID RECIPIT. ⁴SI QUIS AUTEM SORDIDE AUT NEGLEGENTER RES MONASTERII TRACTAVERIT, CORRIPIATUR; ⁵SI NON EMENDAVERIT, DISCIPLINAE REGULARI SUBIACEAT.

1–4 a. The abbot also has the responsibility for questions of material possessions and their administration,[1] here even for the *requisites for work*. Benedict is briefer then the 'Master',[2] but insists very clearly on important points.
b. Those put in charge are to be carefully chosen.[3] In the interests of good *order*, an account must be kept of borrowings and returns of implements, a necessary measure because of the rotation of personnel in the services.[4] The things of the monastery are to be used in the appropriate way and are to be kept clean. Basil, too, requires careful handling of the requisites for work, because they are 'holy goods'.[5]
c. Augustine emphasized a sense of community and love as motives for especial care in the use of things that are not private property: 'Let no one work for his own advantage, but let all your work serve the community. As

far as perseverance and zeal are concerned, let the effort be greater than if you were working for yourselves. For of love it is written, 'it does not insist on its own way'.[6] That means that it places the common good higher than its own advantage, not vice versa. You ought to know: the more you concern your-selves with the interests of the community instead of your own individual interests, the greater progress you will make. Whatever transient needs you may have, in everything everlasting love must have precedence'.[7]

5 The expression 'punishment of the Rule' is not clearly defined. It can mean 'the punishments usually prescribed by the Rule in the monastery'.[8]

NOTES TO CHAPTER 32

1 → 2,33–36; 33,5; 55,16–19; 58,1–4.24–25; cf. RB 22,2; 31,4.15 ; 34,1; 64,17. 2 RB 32,1–2: RM 17,1–4.10–20; RB 32,3: RM 17,5; RB 32,4–5: RM 17,6–9. 3 Cf. RBasRuf 110. 4 Under Pachomius the change-over took place weekly (praec 66). 5 RBasRuf 103–104; → 31,10–12. Careless handling of of the things of the monastery,which are looked on as sacred, is also censured in the 'Rule of the Four Fathers' (R4P 3,29). 6 1 Cor 13:5. 7 Praec 5,2; cf. 1 Cor 13:8. 8 → 24,3; some examples of punishments are to be found in chapter 43.

CHAPTER 33

WHETHER MONKS SHOULD HAVE
ANYTHING OF THEIR OWN

11 Mar
11 July
10 Nov

1 This vice especially is to be cut out from the monastery
   by the roots:

2 let no one presume to give or receive anything
   without a directive from the abbot,

3 nor to have anything of his own,
   absolutely nothing,
   not a book,
   neither writing-tablets nor stylus,
   but nothing at all,

4 for in fact they are not to have their bodies or desires
   in their own will,

5 to hope however for all things necessary from the father
   of the monastery.
   Nor may anything be had which the abbot has not
   given or permitted.

6 And as it is written, let EVERYTHING be COMMON   Acts 4:32
   to all, nor let ANYONE CALL ANYTHING HIS OWN
   or presume it to be so.

7 But if anyone be caught delighting in this most vile
   vice, let him be warned once and a second time;

8 if he do not amend, let him be subjected to correction.

CAPUT XXXIII: SI QUID DEBEANT MONACHI
PROPRIUM HABERE

¹PRAECIPUE HOC VITIUM RADICITUS AMPUTANDUM EST DE MONASTERIO, ²NE QUIS
PRAESUMAT ALIQUID DARE AUT ACCIPERE SINE IUSSIONE ABBATIS, ³NEQUE ALIQUID
HABERE PROPRIUM, NULLAM OMNINO REM NEQUE CODICEM, NEQUE TABULAS,
NEQUE GRAFIUM, SED NIHIL OMNINO, ⁴QUIPPE QUIBUS NEC CORPORA SUA NEC
VOLUNTATES LICET HABERE IN PROPRIA VOLUNTATE; ⁵OMNIA VERO NECESSARIA A
PATRE SPERARE MONASTERII, NEC QUICQUAM LICEAT HABERE QUOD ABBAS NON
DEDERIT AUT PERMISERIT. ⁶OMNIAQUE OMNIBUS SINT COMMUNIA, UT SCRIPTUM
EST, NE QUISQUAM SUUM ALIQUID DICAT VEL PRAESUMAT. ⁷QUOD SI QUISQUAM
HUIC NEQUISSIMO VITIO DEPREHENSUS FUERIT DELECTARI, ADMONEATUR SEMEL ET
ITERUM; ⁸SI NON EMENDAVERIT, CORREPTIONI SUBIACEAT.

1–3 After the chapter about the property of the monastery, Benedict next lays down the rule of complete absence of ownership, which is traditional in monasticism.[1]

4 **a.** As first motif Benedict names the renunciation of the personal right of disposal, which is included in the renunciation of 'one's own will' and of the 'desires of the flesh'.[2] In the matter of absence of ownership, the core of the question is willingness to *renounce oneself*, to conform to Christ in his Kenosis.[3] One wants to belong completely to the Lord and therefore to adopt his attitude.

b. Cassian (d.430) has this formula for it: 'They believe, not merely that they no longer belong to themselves, but also that all that is theirs is consecrated to the Lord.'[4] Basil (d.379) refers to the example of Jesus, who 'laid down his life for his friends, and asks how someone following Christ 'can reserve' anything 'as his own property that does not belong to life'.[5] Jesus is indeed, in his inner disposition of self-denial, in which he has shown solidarity with men, the model of unpretentiousness for every Christian. The 'Rule of the Four Fathers' demands therefore: 'One may keep absolutely nothing for oneself, except the Cross, to which one ought to cling in order to follow Christ.'[6]

c. The aim is the interior attitude of the '*anawim*', whom Jesus calls blessed, because they are 'poor in spirit'.[7] Poverty is primarily a question of interior attitude, before it is a question of possessing. Cassian writes: 'It is no use having no money if the will to possess reigns in us.'[8] Material poverty is not an end in itself. Benedict does not speak of 'paupertas' (poverty), but of individual lack of possessions. Jesus wanted to help the poorest out of their condition of material need. In the monastery, as outside it, want and *destitution are an evil*. Also a lack of means which excludes efficient and socially valuable work, is not automatically a positive thing. What is decisive is the change of direction in one's understanding of oneself. One wants nothing any longer for oneself, nor to control anything for one's own benefit. Love is selfless.

d. Benedict states that renunciation of individual rights and claims in monastic life also includes renunciation of the right to dispose of *one's own body*.[9] The monk does not seek himself or another human being, he 'seeks God'.[10] He expects interior fulfilment from God.[11] Benedict holds steadfastly to the primacy of the spiritual over the material. That is the norm for the abbot[12] as for the craftsman.[13]

5 **a.** As a second motif there emerges trust in the abbot's *fatherly care*. One may 'trustfully ask for' (sperare) all necessities. This formulation is in part reminiscent of Pachomius (d.346). He allows no one to have more 'than what the general rule of the monastery allows', but adds that a person may keep 'what is distributed by the father of the monastery through the priors'.[14] Benedict definitely allows one to ask for what one needs,[15] only on condition that the person involved does not call it his private property. He has culled his relevant formulation from Cassian, without taking on in the process the 'strict' Egyptian ideal of the 'stripping' (nuditas) of all possessions, quoted by the latter.[16] If one may ask for what one 'needs', Benedict is not thinking of a legalistic practice of poverty that permits every luxury by saying it is 'permitted' by the superior. That would stand Benedict's first motif of poverty on its head.[17]

b. The abbot, who takes the place of Christ,[18] is the mediator of God's fatherly care. The monk's 'asking' is, in the last resort, directed to God; it is not a sign of immaturity, but rather of the *freedom* of the children of God. The 'Master' emphasizes that the individual monk, free of 'anxious cares' about material things, can 'seek' the 'Kingdom of God' and need not involve himself in 'worldly affairs'.[19] Benedict, too, possesses an unbroken trust in God's providence, for 'the earth is the Lord's and the fulness thereof'.[20] From the gifts of his creation all should be able to live, especially the poor[21] and the 'servants of God'. This conviction,[22] set out in detail in the 'Rule of the Master', is contained in the first chapter on the abbot. In material difficulties too, the abbot, trusting in God's providence should always know how the priorities are to be set: 'the kingdom of God is first to be sought', 'all these things will be yours as well'; for 'those who seek the Lord lack no good thing'.[23] The priority of the spiritual over the pressures of production or consumption is to be preserved.

c. From the following observations it becomes clear that Benedict, while strongly emphasizing the spiritual element, does not indulge *in airy illusions*:
1. Benedict believes in order, cleanliness and keeping a check on things.[24]
2. In contrast to the 'Master', he permits work in the fields,[25] even when because of it times for prayer must be changed,[26] brothers must be dispensed from participation in them,[27] or rules for fasting must be altered.[28] In questions of sale, he expresses himself cautiously.[29]

6 a. As third motif Benedict gives the example of the primitive, apostolic community, quoting the same text[30] as Augustine (d.430)[31] and Basil (d.373).[32] Augustine has specially developed this theme. His whole concept of poverty proceeds from the fact that the primitive community was of one mind.[33] From this follows the will to have *property in common*, with superiors arranging the provision for individual needs.[34] Augustine takes the holding of property in common as his point of departure. In this tradition, life in community calls for someone in charge, who will care for that community.

b. The perspectives and line of thought of our Rule are different. It *starts* with the 'search for God'[35] and for a 'teacher' and 'father'[36] authorized by God. Around this 'teacher' there is formed a community of brothers, who live without possessions under the responsibility of the abbot. In Benedict's system, as opposed to Augustine's, the community is, as it were, the final point in the development of his understanding of poverty (A. de Vogüé).

c. That Benedict does not merely quote the Acts of the Apostles by chance here, but really has the image of the *primitive community* before his eyes, is shown by the fact that immediately afterwards[37] and later[38] he cites the example of the primitive community, in order to define the relationship to material goods. In Benedict's system, too, one renounces private gains and possession— just as in Augustine's (d.430)—with a view to the community and its tasks. Cassian (d.430) establishes the norm: 'Whatever the individual, by his daily work and sweat, earns in the form of income, he lets accrue to the community. His moderation allows him to support himself and, beyond that, to supply abundantly the necessities of many, without in any way becoming proud of it'.[39]

7–8 The 'most evil vice' that must be avoided, can only be *covetousness*. Cassian (d.430) warned against 'letting this most evil spirit, the seed of new demands, be sown in the heart'.[40] The place of true poverty is the heart. Benedict mentions only the outward procedure against defaulters.

CHAPTER THIRTY-THREE

NOTES TO CHAPTER 33

1 The 'Master' repeatedly mentions the following 'basic principle': 'the monastery's property belongs to all and to no one' (RM 16,61; 2,48). RB 33,1–6: RM 16,58–61; 82; RB 33,7–8: RM 82,26–27. Cf. Cassian, Inst 4,13–15; RBasRuf 29 (The title of RB 33 is from Basil); 106. Also, the image of the operation on the 'root' is well known: → 28,1–5 (in Note 2); cf. RB 2,26; 55,18. 2 → 7,31–32. 3 ib. 4 Inst 4,20. 5 RBasRuf 29. 6 Cf. Phil 2:5–8; R4P 2,32. 7 Cf. Mt 5:3. 8 Inst 4,21. 9 Cf. also RB 58,25. 10 → 58,5–7. 11 → 20,1–3 (in Notes 20–23). 12 → 2,33–36. 13 → 57,1–3. 14 Praec 81. 15 Cf. RB 31,7.13.18. 16 Verse 3; cf. Cassian, Inst 4,13: the individual retains only a few articles of clothing. 17 → 33,4. 18 → 2,1–10. 19 RM 82. He quotes Mt 6:25,33 and 2 Tim 2:4; → 31,1–2. 20 Ps 24: 1. 21 → 4,10–19. 22 → 31,1–2. 23 → 2,33–36,with the quotations: Mt 6:33 and Ps 34:10. 24 → 32,1–4; cf RB 31,3–5. 11–12.18. 25 → 48,7–8.10–12. 26 → 48,6. 27 → 50,1–3. 28 → 39,6–9; 40,5–7; 41,2–4. 29 → 57,7–9. 30 Acts 4:32. 31 Praec 1,2–3. 32 RBasRuf 29. 33 Acts 4: 32:'(they) were of one heart and soul'. 34 Acts 4:35: 'They laid everything' at the apostles' feet; and distribution was made to each as any had need.' 35 RB 58,7. 36 → 2. 37 → 34, 1–2. 38 → 57,4–6 (with a quotation from Acts 5: 1–11: Ananias and Sapphira). 39 Inst 4,14. 40 Inst 7,21.

CHAPTER 34

WHETHER ALL SHOULD RECEIVE
THE SAME AMOUNT OF NECESSARY THINGS

12 Mar
12 July
11 Nov

1   As it is written: Acts 4:35

    DISTRIBUTION WAS MADE TO EACH,

    ACCORDING AS ANY ONE HAD NEED.

2   Here we are not saying   Cf. Rom 2:11
    that there be RESPECT OF PERSONS
    —far from it!—

3   Here let him who needs less
    thank God and not be saddened;

4   for him who needs more,
    let his infirmity keep him humble,
    his exceptions not make him proud,

5   and in this way   Cf. 1 Cor 12:12,26
    all the MEMBERS will be at peace.

6   Above all,
    the evil of murmuring is not to appear
    for whatever cause,
    in any word or sign
    whatever.

7   If he be caught,
    let him undergo stricter punishment.

CAPUT XXXIV: SI OMNES AEQUALITER DEBEANT
NECESSARIA ACCIPERE

¹SICUT SCRIPTUM EST: DIVIDEBATUR SINGULIS PROUT CUIQUE OPUS ERAT. ²UBI NON DICIMUS UT PERSONARUM—QUOD ABSIT—ACCEPTIO SIT, SED INFIRMITATUM CONSIDERATIO; ³UBI QUI MINUS INDIGET, AGAT DEO GRATIAS ET NON CONTRISTETUR, ⁴QUI VERO PLUS INDIGET, HUMILIETUR PRO INFIRMITATE, NON EXTOLLATUR PRO MISERICORDIA; ⁵ET ITA OMNIA MEMBRA ERUNT IN PACE. ⁶ANTE OMNIA, NE MURMURATIONIS MALUM PRO QUALICUMQUE CAUSA IN ALIQUO QUALICUMQUE VERBO VEL SIGNIFICATIONE APPAREAT. ⁷QUOD SI DEPREHENSUS FUERIT, DISTRICTIORI DISCIPLINAE SUBDATUR.

1–2   a. In the 'Rule of the Master' there are no parallels to this chapter, which brings out Benedict's *typical concerns*: impartiality,¹ humanity,² consideration for individual needs.[3] The influence of Augustine (d.430) and Basil (d.379) can be clearly felt.

The starting point is the mention in the Acts of the Apostles of the allocation of what is necessary according to *individual needs*.[4] The relevant passage from the Acts of the Apostles[5] is also quoted by Basil (d.379).[6] While the 'Master' concerns himself more about the common property of the monastery,[7] Benedict is primarily concerned with this consideration for individuals. This willingness to make concessions to individuals is the response to their lack of personal means (A. de Vogüé).

3–5   **a.** Benedict's warnings are aimed in different directions, between which a balance must be established. He seems to take his bearings from Augustine (d.430), who wanted to deal with possible differences between brothers of *rich* and *poor* origin. He wrote: 'Those who were formerly rich ought to rejoice that their possessions become common property. The poor, on the other hand, ought not to seek in the monastery a comfort they never had outside. Everything necessary ought to be given to these poor ones also, to each according to his needs . . . , but they ought not to seek their happiness in better food or clothing. The poor should not hold their heads high now . . . , on the contrary, they ought to lift up their hearts and not strive graspingly after material possessions. Otherwise the monastery will be of advantage only to the rich, not to the poor as well, if that is to say the rich humble themselves, while the poor puff themselves up with pride.'[8]

b. Like Augustine (d.430), Benedict wants each to receive what he needs. Benedict, too, addresses himself to two groups; instead of to the rich and the poor, he turns to the *moderate* and the *demanding*. Like Augustine, Benedict is concerned that exacting monks be humble.[9]

c. Benedict fears that brothers could fall victim to 'sadness'.[10] Instead of showing his ideal only in a negative, contrasting picture[11]—as he does often at other times—here he expressly names the interior *peace* of the monastic community as a chief concern. In the process, Benedict compares the community to a body and its 'members'.[12] The comparison also served in the secular sphere to explain a corporation. Basil (d.379) deduces from it the duty of harmony among the members.[13] In Cassian (d.430) the concept 'body of the brotherhood' (corpus fraternitatis) appears, when he proclaims the 'catholicity' of monasticism, that is, the monastic lifestyle of the cloister practised in the same way 'worldwide', as the norm for all monks.[14]

6–7   'Murmuring', related[15] to sadness, opposed to peace and joy, is a bugbear for Benedict.[16] Augustine writes: 'If questions of garments are for you a reason for strife and murmuring, . . . then you lack the holy garment of the heart, namely humility.'[17]

NOTES TO CHAPTER 34

1 → 2, 16–32. 2 → 31,3–7. 16–19. 3 → 2, 11–15.23–25.27–29.31–32; 5, 1–9; 7,55; 23,5; 27–30. 4 → 33,6. 5 4:35. 6 RBasRuf 111. 7 RM 86. 8 Praec 1 ,4–6. 9 → 31, 13–14. 10 → 31, 3–7. 11 → 31, 10–12 (in Note 56). 12 Cf. Rom. 12:4–5; RB 61,6: 'Body of the monastery'. 13 RBasRuf 3. 14 Inst 1,2,2. 15 → 31,3–7. 16 → 5, 14–19. 17 Praec 5, 1.

CHAPTER 35

OF THE WEEKLY KITCHENERS

13 Mar
13 July
12 Nov

1   Except for sickness,
or if a person is engaged in something of grave importance,
the brethren shall serve one another
so that none shall be excused from duty in the kitchen,

2   because more reward and GREATER LOVE   Cf. Jn 15:13
is thence acquired.

3   Let helpers be provided for the weak,
so that they may not do this work with sadness;

4   but let all have helpers
in keeping with the size of the community
or the location of the place.

5   If the community be larger,
the cellarer shall be excused from the kitchen,
or, as we have said,
if any be engaged in more important matters.

6   All the rest   Cf. Gal 5:13
shall SERVE ONE ANOTHER IN LOVE.

7   The server coming off his week
shall wash up on Saturday.

8   They shall wash the towels
with which the brethren dry their hands and feet.

9   Both the outgoing and the incoming server   Cf. Jn 13:1–20
shall WASH THE FEET of all.

10   He shall hand in the utensils of his MINISTRY   Cf. Acts 6:2–4;
clean and whole to the cellarer;   Rom 15:31; 16:1

11   the latter shall hand them out again
to the incoming server,
so that he may know
what he is giving and what receiving.

14 Mar
14 July
13 Nov

12   When there is only *one* meal,
those who are on for the week
shall each receive some drink and bread
over and above the permitted allowance,

13   so that at the meal-time

they may, without murmuring and heavy work,
serve their brethren.

14 On solemnities however
they shall hold out until the dismissal.

15 On Sunday immediately after Lauds
the incoming and outgoing hebdomadaries
should kneel at the feet of all
asking them to pray for them.

16 The server coming off his week should say this verse: Dan 3:52;
BLESSED ARE YOU, LORD GOD   Ps 86:17
who HELPED ME AND COMFORTED ME.

17 When this has been said three times   Ps 70:2
and the outgoing server has received the blessing,
the incoming server shall follow and say:
O GOD, COME TO MY AID,
O LORD, MAKE HASTE TO HELP ME.

18 And this likewise shall be repeated by all,
and having received the blessing,
let him begin.

CAPUT XXXV: DE SEPTIMANARIIS COQUINAE

¹FRATRES SIBI INVICEM SERVIANT, UT NULLUS EXCUSETUR A COQUINAE OFFICO, NISI AUT AEGRITUDO AUT IN CAUSA GRAVIS UTILITATIS QUIS OCCUPATUS FUERIT. ²QUIA EXINDE MAIOR MERCIS ET CARITAS ADQUIRITUR. ³INBECILLIBUS AUTEM PRO-CURENTUR SOLACIA, UT NON CUM TRISTITIA HOC FACIANT; ⁴SED HABEANT OMNES SOLACIA SECUNDUM MODUM CONGREGATIONIS AUT POSITIONEM LOCI. ⁵SI MAIOR CONGREGATIO FUERIT, CELLARARIUS EXCUSETUR A COQUINA, VEL SI QUI, UT DIXIMUS, MAIORIBUS UTILITATIBUS OCCUPANTUR. ⁶CETERI SIBI SUB CARITATE INVICEM SERVIANT. ⁷EGRESSURUS DE SEPTIMANA, SABBATO MUNDITIAS FACIAT. ⁸LINTEA CUM QUIBUS SIBI FRATRES MANUS AUT PEDES TERGUNT, LAVENT. ⁹PEDES VERO TAM IPSE QUI EGREDITUR QUAM ILLE QUI INTRATURUS EST OMNIBUS LAVENT. ¹⁰VASA MINISTERII SUI MUNDA ET SANA CELLARARIO RECONSIGNET; ¹¹QUI CEL-LARARIUS ITEM INTRANTI CONSIGNET, UT SCIAT QUOD DAT AUT QUOD RECIPIT. ¹²SEPTIMANARII AUTEM ANTE UNAM HORAM REFECTIONIS ACCIPIANT SUPER STATUTAM ANNONAM SINGULAS BIBERES ET PANEM, ¹³UT HORA REFECTIONIS SINE MURMURATIONE ET GRAVI LABORE SERVIANT FRATRIBUS SUIS. ¹⁴IN DIEBUS TAMEN SOLLEMNIBUS USQUE AD MISSAS SUSTINEANT. ¹⁵INTRANTES ET EXEUNTES EBDO-MADARII IN ORATORIO MOX MATUTINIS FINITIS DOMINICA OMNIUM GENIBUS PROVOLVANTUR POSTULANTES PRO SE ORARI. ¹⁶EGREDIENS AUTEM DE SEPTIMANA DICAT HUNC VERSUM: BENEDICTUS ES, DOMINE DEUS, QUI ADIUVASTI ME ET CONSOLATUS ES ME. ¹⁷QUO DICTO TERTIO ACCEPTA BENEDICTIONE EGREDIENS, SUBSEQUATUR INGREDIENS ET DICAT: DEUS, IN ADIUTORIUM MEUM INTENDE, DOMINE, AD ADIUVANDUM ME FESTINA, ¹⁸ET HOC IDEM TERTIO REPETATUR AB OMNIBUS ET ACCEPTA BENEDICTIONE INGREDIATUR.

1–3   a. From selflessness, which proclaims itself in the renunciation of private possessions,[1] Benedict passes on to *self-giving* in the service of the brethren.[2] As motives he names in the same breath 'reward'[3] and 'love'. He does not sense any opposition between a 'morality' of 'reward' and one of 'love', because he knows that, despite the high calling to selfless love, he is 'poor in the eyes of God'[4] and dependent on God's reward, which is a grace.

  b. Service in the kitchen also includes service in the refectory.[5] The 'Master'[6] insists on careful preparation of the refectory and the food, to avoid annoyance and preserve the 'quiet and peace of the cloister'.[7] *Service in the kitchen* was regarded as burdensome, although in the 'Rule of the Master' two in each deanery were assigned to the kitchen.[8] Basil (d.379) also speaks of help which is to be given to the kitchen servers.[9] Benedict wants to prevent any occasion of 'sadness'.[10]

4–5   In this chapter, one notes several *repetitions* (which make things more precise), and overlappings with other chapters.[11] Perhaps practical experiences led to editorial revisions of the text, which appears short in comparison with the detailed and barely ordered text of the 'Master'.

6   Benedict recommends mutual service in love,[12] while the Master mentions only humility as spiritual motive.[13] The invitation to 'service in love' is placed before institutionalized service (A. de Vogüé).[14] Cassian (d.430) lauds the 'spontaneous' will to serve of the monks in Egypt.[15] Inner readiness must inspire outward service.

7–8   The *'weekly service'*,[16] which was widespread except for semi-eremitical settlements of monks in Egypt, was perhaps understood as an analogy to the weekly 'temple service'.[17] Everyday service, too, possesses a cultic character.[18]

9–11   The washing of the feet, envisaged also by other Rules, was, according to Cassian (d.430), undertaken 'in fulfilment of Christ's commandment'.[19] In the serving brother, Christ is present as the one who serves. Immediately following is the expression 'ministerium' (diakonia, service).[20]

12–14   a. An incidental remark is inserted into the explanation of how the weekly duties rotate.—A similar *concession* in view of 'laborious work' is granted by Caesarius of Arles (d.542),[21] while the 'Master' forbids such exceptions.[22]

  b. It is important for Benedict that the service should be rendered with a positive attitude which is constructive towards one's circle, therefore 'without murmuring';[23] Benedict could find a corresponding observation in Augustine (d.430).[24]

  c. For 'Feastdays'[25] Benedict envisages a somewhat different arrangement. Perhaps only 'non-fast-days' (Steidle) are meant, that is, days with two meals,[26] on which people do not rush to table so that the servers did not have to leave church prematurely.[27]

15–18   a. The prayer in common before and after assuming a laborious task for the community[28] is intended to 'recommend to God as "rich holocausts"[29] the services rendered with devotion.'[30] Work therefore is enveloped in an atmosphere of prayer. Thus the devotion in service to the brethren passes over into the sacrificial devotion to God. Here a light falls on Benedict's *work ethic*: work is a 'priestly' activity, a 'sacrifice'.[31]

  b. The *rites* described in detail, correspond more or less to the 'Master's' order; however, Benedict brings forward the much-loved verse, 'O God, come to my aid.'[32]

CHAPTER THIRTY-FIVE

NOTES TO CHAPTER 35

1 → 33,4; cf. Cassian Inst 4,20. 2 → 4,41–50.74.76–77; 5,1–13.14–19; 22,8; 31,8–9; 35,6; 40,1–4. 3 → Prol 48–49; 4,1–9. 10–19.55–58.62–73; 7,67–70. 4 Cf. Mt 5:3. 5 Cf.Pachomius, Praec 44. 6 RB 35,1–2: RM 18:1–12; RB 35,3–4: RM 19,18; RB 35,5–6: RM 18,1–12; RB 35,7–8: RM 19,19–27; RB 35,9; RM 19, 20–31; 30,4–7; RB 35,10–11: RM 16,39–40; RB 35,12–14: RM 21,11–14; RB 35,15–17: RM 25,3–7; RB 35,17–18: RM 19,1–8. 7 RM 21,12–14. 8 RM 18,10–12. 9 RBasRuf 131. 10 → 31,6–7. 11 Cf.RB 31–32. 12 → 22,8; 35,1–3. 13 RM 25,4: 18,8. 14 According to the 'Rule of the Four Fathers', a 'weekly service' is to be organized only in large communities (R4P 3,21). 15 Inst 4,19,1; 4,21; Conl 20,1,3. 16 According to Cassian, it was known in all the monasteries of Mesopotamia, Palestine, and Cappadocia, and in the whole of the Orient, but not in Egypt, where the menu was very simple (Inst 4,19.22). The Pachomian monasteries, too, know weekly service (Jerome, praef in Reg Pach 2). 17 → 17,5; 31,10–12 (esp. Note 58).16–19. 18 Cf. Rom 12:1; 15:15–16; I Cor 6:20 etc.; → 16,1–3. 19 Inst 4,19,2. 20 → 31,8–9. 21 RCaesVirg 14. 22 RM 21,8–10. He gives individual instructions about the reception of Communion by the servers, who must return speedily to their work (RM 21). 23 → 4,34–40; 5,14–19; 31,3–7; 34,6–7. 24 Praec 5,9. 25 Verse 14. 26 → 41,2–4. 27 The meaning of the word 'missas' is not unambiguous here (→ 17,4; 38.10–11). 28 The description of these rites of Sunday would more suitably follow the lines about the completion of the service on Saturday (after verse 11). Verses 12–14 are perhaps an insertion. 29 Ps 20: 4. 30 Cassian, Inst 4,19,2. 31 → 31,10–12 (in Notes 51–53). 32 → 18,1; cf. Cassian, Conl 18,1; this verse was also thrice repeated elsewhere (Cassiodorus, Comm.Ps 69:2; Columban, Reg.coen.9).

CHAPTER 36

OF THE SICK BRETHREN

15 Mar
15 July
14 Nov

1 Before all things
and above all things
care is to be taken of the sick,
so that service be rendered to them
really as to Christ,

2 because he himself said: Mt 25:36
I WAS SICK AND YOU VISITED ME.

3 And: WHAT YOU DID TO ONE OF THESE, THE LEAST,   Mt 25:40
YOU DID TO ME.

4 But the sick themselves too should reflect
that is for the honour of God
that they are being served,
and let them not upset their brothers who are serving them
by their petty, excessive demands.

5 However, they are to be PATIENTLY BORNE WITH,   Cf. Rom 12:12;
because a fuller reward is acquired   Eph 4:2
from such as these.

6 Therefore it shall be the abbot's greatest care
that they do not suffer any neglect.

7 A separate cell shall be set aside
for these sick brethren,
and an infirmarian
who is God-fearing, diligent and assiduous.

8 The use of baths
shall be offered to the sick
as often as is expedient;
to the healthy however
and especially to youths
it shall be offered more reluctantly.

9 But in addition,
the eating of flesh-meat
shall be allowed to the very infirm for their recovery;
but when they are better again,
all shall abstain from flesh-meat in the usual way.

10　It shall however be the abbot's greatest care
that the sick be not neglected
by the cellarers or infirmarians;
and he is accountable
for whatever fault is committed by the disciples.

CAPUT XXXVI: DE INFIRMIS FRATRIBUS

¹INFIRMORUM CURA ANTE OMNIA ET SUPER OMNIA ADHIBENDA EST, UT SICUT REVERA CHRISTO ITA EIS SERVIATUR, ²QUIA IPSE DIXIT: INFIRMUS FUI, ET VISITASTIS ME, ³ET: QUOD FECISTIS UNI DE HIS MINIMIS, MIHI FECISTIS. ⁴SED ET IPSI INFIRMI CONSIDERENT IN HONOREM DEI SIBI SERVIRI, ET NON SUPERFLUITATE SUA CONTRISTENT FRATRES SUOS SERVIENTES SIBI; ⁵QUI TAMEN PATIENTER PORTANDI SUNT, QUIA DE TALIBUS COPIOSIOR MERCIS ADQUIRITUR. ⁶ERGO CURA MAXIMA SIT ABBATI, NE ALIQUAM NEGLEGENTIAM PATIANTUR. ⁷QUIBUS FRATRIBUS INFIRMIS SIT CELLA SUPER SE DEPUTATA ET SERVITOR TIMENS DEUM ET DILIGENS AC SOLLICITUS. ⁸BALNEARUM USUS INFIRMIS QUOTIENS EXPEDIT OFFERATUR, SANIS AUTEM ET MAXIME IUVENIBUS TARDIUS CONCEDATUR. ⁹SED ET CARNIUM ESUS INFIRMIS OMNINO DEBILIBUS PRO REPARATIONE CONCEDATUR; AT UBI MELIORATI FUERINT, A CARNIBUS MORE SOLITO OMNES ABSTINEANT. ¹⁰CURAM AUTEM MAXIMAM HABEAT ABBAS NE A CELLARARIIS AUT A SERVITORIBUS NEGLEGANTUR INFIRMI; ET IPSUM RESPICIT QUIDQUID A DISCIPULIS DELINQUITUR.

1–4　**a.** The questions about the service for the brethren and about their diet[1] give Benedict occasion to concern himself with the care of the *sick*. The chapter is his creation and bears witness to his humanity, which is motivated entirely from the Gospel.
b. Only brief references are to be found in the 'Rule of the Master': one should provide suitable food for genuine sufferers, but not for pseudo-invalids;[2] and brotherly love ought to prove itself in visits to and care of the sick—in this connection the 'Master' calls to mind the scene at the Judgement.[3,4] Basil (d.379) already refers to this scene, which Benedict mentions.[5,6] The *priority* of the care of the sick is emphasized by Benedict alone. The perspective of Christ-service is lacking in the 'Rule of the Master'; in contrast, it is expressly mentioned by Basil: ' . . . serve the sick brothers with the same love as you would the Lord.'
c. Basil urges on the sick *moderation* in their demands on the attendants. He reminds the sick that they are being cared for from a religious motive. Let their attitude be a corresponding one: 'They should distinguish themselves in love for God and his Christ. By their patience and an exemplary behaviour they should show themselves worthy of the good offices of their brothers.'[7] It is typical that Benedict (who adopts Basil to a great degree) should want to prevent ill-humour on the part of the serving brothers.[8] Basil exhorted the sick to allow themselves to be cared for willingly; after all, he added, Peter was not allowed to refuse the service of the Lord at the washing of the feet.[9]

5–6 The exhortation to have patience[11] even in the case of defects of character,[12] which is heard first in Basil (d.379)[10] and frequently in Benedict, is just as Caesarius (d.542) would have it; he urges the abbess to oversee the fulfilment of the community's duties towards the sick.[13]

7–10 **a.** Special *quarters* for the sick and an *infirmarian* are already recorded in the Pachomian monasteries,[14] as well as under Caesarius[15] and Augustine (d.430).[16]
b. Pachomius (d.346) allowed *baths*[17] only for the sick, as Augustine did, basically, who in this connection speaks of public thermae;[18] according to Caesarius.[19] Benedict is comparatively generous.
c. Caesarius lays down that *meat dishes* (chicken) are to be served to the sick, and only to them.[20]
d. The whole chapter shows how Benedict takes his bearings from the cenobitic tradition; also when, in conclusion, he underlines the duty of abbot to exercise care, he is on the same line as Caesarius.[21] The abbot ought to offer his help as 'physician' not only in the spiritual domain,[22] but he must also concern himself with the sick in body and their care; in the one case as in the other, he can or ought to do that through others, as no one at all is free of the duty of caring for others.[23]

NOTES TO CHAPTER 36

1 → 31–35. 2 RM 28,13–18. 3 Cf. Mt 25:36. 4 RM 70,1–3. 5 V.2. Cf. RB 31,9; 53,1. 6 RBasRuf 36 (Mt 25,40). 7 ib. 8 Verse 4. → 31,3–7. 9 RBasRuf 37. 10 ib. 11 → Prol 37–38.50; 4,20–33.62–73; 7,35–43; 31,3–7; 72,5–6. 12 The Master is more concerned with finding out malingerers (RM 28,17). 13 RCaesVirg 42,1–6; cf. RB 36,10. 14 Pachomius, Praec 40–48; cf. Jerome, praef in Pach Reg 5 (special food). 15 RCaesVirg 32;43. 16 Praec 5,8 (the infirmarian); the Master is unacquainted with the office of infirmarian. 17 Praec 92; 93. 18 Praec 5,5.7. 19 RCaesVirg 31. 20 RCaesVirg 71. 21 → 36,5–6 (in Note 13). 22 → 2,1–10.27–28; 27–28; 31,3–7. 23 → 27,1–4 (see above, Note 13).

CHAPTER 37

OF THE OLD MEN AND THE CHILDREN

16 Mar 1 Although human nature of itself
16 July   is drawn to pity
15 Nov   for these times of life,
              that is to say of the old men and the children,
              yet the authority of the Rule
              shall also look after them.
         2 Let their debility always be kept in mind,
              nor shall the rigours of the Rule as regards food
              be in any way applied to them;
         3 but let there be a loving care for them
              and let them forestall
              the times fixed for meals.

CAPUT XXXVII: DE SENIBUS VEL INFANTIBUS

¹LICET IPSA NATURA HUMANA TRAHATUR AD MISERICORDIAM IN HIS AETATIBUS, SENUM VIDELICET ET INFANTUM, TAMEN ET REGULAE AUCTORITAS EIS PROSPICIAT. ²CONSIDERETUR SEMPER IN EIS INBECILLITAS ET ULLATENUS EIS DISTRICTIO REGULAE TENEATUR IN ALIMENTIS; ³SED SIT IN EIS PIA CONSIDERATIO ET PRAEVENIANT HORAS CANONICAS.

1–3 a. A logical sequence of thought leads the 'Master' and Benedict from the sick to the *aged* and *children*. While the 'Master' gives detailed instructions,[1] Benedict, by means of basic reflections, wants to encourage a positive attitude towards the weaker members of the community.
b. He argues at a popular level, putting forward an inclination of human *nature*, which is not viewed pessimistically in this case. Basil (d.379)[2] and Cassian (d.430)[3] also speak of the natural inclination to goodwill. Basil, for example, sees in love and in man's natural 'ability to communicate' a 'power implanted' in us by ... 'the Creator': 'Nothing is more proper to our nature than our reliance on one another, our mutual seeking and the love of the thing sought .. . The seeds of those powers were scattered in us by the Lord ... The (new) Law perfects and beautifies those powers which were implanted inside us by the Creator.'[4]
c. Kindness towards the aged and children (the 'Master' mentions here the twelfth year of age as the limit[5]) is part of the cenobitic 'Rule'.[6] It was cultivated, for instance, in the monasteries of Pachomius (d.346).[7] This concern for individual needs is typical of Benedict.[8]

NOTES TO CHAPTER 37

1 RB 37,1–3: RM 28,19–26. 2 RBasRuf 2. 3 Conl 16,2. 4 RBasRuf 2. 5 RM 28,24. 6 → 1,2; 3,7–11; 7,55; 23,1. 7 Jerome, praef in Pach Reg 5. 8 → 33,6; 34,1–2. Cf. RB 40,3; 48,25; 53,19.

CHAPTER 38

OF THE READER FOR THE WEEK

17 Mar
17 July
16 Nov

1 Reading ought not to be lacking Cf. Lk 4:4
at the meals of the brethren,
nor should anyone who takes up a book at random read there,
but a reader for the week
shall enter on his duty on Sunday.

2 After the final prayers of the Mass and Communion Cf. Ps 51:13
he who is to begin
shall ask all to pray for him
that God may TURN AWAY from him the spirit of pride.

3 And this verse shall be said in the oratory Ps. 51:17
three times by all—he however shall begin it—
LORD, YOU WILL OPEN MY LIPS
AND MY MOUTH SHALL DECLARE YOUR PRAISE.

4 And thus having received a blessing,
he shall enter on the reading.

5 Let there be deep silence
so that no one's muttered criticism,
and no voice except the reader's be heard there.

6 Whatever is needed for eating and drinking
the brethren shall so pass to one another
that nobody need ask for anything.

7 But if something be needed
let it be requested by some audible sign
rather than by the voice.

8 Nor let anyone there presume to raise questions Cf. Eph 4:27;
about the current reading 1 Tim 5:14
or about anything else
lest a pretext be furnished;

9 unless perhaps the superior wish to say something briefly,
for edification.

10 The brother who is reader for the week
shall receive a drink of 'watered wine'
before he begins to read,

on account of the Holy Communion,
and lest it be hard for him to endure the fast.

11 Afterwards he should eat with the kitcheners of the week
and with the servers.

12 The brothers are not to read or sing
each in turn,
but only those who edify listeners.

CAPUT XXXVIII: DE EBDOMADARIO LECTORE

'MENSIS FRATRUM LECTIO DEESSE NON DEBET, NEC FORTUITO CASU QUI ARRIPUERIT CODICEM LEGERE IBI, SED LECTURUS TOTA EBDOMADA DOMINICA INGREDIATUR. 'QUI INGREDIENS POST MISSAS ET COMMUNIONEM PETAT AB OMNIBUS PRO SE ORARI, UT AVERTAT AB IPSO DEUS SPIRITUM ELATIONIS. 'ET DICATUR HIC VERSUS IN ORATORIO TERTIO AB OMNIBUS, IPSO TAMEN INCIPIENTE: DOMINE, LABIA MEA APERIES, ET OS MEUM ADNUNTIABIT LAUDEM TUAM. 'ET SIC ACCEPTA BENEDICTIONE INGREDIATUR AD LEGENDUM. 'ET SUMMUM FIAT SILENTIUM, UT NULLIUS MUSITATIO VEL VOX NISI SOLIUS LEGENTIS IBI AUDIATUR. 'QUAE VERO NECESSARIA SUNT COMEDENTIBUS ET BIBENTIBUS SIC SIBI VICISSIM MINISTRENT FRATRES, UT NULLUS INDIGEAT PETERE ALIQUID. 'SI QUID TAMEN OPUS FUERIT, SONITU CUIUSCUMQUE SIGNI POTIUS PETATUR QUAM VOCE. 'NEC PRAESUMAT IBI ALIQUIS DE IPSA LECTIONE AUT ALIUNDE QUICQUAM REQUIRERE, NE DETUR OCCASIO; 'NISI FORTE PRIOR PRO AEDIFICATIONE VOLUERIT ALIQUID BREVITER DICERE. ''FRATER AUTEM LECTOR EBDOMADARIUS ACCIPIAT MIXTUM, PRIUSQUAM INCIPIAT LEGERE, PROPTER COMMUNIONEM SANCTAM, ET NE FORTE GRAVE SIT EI IEIUNIUM SUSTINERE. ''POSTEA AUTEM CUM COQUINAE EBDOMADARIIS ET SERVITORIBUS REFICIAT. ''FRATRES AUTEM NON PER ORDINEM LEGANT AUT CANTENT, SED QUI AEDIFICANT AUDIENTES.

1 **a.** The succinct opening sentence is justified in the 'Master'[1] with reference to Luke[2] by the saying: 'While the body is being fed, *spiritual food* should never be lacking.'[3]

b. The prescription of *reading at table* is also found in other Rules[4] and, according to Cassian (d.430),[5] probably does not originate in Egypt, where a surprising silence reigned at table,[6] but in Cappadocia.[7] The reading was supposed to prevent quarrelling at table.[8]

2–4 **a.** *A celebration of the Eucharist* was usual in the monasteries on Sunday, as the Rule of Pachomius already attests.[9] The offering of the sacrifice marked out that day as the day of the Lord's resurrection. Everyone had to take part in the celebration. In Benedict's usage the meaning of the expression 'missas' is indeed not defined;[10] here, it has to be related to the Mass;[11] however, the 'dismissal' of the non-communicants, often carried out before the Communion, could be meant.[12]

b. Benedict concerns himself with good order during the reading at table;[13] not everyone at that time was able to read, and even those who were, could not always make themselves understood while reading the manuscripts (scriptura continua!).[14] Because the *duty of reading* was an arduous one, a special blessing is provided for.[15]

c. Benedict is even more concerned with the good *interior dispositions* of the reader; this went beyond the 'Rule of the Master'. A service which presupposes knowledge[16] must also be performed in all humility, like any other work. No one should pride himself on his abilities. Gregory the Great (d.604) relates that the son of a high official, who had become a monk, had once to wait on Abbot Benedict with a light during the evening meal.[17] On thoughts of pride rising up in the young monk: 'Who is this man? ... Who am I!', Benedict, skilled at searching hearts read the thoughts of the young monk and said to him: 'Sign your heart, brother, sign your heart (with the sign of the cross)!' Then Benedict removed the brother from that duty. The latter told the others 'what he had in his heart'.[18]

5–9   a. Benedict leaves on one side the rules about reading at table that had been newly drafted by the 'Master',[19] and consults tradition instead. *Silence* at table is inculcated by Pachomius (d.346) at first as a rule of etiquette: to draw attention 'rather by a sign than by a word' to something needed is a regulation which stems from him.[20] Caesarius (d.542) gives a more profound reason for it: 'When they are sitting at table, let them give their attention in silence to the reading. When the reading ends, let holy meditation not depart out of their hearts.'[21]
b. The 'Master' provides for questions from the brethren and for answers by the abbot, if the reading at table is not understood.[22] That the superior may speak was recorded in older Rules.[23] Benedict limits the scope: no questions, at most a few brief *words from the superior*! Order must reign at table!

10–11   In Benedict's monastery 'watered wine' is drunk,[24] perhaps because the monastery is poor.[25] The explanation of the 'Mixtum' for the reader is in accord with Caesarius;[26] at the same time, Benedict speaks more reverently than the Master[27] about '*Holy Communion*'. The reception of the eucharistic food obviously took place before the beginning of the main meal. Basil (d.379) explains, 'with how much reverence, faith and love we should receive the grace of Christ's Body and Blood': he first quotes relevant passages[28] and then continues: 'Whoever believes in these words interiorly, contemplates the greatness of his (Christ's) glory and admires the excess of his humility (after all, in his unique greatness he became obedient to the Father unto death, and that for our life!), in that person, I believe, a heartfelt love is called forth: the love for God himself, the Father, who spared not his own Son, but sacrificed him for us all; the love for his Only-begotten Son is called forth all the more, because he suffered a most shameful death in order to redeem us.[29] This heartfelt love belongs to the spiritual preparation when someone receives of the Bread and the Cup.'[30] According to the 'Rule of the Master', as well as the celebration of the Eucharist 'on the Lord's Day of the Easter Resurrection', to which they went 'in procession' to the (parish) 'Churches',[31] a daily celebration of Communion before the main meal was customary, at which the (lay) abbot distributed the Sacrament.[32] Benedict himself gives no very clear description of this practice.[33] Once again, he wants to prevent any occasion of displeasure or 'sadness'[34] and provides for all 'servers'.[35]

12   *Exceptions* from the normal order in liturgical services are here declared to be legitimate. The 'Master' had to except illiterates from duty as reader at table.[36] That perhaps was the occasion for this remark of Benedict's; 'singing' hardly comes into question for the refectory, but for the oratory.[37]

NOTES TO CHAPTER 38

1 RB 38,1:RM, 24,1–4; RB 38,2–4: RM 24,6–12; RB 38,8–9: RM 24,19; RB 38,10: RM 24,14; RB 38,11: RM 24,30.40; RB 38,12: RM 24,1–4. 2 4:4: 'Not from bread alone. . .' 3 RM 24,4–5. 4 Justified in almost the same way in Caesarius (RCaesVirg 18), further, with fewer supporting reasons, in the 'Order of the Monastery' (OM7) and in Augustine (Praec 3,2). 5 Inst 4,17: In Tabennisi silence is kept. In Cappadocia, the reading is to prevent 'silly chatter' and especially 'quarrels', which 'easily arise at table'. 6 Pachomius, Praec 33. 7 Cf.Basil, Shorter Rules 180. 8 Cf. Augustine, Praec 3,1. 9 Praec 15–16; 18; → 38,10–11 (in Note 31). 10 → 17,1–4. 11 Cf. RM 45,14.17 and RB 59,2.8; 60,4. 12 Cf. RB 17,4.8.10; 35,12–14 (in Note 27); → 38,2–4. 13 Verse 1. 14 Cf. RM 24,3.18. 15 → 35,15–18. 16 See above, Note 14. 17 That does not correspond to the regulation of RB 41,8. 18 Dial 2,20. 19 Verses 5–7 are without parallel in the 'Master'. He always had his Rule read out, except when 'lay people' were present, who could make fun of the Rule (RM 24,15–30). 20 Verse 7; Cassian, Inst 4,17 is the source of the RB in this case; cf. Pachomius, Praec.33. 21 RCaesVirg 18. 22 RM 24,19. 23 R4P 2,42 (Scripture reading or a few words from the Superior); 2PR 2,46. In V. 9 Benedict uses for the Superior (abbot) the already archaic designation 'Prior', which is later given to the 'Second' in the monastery ('Praepositus'). 24 The 'Master' has unwatered wine served first, and watered wine during the meal (RM 27,1.5); 4,34–40; 40. 25 → 48,7–8. 26 RCaesVirg 14 (tonic); cf. RB 35,12–13. 27 RM 24,14: from fear of a 'spitting out of the Sacrament'. 28 1 Cor 11:29 ('any one who eats and drinks without discerning the body. . .'); Lk 22:19 ('my body which is given for you'); Jn 1:114 ('the Word became flesh. . .we have beheld his glory . . . .ful of grace'); Phil 2:6–8 ('he humbled himself. . .'). 29 With quotation: 2 Cor 5:14. 30 RBasRuf 134. 31 Cf. RM 45,14–17; 81,7. 32 Cf. RM 21–22. 33 → 35,9–10 (Note 22); 38,2–4; 50; 61,1–7; 62,1. 34 → 31,3–7. 35 By the 'servants' in V.11 could be meant: attendants of the sick (RB 36,7.10), assistants to the kitchen servers (RB 35,3) or hired servants, e.g. 'bondsmen' (mancipia), who belong to an estate and work on it. → 48,7–8 (Note 20). 36 Cf. RM 24,3. 37 → 47,2–3.

CHAPTER 39

OF THE RATION OF FOOD

18 Mar
18 July
17 Nov

1 For the main daily meal
whether at the sixth or ninth hour,
two cooked foods are enough, we believe,
at every table,

2 so that he who could not eat of the one,
may make a meal of the other.

3 Therefore two cooked foods shall be enough
for all the brethren;
and should there be fruit or fresh vegetables,
let a third be added.

4 A full pound weight of bread shall be sufficient per day,
whether there be one meal
or a midday and evening meal.

5 If they are to eat in the evening
a third part of this pound should be kept back by the cellarer,
to be served at this meal.

6 But should it happen
that heavier work has been done,
it shall be in the abbot's judgement and power
to add a supplement
if expedient,

7 avoiding above all over-eating
so that indigestion never overtake a monk.

8 Nothing indeed is so unsuited to any Christian
as over-eating,

9 as our Lord says: Lk 21:34
TAKE HEED TO YOURSELVES
LEST YOUR HEARTS BE OVERBURDENED WITH SELF-INDULGENCE.

10 The same amount should not be served
to boys under age,
but less than to their elders:
frugality shall be observed in everything.

11 Except for the very weak sick

all shall together abstain
from eating the flesh-meat of four-footed animals.

CAPUT XXXIX: DE MENSURA CIBUS

ISUFFICERE CREDIMUS AD REFECTIONEM COTIDIANAM TAM SEXTAE QUAM NONAE, OMNIBUS MENSIS, COCTA DUO PULMENTARIA PROPTER DIVERSORUM INFIRMITATIBUS, ²UT FORTE QUI EX ILLO NON POTUERIT EDERE, EX ALIO REFICIATUR. ³ERGO DUO PULMENTARIA COCTA FRATRIBUS OMNIBUS SUFFICIANT ET, SI FUERIT UNDE POMA AUT NASCENTIA LEGUMINUM, ADDATUR ET TERTIUM. ⁴PANIS LIBRA UNA PROPENSA SUFFICIAT IN DIE, SIVE UNA SIT REFECTIO SIVE PRANDII ET CENAE. ⁵QUOD SI CENATURI SUNT, DE EADEM LIBRA TERTIA PARS A CELLARARIO SERVETUR REDDENDA CENANDIS. ⁶QUOD SI LABOR FORTE FACTUS FUERIT MAIOR, IN ARBITRIO ET POTESTATE ABBATIS ERIT, SI EXPEDIAT, ALIQUID AUGERE, ⁷REMOTA PRAE OMNIBUS CRAPULA, ET UT NUMQUAM SUBRIPIAT MONACHO INDIGERIES; ⁸QUIA NIHIL SIC CONTRARIUM EST OMNI CHRISTIANO QUOMODO CRAPULA, ⁹SICUT AIT DOMINUS NOSTER: VIDETE NE GRAVENTUR CORDA VESTRA CRAPULA. ¹⁰PUERIS VERO MINORI AETATE NON EADEM SERVETUR QUANTITAS, SED MINOR QUAM MAIORIBUS, SERVATA IN OMNIBUS PARCITATE. ¹¹CARNIUM VERO QUADRUPEDUM OMNIMODO AB OMNIBUS ABSTINEATUR COMESTIO, PRAETER OMNINO DEBILES AEGROTOS.

1-3 Benedict's directive is, if anything, somewhat stricter than that of the 'Master',¹ who, in addition to the two cooked dishes, provides daily for a third, cold dish and for fruit as well.² Nevertheless, Benedict, like Basil (d.379),³ wishes, where possible, to take account of different *personal requirements*—something that did not concern the 'Master' at all.

4-5 The 'Master' provides for *half a loaf of bread* of about a pound weight,⁴ Benedict, if anything, for more. Both remember Cassian's description of Egyptian usages.⁵

6-9 a. Gregory the Great (d.604) relates that in Benedict's monastery, during a famine, the supply of flour ran out and the brethren became '*disgruntled*'. Then, he says, Benedict mildly reproved them for their 'little faith' and promised succour for the following day, in order to get them out of their bad mood. Next day, we are told, two hundred measures of flour in sacks were found outside the entrance of the monastery, without the benefactor being able to be traced.⁶

b. According to the witness of the Rule, Benedict was always concerned for the health and the contentedness of the monks. Thus, like Basil (d.379), he has a bonus distributed when the *workload* reaches a peak,⁷ whereas the 'Master' has extras (sweets) distributed on feastdays and when guests are present.⁸ Apart from that, Benedict insists on moderation, and quotes the title of 'monk' in support of this (a title mostly avoided by the 'Master'); he believes he can expect more from a monk than from other Christians.

10 According to the 'Master',⁹ a smaller ration of bread is sufficient for children under twelve years of age. Benedict expresses himself less precisely, and, in addition, urges *frugality*.¹⁰

11 At Easter and Christmastide the 'Master' reluctantly (!) permits the *consumption of meat*,[11] which Benedict rejects. In practice, however, Benedict allows fowl. Similar dietary habits are recorded in the monastery of Condat in the Jura region: no meat, apart from fowl and, and if need be, mutton for the sick.[12]

NOTES TO CHAPTER 39

1 RB 39,1–3:RM 26,1; RB 39,4: RM 26,2; RB 39,5:RM 26,3; RB 39,6–9: RM 26,11–13; RB 39,10: RM 26,14; RB 39,11: RM 53,26–33. 2 Benedict's monastery is poorer than that of the 'Master': → 38,10–11; 48,7–8. 3 RBasRuf 89; 91; 94. 4 RM 26,2–3. 5 Inst 4,14; Conl 2,19; 12,15. 6 Dial 2,21. 7 Cf. RBasRuf 94. 8 RM 26,11–12. Caesarius normally provides for three dishes, on feastdays for a fourth, as well as salad and sweet (RCaesVirg 94). 9 RM 24,14. 10 Cf. Cassian, Inst 4,14; → 38,10–11; 39,1–3 (Note 2); 38,7–8. 11 RM 53,26–27. 12 VPJur 66; → 49,4–5.

CHAPTER 40

OF THE AMOUNT OF DRINK

19 Mar
19 July
18 Nov

1 EACH ONE HAS HIS OWN GIFT FROM GOD 1 Cor 7:7
ONE IN THIS WAY, AND ANOTHER IN THAT;
2 and therefore it is with some misgiving
that we are deciding
the amount which others are to eat and drink.
3 Nevertheless, looking at the weakness of the infirm,
we believe that a *hemina* of wine per day
is enough for each.
4 But let those to whom GOD GIVES the endurance Cf. 1 Cor 3:8
to abstain
know that they WILL EACH RECEIVE HIS OWN REWARD.

5 But if the needs of the place Cf. Gal 5:21
or the work or the summer heat demand more
it shall lie within the superior's judgement;
he shall take care in all circumstances
that neither stupefaction nor drunkenness creep in.
6 Although we read that wine is absolutely not for monks, Vitae
but because in our times that cannot be Patrum 5,4,31
brought home to monks,
let us at least agree on this Ecclus 19:2
not to drink to stupefaction, but more temperately,
7 because WINE MAKES APOSTATES EVEN OF THE WISE.

8 But where the needs of the place require it,
that even the measure mentioned above cannot be had,
but much less,
or not even a drop,
let those who live there bless God and not complain.
9 Above all we admonish them not to complain.

CAPUT XL: DE MENSURA POTUS

¹UNUSQUISQUE PROPRIUM HABET DONUM EX DEO, ALIUS SIC, ALIUS VERO SIC; ²ET
IDEO CUM ALIQUA SCRUPULOSITATE A NOBIS MENSURA VICTUS ALIORUM
CONSTITUITUR. ³TAMEN INFIRMORUM CONTUENTES INBECILLITATEM, CREDIMUS
EMINAM VINI PER SINGULOS SUFFICERE PER DIEM. ⁴QUIBUS AUTEM DONAT DEUS

TOLERANTIAM ABSTINENTIAE, PROPRIAM SE HABITUROS MERCEDEM SCIANT. ⁵QUOD SI AUT LOCI NECESSITAS VEL LABOR AUT ARDOR AESTATIS AMPLIUS POPOSCERIT, IN ARBITRIO PRIORIS CONSISTAT, CONSIDERANS IN OMNIBUS NE SUBREPAT SATIETAS AUT EBRIETAS. ⁶LICET LEGAMUS VINUM OMNINO MONACHORUM NON ESSE, SED QUIA NOSTRIS TEMPORIBUS ID MONACHIS PERSUADERI NON POTEST, SALTIM VEL HOC CONSENTIAMUS UT NON USQUE AD SATIETATEM BIBAMUS, SED PARCIUS, ⁷QUIA VINUM APOSTATARE FACIT ETIAM SAPIENTES. ⁸UBI AUTEM NECESSITAS LOCI EXPOSCIT, UT NEC SUPRASCRIPTA MENSURA INVENIRI POSSIT, SED MULTO MINUS AUT EX TOTO NIHIL, BENDICANT DEUM QUI IBI HABITANT ET NON MURMURENT, ⁹HOC ANTE OMNIA ADMONENTES, UT ABSQUE MURMURATIONIBUS SINT.

1–4 **a.** Benedict begins with an *excuse*; perhaps he remembers that Basil (d.379) refuses to give concrete, individual regulations about such questions to the general body.[1]
b. The expression 'Hemina' is found only in Benedict and the 'Master'.[2] Benedict, however, is not interested in the detailed instructions of the 'Master' about drinks, but lays emphasis on different things;[3] *wine* is conceded in principle only to the 'weak';[4] but almost all number themselves among the 'weak'.[5] Although Benedict insists on moderation, he permits what causes joy. Benedict's restraint in the face of individual, personal sensibility is typical.
c. Words of Paul's concerning celibacy serve Benedict here to pick out *abstinence* as a charism. With a further quotation from Paul[6] he points to the corresponding 'reward'.[7]

5–7 *Extra servings* of wine are provided for by the 'Rule of the Master'[8] 'for the sake of love and peace 'on Sundays and holydays, as well as when guests are visiting. When Benedict thinks of exceptions, then it is because of work,[9]—which Basil (d.379) mentions too[10]—, because of 'local conditions' (perhaps a reference to the shortage of labour) and because of oppressive heat. With the 'Master', Benedict warns against 'drunkenness' and 'satiety';[11] while the 'Master' points to the danger of drowsiness at divine service, Benedict recalls the ideals of the earlier monks, who did, in fact, abstain from wine. 'They told Abbot Poimen about a monk who drank absolutely no wine. He said to them "Wine is not meant for monks at all"'[12] It is related of Abbot Lupicinus (d.c.480) in the Jura: 'From the time he had made profession as a monk, he could never be brought to drink even a small taste of wine.'[13] Still, wine came to be tolerated among monks, following the words addressed to Timothy.[14]

8–9 The 'Master' mentions spontaneous abstinence for the benefit of the poor.[15] Benedict thinks of the case in which the monastery itself must feel *poverty*.[16] As in other cases,[17] he counsels moderation, gratitude, and contentment. Augustine (d.430) writes in similar vein: 'They who are stronger in bearing poverty should consider themselves the richer. For it is better to need little than to have much.'[18] A demanding attitude, which reacts swiftly with frustration, and 'murmurs', is especially repugnant to Benedict.[19]

OF THE AMOUNT OF DRINK

NOTES TO CHAPTER 40

1 RBasRuf 9. 2 About a quarter litre (Steidle) of definitely unwatered wine, which was then mixed; → 38, 10–11. 3 RB 40,3: RM 27,39–40; RB 40,4: RM 27,47–51; RB 40,5–7: RM 27,43–46; RB 40,8–9: RM 27,52–54. 4 Cf. 1 Tim 5:23. 5 → Prol 45–50; 73,4–7. 6 Cf. 1 Cor 3:8. 7 Cf. Cassian, Conl 24,2, where 'tolerantia laboris' also is justified by 1 Cor 3:8; → 35,1–3 (Note 2). 8 RM 27,44–45. 9 → 39,6–9. 10 RBasRuf 94. 11 Cf. RM 27,46; RBasRuf 9; Cassian, Inst 5,6. 12 VPatr 5,4,31. 13 VPJur 66; cf. VAnt 6; VPach 6; Pachomius, Praec 45; 54; Cassian, Inst 5,6. 14 1 Tim 5:23 'No longer drink only water, but use a little wine for the sake of your stomach and your frequent ailments.' 15 RM 27,47–53; → 4, 10–19. 16 → 38,10–11; 39,1–3.6–9.10; 48,7–8. 17 → 34,3–5. 18 Praec 3,5. 19 → 4,34–40; 5,14–19; 31, 3–7; 34,6–7; 35,12–14; Cf. RBasRuf 93.

CHAPTER 41

AT WHAT HOURS
THE BRETHREN SHOULD TAKE MEALS

20 Mar 1   From holy Easter up to Pentecost
21 July   the brethren shall have the meal at the sixth hour,
21 Nov   and a supper in the evening.

2   From Pentecost throughout the whole of the summer,
    if the monks have not to work in the fields,
    or if the excessive summer heat does not disturb them,
    they shall fast on Wednesdays and Fridays
    until the ninth hour.

3   On the remaining days they shall have the meal at the sixth
    hour.

4   This sixth hour for the meal shall be maintained
    if they have work in the fields
    or if the summer heat be excessive;
    and it should be for the abbot to foresee this.

5   And let him so time and arrange everything
    that souls may be saved
    and that what the brothers do
    they may do without justifiable complaint.

6   From the 13th of September however until the beginning of
    Lent
    they shall always take their meal at the ninth hour.

7   During Lent however until Easter
    they shall eat at Vesper-time.

8   The Vespers however should be so celebrated
    that they do not need lamplight while eating,
    but let everything be completed
    while it is still daylight.

9   But in every season,
    the hour whether of supper or of the main meal
    should be so timed
    that all be done by daylight.

CAPUT XLI: QUIBUS HORIS OPORTET REFICERE FRATRES

¹A SANCTO PASCHA USQUE PENTESCOSTEN AD SEXTAM REFICIANT FRATRES ET SERA CENENT. ²A PENTECOSTEN AUTEM TOTA AESTATE, SI LABORES AGRORUM NON HABENT MONACHI AUT NIMIETAS AESTATIS NON PERTURBAT, QUARTA ET SEXTA FERIA IEIUNENT USQUE AD NONAM; ³RELIQUIS DIEBUS AD SEXTAM PRANDEANT. ⁴QUAM PRANDII SEXTAM, SI OPERIS IN AGRIS HABUERINT AUT AESTATIS FERVOR NIMIUS FUERIT, CONTINUANDA ERIT ET IN ABBATIS SIT PROVIDENTIA. ⁵ET SIC OMNIA TEMPERET ATQUE DISPONAT, QUALITER ET ANIMAE SALVENTUR ET QUOD FACIUNT FRATRES ABSQUE IUSTA MURMURATIONE FACIANT. ⁶AB IDUS AUTEM SEPTEMBRES USQUE CAPUT QUADRAGESIMAE AD NONAM SEMPER REFICIANT. ⁷IN QUADRAGESIMA VERO USQUE IN PASCHA AD VESPERAM REFICIANT. ⁸IPSA TAMEN VESPERA SIC AGATUR, UT LUCERNAE LUMEN NON INDIGEANT REFICIENTES, SED LUCE ADHUC DIEI OMNIA CONSUMMENTUR. ⁹SED ET OMNI TEMPORE, SIVE CENA SIVE REFECTIONIS HORA SIC TEMPERETUR, UT LUCE FIANT OMNIA.

1 Benedict's arrangement of the meal-times, which is built up chronologically following the course of the year, begins with *Easter*.¹ He provides for two meals in Eastertide, while the 'Master',² whom Benedict rarely follows in this chapter,³ adhered to Egyptian usage⁴ and just brought forward the one meal from evening to midday.⁵

2–4 a. Benedict establishes in principle that during *summer* the monks fast on Wednesdays and Fridays until None, whereas the 'Master' had them fast on five days.⁶ In practice, however, Benedict gives regular dispensations in summer because of the work in the fields, which the 'Master' forbade.⁷,⁸ Thus, the monks have a midday meal on an almost daily basis in summer, although ancient ecclesiastical and older monastic custom always provided for fasting until None on Wednesdays and Fridays.⁹

b. Benedict's solution, mild in practice, is echoed in other Rules of his time,¹⁰ which already found support in the objections of Basil (d.379) and Cassian (d.430) against a plethora of regulations in matters of fasting.¹¹

5 a. For Benedict, the principle of *observing prudent moderation*, or 'discretio' is especially important.¹² The abbot must act as a pastor of souls,¹³ that means having the 'salvation of souls' in view. That excludes a soft line or a showy asceticism—however much one may emphasize moderation.

b. For Benedict a 'legitimate murmuring', clearly *justifiable criticism*, is conceivable.¹⁴ Pachomius (d.346) wrote that, if a person murmured because of being 'overburdened with work', one should make clear to him 'five times that he is murmuring without reason.' If he continues, the work should be taken away from him and he should be treated as a sick person, in order to test whether his complaint was 'justified'.¹⁵

6 In *winter*, Benedict always has fasting 'until None' which, according to Cassian (d.430), was the general rule in Egypt (Saturdays and Sundays were excepted, as was Eastertide).¹⁶ For a correct understanding of this regulation it is important to remember that in Benedict's time, when the natural day and night used to be divided into twelve 'hours' each, in winter the day-hours turned out much shorter than the night-hours. Thus in winter hardly more time

elapsed from rising until the meal-time around the ninth hour (None) than from morning to noon in summer. The stomach did not have to adjust itself too strongly from season to season (A. de Vogüé).—On 13 September incidentally the day is about the same length as at Easter: this explains this date for the change. In Rome, the series of the sixteen Sunday formulae after Pentecost began afresh on the Sunday immediately following; Ember week came straight after (Lentini).

7–9 The monks keep *Lent* as all Christians do; however, Vespers—without over-scrupulous regard for liturgical rules—are fixed at such an early hour that 'everything' can be done 'by daylight',[17] this last perhaps for reasons of economy or in order to preserve the quiet of the night.[18] By the phrase 'that everything be done by daylight', Benedict refers perhaps to the sign quality of light.[19] In any case, the fading of the natural light was an important moment in the life-rhythm of the people of Benedict's time. Cyprian (d.258) writes: 'When the sun sets and the light of day is extinguished, we must of necessity have recourse to prayer; for Christ is the true light and the true day; thus we pray when the sun and the light of this earth are dimmed. Inasmuch as we ask that light should dawn on us anew, we beg for the coming of Christ, who in his mercy will bestow on us eternal light.'[20]

NOTES TO CHAPTER 41

1 Easter is always his starting-point in organizing the daily work in the course of the year: → 48,3. 2 RB 41,1: RM 28,37–40; RB 41,6: RM 28,1–2; RB 41,7: RM 28,8; 53,34; RB 41,8–9: RM 34,12–13; 36,10; 50,70–71. 3 RB 41,2–5 are without corresponding sections in the RM. 4 Cassian, Conl 21,23. 5 RM 28,37–38. 6 RM 28,1–2. 7 → 48,7–8. 8 Cf. also RB 35,12–14; 38,10; 43,19; → 48,5. 9 Cf. Jerome, praef in Pach Reg 5. 10 e.g. RCaesVirg 67 (the abbess shall organize everything according to circumstances); VPJur 31: in summer, the monks eat twice a day, clearly because of the large volume of work; Abbot Eugendus himself, however, confines himself to one single meal. 11 → 49, 4–5 12 → 3,4–6; 7,44–48; 64,12–15. 17–19; 70,4–5. 13 → 2,31–32; 4,41–50; 21,1–4; 23; 27–28; 31, 3–7. 14 Otherwise, murmuring is always a great evil in his eyes: 4,34–40; 5,14–19; 31,3–7; 34,6–7; 35,12–14; 40,8–9. 15 Pachomius, Iud 5; cf.RM 78,11–12: 'justified' complaints by monks about parasitical guests. 16 Inst 2,18; 3,9–12; Conl 21, 17–33; cf. R4P 3,2–5 (only Sunday is an exception). 17 → 17,7–8; 22,4–7. 18 → 42,1. 19 → Prol.8–11.28; 6,2–5; 8,4; 9,1–4; 17,7–8; 22,4–7; 38,2–4. 20 De or. dom. 35.

CHAPTER 42

LET NOBODY TALK AFTER COMPLINE

21 Mar
21 July
20 Nov

1 Monks must apply themselves to silence at all times,
above all however during the hours of the night.

2 And therefore in every season,
whether of fasting or of midday meal:

3 if it be the season of midday meal,
as soon as they have risen from supper
let them all sit down together,
and let one person read the Conferences or the Lives of the
Fathers,
or indeed something which may edify listeners,

4 but not however the Heptateuch or Kings,
because it will not be useful for sick minds
to hear that Scripture at that hour,
but let them be read at other hours.

5 But if it be a fast-day,
when Vespers are over,
after a brief interval
let them go on at once to the reading of the Conferences,
as we have said.

6 And when four or five pages
—or as much as time permits—
have been read,

7 and all have come together during this pause for reading
(if by chance someone was engaged in a task assigned him)

8 all therefore being gathered together as one body,
they shall celebrate Compline, and on going out from Compline,
no one shall be allowed to say anything further to anybody.

9 But if anyone be found to infringe this rule of reserve in speech,
let him undergo severe punishment,

10 unless a need should arise with regard to guests,
or perhaps the abbot should order something to someone.

11 But even this should be done
with all seriousness and the most honourable restraint.

CAPUT XLII: UT POST CONPLETORIUM NEMO LOQUATUR

¹OMNI TEMPORE SILENTIUM DEBENT STUDERE MONACHI, MAXIME TAMEN NOCTURNIS HORIS. ²ET IDEO OMNI TEMPORE, SIVE IEIUNII SIVE PRANDII: ³SI TEMPUS FUERIT PRANDII, MOX SURREXERINT A CENA, SEDEANT OMNES IN UNUM, ET LEGAT UNUS COLLATIONES VEL VITAS PATRUM AUT CERTE ALIUD QUOD AEDIFICET AUDIENTES, ⁴NON AUTEM EPTATICUM AUT REGUM, QUIA INFIRMIS INTELLECTIBUS NON ERIT UTILE ILLA HORA HANC SCRIPTURAM AUDIRE, ALIIS VERO HORIS LEGANTUR. ⁵SI AUTEM IEIUNII DIES FUERIT, DICTA VESPERA, PARVO INTERVALLO MOX ACCEDANT AD LECTIONEM COLLATIONUM, UT DIXIMUS. ⁶ET LECTIS QUATTUOR AUT QUINQUE FOLIIS VEL QUANTUM HORA PERMITTIT, ⁷OMNIBUS IN UNUM OCCURRENTIBUS PER HANC MORAM LECTIONIS, SI QUI FORTE IN ADSIGNATO SIBI COMMISSO FUIT OCCUPATUS, ⁸OMNES ERGO IN UNUM POSITI CONPLEANT, ET EXEUNTES A CONPLETORIIS NULLA SIT LICENTIA DENUO CUIQUAM LOQUI ALIQUID. ⁹QUOD SI INVENTUS FUERIT QUISQUAM PRAEVARICARE HANC TACITURNITATIS REGULAM, GRAVI VINDICTAE SUBIACEAT, ¹⁰EXCEPTO SI NECESSITAS HOSPITUM SUPERVENERIT AUT FORTE ABBAS ALICUI ALIQUID IUSSERIT. ¹¹QUOD TAMEN ET IPSUD CUM SUMMA GRAVITATE ET MODERATIONE HONESTISSIMA FIAT.

1 Night is the time of *silence*, into which the monk withdraws, as Christ withdrew into the silence of solitary prayer and into the desert.[1] Benedict presents an order which is different from the ritualistic arrangement of the 'Master'.[2]

2–7 a. The evening *reading* serves 'to bring all together', something which is mentioned three times[3] and described in detail, perhaps because it is an innovation of Benedict's.[4]

b. The 'Conferences of the Fathers' are *Cassian's* (d.430) 'Collationes', which relate or simulate conversations with Egyptian Fathers. By the 'Lives of the Fathers' are meant various stories about monks, collections of sayings and Lives.[5]—The 'first seven' books of the Old Testament are called the Hepateuch. Cassian recommended that certain readings, which could stimulate sexual fantasies, should be avoided in the evening.[6]

8–11 a. Silence after Compline or '*utmost seriousness*[7] and proper restraint' in a case of 'necessity' draw inspiration from the 'Master' and from Basil (d.379), who requires quiet in the house for the time in which services take place.[8]

b. Pachomius (d.346) was the first to require the *night silence* in the monks' huts,[9] together with other regulations for the protection of chastity.[10] Cassian (d.430) took up the idea.[11] Benedict is concerned with undisturbed rest for the community.[12] The quiet of the night is framed in by the Divine Offices.

NOTES TO CHAPTER 42

1 → 6,2–5 (in Notes 30–31). In the 'Master' the chapter about sleeping appeared here (RM 29). Benedict has already anticipated this subject (RB 22). Taking the keyword 'light' as his cue (→ 22,4–7; 41,7–9) he proceeds now to the night silence. 2 RB 42,1: Rm 30,8–10; 42,8: RM 30,12–13; RB 42,9: RM 30,28–30; RB 42,10: RM 30,24–27.17–22; RB 42,11: RM 30,19.25.25–26. 3 Verses 3.7.8. 4 This usage is not known to the 'Rule of the Master'; however it is briefly mentioned in the 'Order of the Monastery'; (OM 2). 5 Vitae Patrum, Historia Monachorum in Aegypto, Vita Antonii, Vita Pachomii, Vita Honorati, Vitae Patrum Jurensium . . .(→ Introduction 5; 9,8; 73,4–5). 6 Conl 19,16. 7 Gravitas: cf.

RB 6,3; 7,60; 22,6; 43,2; 47,4. 8 RBasRuf 137. 9 Praec 88;94. 10 Praec 92–93; 95. 11 Inst 2, 15,2; cf. verse 11 'proper (honestissima) restraint'. 12 Cf. RB 48,5; 52,2–3.5.

CHAPTER 43

OF THOSE WHO ARRIVE LATE
AT THE WORK OF GOD OR AT TABLE

1 At the hour of Divine Office,
as soon as the signal has been heard,
dropping everything whatever was in hand
let them run at top speed,

2 with seriousness however
so that ribaldry finds no fuel.

3 Nothing therefore shall be given precedence over the Work of
God.

4 But if at night Vigils
someone arrives after the *Gloria* of Psalm 94
—which for this reason we wish to be said
at an absolutely slow pace, with pauses—
let him not stand in his rank in choir,

5 but let him stand last of all
or in a place set apart by the abbot for such negligent persons,
so that he may be seen by him and by all,

6 until, at the end of the Work of God,
he does penance by public satisfaction.

7 We have judged therefore
that they should stand in the last place or apart,
so that being in the view of all,
they may amend for their own very shame.

Cf. Eph 4:27; 1 Tim 5:14

8 For if they were to remain outside the oratory,
there will perhaps be someone of the type who will go back to
bed and sleep,
or at least sit at his ease outside,
passing the time talking nonsense,
and an OPPORTUNITY IS GIVEN to THE EVIL ONE;

9 but let them come in
so that they do not lose everything,
and let them amend for the future.

10 At the Day Hours
he who does not arrive at the Work of God

after the verse and the *Gloria* of the first psalm following the
verse
—by the ruling we have given above,
let them stand in the last place,

11 nor let them presume to join the choir singing the psalms,
before satisfaction,
unless perhaps the abbot, waiving the point, gives permission,

12 in such a way however that the one at fault
does satisfaction for this.

13 At table however he who does not arrive before the verse,
so that all may say the verse together and pray
and all simultaneously go to the table,

14 he who through carelessness or bad will does not arrive,
shall be corrected for this up to twice.

15 If afterwards he do not amend,
he shall not be permitted to partake of the common table.

16 But let him eat alone,
separated from the company of all,
his allowance of wine being withdrawn,
until satisfaction and amendment.

17 He who is not present at the verse said after the meal
shall suffer a similar fate.

18 Not let anyone take it on himself
before or after the appointed time
to take any food or drink of his own initiative.

19 But if someone refuses to take something
offered him by a superior,
he shall receive nothing whatever
until fitting emendation,
at the time when he would like to have what he refused or
something else.

CAPUT XLIII: DE HIS QUI AD OPUS DEI VEL AD MENSAM TARDE OCCURRANT

¹AD HORAM DIVINI OFFICII, MOX AUDITUS FUERIT SIGNUS, RELICTIS OMNIBUS
QUAELIBET FUERINT IN MANIBUS, SUMMA CUM FESTINATIONE CURRATUR, ²CUM
GRAVITATE TAMEN, UT NON SCURRILITAS INVENIAT FOMITEM. ³ERGO NIHIL OPERI
DEI PRAEPONATUR. ⁴QUOD SI QUIS IN NOCTURNIS VIGILIIS POST GLORIAM PSALMI
NONAGESIMI QUARTI, QUEM PROPTER HOC OMNINO SUBTRAHENDO ET MOROSE
VOLUMUS DICI, OCCURRERIT, NON STET IN ORDINE SUO IN CHORO, ⁵SED ULTIMUS

OMNIUM STET AUT IN LOCO, QUEM TALIBUS NEGLEGENTIBUS SEORSUM CONSTITUERIT ABBAS, UT VIDEANTUR AB IPSO VEL AB OMNIBUS, ⁶USQUE DUM CONPLETO OPERE DEI PUBLICA SATISFACTIONE PAENITEAT. ⁷IDEO AUTEM EOS IN ULTIMO AUT SEORSUM IUDICAVIMUS DEBERE STARE UT, VISI AB OMNIBUS, VEL PRO IPSA VERECUNDIA SUA EMENDENT; ⁸NAM SI FORIS ORATORIUM REMANEANT, ERIT FORTE TALIS QUI SE AUT RECOLLOCET ET DORMIT, AUT CERTE SEDIT SIBI FORIS VEL FABULIS VACAT, ET DATUR OCCASIO MALIGNO; ⁹SED INGREDIANTUR INTUS, UT NEC TOTUM PERDANT ET DE RELIQUO EMENDENT. ¹⁰DIURNIS AUTEM HORIS, QUI AD OPUS DEI POST VERSUM ET GLORIAM PRIMI PSALMI QUI POST VERSUM DICITUR NON OCCURRERIT, LEGE QUA SUPRA DIXIMUS, IN ULTIMO STENT, ¹¹NEC PRAESUMANT SOCIARI CHORO PSALLENTIUM USQUE AD SATISFACTIONEM, NISI FORTE ABBAS LICENTIAM DEDERIT REMISSIONE SUA, ¹²ITA TAMEN UT SATISFACIAT REUS EX HOC. ¹³AD MENSAM AUTEM QUI ANTE VERSU NON OCCURRERIT, UT SIMUL OMNES DICANT VERSU ET ORENT ET SUB UNO OMNES ACCEDANT AD MENSAM, ¹⁴QUI PER NEGLEGENTIAM SUAM AUT VITIO NON OCCURRERIT, USQUE SECUNDA VICE PRO HOC CORRIPIATUR; ¹⁵SI DENUO NON EMENDAVERIT, NON PERMITTATUR AD MENSAE COMMUNIS PARTICIPATIONEM, ¹⁶SED SEQUESTRATUS A CONSORTIO OMNIUM REFICIAT SOLUS, SUBLATA EI PORTIONE SUA VINUM, USQUE AD SATISFACTIONEM ET EMENDATIONEM. ¹⁷SIMILITER AUTEM PATIATUR, QUI ET AD ILLUM VERSUM NON FUERIT PRAESENS, QUI POST CIBUM DICITUR. ¹⁸ET NE QUIS PRAESUMAT ANTE STATUTAM HORAM VEL POSTEA QUICQUAM CIBI AUT POTUS PRAESUMERE; ¹⁹SED ET CUI OFFERTUR ALIQUID A PRIORE ET ACCIPERE RENNUIT, HORA QUA DESIDERAVERIT HOC QUOD PRIUS RECUSAVIT AUT ALIUD, OMNINO NIHIL PERCIPIAT USQUE AD EMENDATIONEM CONGRUAM.

1–2 Warnings about *punctuality*, such as are found in the 'Master',[1] in Cassian (d.430)[2] and in the '2nd Rule of the Fathers',[3] are summarized in a basic principle, in which Benedict urges 'gravity'[4] as well as the desired haste. The signal was given by some kind of gong being sounded.

3 The '2nd Rule of the Fathers'[5] states: 'Let nothing be preferred to prayer'. It speaks in this connection of 'praying without ceasing.'[6] Benedict now applies the same formula to the institutionalized divine service. The concept *'Opus Dei'*, which originally designated the whole ascetic life,[7] takes on with Benedict the definite meaning of 'Divine Office'. Just as, according to one's interior disposition, 'nothing' may be preferred to 'the love for Christ',[8] so no other activity is to be prized more highly than the Divine Office, precisely because it is a realization of the summons 'to pray without ceasing'.[9]

4–6 The margin of tolerance[10] provided for in the case of *tardiness* in attending the Divine Office, and the punishments,[11] correspond to Cassian (d.430).[12] A reprimand for latecomers was the custom generally.[13]

7–9 a. Benedict's punishment is aimed at having an educative effect. He trusts the healing power of *community spirit*. The presupposition is that a person has integrated himself in the community and identified himself with it and its standards.

b. The '2nd Rule of the Fathers' expresses the fear that, if the prayer lasts too long, somebody may 'go out' during the readings and 'gossip' outside.[14] Benedict explains in detail his instruction (which does not agree with that of the 'Master'), to let the offenders stay in the oratory in a *place set apart*. His solution is an innovation previously unknown.

c. Gregory the Great (d.604) tells later how Benedict, 'the man of God', realized in prayer that a spiritual *demon of restlessness* was keeping a brother from the common prayer and seducing him to wander about aimlessly. The punishment Benedict imposed on him with the rod healed this monk's 'darkness of heart', and from then on he participated 'zealously and faithfully' in prayer.[15]

10–12 A hymn is not mentioned in the case of the Day Hours.[16] Participation in the 'choir's psalmody' is regarded as a privilege; this, in turn, presupposes an esteem for the community[17] assembled for prayer. In choral psalmody 'we imitate what we shall one day be,' says Cyprian[18] with regard to the communion of saints praising God in the other world.

13–17 a. *Sharing the same table* is a principal element of monastic community life.

b. The *prayer at meals* elevates eating and being together as a community, into a religious atmosphere.—Basil (d.379) has the question posed to him: 'How does someone eat and drink to the glory of God?' Answer: If he thinks of him who is nourishing him, namely God, and if he not only interiorly but also by his bodily posture, proclaims in all that he is rendering thanks to God; one does not demonstrate overweening behaviour while eating, but allows oneself to be fed by God as his workman, in order to strengthen oneself for one's work and for the fulfilment of the commandments.'[19]

c. Once again, Benedict turns his face against *tardiness*. Like Basil[20] he differentiates a justifiable latecoming from 'carelessness'. By 'fault'[21] is to be understood the interior resistance against identification with the community, which expresses itself in tardiness. The procedure for punishment has already been similarly described by Benedict.[22]

18–19 a. The strictly formulated prohibition of eating between meals[23] is reminiscent of Cassian (d.430),[24] who gives as the motive, training towards *self-control* and chastity; it is reminiscent also of other Rules.[25]

b. The 'Master'[26] punishes in like manner an absence from Communion or from table which stems from *false asceticism*. Similarly Basil (d.379) accuses of obstinacy self-willed monks, who refuse what they need.[27]

NOTES TO CHAPTER 43

1 RB 43,1–3: RM 54,1–2; RB 43,4–9: RM 32,9–15; 73,1–5; RB 43,10–12: RM 73,6–7; RB 43,13–16: RM 73,8–10; RB 43,17: RM 73,11; RB 43,18: RM 21,8–10; 30,23; RB 43,19: RM 22,7–8;74. 2 Inst 4,12; → 5,1–9 (in Note 26). 3 2PR 31. 4 → 42,8–11 (Note 7). 5 2PR 31. 6 Cf. 1 Thess 5:17; Lk 18:1. 7 Cf. Horsiesi, Lib 12; 58,5–7 (in Note 33). 8 → 4,20–33 (in Notes 27–28); 72,11. 9 → 4,55–58; 16,1–3. 10 In the night two psalms (counting Ps 3, according to RB 9,2); in the Day Hours one psalm (RB 43,10). 11 They are simpler than in the 'Master' (RM 73,1–5). 12 Inst 3,7; 4, 16,1; Cassian, however, is not speaking of the 'Glory be', but of the Psalm Collect (→ 20,1–5). 13 Pachomius, Praec 9–10; 121 (also with more indulgence in the night); RM 73,2; RCaesVirg 12. 14 2PR 32; 37. 15 Dial 2,4. 16 RB 17,3 is perhaps an insertion (A. de Vogüé); → 9,1–4. 17 → 1,3–5; 16,5. 18 De dom.or.36 19 RBasRuf 57. 20 RBasRuf 97. 21 Verse 15: cf. 2PR 35 (vitium). 22 → 23,2–3; cf. Pachomius, Praec 31–32; RM 73 8–11; RCaesVirg 12. 23 RB 35,12–14; 37,1–3. 24 Inst 4, 18; 5,20. 25 Pachomius, Praec 71–80 (the monks may not climb palm-trees or in any other way look for fruit); Augustine, Praec 3,1 (at least one should not eat between meals, if one does not even fast !); RCaes Virg 30; 41). 26 RM 22,5–8. 27 RBasRuf 96.

CHAPTER 44

HOW THE EXCOMMUNICATED
SHALL MAKE SATISFACTION

1 Those who on account of serious faults
are excommunicated from oratory and table,
shall lie prostrate outside the oratory doors
saying nothing,
at the time when the Work of God is being concluded in the
oratory.

2 Just placing his head on the ground
he shall lie prostrate
at the feet of all
as they come out of the oratory.

3 And he shall do this for so long a time
until the abbot judges satisfaction has been done.

4 When he comes at the abbot's bidding
he shall stretch out at the feet of the abbot himself
and then at the feet of all
that they may pray for him.

5 And then, if the abbot orders it,
he shall be received into choir
or in the place which the abbot has decided,

6 with this proviso however
that he shall not presume to sing or recite alone
psalm, lesson or anything else in the oratory,
unless again the abbot orders it.

7 And at all the Hours,
when the Work of God is being completed,
he shall cast himself on the ground
in the place where he is standing.

8 And he shall do satisfaction in this way
until the abbot orders him
to cease at length from this satisfaction.

9 Those however who on account of minor faults
are excommunicated from the table only
shall do satisfaction in the oratory
until the abbot gives an order.

10 They shall carry out this
until he gives the blessing and says:
'That's enough.'

CAPUT XLIV: DE HIS QUI EXCOMMUNICANTUR QUOMODO SATISFACIANT

'QUI PRO GRAVIBUS CULPIS AB ORATORIO ET A MENSA EXCOMMUNICANTUR, HORA QUA OPUS DEI IN ORATORIO PERCELEBRATUR, ANTE FORES ORATORII PROSTRATUS IACEAT NIHIL DICENS, 'NISI TANTUM POSITO IN TERRA CAPITE, STRATUS PRONUS OMNIUM DE ORATORIO EXEUNTIUM PEDIBUS. 'ET HOC TAMDIU FACIAT, USQUE DUM ABBAS IUDICAVERIT SATISFACTUM ESSE. 'QUI DUM IUSSUS AB ABBATE VENERIT, VOLVAT SE IPSIUS ABBATIS, DEINDE OMNIUM VESTIGIIS UT ORENT PRO IPSO. 'ET TUNC, SI IUSSERIT ABBAS, RECIPIATUR IN CHORO VEL IN ORDINE QUO ABBAS DECREVERIT, 'ITA SANE, UT PSALMUM AUT LECTIONEM VEL ALIUD QUID NON PRAESUMAT IN ORATORIO INPONERE, NISI ITERUM ABBAS IUBEAT. 'ET OMNIBUS HORIS, DUM PERCONPLETUR OPUS DEI, PROICIAT SE IN TERRA IN LOCO QUO STAT. 'ET SIC SATISFACIAT, USQUE DUM EI IUBEAT ITERUM ABBAS, UT QUIESCAT IAM AB HAC SATISFACTIONE. 'QUI VERO PRO LEVIBUS CULPIS EXCOMMUNICANTUR TANTUM A MENSA, IN ORATORIO SATISFACIANT USQUE AD IUSSIONEM ABBATIS. '°HOC PERFICIANT USQUE DUM BENEDICAT ET DICAT: ≪SUFFICIT≫.

0 a. Here[1] Benedict takes up again the theme of *penitential regulations*,[2] speaking first about 'serious faults'.[3]
b. After the 'correction'[4] and the 'exclusion' (excommunication)[5] there follow now the rendering of '*satisfaction*' (i.e. the penitential practice and its duration), as well as the '*taking back*' of the excluded penitent into the community; sometimes the pattern is taken from the 'Master'.[6]
c. Once again, the ancient ecclesiastical order of penance and reconciliation is the model for the monastic procedure.[7] Because Benedict abridges the 'Master's' text,[8] some processes are not clearly recognizable. Without further explanation, for instance, an intervention of the abbot is mentioned nine times (!) in this short chapter. Perhaps Benedict ran up against difficulties in his community with his archaic model of ecclesiastical penitential regulations. That is why he gives such clear prominence to the right and duty of the abbot. He wishes to enable him to act in a pastorally correct way.[9] The difficulties are doubtless connected with the then already general decline of the *ancient ecclesiastical order* of penance and reconciliation,[10] which Benedict wishes to maintain in the monastery, scaled down to a miniature form (A. de Vogüé).
1–3 The 'Rule of the Master'[11] begins similarly, but then gives lengthy confessions of guilt by the penitent and his *request* for prayer, for forgiveness and for the loosing by the abbot of the bands of guilt in the eyes of God.[12] Already Cassian (d.430) has the penitent stretched out on the ground ask for forgiveness.[13]
4–5 When he is to be *taken back*, the penitent is summoned by the abbot (into the oratory). As the Master explains, the 'correction' and the 'promise of amendment' follow[14]; immediately afterwards comes the 'prayer for the penitent'.[15] A

similar alternation of interventions by the abbot and of community prayer is to be found in the reception of novices.[16] A laying on of hands is not provided for in the monastic penitential order. The reception back into the community, the sign of reconciliation with God, takes place by readmission to the 'choir'.

6–8 a. According to this text, the penitent seems to remain initially in the situation of 'minor excommunication' for a period which is not exactly defined.[17] True, forgiveness has occurred, but the purpose of amendment is to be practised, and a lasting penitent state of mind to be called into being.[18] A merely formalistic performance of a 'penance' is sterile. It is probably for this reason that Benedict provides for the repetition of the *penance*, something unknown to the 'Master' or Cassian (d.430). It is not the magnitude of the outward act of penance which is decisive, but rather the state of the heart. The abbot must be able 'to read the heart' and judge rightly;[19] that is his pastoral task.

b. When Abbot Poimen was requested by one who had committed a serious offence, to consign him to a three-year penitential period, he answered: '"Too much!" Also to suggestions of a year-long penance or one of forty days he answered each time: "Too much!" He added: "I believe that, if a man *repents* with his whole heart and resolves not to commit again that for which he is doing penance, God then also accepts a penance lasting only three days."'[20]

9–10 For '*less serious faults*' penance is done in the oratory, perhaps by means of a profound bow.[21] The abbot judges for how long this penance is necessary. The penitential attitude must prove itself in outward behaviour, if one is to be certain of its genuineness.

NOTES TO CHAPTER 44

1 He takes up the theme of 'punishments' mentioned in the foregoing chapter in connection with latecomers at the Divine Office. 2 RB 23–30; → 23,0. 3 → 25,1–2. 4 → 23,2–3. 5 → 24–25. 6 RB 44,1–3: RM 14, 20–22; RB 44,4: RM 14,17; RB 44,6: RM 13,66; 73,17; RB 44,7–8: RM 14,20–22; RB 44,9–10: RM 13,61. 7 → 23,4. 8 Benedict briefly summarizes lengthy disquisitions of the 'Master' about the major (RB 44,1–8) and the minor (RB 44,9–10) penance. 9 → 27–28. 10 → 23,2–3 (Note 14). 4 (Notes 20–23); 27,1–4; 28,1–5 (Note 8). 11 RM 14; for the 'confession of guilt': → 7,44–48. 12 RM 14,17: 'Through your intercession with the Lord, loosen the bonds in which my neglect has ensnared me.' 13 Inst 2,16; 4,16,1. 14 RM 14,24. 15 Verse 4; → 27,1–4.7–9. Cf. RB 27,4; 28,4; 35,15; 58,23. 16 Cf. RB 58,23. 17 Cf. RB 44,9–10; 29,2; 43,4. 18 → 49, 1; 7,59–61. 19 Verse 8; 2,31–32; 3,4–6.7–11; 38,2–4. 20 VPatr 5,10,40. 21 Cf. RM 13,61.

CHAPTER 45

OF THOSE WHO MAKE MISTAKES IN THE ORATORY

25 Mar
25 July
24 Nov

1 Should anyone make a mistake
   in the recitation of
   psalm,
   responsory,
   antiphon,
   or reading,
   unless he be humbled by satisfaction
   there before all,
   he shall undergo a greater punishment,
2 as being in fact
   one who was unwilling
   to correct by humility
   what he had failed in by negligence.
3 The children however shall be flogged
   for such a fault.

CAPUT XLV: DE HIS QUI FALLUNTUR IN ORATORIO

¹SI QUIS DUM PRONUNTIAT PSALMUM, RESPONSORIUM, ANTEFANAM VEL LECTIONEM FALLITUS FUERIT, NISI SATISFACTIONE IBI CORAM OMNIBUS HUMILIATUS FUERIT, MAIORI VINDICTAE SUBIACEAT, ²QUIPPE QUI NOLUIT HUMILITATE CORRIGERE QUOD NEGLEGENTIA DELIQUIT. ³INFANTES AUTEM PRO TALI CULPA VAPULENT.

0 In two chapters,[1] with reference to Pachomius (d.346)[2] and especially to Cassian (d.340),[3] Benedict treats of *lesser faults* in the oratory and at work.
1–2 Benedict tends towards *spontaneous* and immediate satisfaction. Like Cassian,[4] he sees in this admission a sign of humility and a sufficient punishment.[5] Otherwise, 'excommunication' follows. All this shows how important reverence at prayer is for Benedict.
3 Here again we run up against corporal punishment for *children*.[6]

NOTES TO CHAPTER 45

1 RB 45–46. 2 Praec 14: mistakes made while praying. 3 Inst 4, 16, 1 (Breakages, disturbances at the singing of the psalms). 4 Inst 3, 7, 1. 5 → 71, 6–9. 6 → 23,5; 24,3; 30; in verse 3 Benedict is probably relying on RM 14,79–82 (up to fifteen years of age).

CHAPTER 46

OF THOSE WHO ARE AT FAULT
IN ANY OTHER MATTERS WHATSOEVER

1–2 Should anyone commit some fault
or break or lose something
or overstep the mark
in any place whatever
at any work whatsoever
in the kitchen,
in the store-room,
while in service,
in the bakery,
in the garden,
while working at any craft,
3 and does not come immediately
before the abbot and community
doing spontaneous satisfaction,
revealing his fault—
4 should it become known
through someone else,
he shall be chastened more severely.

5 Should however the hidden fault
be a sin of the soul,
let him make it known only to the abbot
(or to the spiritual elders)
6 who will know how to cure
their own and others' wounds,
not uncover and broadcast them.

CAPUT XLVI: DE HIS QUI IN ALIIS QUIBUSLIBET
REBUS DELINQUUNT

¹SI QUIS DUM IN LABORE QUOVIS, IN COQUINA, IN CELLARIO, IN MINISTERIO, IN PISTRINO, IN HORTO, IN ARTE ALIQUA DUM LABORAT, VEL IN QUOCUMQUE LOCO, ALIQUID DELIQUERIT, ²AUT FREGERIT QUIPPIAM AUT PERDIDERIT, VEL ALIUD QUID EXCESSERIT UBIUBI, ³ET NON VENIENS CONTINUO ANTE ABBATEM VEL CONGREGA-TIONEM IPSE ULTRO SATISFECERIT ET PRODIDERIT DELICTUM SUUM, ⁴DUM PER ALIUM COGNITUM FUERIT, MAIORI SUBIACEAT EMENDATIONI. ⁵SI ANIMAE VERO PECCATI CAUSA FUERIT LATENS, TANTUM ABBATI AUT SPIRITALIBUS SENIORIBUS

PATEFACIAT, 'QUI SCIAT CURARE ET SUA ET ALIENA VULNERA, NON DETEGERE ET PUBLICARE.

1–4   **a.** The mention of faults at *work*[1] gives occasion to list some rooms of the monastery.[2]

    b. Benedict adopts a distinction made by Augustine (d.430).[3] The latter distinguished between a 'spontaneous' admission and the discovery of a fault through others.[4] In the second case, the punishment should be more severe. Benedict gives a general application to Augustine's direction, and extends the latter's 'more severe correction' to breakages which occur perhaps by chance. He is concerned above all with *spontaneous* admission. He appeals to the individual's sense of personal responsibility.

    c. The 'Rule of the Master'[5] speaks of faults being reported by others.[6]

5–6   **a.** In other parts of the Rule, Benedict also expresses the wish that secret faults should be *revealed* to the 'spiritual senior' or to the abbot.[7]

    b. In this connection, it is striking that Benedict considers it quite possible that *faults* can also be committed by spiritual advisers.[8] The 'Master' emphasizes that everybody accept his own spiritual state, that is, admit to himself, then however also confess without false shyness to the superiors or the abbot, even when he has 'bad or improper things' to acknowledge. But the abbot, too, must ask the community to pray for him, when he feels the poison of evil in himself. Speaking out and confession eliminate the toxic substances of the spirit.[9]

    c. Cassian (d.430) mentions '*secret faults*', such as the surreptitious pilfering of bread rolls, daily practised by a hungry young monk, or bad thoughts. Cassian underlines the liberating effect of speaking out openly. He emphasizes that a young person's trust must not be betrayed by indiscretions, and interior temptations must not be judged harshly or interpreted as signs that a vocation is lacking.

    d. The counsellor (Cassian continues) must, on the contrary, be aware of his *own weakness*. An uncomprehending counsellor, who reprimands harshly, could drive a good young person almost to despair. Overweening harshness could also lead the counsellor himself to stumble.[10] Thus Benedict demands too that the communication should be made only to competent counsellors. Pastoral, indeed 'medical', therapeutic qualities are presupposed.[11]

    e. By the *healing manifestation of conscience* before the (lay) abbot or before 'spiritual seniors' (an insertion), is not meant a sacramental form of confession, such as belongs to ecclesial penance before the bishop or priest. Basil (d.379) wishes that 'unchaste or improper' things should be confessed only to those who know how to 'heal and correct', just as bodily complaints are allowed to be treated only by doctors 'who are generally regarded as very experienced'.[12] In another passage he writes: 'It is necessary that sins be confessed to those to whom the "stewardship of the mysteries of God"[13] is entrusted. So one finds also that the penitents of old confessed their sins to the saints. In the Gospel it is written that people confessed their sins to John the Baptist,[14] and in the Acts of the Apostles that they confessed them to the Apostles who baptized.'[15]

NOTES TO CHAPTER 46

1 Cf.Pachomius, Praec 125 (breakages); 131 (losses); Cassian, Inst 4, 16,1–2 (breakages; disturbing the psalmody). 2 Cf. RB 7,63. 3 Praec 4,11. 4 Secretly receiving letters from a woman (→ 54,1–5). 5 Verse 4. 6 RM 17,7; 30,29. For the rest, this chapter contains only a few echoes of the Master. 7 → 7,44–48. 8 The plural 'or spiritual *seniores*' (according to RM 15,14 the deans are meant) must be an insertion, because Benedict continues in the singular. 9 RM 15,1–17. 10 Conl 2,11–13; Inst 4,9; 64,12–15 (in Note 33). 11 → 2,26–29.31–32.37–40; 4,41–50.51–54; 27–28; 31,3–7; 41,5; 44,6–8; 64,12–15. 12 RBasRuf 200. 13 1 Cor 4:1. 14 Mt 3:6. 15 Cf. Acts 3:19.

CHAPTER 47

OF TELLING THE TIME FOR THE WORK OF GOD

27 Mar
27 July
26 Nov

1 By day and by night
it shall be the abbot's care
to announce the time for the Work of God;
either by doing it himself,
or by entrusting this charge
to such a careful brother
that everything may be celebrated at the due time.

2 Let those who have been told to do so
sing or recite the psalms and antiphons alone,
in their rank, after the abbot.

3 However let no one presume to sing or read
unless he can fulfil this office
so that listeners can build on it.

4 It shall be done
humbly, gravely, reverently,
and by him who is commissioned by the abbot.

CAPUT XLVII: DE SIGNIFICANDA HORA OPERIS DEI

¹NUNTIANDA HORA OPERIS DEI DIES NOCTISQUE SIT CURA ABBATIS: AUT IPSE
NUNTIARE AUT TALI SOLLICITO FRATRI INIUNGAT HANC CURAM, UT OMNIA HORIS
CONPETENTIBUS CONPLEANTUR. ²PSALMOS AUTEM VEL ANTEFANAS POST ABBATEM
ORDINE SUO QUIBUS IUSSUM FUERIT INPONANT. ³CANTARE AUTEM ET LEGERE NON
PRAESUMAT, NISI QUI POTEST IPSUD OFFICIUM IMPLERE UT AEDIFICENTUR
AUDIENTES; ⁴QUOD CUM HUMILITATE ET GRAVITATE ET TREMORE FIAT, ET CUI
IUSSERIT ABBAS.

1 Establishing the exact *time of day* was a difficult matter in the sixth century.¹
The abbot assumes this important task. He is the person chiefly responsible
for the Divine Office.

2–3 The directives for *chanters*, which follow rather unexpectedly² here, give an
objective criterion for the selection of singers or readers.³

4 Benedict has already referred to reverent behaviour during the *singing of the
psalms*,⁴˒⁵ when he also emphasized the interior disposition of humility. Cassian
(d.430) wrote: 'Beginners, and others who made little progress in interior virtue
and in knowledge, tend to pride themselves on the sound of their voices,

225

because they sing more melodiously than others, or because they perform briskly and energetically, better than others, or because of their prominent or wealthy parents . . ."[6] Dignity of delivery is also important in Benedict's mind.[7]

NOTES TO CHAPTER 47

1 The 'Master' speaks at length about those with responsibility (RM 31,1-9). His order for waking the monks comes before the chapters about the Vigils and other Offices (→ 8,0). 2 In the 'Master', the order for waking the monks precedes the order for the Divine Office (Vigils!), while the rules about singers and readers follow at the end of the order for the Divine Office (RM 46,1-7). The order itself for Divine Office is to be found in an earlier passage in Benedict (→ 8,0), so that now disparate material (order for waking-singers) is found together in our chapter; → 38,12. 3 Benedict has briefly summarized the instruction for him, which is already contained in R4P (2,10-11). However, it is not clear, who in fact now intones. Does an order of precedence exist or does the abbot give instructions? 4 Parallels are to be found in RM47, a chapter which has already served Benedict as a model for RB 19. The latter comes at the end of his order of the Divine Office, brought forward in his text. 5 → 38,12; 7. 6 Inst 11,13. 7 42,8-11 (Note 7).

CHAPTER 48

OF EACH DAY'S MANUAL WORK

28 Mar
28 July
27 Nov

1 Idleness is bad for the soul.
And therefore the brethren must be employed
at certain fixed times
in the work of their hands,
and again at other times—also fixed—
in reading devoted to God.

2 The following plan, we believe,
will adjust the time
for the one and the other.

3 From Easter until the first of October,
going out in the morning
they shall do what needs to be done
from the first until about the fourth hour.

4 From about the fourth hour
until the time they say Sext
shall be reading time.

5 After Sext however on rising from table
they shall rest on their beds
in total silence,
or perhaps should anyone wish to read,
let him read to himself
in such a way as not to disturb another.

6 And let None be anticipated
at the middle of the eighth hour,
and again let them work until Vespers
at what has to be done.

7 Should however the needs of the place or poverty
oblige them to reap the corn themselves
let them not be saddened,

8 because then are they really monks
when they live OFF THE WORK OF THEIR HANDS
just like our Fathers and the Apostles.

Cf. Ps 128:2; 1 Cor 4:12;
9:6,12,15,18; 2 Cor 12:13;
1 Thess 2:9;4,11–12;
2 Thess 3:7–12;
Tit 3:14: Jn 21:2–3;
Acts 18:3: 20:34–35

9 However all shall be done with moderation
on account of the faint-hearted.

29 Mar
29 July
28 Nov
10 From the first of October until the beginning of Lent
reading time goes up to the close of the second hour.

11 Terce is said at the second hour,
and up to None all work at their enjoined tasks.

12 At the first signal for the hour of None
all shall disengage from their work
and be ready when the second signal goes.

13 After the meal they shall occupy themselves
with their readings or the psalms.

14 In the days of Lent however
let them keep at their reading
from morning until the close of the third hour;
and until the close of the tenth hour
they shall carry out the work enjoined them.

15 In these days of Lent
let each receive a separate book from the 'library'
which they shall read through consecutively
from beginning to end;

16 these books are to be given out at the beginning of Lent.

17 Above all one or two seniors shall most certainly be delegated
to do the rounds of the monastery
during the reading hours of the brethren,

18 and see whether perhaps
there be not found a brother who has lost interest,
who is indulging in idleness or chatter
and not concentrating on the reading,
and who is not only useless to himself
but is also a distraction to the others.

19 If such a one—which God forbid—be found,
he shall be corrected once and a second time.

20 Should he not change his ways,   Cf. 1 Tim 5:20
he shall undergo the correction of the Rule in
such a way
THAT THE REST ALSO MAY HAVE FEAR.

21 Nor shall brother associate with brother
at inappropriate times.

30 Mar
30 July
29 Nov
22 On Sunday also let all devote themselves to reading,
except those who are deputed to the various duties.

23 But if someone be so careless and listless
   as not to want to
   or be unable to
   reflect or read
   let him be given a some work to do
   that he be not idle.

24 Brethren who are in poor health
   or who are of delicate constitutions
   shall be allotted a type of task or craft
   that they be neither idle
   nor be overwhelmed by the stress of the work
   or run away.
25 The abbot must remember their debility.

CAPUT XLVIII: DE OPERA MANUUM COTIDIANA

¹OTIOSITAS INIMICA EST ANIMAE, ET IDEO CERTIS TEMPORIBUS OCCUPARI DEBENT FRATRES IN LABORE MANUUM, CERTIS ITERUM HORIS IN LECTIONE DIVINA. ²IDEOQUE HAC DISPOSITIONE CREDIMUS UTRAQUE TEMPORE ORDINARI: ³ID EST: UT A PASCHA USQUE KALENDAS OCTOBRES A MANE EXEUNTES A PRIMA USQUE HORA PENE QUARTA LABORENT QUOD NECESSARIUM FUERIT. ⁴AB HORA AUTEM QUARTA USQUE HORA QUA SEXTAM AGENT, LECTIONI VACENT. ⁵POST SEXTAM AUTEM SURGENTES A MENSA PAUSENT IN LECTA SUA CUM OMNI SILENTIO, AUT FORTE QUI VOLUERIT LEGERE SIBI SIC LEGAT, UT ALIUM NON INQUIETET. ⁶ET AGATUR NONA TEMPERIUS MEDIANTE OCTAVA HORA, ET ITERUM QUOD FACIENDUM EST OPERENTUR USQUE AD VESPERAM. ⁷SI AUTEM NECESSITAS LOCI AUT PAUPERTAS EXEGERIT, UT AD FRUGES RECOLLEGENDAS PER SE OCCUPENTUR, NON CONTRISTENTUR, ⁸QUIA TUNC VERE MONACHI SUNT, SI LABORE MANUUM SUARUM VIVANT, SICUT ET PATRES NOSTRI ET APOSTOLI. ⁹OMNIA TAMEN MENSURATE FIANT PROPTER PUSILLANIMES. ¹⁰A KALENDAS AUTEM OCTOBRES USQUE CAPUT QUADRAGESIMAE USQUE IN HORA SECUNDA PLENA LECTIONI VACENT; ¹¹HORA SECUNDA AGATUR TERTIA; ET USQUE NONA OMNES IN OPUS SUUM LABORENT QUOD EIS INIUNGITUR. ¹²FACTO AUTEM PRIMO SIGNO NONAE HORAE, DEIUNGANT AB OPERA SUA SINGULI ET SINT PARATI, DUM SECUNDUM SIGNUM PULSAVERIT. ¹³POST REFECTIONEM AUTEM VACENT LECTIONIBUS SUIS AUT PSALMIS. ¹⁴IN QUADRAGESIMAE VERO DIEBUS, A MANE USQUE TERTIA PLENA VACENT LECTIONIBUS SUIS, ET USQUE DECIMA HORA PLENA OPERENTUR QUOD EIS INIUNGITUR. ¹⁵IN QUIBUS DIEBUS QUADRAGESIMAE ACCIPIANT OMNES SINGULOS CODICES DE BIBLIOTHECA, QUOS PER ORDINEM EX INTEGRO LEGANT; ¹⁶QUI CODICES IN CAPUT QUADRAGESIMAE DANDI SUNT. ¹⁷ANTE OMNIA SANE DEPUTENTUR UNUS AUT DUO SENIORES QUI CIRCUMEANT MONASTERIUM HORIS QUIBUS VACANT FRATRES LECTIONI, ¹⁸ET VIDEANT NE FORTE INVENIATUR FRATER ACEDIOSUS QUI VACAT OTIO AUT FABULIS ET NON EST INTENTUS LECTIONI, ET NON SOLUM SIBI INUTILIS EST, SED ETIAM ALIOS DESTOLLIT. ¹⁹HIC TALIS SI—QUOD ABSIT—REPERTUS FUERIT, CORRIPIATUR SEMEL ET SECUNDO; ²⁰SI NON EMENDAVERIT, CORREPTIONI REGULARI SUBIACEAT TALITER UT CETERI TIMEANT. ²¹NEQUE FRATER AD FRATREM IUNGATUR HORIS INCONPETENTIBUS. ²²DOMINICO ITEM DIE LECTIONI VACENT OMNES, EXCEPTO HIS QUI VARIIS OFFICIIS DEPUTATI SUNT. ²³SI QUIS VERO ITA NEGLEGENS ET DESIDIOSUS FUERIT, UT NON VELIT AUT NON POSSIT MEDITARE AUT

LEGERE, INIUNGATUR EI OPUS QUOD FACIAT, UT NON VACET. ¹⁴FRATRIBUS INFIRMIS AUT DELICATIS TALIS OPERA AUT ARS INIUNGATUR, UT NEC OTIOSI SINT NEC VIOLENTIA LABORIS OPPRIMANTUR AUT EFFUGENTUR. ²⁵QUORUM INBECILLITAS AB ABBATE CONSIDERANDA EST.

1–2   a. The opening maxim is from Basil (d.379).¹ Benedict's chief concern is an *ascetic* one: a life without sufficient work and activity is exposed to every spiritual danger. In this, Benedict concurs with the 'Master',² who, over and above the ascetic point of view, mentions that of charity: work is to yield what can be 'given to the needy'. 'Good work leads to the dispensing of charity.'³

b. By his cautious formulation,⁴ Benedict hints that his order of the day need not apply at all times and in all places.⁵ His order must be clear and above all contribute to a balanced variation of prayer, work, and reading. In order to achieve a humanly balanced *rhythm*, Benedict changes a number of established traditions. His order of the day is more differentiated than that of the 'Master' of those of earlier Rules.

c. Healthy change and *balance* was always aimed at in the monasteries. Augustine (d.430) writes that he would like 'to do some manual work every day at certain times, as is laid down in well-run monasteries; the rest of the time' he 'would like to have free for reading and prayer or for the explanation of Holy Scripture'.⁶

d. Work itself was regarded in ancient monasticism as an *indispensable obligation*. In the 'Lives of the Fathers' a scene is recorded, which illustrates the dislike of ancient monasticism for sectarian 'prayer-people' (Euchites). These possibly considered themselves 'pneumatics' (bearers of the Spirit), despised the 'sarcians' ('fleshly' men) and wanted to lead a purely 'contemplative' life, that is, not to work, but only to read the Scriptures. The story goes: 'A brother came to Abbot Silvanus on Mount Sinai, saw that the brethren were at work, and said to the Abbot: "Do not labour for the food which perishes!"⁷ 'Mary has chosen the better portion.'⁸ Whereupon the Abbot said to a disciple, 'Fetch Zachary and have this brother conducted to an empty hut (cella). As evening came and it was the ninth hour, the guest waited at the door to see if someone would call him to the meal. But no one was heard. So the guest rose, went to the abbot and said: "Abba, do the brethren not eat today?" The abbot answered: "Indeed they do; they have already had their meal!" So the guest asked: "But why did you not call me?" The abbot then answered: "You are a man of the Spirit (pneumatikos) and do not need such food; but we are fleshly (!) people, and because we want to eat, we work with our hands. You, however, have chosen the better part, spend the whole day reading and do not wish to partake of bodily food." When the guest heard that, he cast himself down on the ground in penance and said: "Forgive, Abba mine!" But the abbot said: "I think Mary depends completely on Martha. Because of Martha, Mary can be praised . . ."'⁹

3–4   a. Benedict begins with *Easter*, when the meal-times change too.¹⁰

b. The *time* for work in summer is especially well-judged and appointed. Though Benedict appoints more time for reading than other Rules, reading occupies only about a quarter of the time, while work occupies three-quarters (A. de Vogüé). Because of the summer heat[11] work is shifted to the cool of the morning, which is in conflict with the usual monastic tradition.[12]

c. Despite all the preference given to the time of work, Benedict still wishes that in every season a *reading* be scheduled before the meal (A. de Vogüé). Work and reading must complement each other, as the Fathers agree in teaching.[13]

5 The rather theoretical case of fasting on Mondays and Fridays in summer[14] is not considered here at all. Benedict brings in several *innovations*: the siesta is longer than in the 'Rule of the Master';[15] the timing and the voluntary nature of the complementary reading period are new; silent reading was not customary with the 'Master' and the ancients.[16]

6 Untroubled, Benedict arranges the *'times for prayer'* somewhat differently to what corresponded to tradition.[17] The reason is the work in the fields, which is necessary in his monastery.[18]

7–8 a. By 'local conditions'[19] is clearly to be understood the lack of *labour* or of 'servants'.[20]

b. Benedict's monastery is *poor*, in contrast to the 'Master's'. The latter forbids work in the fields, in order to preserve peace and quiet for the monks, and so that they must not 'involve' themselves in 'worldly affairs'. The monastery is to lease its holdings and live from the annual rent.' As far as work is concerned, in the monastery handicrafts and horticulture are sufficient'.[21] The 'Master's' monastery is not poor. Since 'the community is perhaps large and the guests numerous', and one does not 'wish to be tightfisted with alms', means must be available, says the 'Master'.[22]

c. Cassian (d.430) has recommended a form of work which does not interfere with asceticism. He is thinking more of the cultivation of the bare necessities of life on the bank of a river, difficult of access and belonging to no one, than of a profitable farm with its compulsion to produce, which could stand in opposition to spiritual fruitfulness.[23] Benedict is neither in the secure position of the 'Master' nor in the semi-eremitical situation of a little settlement in Egypt. The demanding *work in the fields* is in his case a pressing necessity. Because of it he must make concessions in the arrangement of fasting[24] and of the liturgy.[25]

d. Benedict must also *motivate* his monks for laborious work. First of all he hopes that they will not become 'distressed'.[26] The almost contemporary Rule of Ferreolus foresees all excuses, but believes that a 'useful' brother will always find work suited to his powers and capabilities.[27] In order to motivate for work, Benedict points to the command and example of the Apostles and Fathers, as Cassian (d.430) has already done,[28] who sees in work an antidote to 'acedia', that is, spiritual ennui.[29] According to Cassian, the Egyptian Fathers held the basic principle: 'A monk who works is pinched by *one* devil (of work), one who tries to avoid work is attacked by countless demons'.[30] Among the 'Fathers', whose example could have been in Benedict's mind, we must reckon Antony. Of him it is told that he 'rejoiced that he did not have to be a burden to anybody and could live in the desert by the work of his hands, irrigating and cultivating' a piece of land.[31] Augustine insisted with special emphasis that the Divine Office and sacred reading should be accompanied by work. He wishes a balanced lifestyle. A life which is alleged to be 'purely contemplative' he sees as a pretence. A contemplative must also eat and drink, therefore he could work too, perhaps praying while at work.[32] It is recorded of Romanus (d.*c*.463) in the Jura: 'As a true monk he worked for his own living', namely, working in the fields.[33]—Basil (d.379) saw the value of work especially in its charitable and social function. It permits one to serve the Lord in the brethren, and so to practise charity.[34] According to the 'History of the Monks', the brethren worked 'with their own hands, especially at harvest time', so as to be able to help many poor people.[35]

e. Thus the *work ethos* of ancient monasticism takes on a clear outline: ascesis, a balanced lifestyle, earning one's own living, and socio-charitable activity are the traditional motives. Civilizing achievements did not constitute an end in themselves, but emerged as a consequence. Every method of earning one's bread which could be fitted into a 'spiritual life', was permissible. The availability of the monks, who wished to live in obedience, has made possible their insertion in all areas of culture: agriculture, the production of fruit and wine, architecture and art, handicrafts and schools. Demanding work, such as could be required by 'local conditions or poverty' and carried out as a common task, rooted the monastery in a definite place and realized a degree of local stability.[36]

9 The first desire for *moderation* is characteristic of Benedict. Cassian (d.430) relates that John the Evangelist was sought out by a young hunter, a philosopher, while the former was calmly stroking a partridge. Asked why he took time for such a simple relaxation, he asked in turn why a hunter did not always carry about his bow bent. On receiving the answer that the continually overstrung bow must lose its elasticity, John replied that similarly an occasional, brief and simple relaxation promoted the elasticity of the spirit'.[38] The measure must thereby be taken according to individual possibilities. A saying of the Fathers reads: 'Everybody is challenged according to his capacity.'[39]

10–12 a. Certain monasteries of Gaul were contented with *reading* until the second hour in the morning.[40]

b. In *winter*, when it is cold outside, two short morning hours are reserved for reading. Terce, which is mentioned here,[41] is postponed without much ado.[42] Sext is not mentioned. Perhaps it was not celebrated in the oratory, because the monks work at a considerable distance.[43] A first 'signal' must call them home, a second signal (an innovation) then marks the beginning of None (A. de Vogüé).

13 The time for reading *after meals* seems to be rather short, for after None come the meal and then, quite early, Vespers.[44]

14 a. The 'Rule of the Master' does not yet contain a special order of the day for *Lent*. Yet again, (Terce), Sext and None are not mentioned, because the work in the fields at a distance lasts until Vespers.[45]

b. In Lent, Benedict upholds the traditional rule: *reading until the third hour*.[46] This long period of reading was perhaps regarded as a penitential exercise;[47] in any case, the best hours of the day are to be devoted to reading. One is 'to be free for God'.[48] Benedict indeed recommends: 'To listen with pleasure (!) to the holy readings. To prostrate oneself frequently in prayer.'[49] In the process, prayer interrupts meditative reading.[50]

15–16   a. By the word *'library'*, we should, on balance, understand Holy Scripture itself.[51] Apparently everyone does this reading for himself.[52]

b. The Pachomians placed great emphasis on the reading and knowledge of the Scriptures: 'Let us take care to read the Scripture and learn it by heart; let us constantly meditate upon it.'[53] This *scriptural* piety had been taken over from the synagogue.[54]

c. *Meditation* upon Scripture[55] takes place by means of a lengthy oral repetition of individual words or sentences of Scripture, which, humming them to oneself, one thus relishes to the full and makes part of oneself. However, one can also pray quietly to oneself,[56] as, in any case, this 'meditation' is again and again interrupted by intensive prayer.[57]

17–18   a. To devote oneself to *reading* was not popular in a period of decline. 'Two elders'[58] must supervise it. Benedict gives 'spiritual sloth' (acedia) as the reason for this. Cassian (d.430),[59] especially, speaks of this spiritual emptiness, which must be understood as a lack of religious motivation and of sufficient sensitivity to values of intellect and spirit. It makes monks become 'sterile' in what is good.[60] According to Augustine, reading good books should bear fruit, such as awaking the will to work.[61]

b. For Cassian, useful work is an antidote to 'acedia':[62] 'From practical experience, the Fathers in Egypt forbid the monks, especially the younger ones, to be inactive. They measure the zeal of the heart and progress in steadfast patience and in humility by diligence at work. Never do they accept from anyone at all anything for their own support. On the contrary, by their work they maintain the support of visitors and pilgrims. In addition, they collect food and other necessities in large quantities and send them to those areas of Libya suffering drought and famine, as well as to the cities for those languishing in misery and in prisons. In this way they see themselves as offering a true and living sacrifice[63] by the work of their hands'.[64]

c. Cassian (d.430) paints his picture of acedia according to Evagrius (d.399), who writes: 'Acedia imbues him (the monk) with an aversion to the place where he lives, as well as to his lifestyle and to manual work. Acedia suggests to him the idea that love has disappeared from among the brethren, that there is nobody there to say a good word to him . . . As is said, he (the demon of acedia) uses every means to induce the monk to leave his cell and flee from the battlefield. It will be a long time before this demon is followed by another; on the contrary, after the struggle a state of peace and an inexpressible joy establish themselves in the soul.'[65] It is again worth remarking that Evagrius fears the *'demon of work'* less than the demon of ennui and listlessness.

19–20   This punishment is unknown to the 'Master'; Benedict, however, mentions the deterrent effect of punishment in another passage also.[66]

21   This mild prohibition is without parallel in the 'Rule of the Master'. On the other hand, Pachomius (d.346) forbids *visiting* the quarters (cella) of another.[67] In Cassian (d.430) we read that everyone, especially the young, should work in his own cell, not go anywhere else and not withdraw anywhere with another.[68] It is the wish of Basil (d.379) that one should not leave one's workplace[69] in order to be idle and to gossip.[70]

22   On the 'Lord's Day' one should be *'free for God'*; on that day no work is provided for', says the 'Rule of the Four Fathers'.[71] Benedict gives this

'freedom for God' tangible shape as 'being free for (holy) reading'.[72] In the process he lets it be understood that various services remain necessary on Sunday.[73]

23 a. Benedict adopts a severe tone at this point. He must accept that there are those who are *illiterate* through their own fault, and he recommends a solution similar to that of Basil (d.379).[74] The 'Master' simply states that children and illiterates (up to the fiftieth year) learn to read in their deaneries.[75] Under Pachomius (d.346), surprisingly, everybody had to be able to read, indeed to learn the psalms and even large parts of Scripture off by heart.[76] To Benedict's sorrow, this degree of learning could not be generally reached in his time.

b. The recommendation to *study* does not refer to casual reading,[77] but aims primarily at a good knowledge of Holy Scripture. At the same time, the obligation on the monks to read and study led indirectly to a book culture in the monasteries, while the culture of antiquity was in a process of total dissolution.

c. Later, Gregory the Great (d.604) was to relate that Benedict did not want to be counted among the 'learned', and turned his back on studies: 'Of a good family in the province of Nursia, he was sent to Rome to study the liberal arts. When, however, he saw that many, during their studies, got on to the slippery slope of evil habits, he drew back the foot he had already set on the threshold of the world. He did not wish to sample the knowledge of the world, only afterwards to fall into a great emptiness. He had no regard, then, for study and knowledge, left behind his parents' house and possessions, and sought to be a monk from the wish to please God alone. He thus withdrew, knowingly unknowing and wisely unlearned'.[78]

d. With Gregory, reserve towards profane learning is obvious, just as incidentally, such a reserve was retained for a long time in Eastern monasticism. However, we must not ignore the particular drift of Gregory's remarks. Of the same Benedict, who was averse to profane learning, Gregory will later relate that, in his old age, he had become the author of a 'Rule' written 'in a language flooded with light, with a great gift of discernment'. This Rule is to be seen as the fruit of his conscious withdrawal into recollection, ascesis, and seeking the sight of God (A. de Vogüé). In reality, he is not unlearned, but as Augustine (d.430) says of Antony (d.356), 'theodidaktos' (*taught by God*).[79] Similarly, Hilary of Arles (d.449) will say of Honoratus (d.428), the founder of Lérins: 'rather has he been educated in God's own school'.[80]

e. When the monks express reserve with regard to profane learning and reading, they must not be thought of as uncultured in every case. Benedict himself insists on an extensive 'sacred reading'. 'The Lives of the Jura Fathers' make no objection against learning: Eugendus (d.c.510) receives as a boy the basic concepts of knowledge, transmitted by his father, a priest.[81] At the age of seven he enters the monastery, which he never leaves until his death at the age of over seventy. 'As soon as he had accomplished all the tasks entrusted to him by the abbot, he devoted himself to reading (study) with such great zeal, that he was familiar not only with Latin writings but also with Greek rhetoric'.[82] In the Jura monasteries the Western monastic writings were read daily, and, at least in translation, the Eastern too.[83] The work ethos and enthusiasm for work in monasticism early shifted to study and *learning*.

24–25 a. This paragraph repeats in part things already said. Idleness is to be avoided,[84] account is to be taken of a weak state of health.[85] Work must not 'overwhelm' anybody.[86] The 'Master' had written in similar vein: 'Work must help to feed the servant of God, not kill him'.[87] Clearly, the temptation to *hectic work* was not great, for warnings in that direction are rare.[88]

b. Benedict mentions the danger of a monk *leaving*. According to Cassian (d.430), it is 'acedia'[89] which makes one believe one must leave one's 'cella' and the community.[90]

NOTES TO CHAPTER 48

1 RBasRuf 92; cf. Ecclus 33: 28–29. 2 RB 48,1:RM 50,1–7; RB 48,2–6: RM 50,39–69; RB 48,7–9:RM 86; RB 48,10–13: RM 50,8–38; RB 48,22:RM 75,1–7; RB 48,23: RM 50,76–77; RB 48,24–25: RM 50, 75.78. 3 RM 50,7. 4 Verse 2; 31,16–19; 41;48. 5 Cf.RB 18,22; 39,1; 40,3; 55,4. 6 De op.mon.37. 7 Jn 6:27. 8 Lk 10:42. 9 VPatr 5, 10,69. 10 → 41,1. The translation presents difficulties: 'go out early' to work (cf. VPatr 5,6,21) or 'from morning on, coming from Prime, until . . .'? For 'coming from Prime': cf. RB 48,4. 11 → 41,2–4. 12 → 48,14. Only the 'Order of the Monastery' (OM 3) mentions that reading can follow on work. 13 Jerome, ep.22,35,7; Augustine, De op.mon.37; Cassian, Inst 4,12; cf. VPJur 126. 14 → 41,2–4. 15 Cf. RM 50,61–64. 16 Cf. RM 50,12. The ancients used to read to themselves in an undertone in order to manage the 'scriptura continua'. 17 → 41,7–9; cf.47,1; 48,4.11. 18 → 48,10–12. 19 Cf. RB 40,5.8. 20 Cf. 38,11. In Benedict's time, the monasteries could have servants (cf.RF 36) or a 'secular employee' (conductor; RM 86,2). 21 RM 86 (especially 86,27). 22 RM 86,19–20. 23 Conl 24,4; 24,12,14. In connection with this quotation, one thinks of many ancient monastic foundations along the courses of rivers or on islands. 24 → 41,2–4. 25 → 48,6; 11,1–3. 26 → 31,3–7. 27 → RF 28. 28 Conl 24,12, quoting 2 Thess 3:10: 'if any one will not work, let him not eat.' 29 Inst 10,7 9; Conl 24,11–22; 48,17–18. 30 Inst 10,23. 31 VAnt 25. 32 De op.mon. 17–18. 33 VPJur 10. 34 RBasRuf 127; this is also a motif of the 'Master's' (RM 50,7). 35 Hist mon 18. 36 → 58,13–16. 37 Cf. RB 3,4–6; 8,4; 24,1; 25,2; 30,1; 31,12; 41,9; 39; 49,6; 40,2.8; 48,9; 55,8; 68,2; 70,5. 38 Conl 24,21. 39 VPatr 5, 10,78. 40 RCaesVirg 19; 69; 20. 41 Not in RB 48,3.14. 42 → 48,7–8 (in Note 25). 43 → 50,1–2. 44 → 41,7–9. 45 → 48,10–12. 46 Cf. R4P 3,8: 'From the first to the third hour, one is free for God.' 47 → 49,4–5; 48,17–18. 48 See Note 46. 49 → Prol. 1;4,55–58. 50 Cf. Jerome, ep 22,25,7; Augustine, De op.mon.37; → 20,4–5 (Note 26); 48,1–2. 51 An ancient book-list from St.-Gall lays out the separate parts of the Bible under the title 'bibliotheca'. It is divided into: 'Heptateuch' (RB 42,4), 'Kings' (RB 42,4) 'Prophet' (Prol.), 'Evangelia' (11,9), 'Apostolus' (13,11) . . . (Mundò). 73,4–7. 52 → 48,5; in the 'Rule of the Master' reading aloud is carried out in the deanery (RM 50,11). 53 Horsiesi, Lib 51; Pachomius, Praec 3; 6; 28; 36–37; 59–60. 54 The Rule of Qumrân prescribes: Wherever ten are in the same place, there should never be lacking one that 'contemplates the Law day and night', turn by turn, one after the other.' (1 QS 6,6–7). 55 → 6,2–5; 8; 3; 38,5–9. 56 RBasRuf 107. 57 Cf. Note 55. 58 Cf. RB 56,3 (probably 'deans'). 59 Inst 10,2,1 (it prevents reading and work); → Prol. 2; 1,10–11; 7,10–13; 48,7–8. 60 Cf. Tit 3:14; Cassian, Inst 10,2,4. 61 De op.mon.20. 62 See above, Note 29. 63 Cf. Rom 12:1. 64 Inst 10,22; → 31,10–12. 65 Log prakt 12. 66 Cf. RB 70,3. 67 Praec 112; cf.89. 68 Inst 2,15. 69 RBasRuf 101. 70 RBas Ruf 174; cf.RB 48,18. 71 R4P 3,6–7. 72 Cf. the tendency to 'institutionalize': → 7,55, 16,1–3; 35,6. 73 Cf. RM 50,7. 74 RBasRuf 192: 'Whoever is less suited to study or intellectual activity, should be directed to another employment.' 75 RM 50,75 76. 76 Praec 140; 39; 139. 77 RBasRuf 81. 78 Dial 2, introduction (*scienter nescius et sapienter indoctus*). 79 De doctr. christ. 1. 80 VHonor 1. 81 VPJur 125. 82 VPJUR 126. 83 VPJur 174; 73,4–7. 84 → 48,1–2. 85 → 36–37 (the sick, the children, the aged); → 48,23 (in Note 74: the allocation of suitable work). 86 → 31,3–7. 87 RM 50,75–76. 88 → 48,7–8 (in Note 30). 17–18; 7,10–13 (in Note 42). 89 → Prol 2; 1, 10–11; 7,10–13; 48,7–8. 17–18. 90 Inst 10,2.

CHAPTER 49

OF THE OBSERVANCE OF LENT

31 Mar
31 July
30 Nov

1 Although the monk's life
the whole year round
should be an observance of Lent,

2 yet because few have this virtue,
therefore we urge one and all
to keep their lives in total purity
in those days of Lent,

3 and in these holy days
to atone for what was neglected
at other seasons.

4 This will be worthily done
if we abstain from all vice,
if we work at PRAYER WITH TEARS,
at reading and COMPUNCTION OF HEART,
and at ABSTINENCE.

Cf. Heb. 5:7;
Ps 51:19;
Lk 4:18;
Tit 2:12

5 In these days therefore
lest us increase somewhat our ordinary round of service:
prayers on one's own,
abstinence from foods and drink,

6 so that each one of his own will may offer to God
with THE JOY OF THE HOLY SPIRIT
something over and above
the norm required of him.

1 Thess 1:6

7 That is, let him withhold from his body
some food,
some drink,
some sleep,
some chat,
some ribaldry,
and with the joy of spiritual desire
wait for holy Easter.

Cf. Lk 22:15;
Gal 5:17,22

8 But this very thing however
which each is offering,
he shall suggest to his abbot

and do it

with his prayer and goodwill,

9 because what is done without the permission of the spiritual father

will be lodged to the account

of presumption and vain glory, not of reward.

10 All things therefore are to be done with the abbot's goodwill.

CAPUT XLIX: DE QUADRAGESIMAE OBSERVATIONE

'LICET OMNI TEMPORE VITA MONACHI QUADRAGESIMAE DEBET OBSERVATIONEM HABERE, 'TAMEN QUIA PAUCORUM EST ISTA VIRTUS, IDEO SUADEMUS ISTIS DIEBUS QUADRAGESIMAE OMNI PURITATE VITAM SUAM CUSTODIRE OMNES PARITER, 'ET NEGLEGENTIAS ALIORUM TEMPORUM HIS DIEBUS SANCTIS DILUERE. 'QUOD TUNC DIGNE FIT, SI AB OMNIBUS VITIIS TEMPERAMUS, ORATIONI CUM FLETIBUS, LECTIONI ET CONPUNCTIONI CORDIS ATQUE ABSTINENTIAE OPERAM DAMUS. 'ERGO IIIS DIEBUS AUGEAMUS NOBIS ALIQUID SOLITO PENSU SERVITUTIS NOSTRAE, ORATIONES PECULIARES, CIBORUM ET POTUS ABSTINENTIAM, 'UT UNUSQUISQUE SUPER MENSURAM SIBI INDICTAM ALIQUID PROPRIA VOLUNTATE CUM GAUDIO SANCTI SPIRITUS OFFERAT DEO, 'ID EST: SUBTRAHAT CORPORI SUO DE CIBO, DE POTU, DE SOMNO, DE LOQUACITATE, DE SCURRILITATE, ET CUM SPIRITALIS DESIDERII GAUDIO SANCTUM PASCHA EXPECTET. 'HOC IPSUD TAMEN QUOD UNUSQUISQUE OFFERIT, ABBATI SUO SUGGERAT, ET CUM EIUS FIAT ORATIONE ET VOLUNTATE; 'QUIA QUOD SINE PERMISSIONE PATRIS SPIRITALIS FIT, PRAESUMPTIONI DEPUTABITUR ET VANAE GLORIAE, NON MERCEDI. "ERGO CUM VOLUNTATE ABBATIS OMNIA AGENDA SUNT.

1–3 a. On the basis of Scripture,[1] Basil (d.379) recommends a considered and measured fast for the sake of *self-control*, by which he understands chastity and inner freedom from 'unregulated passions' such as 'anger' (aggressiveness) or 'sadness' (ill-humour, depression). Basil acknowledges fasting regulations, but does not hold with itemized rulings to be applied to everybody, since, according to the Acts of the Apostles[2] different needs are present and must be taken account of. Basil's attitude is not one of hostility to the body: 'The weakened body is to be fortified'; harmful excess in eating habits is to be avoided; food-stuffs 'customary in the locality' should be bought, and on no account 'dainties' or selected 'Lenten fare'.[3] Augustine (d.430), too, suggests that individual needs should be considered[4] in the matter of fasting, as does Cassian, who declares in summing up: 'In this question the following direction has come to us from tradition: differences in bodily powers of resistance, in age and sex involve differences in the time of meals and in the quantity and quality of the food; but one and the same rule of asceticism is valid for all: inner self-discipline, serving to strengthen the power of the soul'.[5] According to Cassian, the monks do not fast because they refuse to eat this or that dish,[6] but in order to make themselves capable of living out the essential values, namely 'goodness, patience, and love',[7] in order to attain to 'purity of heart'[8] and apostolic 'love'.[9] b. the Gospel[10] knows of times when Christ 'the Bridegroom is taken from' the disciples; 'then they fast'.[11] Cassian (d.430), however, does not wish to justify *any special time of fasting* by this biblical quotation. In the 'early Church', he says, there was no 'time of fasting' and no 'legal regulations' for it, because 'a fast was maintained unaltered for the whole year'.[12] Now the Rule[13] concedes that theoretically it should be so, that the monks therefore should constantly live out the enthusiasm of the beginnings.[14] But the author knows that among the monks as among the laity, 'few have this strength'. He adopts—in contrast to Cassian—thoughts and formulations from Lenten sermons that Pope Leo I had given to lay people[15]; this is obvious from the style of the chapter, which is like that of a sermon (A. de Vogüé). Monks too are 'neglectful'[16] and need renewal.

4–5 a. The Lenten exercises are *'added to'*[17] the usual obligations; they bear fruit only thanks to God's grace.[18]

b. By the additional *'prayers'* (the works of charity mentioned by Pope Leo are passed over) are meant perhaps communal, silent ('simple' ardent) prayers in the oratory, as are provided for by the 'Master'.[19] Reading or prayer with tears or 'compunction' is often recommended.[20]

6–7 a. While the 'Rule of the Master' speaks of communal exercises, our Rule recommends projects of each individual which are spontaneous 'beyond the measure allocated (to all in common?)', and born of the *'joy of the Spirit'*. Inner joy is alive especially in the time of struggle,[21] that is, already in the time in which one, with Christ, 'crucifies the passions and desires',[22] not just on the day of Resurrection.[23] Expressions that refer to 'joy', to the Holy 'Spirit' and 'spiritual' fathers are usually to be found in those parts of the Rule taken from the 'Master'.[24] There, however, 'gossip' is completely excluded,[25] here one is invited to abstain from it during Lent.

b. The practice of fasting underwent change in the monasteries. In the Jura area, for instance, Abbot Romanus (d.*c.*463) allowed each to fast according to his will-power, while Abbot Lupicinus (d.*c.*480) insisted on each doing everything he could possibly do with God's help.[26] The possibilities listed for self-denial are typical for monastic life.[27]

c. The 'yearning' for the *'holy Passover'* is reminiscent of a saying of the Lord.[28] The author refers to the interior dispositions, in this case towards fasting, whereas the 'Master' describes rites for Lent and Holy Week. Easter, the Passover of the Lord, has a central significance in our Rule in the course of the year[29] and for the basic meaning of a Christian life.[30]

d. As a young hermit, perhaps distanced from the Church, Benedict had forgotten the date of Easter! Following an inspiration, a priest of the *Church* sought him out, in order to treat him to an Easter festive meal. The priest proclaimed: 'Today is Easter, the day of the Lord's resurrection, you are not allowed to fast!' This message brought by a priest draws him out of his cave and makes him become the teacher and father of others. Benedict answers: 'I know it is Easter, because I was allowed to see you!'[31]

8–9 a. It was usual to obtain the blessing of the 'spiritual father' for every project. In this case, the regulation reminds one of a rite described in the 'Rule of the Master', which perhaps reflects an element of the *penitential practice of the primitive Church*: the monk bows down humbly in front of the abbot in the oratory, or kneels before him, reveals to him the state of his conscience and thankfully proclaims his readiness to practice a special penance in Lent.[32]

b. The 'permission' of the abbot is also, however, meant to prevent a *false asceticism*.[33] Basil (d.379), who recommends fasting,[34] warns against an unenlightened, 'self-willed' fasting, which lacks the gift of 'discernment'.[35] Augustine (d.430) wrote: 'Learn to control your bodies through self-denial in eating and drinking, in the measure that health permits'.[36]

c. The author further fears that 'ascetic feats' could lead to 'vain seeking of glory'. This egotistical 'vana gloria' is regarded as an obstacle to openness to God and his glory, to 'being free for God' (vacare Deo).[37] Cassian (d.430) devotes a book of his Institutions to 'kenodoxia'.[38] Vainglory is looked on as a special danger, because it takes possession of the spiritual part of the person and because it can appear in many different forms and spread 'like a fungus': illusions about one's own virtue, and self-deception; wishful thinking arising from feelings of inferiority, aimed at covering up the reality of the situation; careerism or clerical arrogance. Instead of that, we must be centred on 'the royal way', under the leadership of the Lord's Spirit, without deviating to the right in the direction of arrogance or consciously arranged peak performances, or to the left in the direction of vices.[39]

d. Monasticism was sceptical about *outstanding performances in asceticism*. 'Once, three brothers came to a venerable old father in the desert of Scete. The first questioned him and said: "Abba, I have committed the Old and New Testaments to memory!" The old man answered and said "You have filled the air with words!"[40] The second questioned him and said: "I have copied the Old and New Testaments with my own hand!" He spoke also to him: "You have covered the windows with paper!"[41] The third spoke: "Grass has grown over my hearth!"[42] The old man answered and said: "And you have driven out hospitality!"'[43]

10 Finally, there follows once more a reference to the *abbot*, doubtless because the Rule refrains from detailed regulations, in contrast to the 'Master'.[44] The abbot is to order all things.

NOTES TO CHAPTER 49

1 Cf. Mk 9:29; 1 Cor 9:25–27; Acts 13:2–3; 14:23; Rom 13:14. 2 Cf. Acts 4:35. 3 RBasRuf 8–9; 88–91 4 Praec 1,3; 3,1–2. 5 Inst 5,5,1; → 4,10–19.34–40.51–54; 6,8; 7,26–30; 43,18–19. 6 Conl 21,13 quoting 1 Tim 4,3–4. 7 Conl 21,15. 8 Verse 4; → 4,41–50.55–58.59–61; 7,14–18.26–30.35–43.44–48; 20,1–3. 9 Conl 21,16. 10 Mt 9, 15. 11 Conl 21,30. 13 The introduction has no parallel in the 'Rule of the Master'. RB49,4–7: RM 51–53; RB 49,8–10: RM 53,11–15; 74,1–4. In the 'Rule of the Master', chapter 51 begins what was probably a separate 'Regula Quadragesimalis' of its own (RM 51–53). Benedict does not go into the many directions as to ritual found in the 'Rule of the Master'. 14 → 1,3–5. 15 Serm. de Quadr.1–4 (tract. 39,2; 42,1,6). 16 → Prol 46; 18,24–25; 40,5–7; 73,9. 17 Cassian, Col 21,30; Leo, serm. de Quadr. 2,1. 18 Cassian, Inst 12,16. 19 RM 51–52. 20 → 4,55–58; 6,2–5; 7,62–66; 20,1–3; cf. Cassian, Inst 5,14,1; Conl 1,17,2. 21 Cf. Gal 5,16–22; → Prol 2.3.28.29–32.40.45; 5,10–13; 7,35–43. 22 Cf. Gal 5:24. 23 This other view is taken by the 'Master' (RM 53, 19–25). 24 'Joy' or equivalent: RB Prol 19.49; 2,32; 5,14,16; 7,39.69; '(Holy) Spirit': Prol 11; 2,3; 7,70; 'spiritual': 4,46.50.75. 25 Cf. RB 6,8. 26 VPJur 17. 27 'Garrulousness and buffoonery' are inappropriate here, because they were excluded completely in RB 6,8. 28 CF. Lk 22:15: 'I have earnestly desired to eat this passover with you. . .' 29 → 38,10–11; 41,1. 30 → Prol 3.50; 8,4; 11,6–10; 12,1–4; 15; 38,2–4. 31 Gregory, Dial 2,1. 32 RM 53,11–15. 33 → 7,19–25.31–32.35–43; 43, 18–19; 48,1–2. 34 → 49,1–3. 35 RBasRuf 98;88; → 3,4–6.7–11. 36 Praec 3,1. 37 Origen, Ex Hom 8,4. 38 Inst 11. 39 Inst 11, esp. 11,4. 40 When learning by heart, one spoke or hummed sentences to oneself (meditation). 41 A hint of a more sensible use of paper. 42 He fasts as one who eats raw food. 43 VPatr 5,10.94. 44 RM 51–53.

CHAPTER 50

OF THE BRETHREN
WHO ARE WORKING FAR FROM THE ORATORY
OR WHO ARE TRAVELLING

1 Apr
1 Aug
1 Dec

1 The brethren who are working very far off,
and cannot arrive at the right time in the oratory
2 —and the abbot judges that this is in fact so—
3 shall celebrate the Work of God
at the work site,
kneeling down
in the fear of God.

4 Similarly those who are sent on a journey
shall not let the appointed Hours go by,
but, as best they can,
they shall celebrate them by themselves,
and not neglect to offer
their daily stint of service.

CAPUT L: DE FRATRIBUS QUI LONGE AB ORATORIO
LABORANT AUT IN VIA SUNT

¹FRATRES QUI OMNINO LONGE SUNT IN LABORE ET NON POSSUNT OCCURRERE HORA CONPETENTI AD ORATORIUM—²ET ABBAS HOC PERPENDET, QUIA ITA EST—³AGANT IBIDEM OPUS DEI, UBI OPERANTUR, CUM TREMORE DIVINO FLECTENTES GENUA. ⁴SIMILITER QUI IN ITINERE DIRECTI SUNT, NON EOS PRAETEREANT HORAE CONSTITUTAE, SED, UT POSSUNT, AGANT SIBI ET SERVITUTIS PENSUM NON NEGLEGANT REDDERE.

1–2 In Benedict's monastery, work in remote fields has to be done.¹ Whoever works there cannot come to the Office immediately.² These working conditions suggest to Benedict an appropriate solution through prescriptions of the Rule³ and through the abbot⁴: the Offices are abbreviated,⁵ times of prayer shifted slightly⁶ and provisions made for punctual assembly.⁷ Thus, *dispensation* from participation in the communal Office must be granted only *seldom*, only for those who 'work at a great distance'. By this solution, Benedict changes the practice of the 'Master', who grants to those few who worked at a distance of 'fifty paces' from the oratory, a dispensation from participation in the community Office, in order to be able to begin every Office punctually at the appointed time.⁸

3   **a.** Basil (d.379) had already explained: 'Whoever cannot physically come to the place of prayer and be present with the others, should perform his devotions *at the place* at which he finds himself. Attention should be paid, however, as to whether he cannot perform his duties in time and join the others'.[9]

4   **b.** One *bends the knee* for the psalm Collect or the 'Glory be'.[10]
Pachomius (d.346) warns that 'no pretexts should be sought' to be able to stay away 'from psalmody and prayer in community'.[11] But even the person who is away should *not forget* the times of Office: 'Whoever is on board ship, or in the monastery, in the fields, on a journey or engaged in a task, should not let the time of prayer and psalmody go by.'[12]

NOTES TO CHAPTER 50

1 → 48,7–8.10–12 (in Note 43). 2 → 48,10–12. 3 → 48. 4 RB 50,2. 5 → 9,1–4; 10,1–3; 11, 1–3.6–10.11–13; 16, 12–18. 6 → 48,7–8 (in Notes 25 and 42). 7 → 42,2 8 (in Note 3), 48,10–12 (in Note 43). 8 RM 55,2; only on overcast days, when the time cannot be read from the (sun-)dial, are departures from the exact prayer time excusable (RM 56, 18–21). RB 50,1–3: RM 55; RB 50,4:RM 56; 58. 9 RBasRuf 107. 10 RM 53,4–8; → 20,4–5. 11 Praec 141 12 Praec 142.

CHAPTER 51

OF THE BRETHREN
WHO ARE TRAVELLING NO GREAT DISTANCE

1   A brother who is sent
to do any business whatever
and hopes to return to the monastery that same day,
shall not presume to have a meal while out
even if entreated by anyone whatever to do so,

2   unless perhaps his abbot tells him.

3   Should he do otherwise,
let him be excommunicated.

CAPUT LI: DE FRATRIBUS QUI NON LONGE SATIS PROFICISCUNTUR

'FRATER QUI PRO QUOVIS RESPONSO DIRIGITUR ET EA DIE SPERATUR REVERTI AD MONASTERIUM, NON PRAESUMAT FORIS MANDUCARE, ETIAM SI OMNINO ROGETUR A QUOVIS, 'NISI FORTE EI AB ABBATE SUO PRAECIPIATUR. 'QUOD SI ALITER FECERIT, EXCOMMUNICETUR.

1–2   Without taking account of the 'Master's'[1] humane but complicated casuistry, Benedict[2] formulates a succinct *prohibition of eating out*. Perhaps this means that the brother concerned, when he has returned from his journey, can receive Communion fasting, before he eats.[3]

3   a. In other respects Benedict lets the abbot decide and adds a *threat of punishment* not present in his models.[4]

b. According to Gregory the Great (d.604), Benedict, who *knew the hearts of men*, saw through brothers who wished to conceal from him that they had eaten out. When they threw themselves at his feet and confessed their guilt, 'he forgave them immediately, because he was aware that they would not do such a thing in future, since they now knew that he was always present to them in spirit.'[5]

c. According to the account of Gregory the Great (d.604), Benedict insisted on himself not spending any night outside the monastery. Once a year, Gregory relates, Benedict visited his sister Scholastica, who had consecrated herself to God from her youth and lived not far from the monastery. 'The man of God met her on a property belonging to the monastery, not far from the portal . . . They spent the whole night with each other, praising God, and holding spiritual conversations. Even as night's darkness fell, they had their meal together[6] . . . His sister the nun begged him: 'Do not leave me this night! We will speak until morning of the joys of heavenly life.' He answered: 'What is that you are saying, sister? On no account may I stay outside the monastery.' The sky was so clear, that not even the smallest cloud was to be seen. When the nun heard her brother's refusal, she laid her hands with folded fingers on the table and bent her head to touch them in order to pray to the all-powerful God. When she again raised her head, there was such violent thunder and lightning, and such a downpour, that even the venerable Benedict and the brothers who were with him could not set foot outside.' Gregory adds: 'God is *love*';[7] for that reason, the sister in her prayer was able to achieve more than Benedict, who was concerned with *obeying the Rule*.[8] Gregory the Great[9] writes the following about the monk Florentius, who lived in the district of Nursia and whose prayer, it is told, was also heard immediately: 'Because God, by his nature, is absolutely pure and simple, a pure and simple human heart has a very great influence on him.' He is near to God whose heart is simple,[10] he becomes a friend of God and speaks to God with an uninhibited candour (parrhesia) certain of being heard. Three days after Scholastica's prayer had been so miraculously heard, Benedict was permitted to see from his monastery how the soul of his sister, who was 'as a dove, without guile',[11] 'entered' after her death 'into the mystery of heaven' in the shape of a dove. He rendered praise and thanks to God.[12] His sister had reached perfection, love and God.[13]

NOTES TO CHAPTER 51

1 RM 59–61. 2 Similar to OM 8, where it is written: 'No one may eat or drink outside the monastery without being told to do so, because that does not correspond to monastic discipline.' The OM(8) permits excursions only in pairs. 3 Cf. RM 61 T; 38,10 11; 35,9–10 (Note 22); 43,18–19. 4 → 23,4; 24,3. 5 Dial 2, 12. 6 This trait does not correspond to the prescription of the Rule. 7 1 Jn 4:16. 8 Dial 2,33. 9 Dial 3,15. 10 → 20, 1–3 (in Note 11). 11 Mt 10:16. 12 Dial 2,34. 13 → Prol 39.48–49; 4,41–50; 7,67–70.

CHAPTER 52

OF THE MONASTERY'S PLACE FOR WORSHIP

3 Apr
3 Aug
3 Dec

1   The place for worship shall be what it is called:
nothing else shall be done there,
nothing alien to worship stored there.

Cf. Isa 56:7;
Lk 19:46

2   When the Work of God is ended,
all shall go out in deep silence,
and God shall be held in reverence,

3   so that a brother who perhaps may wish to pray on his own,
may not be hindered
by another's impudence.

4   But if at other times
he wishes to pray more secretly by himself,
let him, in all simplicity, go in and pray,
not with a loud voice
but with tears and an attentive heart.

Cf. Mt 6:5–6, 7–8;
1 Sam 1:10–13, 26–27

5   Therefore he who is not similarly engaged
shall not be allowed to stay on in the place for worship
when the Work of God is over,
—as has been said—
lest another suffer hindrance.

CAPUT LII: DE ORATORIO MONASTERII

¹ORATORIUM HOC SIT QUOD DICITUR, NEC IBI QUICQUAM ALIUD GERATUR AUT
CONDATUR. ²EXPLETO OPERE DEI, OMNES CUM SUMMO SILENTIO EXEANT, ET
HABEATUR REVERENTIA DEO, ³UT FRATER QUI FORTE SIBI PECULIARITER VULT
ORARE, NON INPEDIATUR ALTERIUS INPROBITATE. ⁴SED ET SI ALITER VULT SIBI
FORTE SECRETIUS ORARE, SIMPLICITER INTRET ET ORET, NON IN CLAMOSA VOCE,
SED IN LACRIMIS ET INTENTIONE CORDIS. ⁵ERGO QUI SIMILE OPUS NON FACIT, NON
PERMITTATUR EXPLICITO OPERE DEI REMORARI IN ORATORIO, SICUT DICTUM EST,
NE ALIUS IMPEDIMENTUM PATIATUR.

1–3 a. In expressions borrowed from Augustine (d.430),[1] Benedict declares the
oratory to be an especially sacred place. In the prayer room, one may not
engage in any subsidiary occupations—the practice and the religious sensibility of the Egyptian monks were different. They used to perform light
manual tasks and, at the same time, listen to the voice of the psalmist or
reader. They believed that, while performing a simple manual task, they would
'in the purity of their spirit arrive at an even higher spiritual contemplation'.[2]

In the West, therefore, the monastic Office has more of a 'liturgical' character than the 'domestic' one with which Egyptian monasticism was familiar.

b. Benedict inserts an exhortation to silence and *reverence*[3] on leaving after Office.[4] It is borrowed from the 'Master', who forbids the brethren to sing to themselves verses of the psalms they have just heard, as they go out after the end of the Office.[5] Immediately afterwards Benedict returns again to Augustine's[6] recommendation of private prayer in the oratory and of silence in the prayer room.

4 a. Benedict sets out a synthesis of his *teaching on prayer*. He bases it on Scripture, on Cassian (d.430) and the whole tradition. Prayer must not be loud, ostentatious or wordy, but should be a 'prayer in the quiet little room'.[7] Cyprian (d.258) says: 'God hears not the voice, but the heart.'[8]

b. The devout prayer of the heart[9] is a prayer accompanied by 'tears' and 'compunction'.[10] It is that 'pure prayer' that includes remorse, trust and surrender, that stems from burning love and can be thanks or petition.[11] Cassian (d.430) describes ardent prayer[12] as a mystic experience: 'Sometimes, my soul, which has achieved true purity of disposition and begins to take root in it, will perform all the forms of prayer simultaneously, will fly like an intangible, consuming flame from one form of prayer to the other, and thus pour out before God ineffable prayers full of power and purity, which the Spirit himself, interceding for us with unutterable sighs,[13] sends up to God; in that one moment, the soul takes in so much and pours it out in profound prayer before God, as it at other times never could retain in the memory, let alone express with all haste in speech. Whatever the individual 'measure' is, a person can sometimes send forth pure and heartfelt prayers, even though they belong to the first and most humble kind; during that type of prayer one thinks of the judgement to come, is in fear of punishment and in anxiety about the judgement, and experiences compunction only for a short time'.[14] In the final analysis, this purity of heart is identical with the aim itself, with love and contemplation.[15]

5 Benedict *repeats* himself in order to underline what he wants to get across. The liturgical 'Opus Dei' and the prayer of the individual are clearly distinguished from each other. Benedict himself built an oratory of St Martin of Tours[16] at Montecassino on the site of an ancient sanctuary, and erected on the summit of the mountain the oratory of St John the Baptist as a burial place.[17]

NOTES TO CHAPTER 52

1 Praec 2,2. 2 Cassian Inst 2, 12; Pachomius, Praec 5. 3 → 8.0; 19,1–2.3–7; 20,1–3. 4 Verse 2. 5 RM 68. 6 Praec 2,2. 7 Cf. Mt 6:5–8; → 20,1–3; 17,7–8. 8 De or. 4. 9 Prol 4; 4,55–58; 19,3–7; 20,1–3; 31,10–12. 10 Cf. 1 Sam 1:10–13,26–27; Ps 51:19; → 6,2–5; see above, Note 9. 11 Cassian, 9,9–15. 12 → 6,2–5; 19,1–2; 20,4–5; 49,4–5. 'ardent prayer' = preces ignitae. 13 Cf. Rom 8:26. 14 Conl 9,15. 15 Cf. Cassian, Conl 1,7–8; 9,11; 9,15,1; Hist mon 1,397b–398b; see above, Notes 9–10. 16 Gregory, Dial 2,8; → Introduction 7–8. 17 Gregory, Dial 2,37.

CHAPTER 53

ON WELCOMING THE GUESTS

4 Apr
4 Aug
4 Dec

1 All guests who appear
shall be welcomed as Christ
because he will say:
I WAS A GUEST
AND YOU MADE ME WELCOME.

2 And suitable HONOUR shall be SHOWN TO ALL
especially to KINSMEN IN THE FAITH
and to pilgrims.

3 As soon therefore as a guest is announced
let him be met by the Superior and the brethren
with every loving service.

4 And first of all let them pray together
and so join one another in a KISS of peace.

5 This kiss of peace shall not be offered
unless preceded by prayer,
because of the devil's disguises.

6 In this very greeting however
let all humility be shown
to all guests
as they arrive or depart.

7 With head bowed
or with the whole body stretched out on the ground,
let Christ be worshipped in them:
he is being welcomed.

8 Once received the guests shall be led to prayer,
and after this let the superior or someone appointed by him
sit down with them.

9 The Law of God shall be read in the presence
of the guest
for his edification,
and then let all FELLOW-FEELING be shown him.

10 For a guest's sake let the superior break his fast
unless perhaps it should be a major fast day
which may not be infringed.

Mt 25:35

Gal 6:10:cf.
Eph 2:19

Cf. Rom 16:16:
I Pet 2:17; 5:14

Cf. Mt 28:9

Cf. Acts 28:2

11   The brethren however shall continue their customary fasts.

12   The abbot shall pour water on the guest's hands.

13   Both the abbot and the whole community   Cf. Lk 7:44–45
       shall wash the feet of all guests.

14   The washing completed, let them sing this verse: Ps 48:10
       WE HAVE RECEIVED, O GOD, YOUR MERCY
       IN THE MIDST OF YOUR TEMPLE.

15   It is most especially in the reception of the poor   Cf. Mt 25:35
       and of pilgrims that attentive care is to be shown,
       because in them Christ is all the more received.
       Dread is enough of itself to secure honour for the rich.

5 Apr   16   The kitchen for the abbot and the guests
5 Aug   shall be a separate one,
5 Dec   so that guests who turn up at unexpected hours
       —and a monastery is never short of them—
       may not disturb the brethren

17   Two brothers who are capable of carrying out this office well,
       shall take on this kitchen for a year.

18   These shall be given helpers when they need them,
       so that they may serve without a murmur,
       and again,
       when they are less busy
       let them go out to work where they are told to.

19   And not only for them,
       but in all the offices of the monastery
       let this be taken into consideration,

20   that when they need helpers, they are given them,
       and again when they are free, let them obey orders.

21   Similarly, the guest accommodation shall be entrusted to a brother
       of whose soul the fear of God has taken possession.

22   Beds in sufficient numbers shall be made up there.
       And let God's house be served wisely by the wise.

23   No one, who is not authorized to do so,
       shall associate or speak at all with guests;

24   but should he meet or see them,
       let him, as we have said, pass on,

after greeting them most humbly and asking a blessing,
saying that he is not allowed to speak with a guest.

CAPUT LIII: DE HOSPITIBUS SUSCIPIENDIS

¹OMNES SUPERVENIENTES HOSPITES TAMQUAM CHRISTUS SUSCIPIANTUR, QUIA IPSE
DICTURUS EST: HOSPIS FUI ET SUSCEPISTIS ME. ²ET OMNIBUS CONGRUUS HONOR
EXHIBEATUR, MAXIME DOMESTICIS FIDEI ET PEREGRINIS. ³UT ERGO NUNTIATUS
FUERIT HOSPIS, OCCURRATUR EI A PRIORE VEL A FRATRIBUS CUM OMNI OFFICIO
CARITATIS; ⁴ET PRIMITUS ORENT PARITER, ET SIC SIBI SOCIENTUR IN PACE. ⁵QUOD
PACIS OSCULUM NON PRIUS OFFERATUR NISI ORATIONE PRAEMISSA, PROPTER
INLUSIONES DIABOLICAS. ⁶IN IPSA AUTEM SALUTATIONE OMNIS EXHIBEATUR
HUMILITAS OMNIBUS VENIENTIBUS SIVE DISCEDENTIBUS HOSPITIBUS: ⁷INCLINATO
CAPITE VEL PROSTRATO OMNI CORPORE IN TERRA, CHRISTUS IN EIS ADORETUR QUI
ET SUSCIPITUR. ⁸SUSCEPTI AUTEM HOSPITES DUCANTUR AD ORATIONEM, ET POSTEA
SEDEAT CUM EIS PRIOR AUT CUI IUSSERIT IPSE. ⁹LEGATUR CORAM HOSPITE LEX
DIVINA UT AEDIFICETUR, ET POST HAEC OMNIS EI EXHIBEATUR HUMANITAS.
¹⁰IEIUNIUM A PRIORE FRANGATUR PROPTER HOSPITEM, NISI FORTE PRAECIPUUS SIT
DIES IEIUNII QUI NON POSSIT VIOLARI; ¹¹FRATRES AUTEM CONSUETUDINES
IEIUNIORUM PROSEQUANTUR. ¹²AQUAM IN MANIBUS ABBAS HOSPITIBUS DET; ¹³PEDES
HOSPITIBUS OMNIBUS TAM ABBAS QUAM CUNCTA CONGREGATIO LAVET; ¹⁴QUIBUS
LOTIS, HUNC VERSUM DICANT: SUSCEPIMUS, DEUS, MISERICORDIAM TUAM IN MEDIO
TEMPLI TUI. ¹⁵PAUPERUM ET PEREGRINORUM MAXIME SUSCEPTIONI CURA SOLLICITE
EXHIBEATUR, QUIA IN IPSIS MAGIS CHRISTUS SUSCIPITUR; NAM DIVITUM TERROR
IPSE SIBI EXIGIT HONOREM. ¹⁶COQUINA ABBATIS ET HOSPITUM SUPER SE SIT, UT,
INCERTIS HORIS SUPERVENIENTES HOSPITES, QUI NUMQUAM DESUNT MONASTERIO,
NON INQUIETENTUR FRATRES. ¹⁷IN QUA COQUINA AD ANNUM INGREDIANTUR DUO
FRATRES QUI IPSUD OFFICIUM BENE IMPLEANT. ¹⁸QUIBUS, UT INDIGENT, SOLACIA
AMMINISTRENTUR, UT ABSQUE MURMURATIONE SERVIANT, ET ITERUM, QUANDO
OCCUPATIONEM MINOREM HABENT, EXEANT UBI EIS IMPERATUR IN OPERA. ¹⁹ET NON
SOLUM IPSIS, SED ET IN OMNIBUS OFFICIIS MONASTERII ISTA SIT CONSIDERATIO,
²⁰UT QUANDO INDIGENT SOLACIA ADCOMMODENTUR EIS, ET ITERUM QUANDO
VACANT OBOEDIANT IMPERATIS. ²¹ITEM ET CELLAM HOSPITUM HABEAT ADSIGNATAM
FRATER CUIUS ANIMAM TIMOR DEI POSSIDET; ²²UBI SINT LECTI STRATI SUFFICIENTER.
ET DOMUS DEI A SAPIENTIBUS ET SAPIENTER AMMINISTRETUR. ²³HOSPITIBUS AUTEM,
CUI NON PRAECIPITUR, ULLATENUS SOCIETUR NEQUE CONLOQUATUR; ²⁴SED SI
OBVIAVERIT AUT VIDERIT, SALUTATIS HUMILITER, UT DIXIMUS, ET PETITA
BENEDICTIONE PERTRANSEAT, DICENS SIBI NON LICERE CONLOQUI CUM HOSPITE.

1–2 These guiding principles of Benedict's, which are not taken from the 'Master',[1]
resemble the basic principle about the care of the sick.[2] With Benedict, the
emphasis lies on the religiously motivated and honourable reception of all
guests,[3] whereas the Master receives only clerics and stranger monks without
inhibition. This zeal for hospitality takes its model from enthusiastic descrip-
tions of the *hospitality* of Egyptian monks.[4] Almost all earlier monastic Rules
recommend hospitality;[5] with Benedict, the principle of 'honouring all men'[6]
has an especial priority.[7]

3–5 a. While showing all heartfelt kindness for the guests, one should never fail to
'*discern the spirits*'; in the guest one wants to receive Christ into the monastery,

and not to follow illusions, to which monks could be susceptible. Benedict is not lacking in reserve towards outsiders.[8]

b. Prayer is a guarantee of true communion with God, and therefore precedes the kiss of peace, which sets the seal on the prayer (A. de Vogüé). Whether prayer and *contact with the neighbourhood* converge, is an important criterion in approaching the question as to what type and measure of relationships with the outside world are positive for the monastery and the monk.

c. Basil (d.379) assents to the reception of guests into the *'monastery on a temporary basis'*. They draw spiritual profit from it. Some join the monastery. However, Basil warns against watering down the observance of the monastery for the sake of such guests, and against being deceived by swindlers.[9]

6–7 *Prostration* (stretching oneself out on the ground as a sign of humility) before a guest is found only in Benedict.

8–9 **a.** By this prayer Benedict[10] means the Hour which takes place in choir before the meal, rather than the prayer at table.[11] When people have sat down to table after washing their hands,[12] there follows the *reading at table*, because one wishes to exercise an apostolate towards the guests, as we would put it today. At the same time, the guests are 'to be served in a friendly way'.[13]

10–11 **a.** The question as to whether the fast should be broken for the sake of the guests receives varying answers in the monastic Rules. Benedict's solution is simple, and as far as the guest is concerned generous. However, the *observance* of the community must not be disturbed. The general body should not have to constantly make exceptions because visits are frequent.[14]

b. Cassian (d.430) relates that the Egyptian monks infringed the letter of the Rule out of charity to a guest. One of them explained to the visitors: 'Fasting I have always with me; but you I must soon dismiss, and I shall not be able to keep you with me. While fasting is good and necessary, it is still a voluntary sacrificial offering, whereas a commandment imposes this act of charity (hospitality) unconditionally. Since in you *I receive Christ*, I must also feed him. Afterwards, when I let you go your ways, I can replace the hospitality I showed you for his sake, with a strict personal fast.'[15]

12–14 With Benedict, the *reception ceremonies* are organized pretty elaborately; in the 'Rule of the Master' the washing of the feet, for instance, is carried out merely by the two brothers on weekly duty.[16] At that time, hospitality and washing of the feet went together.[17]

15 **a.** This *priority* fixed by Benedict in favour of the 'poor' and 'strangers' is also without parallel in the 'Rule of the Master'.[18] Benedict wishes to be impartial. He gives preference only to those who stand nearer to Christ: the sick, children, the old, strangers, the needy, fellow-believers.[19] Benedict gives proof of solidarity with the poorest and the least among men; he does not seek the protection of the powerful.

b. This passage is reminiscent of the hospitality shown by Honoratus of Lérins (d.428), who 'received everyone with joy and love, so that there was a great *influx of guests*. He had everything distributed to the poor,[20] confident that God would send a benefactor without delay'.[21]

c. For the third time, as in conclusion, it is stated that, in the guest, *Christ is received*.

16 The author starts afresh (an insertion?) and proceeds to treat of some practical problems which the frequent visitors pose (frequent, that is, in comparison with those in the Egyptian desert).[22] Theological considerations are lacking here. The author's chief care is for the undisturbed routine of the community. For its sake, he provides for a certain *sequestration* of the guests, and orders an innovation: the special kitchen for the guests and the abbot. Perhaps he wishes also to help the 'edification' of the guests; they must not come into contact with difficult members of the community.[23]

17–20 Benedict institutes for the care of the guests not only a weekly service,[24] but also an all year-round one by two suitable brothers; this last is an innovation. Since there are two of them and since they often need extra help, Benedict reckons regularly with a large number of guests,[25] who are served from this special kitchen.

21–22 While the 'Master' suspects thieves and parasitical monks among the guests and appoints two monks as custodians of each,[26] Benedict institutes the office of *one person responsible* for the guests. In order that he may fulfil his duty in the desired religious spirit, and not from 'human respect'[27] for instance, he must be 'God-fearing' like the infirmarian.[28] 'Sufficient beds' must always be made up for the obviously numerous guests, and the one responsible must know his job.[29]

23–24 A certain *distance* is to be preserved between the monk and the world outside, even though guests are treated with great respect. In these sentences, influenced not by the 'Master' but by Cassian,[30] Benedict seems to want to prevent too close ties with outsiders; similarly Caesarius (d.542) states that in the monastery one should 'live for Christ and pray for all the people', not cultivate particular ties with the outside world, which Benedict goes to meet with reserve.[31]

NOTES TO CHAPTER 53

1 RB 53,3–4: RM 65,1–8; RB 53,4–5: RM 71,1–10; RB 53,6–7: RM 65,1–8; RB 53,10–11: RM 72; RB 53,13: RM 30,5.26;53,4; RB 53,14: RM 65,9; RB 53,18–20: RM 16,45–46; RB 53,21–22:RM 79. 2 → 36,1–4. 3 Cf.RB 4,8; cf.Rom 12:10. By 'kinsmen in the faith' are probably meant stranger monks,pious folk and others. 4 Historia monachorum in Aegypto 1; 2; 7; 9; 17; 21; Cassian, Inst 5,24. 5 Pachomius, Praec 51–54; RBasRuf 32–33; especially R4P 2,36–42; 2PR 14–16; RCaesVirg 38;40; VPJur 171. A sign that Benedict is drawing on early sources is the designation 'Prior', the 'First', for the abbot (E. Manning). 6 Cf. RB 4,8. 7 Cf. RB 31,9; 56,1–2; 61,1–5.8–11; 66,1–5. 8 Cf. RB 50,4; 51,1–3; 54,1–5; 61,2.6–7; 66,6–7; 67,3–5; for the 'discernment of spirits': → Prol 28. 9 RBasRuf 87. 10 Without parallel in the RM. 11 Cf.RB 43,13; → 50,1–2. 12 Verse 12. 13 'Humanitas': cf.Acts 28:2; Hist mon 17. 14 Verse 16. 15 Inst 5,24. 16 Cf. RM 30,5. 17 Cf. 1 Tim 5:10; RB 53,1–2, 10,11. 18 → 53,1–2. 19 Cf.RB 34; 36–38; 53,2. 20 Cf.Mt 19:21. 21 VIIonor 4,20–21. 22 A new editorial layer? Concerning the numerous guests, cf. in Note 21. 23 Cf.R4P 2,41: for this reason, the guests are to have contact with the abbot only. 24 Cf. RM 79,5–6. 25 The 'Master' provides for two kitchen servers (plus helpers) for a community of about twenty five members (plus guests) (RM 18,1–3; 19.18.20; 53,51–54; A. de Vogüé). 26 RM 79. 27 Verse 15. 28 Cf.RB 36,7. 29 The cellarer and the porter, too, must be 'God–fearing' and 'wise' ('sapiens', cf. 'savoir' faire = 'experienced'): RB 31,1–2; 66,1–4. 30 Inst 4,16. 31 RCaesVirg 40; → 53,3–5; 61,1–4;66,6–7;67,5.

CHAPTER 54

WHETHER THE MONK
SHOULD RECEIVE LETTERS OR ANY THING

6 Apr
6 Aug
6 Dec

1 Without a directive from the abbot
a monk may in no way
accept or give
letters, religious objects or any kind of little gift
from his parents or from anyone else
or from one another.

2 But should something be sent to him
even by his parents
he shall not presume to accept it
unless it be shown to the abbot beforehand.

3 Should he order it to be accepted
it shall be in the abbot's power
to have it given to whom he decides.

4 And let the brother
to whom perhaps it had been sent
not despond,
LEST AN OPPORTUNITY BE GIVEN TO THE DEVIL.

Eph 4:27;
1 Tim 5:14

5 Should anyone presume otherwise
let him undergo the discipline of the Rule.

CAPUT LIV: SI DEBEAT MONACHUS LITTERAS VEL
ALIQUID SUSCIPERE

¹NULLATENUS LICEAT MONACHO NEQUE A PARENTIBUS SUIS NEQUE A QUOQUAM
HOMINUM NEC SIBI INVICEM LITTERAS, EULOGIAS VEL QUAELIBET MUNUSCULA
ACCIPERE AUT DARE SINE PRAECEPTO ABBATIS. ²QUOD SI ETIAM A PARENTIBUS SUIS
EI QUICQUAM DIRECTUM FUERIT, NON PRAESUMAT SUSCIPERE ILLUD, NISI PRIUS
INDICATUM FUERIT ABBATI. ³QUOD SI IUSSERIT SUSCIPI, IN ABBATIS SIT POTESTATE
CUI ILLUD IUBEAT DARI, ⁴ET NON CONTRISTETUR FRATER, CUI FORTE DIRECTUM
FUERAT, UT NON DETUR OCCASIO DIABULO. ⁵QUI AUTEM ALITER PRAESUMPSERIT,
DISCIPLINAE REGULARI SUBIACEAT.

1–5 **a.** After the reception of guests, Benedict deals with the acceptance of *gifts*;¹
remarks about the giving of gifts are inserted.² The theme is to be met with
frequently in monastic writings.³ Benedict adopts phrases from Augustine
(d.430)⁴ verbatim, but transmits only in part what Augustine intended. The

latter wished to ensure that secret correspondences with women would be avoided,[5] and wanted gifts, e.g. clothes, kept for the genuinely needy. Benedict passes over in silence the justification that is so important for Augustine: in the monastery, following the model of the primitive Christian community, all property is 'in common',[6] and 'necessaries must be allocated according to need'.[7] Perhaps Benedict especially wants to prevent blood or other personal relationships leading to individual members of the community becoming privileged in practice.

b. Instead, Benedict warns against *'occasions'*[8] of sin and threatens a punishment.[9] The mention of the blessed tokens is reminiscent of Caesarius (d.542),[10] the warning against being distressed of Augustine.[11] Thus, into this chapter Benedict has compressed, briefly and not very logically, various practical rules of behaviour.

NOTES TO CHAPTER 54

1 He differs in this from the 'Master', who in another passage speaks of the acceptance of consecrated gifts which the bishop or a priest sends (RM 76). 2 The insertions, which are perhaps later, are not mentioned as contents in the title, and fit in badly from a gramatical point of view 3 Pachomius, Praec 53;106; Basil,RBasRuf 31; 98; 105; Cassian Inst 4, 16, 2; Caesarius, RCaesVirg 25; 43; 54; cf. VPJur 172. 4 Verses 1.3; cf. Augustine, Praec 4,11;5,3. 5 → 25,1–2. 6 Cf.Acts 4:32. 7 Cf. Acts 4:35. 8 Cf.RBasRuf 31. 9 → 23,4. 10 consecrated bread-rolls; RCaesVirg 25; → 66,6–7. 11 Praec 1,4; → 31,3–7.

CHAPTER 55

OF THE CLOTHES AND FOOTWEAR OF THE BRETHREN

7 Apr
7 Aug
7 Dec

1 Clothes shall be given out to the brethren
in keeping with the nature of the places where they live
and the weather;

2 because in cold regions more is needed,
in warm regions less.

3 It is for the abbot to judge this.

4 For our part however we believe   Cf. Lk 3:11
that in average places
a cowl and a tunic are enough for each single monk

5 —in winter a cowl that is woolly
in summer one that is light or not new—

6 and a scapular for work,
shoes and boots.

7 Let the monks not make an issue
of the colour or coarseness of all these garments,
but such as can be found in the province where they live,
or what can be bought more cheaply.

8 The abbot however shall see to the cut
that the clothes be not too short for the wearers,
but the right fit.

9 On receiving new ones
let them always personally hand in the old,
to be stored in the clothes-room for the poor.

10 It is enough for the monk to have two tunics and two cowls
on account of night wear and washing;

11 what is over and above this is superfluous;
it must be cut off.

12 And footwear and whatever is old
they shall hand in when they receive the new.

13 Those who are sent on a journey
shall receive underwear from the clothes-room;
they shall hand it back, washed, on their return.

14 Both cowls and tunics shall be somewhat better

than what they usually wear;
they shall receive them from the clothes-room when setting out,
and hand them back on their return.

8 Apr
8 Aug
8 Dec

15 To furnish the beds
let a straw pallet, a light covering, a heavy covering and a pillow
be enough.

16 These beds however are to be frequently searched by the abbot
on account of private property, lest it be discovered.

17 And should something be discovered with anyone,
which he did not receive from the abbot,
let him undergo the severest discipline.

18 And in order to cut out this vice of private ownership by the roots,
let everything necessary be provided by the abbot:

19 that is to say, the tunic, the shoes, the boots, the belt, the knife,
the stylus, the needle, the handkerchief, the writing tablets,
to take away every excuse of need.

20 The abbot himself however must always reflect   Acts 4:35
on that sentence of the Acts of Apostles:
DISTRIBUTION WAS MADE TO EACH,
ACCORDING AS ANYONE HAD NEED.

21 Therefore let abbot similarly keep in mind
the weaknesses of those in need,
not the evil will of those who are jealous.

22 In all his decisions however
let him ponder on God's judgement.

CAPUT LV: DE VESTIARIO VEL CALCIARIO FRATRUM

¹VESTIMENTA FRATRIBUS SECUNDUM LOCORUM QUALITATEM UBI HABITANT VEL AERUM TEMPERIEM DENTUR, ²QUIA IN FRIGIDIS REGIONIBUS AMPLIUS INDIGETUR, IN CALIDIS VERO MINUS. ³HAEC ERGO CONSIDERATIO PENES ABBATEM EST. ⁴NOS TAMEN MEDIOCRIBUS LOCIS SUFFICERE CREDIMUS MONACHIS PER SINGULOS CUCULLAM ET TUNICAM—⁵CUCULLAM IN HIEME VELLOSAM, IN AESTATE PURAM AUT VETUSTAM—⁶ET SCAPULARE PROPTER OPERA, INDUMENTA PEDUM PEDULES ET CALIGAS. ⁷DE QUARUM RERUM OMNIUM COLORE AUT GROSSITUDINE NON CAUSENTUR MONACHI, SED QUALES INVENIRI POSSUNT IN PROVINCIA QUA DEGUNT AUT QUOD VILIUS CONPARARI POSSIT ⁸ABBAS AUTEM DE MENSURA PROVIDENT UT NON SINT CURTA IPSA VESTIMENTA UTENTIBUS EA, SED MENSURATA. ⁹ACCIPIENTES NOVA, VETERA SEMPER REDDANT IN PRAESENTI REPONENDA IN VESTIARIO PROPTER PAUPERES. ¹⁰SUFFICIT ENIM MONACHO DUAS TUNICAS ET DUAS CUCULLAS HABERE PROPTER NOCTES ET PROPTER LAVARE IPSAS RES; ¹¹IAM QUOD SUPRA FUERIT SUPERFLUUM EST, AMPUTARI DEBET. ¹²ET PEDULES ET QUODCUMQUE EST VETERE REDDANT, DUM ACCIPIUNT NOVUM. ¹³FEMORALIA HII QUI IN VIA DIRIGUNTUR DE VESTIARIO

ACCIPIANT, QUAE REVERTENTES LOTA IBI RESTITUANT. "ET CUCULLAE ET TUNICAE
SINT ALIQUANTO A SOLITO QUAS HABENT MODICE MELIORES; QUAS EXEUNTES IN
VIA ACCIPIANT DE VESTIARIO ET REVERTENTES RESTITUANT. "STRAMENTA AUTEM
LECTORUM SUFFICIANT MATTA, SAGUM ET LENA ET CAPITALE. "QUAE TAMEN
LECTA FREQUENTER AB ABBATE SCRUTINANDA SUNT PROPTER OPUS PECULIARE, NE
INVENIATUR. "ET SI CUI INVENTUM FUERIT QUOD AB ABBATE NON ACCEPIT,
GRAVISSIMAE DISCIPLINAE SUBIACEAT. "ET UT HOC VITIUM PECULIARIS RADICITUS
AMPUTETUR, DENTUR AB ABBATE OMNIA QUAE SUNT NECESSARIA: "ID EST
CUCULLA, TUNICA, PEDULES, CALIGAS, BRACILE, CULTELLUM, GRAFIUM, ACUM,
MAPPULA, TABULAS, UT OMNIS AUFERATUR NECESSITATIS EXCUSATIO. "A QUO
TAMEN ABBATE SEMPER CONSIDERETUR ILLA SENTENTIA ACTUUM APOSTOLORUM,
QUIA DABATUR SINGULIS PROUT CUIQUE OPUS ERAT. "ITA ERGO ET ABBAS
CONSIDERET INFIRMITATES INDIGENTIUM, NON MALAM VOLUNTATEM
INVIDENTIUM. "IN OMNIBUS TATEM IUDICIIS SUIS DEI RETRIBUTIONEM COGITET.

1–3   While the 'Master' presents an outfit which varies according to the season,[1]
Benedict concerns himself with the question of different *climatic* conditions.[2]
As usual, he consigns questions of detail to the responsibility of the abbot.

4–6   Benedict's monks are provided with fewer and with 'more traditional' *articles
of clothing* than those of the 'Master'. The Rule formulates the matter
cautiously,[3] perhaps out of respect for the Lord's words about having only
two tunics.[4] The 'tunica' is a garment next the skin, the 'cowl' an over-garment
like a coat, worn over the tunic, and with a hood (a 'cape'); the 'scapular'[5] is
an abbreviated cowl, which is merely an over-garment (a 'shepherd's shirt' open
at the sides with a hood).—Basil (d.379) also provides for special winter clothing.[6]
The terms for footwear are not very clear.[7]

7–8   a. Basil (d.379) had recommended types of food 'that are to be bought *more
cheaply* . . . in the province'.[8] Benedict applies this advice here in another
matter.
b. The frequently repeated keyword 'suffice'[9] shows that *moderation* is the
leitmotiv of this chapter. In this, Benedict is again under the influence of
Basil (d.379),[10] not of the 'Master'. Basil advises that one should be content[12]
with what is 'necessary',[11] in order to cover one's nakedness and protect oneself from the cold.[13] He recommends durable, but otherwise cheaper clothes
than usual, because monks wish to be the 'last'. 'In no way let voluntary
poverty be infringed.' According to Basil (d.379),[14] as according to Benedict
later,[15] the monks' clothing, as far as the outward form is concerned, differs
little from what ordinary people wear. In this sense, Basil was already familiar
with that he called '*Christian*' or '*monastic*' dress:[16] 'Let our dress be common
to all, the same and uniform for everybody. The first glance, even, must already
pick out the Christian (!) . . . For the weak, a form of dress corresponding to
the religious calling is like a guide; it holds back even the most restless from
indecorous and inappropriate behaviour.'[17] Benedict seems to be thinking of
Basil also when he warns of dissatisfaction with 'ill-fitting clothes' and asks for
a correct 'measurement'.[18]

9–12   The clothes room (Vestiarium) is mentioned by Augustine (d.430).[19] Caesarius
(d.542) also, has clothes which are no longer needed passed on to the poor or

to new entrants.[20] Clearly, Benedict does not wish to see the monks wholly destitute, however much he wants to practise solidarity with the poor.[21] Still, moderation is important to him. Horsiesi (d.c. 380) saw in the poverty of the monks a sign of the following of Christ: 'What is harder than the cross of Christ?'[22] Benedict refrains from a more detailed symbolic interpretation of monastic dress.[23]

13–14   Usually, Benedict keeps to the *traditional* articles of clothing,[24] while remaining open to new customs and the conventions of public life.

15   There is a similar enumeration in the 'Rule of the Master'.[25]

16–19   Benedict imparts an instruction to the abbot in order to check the tendency to *private ownership*.[26] In addition, things already said are repeated.[27]

20–22   Benedict repeats himself again.[28] He does not exhort the community directly, but the abbot,[29] and incorporates the tendency of Augustine to pay due regard to *strong* and *weak* at the same time.[30] Consideration for individuals and regard for their differing needs are very important to Benedict. Perhaps that is the reason for the repetition, while the reference to the Judgement is intended to prevent any partiality.[31]

NOTES TO CHAPTER 55

1 RB 55,4–6:RM 81,1–30; RB 55,13–14: RM 81,7; RB 55,15:RM 81,31–32; RB 55,16–17: RM 81,23–31; RB 55,18–19: RM 82,1–22. 2 Cf. Cassian, Inst 1,10, what is necessary is different in Gaul from in Egypt. 3 → 39,1–3;40,1–4. 4 Cf. Lk 3:11: 'He who has two coats, let him share with him who has none!' This saying pierced Basil to the core (RBasRuf 129). 5 The expression occurs otherwise only in VPJur 127, meaning a light working garment that replaces the cowl in summer. 6 RBasRuf 143 (also for day and night, for winter and summer). 7 According to the 'Master', 'pedules' are footwear of hide for night choir in winter; the 'caligae' in the 'Rule of the Master' are hobnailed shoes used during the day; besides them, the 'Master' also mentions light sandals (RM 81,25–30). 8 RBasRuf 9. 9 Verses 4.10.15. 10 Cf. RBasRuf 11 (three times: 'suffice'). 11 Cf. verses 18–20. 12 Cf. 1 Tim 6:8. 13 RBasRuf 11; cf. Cassian, Inst 1,2,1. 14 RBasRuf 11. 15 Verse 9: The clothes can be passed on to the poor. 16 Significantly, he uses the words synonymously. 17 RBasRuf 11. 18 RBasRuf 95. 19 Praec 5,1; appropriate regulations about clothing: Pachomius, Praec 42; 65; 70;81; 105; Leges 15; Jerome, praef in Pach reg 4; Cassian, Inst 4,10. 20 RCaesVirg 43. 21 → 53,15. 22 Lib 22. 23 Cf. Cassian, Inst 1,3–5.7–8 (Sign of mortification, the Cross, innocence, spiritual power). 24 Trousers are the article of clothing which was brought to Rome only by the 'barbarians'. In contrast to Benedict's monastery, this article of clothing had already been constantly worn for a long time in that of the 'Master' (RM 81,7). The situation in Montecassino was a different one. 25 RM 81,31–32 (without 'pillows'). 26 The 'Master' motivates the 'spiritual' person with 'abstention' from temporal cares.—On punishment:RCaesVirg 30.— In a Jura monastery somebody concealed a hoe in his bed (VPJur 70).— 'Opus peculiare'would really mean 'special work'; cf. Cassian, Inst 4,14; 4,16,3; 7,7,3. 27 Cf. RB 33,1–3 (the 'needle' is perhaps a clasp for the tunic); the list of objects in use is longer here. 28 → 34 (with the quotation: Acts 4:35): Directions for the strong and the weak. 29 Cf. RBasRuf 94; → 3,4–5.Cf. 2,34; RB 34,2; 37,2–3; 63,3. 30 Praec 1,4–8; 3,3–5; 6–7; → RB 64. 31 → 3,11;65,22; cf.RB 36,10.

CHAPTER 56

OF THE ABBOT'S TABLE

1 The abbot's table shall always be with the guests and the
pilgrims.

2 As often however as there are no guests
it shall be in his power
to invite whom he wishes
from among the brethren.

3 Let one or two seniors however always be left with the
brethren for the sake of good order.

CAPUT LVI: DE MENSA ABBATIS

¹MENSA ABBATIS CUM HOSPITIBUS ET PEREGRINIS SIT SEMPER. ²QUOTIENS TAMEN MINUS SUNT HOSPITES, QUOS VULT DE FRATRIBUS VOCARE IN IPSIUS SIT POTESTATE. ³SENIOREM TAMEN UNUM AUT DUO SEMPER CUM FRATRIBUS DIMITTENDUM PROPTER DISCIPLINAM.

1–2 The author wishes to allocate a *place of honour* to the guests and assign their care in a special way to the abbot.¹ The brethren should not make contact with the guests indiscriminately.² The abbot's table, however, is indeed located in the common refectory, for on certain days the abbot speaks 'words of edification' to the brethren.³ According to the 'Master', too, the abbot has his own table, to which he invites elders, guests, and 'experts in the psalter', while the deans remain at the tables of their charges in the same refectory.⁴ On fast days the abbot eats alone with the guests, at an early hour, at his table in the refectory.⁵ Abbot Eugendus (d.c. 510) of the Jura refused a special table or special dishes for himself. The author of his biography comments that he has 'recently heard' that some practised this.⁶

3 Proper *order* is, according to the 'Master', 'God's business, namely silence and seriousness'.⁷

NOTES TO CHAPTER 56

1 The author (an insertion?) takes up RB 53,16.—Cf R4P 2,41; the abbot 'edifies' the guests. 2 → 53,10–11.16.23–24. 3 Cf.RB 38,9. Cf. however RB 58,5: the novices eat in their own quarters, and RB 53,16.21–22: the guests have their own accommodation. 4 RM 84. 5 → 53,10 6 VPJur 170. 7 RM 84,3.

CHAPTER 57

OF THE MONASTERY CRAFTSMEN

10 Apr
10 Aug
10 Dec

1 If there are craftsmen in the monastery
they shall, with all humility, exercise these crafts,
if the abbot gives permission.

2 Should one among them
pride himself on his mastery of his craft,
because he seems to be doing something for the monastery,

3 let such a person be removed from the craft
nor let him undertake it again,
unless perhaps he humbles himself
and the abbot gives him a new mandate.

4 If anything produced by the craftsmen is to be sold,
let those who handle the transaction
not dare to cheat in any way.

5–6 Let them always remember Ananias and Sapphira,   Cf. Acts 5:1–11
lest they or all who cheat from the goods of the
  monastery
should suffer in the soul
the death that these underwent in the body.

7 In the prices let not evil of avarice steal its way in,
8 but let the offer always be a shade lower
that what can be made by others, the seculars,
9 SO THAT IN ALL THINGS GOD MAY BE GLORIFIED.   1 Pet 4:11

CAPUT LVII: DE ARTIFICIBUS MONASTERII

¹ARTIFICES SI SUNT IN MONASTERIO CUM OMNI HUMILITATE FACIANT IPSAS ARTES, SI PERMISERIT ABBAS. ²QUOD SI ALIQUIS EX EIS EXTOLLITUR PRO SCIENTIA ARTIS SUAE, EO QUOD VIDEATUR ALIQUID CONFERRE MONASTERIO, ³HIC TALIS ERIGATUR AB IPSA ARTE ET DENUO PER EAM NON TRANSEAT, NISI FORTE HUMILIATO EI ITERUM ABBAS IUBEAT. ⁴SI QUID VERO EX OPERIBUS ARTIFICUM VENUNDANDUM EST, VIDEANT IPSI PER QUORUM MANUS TRANSIGENDA SINT, NE ALIQUAM FRAUDEM PRAESUMANT. ⁵MEMORENTUR SEMPER ANANIAE ET SAFIRAE, NE FORTE MORTEM QUAM ILLI IN CORPORE PERTULERUNT, ⁶HANC ISTI VEL OMNES QUI ALIQUAM FRAUDEM DE REBUS MONASTERII FECERINT, IN ANIMA PATIANTUR. ⁷IN IPSIS AUTEM PRETIIS NON SUBRIPIAT AVARITIAE MALUM, ⁸SED SEMPER ALIQUANTULUM VILIUS DETUR QUAM AB ALIIS SAECULARIBUS DARI POTEST, ⁹UT IN OMNIBUS GLORIFICETUR DEUS.

1–3 **a.** This chapter is for the most part Benedict's own creation, even though he remains within the ambit of tradition. He is less concerned than the 'Master' is about production and sale,[1] and more about the people involved and their *interior* dispositions. Benedict demands from the craftsmen humility as well as obedience, just as he does from the office-holders;[2] these basic dispositions are more important to him than all material values.[3]

b. Benedict seems to carry over on to the possible *arrogance* of professionals who presume on their works, a warning of Augustine's (d.430) to rich men who presume on the riches they have brought into the monastery.[4] Cassian (d.430)[5] also warns against such a pride, and recommends that in 'love' and 'nakedness' (nuditas), one should discard all private possessions, whereby he reminds us of the Crucified and his self-renunciation. The monk 'conducts himself like a pilgrim and stranger on the earth'.[6] The eschatological motive[7] is also sufficient ground for Basil (d.379) to be willing to train for a certain profession or take on a task, not at one's discretion, but only in obedience.[8]

c. In contrast to the 'Rule of the Master', for Benedict the existence of *craftsmen* in the monastery seems to be only an eventual possibility. The 'Master' usually leaves them at their professional work and calls them away only for urgent commissions.[9] The idea of a kind of removal from office, which resembles a temporary 'excommunication',[10] does not occur to him.

4–6 The 'Master' gives practical directions in the matter of price. The abbot is to fix the prices. Benedict, on the other hand, warns all concerned against *fraud* in business dealings, declares that they are responsible, brings forward the traditional example from the Acts of the Apostles,[11] and speaks of a mortal sin. *The Order of the Monastery* states simply this about buying and selling: 'they are to act conscientiously and loyally as servants of God'.[12]

7–9 **a.** The warning against *avarice* is expressed quite briefly in the Rule of Benedict, for in this regard he has hardly any difficulties in his poor monastery.[13] One remarks also that he expresses himself less strongly than the 'Master': sell 'somewhat more cheaply'![14]

b. By concluding with a terse scriptural quotation, Benedict restates the primacy of the spiritual order in the monastery. As the care of the guests is seen as an apostolate,[15] so, too, the commercial behaviour of the monastery should proclaim the *glory of God* to those outside. Work, in Benedict's eyes, is a sacrifice, a realization of the general priesthood.[16] This explains why Benedict emphasizes so strongly the inner dispositions of the craftsmen.[17]

NOTES TO CHAPTER 57

1 The 'Master' has a special chapter on this subject: RM 85. RB 57,4–6: RM 85,8–11; RB 57,7–9: RM 85,1–7; → 35,5. 2 → 21,2–5; 31,4–7.12–16; 65,1–6.13–21. 3 → 5;7. 4 Praec 1,7. 5 Inst 4,17. 6 Cf 1 Pet 2:11. 7 Cf. Lk 12:40. 8 RBasRuf 67; 102; 105; cf. RCaesVirg 8. 9 RM 50,73–74; 57,14–16. 10 → 44,1–8. 11 Cf. Acts 5:1–11; cf. Cassian, Inst 7,30; VPJur 31 and passim. 12 OM 8. 13 Compared to the 'Master' and to verses 4–6; → 2,33–36; 38,10–11; 39,1–3 (Note 2). 6–9; 40,8–9; 48,7–8; 64,17–19. 14 → 33,5. 15 → 53,8–9.21–22. 16 → 31,10–12; 35,15–18. 17 Verses 1–3.

CHAPTER 58

OF THE RULING FOR ACCEPTING BRETHREN

11 Apr
11 Aug
11 Dec

1 No easy entrance shall be offered
to a person newly come to the monastic life

2 but as the Apostle says:
TEST THE SPIRITS WHETHER THEY ARE OF GOD.

1 Jn 4:1

3 Therefore if the newcomer PERSEVERES KNOCKING,
and is seen after four or five days
TO BEAR PATIENTLY the insults offered him
and the difficulty made about entry,
and to persist in his petition,

Cf. Lk 11:8;
Acts 12:16;
Rom 12:12;
cf. Rev 2:3

4 let entry be granted him
and let him be in the room for guests for a few days.

5 After this he shall be in the room where the novices
learn to reflect,
take their meals,
and sleep.

6 And a senior shall be appointed to them
who has the gift of WINNING souls
and who shall observe them
through and through.

Cf. Mt 18:15;
1 Cor 9:20

7 And care shall be taken
whether he is really SEEKING GOD
whether he is careful
about the Work of God,
about obedience,
about reproaches.

Cf. Zeph 2:3 (and 3:12);
Ps 14:2; 24:6;
and passim

8 All the hard and bitter things
through which one GOES to God
shall be told him in advance.

Cf. Mt 7:14

9 If he shall have promised
perseverance in his stability,
after the lapse of two months
this Rule shall be read out to him in full,

10 and he shall be told:
'This is the law under which you wish to serve;

Cf. Jn 6:67

if you can observe it, come in;
if you cannot, freely DEPART.'

11 If he still stands,   Cf. 2 Tim 4:2
let him be brought to the novices' room mentioned above,
and let him be tested again IN ALL PATIENCE.

12 And after six months have gone round
let the Rule be read out to him,
so that he knows what he is coming in to.

13 And if he still stands,
after four months
the same Rule shall be re-read to him.

14 And if after having weighed it up to himself
he promises to keep it all
and carry out all the orders he gets,
then let him be received into the community,

15 aware that he is bound by the law of the Rule
and that from that day on he may not leave the
monastery,

16 nor wriggle out his neck   Cf. Mt 11:29–30
from under the YOKE of the Rule,
which, under such long-drawn out reflection,
he had been free
either to refuse or to take on.

12 Apr 17 He who is to be received however
12 Aug   shall promise in the presence of all in the oratory
12 Dec   his stability,
the conversion of his ways,
and obedience

18 before God and his saints,   Cf. Gal 6:7
so that if he should ever do otherwise
he shall know that he will be condemned
by him whom HE IS MOCKING.

19 He shall make a written petition of this promise
in the name of the saints whose relics are there
and in the name of the abbot present.

20 He shall write this petition in his own hand
—or indeed if he be illiterate
another shall write it at his request—
and the novice shall put his mark on it,

and place it by his own hand
on the altar.

21 When he has placed it,   Ps 119:116
    the novice himself shall intone this verse:
    RECEIVE ME LORD
    ACCORDING TO YOUR WORD
    AND I SHALL LIVE;
    AND DO NOT PUT MY HOPE
    TO SHAME.

22 The whole community repeats this verse three times
    adding: *Glory be to the Father.*

23 Then the novice brother
    prostrates himself at the feet of each one
    that they may pray for him;
    and now from that day on
    he is considered one of the community.

24 If he has property   Cf. Mk 10:21
    let him either give it away beforehand to THE POOR,
    or by a solemnly attested donation
    bestow it on the monastery,
    keeping nothing back for himself out of it all,

25 for indeed he knows   Cf. 1 Cor 7:4
    that from that day on
    he will not even have POWER OVER HIS OWN BODY.

26 Immediately then he is to be stripped in the oratory   Cf. Eph 4:22
    of his own clothes which he is wearing,
    and he is to be dressed in the monastery's clothes.

27 The clothes of which he was stripped
    shall be put for safe keeping in the clothes room

28 so that—God forbid!—
    should he ever consent to the devil's persuasion
    to leave the monastery,
    then let him be thrown out,
    stripped of the monastery's clothes.

29 That petition of his however
    which the abbot took from off the altar,
    he shall not get,
    but it shall be kept in the monastery.

CAPUT LVIII: DE DISCIPLINA SUSCIPIENDORUM FRATRUM

¹NOVITER VENIENS QUIS AD CONVERSATIONEM, NON EI FACILIS TRIBUATUR INGRESSUS, ²SED SICUT AIT APOSTOLUS: PROBATE SPIRITUS SI EX DEO SUNT. ³ERGO SI VENIENS PERSEVERAVERIT PULSANS ET INLATAS SIBI INIURIAS ET DIFFICULTATEM INGRESSUS POST QUATTUOR AUT QUINQUE DIES VISUS FUERIT PATIENTER PORTARE ET PERSISTERE PETITIONI SUAE, ⁴ANNUATUR EI INGRESSUS ET SIT IN CELLA HOSPITUM PAUCIS DIEBUS. ⁵POSTEA AUTEM SIT IN CELLA NOVICIORUM UBI MEDITENT ET MANDUCENT ET DORMIANT. ⁶ET SENIOR EIS TALIS DEPUTETUR QUI APTUS SIT AD LUCRANDAS ANIMAS, QUI SUPER EOS OMNINO CURIOSE INTENDAT. ⁷ET SOLLICITUDO SIT SI REVERA DEUM QUAERIT, SI SOLLICITUS EST AD OPUS DEI, AD OBOEDIENTIAM, AD OBPROBRIA. ⁸PRAEDICENTUR EI OMNIA DURA ET ASPERA PER QUAE ITUR AD DEUM. ⁹SI PROMISERIT DE STABILITATIS SUAE PERSEVERANTIA, POST DUORUM MENSUUM CIRCULUM LEGATUR EI HAEC REGULA PER ORDINEM, ¹⁰ET DICATUR EI: «ECCE LEX SUB QUA MILITARE VIS; SI POTES OBSERVARE, INGREDERE; SI VERO NON POTES, LIBER DISCEDE». ¹¹SI ADHUC STETERIT, TUNC DUCATUR IN SUPRADICTAM CELLAM NOVICIORUM ET ITERUM PROBETUR IN OMNI PATIENTIA. ¹²ET POST SEX MENSUUM CIRCUITUM LEGATUR EI REGULA, UT SCIAT AD QUOD INGREDITUR. ¹³ET SI ADHUC STAT, POST QUATTUOR MENSES ITERUM RELEGATUR EI EADEM REGULA. ¹⁴ET SI HABITA SECUM DELIBERATIONE PROMISERIT SE OMNIA CUSTODIRE ET CUNCTA SIBI IMPERATA SERVARE, TUNC SUSCIPIATUR IN CONGREGATIONE, ¹⁵SCIENS ET LEGE REGULAE CONSTITUTUM QUOD EI EX ILLA DIE NON LICEAT EGREDI DE MONASTERIO, ¹⁶NEC COLLUM EXCUTERE DESUB IUGO REGULAE QUEM SUB TAM MOROSAM DELIBERATIONEM LICUIT AUT EXCUSARE AUT SUSCIPERE. ¹⁷SUSCIPIENDUS AUTEM IN ORATORIO CORAM OMNIBUS PROMITTAT DE STABILITATE SUA ET CONVERSATIONE MORUM SUORUM ET OBOEDIENTIA, ¹⁸CORAM DEO ET SANCTIS EIUS, UT SI ALIQUANDO ALITER FECERIT, AB EO SE DAMNANDUM SCIAT QUEM INRIDIT. ¹⁹DE QUA PROMISSIONE SUA FACIAT PETITIONEM AD NOMEN SANCTORUM QUORUM RELIQUIAE IBI SUNT ET ABBATIS PRAESENTIS. ²⁰QUAM PETITIONEM MANU SUA SCRIBAT, AUT CERTE, SI NON SCIT LITTERAS, ALTER AB EO ROGATUS SCRIBAT ET ILLE NOVICIUS SIGNUM FACIAT ET MANU SUA EAM SUPER ALTARE PONAT. ²¹QUAM DUM INPOSUERIT, INCIPIAT IPSE NOVICIUS MOX HUNC VERSUM: SUSCIPE ME, DOMINE, SECUNDUM ELOQUIUM TUUM ET VIVAM, ET NE CONFUNDAS ME AB EXPECTATIONE MEA. ²²QUEM VERSUM OMNIS CONGREGATIO TERTIO RESPONDEAT, ADIUNGENTES: GLORIA PATRI. ²³TUNC ILLE FRATER NOVICIUS PROSTERNATUR SINGULORUM PEDIBUS UT ORENT PRO EO; ET IAM EX ILLA DIE IN CONGREGATIONE REPUTETUR. ²⁴RES SI QUAS HABET, AUT EROGET PRIUS PAUPERIBUS AUT FACTA SOLLEMNITER DONATIONE CONFERAT MONASTERIO, NIHIL SIBI RESERVANS EX OMNIBUS, ²⁵QUIPPE QUI EX ILLO DIE NEC PROPRII CORPORIS POTESTATEM SE HABITURUM SCIT. ²⁶MOX ERGO IN ORATORIO EXUATUR REBUS PROPRIIS QUIBUS VESTITUS EST, ET INDUATUR REBUS MONASTERII. ²⁷ILLA AUTEM VESTIMENTA QUIBUS EXUTUS EST REPONANTUR IN VESTIARIO CONSERVANDA, ²⁸UT SI ALIQUANDO SUADENTI DIABOLO CONSENSERIT UT EGREDIATUR DE MONASTERIO— QUOD ABSIT—TUNC EXUTUS REBUS MONASTERII PROICIATUR. ²⁹ILLAM TAMEM PETITIONEM EIUS, QUAM DESUPER ALTARE ABBAS TULIT, NON RECIPIAT, SED IN MONASTERIO RESERVETUR.

1–4   **a.** Benedict presents a *carefully-constructed* chapter on the reception of novices, whereas the 'Master' deals with the same matter over four chapters in a very diffuse way.¹

b. In Benedict's time, the monasteries were overcrowded; for in the monasteries one was always certain to find food on the table.[2] Thus, Benedict presses for a marked *reserve* to be cultivated towards the candidates, as in the large Egyptian monasteries. Those who arrive are at first left to wait for a few days before the monastery gate;[3] they are treated badly.[4] Out of responsibility towards God, neither the monastery nor the new entrant should take a step which has not been well thought over.[5]

c. With a quotation from Scripture[6] Benedict makes it clear that there must be an aptitude test for everyone who wishes to 'convert'. This is to test whether the candidate is 'inspired' by the *good spirit* or not. The 'discernment of spirits' is necessary. 'Do not believe every spirit',[7] says the Master.[8] Proper to the good Spirit of God are the gifts of grace: patience, fortitude, endurance, constancy and 'perseverance'.[9] One who is called, possesses them. Where this 'strength', the 'comfort' of the Spirit, is lacking, a presumed vocation will not stand the test.[10] As early a document as the 'Rule of the Four Fathers' insisted that a candidate be tested as to whether he could be 'patient in the face of trials', that he be confronted with difficulties, but that he might be received if he 'continued to knock insistently'.[11]

d. Benedict presupposes—as he does in the case of all who encounter others in a pastoral context[12]—the 'gift of discernment' or *discretion* given by the Spirit, in those who receive a newcomer. Perhaps it is this challenge of 'discerning the spirits' which causes Pope Gregory to praise the 'discretion' of the Rule of Benedict.[13] Gregory the Great (d.604) has indeed no one but Benedict in mind when he refers to the 'best master of the ascetic life and learned disciple of the highest truth'. The latter demands: 'Test the spirits, to see whether they are from God!',[14] likewise: 'He should be clearly told all the hardships and difficulties,[15] so that he knows what he is about when he enters'.[16] Gregory continues: 'Strong superiors should not receive soft people readily. An over-hasty conversion to monastic life stems mostly from a precipitate consideration, nor from a genuine growth in piety. When weak people promise something strong, it does not spring from experience and the strength of soul, but from a confused 'gift of discernment' . . . Monastic life is a formidable undertaking. Whoever within it is in charge of others, must, when receiving others who have converted to this life, proceed with a so much greater gift of discernment, the more profitable it is to know in advance whether the request for entry stems from strength of soul or from a hasty decision of the will . . . '[17]

e. The time of testing was very hard in the case of the Pachomians, but by today's standards was unusually *short*. The following text describes what it might well have been like: 'When the great Macarius heard of the extra-ordinary way of life of the monks of Tabennisi, he changed his clothes and dressed as an ordinary labourer. After a desert journey of fourteen days he came to the Thebaid. When he came to the monastery of the monks of Tabennisi, he had their abbot, named Pachomius, called . . . and said: "I ask you, sir, receive me into your monastery, that I may become a monk." The great Pachomius said to him: "You are already of advanced age. How are you going to learn the monks' asceticism now? The brethren here have cultivated an ascetic way of life from their youth. They endure (!) the labours. At your age, you will not be able to pass the tests of asceticism. You will feel that too much is being demanded of you, you will go away and speak evil of us." Thus, he did not receive him, neither on the first day, nor on the second, and so on until the seventh day. The latter, however, remained constant (!), although he was left to fast. But then Macarius pleaded: "Receive me, O Abbot, and if I do not fast like the others or do not work like the others, command me to be sent away from the monastery" Then the great Pachomius advised the brethren to receive him.'[18] Thus, the first, hard, week-long period of probation was followed in Pachomius' (d.346) monastery immediately by the renunciation of private property, the clothing as a monk and the storing of the secular garb.[19]

f. According to Cassian (d.430), he who has already been definitively received in this way is first of all, 'for the space of a year', entrusted to an 'elder', who is in charge of the *guest house* in front of the entrance to the monastery, so that the novice can be properly introduced to the monastic life and can still be tested by the community. Only after *one year* has elapsed is he inducted into a deanery of the community.[20]

g. A later text relates that, according to the so-called 'Angelic Rule', a *three-year* probationary period was in force in the monastery of Tabennisi: 'Whoever has entered in order to remain with them, must not be allowed into the sacred area (to study Scripture!) for the space of three years. Only when he has worked hard may he be allowed in after three years.'[21]

h. We meet these periods of time, 'some days', 'one year', 'three years', again and again later in Church *law*[22] (A. de Vogüé), as we do in Benedict. Just as certain structures of the catechumenate were developed in the ancient Church,[23] so also there developed a monastic reception procedure (RB 1980).

5–7 a. The *noviciate quarters* (cella) are an innovation on the part of Benedict. The novices there seem to be more definitively separated from the community than are the guests, who are catered for in the common refectory,[24] while the novices manifestly eat in their own noviciate quarters. Profession then appears clearly as the real entry into the community.

b. An author as early as Cassian (d.430) entrusts the responsibility for the novices to a 'senior'.[25] Caesarius (d.542) speaks of a 'novice mistress'.[26] The *novice master*, according to Benedict, performs tasks that previously were the responsibility of the abbot, for example in the 'Master's' monastery, or in Lérins. There the founder, Honoratus (d.428) is supposed 'to have joined himself' to the newly entered, observing the same law'.[27]

c. The novice master has not only to warn of difficulties, but also 'to win souls'. Benedict has the habit of accompanying every mention of rigour with a word of consolation.[28]

d. According to Basil (d.379), Jesus' words of invitation are to be acted upon: 'Come to me, all who labour and are heavy laden, and I will give you rest'.[29] A candidate should neither be 'ruthlessly sent packing', nor received without being tested.

e. Basil (d.379) requires further that is should first be made clear whether the candidate has 'spent' his earlier life 'well', or whether he is not perhaps coming 'as a hypocrite', with the wrong inner motivation.[30] This basic question about the genuineness of the religious motives has found expression in Benedict's formula: 'whether a person truly (revera) *seeks God*'. 'To seek God' means to want to belong to the 'Anawim', that is to the people of the Sermon on the Mount, of the Beatitudes.[31] Basil (d.379) gives a whole list of criteria that can be helpful in assessing the motives. They appear in Benedict's text. He brings the motive mentioned last by Basil to the first place, and in doing so, slightly alters its sense; for Basil wrote: 'For those who wish to enter into the service of God at a mature age, their previous life is to be examined, as I have said, and then this one criterion is sufficient: that they plead persistently to be admitted and that their longing for the work of God (*Opus Dei*) be true and warm.'[32] While Basil understands by the term 'Opus Dei' the whole ascetic life or the 'service of God', for Benedict the term means 'Divine Office'[33] and is at the heart of monastic life.

f. As further criteria of a vocation Basil names *obedience*:[34] 'It must be estab-lished whether he performs tasks gladly, freely (!) and loyally'.[35] Basil asks further whether the person is prepared to practise 'all *humility*' and 'whether he will not become fractious if he must devote himself to the simplest and lowliest services, when they can be reasonably demanded'.[36] Because of this, Benedict demands readiness for 'humiliations'.[37] In late antiquity, work, as a 'servile' occupation, was a 'humiliation' for a free man. But already Basil demands readiness to be 'industrious' at hard '*work*'.[38]

g. However, like Basil (d.379), Benedict sees the decisive basic challenge not in exterior achievements, but in the 'search for God'. The Cappadocian speaks of a 'burning longing to please God' that 'can never be stilled'.[39] The fulfilment of this central desire is brought about by the '*search*, that is the perception through which, in a deep, inner sense, we are allowed to behold and contem-plate the greatness of God's glory, in the holy and pure remembrance of the goodness of God which we have experienced'. From that grows the love we have for God, a love which seeks him with longing.[40] The 'search for God' is the antithesis of a practical atheism; it is the core of an 'alternative life'; it is the consciousness of being addressed by God; it is an intuition of the over-whelming greatness as well as of the fascinating lovableness of God.[41]

h. 'God-seekers' is the name given in the Life of the founder of Lérins to those who seek out the cloister because they '*long for Christ*'; he is the Mediator between God and man.[42]

8   The 'Rule of the Master', too, emphasizes that the difficulties are to be *made known in advance*.[43] Cassian (d.430) remarks: 'According to the pure and true teaching of the Lord, the royal road is mild and light, even though it seems hard and strict.'[44]

9–10 **a.** A first promise[45] refers to perseverance and *stability*, that is to an inner 'constancy' brought about by the spirit.[46] This promise is made at the begin-ning (or at the end?) of a two-month period of reflection, after the Rule has been read to him.[47] The novice engages himself to keep the Rule, which is the institutional basis of monastic life and presupposes the 'teaching of Christ' as basic law.[48]

b. It is striking that here, as in other places,[49] the Rule is designated as basic norm and is called '*law*' in juridical phraseology. It is regarded as an authentic interpretation of the 'divine law', namely of Scripture.[50] Someone as early as Pachomius (d.346) uses juridical phraseology for his rules: 'decrees, verdicts, laws'. Rufinus of Aquileia (d.410) says that the Basilian Rules contain the 'answers of the divine law', namely from the Bible.[51] For the monastic move-ment, arising spontaneously in the Church, the enthusiasm of the new begin-nings also involved a certain risk. Zealots or eccentrics could fall into extremes.[52] Bishops and fathers of monks sought therefore to put order into the monastic movement in the spirit of Scripture. They use words like 'law', 'order', 'discipline'.[53] They do not mean by this the imposing of a yoke on people, but the teaching and the Gospel of Christ, and also the experiential knowledge of monasticism and of the previous Christian generations. In this strain Bishop Ferreolus of Uzès (d.581) writes in the dedicatory letter of his Rule: 'I wanted to lay upon the new people, as it were, the yoke of a new law. Not in order to weigh down their shoulders, but in order to bend their spiritual neck have I written this Rule, which is to be observed by them as a law'[54] (Frank).

c. The whole procedure aims at ensuring on the part of the novice a *free* and responsible decision, which has been well thought over and takes account of all obligations; the novice himself is taken completely seriously as a person. The testing is clearly a reciprocal one.[55]

11 It is striking that there now follows the '*introduction* into the above-mentioned dwelling (cella) of the novices'.[56]

12 After six months in the 'noviciate', a second reading of the Rule takes place. This repeated reading of the Rule to the novice, who is turning to the monastic life,[57] is reminiscent of the 'conferring' on the candidates for baptism of the Creed, Our Father, etc., which takes place in *stages*.[58] The assimilation of monastic procedures to ecclesiastical practices, in this case of conversion, novi-ciate, and profession to catechumenate and baptism, is frequent with Benedict.[59]

13–16 a. After a further four months in the noviciate there follows a third reading of the Rule and a second promise, which refers to the *Rule* and to *obedience* in respect of all commands.[60] This second and third reading of the Rule, and the second promise (procedures introduced for the first time by Benedict) are aimed at encouraging a conscious and free commitment.

b. *Stability*, which goes with the acceptance of the Rule, was supported espe-cially by Caesarius (d.542) as a pupil of Lérins; he did this also at councils[61] that gave ecclesiastical sanction to stability. Nevertheless, 'stability' is not an invention of the monks of Lérins.[62] Its core is the gift of grace called fortitude, which is patient steadfastness, 'perseverance' or 'endurance'.[63] This 'power' of the Spirit, often mentioned in the New Testament, was given to the martyrs.[64] It is now the supporting foundation of 'stability'.[65] 'The monk's charism is fidelity' (A. de Vogüé). There are many God-given gifts of grace. One of them is this charism of stability. 'For the gifts and call of God are irrevo-cable'.[66] These words, spoken about the covenant of God with his people, are also valid for the fidelity to the baptismal confession and similarly for the promise of 'stability'. Already in Scripture there are references to the esteem for such fidelity.[67]

c. 'Stability' is realized in being bound to a particular community, in being rooted in a 'place', in the 'house of God'.[68]

d. The image of the *yoke* of the Rule is a traditional reference to the 'easy yoke' of Christ.[69] With remarkable emphasis there is postulated on the one hand the freedom of the person's assent to the vocation, on the other there is presupposed that, once the choice has been made, the 'help' of God will not be lacking, that there will, then, be supplied from God's side a lasting charism, and thus there will be the possibility that in the assent of his profession a person commits himself completely and irrevocably to Christ. One stays in the monastery because one wishes to 'remain' with Christ[70] (von Balthasar). It is perseverance in the new way.[71]

17–18   a. In this section, the *ceremony of profession* is described briefly;[72] it probably took place at the preparation of the gifts during the eucharistic celebration.[73] Questions and answers between the abbot and the candidate are not expressly mentioned.[74] The content of the promise is rendered in three concepts; stability[75] and obedience[76] were already contained in a promise.

b. A new element is the promise of the '*conversatio morum*'. It contains the renunciation of the former 'worldly' way of life, and the assent to Christ whom one wishes to serve in a certain monastery according to the Rule which was read beforehand. It contains the rule of life for the particular monastery.[77] 'To lead a monastic life' means in practice to live in obedience and humility, as well as to cultivate the traditional asceticism (Divine Office, silence, reading, work, fasting),[78] as it is specific to a given monastery. Poverty and chastity are necessarily part of this 'monastic way of life'.[79] In Benedict's time people were not yet thinking of three or more formal 'vows'; the candidate wished, through the profession-promise, to make himself completely available for the 'service of God'.[80] However, already about that time, the Church began to protect the monastic promises by sanctions;[81] they are not of a purely 'private' nature.

c. The vow is taken *before God* and his saints.[82] It is more than a promise to the community or to the abbot; however, he who is making profession may legitimately see in the abbot and in the community of the brethren the representatives of Christ, whom he wishes to serve and who alone suffices him.[83] Christ is for him both poverty and fulfilment. Fulfilment above all in the brotherly love of the community.[84] The 'Master' mentions at this point the rendering of accounts at the Judgement and the promised 'crown';[85] Benedict speaks of the danger of damnation.

19–20   a. The 'petition' is a document. It contains, of course, the 'donation' of eventual goods,[86] but especially the power of disposal over one's own person, which in its poverty surrenders itself to God in the monastery.[87] In his own surrender of self,[88] the one making profession imitates the self-renunciation of Christ.[89]

21–23   b. Benedict is the first to mention the case of an illiterate person.

The promise of profession is completed by the *prayer* of the candidate himself, who calls to Christ in the words of a psalm, and by the prayer of the brethren (vocation and perseverance are gifts of the Spirit, which come 'from God'[90]) together with an assent, in which the essence of the person expresses itself fully and irrevocably. That which is 'from God' is offered to God with a humble and confident prayer that it be accepted. The candidate trusts that his 'sacrifice'[91] is pleasing to God. This understanding of offering is that of the eucharistic celebration, where the sacrifice flows into the doxology, the praise of God, and leads to the 'communio', as the profession here leads to the reception into the community.

24–25   a. This is a kind of digression on Benedict's part; the distribution to the poor or the 'donation' took place beforehand.[92] Unlike the 'Master',[93] Benedict can be brief. According to the 'Master', the ancient law[94] still prevails for a 'donation', while for Benedict a laying down of the law on this form of donation is now mostly superfluous; for Justinian (527–565) decreed in the meantime that anyone could dispose freely of his property before entering a monastery, but that afterwards he can no longer possess property.[95] (R. Kay)

b. Benedict is concerned with the fulfilment of the *Lord's command*: 'If you would be perfect, go, sell what you possess and give to the poor, and you will have treasure in heaven; and come, follow me'.[96] As we know, Antony (d.356) as a young man is supposed to have arrived at Mass as these words were read out. He is said to have felt that they were meant for him personally, and to have begun straight away to put them into practice.[97]

c. Basil (d.379) requires a careful procedure for the *declaration of renunciation* of private property, so that relatives will not later make unjustified demands.[98]

d. Benedict again makes the statement that complete renunciation of possessions and the right of disposal over goods, also includes chastity. The monk's own body is not at his disposal. In the matter of being without property, Basil (d.379) refers to the love of the Lord, who laid down his life for those whom he loved. 'If he laid down his life for his friends,[99] how can we then keep for ourselves something which is not life?'[100] Basil expresses himself similarly to Benedict when he says that a monk no longer freely disposes of 'his limbs'.[101]

e. In these texts neither the material nor the biological good things are declared to be worthless. But for his 'friends' the Lord himself is more important. In their devotedness they wish to become like the Lord on the Cross, who was stripped of everything.[102] This renunciation includes chastity. Benedict does not go into more detail on the question of celibacy, perhaps so as not to provoke the accusation of *despising marriage*. Cassian (d.430) had to defend himself against such charges.[103]

26 a. Taking off one's own clothes, and putting on the clothes of the monastery[104] has also, according to Cassian, a sign value. He speaks of 'putting off worldly pomp', of 'descending to the poverty of Christ' and of belonging to the 'poor', that is to the community of Christ's brethren, who keep themselves free of anxious care about food and clothing.[105] The echoes of *baptism* with the renunciation of worldly pomp, stripping, and the descent into the baptismal water, are clear. Cassian speaks repeatedly of the *aktemosyne*, i.e. the complete stripping (*nuditas*) of all private possessions.[106] In view of Christ's sufferings, his yoke is light, Cassian thinks. 'The renunciation of his own possessions does not grieve him who, splendid in his complete nudity, denies himself all the pomp of this world for Christ's sake.'[107]

b. The thought of baptism or of the baptismal garment probably plays a role in the conferring of the *monastic habit*, which to some degree is already assuming 'sacral' characteristics.[108] In the 'Sayings of the Fathers' we read: 'A great one from among the seers answered, saying: "The power that I saw resting over baptism,[109] I saw too over the monk's clothes at the reception of the spiritual habit".'[110] Thus, profession is seen in an analogy with baptism.[111] According to Caesarius (d.542),[112] the 'Master',[113] and Benedict, the clothing follows at the end of the probationary period.[114] Benedict himself, as a young hermit, had the claustral monk Romanus confer on him 'the habit of the holy monastic life',[115] and thus entered into the monastic tradition. From the beginnings of monasticism, the monastic habit was conferred on each new monk, at that time immediately on entry.

27–28 The *storing* of the previous clothing is mentioned by Cassian (d.430) and similarly justified. In the case of a monk leaving or being dismissed, which were seen as disgraceful, the clothes were given back to him.[116]

29 The retention of the *chart* serves to secure the abbot and his successor legally (and economically) against charges which might be brought later, or in case someone leaving might make claims.[117]

NOTES TO CHAPTER 58

1 RB 58,1–4: RM 87,2; 90,1–71; RB 58,8: RM 87,4; 90,3–67; RB 58,9: RM 88; RB 58,9–10: RM,87,3–4; RB 58,12: RM 89,1; RB 58,13: RM 89,1; RB 58,14: RM 90,67; RB 58,15–16: RM 90,66; RB 58,17–23: RM 89,3–28; RB 58, 24–25: RM 87,5–75; RB 58,26: RM 90,80; RB 58,27: RM 90,83; RB 58,28: RM 90,84–87; RB 58,29: RM 89,27; 90,88–95. 2 After the first two young men from Nyon (VPJur 13), very many candidates presented themselves to Romanus (d. *c.* 463) in the Jura. Romanus received everybody, but many left. Still, Laucon soon had 150 monks, La Balme 105 nuns (VPJur 24–25). Abbot Lupicinus (d. *circa* 480) had to hasten to the assistance of his excessively mild brother, and was able, only by means of a vigorous bout of fasting, to get rid of the many who had no vocation (VPJur 36–40). The *Life* of Caesarius speaks of 200 nuns. 3 Pachomius, Praec 49. 4 Cassian, Inst 4,3,1 (10 days); cf. R4P 2,25–28 (a week); VPachom 6–7. 5 Cassian, Inst 4,32–33. 6 1 Jn 4:1. 7 ib. 8 RM 90,71: One must beware of the 'wolf in sheep's clothing' (cf. Mt 7:15; RM 90,72). 9 → Prol 37–38.48–49.50; 4,20–33.62–73; 5,10–13; 7,35–43; 31,3–7; 35,5–6; 48,17–18; 49,1–3; 72,4–12 (Notes 14.53). 10 One is reminded of accounts from the Age of Martyrs about Christians who elbowed their way to the front in order to appear important, but did not stand the test, while others were fearful, but with the help of Christ suffered martyrdom steadfastly. 11 2,26; cf. Rom 12:12 (hypomone). 12 → Prol 28; 3,4–6.7–11; 4,41–50; 27,1–4; 31,3–7.16–19; 49,8–9; 53,3–5; 64, 17–19. 13 Dial 2,36; 9,8 (Note 21). 14 1 Jn 4:1; RB 58,2. 15 RB 58,8. 16 RB 58,12. 17 In 1 Reg 4,70. 18 Historia lausiaca 19–20 (PG 34,1057). 19 Cassian, Inst 4,3–6 (10 days); cf. R4P 2,25 (a trial period of one week); cf. RB 58,24–28. 20 Cassian, Inst 4,7. A one–year trial period is also envisaged in Qumrân. The novice gets to know the Rule, and after a further year is admitted to community of goods and the common council (IQS 6,13–23). 21 Verses 3–4; 58,26. 22 Justinian, Nov.5,2 (535); Nov.123,35 (546). The Council of Orleans (V., 549) mentions one or three years as a probationary period. The current Canon Law for religious provides for a postulancy, a one–year noviciate, a temporary commitment lasting at least three years, and only then the final profession. 23 Cf. Hippolytus (235), Traitio apostolica 15–20. 24 → 56,1–2. 25 Inst 4,7: he takes care of the guests. Cf.VPach 25. 26 RCaesVirg 7. 27 VHonor 4,18. 28 → Prol 46–49; 2,32. 29 Mt 11:28. 30 RBasRuf 6. 31 → 33,4.4; cf. Wisd 1:1: 'Seek him with sincerity of heart'; cf. Mt 5:3,8: 'Blessed are the poor in spirit . . . the pure in heart, for they shall see God.' 32 RBasRuf 7. 33 → 43,3. 34 → Prol 2; 5; 7,34; 71,2. 35 RBasRuf 7. 36 ib. 37 → Prol 45; 7,35–43. 38 RBasRuf 6; 1,10–11; 48,1–2. 39 RBasRuf 14. 40 ib. 41 → Prol 18–20; 7,5–9.10–13.14–18.19–25.62–66. 42 VHonor 3,17; cf. I Tim 2:5. 43 RM 87,4; 90,3–67. 44 Conl 24,25,2. 45 Cf. RM 89,1. 46 See above, in Note 9. 47 Cf. RM 89,1. 48 → 1,2; the 'Rule' has a pre–eminent significance for the monks of Lérins (cf. RCaesVirg 58; read out 'frequently'; cf.RB 66,8). 49 → 2,1–10 (Note 17); cf.RB 1,2; 3,7; 7,55. 50 Cf. RB 53,9; → Prol 45–50.45; 1,2. 51 'Responsa sacri iuris' (in the accompanying letter to Abbot Urseus). In the prologue to his Rule Basil explains that he to whom is entrusted 'the service to the Word', wishes to instruct all 'in the commandments of God in the public hall of the church'; he intends to instruct a few 'seekers' (cf.RB 58,7) 'privately' in more detail about the way to perfection. 52 We think, for example, of the judgement on Eustathius of Sebaste (d.after 377, Basil's teacher (→ Introd 4), and of Benedict himself as a young man (→ 49,6–7, in Note 31; 58,1–4); → Prol 46; 1,6–9. 53 In the early Church writings, the Church is the house of 'disciplina', Christ is the teacher (paidagogos, the disciples are the pupils. 'Discipline' means more or less 'pedagogics'. In RB the word 'discipline' appears about twenty two times, → 23,2–3 (in Note 14), often in a very general sense as 'behaviour' or as 'measure' (punishments!). 54 Mt 11:29–30. → Prol 21.45–50.45; 1,2; 2,1–10. 55 In contrast to Cassian: → 58,1–4 (in Note 20); cf.RM 88,5. 56 Are verses 5–7 a later insertion? Are the 'few days in the room for guests' (RB 58,4) identical with the 'two months' (RB 58,9)? (A.de Vogüé). The quarters (cella) of the novices resemble the special quarters (cella) of the sick and the accommodation for the guests (cf. RB 53,16.21–22; 56). 57 Verse 1. 58 They were also called 'petentes' (cf. RM 87,1 for the monastic candidate). Benedict uses the word 'petitio' (request, petition, document) in connection with the profession (Verses 19.29; RB 59,2) 59 → 21,1–4; 23,4; 31,1–2.8–9; 49, 8–9. 60 → 58,5–7 (in Note 36). 61 RCaesVirg 2 ('until death'); 36–40

270

(enclosure); similarly under Caesarius and, after him, Councils of Gaul: Agde (506),c.27; Orleans I. (511),c.19. **62** Even a writer as early as Horsiesi wishes that the monks 'stand by the decision once they have taken it' (Lib 12). Cassian warns against the illusion of believing one will find more peace by moving to another place (Conl 24,13,9). **63** See above, Note 9. **64** → Prol 28; 47; 4,20–33.62–73; 5,10–13; 7,35–43; 9,8; 14,1–2. **65** → 1,10–11; 4,78; 5,1–9.14–19; 6,2–5;48,7–8.17–18; 58,17–23. **66** Rom 11:29. **67** Cf. 1 Tim 5:12 (young 'widows', who were 'unfaithful to their promise'). **68** RB 31,19; 53,22;64,5. **69** Cf.Mt 11:30; Horsiesi, Lib 7; Cassian, Conl 24,23–24; Teridius, ep. hortat.3; RF praef; Versus Simplicii; see Note 48. **70** Jn 1:39. **71** Cf. RB Prol 2.13.22–27.44.48–49. **72** With variations as against the 'Master's' longer text (RM 89,3–28). **73** Cf.RB 59,2.8; the 'Master' had the promise made after Prime (RM 89,3). **74** RM 89,6–16. **75** → 58,9–10. **76** → 58,13–16. **77** The 'Master' uses the following formulations (RM 90,1): 'When a newcomer withdraws from the world to the service of God in the monastery, and declares, that he wishes to be converted. . .' (on 'the service of God': see above, in Note 32; on 'convert': in Notes 57–58; → Prol 3.45; 4,20–33.) A request that the 'petitioner' or 'applicant' (*petitor*, see Note 58) makes to the abbot runs (RM 89,8): 'I wish to serve God according to the discipline of the Rule of your monastery, which was read to me. **78** Origen already had named the following as characteristics of an ascetic life: vigils, Scripture reading, meditation, fasting (Ex Hom 13,5; Ps Com 34,13; Gen Hom 10,3). Horsiesi writes: 'We wish to follow the way of life (*conversatio*) of our fathers and brothers, who went before us in the Lord; they renounced the world, went to meet the Lord with unerring tread, and now possess his heritage' (Lib 47). Cf. VPach 16. **79** See above Note 77. **80** → 33,4; 58,24–25. **81** E.g. the Council of Orleans I.(511), c.21(chastity). **82** Benedict expresses himself somewhat more 'personally' than the 'Master': 'To God and to this oratory and to this holy altar' (RM 89,11). **83** Cf. RM 89,20–23 (with quotations: Lk 10:16; Phil 1:21). **84** → 72,4–7; 1,2.3–5; 5,14–19; 36,1–4. **85** RM 89,11–16. **86** Verse 24; cf. RM 89,17; RB 59,3. **87** These expressions are used by the 'Master' (RM 87,35; 89,18–19). For that reason, the chart is also required when someone does not possess any goods (verse 24). **88** → 7,51–54; 33,4; 35,1–3.6. **89** → 5,10–13; 7,5–9.31–32.34; 38,10–11; 57,1–3. **90** Verse 2; 58,1–4.13–16. **91** Cf. RB 59,8: 'oblatio'. **92** → 58,19–20. **93** RM 87. **94** 'donatio (mortis causa)'. **95** Nov. 5,4–5. **96** Mt 19:21. **97** VAnt 2. **98** RBasRuf 5. **99** Cf. Jn 15:13. **100** RBasRuf 29. **101** RBasRuf 106; cf.Cassian, Inst 2,31; RF 10. **102** → Prol 50; 4,59–61; 33,4; 55,9–12. **103** Conl 21,10. On chastity: → 4,62–73; 22,4–7; 33,4; 42,8–11; 43,18–19; 58,17–18. The accusation of 'despising marriage' had already been made by the hierarchy against Eustathius of Sebaste (→ Introd 4). **104** Cf. Pachomius, Praec 49. **105** Inst 4,5. **106** Conl 18,17. **107** Conl 24,23. **108** Cf. RCaesVirg 4; RM 90,83–87. **109** Cf. Mt 3:16: 'And when Jesus was baptized, he went up immediately from the water, and behold, the heavens were opened, and he saw the Spirit of God descending like a dove and alighting on him.' → Prol 48–49.50; 1,2; 7,26.30. **110** VPatr 6,1,19. **111** See Notes 44–45. **112** RCaesVirg 4. **113** RM 90,80. **114** In contrast to earlier (→ 58,1–4, in Note 19) and present-day usages. **115** Gregory, Dial 2,1. **116** Inst 4,6; RM 90,83–87. **117** Cf. RM 89,31–35; 90,88–95.

CHAPTER 59

OF SONS OF THE NOBILITY OR OF THE POOR
WHO ARE OFFERED

13 Apr
13 Aug
13 Dec

1 Should anyone of the nobility perhaps   Cf. 1 Sam 1:21–28
offer his son to God in the monastery,
if the boy himself be under age
his parents shall make the petition
which we have spoken of above.

2 They shall wrap the petition and the boy's hand
in the altar-cloth
with the offering;
that is how they shall offer him.

3 With regard to their property
they shall either promise under oath in the present petition
that never by themselves
nor through a third party
nor in any way whatever
will they ever give him anything,
or give him the opportunity of having anything.

4 Or indeed if they do not wish to do this
and want to offer something as an alms to the monastery
for their own reward,

5 let them make a gift to the monastery
from what they want to give,
reserving to themselves if they so wish, the income.

6 And in this way all will be blocked
so that not the faintest hope will remain to the boy
by which—God forbid—he could be deceived and perish,
a thing we have learned by experience.

7 Those less well-off shall do the same.
8 But those who have nothing at all
shall simply make the petition,
and with the offering
they shall offer their son in the presence of witnesses.

CAPUT LIX: DE FILIIS NOBILIUM AUT PAUPERUM QUI OFFERUNTUR

¹SI QUIS FORTE DE NOBILIBUS OFFERIT FILIUM DEO IN MONASTERIO, SI IPSE PUER MINOR AETATE EST, PARENTES EIUS FACIANT PETITIONEM QUAM SUPRA DIXIMUS, ²ET CUM OBLATIONE IPSAM PETITIONEM ET MANUM PUERI INVOLVANT IN PALLA ALTARIS, ET SIC EUM OFFERANT. ³DE REBUS AUTEM SUIS AUT IN PRAESENTI PETITIONE PROMITTANT SUB IUREIURANDO, QUIA NUMQUAM PER SE, NUMQUAM PER SUFFECTAM PERSONAM NEC QUOLIBET MODO EI ALIQUANDO ALIQUID DANT AUT TRIBUUNT OCCASIONEM HABENDI; ⁴VEL CERTE SI HOC FACERE NOLUERINT ET ALIQUID OFFERRE VOLUNT IN ELEMOSINAM MONASTERIO PRO MERCEDE SUA, ⁵FACIANT EX REBUS QUAS DARE VOLUNT MONASTERIO DONATIONEM, RESERVATO SIBI, SI ITA VOLUERINT, USUM FRUCTUM. ⁶ATQUE ITA OMNIA OBSTRUANTUR UT NULLA SUSPICIO REMANEAT PUERO PER QUAM DECEPTUS PERIRE POSSIT—QUOD ABSIT—QUOD EXPERIMENTO DIDICIMUS. ⁷SIMILITER AUTEM ET PAUPERIORES FACIENT. ⁸QUI VERO EX TOTO NIHIL HABENT, SIMPLICITER PETITIONEM FACIANT ET CUM OBLATIONE OFFERANT FILIUM SUUM CORAM TESTIBUS.

The 'Master'[1] discusses the case of a *son of a noble family* who hastens to enter the monastery on his own initiative. The abbot then summons the parents, so that they may confirm the young person's decision, if he sticks to it, and 'offer' him at the same time. Following up that, the question of the inheritance has to be settled. Donations to the poor or to the monastery are advised. Concessions to the family remain possible, if only the son follows Christ without possessions and with trust in God's paternal benevolence.

1–2 **a.** By contrast, Benedict is thinking of *dependent children* of perhaps tender years[2] who are 'offered' by the parents.[3] As in the ceremony of profession, a chart which also settles the matter of the personal fortune, is deposited on the altar. This takes place at the Preparation of Gifts in the eucharistic celebration.[4]
b. The parents have acted for the child, but the 'offering' has an irrevocable effect for the latter. This is a *questionable innovation* on Benedict's part. Basil (d. 379) is indeed of the opinion that it is advantageous to introduce children 'from an early age to the fear of God and the Lord's teaching'; he declares however that the 'decision to remain a virgin' (professio virginitatis) would become 'valid' (firma) only at a 'mature, marriageable age'. Basil continues: 'Children who are offered at the will or with the agreement of the parents, or by the parents themselves, should be received before many witnesses', so that 'difficulties' would not be experienced later 'with malicious persons'. Basil then proceeds to insist that the children should be scrupulously cared for by educators of proved 'patience'.[5] As Basil describes, it, the child is 'received' by the monastery in the act of 'offering'. When he reaches marriageable age, the young person can ratify the option for celibacy. The proviso is not clearly formulated by Basil.[6] However he is obviously following the line of free choice of celibacy traced by Paul.[7]
c. The 'offering' with elements of a profession made before God, has a more 'sacral' character with Benedict than with Basil, where it simply means 'the reception into the community'. Therefore it can hardly be assumed that

Benedict also silently presupposed Basil's proviso. He regards the offering as *irrevocable*. In this matter he is doubtless influenced by the ecclesiastical legislation of the sixth century in Gaul. In it we find regulations which specify that children who are received into the status of clerics belong permanently to that class. They were free to marry, however, if they renounced the prospect of higher Orders; or, in monasteries, a probationary period was allowed after the 'oblation', so that a later choice remained open.[8] Benedict's new solution was practised for some centuries in the West.

3–6 a. Benedict, who had unpleasant experiences in this context, seeks to ensure the 'permanence' of the dedication to God by using precise *juridical* formulae.[9] In contrast to the 'Master', he wishes primarily an 'alms' for the monastery, not for the 'poor'.[10] He does not seem to have very great hopes. The main thing is: 'One may keep absolutely nothing for oneself, except the cross, which one takes upon oneself in order to follow Christ'.[11]

7–8 The monastery receives people of every social origin, also those of *'slender means'* and of *'none at all'*. These two cases are unknown to the 'Master'; they look as if they were tacked on afterwards.[12] The witnesses, with whom we are already familiar from Basil (d.379),[13] are mentioned because 'difficulties for the monastery' are feared; for that reason, the 'Master' makes witnesses 'sign'.[14]

NOTES TO CHAPTER 59

1 RM 91. 2 → 37; 39,10;63,18–19. 3 The case in which the monastery receives orphaned children is not mentioned; → 59,7–8. 4 A part of the altar cloth is folded round the boy's hand and round the gifts (which was customary; from the two parts of the cloth there developed the 'corporal' and the 'pall'). 5 RBasRuf 7. 6 It can be inferred from this that at a mature age the 'professio virginitatis' would automatically become'valid'. The insertion of this clause would have no sense, however. 7 Cf. 1 Cor 7:7. 8 Cf. V.Council of Orleans (549) c.19; RCaesVirg 6–7. 9 → 58,13–16.17–23. 10 → 58,0; on the poverty of his monastery: → 48,7–8; 57,7–9. 11 R4P 2,32; cf.Mt 16:24. 12 They are not mentioned in the title. The arrangement for them is not new, so that really these cases could have been dealt with above as well (A. de Vogüé). 13 RBasRuf 7. 14 RM 87,34.36.

CHAPTER 60

OF THE PRIESTS WHO PERHAPS MAY WISH
TO LIVE IN THE MONASTERY

14 Apr
14 Aug
14 Dec

1 If someone of the order of priests
asks to be received in the monastery,
consent indeed shall not be granted him too quickly.

2 Nevertheless,
should he absolutely persist in this application,
let him realize he will have to keep the full discipline of the
Rule,

3 nor will anything be mitigated for him   Mt 26:50
so that what is written will apply:
FRIEND,
FOR WHAT HAVE YOU COME?

4 Let him however be allowed
to stand next to the abbot
and to bless,
and to celebrate Mass,
if however the abbot orders him.

5 Otherwise let him presume nothing
knowing that he is subject to the discipline of the Rule,
and let him rather give examples of humility to all.

6 And should there be question in the monastery
of an appointment to office
or of some other matter of business,

7 let him think of his place by his date of entry into the
monastery,
not of the place conceded to him
out of reverence for the priesthood.

8 Should anyone of the clerics
have the same desire
to be incorporated in the monastery
let them be placed in a middle rank;

9 and they too however
if they promise
observance of the Rule
and their own stability.

CAPUT LX: DE SACERDOTIBUS QUI FORTE VOLUERINT IN MONASTERIO HABITARE

¹SI QUIS DE ORDINE SACERDOTUM IN MONASTERIO SE SUSCIPI ROGAVERIT, NON QUIDEM CITIUS EI ADSENTIATUR. ²TAMEN, SI OMNINO PERSTETERIT IN HAC SUPPLICATIONE, SCIAT SE OMNEN REGULAE DISCIPLINAM SERVATURUM, ³NEC ALIQUID EI RELAXABITUR, UT SIT SICUT SCRIPTUM EST: AMICE, AD QUOD VENISTI? ⁴CONCEDATUR EI TAMEN POST ABBATEM STARE ET BENDICERE AUT MISSAS TENERE, SI TAMEN IUSSERIT EI ABBAS. ⁵SIN ALIAS, ULLATENUS ALIQUA PRAESUMAT, SCIENS SE DISCIPLINAE REGULARI SUBDITUM, ET MAGIS HUMILITATIS EXEMPLA OMNIBUS DET. ⁶ET SI FORTE ORDINATIONIS AUT ALICUIUS REI CAUSA FUERIT IN MONASTERIO, ⁷ILLUM LOCUM ADTENDAT QUANDO INGRESSUS EST IN MONASTERIO, NON ILLUM QUI EI PRO REVERENTIA SACERDOTII CONCESSUS EST. ⁸CLERICORUM AUTEM SI QUIS EODEM DESIDERIO MONASTERIO SOCIARI VOLUERIT, LOCO MEDIOCRI CONLOCENTUR; ⁹ET IPSI TAMEN SI PROMITTUNT DE OBSERVATIONE REGULAE VEL PROPRIA STABILITATE.

1-7 a. In the context of questions about the reception of members into the monastic community and about rank,¹ Benedict concerns himself with the *priest* in the monastery. Originally, ascetics and monks came together in specifically lay communities. The 'Life of Pachomius' reflects the general attitude of early monasticism when it describes how Pachomius behaved in his larger community: 'When, as usual, the feastday required participation in the heavenly mysteries, they called presbyters together from the nearest villages, who provided for them the full spiritual joy of the feast. The old man (Pachomius) did not tolerate any cleric among themselves.' He feared that a monk's striving after the priestly office could lead to arrogance and strife in the community, but declared: 'In all simplicity and purity we must preserve community with the churches of Christ and honour the clerics; that is fitting for monks, who, on the contrary, are not permitted to strive after the priestly dignity. When, however, monks have already been ordained clerics by bishops, we accept their service.' In connection with this it is related that Pachomius required that stranger priests should not be met with suspicion, 'since we urgently request them to celebrate the heavenly mysteries', and that if suspicion should arise, they should not be judged, since that was a matter for the bishops.²
b. As regards Benedict, it is noticeable that he displays *reserve* towards priests who ask to be received, just as he does towards laymen.³ In contrast with other Rules he is, however, prepared to receive a priest.⁴ But he demands from the priest stability, obedience to the Rule and the abbot, and also humility.⁵
c. The different stages of a noviciate are not mentioned in the case of clerics. However, they must make a *promise*.⁶ In this way they become members of the community.
d. 'To stand in the place behind the abbot'⁷ was, according to the 'Master', the role of the 'second' destined to succeed him.⁸ This is perhaps an indication that Benedict is reckoning with the then frequent case in which a priest is installed as abbot (A. de Vogüé). If the *abbot* was a layman, a good relationship could grow up between him and a priest in the monastery by a

division of labour. 'When a cleric came to him (Pachomius) in order to live under his Rule, Pachomius displayed in the church the respect due to the priest; the cleric however lived according to the custom of the monks and placed himself in all humility under the abbot as under a father'.[9] The comparative anomaly in having a layman acting as teacher and pastor in the community, while the priest exercised only the functions of a liturgical figure in divine worship, was mitigated by the fact that pastoral work and 'proclamation' had a markedly individual character;[10] a 'spiritual' man knew himself called to this service from person to person.

e. Problems arose nevertheless. For instance, the lay Abbot Eugendus (d.c. 510) sought to settle cases of conscience among the brethren himself; he did not take the priest into confidence, in order not to unloose a Church excommunication from the Eucharist.[11] The main worry, however, was the fear of *ambitious* careerism and of rivalries among the monks. Because of this, Abbot Eugendus did not have himself ordained priest, while Abbot Romanus (d.c. 463) 'presided at the sacrifice only on a feastday. On the other days he showed himself as a monk to the monks, and bore no sign of his priestly dignity'.[12] Humility[13] is emphasized very strongly by Cassian (d.430) as an indispensable characteristic of the monk-priest.[14]

8–9 The section on *other clerics* is peculiar to Benedict. He is open to a development which allows the number of clerics in the monastery to increase, so that the community is not dependent on the services of outside priests or has to resort to their churches. Like the priests, so 'they too' (the clerics) have to make the promise of stability[15] and 'observance of the Rule', by which we have to understand the monastic 'observance', that is, the 'monastic life'.[16]

NOTES TO CHAPTER 60

1 RB 58–59 and RB 60–62. 2 VPach 24 3 → 58,1–4. According to the monastic Rule of Augustine, the 'Presbyter' was an external agent (of the bishop), to whom the overall supervision of the community was entrusted (Praec 4,9; 7,1–2). By contrast, Augustine had set up a community of clerics in the episcopal residence of Hippo.—The 'Rule of the Four Fathers' allows clerics into the monastery only on a visit (R4P 4,14–19). The 'Master' tolerates priests only as guests in the monastery, insofar as they work, and notwithstanding all honours shown to them, do not arrogate any authority to themselves (RB 60,1–7: RM 83). 5 → 58. 6 → 60,8–9. 7 Verse 4. The expression 'missas tenere' means 'to say the concluding prayer of an Office' or 'to *celebrate* Mass'. 8 RM 92–93. 9 VPach 24. 10 → 2,31–32.37–40; 4,41–50.51–54; 21,1–4; 27–28; 31,3–7; 46,5–6. 11 VPJur 151. 12 VPJur 133–134.19. 13 Verse 5. 14 Conl 4,20; 5,12; → 62. 15 → 58,1–4.13–16. 16 → 58,17–18.

CHAPTER 61

OF PILGRIM MONKS: HOW THEY ARE TO BE RECEIVED

15 Apr　1　Should some pilgrim monk appear
15 Aug　　　　from distant parts,
15 Dec　　　　and wish to live as a guest in the monastery
　　　　2　and is pleased with the customs of the place as he finds them,
　　　　　　and does not perhaps upset the monastery by his demanding
　　　　　　ways,
　　　　3　but is simply pleased with what he finds,
　　　　　　let him be received for as long as he wants.
　　　　4　Should he,
　　　　　　reasonably and with humble charity
　　　　　　criticize or draw attention to some matters,
　　　　　　let the abbot prudently reflect
　　　　　　whether it was not perhaps for this
　　　　　　that the Lord had sent him.
　　　　5　If moreover afterwards
　　　　　　he should wish to fix his stability,
　　　　　　such a wish is not to be refused,
　　　　　　and especially because his life could be discerned
　　　　　　while he was a guest.

16 Apr　6　But if while he was a guest
16 Aug　　　　he was found to be exacting or sinful,
16 Dec　　　　not only should he not be incorporated
　　　　　　into the body of the monastery,
　　　　7　rather let him be frankly told to go away,
　　　　　　lest others also be infected by his disease.
　　　　8　But if he be not of the type
　　　　　　who deserves to be thrown out,
　　　　　　not only if he asks
　　　　　　should he be received
　　　　　　to be incorporated into the community,
　　　　9　rather let him be induced to stay,
　　　　　　so that others might learn from his example,
　　　10　since too in every place
　　　　　　one Lord is served,
　　　　　　one King is fought for.

11 Moreover the abbot may place him
in a somewhat higher rank,
should he judge him to be fit for it.

12 Not only as regards a monk
but also from the above-mentioned grades of priests and clerics,
the abbot may establish in a higher place
than their place of entry,
should he see their life to be such.

13 Let the abbot however take care
never to accept a monk
from another known monastery
as a member of the community
without the consent of his abbot
or letters of commendation,

14 because it is written: Tob 4:15; Mt 7:12
WHAT YOU DO NOT WANT
DONE TO YOU,
DO IT NOT TO ANOTHER.

CAPUT LXI: DE MONACHIS PEREGRINIS QUALITER SUSCIPIANTUR

¹SI QUIS MONACHUS PEREGRINUS DE LONGINQUIS PROVINCIIS SUPERVENERIT, SI PRO HOSPITE VOLUERIT HABITARE IN MONASTERIO ²ET CONTENTUS EST CONSUETUDINEM LOCI QUAM INVENERIT, ET NON FORTE SUPERFLUITATE SUA PERTURBAT MONASTERIUM, ³SED SIMPLICITER CONTENTUS EST QUOD INVENERIT, SUSCIPIATUR QUANTO TEMPORE CUPIT. ⁴SI QUA SANE RATIONABILITER ET CUM HUMILITATE CARITATIS REPREHENDIT AUT OSTENDIT, TRACTET ABBAS PRUDENTER NE FORTE PRO HOC IPSUD EUM DOMINUS DIREXERIT. ⁵SI VERO POSTEA VOLUERIT STABILITATEM SUAM FIRMARE, NON RENNUATUR TALIS VOLUNTAS, ET MAXIME QUIA TEMPORE HOSPITALITATIS POTUIT EIUS VITA DINOSCI. ⁶QUOD SI SUPERFLUUS AUT VITIOSUS INVENTUS FUERIT TEMPORE HOSPITALITATIS, NON SOLUM NON DEBET SOCIARI CORPORI MONASTERII, ⁷VERUM ETIAM DICATUR EI HONESTE UT DISCEDAT, NE EIUS MISERIA ETIAM ALII VITIENTUR. ⁸QUOD SI NON FUERIT TALIS QUI MEREATUR PROICI, NON SOLUM SI PETIERIT, SUSCIPIATUR CONGREGATIONI SOCIANDUS, ⁹VERUM ETIAM SUADEATUR UT STET, UT EIUS EXEMPLO ALII ERUDIANTUR, ¹⁰ET QUIA IN OMNI LOCO UNI DOMINO SERVITUR, UNI REGI MILITATUR. ¹¹QUEM SI ETIAM TALEM ESSE PERSPEXERIT ABBAS, LICEAT EUM IN SUPERIORI ALIQUANTUM CONSTITUERE LOCO. ¹²NON SOLUM AUTEM MONACHUM, SED ETIAM DE SUPRASCRIPTIS GRADIBUS SACERDOTUM VEL CLERICORUM STABILIRE POTEST ABBAS IN MAIORI QUAM INGREDIUNTUR LOCO, SI EORUM TALEM PERSPEXERIT ESSE VITAM. ¹³CAVEAT AUTEM ABBAS, NE ALIQUANDO DE ALIO NOTO MONASTERIO MONACHUM AD HABITANDUM SUSCIPIAT SINE CONSENSU ABBATIS EIUS AUT LITTERAS COMMENDATICIAS, ¹⁴QUIA SCRIPTUM EST: QUOD TIBI NON VIS FIERI, ALIO NE FECERIS.

1–4   **a.** *Strangers*, even when they happen to be travelling monks,[1] are initially received into the guest quarters, where they are to be tested,[2] especially as to whether they are undemanding.[3]

      b. Benedict assumes that a guest, too, can be the bearer of a mission from the Lord. It depends, however, on the abbot to judge with the gift of *discernment*.[4] As criteria Benedict mentions—corresponding with his ideal—peaceableness, 'love and humility'.

5–12   **a.** The reception procedure seems to be shorter in the case of monks than in that of laymen.[5] While the 'Master' mentions conditions of an economic nature,[6] Benedict lists spiritual *criteria for testing*: fear of 'infection', hope of edification, general conduct. An eventual invitation to remain must also be spiritually motivated. In this context, the whole of monastic life is characterized as service of the Lord.[7]

      b. The expression 'to be admitted as a member of the corporate body of the monastery'[8] is reminiscent of Cassian (d.430), who remarks in connection with the putting off of secular clothing and the giving of the monastic habit: 'a person should not be ashamed to become like the poor, that is, the community of the brethren. Christ was not ashamed to be counted one of them and to be called their brother. Therefore one should rejoice all the more to become one of his household'.[9]

      c. Typical of Benedict is his interest in the reception of *priests and clerics*;[10] however, he mentions only conduct, and not office, as a justification for a higher rank.[11]

13–14   For the reception of monks from other known monasteries, Benedict reproduces the ancient ecclesiastical regulation for clerics,[12] which was taken up into the monastic Rules.[13] The concern here is for peace between different monasteries. Benedict would seek to help monks from unknown monasteries—'gyrovagues'[14] —to achieve 'stability'.

NOTES TO CHAPTER 61

1 → 1,10–11. 2 RB 61,1–4: RM 79,29–34; RB 61,5–10: RM 79,23–28; → 53,23–24. 3 → 7,49–50; 31,3–7; 33,4.5.6; 34,3–5; 40,1–4.8–9; 55,7–8.9–12. 4 Cf. 53,.1.7.15 (Christ in the guest). Something similar is said of the advice of a young monk (cf.RB 3,2–3: the abbot has to reflect on it). 5 → 58; 60,1–7. 6 RM 79,23: a long stay, willingness to work. 7 → Prol 3.45; 1,2; 58,17–18. 8 Verse 6; 34,5–6. 9 Inst 4,5; RF 10 gives a similar expression, as does RBasRuf 192. 10 → 60;62. 11 Verse 12. 12 Cf. Council of Chalcedon,c.11; 13. Councils held in Gaul transfer this ruling to the monks. For instance, the Council of Agde(506), presided over by Caesarius, issued the regulation which Benedict lays down here (can 27;38); cf. First Council of Orleans, 511, can.59. 13 R4P 4,1–13: 'for the sake of secure peace between the monasteries' RF6: the same provision as RB, with the same form of words and with the quotation of the 'golden Rule' (Mt 7:12); Ferreolus declares that ignoring it leads to endless disputes between the monasteries, and he regards it as unlikely that a monk will be transferred peaceably. 14 See Note 1.

CHAPTER 62

OF THE PRIESTS OF THE MONASTERY

17 Apr
17 Aug
17 Dec

Cf. Ecclus 45:19 (lat.)

1 If an abbot petitions
that a priest or deacon
be ordained for him,
let him choose from among his own
one who may be worthy
TO PERFORM THE PRIEST'S OFFICE.

2 Let the ordained priest however
be on his guard against vanity or pride,

3 nor let him take on anything
except what is commanded him by the abbot,
knowing that he must be all the more subjected
to the discipline of the Rule.

4 Nor let him by reason of the pricsthood
forget the obedience and discipline of the Rule
but more and more draw closer to God.

5 Let him always think of that place which is his
by his date of entry into the monastery

6 apart from the office of the altar,
and if perhaps
the choice of the community and the will of the abbot
wishes to promote him for merit of life.

7 He must know however
that he has to keep the ruling laid down
for deans and priors.

8 Should he presume to do otherwise,
he shall be judged to be in rebellion,
not a priest.

9 And if frequently admonished
he has not changed,
even the bishop shall be called in as witness.

10 But if even then there is no amendment,
and his faults are glaring,
let him be thrown out of the monastery,

11   should his stubbornness be such
       that he is unwilling to be subject
       or to obey the Rule.

CAPUT LXII: DE SACERDOTIBUS MONASTERII

¹SI QUIS ABBAS SIBI PRESBYTERUM VEL DIACONEM ORDINARI PETIERIT, DE SUIS ELEGAT QUI DIGNUS SIT SACERDOTIO FUNGI. ²ORDINATUS AUTEM CAVEAT ELATIONEM AUT SUPERBIAM, ³NEC QUICQUAM PRAESUMAT NISI QUOD EI AB ABBATE PRAECIPITUR, SCIENS SE MULTO MAGIS DISCIPLINAE REGULARI SUBDENDUM. ⁴NEC OCCASIONE SACERDOTII OBLIVISCATUR REGULAE OBOEDIENTIAM ET DISCIPLINAM, SED MAGIS AC MAGIS IN DEUM PROFICIAT. ⁵LOCUM VERO ILLUM SEMPER ADTENDAT QUOD INGRESSUS EST IN MONASTERIO, ⁶PRAETER OFFICIUM ALTARIS, ET SI FORTE ELECTIO CONGREGATIONIS ET VOLUNTAS ABBATIS PRO VITAE MERITO EUM PROMOVERE VOLUERINT. ⁷QUI TAMEN REGULAM DECANIS VEL PRAEPOSITIS CONSTITUTAM SIBI SERVARE SCIAT. ⁸QUOD SI ALITER PRAESUMPSERIT, NON SACERDOS SED REBELLIO IUDICETUR. ⁹ET SAEPE ADMONITUS SI NON CORREXERIT, ETIAM EPISCOPUS ADHIBEATUR IN TESTIMONIO. ¹⁰QUOD SI NEC SIC EMENDAVERIT, CLARESCENTIBUS CULPIS, PROICIATUR DE MONASTERIO, ¹¹SI TAMEN TALIS FUERIT EIUS CONTUMACIA UT SUBDI AUT OBOEDIRE REGULAE NOLIT.

1   **a.** The basic principle which introduces this chapter¹ agrees with the 'Monastic Rule of Aurelian':² 'Let no one receive the dignity of the presbyterate or diaconate, except the *abbot* wishes the ordination of a presbyter, *one* deacon, or a subdeacon. It is his right to pick out whom he will and have him ordained when he wants to.'³ The monks of Lérins insisted on this regulation:⁴ the bishop may not confer Orders over the abbot's head. He must not alienate monks from their community by ordaining them for service in the diocese; only the call to a bishopric gives the right to leave the monastery.⁵
b. In pre-Benedictine monasticism the rule obtained that the monk in his *humility* must flee the 'dignity of the priesthood' and that notwithstanding all due respect towards the priest.⁶ Cassian (d.430), who had grown up with a sister and had received the bishop's laying on of hands at his ordination to the priesthood, states wryly: 'From of old and even to the present day the Fathers keep to the following principle, which I repeat to my shame, since I could neither shun my sister nor escape the hands of the (ordaining) bishop: "A monk must at all costs flee from women and bishops". For neither the former nor the latter, as soon as he has fallen into their company, will allow him to remain quietly in his cell or to devote himself with great purity of heart to religious contemplation and beholding God'.⁷
c. In response to pressure from the Church, however, these monks showed themselves to be *prepared to serve*, for example Honoratus of Lérins (d.428), who avoided the priestly dignity for a long time, and later 'in the priesthood preserved the humility of the monk'.⁸ In Benedict's Rule the community normally includes one or two priests and deacons, a fact which points to an increasing significance of the sacramental life within the monastery itself.⁹ In

the monasticism of an earlier age the sacramental life appears more as the unique, dominant climax of the week. 'Abbot Poimen said: "As a hart longs for flowing streams, so longs my soul for thee, O God."[10] The gazelles in the desert often tread on snakes. When the poison of the latter makes them over-heated, they long to get to water; when they then drink, the fever heat caused by the snake venom has a purgative effect. In like manner the poison of evil spirits overheats the monks, who lead a life of solitude; therefore they long to come on the sabbath of the Lord to the springs of water, that is, to the Body and Blood of our Lord Jesus Christ, in order to be purified from all evil spirits of bitterness.'[11] The ardour of communion with Christ cleanses the heart.

2–7   a. Benedict is more inclined to ascribe *sacral* functions to the priest in the monastery;[12] the abbot, as 'teacher', performs the service of the Word;[13] this, however, did not exclude the important individual pastoral care by other 'spiritual fathers'.[14]

b. Benedict's main concern is not with precedence, but especially with the interior attitude of the priest. As he has already done previously,[15] he lays the emphasis on obedience and humility, in other words, on the disposition to self-denial and the evangelical simplicity of the Sermon on the Mount.[16]

c. The priesthood is not an opportunity to strive for power of dominance, but a motive for living out in an exemplary fashion the basic disposition of self-giving in love. Benedict gives a formula that is already to be found in Cyprian:[17] 'Let him walk on and on towards God'.[18] Cyprian (d.258) directed this exhortation to 'confessors', who had remained constant under persecution, but did not retain the high degree of respect they had previously won as confessors of Christ. Benedict transfers to priests the declaration made then to such lay people. Thus he demands from them no other *spirituality* than that based on baptism; but it is to be lived out in an exemplary fashion (A. de Vogüé). The object is to get nearer to Christ, to follow him, to lead to him, that is, 'to walk on and on towards God'.

d. The priest's presence in the community reminds the other brethren of the task of the *general priesthood*.[19] For Augustine (d.430), this task is 'sacrum facere', that is, to lead to an increase in 'being happy' (beatius esse), or to being nearer 'to God', who is the fullness of being and blessedness. 'Thus a true sacrifice (sacrificium) is every deed that is done so that we may join ourselves in sacred communion with God. The sacrifice is directed towards that (greatest) good, through which we can in truth be happy'.[20] For Augustine, the complete sacrifice is not just an individual action, but a process that includes the community: 'the whole redeemed city (of God), that is, the assembly and community of the saints is the universal sacrifice', in its complete openness towards God.[21]

8–11   e. For the rest, the Rule makes the same demands of the superiors and the priests with regard to *worthy* conduct.[22]

The particular procedure against the *unworthy priest* is outlined using juridical concepts. Essentially, laymen, whether brethren or abbot, may not judge a priest;[23] for this reason the bishop is brought into the process; only when there is no prospect of improvement and the fault is notorious does excommunication follow.[24]

CHAPTER SIXTY-TWO

NOTES TO CHAPTER 62

1 The 'Master' has no corresponding passage. 2 Aurelian was Bishop of Arles 546–551, the second successor of Caesarius. 3 C.46. 4 The Council of Agde (506 under Caesarius),c.27: 'If it is necessary to ordain one of the monks as cleric, let the bishop do this only at the will and with the agreement of the abbot.' Cf.Vita Caesarii 1,11: The abbot of Lérins is asked for permission to ordain Caesarius to the diaconate and the priesthood. Caesarius remains true to the usages of Lérins. 'As far as humility, love, willingness to serve, and the Cross are concerned, he remains a monk.' 5 Monastic Rule of Aurelian,46. 6 Cassian, Inst 11,14; VPatr 7,33,7; → 60,1–7. 7 Inst 11,18. 8 VHonor 3, 16. 9 → 38, 10–11; 60,8–9; 61,5–12. 10 Ps 42:2. 11 VPatr 5,18,17. 12 Verse 6: 'service at the altar'; RB 60,4:'to give blessings and to say the concluding prayers' ('missas tenere'). 13 2,1–10.11–15; 64,9. 14 → 60, 1–7. 15 → 60, 1–7; 61, 5–12. 16 → 5; 7 and *passim*. 17 Ep. 13,6. In the RB we often find the idea of progress or of spiritual ascent: cf.RB 2,25 (similar formulation); Prol 45 (a 'school'!) Prol 49; 7 ('rungs'!); 73,9. 18 Verse 4. 19 → 4,55–58.62–73; 31,10–12; 35,15–18; 57,7–9. 20 De civ. Dei 10,6. 21 ib. 22 → 21,5–6; 60,1–7; 61,5–12: as in the selection, the question is asked whether he is 'worthy' (dignus). 23 Cf. VPach 24 (→ 60,1–7, in Note 2). 24 21,5–6; 65,18–21.

CHAPTER 63

OF RANK IN COMMUNITY

18 Apr
18 Aug
18 Dec

1 They shall keep to their ranks in the monastery
as determined by their time of entry into the monastery
their merit of life,
and the abbot's decision.

2 He, the abbot, shall not disturb   Cf. 1 Pet 5:1–5
the FLOCK committed to him,
as if he could arrange anything unjustly
by exercising arbitrary power,

3 but let him always reflect   Cf. Phil 2:11; Rom 8:15
that he will be rendering an account to God
of all his decisions and doings.

4 Therefore it is according to the ranks
which he has established
or which the brethren have of themselves
that they come to the Pax,
to Communion,
to reciting a psalm,
to standing in choir.

5 And absolutely everywhere
age shall neither determine nor prejudice rank,

6 since it was as boys   Cf. 1 Sam 3: Dan 13
that Samuel and David judged the elders.

7 Therefore, except for those whom, as we have said,
the abbot, for a deeper reason
has promoted or degraded
for some definite cause,
all the rest shall take their place according to their time of entry.

8 Thus, for example, a person who came to the monastery
at the second hour of the day
must know that he is junior to one
who came at the first hour,
irrespective of age or dignity.

9 Children are to be kept under discipline
in everything
by all.

19 Apr
19 Aug
19 Dec

10 Let the young honour their elders,
   let the elders love their juniors.

11 In addressing by name
   nobody shall be allowed to call another by mere name

12 but the elders are to call the juniors 'brother'
   the juniors call the elders 'nonnus'
   which is to be understood as reverence for a father.

13 The abbot however,
   because he is believed to act the part of Christ,
   shall be called 'LORD' and 'ABBOT',
   not by his own usurpation,
   but by the honour and love of Christ.

14 Let him however think over this
   and show himself to be such
   that he is worthy of such honour.

15 Wherever brethren meet one another
   the junior shall ask a blessing from the senior.

16 When a senior passes by   Cf. Lev 19:32
   the junior SHALL RISE and offer him a seat
   nor let the junior presume to sit along with him
   unless his senior bid him,

17 so that what is written may take place: Rom 12:10
   FORESTALLING ONE ANOTHER WITH HONOUR.

18 Small boys and growing youths
   shall keep their ranks with discipline
   in the oratory and at table.

19 Out of doors or wherever
   let them have both supervision and discipline
   until they reach the age of reason.

CAPUT LXIII: DE ORDINE CONGREGATIONIS

¹ORDINES SUOS IN MONASTERIO ITA CONSERVENT UT CONVERSATIONIS TEMPUS, UT
VITAE MERITUM DISCERNIT UTQUE ABBAS CONSTITUERIT. ²QUI ABBAS NON
CONTURBET GREGEM SIBI COMMISSUM NEC, QUASI LIBERA UTENS POTESTATE,
INIUSTE DISPONAT ALIQUID, ³SED COGITET SEMPER QUIA DE OMNIBUS IUDICIIS ET
OPERIBUS SUIS REDDITURUS EST DEO RATIONEM. ⁴ERGO SECUNDUM ORDINES QUOS
CONSTITUERIT VEL QUOS HABUERINT IPSI FRATRES, SIC ACCEDANT AD PACEM, AD
COMMUNIONEM, AD PSALMUM INPONENDUM, IN CHORO STANDUM. ⁵ET IN OMNIBUS
OMNINO LOCIS AETAS NON DISCERNAT ORDINES NEC PRAEIUDICET, ⁶QUIA SAMUHEL
ET DANIHEL PUERI PRESBYTEROS IUDICAVERUNT. ⁷ERGO, EXCEPTO HOS QUOS, UT

DIXIMUS, ALTIORI CONSILIO ABBAS PRAETULERIT VEL DEGRADAVERIT CERTIS EX
CAUSIS, RELIQUI OMNES UT CONVERTUNTUR ITA SINT, ⁸UT VERBI GRATIA QUI
SECUNDA HORA DIEI VENERIT IN MONASTERIO IUNIOREM SE NOVERIT ILLIUS ESSE
QUI PRIMA HORA VENIT DIEI, CUIUSLIBET AETATIS AUT DIGNITATIS SIT, ⁹PUERIS PER
OMNIA AB OMNIBUS DISCIPLINA CONSERVATA. ¹⁰IUNIORES IGITUR PRIORES SUOS
HONORENT, PRIORES MINORES SUOS DILIGANT. ¹¹IN IPSA APPELLATIONE NOMINUM
NULLI LICEAT ALIUM PURO APPELLARE NOMINE, ¹²SED PRIORES IUNIORES SUOS
FRATRUM NOMINE, IUNIORES AUTEM PRIORES SUOS NONNOS VOCENT, QUOD
INTELLEGITUR PATERNA REVERENTIA. ¹³ABBAS AUTEM, QUIA VICES CHRISTI
CREDITUR AGERE, DOMINUS ET ABBAS VOCETUR, NON SUA ADSUMPTIONE SED
HONORE ET AMORE CHRISTI; ¹⁴IPSE AUTEM COGITET ET SIC SE EXHIBEAT UT DIGNUS
SIT TALI HONORE. ¹⁵UBICUMQUE AUTEM SIBI OBVIANT FRATRES, IUNIOR PRIOREM
BENDICTIONEM PETAT. ¹⁶TRANSEUNTE MAIORE MINOR SURGAT ET DET EI LOCUM
SEDENDI, NEC PRAESUMAT IUNIOR CONSEDERE NISI EI PRAECIPIAT SENIOR SUUS, ¹⁷UT
FIAT QUOD SCRIPTUM EST: HONORE INVICEM PRAEVENIENTES. ¹⁸PUERI PARVI VEL
ADULESCENTES IN ORATORIO VEL AD MENSAS CUM DISCIPLINA ORDINES SUOS
CONSEQUANTUR. ¹⁹FORIS AUTEM VEL UBIUBI, ET CUSTODIAM HABEANT ET
DISCIPLINAM, USQUE DUM AD INTELLEGIBILEM AETATEM PERVENIANT.

1–9 **a.** The 'Master' does not allow any order of precedence to arise among the
brethren, but organizes among them a kind of 'contest of virtue', with the
promise to make the best one from among them his successor.¹ We find nothing
in the Rule of Benedict of this solution which is pedantic and must tempt
people to put on a show. Benedict advocates a *definite order of precedence* among
the brethren, which is a tradition of Jewish monasticism,² and in a specially
pronounced degree of the Pachomian monasteries, the regulation of which
Benedict reproduces.³ The Syrian 'Didascalia of the Apostles' (early third
century) warns the bishops: 'In your assemblies in the holy churches, hold
your meetings in a decorous fashion and arrange the places for the brethren
with respect.'⁴

b. A definite order of precedence was not entirely without its problems in all
Christian monastic communities. Basil (d.379) reveals discreetly that from time
to time, with direct reference to the Lord's warning 'not to seek out the place
of honour',⁵ there could be a regular scramble for the 'lowest place'. He therefore proposes: 'It must be conceded to him on whom the responsibility is
conferred that he orders all things; one should keep to the seating order and
obey him, so that the word may be fulfilled: "With you, everything must be
done with propriety and order."'⁶,⁷

c. For Benedict, *order* is an important factor in community life.⁸ The abbot
himself must keep to the order of precedence decided by the time of profession. He can, it is true, make changes, especially having in mind individual
conduct;⁹ but Benedict exhorts the abbot (!)—something typical of him¹⁰—to
maintain peace in the community and not to exercise power in an arbitrary
fashion,¹¹ but to let an existing order stand. In Benedict's words Augustine
(d.430) can be heard, who wrote about the superior: 'Let him consider himself
fortunate if he does not exercise an authority based on force, but serves in
love, keeping always in his thoughts the account he has to give for you before
God.'¹²

d. Benedict does not allow himself to be guided merely by considerations of group sociology. In this section about the order of precedence (!) he recognizes absolutely *no social distinctions*.[13] As he has already explained,[14] he keeps to Pauline instructions.[15] Paul had understood the complete equality and unity of all, based on baptism, in a predominantly mystical sense; it was only in the group assembled for divine worship that all distinctions between slave and free fell away,[16] not at other times or in other places.[17] As far as Benedict is concerned, profession justifies the removal of all differences of rank based on natural age or previous position (A. de Vogüé). Community life in the monastery has a sacral character, such as is normally proper to the Christian worshipping assembly.[18]

10–17 It is not only the relationship between abbot and monk that interests Benedict, but also the relationship of the brethren among themselves.[19] The question of precedence, which is meant to prevent quarrels and serve *peace*, is an occasion for him in what follows[20] often to enter into particulars on community life and brotherly love.

10 The exhortation to love the *younger* brethren and honour the *older* is to be found also in Benedict's 'spiritual art',[21] but not in the corresponding text of the 'Master'. Love descends from the elders, honour ascends to them. This double movement is reminiscent of the relationship Christ-Church,[22] parents-children,[23] president-congregation[24] (A. de Vogüé). The community life of the monastery orients itself by the biblical and ecclesial ideal of community.

11–12 Benedict lays emphasis on the Christian *name of 'brother'*. The monastery must be like the primitive Church, in which all regarded themselves as 'brethren'. Basil (d.379) justified addressing others as 'Father' or 'Brother' from the Bible: 'One will regard those more as fathers who have begotten us through the Gospel,[25] as brethren, however, those who have received the same spirit of sonship'.[26] Not only the individual vocation, but also the fraternal community as a whole is a work of the Spirit. The inner, religiously motivated disposition of brotherliness is more important than the use of the title 'Brother' or Nonnus' before the proper name.[27]

13–14 The form of salutation used towards the abbot appears as an intensification of the honour which is shown to the elder brethren. The ascending curve (A. de Vogüé) leads on to Christ.[28] The abbot is only his representative, as was already explained in the first chapter on the abbot.[29] The double name 'lord' and 'abbot'[30] corresponds to the 'honour' and 'love' shown to him for the sake of *Christ*.

15–16 In a period of decline, Benedict calls to mind traditional biblical and ecclesiastical rules of good behaviour: the asking for a blessing[31] and standing up before an elder.[32] The re-adopting of values and norms of the earlier Church is typical of Benedict. He has been called a *'conservative reformer'*.

17 **a.** The words of the Apostle concerning the *showing of mutual respect*[33] are repeatedly quoted and interpreted by Benedict.[34] He speaks twice as often of respect as of love, but the display of esteem and respect towards the person of the other must be a 'mutual' one.[35] This living together in conscious 'mutuality' is unthinkable without 'brotherly love'.[36] This love is mentioned by Paul in the same breath with 'mutual esteem',[37] and by Benedict twice together with the showing of respect towards others.[38]

b. *Community life* may not infringe the dignity of the person. The sense of order, which lends an air of distinction to the Benedictine monastery, protects especially the rights of the person. Tact and respect must be combined with brotherly love.

c. Not speaking to '*old* and *young*', but to those previously 'rich and poor', Augustine (d.430) addressed all as 'brothers', without differentiation arising out of social origin. Those previously poor must not 'throw back their heads', but 'lift up their hearts' (sursum corda), those previously rich must not despise their formerly poor 'brethren'. 'Live, all of you, at one in heart and soul, and honour God in each other, since you became his temples.'[39]

18–19 This postscript shows that natural age does in fact have its significance: towards *children* under fifteen[40] all have a responsibility, such as otherwise only the abbot and his deputy exert.[41]

NOTES TO CHAPTER 63

1 RM 92. 2 1 QS 6,2.9.11. 3 Verses 1.4–5. The custom of the Pachomians was: whoever enters first takes the first place when sitting and walking, reciting the psalms and receiving communion. 'Among them it is not age that is observed, but the time of profession' (Jerome, praef in Pach Reg 3; Pachomius, Praec 20; 59)); R4P 10–13. 4 2,57,2. 5 Cf. Lk 14:7–11. 6 Cf. 1Cor 14:40. 7 RBasRuf 10. 8 → 5,14–19; 7,55; 32,1–4; 35,5; 38,5–9; 43; 48,1–2; 53,10–11.16; 56,3. 9 Cf.RB 21,5–7;60,4; 61,11–12; 65,18–20 10 Cf.RB 2,34: 'Let him keep before his mind' (cogitet). 11 The 'Didascalia Apostolorum', (early third century) also warns the 'bishops' not to be 'tyrannical' (2,57,1). 12 Praec 7,3; cf. 1 Pet 5:1–5; → 27,5–6; cf.RB 65,2. 13 Verse 8. 14 → 2,16–22. 15 Cf.Eph 6:8; Rom 2:11; 10:12; Gal 3:28; Col 3:11,18. 16 Cf. 1 Cor 11:21–22; James 2: 1–9. 17 1 Pet 2:18–3:7. 18 → 2,33–36; 31,10–12; 32,1–4; 52,1–3. 19 → 1,1.2.3–5; 5,14–9; 22,8; 35,1–3; 36,1–4; 48,17–18;58,17–18. 21–23; 61,5–12. 20 → 69–72. 21 RB 4,70–71. 22 Eph 5:22–23; Col 3:18–19. 23 Eph 6:1–4; Col 3:20–21. 24 1 Pet 5:1–5. 25 Cf. 1 Cor 4:15. 26 Cf. Rom 8:15; RBasRuf 4; cf.Note 19. 27 Originally, 'Brother' was not always put before the proper name; cf. Jn 11:43; 14:18; 21:15; 1 Tim 6:20; Acts 1:1. The custom arose in Benedict's time out of nostalgia for the primitive Church. The expression 'Nonnus' has maintained itself in German as 'Nonne' (in English: nun), and in Italian as 'nonno' (grandfather). 28 → 72,8.9–10.11. 29 → 2,1–10. 30 Cf. VHonor 4,19: 'All called him lord, all father.' 31 The prayer for blessing was: 'Benedic(ite)!— Bless!; the answer: 'Deus (te benedicat)!— God (bless you)!'; cf.RM 23,18.29; 27,8. 32 Standing up at the approach of the bishop or the priest was a custom of the ancient Church (Cyprian, Test.3,58); cf. Lev 19:32. 33 Rom 12:10. 34 Cf.RB 72,4; → 4,1–9; 53,1–2. 35 The expression 'mutual' occurs ten times in the Rule. 36 Cf. 72,8: 'caritas fraternitatis'. 37 Cf.Rom 12:10. 38 Cf. RB 72,4.8. 39 Praec 1,6–7; 34,3–5; 55,20–22; cf. RCaesVirg 21. 40 Cf.RB 70,4. 41 Cf.RB 63,9; 22,7.

CHAPTER 64

OF THE APPOINTING OF AN ABBOT

20 Apr
20 Aug
20 Dec

1 In the appointing of an abbot
let this principle always be kept in mind:
that he be installed
whom the whole community in the fear of God,
or even a part of the community—even though small—
will have ELECTED by sounder judgement.

Cf. Ps 33:12; 132:13; 135:4

2 Let him who is to be appointed,
be elected
for merit of life and wise doctrine,
even were he last in rank in the community.

Cf. Jer 3:15:
Acts 2:42;
Tit 1:9;2:7

3 But even should the whole community
—God forbid—
unanimously elect
a person who connives at their vices

4 and these vices somehow come to the knowledge
of the bishop to whose diocese the place belongs,
or become obvious to the local abbots and Christians,

5 let them prevent the consensus of the wicked
from having its way.
Rather let them APPOINT
A WORTHY STEWARD for the HOUSE OF GOD,

Cf. Ps 105:21;
Lk 12:42;
cf. Heb 10:21;
1 Tim 3:4

6 knowing that they will receive a good reward for this
if they do it chastely, with the zeal of God,
just as on the contrary
a sin if they neglect it.

21 Apr
21 Aug
21 Dec

7 Once appointed
let the abbot always be thinking
of what a burden he has taken on,
and to whom he will be rendering
THE ACCOUNT OF HIS STEWARDSHIP.

Lk 16:2

8 And let him realize
that he has to help
more than to rule.

9 Therefore he has to be learned in God's law

Mt 13:52;

to know from where

cf. 1 Tim 3:2;

TO DRAW OUT

Tit 1:7–9; 2:2, 4–5;

THINGS NEW AND OLD,

to be CHASTE, SOBER, MERCIFUL,

10 and let him always

James 2:13; Mt 5:7

TREASURE MERCY ABOVE JUSTICE

so that he himself may RECEIVE the same.

11 Let him hate vices,

but love the brethren.

12 In the very act of correction

let him act prudently

and not go too far,

lest while he is overanxious to scour the rust,

the vessel crack.

13 Let him always distrust his own weakness

Isa 42:3; Mt 12:20

and let him remember

THE BRUISED REED IS NOT TO BE BROKEN.

14 We do not imply by this

that he should allow vices to thicken

but that he should cut them off

prudently and lovingly,

as he shall see best for each person,

as we have already said,

15 and let him set himself

to be loved rather than feared.

16 He should not be

Cf. Isa 42:2

restless and a worrier,

excessive and stubborn,

jealous and over-suspicious,

because he will never be in repose.

17 Far-seeing and considerate

in his very commands,

and whether the works he enjoins

be of God or of the world,

let him be discerning and moderate,

18 reflecting on the discretion of holy Jacob who is saying:

Gen 33:13

IF I SHOULD CAUSE MY FLOCKS TO BE OVER-DRIVEN,

IN ONE DAY

ALL WILL DIE.

19 Taking up these
and other examples of discretion,
the mother of virtues,
let him so attune everything
that there be both scope
for the strong to want more,
and the weak do not turn tail.

20 And most importantly
that he keep this present Rule in all points,

21 so that after ADMINISTERING WELL,
he may hear from the Lord
what the GOOD SERVANT heard
who gave his fellow-servants wheat in due season:

Cf. 1 Tim 3:13;
Mt 24:45; 25:21;
Mt 5:7

22 AMEN I SAY TO YOU,
he says,

HE WILL PLACE HIM OVER ALL HIS GOODS.

Mt 24:47

CAPUT LXIV: DE ORDINANDO ABBATE

¹IN ABBATIS ORDINATIONE ILLA SEMPER CONSIDERETUR RATIO, UT HIC CONSTI-
TUATUR QUEM SIBI OMNIS CONCORS CONGREGATIO SECUNDUM TIMOREM DEI, SIVE
ETIAM PARS QUAMVIS PARVA CONGREGATIONIS SANIORE CONSILIO ELEGERIT. ²VITAE
AUTEM MERITO ET SAPIENTIAE DOCTRINA ELEGATUR QUI ORDINANDUS EST, ETIAM
SI ULTIMUS FUERIT IN ORDINE CONGREGATIONIS. ³QUOD SI ETIAM OMNIS CON-
GREGATIO VITIIS SUIS—QUOD QUIDEM ABSIT—CONSENTIENTEM PERSONAM PARI
CONSILIO ELEGERIT, ⁴ET VITIA IPSA ALIQUATENUS IN NOTITIA EPISCOPI AD CUIUS
DIOCESIM PERTINET LOCUS IPSE VEL AD ABBATES AUT CHRISTIANOS VICINOS
CLARUERINT, ⁵PROHIBEANT PRAVORUM PRAEVALERE CONSENSUM, SED DOMUI DEI
DIGNUM CONSTITUANT DISPENSATOREM, ⁶SCIENTES PRO HOC SE RECEPTUROS
MERCEDEM BONAM, SI ILLUD CASTE ET ZELO DEI FACIANT, SICUT E DIVERSO
PECCATUM SI NEGLEGANT. ⁷ORDINATUS AUTEM ABBA COGITET SEMPER, QUALE
ONUS SUSCEPIT ET CUI REDDITURUS EST RATIONEM VILICATIONIS SUAE, ⁸SCIATQUE
SIBI OPORTERE PRODESSE MAGIS QUAM PRAEESSE. ⁹OPORTET ERGO EUM ESSE
DOCTUM LEGE DIVINA, UT SCIAT ET SIT UNDE PROFERAT NOVA ET VETERA,
CASTUM, SOBRIUM, MISERICORDEM, ¹⁰ET SEMPER SUPEREXALTET MISERICORDIAM
IUDICIO, UT IDEM IPSE CONSEQUATAR. ¹¹ODERIT VITIA, DILIGAT FRATRES, ¹²IN IPSA
AUTEM CORREPTIONE PRUDENTER AGAT ET NE QUID NIMIS, NE DUM NIMIS ERADERE
CUPIT AERUGINEM FRANGATUR VAS. ¹³SUAMQUE FRAGILITATEM SEMPER SUSPECTUS
SIT, MEMINERITQUE CALAMUM QUASSATUM NON CONTERENDUM. ¹⁴IN QUIBUS NON
DICIMUS UT PERMITTAT NUTRIRI VITIA, SED PRUDENTER ET CUM CARITATE EA
AMPUTET, UT VIDERIT CUIQUE EXPEDIRE SICUT IAM DIXIMUS, ¹⁵ET STUDEAT PLUS
AMARI QUAM TIMERI. ¹⁶NON SIT TURBULENTUS ET ANXIUS, NON SIT NIMIUS ET
OBSTINATUS, NON SIT ZELOTIPUS ET NIMIS SUSPICIOSUS, QUIA NUMQUAM
REQUIESCIT; ¹⁷IN IPSIS IMPERIIS SUIS PROVIDUS ET CONSIDERATUS, ET SIVE
SECUNDUM DEUM SIVE SECUNDUM SAECULUM SIT OPERA QUAM INIUNGIT,
DISCERNAT ET TEMPERET, ¹⁸COGITANS DISCRETIONEM SANCTI IACOB DICENTIS: SI
GREGES MEOS PLUS IN AMBULANDO FECERO LABORARE, MORIENTUR CUNCTI UNA
DIE. ¹⁹HAEC ERGO ALIAQUE TESTIMONIA DISCRETIONIS MATRIS VIRTUTUM SUMENS,

SIC OMNIA TEMPERET UT SIT ET FORTES QUOD CUPIANT ET INFIRMI NON REFUGIANT. "ET PRAECIPUE UT PRAESENTEM REGULAM IN OMNIBUS CONSERVET, "UT DUM BENE MINISTRAVERIT AUDIAT A DOMINO QUOD SERVUS BONUS QUI EROGAVIT TRITICUM CONSERVIS SUIS IN TEMPORE SUO: "AMEN DICO VOBIS, AIT, SUPER OMNIA BONA SUA CONSTITUIT EUM.

1–6 **a.** This second chapter on the abbot completes the first, initially by a short instruction for the *choice of the abbot* by the community. It is assumed that the procedure is already known, whereas the 'Master' speaks in detail about the appointment of the most worthy brother by the predecessor.[1] The whole interest centres on choosing one worthy of the office;[2] and that corresponds to the tradition of the Church. Two qualities above all are expected: exemplary 'conduct'[3] and 'wisdom in teaching', for the abbot must be spiritual father, teacher, and physician.[4] In contrast with a widely prevailing practice,[5] natural age or rank in the community are not valid as criteria.[6] Our text is in accordance with a brief of Pelagius I from the year 559, which is based on decrees of Justinian from 546.[7]
b. Desirable preconditions for a good election are the *unanimity* of the community and the electors' '*fear of God*', that is, on the one side a 'spiritually inspired consensus' (Origen),[8] and on the other the lively consciousness of personal responsibility before God.[9] These spiritual factors must be the decisive ones for the election, not democratic majorities.[10]
c. A legal uncertainty or insoluble practical difficulties because of a possible right to resist on the part of the defeated are not anticipated. For the process of 'election' is followed by a second, not merely formal step: the 'ordinatio' or induction into office of the chosen candidate by the bishop. Here it becomes clear that the monastery is integrated into the local Church. The bishop must make sure that the monk to be installed as abbot is worthy. The author reckons realistically with the possibility of abuses. Here one thinks of the community of Vicovaro, which had wished Benedict as its abbot, but wanted to poison him because of his efforts to reform it.[11] Abbots or Christians of the surrounding area must draw the bishop's attention to abuses. According to this remark, not only the bishop, but also the other members of the *local Church* share the responsibility for the welfare of the religious communities in their own area. Thus it is presupposed that lay people can be more perfect than monks. In any case, it is for the bishop to install a 'worthy administrator'[12] in place of the elected unworthy monk. The monastery is defined as the 'house of God', an expression which occurs three times in the Rule.[13] It seems that the Rule is observed in different dioceses[14] and is known to the bishops.[15]

7–22 Benedict is more interested in explaining to the abbot how he should exercise his office than in the procedure of the abbatial election. Whereas in the first chapter on the abbot, which is taken almost completely from the 'Master',[16] Benedict remains chiefly under the influence of the teacher-pupil (disciple) relationship, he develops here a picture of the abbot that integrates the most diverse features of the *ecclesiastical superior*.[17] Benedict corrects or completes the picture of the superior originating from Cassian (d.430) and from the

'Master' and influenced by the figure of the abba in the semi-eremitical settlements of Lower Egypt.[18] The understanding of the monastery proceeding more from the 'koinonia' or 'life-long community' of the brethren in Christ, prevailed more in Cappadocia,[19] in the Pachomian monasteries[20] and with Augustine (d.430) whose 'paragraph on the object' of the monastery reads: 'You are brought together into *one* community, chiefly in order to live at one in one house,[21] to be of one heart and one mind . . . '[22] In this tradition, the superior possesses the characteristics of the ecclesiastical leader who stands in the middle of his community as one who serves, but also, as 'epi-skopos' (overseer), forms the 'eye' of the community, that is, judges and orders all things with foresight and care.[23]

7–8   **a.** Benedict begins a second *catalogue of duties* of the abbot, which without doubt reflects the experience of a whole life. He starts with a reference to the Judgement.[24] As 'representative', the abbot must render an account to the real head of the monastery, namely to Christ.

b. In a well-formulated maxim[25] the *serving* character of the office is clearly expressed. This is a complementary aspect of obedience,[26] which, in the Christian and ecclesial understanding of it, is never viewed according to the pattern of political power structures.

9–10   The abbot must be *acquainted with the Scriptures* and possess a knowledge that permits him to teach the community and be its 'eye'. Apart from that, Benedict wishes the abbot to have qualities which are expected of Church leaders or servants in the Pastoral Epistles.[27] Benedict envisages neither monarchical nor democratic authority structures, but simply the ecclesial concept of service. In particular, the healing means of mercy in the light of the Sermon on the Mount is recommended, not legalism or obsession with principles.

11   The maxim about hating evil and *loving* the brethren is modelled on Horsiesi (d.*c*.380)[28] and above all on Augustine (d.430): 'For the discovery . . . and punishment of every fault let the principle be: let it be carried out with hatred for evil and love for men.'[29]

12–15   **a.** The popular saying 'shun excess'[30] serves as an exhortation to proper balance. It was said of the founder of Lérins that he ensured 'in a kind and careful way' that neither 'too much work' nor 'too much rest' harmed anybody.[31]

b. A sense of proportion, care and regard for others are necessary above all in the *correction* of defaulters. The superior must remain conscious of his own weakness. Benedict remembers at this point a story of Cassian's (d.430): 'A genuinely zealous young man went to an old father to find healing for his difficulties. He admits simply that his sex drive and the spirit of unchastity are plaguing him. In the prayer of the elder he hopes to find a soothing consolation in his struggle and an unction for his wounds. The elder, however, scolds him with bitter anger and declares he is a miserable good-for-nothing and unworthy to bear the name of a monk if he is tempted by such lusts and vices. The old man really hurts him very deeply with this reprimand. He drives the young monk to the deepest despair and dismisses him from his dwelling completely crushed and in a state of deadly depression. In this bitter depression the young monk thinks no more of interior peace, but mulls over thoughts of how he could live out his desires. Then he meets Abbot Apollo, an experienced elder. The latter reads the interior struggle and the violent temptation in the young man's features and asks the reason for the difficulties. Apollo puts the question with all kindness, but the young monk cannot answer. Abbot Apollo senses ever more clearly that a certain inhibition is causing the young man to remain silent about the reason for his deep depression, even though just a look at him reveals that there are problems. Apollo does not give up and enquires with concern about the reasons for his great sadness. Embarrassed, the young man now confesses that he must return to his village; for, according to the statement of that senior, he is not capable of being a monk, incapable of harnessing his sex drive and unable to find a remedy for his temptation. So he is now turning his back on the cloister, going back into the world and taking unto himself a wife. Then Abbot Apollo begins lovingly to console him and set him at rest. Apollo explains that the same stirrings of lust also beset himself daily and inflame his imagination. He tells the young monk that in no way must he abandon himself to despair, and he must not be surprised if a temptation is violent. The latter must be overcome, not so much by his own efforts, but through the grace and mercy of God.' A little later Apollo then discovers that the old firebrand is himself incapable of resisting a temptation. He preaches him a stiff sermon on the loving patience with which one must stand by young people, and quotes in that connection the words of Scripture about the bruised reed that one may not break.[32] Only the 'grace of God' can help 'our weakness'.[33] It is typical what significance Benedict assigns to *individual pastoral care*,[34] in this case in an exhortation to the abbot.

c. Benedict has moved on from the folk wisdom of 'shunning excess' to a deeper biblical insight, for with the Scripture passage just quoted he presents the picture of the Suffering Servant from Isaiah,[35] that is, the picture of Christ.[36] Jesus, of whom it is said in the pericope of the *Suffering Servant*: 'he healed all the sick',[37] is the model for the abbot as physician of souls. In contrast with his general tendency towards brevity, and otherwise than in the first chapter on the abbot,[38] to which he wishes to add complementary aspects, Benedict lingers long over the theme of mild kindness and wise consideration. Also, the tendency to reject simultaneously exaggeration in one direction or the other, is typical of Benedict.[39]

d. The maxim 'to be *loved more than feared*' is traditional and is reminiscent of Augustine's (d.430) exhortation to the superior: 'Let him love order, and support it with authority; and although both are necessary, let him seek nevertheless to be more loved than feared by you, always remembering the account he must render to God for you.'[40]

16 The list of *negative* features in the picture of the abbot is opened with a statement that reminds us of what the Suffering Servant is not like (A. de Vogüé). Benedict's portrait of the abbot manifests the features of the mild and tranquil Suffering Servant,[41] not those of an autocratic monarch, of a Roman paterfamilias, of a feverishly active manager or of a suspicious overseer.

17-19 a. Benedict now speaks expressly about the abbot's task of being the *'eye' of the community*. Foresight and circumspection are the fruits of 'discretion', that is, the gift of discernment[42] and of a sense of proportion or moderation.[43] The power 'to distinguish the spirits' is 'given to us by the Spirit'.[44] For Cassian (d.430) this 'discretion' is the gift of 'counsel'. 'According to the explanation of blessed Antony and all others, it leads the monk with unerring tread to God, without the monk having to fear anything . . . It is mother, protectress and measure of all virtues.'[45]

b. In the name of discretion, which Cassian considers indispensable for a sensible 'self-control' and for progress in the interior life, he rejects '*exaggerations in one direction or the other*' with the old saying 'les extrêmes se touchent',[46] for example in the question of fasting.[47] However, Cassian draws attention to the fact that 'discretio' is not a comfortable, bourgeois mediocrity, but 'one of the finest gifts of the Spirit'[48] . . . for distinguishing the spirits that rise up from inside us.[49] It presupposes humility, that is, the essential touching of the person's core by the presence of God.[50]

c. It is noticeable that the same abbot who is seen as a spiritual man also allots '*worldly tasks*'.[51]

d. Benedict treats here of the theme of the '*strong*' and the '*weak*', which is important for him.[52] His basic principle of pointing out to the 'strong' an attractive and demanding ideal, but of not overtaxing the 'weak' and provoking someone to leave,[53] should not be misinterpreted as opportunism. The ability to accept a certain pluralism and to show tolerance towards the 'weak', is evidence of a 'wide heart'.[54] Basil (d.379) has devoted to this attitude its own question and answer: 'Question: How are the stronger brethren able to bear the weaknesses of the difficult brethren? Answer: "To bear" means "to take upon oneself" and "to heal", according to the words of Scripture: "Surely he has borne our griefs and carried our sorrows."[55] Not that he himself fell victim to the weaknesses! He relieved their bearers of them and healed them. So in our case too the weak can be healed by a conversion, namely by the lasting constancy and health of the strong. Of them it can be said[56] that they "bear" the others, i.e. they relieve the weak of their difficulties and bear them away.'[57] The Suffering Servant is the model of the abbot and of all who are called to show that tolerance from which Benedict hopes for a therapeutic effect.

20–22 This summons to be true to the Rule is connected with the theme of the reward for the *faithful servant*;[58] once again we see the biblical features of the Benedictine picture of the abbot and of the Benedictine understanding of authority. Authority is service of the Lord, who encounters us in the brethren. They are not called subordinates, but 'fellow-servants'.[59] Fidelity to the Rule was encouraged above all in the circle of Lérins.[60]

NOTES TO CHAPTER 64

1 RB 64,1–6: RM 92–93; RB 64,7–22: RM 93,15–23. The appointment of the bishop by his predecessor occurred in sixth-century Rome. → Introd 8. In the *Life* of Pachomius we read of the brethren abstaining from voting and the naming of Petronius by the dying Pachomius, and also of the naming of Horsiesi by Petronius (VPach 53). Cassian mentions the recommendation of a dying abbot as to who should be chosen as his successor (Inst 4,28). The naming of a successor by a predecessor also occurred in the Jura monasteries (VPJur 115;132). 2 Verse 5 cf. RB 2,1; 21,6;62,1; 63,14; 65,20. 3 → 21,1–4;5–6; 60,1–7; 61,5–12; 62,8–11. 4 → 2, 1–10. 11–15;27–28; 60, 1–7. 5 Cf. Cassian, Conl 21,1. 6 Cf. RB 21,4. 7 Pelagius I., ep.28 Justinian, Nov.123,c.34 (of 1 May 546). The order of precedence among the monks is not to be considered in making the choice, but their conduct is. The one chosen must be worthy. The local bishop installs him. Earlier laws of Justinian have a similar tone (Codex 1,3,46 of 17 November

530; Nov 5,9 of 20 March 535. **8** → 3,1–3 (in Note 15); 4,62–73. **9** → 5,1–9; 7,10–13.26–30.62–66. **10** → 3,1–3. **11** Dial 2,3. **12** Cf. RBasRuf 15: 'stewards of the mysteries of God' (1 Cor 4:1). **13** RB 31,19; 53,22; Verse 5; → 2,1–10. The concept 'school of the Lord's service' is, by contrast, to be found only in the longer version of the conclusion of the Prologue that was taken over from the 'Master' (Prol 45). **14** → 7,55;18, 22–25, 5; 55,1–3; 7–8. **15** Occasionally a Monastic Rule is preceded by a letter of dedication to a bishop (RF praef). **16** RB 2. **17** 'Didascalia Apostolorum' (early third cent.) 2,20–21; 28,1–5 (in Note 8). **18** → Prol 45–50; 1,2; 2,11–15. **19** RBasRuf 3; → 1,2. **20** Horsiesi, Lib 50. **21** See above, in Note 13. **22** Praec 1,2. **23** → 27,7–9 (in Note 24); 64,12–15.17–19. **24** Cf. Horsiesi, Lib.10–11. **25** Verse 8: It is difficult to reproduce the play on words, 'magis prodesse quam praeesse': 'to help more than to rule'. It has an Augustinian ring (cf.sermo 340; 1; De civ.19,19). **26** → Prol 45;2,31–32; 4,59–61.62–73; 7,35–43 and *passim*. **27** See the scriptural quotations in relation to verse 9. **28** Lib 9: 'Be careful above all not to love the one and hate the other' (cf. Lib.16). **29** Praec 4,10; sermo 49,50; cf. RCaesVirg 24. **30** 'Ne quid nimis' (be wisely moderate). **31** VHonor 4,18. **32** Mt 12:20. **33** Conl 2,13; cf. verse 13 ('fragilitas'; Mt 12:20). **34** → 2,31–32.37–40; 4,41–50.51–54; 21,1–4; 23,1; 27–28; 31,3–7; 41,5; 44.0.6–8; 46,5–6; 60,1–7; 62,2–7. **35** 42,3. **36** Cf. Mt 12:20. **37** Cf. Mt 12: 15–21. **38** Cf. the reprimand in verse 14. The first chapter on the abbot (RB 2) through abbreviations and additions has become clearly more severe than that of the 'Master' (RM 2); → 2;26–29; Note 34. **39** → Prol 46.47; 3,4–6; 41,5; 48,9. **40** Praec 7,3; cf. VHonor 3,17: 'Nobody was simultaneously loved and feared as he was'; 7,30: 'He sought to lead more by love than by fear'. **41** See Note 23; → Prol 45–50; 7,26–30. **42** → Prol 28; 3,4–6.7–11; 4,41–50; 49,8–9; 53,3–5; 58,1–4. **43** → 3,4–6; 41,5; 48,9. **44** Cf. 1 Jn 3:24–4:6. **45** Conl 2,4. **46** 'Akrótetes isótetes'—('nimietates aequales sunt'). **47** Conl 2,16–17. **48** Cf. 1 Cor 12:10. **49** Conl 2,1. **50** Conl 2,16; → 7,10–13.26–30.52–66. **51** Verse 17; → 2,33–36; 41,4–5. **52** Verse 19; → 55,20–22; 18,1; 27,7–9; 31,3–7; 36–37; 40,1–4; 49,1–3. **53** Cf. Cassian, 2,13; → Prol 48; 29; 48,17–18.24–25; 62,1; 64,12–15. 17–19. **54** → Prol 48–49; 20,1–3; 72,1–3.5–6. **55** Isa 53:4. **56** Cf. Col 3:13. **57** RBasRuf 177. **58** → 5,14–19; 22,4–7; 57,4–6; 61,5–12. **59** Cf. Mt 24:49; Horsiesi, Lib 14; 15,1–4; 35,5; 48,24–25; 58,5–7.17–23; 61,5–12; 64,1–6. **60** → Prol 1; 1,2; 3,7–11; 4,75; 23,1; 37,1–3; 48,23; 51,3; 53,10–11; 58,9–10.12–13; 60,1–7; 65,18–21; cf.RM 93,13–15; R4P 6,1; RCaesVirg 61: 'All of you choose unanimously and under the inspiration of Christ a holy and truly spiritual abbess, who can be an effective custodian of the Rule of the monastery'; RCaesVirg 35: Abbess and prioress must 'seek to uphold the discretion of the Rule with love and kindness.'

CHAPTER 65

OF THE PRIOR OF THE MONASTERY

22 Apr
22 Aug
22 Dec

1 It happens rather often indeed
    that serious scandals in monasteries
    arise out of the appointment of a prior.

2 For there are some,
    bloated by the evil spirit of pride,
    and looking on themselves as second abbots
    take on a tyranny,
    nurture scandals
    and make factions in community.

3 This especially in those places
    where the prior is also appointed
    by the same bishop
    or by those abbots
    who appointed the abbot.

4 How absurd this is
    can be easily understood
    because matter for pride is furnished him
    right from the beginning of his appointment;

5 his own thinking suggests to him
    that he is free from his abbot's ruling power:
    'because you also
    have been appointed
    by the very same persons
    as the abbot.'

7 From out of this are stirred up
    ENVYINGS,
    QUARRELS,
    DETRACTIONS,
    ANIMOSITIES,
    DISSENSIONS,
    DISORDERS;

8 with abbot and prior at odds with each other,
    their own souls, of necessity,
    run into danger
    in the course of this dissension,

Cf. 2 Cor 12:20;
Gal 5:20–21

9 and those under them
playing up to party spirit
go to ruin.

10 This dangerous evil
lies first of all
with those who made themselves authors of such a disorder.

23 *Apr*
23 *Aug*
23 *Dec*
11 Therefore we see it expedient
that the abbot
have in his discretion
the running of his monastery,
in order to keep the peace
and safeguard love.

12 And if possible,
let everything useful for the monastery be done by deans,
as the abbot shall arrange
(as we laid down earlier),

13 so that, shared out among many,
no individual becomes proud.

14 But should the place require it,
and the community
reasonably and humbly ask for it,
and the abbot judge it expedient,

15 let the abbot appoint as his prior
whomsoever he chooses
with the advice of brethren who fear God.

16 This prior however
shall carry out respectfully
what the abbot enjoins him,
undertaking nothing against the abbot's will or directive,

17 because the more he is up in front of others
all the more carefully should he carry out the precepts of the
Rule.

18 Should this prior be found to have vices
or, taken in by vanity, to become proud,
or be proven to hold the holy Rule in contempt,
let him be corrected verbally up to four times.

19 If he does not amend,
let him undergo the correction of regular discipline.

20 Should he not amend even thus,
then let him be sacked from the priorship
and another who is worthy
be substituted in his place.

21 But also if subsequently
he be not quiet and obedient in community
let him even be driven away from the monastery.

22 Let the abbot however reflect
that he is giving an account of all his decisions to God,
lest perhaps the flame of jealousy or of envy
singe his soul.

CAPUT LXV: DE PRAEPOSITO MONASTERII

'SAEPIUS QUIDEM CONTIGIT, UT PER ORDINATIONEM PRAEPOSITI SCANDALA GRAVIA IN MONASTERIIS ORIANTUR, 'DUM SINT ALIQUI MALIGNO SPIRITU SUPERBIAE INFLATI ET AESTIMANTES SE SECUNDOS ESSE ABBATES, ADSUMENTES SIBI TYRANNIDEM, SCANDALA NUTRIUNT ET DISSENSIONES IN CONGREGATIONES FACIUNT, 'ET MAXIME IN ILLIS LOCIS UBI AB EODEM SACERDOTE VEL AB EIS ABBATIBUS QUI ABBATEM ORDINANT, AB IPSIS ETIAM ET PRAEPOSITUS ORDINATUR. 'QUOD QUAM SIT ABSURDUM FACILE ADVERTITUR, QUIA AB IPSO INITIO ORDINATIONIS MATERIA EI DATUR SUPERBIENDI, 'DUM EI SUGGERITUR A COGITATIONIBUS SUIS EXUTUM EUM ESSE A POTESTATE ABBATIS SUI, 'QUIA AB IPSIS ES ET TU ORDINATUS A QUIBUS ET ABBAS. 'HINC SUSCITANTUR INVIDIAE, RIXAE, DETRACTIONES, AEMULATIONES, DISSENSIONES, EXORDINATIONES, 'UT DUM CONTRARIA SIBI ABBAS PRAEPOSITUSQUE SENTIUNT, ET IPSORUM NECESSE EST SUB HANC DISSENSIONEM ANIMAS PERICLITARI, 'ET HII QUI SUB IPSIS SUNT, DUM ADULANTUR PARTIBUS, EUNT IN PERDITIONEM. ''CUIUS PERICULI MALUM ILLOS RESPICIT IN CAPITE QUI TALIUS INORDINATIONIS SE FECERUNT AUCTORES. ''IDEO NOS VIDIMUS EXPEDIRE PROPTER PACIS CARITATISQUE CUSTODIAM IN ABBATIS PENDERE ARBITRIO ORDINATIONEM MONASTERII SUI. ''ET SI POTEST FIERI PER DECANOS ORDINETUR, UT ANTE DISPOSUIMUS, OMNIS UTILITAS MONASTERII, PROUT ABBAS DISPOSUERIT, ''UT DUM PLURIBUS COMMITTITUR, UNUS NON SUPERBIAT. ''QUOD SI AUT LOCUS EXPETIT AUT CONGREGATIO PETIERIT RATIONABILITER CUM HUMILITATE ET ABBAS IUDICAVERIT EXPEDIRE, ''QUEMCUMQUE ELEGERIT ABBAS CUM CONSILIO FRATRUM TIMENTIUM DEUM ORDINET IPSE SIBI PRAEPOSITUM. ''QUI TAMEN PRAEPOSITUS ILLA AGAT CUM REVERENTIA QUAE AB ABBATE SUO EI INIUNCTA FUERINT, NIHIL CONTRA ABBATIS VOLUNTATEM AUT ORDINATIONEM FACIENS, ''QUIA QUANTUM PRAELATUS EST CETERIS, ITA EUM OPORTET SOLLICITIUS OBSERVARE PRAECEPTA REGULAE. ''QUI PRAEPOSITUS SI REPERTUS FUERIT VITIOSUS AUT ELATIONE DECEPTUS SUPERBIRE, AUT CONTEMPTOR SANCTAE REGULAE FUERIT CONPROBATUS, ADMONEATUR VERBIS USQUE QUATER. ''SI NON EMENDAVERIT, ADHIBEATUR EI CORREPTIO DISCIPLINAE REGULARIS. ''QUOD SI NEQUE SIC CORREXERIT, TUNC DEICIATUR DE ORDINE PRAEPOSITURAE ET ALIUS QUI DIGNUS EST IN LOCO EIUS SUBROGETUR. ''QUOD SI ET POSTEA IN CONGREGATIONE QUIETUS ET OBOEDIENS NON FUERIT, ETIAM DE MONASTERIO PELLATUR. ''COGITET TAMEN ABBAS SE DE OMNIBUS IUDICIIS SUIS DEO REDDERE RATIONEM, NE FORTE INVIDIAE AUT ZELI FLAMMA URAT ANIMAM.

1–10   a. *'Praepositus'* (provost) was initially the name of the 'first man' in the monastery; the word means nothing other than 'superior'. In Benedict's time the custom had spread of calling the 'second man' praepositus; later, the name 'prior' established itself for him. The office is found in Caesarius' (d.542)[1] work, whereas the 'Master' will not tolerate any 'second'.[2]

b. The rejection of every kind of 'tyrannical' *abuse of power* is not new;[3] it represents the opposite pole to 'serving in love and humility'.[4]

c. *'Splits'* in the community are in contradiction to the essence and meaning of a monastery.[5] The danger of such splits exists if a monastery has two abbots, something which happens if the abbot is incapable, whereas the prior is completely on top of his job;[6] or in the case of interference from outside, especially if the bishop or other abbots[7] install both the abbot and the prior. Gregory the Great (d.604) relates, as it happens, of Benedict that he installed the abbot and the prior in the new foundation of Terracina.[8] Pope Gregory, too, if he had to intervene in monasteries because of abuses, repeatedly filled both offices with new men.[9] (A. de Vogüé)

d. Benedict declared himself unambiguously for the system of 'deans', who were called 'praepositi' by the 'Master', who equally emphatically rejected a 'second man' after the abbot. In this chapter the *office of prior* (praepositus) is now introduced, relying on a tradition attested to by Gregory the Great (d.604). The chapter is also remarkable because of its peculiarities of language. It is supposed (!) that the abbot of the monastery in the Lateran intended to provide for and institute the office of a prior on the model of Gregory's monastery of St. Andrew nearby, and therefore replaced the earlier regulations of this chapter of the Rule (E. Manning), or that Gregory himself interfered with this chapter (B. Steidle).

11–13   The maintenance of *peace* and *love* in the community is the motive for referring the appointments to the offices in the monastery exclusively to the abbot.[10] Benedict's inclination is really to the system of 'deans'; the relevant chapter is specifically recalled.[11]

14–15   The author is prepared to leave his theory and ideal solution to one side and to discuss things. Because of 'local conditions', by which probably the numerical size of the community is meant,[12] initiatives towards changes in the system are permitted. One can 'humbly' make 'a reasonable request' of the abbot.[13] He wishes to listen to the 'counsel of the brethren'.[14]

16–17   The requirement of obedience in the 'second man' corresponds to the general rules. The motive of *good example* is traditional: 'You who are the "second men" in the monastery should show yourselves to be the "first" in the virtues.'[15]

18–21   The procedure against an *unworthy* prior, who is a 'despiser of the holy Rule',[16] should be carried through with a sense of justice.[17] If it comes to a removal from office, the author presupposes the appointment of a new prior, as if that went without saying. He seems to have forgotten his previously expressed, rather theoretical reservations towards the system of the prior. In reality, the 'prior' must have already been established for a long time. The tone of the whole chapter is nervous. The author even contemplates the possible 'expulsion' of an unworthy prior.[18] Practical experiences of a corresponding nature[19] most probably constitute the background to this presentation. Only here do we find a fourfold warning.

22 The author reckons with possible errors on the part of the abbot (something the 'Master' would not do!).²⁰ In the Rule, the necessity of *conscientiousness* is repeatedly emphasized.²¹

NOTES TO CHAPTER 65

1 The prioress is the substitute for the extremely busy abbess (RCaesVirg 25; 35; 42,44; 47). Cf. RF 17: 'Help for the abbot'. 2 RB 65,1–10: RM 92–93; RB 65,11–13: RM 92; RB 65,14–15:RM 93,56–68; RB 65,16–17: RM 93,69–70. The 'Master' calls the two 'seniores' of a deanery (decada) 'praepositi'. The Rule of Benedict has no fixed terminology, a sign of the use of various models or of different editorial strata. 3 → 27,5–6; 63,1–9; 64,1–9 (in Note 11); cf. Horsiesi, Lib 13 (out of 'pride'). 4 → 35,1–3.6; 57,1–3; cf Augustine, Praec 7,3. 5 → 1,1.2. 3–5 and *passim*. 6 Cf. Gregory, Dial 1,2,7. 7 → 64,1–6. 8 Dial 2,22. 9 Ep 11,48; 5,6. 10 → 21,1–4; 62,1. 11 RB 21. Only in RB 62,7 does the word 'deans' reappear; otherwise they are always called 'seniores'. 12 Cf.RB 35,4. 13 Cf. RB 31,5; 61,4; 68,2–3. 14 → 3.15 → Horsiesi, Lib 14. Caesarius,who expects fidelity to the Rule from abbess and prioress, sees those more highly placed as exposed to greater dangers (RCaesVirg 35). → 7,55; 23,1. 16 → 64,20–22 (in Note 60). 17 The prescriptions of RB 21,5–6 are repeated. Guilt must be proved. The number of reprimands is higher than usual (→ 21,5–6). 18 Cf. RB 62,10. 19 Verse 1. 20 3,7–11; 4,59–61; 65,22. 21 'Cogitet': cf. RB 2,34; 55,22; 63,3.14; 64,7; 65,22.

CHAPTER 66

OF THE GATEKEEPERS OF THE MONASTERY

24 Apr
24 Aug
24 Dec

1 Let a wise old man be stationed
at the gate of the monastery:
he will know
how to give and receive a message;
his maturity will prevent his wandering about.

2 This porter must have a cell alongside the gate
so that those who come
will always find someone to answer them.

3 And as soon as anyone knocks
or a poor man calls out,
let him reply
'Thanks be to God' or
'A blessing to you,'

4 and immediately   Cf. 2 Cor 5:14
let him answer quickly
WITH FERVENT LOVE
and with all the meekness of the fear of God.

5 Should this porter need an assistant
let him get a junior brother.

6 If possible however
the monastery should be so set up
that everything necessary is carried on within the monastery,
that is,
the water,
the mill,
the garden,
and the various crafts

7 so that there be no necessity for the monks
to be wandering about outside:
this is absolutely not good
for their souls.

8 We wish moreover
that this Rule be frequently read out
in community,

lest any brother make excuses
about not knowing it.

CAPUT LXVI: DE HOSTIARIIS MONASTERII

¹AD PORTAM MONASTERII PONATUR SENES SAPIENS, QUI SCIAT ACCIPERE RESPONSUM
ET REDDERE, ET CUIUS MATURITAS EUM NON SINAT VACARI. ²QUI PORTARIUS
CELLAM DEBEBIT HABERE IUXTA PORTAM, UT VENIENTES SEMPER PRAESENTEM
INVENIANT A QUO RESPONSUM ACCIPIANT. ³ET MOX UT ALIQUIS PULSAVERIT AUT
PAUPER CLAMAVERIT, «DEO GRATIAS» RESPONDEAT AUT «BENEDIC», ⁴ET CUM
OMNI MANSUETUDINE TIMORIS DEI REDDAT RESPONSUM FESTINANTER CUM
FERVORE CARITATIS. ⁵QUI PORTARIUS SI INDIGET SOLACIO IUNIOREM FRATREM
ACCIPIAT. ⁶MONASTERIUM AUTEM, SI POSSIT FIERI, ITA DEBET CONSTITUI UT OMNIA
NECESSARIA, ID EST AQUA, MOLENDINUM, HORTUM VEL ARTES DIVERSAS INTRA
MONASTERIUM EXERCEANTUR, ⁷UT NON SIT NECESSITAS MONACHIS VAGANDI FORIS,
QUIA OMNINO NON EXPEDIT ANIMABUS EORUM. ⁸HANC AUTEM REGULAM SAEPIUS
VOLUMUS IN CONGREGATIONE LEGI, NE QUIS FRATRUM SE DE IGNORANTIA
EXCUSET.

1–5 Many monastic writings mention the *porter* of the monastery,¹ and the
'Master' draws up a detailed catalogue of duties for him.² Benedict is concerned
with the mature age and above all with the human and spiritual qualities of
the porter. He must not 'roam about' outside;³ he should always be available.
The mention of the 'visitors' and the 'poor', who could be numerous,⁴ gives
Benedict occasion to call for 'friendliness'⁵ and attentive love towards them. In
them Christ is received.⁶

6–7 a. As in the chapter on the guests,⁷ here also the influence of the '*History of
the Monks in Egypt*' is to be felt: 'In the Thebaid we have also seen the well-
known monastery of Isidore. It is bound in by extensive walls, so that it offers
spacious accommodation to those who live there. Within the monastery there
are several springs, watered gardens, various orchards and gardens with trees.
All needs are sufficiently or generously catered for, so that none of the monks
there needs to go out in order to get anything. A worthy elder, who was chosen
by the seniors, sits at the door. His task it is to receive the visitors . . . Nearby
there is a guesthouse, in which he receives the visitors and waits on them in
all friendliness.'⁸

b. Gregory the Great (d.604) describes Benedict himself as porter sitting *in
front of the monastery gate* (!): 'A Goth named Zalla . . . was one day torturing
a peasant in a predatory and cruel way. Compelled by the tortures he had
been subjected to, the peasant confessed that he had entrusted himself and his
possessions to Benedict, the servant of God. If the torturer believed him and
stopped plaguing him for a while, the peasant could gain a few short hours of
life. Zalla stopped maltreating the peasant, but bound his arms securely and
began driving him before his horse, so that he might show him, who this
Benedict was, who had taken over his possessions. With his arms bound, the

peasant went before Zalla and led him to the holy man's monastery. The peasant said to the raging Zalla, who was following him: "Look, here is the man of whom I spoke to you: Benedict, the father!" Zalla looked at him, and, snorting with rage, he thought, in his sick state of mind, that he would terrorize Benedict in the way he had often practised. Loudly bawling he shouted at Benedict: "Up! Stand up! Out with this peasant's things, which you have received!" On hearing this shout, Benedict at once raised his eyes from his reading, looked steadily at Zalla, then noticed also the fettered peasant and looked at his bound arms. Then the bonds were loosed with wonderful swiftness . . . Terrified, Zalla fell to the ground. The hard and cruel man bent his neck to Benedict's feet and recommended himself to his prayers. The saint remained seated with his book, but he called brethren to take Zalla inside and give him a blessed loaf. When he was brought before him again, Benedict exhorted him to drop his perverted cruelty'.[9] Subsequently Pope Gregory explains that Benedict had been given a 'power'.[10] Empowered by this inner, spiritual authority, received during the 'lectio divina', he was able to loosen bonds and heal one who was shouting like one possessed.

c. The 'Master' regards going out as harmful, because, outside, the monks are sometimes looked on as saints and sometimes ridiculed![11] Basil (d.379) attempted to justify a certain seclusion or a *distance from one's surroundings*: 'Above all, in order to be able to devote oneself to prayer, one must withdraw into solitude . . . In this way we break with old habits . . . We must take on the Cross of Christ and follow him . . . It is difficult, if not impossible, to leave everything in life as it was, and nevertheless to change and better oneself.'[12] Thus, Christ is the reason for turning to people[13] as well as for distancing oneself from them.[14]

8 a. The 'Rule of the Master' ends with the chapter on the 'Doorkeepers of the Monastery'.[15] The *final sentence* of Benedict's chapter on the porter must have formed the conclusion of his Rule in a certain phase of its editing.

b. An exhortation to *fidelity to the Rule* is also found at the conclusion of the Rule of Augustine: 'The Lord grant you the strength to keep all that in love, because you love spiritual beauty, and because there rises from you, thanks to your way of life, the aroma of Christ.[16] You are not placed like slaves under the Law,[17] but like freemen under grace.[18] So that you can examine yourselves in this writing as in a mirror, and so that you forget or neglect nothing, read it every week.'[19] A Christian life that gladdens God and men, that is free and harmonious, must be the fruit of fidelity to the Rule.

NOTES TO CHAPTER 66

1 Pachomius, Praec 53–54; Cassian, Inst 4,7. 2 RB 66,1–5: RM 95,1–3; RB 66,6: RM 95,17; RB 66,7:RM 95,18–21; RB 66,8: RM 95,24; 24,15–17.26–27.31–33. 3 Or 'be idle'? cf. verse 7. 4 → 53,16.17–20. 5 → 6,2–5; 7,59–61; 31,3–7; 53,8–9. 6 Cf. RB 53,1.7.15. 7 → 53,1–2. 8 Hist mon 17,2. 9 Dial 2,31. 10 Cf. Mk 3:15: 'and have authority to cast out demons'; Mt 16:19: 'what you will loose upon earth' Lk 13:16; → 6,2–5 (in Note 23). 11 RM 95, 17–21. 12 RBasRuf 2. 13 → 31,8–9; 53,3–5.15; 61,1–4. 14 → 6,2–5; 51,1–2; 53,3–5.23–24; 27,1–4; cf. 2 Tim 2:4. 15 RM 95:24: 'Conclusion of the Rule of the Holy Fathers'. 16 Cf. 2 Cor 2:14–15. 17 Cf. Gal 5:18. 18 Cf. Gal 4:22–31. 19 Praec 8,1–2; cf.R4P 3,30.

CHAPTER 67

OF THE BRETHREN SENT OUT ON A JOURNEY

1   The brothers being sent on a journey
are to recommend themselves
to the prayer of all the brethren and the abbot;

2   and a commemoration of all those absent
shall always be made
at the concluding prayer of the Work of God.

3   On the same day on which they return,
the brethren who come back from travel,
shall lie prostrate on the floor of the oratory
at all the canonical hours
when the Work of God is being completed,

4   they shall ask a prayer from all
on account of transgressions
which may have crept in on the road:
seeing or hearing some bad thing, or idle talk.

5   Nor let anyone dare recount to another
whatever he may have seen or heard outside the monastery:
it is absolutely ruinous.

6   Should someone presume to do this,
let him undergo the punishment of the Rule.

7   Similarly, anyone who presumes
to go out of the monastery enclosure,
or go anywhere,
or without the mandate from the abbot
to do anything
no matter how small.

CAPUT LXVII: DE FRATRIBUS IN VIAM DIRECTIS

¹DIRIGENDI FRATRES IN VIA OMNIUM FRATRUM VEL ABBATIS SE ORATIONI CONMENDENT, ²ET SEMPER AD ORATIONEM ULTIMAM OPERIS DEI COMMEMORATIO OMNIUM ABSENTUM FIAT. ³REVERTENTES AUTEM DE VIA FRATRES IPSO DIE QUO REDEUNT PER OMNES CANONICAS HORAS, DUM EXPLETUR OPUS DEI, PROSTRATI SOLO ORATORII ⁴AB OMNIBUS PETANT ORATIONEM PROPTER EXCESSOS, NE QUI FORTE SUBRIPUERINT IN VIA VISUS AUT AUDITUS MALAE REI AUT OTIOSI SERMONIS. ⁵NEC PRAESUMAT QUISQUAM REFERRE ALIO QUAECUMQUE FORIS MONASTERIUM VIDERIT AUT AUDIERIT, QUIA PLURIMA DESTRUCTIO EST. ⁶QUOD SI QUIS

PRAESUMPSERIT, VINDICTAE REGULARI SUBIACEAT. ⁷SIMILITER ET QUI
PRAESUMPSERIT CLAUSTRA MONASTERII EGREDI VEL QUOCUMQUE IRE VEL QUIPPIAM
QUAMVIS PARVUM SINE IUSSIONE ABBATIS FACERE.

1–4 a. Like the 'Master',[1] but more briefly, Benedict describes how one recommends oneself to *prayer* before and after a journey. The 'Master' recommends the pause for prayer after the psalm for this purpose.[2]

b. The warning against *bad impressions* on the journey appears with verbal reminiscences in the 'Lives of the Jura Fathers',[3] and there are corresponding passages in the works of Augustine (d.430).[4]

c. Benedict always speaks of travellers in the plural; according to Pachomius (d.346),[5] monks go out *in pairs*. According to the 'History of the Monks', two elders look after affairs with the outside world.[6] Travelling was regarded as 'burdensome'. Craftsmen were dispensed by the 'Master';[7] it happened that someone became arrogant and refused to go outside because of a commission.[8]

5 Pachomius (d.346) already recommends that outside *experiences* should not be spoken about;[9] Benedict adds a warning about 'harm'.

6–7 a. There is no threat of punishment in the earlier material, only in Benedict's Rule;[10] he insists that the abbot check everything. Perhaps in Benedict's time the abbatial authority could get itself accepted only *with difficulty*.[11] With the way he puts it, Benedict can spare himself individual regulations such as the prohibition of the pleasures of the chase, which his contemporary Ferreolus cites with verbal reminiscences.[12]

b. The prohibition of *excursions* for which permission has not been granted appears also in the writings of Pachomius (d.346)[13] and in the 'History of the Monks',[14] as well as in the work of Basil (d.379).[15] Instead of getting involved in casuistry, Basil mentions a criterion based on the Gospel:[16] One may with the permission of the superior go on visits outside in order to promote 'the good of the Faith', not 'because of the mere favour of men'.—Caesarius (d.542), finally, describes a kind of 'enclosure' in his monastery of women.[17]

NOTES TO CHAPTER 67

1 RB 67,1: RM 66,1–4; RB 67,2:RM 20,2–13; 67; RB 67,3–4: RM 66,5–7. 2 Cf. verse 2; RM 76,3; 20,4–5. 3 VPJur 50. 4 Praec 4,2–11. 5 Praec 5–6; cf. OM 8. 6 Hist mon 17; → 66,6–7. 7 RM 50,72. 8 RM 57,14–15. 9 Praec 57; 86. 10 → 24,3. 11 → 6,6–7; 64,12–19; 65,14–15. 12 RF 22. 13 Praec 54–55; 84. 14 Hist mon 17; see Note 6. 15 RBasRuf 80. 16 Cf. Lk 9:59–60. 17 RCaesVirg 2;50 (never to leave the monastery of one's own will until death; not even in order to go into the basilica); 36(no entry for men, with the exception of the bishop, the administrator, priest, deacon, subdeacon, about two readers, and workers); 38–39 (conversations in the company of an older sister in one's own parlour).

CHAPTER 68

IF IMPOSSIBLE THINGS
ARE ENJOINED ON A BROTHER

26 Apr
26 Aug
26 Dec

1   If some things,
    perhaps burdensome or impossible,
    are enjoined on a particular brother,
    let him, in all meekness and obedience,
    take on what is commanded
    by the person in charge.

3   But when he sees
    that the weight of the burden
    altogether surpasses the capacity of his powers,
    let him point out
    to the one in charge of him,
    with patience and a good moment,
    the reasons for his impossibility,

3   not with pride,
    nor with resistance
    nor with contestation.

4   But if after his statement
    the superior's command continues the same,
    let the junior know
    that this is best for him,

5   and out of love,
    trusting in God's help,
    let him obey.

CAPUT LXVIII: SI FRATRI INPOSSIBILIA INIUNGANTUR

¹SI CUI FRATRI ALIQUA FORTE GRAVIA AUT INPOSSIBILIA INIUNGUNTUR, SUSCIPIAT
QUIDEM IUBENTIS IMPERIUM CUM OMNI MANSUETUDINE ET OBOEDIENTIA. ²QUOD SI
OMNINO VIRIUM SUARUM MENSURAM VIDERIT PONDUS ONERIS EXCEDERE,
INPOSSIBILITATIS SUAE CAUSAS EI QUI SIBI PRAEEST PATIENTER ET OPORTUNE
SUGGERAT, ³NON SUPERBIENDO AUT RESISTENDO VEL CONTRADICENDO. ⁴QUOD SI
POST SUGGESTIONEM SUAM IN SUA SENTENTIA PRIORIS IMPERIUM PERDURAVERIT,
SCIAT IUNIOR ITA SIBI EXPEDIRE, ⁵ET EX CARITATE, CONFIDENS DE ADIUTORIO DEI,
OBOEDIAT.

1–3   **a.** In the concluding part of his Rule, Benedict brings in some *supplements*, here a complementary point of view on the theme of obedience. He rounds off the 'Master's' somewhat one-sided concept of obedience, which he had adopted almost unchanged in the first chapters.[1]

b. First of all, Benedict holds fast to the obligation to obey. That is the traditional view. Cassian (d.430) praises the *unconditional* obedience of the 'disciples': 'They accept even impossible commands trustingly and willingly . . . and, out of respect for the "senior", do not weigh up whether and how far the command be impossible.'[2] Cassian does not seem to be conscious of the fact that unconditional obedience has its problems, if it means switching off one's own conscience.

c. Basil (d.379) advocates a *more balanced* understanding of obedience. At first he insists on an obedience without reservations, which models itself on Jesus readiness to obey 'unto death'.[3,4] Whoever seeks his own way, avoiding obedience, estranges himself from the mind of Jesus, from his self-sacrifice. He adopts an attitude of opposition and draws others after him. Then Basil continues: 'If, however, there is a definite ground for excuse, which really seems to excuse someone from his task, let him lay this ground before the superior and leave the matter to his judgement, so that the latter may establish whether the excuse presented is justified.'[5] From Basil's long 'answer' Benedict adopts only this concluding section (with word-for-word echoes),[6] because it examines the problem of a possible interior conflict, which he sees as important. Benedict views the problem from the side of the subordinates, as it were, and proceeding from their interior situation (A. de Vogüé). He accepts that in a certain case it is not only the abbot who can be a bearer of a command of the Lord.[7] One's own view may be expressed, and an interior conflict must *not be passed over in silence*. With a great capacity for psychological sensitivity, Benedict feels that mere silence would be no solution. The individual is permitted to present his difficulty in a confidential discussion with the superior. He is allowed to make credible suggestions. Only a destructive lust for opposition, which stems from a negative attitude[8] or from arrogance, is inadmissible.

4–5   Benedict makes a special point of bringing into his short Rule the reference to the necessity for dialogue; but he does not want a discussion deliberately prolonged until the superior gives way. Like Basil (d.379) he presupposes that the superior can more clearly distinguish what is better.[9] Benedict speaks of the decisive *word of the superior*, in a way in which, in other passages, he speaks of the word of the Lord or the Apostle.[10] Obedience towards the abbot as God's steward and Christ's representative[11] is not levelled down to a merely horizontal relationship, nor to a merely functional understanding in the sense of a sociological or organizational necessity. In the final analysis Benedict wants to lead to a loving obedience,[12] which Basil bases on the Lord's call to serve[13] and on Paul's words: 'Through love be servants of one another!'[14] With Benedict, this power of the Spirit becomes the 'help of God', with whom 'nothing' is 'impossible'.[15]

NOTES TO CHAPTER 68

1 → Prol 2.45; 2,31–32; 4,59–61.62–73; 5; 6,1.2–5; 7,5–9.35–43. **2** Inst 4,10. **3** Cf. Phil 2:5. **4** RBasRuf 65. **5** RBasRuf 69. **6** It is only in this passage of the Rule that the superior is described as 'is qui praeest' (he who presides), exactly as in the text of Basil which is quoted. **7** → 3,1–3;61,1–4; 65,14–15. **8** → 4,34–40; 5,14–19; 34,6–7; 35,12–14; 41,5. **9** Verse 4; cf. RBasRuf 69. **10** 'Sententia': cf.RB 5,13; 25,3; 55,20. **11** → 2,1–10; 5,1–9.10–13; 58,17–18; 63,13–14. **12** Verse 5; 5,10–13. **13** Cf. Mt 20:27–28. **14** Gal 5:13; RBasRuf 65. **15** Lk 1:37.

CHAPTER 69

THAT IN THE MONASTERY
NO ONE PRESUME TO DEFEND ANOTHER

27 Apr
27 Aug
27 Dec

1 Every precaution must be taken
that under no circumstances
one monk presume to defend another in the monastery
or to exercise a kind of patronage over him,

2 even were they bonded
by any degree of blood relationship.

3 Nor shall it be presumed by monks
in any way whatever,
because a most serious circumstance for scandals
can originate from this.

4 But if anyone transgresses in these things
let him be corrected more sharply.

CAPUT LXIX: UT IN MONASTERIO NON PRAESUMAT
ALTER ALTERUM DEFENDERE

¹PRAECAVENDUM EST NE QUAVIS OCCASIONE PRAESUMAT ALTER ALIUM DEFENDERE
MONACHUM IN MONASTERIO AUT QUASI TUERI, ²ETIAM SI QUALIVIS CONSANGUINI-
TATIS PROPINQUITATE IUNGANTUR. ³NEC QUOLIBET MODO ID A MONACHIS
PRAESUMATUR, QUIA EXINDE GRAVISSIMA OCCASIO SCANDALORUM ORIRI POTEST.
⁴QUOD SI QUIS HAEC TRANSGRESSUS FUERIT, ACRIUS COERCEATUR.

1–3 a. Basil (d.379) had expressed the opinion that whoever defended (!) another's
sin, strengthened him in that way and provoked others, deserved a sterner
judgement than those who caused 'scandals' (!).¹ Benedict seems to recall this
text of Basil's. However, it is not clear that he condemns the *abetment* of the
sin. He argues on the interpersonal level. Corresponding texts are also to be
found in the Pachomian writings.²
b. When Benedict seeks to block *encroachments* on the part of 'blood relations',
he seems to speak from 'experiences', such as he has already hinted at in the
case of the 'sons of prominent or poor people'.³ Clearly, even in Benedict's
time, a clan or the 'godfathers' of a Mafia-type association could draw attention in a very unpleasant way to what they considered to be their rights.

4 As he often does, Benedict appends an unspecified threat of punishment.

NOTES TO CHAPTER 69

1 RBasRuf 26. 2 Pachomius, Iud 16; Horsiesi, Lib 24 (the advocate and defender of another is condemned, because he gives scandal). 3 Cf. RB 59,6.

CHAPTER 70

THAT NO ONE PRESUME
TO STRIKE INDISCRIMINATELY

1   In the monastery
every occasion for presumption shall be avoided,

2   and we lay down
that nobody is allowed to excommunicate or strike
any of his brethren,
unless it is permitted him by the abbot.

3   LET THOSE WHO SIN however   1 Tim 5:20
BE REBUKED IN THE PRESENCE OF ALL,
THAT THE REST ALSO
MAY HAVE FEAR.

4   All shall exercise diligence and supervision
of the children up to fifteen years of age;

5   but this too with all moderation and reason.

6   He who, without the abbot's mandate,
presumes in any degree with an older person,
or who flares up without discernment with the children,
shall be subjected to the discipline of the Rule,

7   because it is written: Tob 4:16; Mt 7:12
WHAT YOU DO NOT WANT
DONE TO YOU,
DO IT NOT TO ANOTHER.

CAPUT LXX: UT NON PRAESUMAT PASSIM
ALIQUIS CAEDERE

¹VITETUR IN MONASTERIO OMNIS PRAESUMPTIONIS OCCASIO; ²ATQUE CONSTITUIMUS
UT NULLI LICEAT QUEMQUAM FRATRUM SUORUM EXCOMMUNICARE AUT CAEDERE,
NISI CUI POTESTAS AB ABBATE DATA FUERIT. ³PECCANTES AUTEM CORAM OMNIBUS
ARGUANTUR UT CETERI METUM HABEANT. ⁴INFANTUM VERO USQUE QUINDECIM
ANNORUM AETATES DISCIPLINAE DILIGENTIA AB OMNIBUS ET CUSTODIA SIT; ⁵SED
ET HOC CUM OMNI MENSURA ET RATIONE. ⁶NAM IN FORTIORI AETATE QUI
PRAESUMIT ALIQUATENUS SINE PRAECEPTO ABBATIS VEL IN IPSIS INFANTIBUS SINE
DISCRETIONE EXARSERIT, DISCIPLINAE REGULARI SUBIACEAT, ⁷QUIA SCRIPTUM EST:
QUOD TIBI NON VIS FIERI, ALIO NE FECERIS.

1–2 Benedict seeks to secure the abbot's authority[1] and his exclusive competence in matters involving punishment, against 'encroachments'.[2] A norm for this *right of the abbot to control things* is to be found elsewhere only in the writings of Pachomius (d.346).[3] Benedict decisively rejects the use of strong-arm methods and taking the law into one's own hands.

3 By these 'sinners' are presumably meant brethren who became guilty of *'encroachments'* or resort to physical force.[4]

4–5 a. Benedict makes everybody responsible for the care and supervision of the *children*, whereas otherwise he always seeks to protect the competence of the abbot or his deputies. Natural age, which otherwise plays no role, justifies a special ruling for children.[5]

b. Benedict differs from Basil (d.379) to some extent; the latter entrusts responsibility for the boys not to the community, but to selected brethren who distinguish themselves by *patience* and are capable of keeping to a proper measure of punishment.[6] Benedict trusts the community to be discreet and understanding.[7]

6–7 At the end of the chapter it is no longer only the maintenance of the abbot's authority that is in question, but also *mutual relationships*. Benedict demands consideration and respect for one another[8] and mutual love, as he puts before the monk the 'golden rule' valid for every Christian.[9] Respect for one another and brotherly love are the theme of the concluding chapters.[10]

NOTES TO CHAPTER 70

1 Evidently it was not uncontested in his monasteries. 2 → 65,1–10.11–13; 67,6–7. In RB 69–70 the expression 'to presume' in the sense of arrogance, encroachment, occurs six times! 3 Inst 5. 4 Cf T. and RCaesVirg 26; 33. 5 → 63,1–10; 18–19; 37,1–3. 6 RBasRuf 7. 7 → 2,33–36; 41,5; 64,12–5.17–19. 8 → 8.0; 53,1–2.21–22; 55,1–2; 63,10.13–14.17. 9 Cf. Tob 4:16Vg; RB 4,9; 61,4. 10 RB 63; 67–72.

CHAPTER 71

THAT THEY BE OBEDIENT ONE TO THE OTHER

29 *Apr*
29 *Aug*
29 *Dec*

1 The good thing that obedience is
  shall be shown by all
  not only to the abbot,
  but also let the brethren similarly obey each other mutually

2 knowing it is by this way of obedience
  that they will go to God.

3 The abbot's order and that of the persons put in charge by him
  being dealt with first
  —nor do we permit private orders to come before this—

4 for the rest let all the juniors obey their elders
  with all loving solicitude.

5 But if a person be found to be CONTENTIOUS   Cf. 1 Cor 11:16
  let him be corrected.

6 If any brother
  for any tiny reason at all
  be corrected in any way
  by the abbot or by any of his elders

7 or if he feels that the souls of any elder whatever
  to be slightly irritated against him, or upset even if a little,

8 immediately
  without delay
  let him lie, prostrate on the ground at his feet,
  doing satisfaction,
  until this upset is healed by a blessing.

9 Should he despise to do so,
  either let him be subjected to physical punishment,
  or if he be rebellious,
  let him be expelled from the monastery

CAPUT LXXI: UT OBOEDENTES SIBI SINT INVICEM

¹OBOEDIENTIAE BONUM NON SOLUM ABBATI EXHIBENDUM EST AB OMNIBUS, SED
ETIAM SIBI INVICEM ITA OBOEDIANT FRATRES, ²SCIENTES PER HANC OBOEDIENTIAE
VIAM SE ITUROS AD DEUM. ³PRAEMISSO ERGO ABBATIS AUT PRAEPOSITORUM QUI AB
EO CONSTITUUNTUR IMPERIO, CUI NON PERMITTIMUS PRIVATA IMPERIA PRAEPONI,

'DE CETERO OMNES IUNIORES PRIORIBUS SUIS OMNI CARITATE ET SOLLICITUDINE OBOEDIANT. 'QUOD SI QUIS CONTENTIOSUS REPPERITUR, CORRIPIATUR. 'SI QUIS AUTEM FRATER PRO QUAVIS MINIMA CAUSA AB ABBATE VEL A QUOCUMQUE PRIORE SUO CORRIPITUR QUOLIBET MODO, 'VEL SI LEVITER SENSERIT ANIMOS PRIORIS CUIUSCUMQUE CONTRA SE IRATOS VEL COMMOTOS QUAMVIS MODICE, 'MOX SINE MORA TAMDIU PROSTRATUS IN TERRA ANTE PEDES EIUS IACEAT SATISFACIENS, USQUE DUM BENEDICTIONE SANETUR ILLA COMMOTIO. 'QUOD QUI CONTEMPSERIT FACERE, AUT CORPORALI VINDICTAE SUBIACEAT AUT, SI CONTUMAX FUERIT, DE MONASTERIO EXPELLATUR.

1-4 **a.** Benedict feels the need to supplement the 'Master's' understanding of obedience, which he had adopted at the beginning of the Rule.' Whereas, in the first sentences of the Rule, obedience is seen from the ascetical point of view and designated as 'toil' or 'labour',² it is seen at the end of the Rule as a *'value'* or *'good'* (E. Manning).

b. This positive and theologically motivated view of obedience (hypakoe) is to be found already in the writings of Irenaeus (d.c.202); 'Man received the "knowledge of good and evil".³ *Good* it is, however to obey God, to believe him and to observe his commandments; and that is man's life . . . Because God showed himself generous, therefore, man learned the *good of obedience.'⁴* Man finds his 'life'⁵ in becoming like God, not in disobedience. Cassian (d.430) spoke explicitly of the 'value of obedience' as a stage in the ascent to perfection, that is, to the fullness of love and thus to God.⁶ Benedict now draws a parallel: as the abbot is to be obeyed, so (ita) is mutual, serving obedience necessary (Manning).

c. Whereas in the previous chapter, Benedict delimited the rights of the 'elder' brethren he now speaks about the behaviour of the younger (A. de Vogüé). He repeats an invitation of Basil to spontaneous, mutual obedience or *'listening to each other'.⁷* Without bringing in the problem of rank or age, Basil (d.379) wishes all to obey each other 'as to their masters', with Jesus' willingness to serve.⁸ He quotes the words of the Apostle: 'Serve one another in the love of the Spirit.'⁹ Basil emphasizes spontaneous obedience, which is to be shown not only to the superiors. He is also very aware, however, of the indispensable function of personal conscience: 'If someone tells us to do something that is consistent with God's command and contributes to the person's salvation, let us willingly accept such a command as God's will in love and thus fulfil the words: "Obey one another in the love of Christ."¹⁰ If, however, someone tells us to do something that is against the commandments of God, corrupts or waters them down, then it is time to say: "One must obey God more than men." '¹¹

d. Benedict re-echoes the motive of spontaneous, loving obedience, whereas the conscience clause is missing. Because he sees the order of precedence as important,¹² he speaks here, too, of graded degrees of competence and authority, which reminds us of the *'order in love'* mentioned by Cassian (d.430): 'A rightly ordered love hates nobody, but loves especially those who lead a worthy life. It loves all without exception, but proposes to treat some with very special affection, while among them again a few take the highest of all in love and, in comparison with others, enjoy most affection.' Cassian is thinking in this context of the particular, but not exclusive love for 'parents, spouses, brothers, children', of Jacob's love for his son Joseph, of Jesus' love for John.[13] Thus Benedict desires generally this 'listening to each other', but especially that the younger brethren be biddable towards the elder. In principle, every elder is entitled to give commands (something the 'Master' would never have said).

e. Cassian (d.430) relates from his own experience that, in his early years, 'in questions of morals and Scripture' he often emphatically advocated 'theses' which, only 'after' he had '*discussed* and examined' them 'together' in dialogue with others, he recognised as false and harmful. He had to learn to keep to the saying of the Fathers, 'that nobody ought to rely more on his own judgement than on that of his brother'. One presumes that the other has 'the gift of discernment to a greater degree than oneself'. The judgement 'of an experienced brother or a tried and tested elder' protects one from self-deception.[14]

f. Benedict is concerned about the disposition in which mutual obedience is rendered. Together with Basil (d.379) he mentions 'love and willingness.'[15] 'The value of love, peace and patience' is explained at length by Cassian (d.430). Quoting from the Psalms,[16] he rates brotherly love so highly that we: 1. may prefer no personal possession; 2. may not remain prisoners of our own wills, but must obediently attend to the others' views; 3. must prefer the good of peace to private interests; 4. must beware of aggressiveness; 5. must help another, who is aggressive, to find peace; 6. may not insist on secondary values or persevere in negative moods.[17]

g. Almost all those statements recur in Benedict's Rule, especially in this and in the following chapter. Cassian motivates his teaching on brotherly love by the example of the primitive apostolic community,[18] by the obedience and self-emptying of Jesus,[19] and by the commandment of love by which the disciples are recognized.[20] The requirement of obedience has not got a negative, anti-person point, but aims at '*perfection in the Spirit*'.[21] This perfection is not understood in an individualistic sense, as if it were a question of breeding a 'pneumatic' preoccupied with himself and his own virtuousness. 'Perfection of the Spirit', on the contrary, consists in undivided '*communio*' and the 'will to consensus'. It is 'unity of heart that stems not from love that desires, but from the apostolic caritas-love.[22] With the Apostle John, Cassian says that this love is 'God'.[23] It is 'poured out' through the Holy Spirit into our hearts, where that Spirit prays for us and thus unites us with God.[24] Whoever 'truly seeks God,'[25] seeks this love, which is fraternity in the fellowship of the Spirit. It is the Benedictine 'pax'; 'peace is in God'.

5–8 a. The correction of aggressive and querulous members of the community is no longer reserved to the abbot, who, in the earlier chapters, appears as the only authority in penal matters.[26] The author goes into the question of correction in general and into possible differences between abbot[27] or elders and younger monks.[28] Benedict turns especially to the younger ones and explains to them how they must accept a '*fraternal correction*'.[29]

b. Cassian (d.430) teaches that aggressive emotions can suddenly be transformed into a depression or 'sadness'. One must not intensify such emotions though inflammatory behaviour, but must 'soothe' them by means of a '*dialogue* and a humble satisfaction'.³⁰ Cassian recommends a 'speedy satisfaction', even if a 'merely light and trivial matter has caused the excitement.'.³¹

c. Benedict clearly takes up these thoughts of Cassian³² and seeks, by means of general prescriptions, to include all possible individual cases. The effects of the immediate '*satisfaction*' resemble the re-establishment of fraternal unity brought about by the ending of an 'excommunication,'³³ even though the satisfaction is simpler in its form too³⁴ (A. de Vogüé).

9 The punishment for an obstinate irreconcilability hostile to the community is severe. According to Cassian (d.430), the irreconcilable type is possessed by the '*rebellious spirit*.'³⁵ Dismissal from the monastery is also provided for in the case of the priest proved to be 'rebellious'.³⁶

NOTES TO CHAPTER 71

1 → 68,1–3. 2 Prol 2. 3 Gen 3:22. 4 Adv haer 4,39,1. 5 → 5,1–9 (Notes 18–19). 6 Cassian, Inst 12,31; 4,30,1; Conl 16,3 → 72,1–3.8.9–10; 73,2.8–9. 7 'Invicem ob-audire': T. and V.1; cf. RBasRuf 64. 8 Cf. Mt 20:27–28. 9 Cf. Gal 5:13, 10 A free quotation; cf. Eph 4 :2,32; 5:2; 6:1. 11 Acts 5:29; RBasRuf 13. 12 → 2,16–22; 29,1–2; 38,12; 43,7–9; 47,2–3 (Note 3); 60,1–7; 61,5–12; 62,2–7; 63; 64,1–6. 13 Conl 16:14; on aggressiveness: 4,20–33.62–73; 5,1–9; 7,26–30; 31,3–7; 49,1–3. 14 Conl 16,10–13; Cassian quotes in this context Rom 12:10: 'outdo one another in showing honour!' (cf. RB 63,17; 72,4). 15 Verse 4; cf. RBasRuf 64 (see Note 7). 16 Ps 133:1: 'Behold, how good and pleasant it is when brothers dell in unity!' Ps 67:7: 'They live in unity in the house.' 17 Conl 16,5–6. 18 Acts 4:32: 'The company of those who believed were of one heart and soul.' 19 Mt 26:39: 'not as I will, but as thou wilt'; Jn 6: 38: 'not to do my own will'. 20 Jn 13 :35; also: Mt 5:22–24; Eph 4:26; 1 Tim 2:4. 21 Conl 16,5: 'spiritalis perfectio'. 22 Cf. Conl 16,12.28. 23 Cf. 1 Jn 4:16. 24 Cf.Rom 5:5; 8:26–27; Cassian, Conl 16,13 → 1,2. 25 → 58,5–7. 26 Cf.RB 24,2; 25,5; 26,1; 27–28; 43–44; 69–70. 27 → 68. 28 → 3,1–3; 4,62–73; 7,63–66; 37; 63,10.17.18–19; 64,1–6;66,1–5;70,4–5. 29 Cf. Mt 18:15; 1 Thess 5:14; 2 Thess 3:15; Col 3:16; 2 Tim 2:25. 30 Conl 16,15. 31 Conl 16,16. 32 Verses 6–8. 33 → 44,6–8.9–10. 34 Cf. Cassian, Inst 4,16,1–2: Confession of guilt before the community after committing faults. 35 Conl 16,16; the Devil is meant. 36 → 62,8–11; 65,18–21.

CHAPTER 72

OF GOOD ZEAL WHICH MONKS MUST HAVE

30 Apr
30 Aug
30 Dec

1 Just as there is an evil BITTER ZEAL
which separates from God
and LEADS to hell,

Cf. James 3:14;
Mt 7:13; 1 Cor 3:3;
cf. Gal 4:17–18

2 so there is a good zeal
which separates from vices
and LEADS to God and TO EVERLASTING LIFE.

Cf. Mt 7:14; Jn 2:17;
Gal 4:17–18

3 Let monks therefore
exercise this zeal with burning love,

Cf. Rom 12:10a

4 that is,
LET THEM ANTICIPATE ONE ANOTHER WITH HONOUR.

Rom 12:10b; cf. 15:7

5 And WITH utmost PATIENCE
BEARING their weaknesses
whether of bodies or of characters

Cf. Rom 12:12;
Eph 4:2

6 let them vie with one another
in rendering mutual OBEDIENCE.

Cf. 1 Pet 1:22

7 LET NO ONE SEEK HIS OWN INTERESTS
BUT THOSE OF HIS NEIGHBOUR.

Cf. 1 Cor 10:24,33;
Phil 2:4

8 LET THEM WITH PURITY,
OFFER THE LOVE OF BROTHERHOOD.

Cf. 1 Pet 1:22; 2:17; Rom 12:10a;
1 Thess 4:9; Heb 13:1

9 LET THEM FEAR GOD lovingly.

Cf. 1 Pet 2:17

10 Let them cherish their abbot
with TRUE and HUMBLE love.

Cf. Eph 4:15; 1 Cor 4:21

11 Let them prefer absolutely nothing to Christ.

12 May he bring us all alike to everlasting life.

CAPUT LXXII: DE ZELO BONO QUOD DEBENT
MONACHI HABERE

¹SICUT EST ZELUS AMARITUDINIS MALUS QUI SEPARAT A DEO ET DUCIT AD
INFERNUM, ²ITA EST ZELUS BONUS QUI SEPARAT A VITIA ET DUCIT AD DEUM ET AD
VITAM AETERNAM. ³HUNC ERGO ZELUM FERVENTISSIMO AMORE EXERCEANT
MONACHI, ⁴ID EST UT HONORE SE INVICEM PRAEVENIANT, ET ⁵INFIRMITATES SUAS
SIVE CORPORUM SIVE MORUM PATIENTISSIME TOLERENT, ⁶OBOEDIENTIAM SIBI
CERTATIM INPENDANT; ⁷NULLUS QUOD SIBI UTILE IUDICAT SEQUATUR, SED QUOD
MAGIS ALIO; ⁸CARITATEM FRATERNITATIS CASTE INPENDANT. ⁹AMORE DEUM
TIMEANT. ¹⁰ABBATEM SUUM SINCERA ET HUMILI CARITATE DILIGANT. ¹¹CHRISTO
OMNINO NIHIL PRAEPONANT, ¹²QUI NOS PARITER AD VITAM AETERNAM PERDUCAT.

1–3   **a.** The final chapters speak of the objective of the 'ascent'.[1] In the process, the theme of the 'two ways' appears.[2] Irenaeus (d.*c*.202) had already expressed it in similar terms: 'That way (in light) unites man with God and leads to the heavenly kingdom, those (many ways of the blinded) separate man from God and lead down to death.'[3]

b. The expression 'zeal for the good' admittedly is also found in the 'Rule of the Master'. However, Benedict's *'good zeal'* has nothing to do with the 'competition in virtue' organized by the 'Master' in the monastery.[4] Benedict, on the contrary, is thinking of the 'good zeal in the Holy Spirit',[5] namely of love. This comes to light in his contrasting of 'bitter zeal' and 'good zeal'.[6]

c. Similarly, Cassian (d.430) distinguishes between 'love and peace' on the one hand, fear or depression (tristitia) and aggression (ira, a result of fear!) on the other.[7] Cassian warns against provoking further by means of 'dismissive gestures', a 'closed expression', hurtful behaviour or 'bitter silence' (amara taciturnitate) someone who is emotionally excited. Otherwise (he thinks) a brother will become victim of still greater states of anxiety (tristitia); outbursts will be unleashed and the 'bitter mood of aggressiveness' (amaritudo irae). A brother should not be left to himself either; one should not irritate him beyond endurance with a 'hostile silence' or with 'feigned patience'.[8] As the opposite of such 'bitter zeal'[9] Benedict puts the 'good zeal', namely the 'ardent love'[10] that leads to God. Cassian speaks of a heroic 'patience', which must 'not be just carried on the lips', but 'hidden in the secret depths of the psyche'. The aim consists in helping the other person also to gain inner peace, thus 'to overcome evil with good'.[11]

4–12   The following maxims for community life were prepared in the preceding chapters, which were not taken from the 'Rule of the Master'.[12] At the end of the Rule the principles of order, precedence in rank and subordination to the elders, which are normally given such weight, take second place to the dominant theme of love. Other leading themes of the Rule are grouped as maxims around this central theme. As with the 'tools of the Art of the Spirit',[13] we have here a *moral catechesis of the early Church* or exhortation to the faithful,[14] with a single supplement for the monks.[15]

4   For Benedict, mutual love necessarily presupposes respect for the *person* of the other, as he emphasizes in many passages.[16] He likes to quote the words of the Apostle: 'Outdo one another in showing honour!'[17]

5–6   **a.** The first sentence is reminiscent of the chapter on the care of the sick[18] and of the many exhortations to show consideration for the *weak*.[19] The second sentence takes up from the preceding chapter the theme of mutual obedience or of 'listening to each other'. Cassian explains: 'Whoever submits his will to that of a brother is generally the stronger partner than he who obstinately sticks to his claims and defends them. Whoever puts up with and bears with the other shows he is strong; on the other hand, whoever tends to be weak, almost pathological, must be treated carefully and gently; sometimes, for the sake of his quietness, his peace and his salvation, one must give way to the other even in essential matters. Nobody ought then to believe that he has lost something of his perfection because he entered on a compromise against his will; on the contrary, he must realize that he has acquired the gift of long-suffering patience[20] ... For the weak person never puts up with a strong person. Apart from that, it must be said that the weak are by nature always only too ready to insult others or unleash a conflict, but themselves can tolerate not even the shadow of a wrong.'[21] As a model for putting up with injustice Cassian presents 'the sufferings of the Lord and of the saints (martyrs)'.[22]

b. Benedict speaks here of spontaneous, mutual obedience, without introducing clauses in favour of the superiors or the elders.[23] The aims of community obedience[24] are the solidarity and peace of that community.

7 Only in this passage of the Rule is *selflessness* so explicitly demanded, and specifically linked to a saying of an Apostle.[25] Cassian (d.430) calls this selfless love, which seeks the other's advantage, 'apostolic charity'.[26] In essence, however, the self-giving and self-surrender of Jesus is very often, even in earlier chapters, the model for the behaviour expected in each case.[27] Unselfish readiness to serve others is a basic virtue of community, as Basil (d.379) above all has shown.[28]

8 a. Immediately before love for God, there is mention of *brotherly love*, which is to be rendered selflessly (caste). Corresponding to the writings and practice of the early Church, this brotherly love—so highly valued—is at the core of Christian and monastic life. Athanasius (d.373) had already written about Antony (d.356): 'He led his life in such a way that all the brothers loved him with genuine affection; he went to all, in order to learn from them, that is, in order to obey. Thus he drew from each brother's gifts of grace: from one he learned self-control, from another joy, from that one friendliness, from this one watchfulness . . . He was permitted to experience everybody's love in return and took it into himself.'[29] If Benedict, drawing on Cassian (d.430) and the 'Master', emphasizes strongly the 'master' (abbot)—'disciple' relationship, then this relationship of leading and listening or obeying includes selfless, mutual love, as may be deduced from the text just quoted from the Life of Antony.

b. In the Pachomian monasteries, 'community' is expressly regarded as the central motive power of the monastery: 'The circle of "koinonia", which binds us together, comes from God.'[30] Similarly in the case of Basil (d.379), 'brotherliness' takes precedence a long way before the relationship 'superior'—'disciple';[31] in the case of Augustine (d.430), too, his understanding of the monastery carries the unmistakable stamp of the community ideal of the primitive Church.[32] As in the 'art of the Spirit'[33] the Alpha of the love of God is followed immediately by love of one's neighbour, so here brotherly love immediately precedes the Omega of the love of God.

c. Admittedly, Benedict thinks somewhat less systematically than the model of ascent would really require. He uses the concept of 'charity' on a large scale before the goal is reached, with regard to relationship to outsiders: the excommunicated,[34] the guest,[35] visitors.[36] The community must not revolve about itself and fall victim to a kind of group egoism. Love opens itself to the world round about, especially to the poor.

d. Love is for Benedict the *inner motive* of mutual service,[37] of obedience,[38] of asceticism,[39] of the measures for the betterment of defaulters[40] and of conditions generally,[41] as it is also the criterion for the exercise of authority.[42]

9–10   **a.** The thought of the *fear of God*, that is of the personal, inner apprehension of the presence of God,[43] is bound up with the *love of God*. In the
chapter on humility, the perfect love of God, which casts out fear,[44] stood
on the peak of the ascent. Here, fear accompanies love. Cassian explains
the apparent antithesis. The aim is to progress from fear to hope and to
love.[45] In the final analysis, however, in Cassian's eyes, fear and love become
one: 'Neither fear of punishment or desire for reward, but only generous
affection is capable of giving birth to fear-love ... Because of it, friends or
spouses shy away from clouding mutual love even in the slightest ... Let
us move forward from the fear of punishment to the full freedom of love
and to the trust of the children and friends of God'.[46] Benedict has to be
understood in this sense when he brings together here the twin concepts
often used by Augustine, 'fear' and 'love.'[47,48]
  b. If one loves Christ in one's brother, in the sick person, in the guest,
and especially in the poor, then one does so as well particularly in the
abbot.[49] He has to fulfil a unifying function in the community, and is
mentioned here for about the 130th time, in this case in a chapter devoted
to fraternal community. The person to whom the monks really relate
however is Christ himself, the abbot is a representative.[50]

11   The motto '*Let them prefer absolutely nothing to Christ*', stems from the
Age of the Martyrs;[51] it is found in the same form and in a similar context
in the writings of Cyprian (d.258):[52] 'To be able to put up with a wrong,
to keep the peace among the brethren, to be devoted to God with one's
whole heart, to love him as a father, to fear him as God, to prefer nothing
whatever to Christ, because he has preferred nothing to us; to remain
inseparably bound up in his love; to stand under his cross with fortitude
and faith; if it comes to a dispute about his name and his honour, in one's
speech to give unshakeable witness (constantia), to respond without fear
when questioned (fiducia—parrhesia), to preserve patience when dying
(patientia—hypomone), so as to receive the crown—that is what it means
to want to be a "coheir of Christ"'. These gifts of the Spirit, which are
mentioned frequently in the New Testament and which belonged existentially to the Christian experience of life in the Age of the Martyrs, are also
often mentioned by Benedict.[53]

12   In an earlier phase, the whole Rule probably closed with this sentence.
Christ, the Redeemer, the Abbot proper,[54] in his grace leads the brothers to
the end of a long road (E. Manning). All enter into eternal life together, as
a community (A. de Vogüé). The ascent led through the stages of humility
and obedience, asceticism, readiness to serve and brotherly love, and now
reaches the end of the search for God,[55] the *Kingdom of God*.[56] Following
Cassian (d.430), one can say that this whole chapter treats of the last stage
of the journey or of the 'home straight' immediately before crossing the
line into perfection: 'The end of our calling is the Kingdom of God; nobody
can reach the end if he does not enter the home straight,[57] that is, if he
does not achieve "purity of heart",[58,59] which even in this life, "consists in
love"'.[60]

NOTES TO CHAPTER 72

1 → Prol 48–49; 4,1–9.76–77;71,1–4.5–9.26–30.31–32.55; 72,9–10; 73,8–9. 2 → Prol 48–49 (in Note 153). 3 'The Demonstration of the Apostolic Preaching'; Introd I; → Prol 8–11 (in Note 49). 4 RM 92,51 (together with the positively graded 'striving after the conferring of honours', i.e. the possible promotion to abbacy. A faint echo is found in verse 6 :'excel each other'; cf. RB 61,1.7; VHonor 2,9. 5 Cf. RCaesVirg 65. 6 The biblical turns of phrase bring to mind the differentiation, frequent in the writings of the early Fathers, of the 'two ways' (Clement of Rome, *circa* 96, ep.ad Cor 9; Didache). 7 Conl 16,6–7. 8 Conl 16,18. 9 Basil understands by 'bitterness' a clever nastiness, which is orchestrated with others (RBasRuf 159). Hilary of Arles writes: 'Bitterness, crudeness and unreasonableness gave way to the freedom that Christ has brought' (VHonor 3,17). → 4,62–73. 10 → 71,1–4. 11 Rom 12:21; Conl 16:22. 12 Cf. RB 64:15; 66,4; 68,1–2; 70,7; 71,1–4 (A.de Vogüé). 13 → 4. 14 Thus, Cyprian, for example (De or.dom.5) writes in the same breath about love and fear of God (cf.verse 9). Cyprian uses the sentence word for word: 'Nothing may be preferred to Christ!' (cf. verse 11; RB 4,21). He speaks of putting up with others (verse 5), of peace among the brethren (cf.verse 8), of humility (verse 10) and patience (verse 5). 15 Verse 10. 16 → 70,6–7 (Note 8). 17 Rom 12:10; cf.63:17. He has this quotation in mind in other passages about showing respect (see Note 16); in verse 3, Rom 12:10a is echoed, in verse 5 Rom 12:12. 18 → 36. 19 → 27,7–9; 31,3–7; 37; 40,1–4; 49,1–3; 55,20–22; 64,12–15.17–19. 20 Cassian quotes here Rom 15:1 and Gal 6:2. On the gifts of grace of 'patience' and 'long–suffering': → Prol 37–38.50; 4,20–33. 62–73; 7,35–43; 31,3–7; 36,5–6; 48,17–18; 49,1–3; 58,1–4; 59,1–2. 21 Conl 16,23–24, 22 Inst 12,33,1; cf. Conl 6,3. 23 → 71,1–4 24 → 5,14 19; 7,35–42. 25 Cf.1 Cor 13:5. 26 Conl 16:22. 27 → 5,10–13; 7,5–9.31–31.34.51–54; 33,4; 35,1–3; 38,10–11; 57,1–3; 58,19–20; 62,2–7; 68,1–3; 71,1–4. 28 RBasRuf 3; 12; → 1,3–5 (in Note 56). 29 VAnt 3. 30 Horsiesi, Lib 50; 1,2. 31 RBasRuf 3; cf. Note 28. 32 Praec 1,1–3. 33 RB 4,1–2. 34 RB 27,4. 35 RB 53,3 (with preference for the poor and pilgrims). 36 RB 66,4. 37 RB 35,2.6. 38 RB 68,5; 71,4. 39 RB Prol 47. 40 RB 64,14. 41 RB 61,4. 42 RB 2,22;65,11. 43 → 5,1–9; 7,5–9.10–13.26–30.62–66; 19,1–2.5–7; 58,5–7;64,1–6. 44 → 7,67–70; cf.Cassian, Inst 4,39.3. 45 Cf. Conl 11,7. 46 Conl 11,13. 47 Praec 7,3. 48 → 7,67–70. 49 → 2,1–10; 68,4–5. 50 → 2;64. 51 Cf.4,21; Prol 3; 61,10. 52 De or.dom 5; → 72,1–3 (in Note 14). 53 Virtus, fortitudo (dynamis)—power or fortitude: RB Prol 3; 1,13; 4,19; 73,9; patientia, sustinere (hypomone), tolerantia—patience, stead-fastness, endurance: RB Prol 37.50; 2,25; 4,30; 7,35.42; 36,5; 40,4; 58,3.11; 68,2; 72,5; fiducia (parrhesia)—openness, trust: RB 68,5; patientia/longanimitas. (makrothymia)—long-suffering: cf. RB Prol 37–38i temperantia, continentia (enkrateia)—self-control: RB 49,4; 64,17–19; perseverantia, constantia, stabilitas (karteria)—perseverance, constancy, stability: RB Prol 50; 7,36; 58,3.9.17. 54 → 2; 64. 55 → 58,5–7. 56 → Prol 22–27. 57 Skopos, destinatio; → 7,5–9; 20,1–3. 58 Cf. Mt 5:8; → 4,41–50.55–58.59–61; 6,2–5; 7,5–9.14–18.26–30.35–43.44–48.62–66; 20,1–3; 31,10–12; 49,1–3;52. 59 Conl 1,4. 60 Cassian, Conl 1,4.

CHAPTER 73

OF THE FACT THAT THE OBSERVANCE
OF THE WHOLE OF RIGHTEOUSNESS
IS NOT LAID DOWN IN THIS RULE

Cf. Mt 3:15:5:6,10

1 May
31 Aug 1 We have composed this Rule however
31 Dec   so that by its observance in monasteries
   we could prove that we have at least
   some decency of behaviour
   and a first beginning in monastic life.

2 For the rest,
   for one who hastens to the perfection of monastic life
   there are the teachings of the Holy Fathers,
   the observance of which lead a man
   to the height of perfection.

3 For what page or phrase of divine authority   Cf. 2 Tim 3:16;
   of the Old and New Testament   2 Pet 1:20
   is not the straightest norm for a human life?

4 Or what book of the holy Catholic Fathers
   does not re-echo
   how we may reach our Creator
   in a straight run?

5 And the 'Conferences' of the Fathers
   and their 'Institutes' and 'Lives',
   and the Rule too of our holy Father Basil,

6 what else are they but tools of virtues
   of good-living and obedient monks?

7 But it is DOUBLE CONFUSION AND SHAME   Cf Isa 45:16; 61:7
   for us, the lazy, the evil-living, the negligent ones.

8 Whoever you are therefore   Cf. Heb 4:11; 11:14–16
   who are HASTENING TO THE HOME COUNTRY
     OF HEAVEN,
   carry out this very small beginners' Rule,
   with Christ to help you;

9 and then,
   under God's protection,
   you will arrive

at those greater peaks of doctrine and of virtues
which we have spoken of above. Amen.
Here ends the Rule (for monks).

CAPUT LXXIII: DE HOC QUOD NON OMNIS IUSTITIAE OBSERVATIO IN HAC SIT REGULA CONSTITUTA

¹REGULAM AUTEM HANC DESCRIPSIMUS, UT HANC OBSERVANTES IN MONASTERIIS ALIQUATENUS VEL HONESTATEM MORUM AUT INITIUM CONVERSATIONIS NOS DEMONSTREMUS HABERE. ²CETERUM AD PERFECTIONEM CONVERSATIONIS QUI FESTINAT, SUNT DOCTRINAE SANCTORUM PATRUM, QUARUM OBSERVATIO PERDUCAT HOMINEM AD CELSITUDINEM PERFECTIONIS. ³QUAE ENIM PAGINA AUT QUI SERMO DIVINAE AUCTORITATIS VETERIS AC NOVI TESTAMENTI NON EST RECTISSIMA NORMA VITAE HUMANAE? ⁴AUT QUIS LIBER SANCTORUM CATHOLICORUM PATRUM HOC NON RESONAT UT RECTO CURSU PERVENIAMUS AD CREATOREM NOSTRUM? ⁵NECNON ET COLLATIONES PATRUM ET INSTITUTA ET VITAS EORUM, SED ET REGULA SANCTI PATRIS NOSTRI BASILII, ⁶QUID ALIUD SUNT NISI BENE VIVENTIUM ET OBOEDIENTIUM MONACHORUM INSTRUMENTA VIRTUTUM? ⁷NOBIS AUTEM DESIDIOSIS ET MALE VIVENTIBUS ATQUE NEGLEGENTIBUS RUBOR CONFUSIONIS EST. ⁸QUISQUIS ERGO AD PATRIAM CAELESTEM FESTINAS, HANC MINIMAM INCHOATIONIS REGULAM DESCRIPTAM ADIUVANTE CHRISTO PERFICE; ⁹ET TUNC DEMUM AD MAIORA, QUAE SUPRA COMMEMORAVIMUS, DOCTRINAE VIRTUTUMQUE CULMINA DEO PROTEGENTE PERVENIES. AMEN. EXPLICIT REGULA (MONACHORUM)

o **a.** The Epilogue is, as it were, Benedict's statement of account[1] on his work or his *statement of intent*[2] on the entire Rule. The Epilogue informs clearly about the intentions of the author as well as about the most important 'sources' and the monastic writings to which he feels himself indebted. He thereby himself gives the key to the interpretation of the Rule.

b. Gregory the Great (d.604) writes about the *Rule* of Benedict: 'He composed a monastic Rule with an outstanding talent for discernment and in luminous language. If anyone wishes to acquaint himself more closely with his way of life, he can find everything in this Rule and its directives: his teaching and its realization;[3] for the holy man could not possibly teach other than he lived.'[4]

c. It is a 'luminously' written Rule. Gregory mentions it immediately after he has shown that Benedict, in a mystic rapture, was 'inwardly seized' and exalted even into the 'light' of God, could behold the world and its bounds in that light.[5] Gregory wants to show that Benedict was able to become the author of this Rule because he led an ascetical life, because he was a 'bearer of the Spirit' (which is borne out by 'proofs of power'), and because the man of God was a contemplative 'seer'. Pope Gregory's high praise for Benedict and his Rule has given this Rule of the 'Roman Abbot'[6] an incomparable standing. That praise, unique of its kind, is deserved, whether one considers Benedict's power of synthesizing Scripture and traditional spirituality of East and West,[7] or his ability to produce a *new concept*[8] of monasticism that is both forward-looking[9] and flexible.[10]

d. The decisive core of the Rule is Holy Scripture. This is already hinted at by the title of this chapter and by the echoes of the Gospel that it contains: not the Rule, but Jesus himself fulfils *all righteousness*; people of the Beatitudes long for this righteousness. The Rule offers basic directions for this way.[11]

1 **a.** The very reserved assessment of the Rule by the author himself is in striking contrast to its inner value, which subsequent history demonstrates and certifies. What has been said before is repeated here: that the Rule is meant for *beginners*, who are taking up monastic life.[12] Whereas the 'Master' puts his Rule in the same class as that of the holy Fathers,[13] Benedict defines his Rule as meant for the 'beginners' in monastic life. He understands this last as a dynamic process, since he distinguishes a 'beginning',[14] an 'advance'[15] and a 'perfection'[16] in the monastic way, which, following the Alexandrian school, he compares to an 'ascent' to love.[17]

b. Benedict speaks of a 'beginning in the way of conversion'.[18] Cassian (d.430) insisted that at the beginning of the way, conversion was indispensable: 'The beginning and guardian of our salvation is the fear of the Lord. It is the *beginning of conversion*, and consists in the purging of faults and the practice of a positive, worthwhile life, for all who strive in the way of perfection.'[19]

c. The monks of old were conscious of the fact that an *initiation* into monastic life was indispensable. 'A brother forsook the world, took the habit, withdrew totally into solitude and declared: "I want to be a hermit." When the venerable Fathers of the neighbourhood heard of this, they expelled him. They told him to pass in front of all the dwellings of the brethren, to do penance before every single one and say: "Forgive me, I am not a hermit. It is only a short time since I made a beginning as monk."'[20] 'Some Fathers said: If you see a youth who in wilfulness wants to climb up to heaven, then grab him by the foot and bring him down to earth. Everything else is harmful for him.'[21]

d. By '*some decency of behaviour*' we must understand a real Christian life. Cassian speaks in the same sense of 'practical knowledge', which is a preliminary stage of contemplative or 'theoretical' knowledge. 'Active (practical) knowledge consists in an amended life and in purging of faults,[22] contemplative (theoretical) knowledge consists in the contemplation of divine realities and in insight into the most sacred interpretations (of Holy Scripture).'[23]

e. The Rule seems to be meant for a number of 'monasteries'.[24] Did this '*Epilogue*' originally have the function of a covering letter?[25] (E. Manning).

2 **a.** The search for *perfection* appears as an initiative which is prescribed, but freely chosen. Cassian (d.430) explains: 'Christ does not force anybody to climb the high peaks of virtue, but appeals to our free will, sensitizes us with his good counsel and kindles in us a longing for perfection.'[26] Through asceticism and a worthy, positive life, one comes into the home straight even in this life, just before the finishing line beyond which lies heavenly perfection:[27] 'In purity of heart one achieves the perfection of apostolic love.'[28] This perfection is unattainable without 'the grace of God.'[29]

b. Benedict wrote an 'open' Rule. It points beyond itself to the '*holy Fathers*'. Caesarius (d.542) repeats frequently that he has 'followed the directives of the ancient Fathers.'[30] The Pachomians had already venerated

the 'holy Fathers' of the generation that had passed into eternity: 'Since
we are now living together in coenobitical communities and are united with
each other in mutual love, let us take pains to see that, as we are permitted
to enjoy the company of the holy Fathers here below, we shall also be able
to be with them in the next life. At the same time, we must keep in mind
that the Cross is the foundation of our life and of our teaching.'[31] For the
sisters of his convent Caesarius expresses the wish that they 'may receive
the crown of glory with holy *Mary* and all other *virgins*'.[32]

3   a. One's attention is drawn to the series of rhetorical questions, which
begins with praise of *Holy Scripture*. Benedict sees an ascetical life and
monasticism as originated from Holy Scripture.[33] The way he puts it is
reminiscent of Cassian (d.430), who proclaims Scripture as the point of
reference and orientation, as norm and guideline for life: 'We must turn
our gaze completely to the home straight,[34] and set our course carefully
and exactly towards that clear line. If our thoughts wander from it in any
way, then we must fix it with our eyes once again. We have to turn about
and correct our course according to that guideline.'[35]
b. Benedict himself composes all important chapters of the Rule from a
tissue of words and sentences from the Bible. It is his practice to relate the
words of Scripture to *the present situation* and to use them in a metaphorical
or 'spiritual' sense.[36] In the power of the Spirit, the 'hidden' sense of a
scriptural quotation is interpreted, or Benedict believes that with the
assistance of the Spirit, he is permitted to take a saying of Scripture, to
proceed from it and to apply it to new contexts.
c. With his scriptural knowledge and piety based on it, and with his
tendency to a '*spiritual*' *interpretation* of Scripture, Benedict shows that he
is very much under the influence of the Alexandrian school of theology.
Origen, for example, wrote: 'We have often emphasized that there is in
Scripture a threefold way of understanding: a "historical", a "moral", and
a "mystical", so that we can also see that Scripture consists of "body",
"soul", and "spirit"'.[37] Cassian became acquainted in Egypt with this way
of looking at Scripture: 'Contemplation consists in the recognition of the
divine realities and in the recognition of the holy, hidden meaning (of
sacred Scripture).'[38] Contemplation[39] is twofold: 'historical interpretation
and spiritual insight.' Spiritual knowledge is of three kinds: 1. tropology
(for example Jerusalem, 'historically' the city of the Jews,[40] as the spiritual
condition of man), 2. allegory (for example Jerusalem[41] as Christ's Church,
3. anagoge (for example Jerusalem[42] as the heavenly City of God).[43] 'Whoever presses on in this way[44] will ascend from the contemplation (of the
example of the saints) to the ONE, that is, to the intuitive contemplation
of the one and only God, with the help of his grace, ... and thus live on
the beauty and knowledge of God alone.'[45] The interpretation of the Rule
cannot devote enough attention to its biblical background, to its echoes of
Scripture and to the corresponding terminology. Only in that way does
one remain within Benedict's sphere of understanding. He is someone
who has absorbed Scripture completely into himself.[46]

4–7   a. Benedict refers to the 'holy *Catholic Fathers*'.[47] In this, too, he is the
pupil of Cassian (d.430). Cassian states: 'The catholicity of the Faith moved

me to travel through the other provinces also.'[48] As Cassian is solicitous about the 'Catholica' and wants to describe the authentic monasticism spread through all provinces so Benedict, too, simply knows he belongs to the Church and wants essentially to summarize in his Rule the teaching common to the 'Catholic Fathers'. Benedict himself would be somewhat at a loss if he suddenly saw himself confronted with our present-day terms: 'Benedictine', 'Augustinian', 'Basilian', etc. In his time—as still today in the East—one had the writings and Rules of various 'Catholic Fathers' to hand, and sought in them the answer to one's own questions concerning the right monastic way of life. One knew that within a 'Catholic' framework one was entitled to draw on one or other source, or on the practice of well-known monasteries. There thus developed under the leadership of an abbot, a monastery's practical way of life, an unwritten Rule, or even one put in writing, which always remained open to further development or rewording (E. Manning).

b. Which monastic writings did Benedict know and use? The way he expresses himself in this passage is reminiscent of a sentence in the 'Lives of the Jura Fathers', the author of which (about 515) draws up the following *dossier*: 'the Institutions which were issued by the great and holy Basil, the bishop of the capital of Cappadocia, by the holy Fathers of Lérins, also by the holy Pachomius, an early abbot of the Syrians (!), and in more recent times by the worthy Cassian.'[49] Benedict cites Basil by name out of this list. By the 'Conferences' and 'Institutions' are meant Cassian's work, but also other writings from the circle of the 'holy Fathers' of Lérins and from the Jura; in this connection we must also think of the 'Rule of the Master' or of its early stages of development. Along with Pachomius, Augustine (whom he does not mention by name) plays an important role for Benedict. In the introduction and in the whole of the commentary, these writings were referred to, as were the 'Lives of the Fathers' and the sayings of the Fathers; that is the spiritual reading which Benedict recommends. He clearly makes the point that contemporary monasticism is no longer up to the standard of the Fathers.[50]

8–9   **a.** Benedict is writing for 'beginners',[51] who as 'people of the Exodus'[52] are on the journey to their future homeland.[53] For them he writes a 'modest' or 'brief' Rule, or one 'containing *minimal demands*.'[54] This Rule is not meant to overtax anybody; but at the same time Benedict recommends fidelity to the Rule.[55]

b. As *the grace of Christ* is indispensable for the beginning,[56] more than ever is this the case for finishing. Cassian (d.430) writes: 'Let him who ascends to the peak of evangelical perfection . . . be aware that he stands in the grace of the Redeemer.'[57]

c. The Rule contains as a guide for beginners above all the so-called 'practical (ascetical) knowledge',[58] but it also directs one's gaze again and again towards perfection.[59] The Rule is not a closed system; it points to things beyond itself.[60] The purpose is to facilitate a dynamic progress (so called because it is carried in the 'power' or 'dynamis' of the Spirit), or an 'ascent',[61] the aim of which is love, which is achieved in communion with Christ.[62]

d. By the 'greater peaks of *doctrine*' we have to understand first of all not some secret knowledge, but a profound knowledge of Scripture, which leads to contemplation.[63] The 'doctrine' is here, as at the conclusion of the Prologue, none other than that of the first Christian community, of which it is written: 'And they devoted themselves to the apostles' teaching and fellowship, to the breaking of bread and the prayers.'[64] We shall have to understand the 'greater peaks of virtues' (virtutum) in the same biblical sense. In this concept of the 'virtues' (virtutes) there re-echoes still the biblical '*dynameis*' (evidence of power). Thus it is written: 'And with great power (dynamis) the apostles gave their testimony to the resurrection of the Lord Jesus, and great grace (charis) was upon them.'[65] It is the power of the Spirit, which rests over the community of believers, and is active in many gifts and charisms.[66] To sum up, it may be said that the purpose of the Rule of Benedict is to form people of the Church, people of the Beatitudes.[67]

NOTES TO CHAPTER 73

1 Did the Epilogue once follow immediately on the chapter about the porter, with which the Rule ended in an earlier editorial phase? (→ 66,8). The Epilogue begins 'Regulam autem . . .' just as at the end of the chapter on the porter it is said: 'Hanc autem Regulam. . .' (RB 66,8) (A. de Vogüé). 2 Occasionally this 'Epilogue' is found immediately after the Prologue, before the first chapter (Concordia regularum!). The title of the Epilogue speaks of 'righteousness'; it is worth remarking that, according to RM 11,1 the 'records of justice' were dealt with in the first pages of the Rule. 3 'Actus' must be translated perhaps as 'documentation' or 'record'. 4 Dial 2,36. 5 Cf. Dial 2,35; Prol 48–49. 6 In various MSS. of the Rule, Benedict is designated as 'abbas romensis'. 7 → 73,3.4–7. 8 → 48,7–8.23. 9 → 18,22–25; 48,1–2; 55,1–3; cf.RB 40,5.8. 10 → 3,1–3.12 13; 7,55, 8,1–2; 11,1–3.6–10; 18,0.2–6.12–18. 22–25; 21,7; 43,7–9; 48,1–2.3–4.5.6; 50,1–2; 53,16.17–20.21–22; 55,13–14; 56,1–2; 59,1–2; 65,1–10.14–15. 11 Cf. Mt 3:15; 5:6,10. → Introd 1 (Note 2). The 'righteousness' preached in the Sermon on the Mount is a fundamental concept of the Bible, and designates God's holy and healing righteousness. 12 → Prol 1–4,48–49; Verses 1.8. 13 RM 'explicit regula sanctorum patrum'. 14 RB 73,1:'initium'. 15 RB Prol 49: 'processu'. 16 RB 73,2:'perfectio'. 17 → Prol 48–49; 4,1–9.55–58.76–77; 5,10–13; 6,2–5; 7,1–4.5–9. 26–30.31–32.55; 72,5–6.12; 73,8–9. 18 Verse 1 :'conversatio' means the monastic way, observance (→ 58,17–23); still, in certain passages, one can also hear overtones of 'conversio'—conversion. 19 Inst 4,39,1; on 'fear': → 7,5–9.10–13.62–66. 20 VPatr 5,10,110. 21 VPatr 5,10,111. 22 → 72,12 (Note 58); Prol 47; 7,55. 23 Conl 14,1. 24 See Note 9. 25 → 64,1–6 (Note 15). 26 Conl 21,5,4. 27 → 72,12 (Note 57). 28 Cassian, Inst 4,43; → 72,7. 29 Cassian, Conl 23,10. 30 Or he made a selection from them for the convents (RCaesVirg 1; 2; 63; 65); cf. RM explicit; → 72,1 (Note 14). 31 Horsiesi, Lib 50. 32 RCaesVirg 63 33 → Prol 1.8 11.18–20.45.50; 18,7–11; 4,55–58; 27,1–4; 38,1; 42,2–8; 48,15–16.17–18.22; 49,8 9; 58,1–4; 64,9–10; 71,1–4. 34 → 72,12 (Note 57). 35 Conl 1,4. 36 → Prol 8–11; 19,3–7. 37 Lev Hom 5,5. 38 Conl 14,3; → 73,1 (in Note 23). 39 theoria (theoretical knowledge), vision, intuition, insight. 40 Gal 4:22. 41 Gal 4:24–25. 42 Gal 4:26–27. 43 Conl 14,8. 44 'Progress'. Anagoge means 'leading up to'. 45 Conl 1,8. We have to do here with Neoplatonic categories, which, however are used only as tools, in order to give expression to the biblical piety which is experienced existentially. 46 → 48,15–15. 47 Verse 4. 48 Conl 18,7. 49 VPJur 174; see Introd, Note 12. 50 Verse 7; see Introd Note 64. On the 'Fathers': → Introd 4; 9,8; 42,2–7; 73,4–5. 51 → 73,1. 52 Cf. Cassian, Conl 18,5 (recessores): → 1,3–5 (in Note 40). 53 Cf. Heb 11: 14. 54 'Hanc minimam inchoationis regulam descriptam.' The double occurrence of 'describere' (verse 1) and 'descriptam' has given rise to the question as to whether the Rule should be explained as a 'transcript' from the 'Rule of the Master' (Prol 1). 55 → 3,7–11; 64,20–22; 66,8. 56 → Prol 4.22–27.29–32.41.47.48–49; 1,3–5; 4,62–73; 37,1–3; 64,12–15. 57 Conl 21,33. 58 → 73,1 (in Note 22). 59 → Prol 39.48–49; 4,41–50.55–58; 6,2–5; 7,67–70; 51,3; 64,1–6; 71,1–4; 72,5–6.12. 60 Verses 1–6.9; → 3,7–11. 61 → 73,1 (Note 17). 62 → 72,11–12. 63 → 73,3 (in Notes 37–45). 64 Acts 2:42; Prol 50. 65 Acts 4:33; cf. 1 Cor 2:4 ('demonstration of the Spirit and power'). 66 → Prol 50; 1,3–5; 2,31–32.33–36; 3,1–3.4–6; 4,62–73; 5,1–9; 7,31–32.33–36.37 43.67–70; 18,1; 31,3–7; 58,13–16.21–23; 61,1–4; 64,17–19; 66,6–7; 68,4–5; 72,4–12 (Notes 14.53). 67 → Introd 1 (in Note 2).

APPENDIX

This list of chapter headings or titles occurs in the manuscripts of the RB after the Prologue, the latter not being included in the list. The headings of individual chapters within the RB occasionally differ slightly from this list. It should be noted that the list of chapter headings usually corresponds more closely with the wording of the text of the RM (in which the list is placed before the Prologue) than with the wording of individual chapter headings within the RB (A. de Vogüé).

INCIPIUNT CAPITULA (REGULAE MONASTERIORUM)

I	De generibus vel vita monachorum
II	Qualis debeat esse abbas
III	De adhibendis ad consilium fratribus
IV	Quae sunt instrumenta bonorum operum
V	De oboedientia discipulorum qualis sit
VI	De taciturnitate
VII	De humilitate
VIII	De officiis divinis in noctibus
IX	Quanti psalmi dicendi sunt nocturnis horis
X	Qualiter aestatis tempore agatur nocturna laus
XI	Qualiter dominicis diebus vigiliae agantur
XII	Qualiter matutinorum sollemnitas agatur
XIII	Privatis diebus qualiter matutini agantur
XIV	In natale sanctorum qualiter vigiliae agantur
XV	Alleluia quibus temporibus dicatur
XVI	Qualiter divina opera per diem agantur
XVII	Quanti psalmi per easdem horas dicendi sunt
XVIII	Quo ordine psalmi dicendi sunt
XIX	De disciplina psallendi
XX	De reverentia orationis
XXI	Decani monasterii quales debeant esse
XXII	Quomodo dormiant monachi
XXIII	De excommunicatione culparum
XXIV	Qualis debeat esse modus excommunicationis
XXV	De gravioribus culpis
XXVI	De his qui sine iussione iunguntur excommunicatis
XXVII	Qualiter debeat abba sollicitus esse circa excommunicatos
XXVIII	De his qui saepius correpti emendare noluerint
XXIX	Si debeant iterum recipi fratres exeuntes de monasterio
XXX	Pueri minore aetate qualiter corripiantur
XXXI	Qualis debeat esse cellararius monasterii
XXXII	De ferramentis vel rebus monasterii

APPENDIX

This list of chapter headings or titles occurs in the manuscripts of the RB after the Prologue, the latter not being included in the list. The headings of individual chapters within the RB occasionally differ slightly from this list. It should be noted that the list of chapter headings usually corresponds more closely with the wording of the text of the RM (in which the list is placed before the Prologue) than with the wording of individual chapter headings within the RB (A. de Vogüé).

LIST OF CHAPTER HEADINGS

1   On the Types of Monks and their Lives
2   What the Abbot should be like
3   On calling the Brothers for Consultation
4   The Tools with which Good is done
5   On the Obedience of the Disciples: what its Characteristics should be
6   On Silence
7   On Humility
8   On the divine Offices at Night
9   How many psalms are to be sung at Prayers during the Night
10 How praise at Night is to be celebrated during the Summer
11 How Vigils on Sundays are to be celebrated
12 How Lauds are to be celebrated
13 How Lauds are to be celebrated on ordinary Days
14 How Vigils are to be celebrated on the Feast of a Saint
15 At what times the *Alleluia* is to be sung
16 How the Work of God is to be celebrated during the Daytime
17 How many psalms are to be sung during these Hours
18 The Order in which the psalms are to be sung
19 On Behaviour during the Singing of the psalms
20 On Reverence at Prayer
21 What the Deans of the Monastery should be like
22 How the Monks sleep
23 On Exclusion for Offences
24 The Form Exclusion is to take
25 On grave Offences
26 On unpermitted Contact with the Excluded
27 How the Abbot should care for the Excluded
28 On those who, though often corrected, do not amend
29 Whether Brothers who have left the Monastery should be received again
30 How young Boys are to be punished
31 What the Cellarer of the Monastery should be like
32 On the Tools and Property of the Monastery

[Expliciunt Capitula]

BIBLIOGRAPHY

This bibliography is confined to a few publications, most of which contain detailed references to literature available.

SOURCES, TRANSLATIONS AND COMMENTARIES

Bacht, H., *Das Vermächtnis des Ursprungs (Liber Horsiesii) (Würzburg 1972)*

Basilius von Caesarea, *Die Mönchsregeln. Hinführung und Übersetzung von K. Suso Frank* (St. Ottilien 1982)

Battle, C.M., *Pelagii I Papae epistolae* (Montserrat 1956) 83

De Bruyne, D., 'La première Règle de S. Benoît (ed.: OM; Augustini Praecepta)' *Rev. Bén.* 42 (1930) 318–326

Fässler, F., *Die Regel des heiligen Benedictus: H.U. v. Balthasar, Die großen Ordensregeln* (Einsiedeln, 3rd ed., 1974) *185–192*

Funk, F.X., (ed.), *Didascalia* . . . (Paderborn 1905)

Guy, J.C., (ed.) *Jean Cassien, Institutions (Lat-Fr): Sources chrétiennes 109 (Paris 1965)*

Goutagny, E., *Commentaire de la Règle de S. Benoît* (Dombes, 2nd ed., 1978)

Guillaumont, A. & C., (ed.) *Evagre le Pontique, Traité pratique II (Logos praktikos); Sources Chrétiennes 171* (Paris 1971)

Hanslik, R., *Benedicti Regula: Corpus Scriptorum ecclesiasticorum latinorium* (Vienna, 2nd ed., 1977)

Holste-Brockie-Migne, *Codex Regularum . . . collectus olim a S. Benedicto Anianensi abbate* (PL 103, 339–664)

Kleeba, E., *Irenäus*, Ausgew. Schriften: *Bibl. d. Kirchenväter* (Kempten 1912)

Lentini, A., S. *Benedetto, La Regola* (Montecassino , 2nd ed., 1980)

Martine, F., (ed.), *Vie des Pères du Jura (Lat-Fr): Sources chrétiennes 142* (Paris 1968)

Morin, G., S. *Caesarii . . . opera omnia I–II* (Maretioli 1937/1942)

Pichery, E., *Jean Cassien, Conférences (Lat-Fr): Sources chrétiennes 42. 54. 64* (Paris 1955/1958/1959)

Rochais, H. and Manning, E., *Règle de S. Benoît* (Rochefort/now: Abtei Oelenberg, F-68950 Reiningue, 2nd ed., 1980)

RB 1980, *The Rule of St. Benedict* (Collegeville/Minn., 1981)

Rosweyd-Migne, *Vitae Patrum* (PL 73)

Steidle, B., *Die Benedikrusregel (Lat.-Germ.)* (Beuron, 4th ed., 1980)

Turbessi, G., *Regole monastiche antiche* (Roma 1974)

Valentin, M. D. (ed.), *Hilaire d'Arles, Vie de S. Honorat: Sources chrétiennes 235* (Paris 1977)

Vogüé, A. de, *La communauté et l'abbé* (Paris 1961)

——, *La Règle du Maître I–III: Sources chrétiennes 105–107* (Paris 1964–1965)

——, *La Règle de S. Benoît I–VII: Sources chrétiennes 181–186* (Paris 1972–1977)

——, *Grégoire le Grand, Dialogues I–II: Sources chrétiennes 251. 260* (Paris 1980). German translation, E. Jungclaussen, Benedictus, (Ratisbon 1980)

SPECIAL STUDIES AND OTHER ARTICLES

Braulik, G., (ed.), *Herausforderung der Mönche* (Vienna 1979)

Fabbi, A., *Norcia* . . . (1980)

Fischer, B., 'Das Verhältnis von festgelegtem Gemeinschaftsgebet und freiem Gebet des einzelnen in der Regel des heiligen Benedikt', *Trierer Theol. Zeitschrift 90* (1981) 1–18

Frank, K.S., *Siehe das Gesetz* . . . *Erbe und Auftrag* 56 (1980) 427–440

Gindele, C., *Zur Offiziumsordnung der Regula: Erbe und Auftrag* 37–38 (1961–1962)

Gregor d. Gr., *Leben des Benedictus. Übers. u. eingel. v. Fr. van der Meer u. G. Bartelink* (St. Ottilien 1979)

Hallinger, K., *Papst Gregor d. Gr. und der hl. Benedikt: Studia Anselmiana* 42 (1957) 231–319 (ed., B. Steidle)

Heufelder, E., *Der Weg zu Gott nach der Regel des heiligen Benedikt* (Würzburg, 2nd ed., 1964)

——, *Weite des Herzens. Meditationen über den Geist der Benediktusregel* (Ratisbon 1971)

Hume, B. Cardinal, *Searching for God* (London, 5th ed., 1978)

Jaspert, B. - Manning, E., *Regulae Benedicti Studia. Annuarium internationale* I–IV (Hildesheim 1972–1975)

——, *Regulae Benedicti Studia. Supplementa I–II (Hildesheim 1974–1975)*. A bibliography on current scholarly research on the Rule is provided in the *Regulae Benedicti Studia.*

Kay, R., Benedict, 'Justinian, and donations "mortis causa" in the Regula Magistri; *Rév. bén.* 90 (1980) 169–193

Kleiner, S., *Dieu premier servi* (Paris 1974)

Mundò, A., 'Bibliotheca' *Rev. Bén.* 60 (1950) 65–92

——, 'Les anciens synodes abbatiaux . . . ' *Studia Anselmiana* 44 (1959) 107–125

Nigg, W.-Loose, H.N., *Benedikt von Nursia* (Freiburg im Br. 1979)

Penco, G., *Storia della chiesa in Italia I* (Milan 1977)

Prinz, F., *Frühes Mönchtum im Frankenreich* (Munich and Vienna 1965)

Van Parys, M., 'L'accès à l'Orient monastique chez S. Benoît' *Irenikon* 47 (1974) 48–58

Rees, D. (ed.), *Consider your call. A theology of monastic life today* (London 1978)

Schmitz, P., *Histoire de l'Ordre de Saint Benoît*. 7 vols. Maredsous 1942.

Tschudy, F.J. and Renner, F., *Der heilige Benedikt und das benediktinische Mönchtum* (St. Ottilien 1979)

Vogüé, A. de, *Saint Benoît. Sa vie et sa Règle* (Abbaye de Bellefontaine 1981)

INDEX

The numbers following the arrow (→) refer to the Commentary
(chapter and verses), or to the Introduction (paragraphs).